Fodor's

WALT DISNEY WORLD

WELCOME TO WALT DISNEY WORLD

Orlando vacations are events that often become part of family legend. Kids and parents swap Disney or Universal stories for years, fondly reliving favorite moments such as the first Butterbeer in Hogsmeade, the "Be Our Guest" dance with Belle, or the final battle between Buzz Lightyear and Zurg. Beyond the Wizarding Worlds and Fantasylands, there is a lot more to see in Orlando. Towns such as Mount Dora, Kissimmee, and Winter Park lure travelers away from the theme parks with fascinating museums, great shopping, and tempting freshwater lakes.

TOP REASONS TO GO

★ **Walt Disney World:** Quite simply, the magic of the Disney parks touches all who visit.

★ **Universal Orlando:** Islands of Adventure and Universal Studios are high-energy fun.

★ **Resorts:** Elaborately themed resorts offer visitors fun and memorable experiences.

★ **International Drive:** Bustling strip with attractions like Fun Spot and Acquatica.

★ **Downtown Orlando:** Top restaurants, theater, and music create a thriving scene.

★ **LEGOLAND Florida:** A unique family-friendly theme park with fun rides, shows, and attractions.

25 ULTIMATE EXPERIENCES

Walt Disney World offers terrific experiences that should be on every traveler's list. Here are Fodor's top picks for a memorable trip.

1 Watch IllumiNations

The laser and fireworks show at Epcot is one of Walt Disney World's most popular evening showstoppers. Visible from almost everywhere in the World Showcase (not to mention from some spots outside the park, it's a celebration of the unified spirit of humankind. *(Ch. 2)*

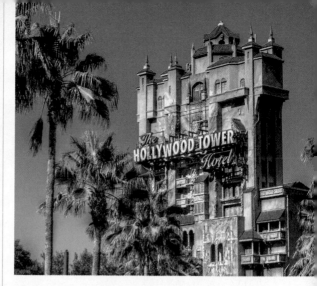

2 Ride the Tower of Terror

This classic takes you to 1930s Tinseltown at the Hollywood Tower Hotel and a stomach-flipping elevator ride into the Twilight Zone. The best part? It's different every single time you ride it. *(Ch. 2)*

3 Channel Your Inner Child

Dedicated to your favorite building blocks, this sprawling theme park 45 minutes from Orlando is a great non-Disney option if you have younger kids who can't ride the thrill rides at Universal Orlando. *(Ch. 4)*

4 Let It Go

After you've ridden Frozen Ever After, you can meet Anna and Elsa at Royal Summerhus or sing along with the whole cast at For the First Time in Forever in Disney's Hollywood Studios. *(Ch. 2)*

5 Rivers of Light

If you're looking for a seated and more understated way to end your day, Rivers of Light captures the conservation ethos of Animal Kingdom with beautiful music and visuals. *(Ch. 2)*

6 Experience Pandora—The World of Avatar

Animal Kingdom's newest section includes the world's best ride, Avatar Flight of Passage in addition to the otherwordly beauty of Pandora's bioluminescent flora and fauna. *(Ch. 2)*

7 Visit Winter Park

Winter Park is one of Orlando's hidden gems, a great place to spend some quality family time in a lovely small town and take a scenic boat ride across the town lake. *(Ch. 4)*

8 Ride Jurassic Park

At Universal Islands of Adventure, you can ride on a river past dinosaurs both gentle and scary, ending your journey with an 85-foot plunge. You will get wet. *(Ch. 3)*

9 A Night at CityWalk

Like Disney Springs, this outdoor mall is full of shops, restaurants, and entertainment, but the experience feels more Las Vegas than Orlando. *(Ch. 7, 8)*

10 Kayak the Wekiva River

Wekiwa Springs State Park, an hour from Orlando, gives you a break from the go-go-go vibe in all the parks, with plenty of space to enjoy a quiet river adventure. *(Ch. 4)*

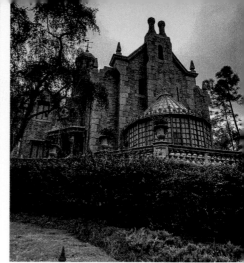

11 Stroll Down a Garden Path

If theme parks aren't your thing, you can relax in over 50 acres of lush greenery at the Harry P. Leu Gardens, which offers flora and fauna from all over the world. *(Ch. 4)*

12 Get Spooked

No matter what time of year, the Haunted Mansion is a classic that can't be missed. It's more fun than spooky and definitely good for the whole family. *(Ch. 2)*

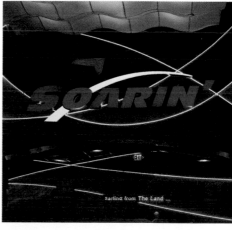

13 Stay at a Disney Resort

Staying at a Disney-owned resort gives you free transportation, early access to reservations, extra time at the parks, and a free Magic Band regardless of the price point. *(Ch. 6)*

14 Soar Over the World

Soarin' lets you travel around the world on a simulated hang-glider, offering 180-degree panoramas and other special effects; you'll feel like you're really flying. *(Ch. 2)*

15 Ride the Waves

If you'd rather cool your heels and the rest of you in the waves, try one of Disney's two water parks or the new Volcano Bay at Universal. *(Ch. 2, 3)*

16 Get Happily Ever After

For the quintessential Disney fireworks experience, the Magic Kingdom has a new animated fireworks spectacular that provides a fitting end to a fun day. *(Ch. 2)*

17 Be Their Guest

The Magic Kingdom's most popular restaurant is worth the time and trouble for a great prix-fixe breakfast, lunch, or dinner. Try the grey stuff—it's delicious! *(Ch. 5)*

18 A Night at Disney Springs

Disney's expanded and reinvigorated dining and shopping mega-complex is a fitting way to end your day with a meal, a movie, or a stroll. *(Ch. 7, 8)*

19 Explore Everest

Journey to the summit of the world's highest peak at Animal Kingdom's exciting thrill ride, which moves both backward and forward. *(Ch. 2)*

20 Dine (or Drink) Around the World

With 8 restaurants in Future World and more than 25 in World Showcase, Epcot allows you to eat a wide variety of cuisines, from American to Mexican to Moroccan. *(Ch. 5)*

21 Use the Force

While the new Star Wars experience doesn't open at Hollywood Studios until 2019, there are lots of ways you can journey to a galaxy far, far away right now. *(Ch. 2)*

22 Meet the Characters

One of the best parts of going to Disney? Meeting your favorite characters and getting a hug and an autograph, from Minnie and Mickey to your favorite princess. *(Ch. 2)*

23 Putt Putt Your Way to Victory

If you're looking to hit the links but limit yourself to a putter, Orlando has you covered from Walt Disney World to International Drive with over a dozen courses. *(Ch. 9)*

24 Ride the Mega-Coasters

Universal Orlando is home to two of the country's biggest and most exciting rollercoasters: The Incredible Hulk Coaster and the Hollywood Rip Ride Rockit. *(Ch. 3)*

25 Get the Harry Potter Experience

Harry is the biggest draw at Universal Orlando Resort, whether you're going to Hogsmeade at Islands of Adventure or Diagon Alley at Universal Studios. *(Ch. 3)*

Fodor's WALT DISNEY WORLD

Editorial: Douglas Stallings, *Editorial Director*; Margaret Kelly, Jacinta O'Halloran, *Senior Editors*; Kayla Becker, Alexis Kelly, Amanda Sadlowski, *Editors*; Teddy Minford, *Content Editor*; Rachael Roth, *Content Manager*

Design: Tina Malaney, *Design and Production Director;* Jessica Gonzalez, *Production Designer*

Photography: Jennifer Arnow, *Senior Photo Editor*

Maps: Rebecca Baer, *Senior Map Editor*; Mark Stroud (Moon Street Cartography) and David Lindroth, *Cartographers*

Production: Jennifer DePrima, *Editorial Production Manager*; Carrie Parker, *Senior Production Editor*; Elyse Rozelle, *Production Editor*

Business & Operations: Chuck Hoover, *Chief Marketing Officer*; Joy Lai, *Vice President and General Manager*; Stephen Horowitz, *Director of Business Development and Revenue Operations;* Tara McCrillis, *Director of Publishing Operations;* Eliza D. Aceves, *Content Operations Manager and Strategist*

Public Relations and Marketing: Joe Ewaskiw, *Manager;* Esther Su, *Marketing Manager*

Writers: Jennifer Greenhill-Taylor, Joseph Hayes, Gary McKechnie

Editor: Douglas Stallings

Production Editor: Carrie Parker

9th Edition

ISBN 978-1-64097-046-5

ISSN 1531–443X

All details in this book are based on information supplied to us at press time. Always confirm information when it matters, especially if you're making a detour to visit a specific place. Fodor's expressly disclaims any liability, loss, or risk, personal or otherwise, that is incurred as a consequence of the use of any of the contents of this book.

SPECIAL SALES

This book is available at special discounts for bulk purchases for sales promotions or premiums. For more information, e-mail SpecialMarkets@fodors.com.

PRINTED IN THE UNITED STATES OF AMERICA

10 9 8 7 6 5 4 3 2 1

CONTENTS

CONTENTS

MAPS

ABOUT THIS GUIDE

Fodor's Recommendations

Everything in this guide is worth doing—we don't cover what isn't—but exceptional sights, hotels, and restaurants are recognized with additional accolades. **Fodor's** Choice★ indicates our top recommendations. Care to nominate a new place? Visit Fodors.com/contact-us.

Trip Costs

We list prices wherever possible to help you budget well. Hotel and restaurant price categories from **$** to **$$$$** are noted alongside each recommendation. For hotels, we include the lowest cost of a standard double room in high season. For restaurants, we cite the average price of a main course at dinner or, if dinner isn't served, at lunch. For attractions, we always list adult admission fees; discounts are usually available for children, students, and senior citizens.

Hotels

Our local writers vet every hotel to recommend the best overnights in each price category, from budget to expensive. Unless otherwise specified, you can expect private bath, phone, and TV in your room. For expanded hotel reviews visit Fodors.com.

Top Picks	Hotels &
★ **Fodor's** Choice	**Restaurants**
	⬚ Hotel
Listings	⬚ Number of
⬚ Address	rooms
⬚ Branch address	⬚ Meal plans
⬚ Telephone	✗ Restaurant
⬚ Fax	⬚ Reservations
⬚ Website	⬚ Dress code
⬚ E-mail	⬚ No credit cards
⬚ Admission fee	$ Price
⬚ Open/closed times	**Other**
Ⓜ Subway	⇨ See also
⬚ Directions or Map coordinates	☞ Take note
	⬚ Golf facilities

Restaurants

Unless we state otherwise, restaurants are open for lunch and dinner daily. We mention dress code only when there's a specific requirement and reservations only when they're essential or not accepted.

Credit Cards

The hotels and restaurants in this guide typically accept credit cards. If not, we'll say so.

EUGENE FODOR

Hungarian-born Eugene Fodor (1905–91) began his travel career as an interpreter on a French cruise ship. The experience inspired him to write *On the Continent* (1936), the first guidebook to receive annual updates and discuss a country's way of life as well as its sights. Fodor later joined the U.S. Army and worked for the OSS in World War II. After the war, he kept up his intelligence work while expanding his guidebook series. During the Cold War, many guides were written by fellow agents who understood the value of insider information. Today's guides continue Fodor's legacy by providing travelers with timely coverage, insider tips, and cultural context.

EXPERIENCE ORLANDO AND THE PARKS

WHAT'S NEW IN ORLANDO AND THE PARKS

Prior to 1971, Orlando was a quiet town whose main industry was citrus. There was a new interstate highway and a nature park where you could see alligators, but that was about it. But then came Walt Disney World. The boom in tourism meant the city needed a more modern airport and new hotels. That, of course, meant Orlando would need more workers, which meant more housing and successively more theme parks, malls, as well as arts, culture, and industry to keep things going. The city you saw in 2010 is even more different than the city you see today as the pace of growth increases. As of this writing, the Orlando International Aiport is in the midst of expansion as people movers and new international arrivals hall are built to accommodate more flights. The Dr. Phillips Center for the Performing Arts, which opened in 2014, continues to expand and elevate its status as the core of Orlando culture. On tourist-rich International Drive, the Coca-Cola Orlando Eye likewise raised the city's profile when it opened in 2015. At 400 feet, it's the sixth-tallest observation wheel on earth.

And there are always new shows, events, and attractions at the theme parks as creative teams at Disney and Universal try to out-tech and out-dazzle the other—as evidenced in the open rivalry between the Wizarding Worlds at Universal and Disney's new-in-2017 world of Pandora. Both companies, too, have latched onto new technology that allows guests to pre-plan portions of their vacations and make things easier while they're in the parks. At Disney, you can see it in online apps like My Disney Experience (which allows guests to set up reservations at attractions) and in the MagicBand (wrist bands that can be linked to an account). A swipe of the hand can charge meals and merchandise or unlock your resort room door. Universal offers a similar service with Universal Express, which ushers guests into shorter lines. At Universal's new-in-2017 Volcano Bay water theme park, the Tapu-Tapu wristband can hold your place in a virtual line while you wait to ride most thrill rides as you laze on the beach. The band can sync up souvenir photos shot at tiki totems, unlock lockers, and help you pay for your meals.

Walt Disney World

Just as Universal holds a monopoly on the highly creative (and lucrative) Harry Potter lands, Disney now has the wildly popular Pandora–The World of Avatar at Animal Kingdom as well as an ever-increasing number of attractions devoted to Marvel and Star Wars, in addition to its already impressive heritage of classic Disney characters.

But more happened in 2018. A new Toy Story Land opened in late June at Disney's Hollywood Studios, including a Slinky Dog roller coaster and the Alien Swirling Saucers, similar to the Magic Kingdom's teacups. The Great Movie Ride, which was the centerpiece of the park for more than 25 years, is being replaced by the park's first "Mickey-centric" attraction, to be called "Mickey and Minnie's Runaway Railway" (which will open sometime in 2019). Also under construction at the park is "Star Wars: Galaxy's Edge," which will arrive at Disney's Hollywood Studios in 2019 to give riders the chance to board a Star Destroyer or the Millennium Falcon. Each experience will immerse riders in the action—and word is they'll even be able to take control of the Falcon.

Elsewhere at Disney, Epcot has said goodbye to Ellen's Energy Adventure and will welcome a Guardians of the Galaxy roller coaster (perhaps not until 2019); also expected is a *Ratatouille*-themed ride in the France pavilion. At the Magic Kingdom, a TRON-themed roller coaster will be neighbors with the classic Space Mountain attraction, while Main Street USA will see a new theater. No word yet on exact dates, but some expect most of these new attractions to arrive around 2021, the 50th anniversary of Walt Disney World.

A further example of the perpetual enhancements is **Disney Springs**, which itself was modified from what was Downtown Disney. In 2017, Cirque du Soleil retired its long-running La Nouba show, and the DisneyQuest interactive video game center was also shuttered to make room for an NBA-themed attraction. Time will tell what will come next, but as time and tastes change, so does Disney.

Universal Orlando

Following the premiere of The Wizarding World of Harry Potter–Hogsmeade in 2010 at Islands of Adventure, it was clear that Universal Studios needed a similar land. So in 2014 Universal Studios opened The Wizarding World of Harry Potter–Diagon Alley. Noticing the appeal of both lands, expansion seems to be the magic formula. In 2017 the popular Dueling Dragons roller coaster at Islands of Adventure was scuttled to make room for a new Potter-themed attraction. Also in 2017, Universal introduced a new water park, Volcano Bay, and razed America's first water park—Wet n' Wild—on nearby International Drive, later revealing plans that the now-vacant 64 acres would accommodate two new Universal resort

hotels: one with 2,050 rooms, the other with 750. Although they'll be distant from the theme parks, the rumored price point (less than $100) should make them an attractive option.

Tracking Universal the way they track Disney, theme park insiders assume that the cutting-edge, high-tech attraction Super Nintendo World scheduled to premiere at Universal Studios Japan in 2020 will subsequently come to Universal Orlando. But will it? You'll just have to plan a vacation and see.

Beyond the Theme Parks

Not all the local developments are happening at the city's two largest theme parks. On International Drive near the Orange County Convention Center, the Coca-Cola Orlando Eye (an observation wheel) opened in 2015, giving guests a round-trip view of Orlando from a peak altitude of 400 feet. Nearby, TopGolf made its debut, bringing a cutting-edge approach to the old-fashioned driving range. Once you tee off with a micro-chipped golf ball, a computer tracks it and almost instantly displays on a big-screen monitor the altitude, speed, and distance of the shot. Right next door, race legend Mario Andretti lent his name to Andretti Indoor Karting & Games which includes high-speed kart racing, boutique bowling, laser tag, pro racing simulators, hologram virtual reality games, and a sky trails ropes course with a curved zipline.

WHAT'S WHERE

1 Walt Disney World. Walt Disney World Resort, which covers an area roughly the size of San Francisco, is not technically in Orlando, but it is adjacent, about 30 minutes by car southwest of town. The resort's four theme parks (Magic Kingdom, Epcot, Disney's Hollywood Studios, Animal Kingdom) and more than two dozen hotels with a total of approximately 26,000 rooms, are the primary reason Orlando is the booming city it is today.

2 Universal Orlando. Universal Orlando is in the heart of Orlando, right off busy International Drive. In addition to two theme parks (Universal Studios and Islands of Adventure) and a new water park (Volcano Bay), it has several resort hotels and is expanding even further in the coming years.

3 Orlando & Environs. The greater Orlando area encompasses both Orlando proper and several surrounding communities, which include Kissimmee, Lake Buena Vista, and Winter Park. Most of these are east of Walt Disney World.

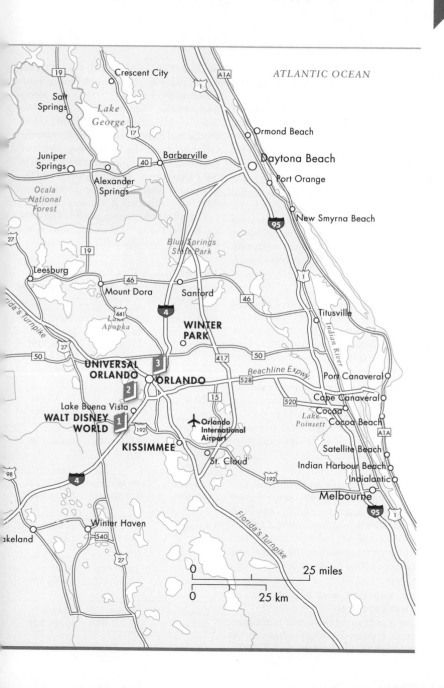

ORLANDO TRANSPORTATION PLANNER

Getting Here

Among America's top 15 busiest airports, all the major and most discount airlines fly into **Orlando International Airport** (**MCO**). About 30 minutes north of town, the **Orlando-Sanford Airport** (**SFB** is a far smaller but far more manageable option.

Magical Express

If you're staying at a Disney hotel and flying on certain airlines, this free service will deliver your luggage from your home airport to your hotel (and back again) *and* shuttle you to and from your resort, albeit slowly. You must book before departure (☎ *866/599–0951* ⊕ *www.disneysmagicalexpress.com*).

Getting Around

If you'll be on Disney property, you can use its buses, trams, boats, and monorails—which are free. Off-property, some hotels also have shuttles to and from Universal and SeaWorld, which don't have transit systems.

From the airport, the Beachline Expressway, aka State Road 528, is a toll road that gets you from the airport to the area attractions. If you need to pay cash, make sure you follow the signs and stay in the correct lane.

CAR RENTAL

Rates vary seasonally and can begin as low as $30 a day or $149 a week for an economy car (excluding 6.5% rental-car tax). ■TIP→ If you're returning a car to MCO, definitely fill up several miles from MCO. Some stations near the airport rip off unsuspecting travelers by doubling the price of a gallon.

CABS, SHUTTLES, AND PUBLIC TRANSPORTATION

Many non-Disney hotels offer free airport shuttles. If yours doesn't, cabs from the airport to the Disney area run $55–$75. Try **Star Taxi** (☎ *407/857–9999*), **Yellow Cab Co.** (☎ *407/422–2222*), or **Town & Country Transportation** (☎ *407/828–3035*). The **Mears Transportation Group** (☎ *407/423–5566* ⊕ *www.mearstransportation.com*) offers shuttle and charter services throughout the Orlando area. The **I-Ride Trolley** (⊕ *www.iridetrolley.com*) serves most attractions in the I-Drive area. It won't get you to Disney, but it does have a stop about a half mile from Universal. A one-way trip is $2, but an all-day pass costs just $5. The **LYNX** (☎ *407/841–5969* ⊕ *www.golynx.com*) bus system provides service in Orlando.

Airport Transit Times and Costs

AIRPORT TO:	BY SHUTTLE (PER PERSON)	BY TAXI/ CAR
Magic Kingdom	30–45 mins; $37 round-trip (RT); $23 one way (OW)	35 mins; approx. $70 (taxi fare for up to 7 people)
Disney Springs	N/A	25–30 mins; approx. $60
Animal Kingdom/ Hollywood Studios	30–45 mins; $37 RT; $23 OW	35 mins; approx. $58
Universal Orlando	30–40 mins; $33 RT; $21 OW	20 mins; approx. $48
Kissimmee	30–45 mins; $37 RT; $23 OW	30 mins; approx. $59
I-Drive (midway)	30–40 mins; $33 RT; $21 OW	20 mins; approx. $36
Downtown Orlando	30 mins; $32 RT; $21 OW	20 mins; approx. $34

Transit Times and Costs in and around Walt Disney World

MAGIC KINGDOM TO:	BY SHUTTLE	BY TAXI/ CAR
Disney Springs	N/A (use Disney transportation)	10–15 mins; approx. $18
Animal Kingdom/ Hollywood Studios	N/A (use Disney transportation)	15 mins; approx. $22
Universal Orlando	25 mins; $20 RT	25 mins; approx. $43
Kissimmee	N/A	25–30 mins; approx. $33
I-Drive (midway)	N/A	30 mins; approx. $41
Downtown Orlando	N/A	40 mins; approx. $61

Transit Times and Costs in and around Universal Orlando

UNIVERSAL CITY WALK TO:	BY SHUTTLE	BY TAXI/ CAR
Magic Kingdom	N/A	25 mins; approx. $43
Disney Springs	N/A	20 mins; approx. $30
Animal Kingdom/Hollywood Studios	N/A	30 mins; approx. $40
Kissimmee	30 mins; $37 RT; 23 OW	25 mins; approx. $38
I-Drive (midway)	25 mins; $18 RT	5–10 mins; approx. $10
Downtown Orlando	N/A	10 mins; approx. $23

Orlando Driving Routes

Beachline Expressway: Toll road from the airport to I-Drive and Disney ($2.25). Also good for Universal, SeaWorld, and Space Coast.

Interstate 4: Main east–west highway between Tampa and Daytona; it follows a north–south track through Orlando, making for a little confusion. ■TIP→ Think north when Interstate 4 signs say east (toward Daytona, say), and south when they say west (toward Tampa).

Key exits:

–Exit 64B: Magic Kingdom/U.S. 192; *heavy* peak-season traffic near this exit

–Exit 65: Animal Kingdom, ESPN Wide World of Sports

–Exit 67: Epcot/Disney Springs, Typhoon Lagoon, Universal; less-congested exit

–Exit 68: Disney Springs, Typhoon Lagoon

–Exits 71 and 72: SeaWorld

–Exits 72, 74A, and 75A: I-Drive

–Exits 74B and 75A: Universal Orlando Resort

Semoran Boulevard: One of the main roads to Orlando and Winter Park from the airport. Heavily traveled but moves well; plenty of amenities.

Spacecoast Parkway or Irlo Bronson Memorial Highway (U.S. 192): Runs east–west to Kissimmee. Continues east to the coast at Melbourne. Crosses Interstate 4 at Exits 64A and 64B.

ROAD SERVICE

The **AAA Car Care Center** (☎ *407/824– 0976*) near the Magic Kingdom provides emergency services, including free towing on Disney property, even for non-AAA members. Elsewhere, dial 511.

SEASONAL AND HOLIDAY EVENTS

If you've been to Orlando and its parks and enjoyed the top attractions at least once, consider a special trip around one of the many festivals and events.

The year-end holiday season is particularly festive. Decorations go up and events begin around Thanksgiving and continue through early January. It pays to book a trip during the first few weeks of December, when there's a lull between Thanksgiving and Christmas crowds.

Winter

Candlelight Processional. Each holiday season between Thanksgiving and New Year's, a succession of celebrity narrators visit Disney to retell the story of Christmas before a full orchestra and large choir comprised of guest singers from local schools and churches. Presented at Epcot's American Gardens Theatre, the show is truly a spectacular with sing-along carols and a stirring performance of the Hallelujah Chorus from Handel's *Messiah*. The performance is free with admission (although you'll wait in a very, very long line)—or you can opt for the Candlelight lunch or dinner package, which includes a meal at one of Epcot's pavilions as well as VIP early-access seating. Prices change often; call in advance. ⊠ *World Showcase, America Gardens Theatre, Epcot* ☎ 407/939–3463.

Christmas in The Wizarding World of Harry Potter. Already steeped in magic, Universal's dual Wizarding Worlds take on a winter veneer during the holidays; transformed with lights and festooned with Christmas decor and ornaments. In Universal Studios' Diagon Alley, buskers sing holiday songs at King's Cross Station, and Celestina Warbeck and the Banshees (a popular singing group) change up their set with holiday favorites. At Islands of Adventure, Hogsmeade takes on even more the look of a traditional English village, with Hogwarts Castle lit for the season and each shop decorated in a garland. In the evening the castle becomes a towering screen for "The Magic of Christmas at Hogwarts," an elaborate special-effects projection that brings the castle to life with an assortment of dazzling film clips and images. ⊠ *Islands of Adventure* ☎ *407/363–8000* ⊕ *www.universalorlando.com/web/en/us/things-to-do/events/holidays-at-universal/index.html#the-wizarding-world-of-harry-potter.*

Grinchmas Wholiday Spectacular. The holiday season takes a curmudgeonly turn at Seuss Landing during Grinchmas, an Islands of Adventure stage show based on the Dr. Seuss classic *How the Grinch Stole Christmas*. An original Mannheim Steamroller musical score backs up a half-dozen songs by an energetic and colorful cast including the Grinch and the Whos from Whoville. The stage show is only part of it. Stick around and this festive "Whobilation" and the Grinch (as well as several Whos) will be out on curving Seussian streets to say hello and pose for souvenir snapshots. ⊠ *Islands of Adventure.*

Mickey's Jingle Bell, Jingle BAM! Held at Disney's Hollywood Studios, the park's buildings and rooftops come alive with scenes from *Mickey's Christmas Carol, Beauty and the Beast, Pluto's Christmas Tree*, and Tim Burton's *The Nightmare Before Christmas*; this all builds to a festive finale that must be seen—and heard—to be believed. The seasonal show features scenes from animated Disney classics, special effects, holiday songs, a little snow, and fiery display of fireworks (hence, the BAM!). ⊠ *Disney's Hollywood Studios.*

Mickey's Very Merry Christmas Party. Disney's Magic Kingdom is just that: magic. Come here during scheduled evenings in November and December, and you'll discover Mickey's Very Merry Christmas Party spreads even more holiday cheer. On these evenings, add to the park's twinkling lights, fantasy architecture, and grandeur of Cinderella Castle a holiday parade, seasonal stage shows, fireworks, "snow" on Main Street, U.S.A., and platters of hot cocoa and cookies, and you've set the stage for some wonderful photographs as well as lifelong memories. Since this is an evening event only, it's priced lower than a single day's park admission. Guests inside the park without the requisite "Christmas Party" wristband will be asked to exit, leaving the park clear for the guests arriving for the holiday event. ⊠ *Magic Kingdom.*

Walt Disney World Marathon. Celebrating its 25th anniversary in 2018, the Walt Disney World Marathon Weekend attracts nearly 50,000 athletes from around the globe who compete in several races over several days. The most popular race of all is Sunday's 26.2-mile marathon, which takes runners through four theme parks and the ESPN Wide World of Sports Complex, and keeps runners motivated with entertainment and Disney magic along the way. Saturday is reserved for the 13.1-mile half marathon (through the Magic Kingdom and Epcot); "Goofy's Race and a Half" is a two-day (Saturday and Sunday), 39.3 mile race through four theme parks. A 10K race on Friday and a 5K race on Thursday completes the calendar. So run, don't walk, and sign up now. ⊠ *Walt Disney World* ⊕ *www.rundisney.com.*

Spring

Mardi Gras at Universal Studios. One of the year's most popular events, Mardi Gras at Universal Studios is held on select evenings between February and April), bringing the spirit of New Orleans to Orlando in a family-friendly festival. In addition to colorful floats, stilt walkers, New Orleans–style food and drinks, zydeco bands, and the distribution of nearly two million beads, there is a full calendar of concerts with groups like Heart, Styx, the B52s, Kelly Clarkson, and Olivia Newton John. Best of all, all of it—the parades, shows, and performances—is free with park admission. ⊠ *Universal Studios* ⊕ *https://www.universalorlando.com/ Events/Mardi-Gras/.*

Winter Park Sidewalk Art Festival. Let the theme parks have their high-tech attractions. For locals, it is this low-key community event that captures their hearts. Since 1960, the juried Winter Park Sidewalk Art Festival has found posh Park Avenue and oak-shaded Central Park filled with paintings, sculptures, and myriad works of art displayed by more than 225 artists and exhibitors. In 2016 the Art Fair Calendar ranked it No. 4 among the year's Best Art Fairs, and other accolades include the Art Fair Source Book's listing in their Top 10 Fine Art Shows, 2016 and Sunshine Artist Magazine's Top 100. Taking place during the third weekend of March, an estimated 350,000 visitors peruse this outdoor gallery, enhanced by food vendors, art workshops for children and adults, and the upscale shops of peaceful Park Avenue. If you're in the neighborhood, this art festival is a must. ⊠ *Park Ave. and Central Park, Winter Park* ⊕ *www.wpsaf.org.*

Summer

City of Kissimmee July 4th Celebration. Starting at 5 pm on the shores of Kissimmee's Lake Tohopekaliga (aka Lake Toho), the city makes the most of the Fourth of July and its Lakefront Park with live music by artists you would recognize, entertainment, food, and children's events and activities. Just after 9 pm, the sky explodes with thunderous and colorful fireworks that rattle this still slow-paced cattle community on the doorstep of Disney. ⊠ *Kissimmee.*

Fireworks at the Fountain. The focal point of Orlando isn't Cinderella Castle, it's the Rainbow Fountain at Downtown's Lake Eola, which was built in 1957 and, after being struck by lightning in 2009, was given a $2 million makeover to reflect Orlando's origins as "The City Beautiful." The fountain is so beloved by residents that the city used its profile as Orlando's official logo. On all other nights of the year, the fountain is illuminated with a choreographed six-minute show set to music, with the colors and songs changing with the season. But on the Fourth of July, the main event is a free celebration that begins in the afternoon with games, food, and live entertainment. Encircling the picturesque lake is a one-mile promenade that gives everyone a perfect vantage point to watch fireworks burst high above Lake Eola Park. ⊠ *Lake Eola Park, Downtown Orlando* ⊕ *www.cityoforlando.net/fireworks/.*

A Sci-Fi 4th of July. The Disney-planned community of Celebration teamed up with MegaCon (the renowned comic book, fantasy, gaming, and sci-fi convention) to create the Sci-Fi 4th of July; a festival-themed costume contest tied to a science fiction theme. The community celebration also features live music, dancing, games, activities for kids, costume contests, and fireworks. ⊠ *Celebration* ⊕ *celebrationtowncenter.com/events/.*

Gay Days Orlando. In early June, Gay Days Orlando brings more than 150,000 members of the gay, lesbian, bisexual, and transgendered community to Orlando, primarily arriving to visit theme parks—although Disney makes a point to say they don't "officially sponsor or promote" the event. Started in 1991 as a single day when participants wore red shoes as an identifier, it gathered steam and is now the largest such gathering in the world. The weeklong Gay Days event includes DJ parties, pool parties, music, and events throughout the metro area. ⊠ *Orlando* ☎ *407/896–8431* ⊕ *www.gaydays.com.*

Fall

Epcot International Food & Wine Festival. A must for foodies, for six weeks (late September through mid-November) the Epcot International Food & Wine Festival transforms the park into a food-and-wine wonderland with tasting seminars, culinary demonstrations, and a constant stream of celebrity chefs. Dine around the world at international marketplaces selling tasty bites, or splurge on wine schools and signature dinner events. Adding to the epicurean event is the Eat to the Beat concert series, featuring popular hit makers such as The Commodores, Pointer Sisters, Christopher Cross, and Squeeze. ⊠ *World Showcase, Epcot* ⊕ *https://disneyworld. disney.go.com/events-tours/epcot/epcot-international-food-and-wine-festival/.*

Halloween Horror Nights. Much more intense than your average haunted house, this extremely popular event incorporates all the special effects and movie make-up skills you'd expect from one of the leaders in the horror genre. Each evening, the streets of Universal Studios are transformed into chill-inducing haunted houses and scare zones populated by characters from your worst nightmares. A new theme is introduced each year, but at heart this terror-rific event has a simple purpose: to attract teens and young adults who can't get enough of its heart-pounding horrors. Admission for this after-park-hours event is less than the price of regular park admission. ⊠ *Universal Studios* ⊕ *www. halloweenhorrornights.com.*

Macy's Holiday Parade. In New York, you can experience Macy's famous parade just once a year. Come to Universal Studios between November and into early January and you can take in an abridged version of the parade every day of your visit. Featuring Macy's floats and balloons shipped to Orlando following the Big Apple event, the Universal Studios version features marching bands from across America, a Christmas tree lighting ceremony, and shines a spotlight on Barney, the Blues Brothers, and other Universal celebs. ⊠ *Universal Studios* ⊕ *www. universalorlando.com.*

Mickey's Not-So-Scary Halloween Party. As a marked contrast to Universal's Halloween Horror Nights, at Disney's Magic Kingdom kids in costumes own the streets during their quest for treats (no tricks!) at Mickey's Not-So-Scary Halloween Party. The gently spooky celebration takes place on scheduled evenings throughout September and October. Party tickets are priced below regular park admission, and it's easier to meet the characters and avoid ride queues. ⊠ *Magic Kingdom.*

WALT DISNEY WORLD GREAT ITINERARIES

Walt Disney World can be overwhelming. Take a breath, relax, and consider this approach.

If You Have One Day

If you have only one day to experience the essence of Disney, there's only one way to do it: visit the Magic Kingdom. Walt Disney's genius is on full display in this park adapted from his original at California's Disneyland, and you'll feel the pixie dust as soon as you step through the turnstiles.

Main Street, U.S.A. is a step into the past with horse-drawn streetcars rolling past, a barbershop quartet, and turn-of-the-20th-century buildings.

Ahead, the draw is Cinderella Castle, the focal point of the park. On your left Adventureland features two must-sees: the Jungle Cruise and its wisecracking skippers and Pirates of the Caribbean, an entertaining boat ride that inspired the movie franchise.

Continue your clockwise walk and enter Frontierland where the standouts are the Big Thunder Mountain Railroad, a roller coaster mine train; Splash Mountain, a water flume ride through scenes from *Song of the South*; and the Country Bear Jamboree, the classic attraction featuring a band of hillbilly bears. Liberty Square adjoins Frontierland with two more Disney classics: spooky Haunted Mansion and the inspiring Hall of Presidents.

A new and improved Fantasyland is next. Completed in 2014, a $400-million renovation (which, incredibly was the entire cost of the Walt Disney World resort when it opened in 1971) added new attractions including the Beast's Castle, Princess Fairytale Hall, and the Seven Dwarfs Mine Train to join It's a Small World and Dumbo the Flying Elephant, Under the Sea–Voyage of the Little Mermaid, and Prince Charming's Regal Carousel.

Tomorrowland offers a retro-futuristic look in favorites like the Speedway and Space Mountain. Your round-trip complete, be sure to include time to watch a parade or circle the park via an authentic steam train.

If You Have Four Days

If you have the good fortune to spend four days at Disney, you have to see each of its four theme parks. After visiting the Magic Kingdom on Day One, you can slow down the pace at Epcot—but be prepared for a lot of walking. The park is divided into two sections: Future World and the World Showcase, with the former—at the entrance to the park—opening an hour earlier than its neighbor. Although it lacks the magic of the Magic Kingdom, Future World can be entertaining with high-tech demonstrations in the Innoventions areas and the virtual hang-gliding adventure at Soarin'.

But what most Epcot visitors talk about is exploring the World Showcase. If travel abroad is out of your budget, you can test drive visits to exotic locations. At nearly every international pavilion—Canada, Great Britain, France, Morocco, Japan, United States, Italy, Germany, China, Norway, Mexico—there is usually entertainment (a movie, live show, street theater), a restaurant, art gallery, and a variety of gift shops. That evening, stick around for the grand finale. IllumiNations: Reflections of Earth is an over-the-top fireworks and laser show that wraps up the day with a dazzling finish.

On Day Three, plan a day at Disney's Hollywood Studios. Inspired by the golden age of the silver screen, the park ushers you in past classic Tinseltown landmarks. Must-sees here include the Muppet*Vision 3D, Star Tours: The Adventure Continues, Indiana Jones Epic Stunt Spectacular!, and the mind-blowing Twilight Zone Tower of Terror. After dark, thousands of park guests flood into the Hollywood hills to watch the final show of the evening, Fantasmic!, a celebration of classic Disney films and characters accompanied by music, songs, water effects, and fireworks.

Day Four brings you to the Disney's Animal Kingdom, one of the most interesting parks you'll find. Two continents—and a new world—create the park. Just off the Oasis (the junglelike area just past the turnstiles), is Pandora–The World of Avatar. New in 2017, it turns the two-dimensional film blockbuster into a three-dimensional world with upside-down trees and a chance to fly on the back of a mountain banshee. In the center of the park, the Tree of Life conceals the don't miss 4-D film *It's Tough to Be a Bug!*, a comedy that shows how insects affect our lives and includes sensations that'll make you shiver—and laugh.

Farther inside the park, you'll enter Africa, where you'll find the Kilimanjaro Safari is extremely popular, since it offers a chance to see hippos, lions, giraffes, baboons, and more. But get there early because the wildlife is more active in the morning before the day gets too hot. Asia is filled with photo ops—and one incredible coaster. Expedition Everest takes you high into the Himalayas in search of the fabled yeti, and at the very peak of the mountain a surprise twist finds the entire coaster racing backward through the hills. Nearby, the Kali River Rapids offers similar thrills but via a whitewater raft ride. Look for shows, animal encounters, street performers, and the retro amusement park thrills of DinoLand U.S.A. and you'll easily pack in a full day.

If You Have Seven Days

If you can spend a full week at Walt Disney World, you'll enjoy a vacation that few have had the privilege to experience.

Follow the Day Four suggestions (above), then take the fifth to recharge and relax. That evening, head to Disney Springs, take in a movie, go bowling at Splitsville, or watch a live concert at the House of Blues.

Wherever you place your "free day," you're now up to Day Six—and this is a good time to pay a return visit to your favorite theme park, especially if you purchased a multiple-day "all-parks" pass. Since you have a full day to explore, consider splitting up your time between two parks—perhaps Animal Kingdom for an early morning safari and Epcot or the Magic Kingdom to see that evening's fireworks display.

On Day Seven, start to wind things down. Theme parks are still an option, but it's also a good time to review the list of souvenirs you need to take home. That evening, make a reservation for dinner at the California Grill atop the Contemporary Resort (which is also a wonderful vantage point to watch fireworks over the Magic Kingdom), or go all out and dine at Victoria & Albert's at the Grand Floridian—one of the rare AAA Five Diamond restaurants in Florida.

What a week! Thanks, Walt!

ORLANDO GREAT ITINERARIES

AWAY FROM THE THEME PARKS

If you need a break from theme parks, or if you have people in your group who aren't interested in them—or if have an extra day or week—keep in mind that it's easy to get out and explore Central Florida. You'll find plenty of things to do and see outside the parks, particularly since Orlando is just one hour from the Atlantic Ocean and 90 minutes from the Gulf of Mexico.

If You Have One Day

If you head east from Orlando via SR528 (the Beachline Expressway, a toll road), you can be at the Kennedy Space Center in about an hour. It's an easy drive if you have a car, but you can also take an organized tour for about $100 per person. The exhibitions on American space travel and the pioneer astronauts who were launched into space from the Cape have enthralled visitors from around the world. The IMAX 3-D films and Shuttle Launch Experience are highlights, but the two most impressive sights are the space shuttle Atlantis, which takes center stage at the wonderfully educational and entertaining Atlantic Exhibit (enhanced by movies, simulators, and hands-on experiments). A bus tour will take you to the Saturn V Center, where there's an actual Saturn V built for an Apollo mission that was never launched, as well as early spacesuit protoypes, the Apollo XIV capsule, and even a moon rock you can touch. With the right timing, you may even see an actual SpaceX or Delta rocket rising from the nearby launch pads. On an overnight stay, you can lounge on the blissful beaches of Canaveral National Seashore, catch a wave like surfing legend (and local hero) Kelly

Slater, or explore the adjacent 140,000-acre Merritt Island National Wildlife Refuge. There are also opportunities for horseback riding, hiking, bird-watching, and fishing. Cape Canaveral and Cocoa Beach make great bases if you want to explore the region further.

If it's Saturday and you're looking for a quieter alternative, head out early so you can start your spree at the Winter Park Farmers' Market, where there's free valet parking. Stalls sell locally sourced foods—including breakfast—and crafts. Regardless of the day, Park Avenue's boutiques and galleries—including Ten Thousand Villages and Timothy's—beckon. They line the east side, opposite an oak-shaded park. An alfresco lunch will carry you through an afternoon of still more shopping. In the evening, head to Orlando's Sand Lake Road for a plethora of multicultural cuisines—from Italian and Mediterranean to Thai, Mexican, Indian, and Hawaiian fusion.

If You Have Four Days

Spend a day at Kennedy Space Center, but then explore Orlando itself. Among the highlights here are the Mennello Museum of Folk Art in Loch Haven Park. If you have kids, the Orlando Science Center, across the street, is a great alternative, and you can check to see what's playing at the adjoining Orlando Shakespeare Theater. If it's a nice day, explore the 50-acre Harry P. Leu Gardens, home to subtropical flora and a huge Floral Clock from Scotland. Arrive for one of the day's first guided tours (they start at 10) of the Leu House Museum.

Before returning to your hotel, a stroll around Downtown's tranquil and beautiful Lake Eola Park brings views of the resident swans and waterbirds, along with the centerpiece fountain. Have a snack in the park's Relax Grill or at one of the many eateries in trendy Thornton Park. Afterward there are many happy hours at the bars or clubs of Orange Avenue. The Dr. Phillips Center for the Performing Arts showcases A-list musicians, bands, and stage shows.

On your remaining three days, you can continue your exploration of the museums at the Orlando Museum of Art in Loch Haven Park, with its stunning permanent collection of pre-Columbian artifacts from South and Central America. Downtown's Orange County Regional History Museum offers several floors of family-friendly and gently educational local history. Winter Park's crowning jewel, the Charles Hosmer Morse Museum of American Art, houses the world's most complete collection of Tiffany windows, art glass, and ceramics. If you need some time outdoors, take a picnic on Winter Park's scenic boat tour, which offers a pleasant two-hour voyage through lakes and canals, past luxurious homes and the campus of Rollins College, the Southeast's oldest hall of academe. Central Florida's subtropical ecosystem contains lush natural greenery and wildlife that can be observed at several nearby state and local parks. The Audubon Center for Birds of Prey in Maitland houses injured eagles, hawks, owls, vultures, and more who cannot return safely to the wild. Just to the north is Wekiwa Springs State Park, where you can swim in crystal clear waters that power up from the Florida Aquifer, or rent a canoe to slip silently along the river, to glimpse alligators, turtles, herons, eagles, cranes, deer, and even bears. Blue Spring State Park, a few miles farther north, is winter home to hundreds of manatees. A raised boardwalk meanders along the river to the springhead so you can observe the manatees, without disturbing them.

If You Have Seven Days

Expanding your range, one of Florida's most charming towns is Mount Dora, about 40 minutes northwest of Walt Disney World. The New England–style community rests on the shores of 4,500-acre Lake Dora and is centered around a historic shopping village filled with boutiques, gift shops, bakeries, bookstores, sidewalk cafés, and quiet parks. You could also spend a day shopping at one of Orlando's many outlet malls, explore the old-time Florida attraction Gatorland in nearby Kissimmee, drive out to Lake Wales to see beautiful Bok Tower Gardens, or head to Sanford along the St. John River, where you can visit the Central Florida Zoo & Botanical Gardens.

ORLANDO WEDDINGS AND HONEYMOONS

Orlando and its theme parks have become increasingly popular shower, wedding, and honeymoon destinations. The area appeals to starry-eyed young couples and, more and more, older couples, some marrying for the second time and many bringing family and friends in for the wedding-vacation-reunion of a lifetime. They come from across the United States and throughout the world, and their ideas of the perfect wedding vary greatly.

Disney has created a cottage industry from weddings. Just visit ⊕ *www.disneyweddings.com* and you can begin designing the wedding of your dreams, picking and choosing among hundreds of locations and enhancements until your imagination (or bank account) runs dry. One bride made an entrance in Cinderella's glass coach; her groom rode in on a white horse. A thrill-seeking couple took the free-fall plunge on the Tower of Terror at Disney's Hollywood Studios. Two couples, on separate occasions, tied the knot in the middle of their Walt Disney World Marathon run, exchanging vows in front of Cinderella Castle at the Magic Kingdom. Moonlight on the Ritz-Carlton lawn set the scene for another couple's romantic vow exchange, and a rooftop Orlando wedding wowed yet another couple's guests with a 360-degree view of the Downtown skyline and scenic Lake Eola Park.

Prewedding Events

Showers and bachelor and bachelorette parties are easy to arrange in a city where there's so much to do—provided you have much money to spend. At Disney the Mad Hatter can show up for a bridesmaids' tea event at the Grand Floridian. Parties can begin with dinner and a wine tasting at Hannibal's wine cellar in Winter Park

before moving on to a local nightclub. Grooms who stay at Portofino Bay like to party at Universal CityWalk because no driving is required—a ferry will shuttle them back to the hotel.

For rehearsal dinners (or wedding receptions or honeymoons), Disney pulls out the stops to stage events ranging from an after-hours reception in one of the theme parks to an internationally themed event at one of the World Showcase countries in Epcot.

Weddings

You can opt for a traditional ceremony at Disney's Wedding Pavilion on the Seven Seas Lagoon by the Grand Floridian Resort & Spa. Designed with the charming features of a Victorian summerhouse, the pavilion is an airy room with a view of Cinderella Castle just across the lagoon. Alternatively you can plan an informal beachside vow exchange at a lakeside Disney resort; a garden or gazebo ceremony; an over-the-top, Cinderella-style wedding; or a Broadway-themed blowout.

Downtown Orlando and historic Winter Park are popular wedding destinations as well. Elegant, yet, affordable, lakefront ceremonies are popular, with a variety of waterfront pavilions and gardens available in picturesque city and county parks and botanical gardens.

Other top wedding spots are Downtown's Orange County Regional History Center; the Mennello Museum of American Art in the city's Loch Haven area; and Casa Feliz, a historic Spanish home–museum in Winter Park.

Another factor that makes Orlando the perfect choice for a wedding is the city's wealth of entertainment and resort hotels. Theme-park musicians and other performers often hire out for receptions t reasonable prices, and there's a lot of diversity, from zydeco and salsa bands to groups that specialize in swing music. Resort hotels like the Four Seasons, the Ritz-Carlton, Waldorf Astoria, and Portofino Bay at Universal feature romantic backdrops for the ceremony plus smaller ballrooms ideal for receptions. The hotels can also support activities ranging from spa parties to golf outings for those in the wedding party.

Honeymoons

Central Florida resorts cater to honeymooners with special packages. Honymoon suites with whirlpools and other amenities create the backdrop for romance that's enhanced with extras like champagne and chocolate-covered strawberries. Resort pools with cabanas, beaches, waterfalls, swaying palms, and poolside margarita delivery make the subtropical setting seem as exotic as a tropical island.

Disney's Fairy Tale Honeymoons division helps you customize a vacation package and even offers a Honeymoon Registry if your guests wish to contribute to your postwedding getaway rather than give a traditional gift. There are package deals to be had at Walt Disney World resorts and at Disney's Vero Beach Resort. Some couples make their wedding dreams or vow renewals come true at sea, where the honeymoon follows immediately.

Planning Tips

If you're dreaming about a Central Florida wedding, keep these tips from the experts in mind:

■ If your budget can handle the expense, hire a reputable planner long before the big date. Though you'll pay a fee for your planner, he or she will be an advocate with barter power when dealing with vendors.

■ For a destination wedding, build in plenty of time to book travel arrangements and accommodations for all who plan to attend.

■ If your budget is tight, plan your Orlando wedding between Monday and Thursday during nonpeak season for the lowest hotel rates.

■ Split the wedding-planning tasks with your partner. If the groom is focused more on the reception's music, food, and beverages, the bride can focus on, say, wedding flowers and photography.

■ Let your wedding planner arrange romantic escapes from your guests, especially if you plan to wed and honeymoon in Orlando. If everyone's staying at the Gaylord Palms Resort or the Hard Rock Hotel, have your wedding planner book you a spa package at the Waldorf Astoria or Ritz-Carlton.

■ Start your research by visiting several Orlando-area wedding-planner websites: Visit Orlando at ⊕ www.visitorlando.com/weddings, and Disney's Fairy Tale Weddings & Honeymoons at ⊕ www.disneyweddings.disney.go.com.

DISNEY CRUISES

When Disney first went to sea in 1998, some assumed their single ship—the *Disney Magic*—would be the lone vessel in its fleet. But the *Disney Wonder* made its debut the following year. Very quickly passengers found the experience of sailing with Disney's level of style, class, characters, and theming proved so popular that Disney Cruise Line (DCL) leaped to the top of cruise passenger favorites. As a result, two more ships joined the fleet—the *Disney Dream* in 2011 and the *Disney Fantasy* in 2014, with three more ships scheduled to set sail in 2021, 2022, and 2023.

Disney Cruise Line. To book any Disney cruise or to check into vessels, staterooms, shore excursions, and more, contact the Disney Cruise Line. ☎ *800/370–0097* ⊕ *www.disneycruise.com.*

For Guests with Disabilities
Accessible staterooms for people with disabilities have ramps, handrails, fold-down shower seats, and handheld showerheads; special communications kits are available with phone alerts, amplifiers, and text typewriters. Assisted-listening systems are available in the ships' main theaters, and sign-language interpretation is offered for live performances on specified cruise dates.

Adult Activities
Poolside games, wine tastings, and behind-the-scenes seminars are among the adults-only diversions. Each ship's spa is a don't-miss for those who need some pampering—book early!

For a romantic dinner, the intimate, adults-only **Palo** (*all ships*) offers sweeping ocean views. Expect a fantastic wine list and dishes such as grilled salmon with creamy risotto and grilled filet mignon with a port-wine reduction and Gorgonzola cheese sauce. Reserve early for this hot ticket. The champagne brunch is another great Palo dining event.

The decor in the *Dream*'s and *Fantasy*'s exclusive 80-seat restaurant, **Remy,** is a nod to the movie *Ratatouille,* and, of course, the cuisine is French inspired. The eight or nine tasting dishes served each night might include Kurobata pork tenderloin and belly with corn ragout and wild turbot with lemon, capers, and spinach. Wine pairings are amazing; so are the pastries. Remy also has a champagne brunch. Book as far ahead of your trip as possible.

Children's Activities
More than a few prospective passengers have passed on DCL, assuming the decks would be cluttered with kids. On the contrary—on all four ships, there's nearly an entire deck reserved for kids and you may enjoy a complete voyage without ever noticing them. Making it better for parents—and even better for the kids—are activity centers divided by age groups, from kids 10 and younger, for "tweens" 11–14, and for older teens ages 14–17. Counselors keep them focused with a wide-ranging assortment of activities including playrooms, rope bridges, scavenger hunts, science experiments, sports challenges, karaoke games, video games, trivia contests, and evening dance parties. While you're having fun with other adults, kids are literally have a ball on their own level. To help stay in touch, an onboard mobile phone service keeps you connected with activities counselors.

Restaurants
Dining is one of the most anticipated experiences aboard the Disney ships, and the **Animator's Palate** is a favorite. Scenes featuring Disney characters

change from black-and-white to Technicolor as the meal progresses on the *Magic* and *Wonder*; on the *Dream* and *Fantasy,* diners are surrounded by an artist's studio where famous film scenes line the walls and fiber-optic "brush pillars" paint oversize ceiling "palettes" in vibrant colors. Dining is slightly more formal at **Lumiere's,** on the *Magic,* where beef tenderloin, lamb shank, and other entrées are served French style in a classic ocean-liner-style dining room.

At **Triton's,** on the *Wonder,* seafood, roast duck, pasta, and other selections are served in an elegant, art deco, under-the-sea-themed dining room. The *Dream's* **Royal Palace** and the *Fantasy* 's **Royal Court** are inspired by Disney's princess films, with menus that may include crowned rack of lamb, beef Wellington, and other royal dishes. At the Caribbean-themed **Parrot Cay** restaurant (*Wonder*) and the new Rio de Janeiro–themed **Carioca's** (*Magic*), the mood is casual and festive. On the *Fantasy* and *Dream*, **Enchanted Garden** is the whimsical, more informal rotation restaurant. Character breakfasts are offered one morning on most seven-nights-or-longer sailings.

After-Dark Entertainment

Few can out-do Disney entertainment, and the level of stage shows, on-deck performances, and character greetings—Disney, Star Wars, and Marvel superheroes among them—is spectacular. **Lavish shows** and variety acts entertain families every night of every cruise. The over-the-top theatricals with Broadway-quality sets and staging are often musicals based on Disney's biggest blockbuster hits. You may see a *Toy Story* musical or an extravaganza based on *Frozen, Tangled, The Little Mermaid, Aladdin,* or *Beauty and the Beast*. Whatever is playing, prepare to be dazzled. The Golden Mickeys on the *Wonder* is a high-tech salute to the animation of Walt Disney in the form of a Hollywood-style awards ceremony. *Twice Charmed: An Original Twist on the Cinderella Story* is a Broadway-style production on *Magic* that begins where the original Cinderella story ended.

Each ship also has a **cinema** screening classic Disney films, and every guest has the opportunity to experience a show or film featuring digital 3-D enhancements.

In addition to shows and shore excursions, a wide assortment of bars, lounges, dance clubs, piano bars, Irish pubs, sports bars, and nightclubs across the four ships appeals to adults. The best way to find one you prefer is to spend a few hours exploring the ship, checking the maps, and circling the decks to get your bearings and finding the places that are perfect for you and the mood you're in. Everyone, it seems, is in the mood for the **Pirate Night event** when swashbuckling servers dish up Caribbean and Bahamian taste treats, a cup of grog, and (on seven-night cruises) a pirate bandanna for every dinner guest. After dinner, you head off to a deck party where Captain Hook, Mr. Smee, and others appear for some high-spirited action, dancing, and fireworks.

Castaway Cay

Disney's own private Bahamian island, Castaway Cay, is paradise found. When the ship docks and passengers go ashore, they step into a land of white-sand beaches, towering palms, swaying hammocks, and abundant food. You can relax on the beach or join a snorkeling or parasailing excursion.

DID YOU KNOW?

Mickey Mouse was the inspiration for the Disney ships' colors—black hull, white superstructure, yellow trim and lifeboats, and giant red funnels (a color scheme that took some conversation with the government agencies who had rules in place regarding lifeboat colors). The ships recall classic ocean liners of the 1930s, and when the captain hits the horn, it plays the first seven notes of "When You Wish Upon a Star."

DOING ORLANDO AND THE PARKS RIGHT

by Jennie Hess

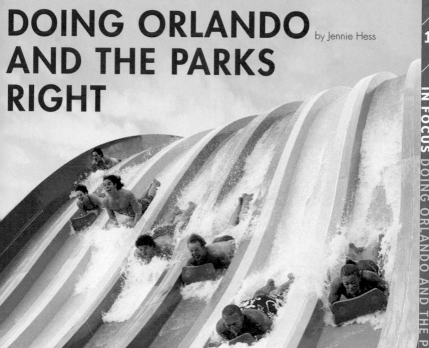

aumata Racer, Aquatica

You don't have to wish upon a star to make all your Orlando vacation dreams come true. Your trip will be memorable, whether you're traveling with small children, tweens, teens, or the whole gang of friends or family; whether you're on your honeymoon or flying solo.

Gather (or cyber-gather) all your travel companions together to create a wish list. Then, as you create your itinerary, consider everyone's needs and plan accordingly.

Got small children? Know their theme-park limits to prevent meltdowns, and factor in time away from crowded parks for a laid-back visit to smaller attractions. And, to avoid disappointments, don't wait to get to the parks to determine ride height restrictions.

Teens and tweens may want to head for some rides on their own. Determine theme-park meeting locations, and be sure everyone carries a cell phone in case they encounter longer ride lines and delays.

If the guys are planning to hit the links and the gals want a spa day, don't wait until you're in town to reserve a tee time or a facial-mani-pedi package.

What follows are suggestions (and a few quick tips) on how you can do Orlando and the parks right—regardless of who's in your group. For more planning tips and insights, check out Chapter 1.

Shamu's Happy Harbor play area, SeaWorld

Pirates of the Caribbean, Magic Kingdom

FAMILIES WITH SMALL KIDS

Things will go more smoothly if you stick to routines. It's easier than you think. During naptime, for instance, you can relax on a bench while your toddler snoozes in her stroller and the rest of the family heads for a park attraction. Finding sights for wee ones is easy in the parks and outside.

Magic Kingdom. This is the top Disney destination for families with tots. Fantasyland has a treasure trove of age-appropriate attractions. Tom Sawyer Island lets squirmy kids burn up some energy.

SeaWorld. Dolphins, whales, and other marine mammals mesmerize young children. Most shows are captivating, and Shamu's Happy Harbor is a wet, wonderful play area.

Typhoon Lagoon. It sets an idyllic water-park scene for families with small children. Ketchakiddie Creek is a favorite splash zone.

Orlando Science Center. Exhibits—many of them interactive—at this center near downtown Orlando let kids experience science and the world around them.

Disney Springs. A kiddie carousel, splash fountains, a LEGO Imagination Center, Bibbidi Bobbidi Boutique (think princess makeovers) are among the attractions for kids.

FAMILIES WITH TWEENS

You and your tweens will have more fun together if you involve them in pre-trip planning. Let each child scope out best bets on Orlando- and theme-park Web sites, then gather to compare notes and create a rough itinerary. Here are a few suggestions to jumpstart the research.

Magic Kingdom. Who ever really outgrows this classic? Tweens love rides ending in "mountain"—Space, Splash, and Big Thunder. The Haunted Mansion and Pirates of the Caribbean are both cool.

Islands of Adventure. This theme-park will be a hit with tweens who love thrill rides and/or superheroes like Spider-Man. For muggle fans of J.K. Rowling's books, the Wizarding World of Harry Potter is a must-see.

Disney's Animal Kingdom. The exotic animals and safari are highlights, but so are scream-inducing Expedition Everest, DINOSAUR, Kali River Rapids, and Avatar Flight of Passage.

Hollywood Studios. The addition of Toy Story Land has brought a new family coaster (Slinky Dog Dash) and Alien Swirling Saucer.

Fun Spot. Tweens love the go-kart racetrack best, but the carnival-style rides and arcades are a big draw, too.

WonderWorks. Tweens can "build" their own coaster, and then ride it; lie on a bed of nails; and pilot a simulated fighter jet.

Incredible Hulk Coaster, Islands of Adventure

Sleuths Mystery Dinner Show, Orlando

FAMILIES WITH TEENS

Let teens make their own "gotta do" list and head out on their own. (Chances are at least some of the sights below will make it to every list.) Stay in touch by texting updates and meeting for meals.

Disney's Hollywood Studios. Teens rave about The Twilight Zone Tower of Terror and Rock 'n' Roller Coaster Starring Aerosmith. Competing in Toy Story Midway Mania! is another cool option.

Islands of Adventure. Older kids are drawn to the action here—from the Amazing Adventures of Spider-Man to the Incredible Hulk Coaster.

Universal Studios. Teens love Hollywood Rip Ride Rockit, Revenge of the Mummy, and The Wizarding World of Harry Potter.

Blizzard Beach and Volcano Bay. Blizzard stands out for its wintry theme, mix of thrills, and laid-back "beach" scene. Volcano Bay has loud music and big-thrill slides.

Universal CityWalk. It gets high marks for trendy shopping, movie theaters, and concerts. The theatrics of Blue Man Group is a big teen draw around the corner.

Spa with Mom. Mother-daughter facials and pedicures make for a fun morning or afternoon at Orlando spas like the Buena Vista Palace or Disney's Grand Floridian.

LARGE, MIXED GROUPS

Look into Disney's vacation-planning program, Grand Gatherings. Just remember that group members will be happier campers with some "me" time factored in. Here are some suggestions for shared and individual experiences.

Behind-the-Scenes Park Tours. Tours at SeaWorld, Magic Kingdom, Epcot, and Animal Kingdom are great shared experiences. Note that the more people you have on the expensive but oh-so-cool VIP tour at Universal, the better value it is.

Dinner shows. Some area favorites are Medieval Times in Kissimmee, Sleuths Mystery Dinner Show on I-Drive, and Disney's Hoop-Dee-Doo Revue.

Discovery Cove. Book a "beach" day here to share the experience of swimming with the dolphins. Meals and snacks are included.

Epcot. Everyone can fan out here to take in the attractions of Future World or World Showcase and then gather for dinner at a reserved table to share experiences.

Spa Visits and Golf Expeditions. These are perfect "breakaway" activities. And there are options for both at Disney and in the greater Orlando area.

Spring Training. In March, it's easy to arrange a group outing to a ballgame in one of several central Florida locations.

Islands of Adventure

Disney's Boardwalk

COUPLES

Let us count the ways to be romantic in Orlando . . . there are too many to list here. Even if the kids are along for the trip, you can carve out time together by using a hotel's sitter service or by packing the children off to a resort kids' club.

Victoria & Albert's. Splurge on a dinner fit for royalty at the Grand Floridian's elegant eatery, central Florida's only AAA Five-Diamond restaurant. Reserve months ahead.

Spa Treatments for Two. Top spas for couples pampering include those in the Ritz Carlton, Waldorf Astoria, Grand Floridian, Portofino Bay, Gaylord Palms, and Walt Disney World Dolphin, and the Four Seasons.

Wekiwa Springs State Park. Escape here for a picnic and/or to rent a canoe and share quiet time on the river.

Islands of Adventure and CityWalk. Plan a wild and crazy evening of roller-coaster thrills and then belly up to the bar for a cheeseburger in paradise at Jimmy Buffet's Margaritaville.

Lake Eola. Paddle a swan-shaped boat together at this lake in downtown Orlando. Then share flatbread and sip champagne at Eola Wine Company across the street.

SINGLES (OR GROUPS OF FRIENDS)

It's nice to have a traveling companion, but there's an advantage to visiting on your own—you can cover a lot more territory. Single but traveling with friends? You still may want to split up to sample from your own play list.

Animal Kingdom. Animal-loving singles can linger longer at this park to watch behaviors of many exotic creatures. Rough it on the excellent Wild Africa Trek for a fee.

Winter Park. On a day trip to this this town you can shop Park Avenue, take a scenic boat tour, and see the huge Tiffany collection at the Morse Museum of American Art.

Disney's Boardwalk. Let nostalgia take hold on a lakeside stroll. Or hop into a surrey or onto a bicycle built for two. Watch dueling pianos at Jellyrolls or a game at ESPN Club.

Run through the parks. Plan your visit in January and compete in the Walt Disney World Half- or Full Marathons—run both, and you'll go home with a Goofy medal as well as a Donald (half) and a Mickey (full)!

Tour new Worlds. Spend seven hours on Disney's Backstage Magic Tour of Magic Kingdom, Epcot, and Hollywood Studios. Or take one of SeaWorld's Spotlight tours into the penguin or dolphin backstage habitats.

EXPLORING WALT DISNEY WORLD

WELCOME TO WALT DISNEY WORLD

TOP REASONS TO GO

★ **Nostalgia:** Face it— Mickey and Company are old friends. And you probably have childhood pictures of yourself in front of Cinderella Castle. Even if you don't, nobody does yesteryear better: head to Main Street, U.S.A., or Hollywood Boulevard and see.

★ **Memories in the Making:** Who doesn't want to snap selfies on the Dumbo ride or of Junior after his Splash Mountain experience? The urge to pass that Disney nostalgia on to the next generation is strong.

★ **The Thrills:** For some this means hopping on the back of a Banshee and screaming down a cliff-face, or roller coasting to an Aerosmith sound track, or simulating space flight; for others it's about going on safari.

★ **The Chills:** If the Pirates of the Caribbean cave doesn't give you goose bumps, try the Haunted Mansion or Twilight Zone Tower of Terror.

★ **The Spectacle:** The list is long: fireworks, laser-light displays, arcade games, parades …

Walt Disney World straddles Orange and Osceola counties to the west of Interstate 4. Four exits will get you to the parks and resort areas: 64B, 65, 67, and 68. To reach hotels along I-Drive, use Exit 72, 74A, or 75A.

1 Magic Kingdom. Disney's emblematic park is home to Space Mountain, Pirates of the Caribbean, Fantasyland, and the iconic Cinderella Castle.

2 Epcot. Future World's focus is science, technology, and hands-on experiences. In the World Showcase, you can tour 11 countries without getting jet-lagged.

3 Disney's Hollywood Studios. Attractions at this park are focusing more on Star Wars and Toy Story, which will eventually be two new lands within the park. For now, Twilight Zone Tower of Terror and Rock 'n' Roller Coaster are still the source of screams.

4 Disney's Animal Kingdom. Amid a 403-acre wildlife preserve are an Asian-themed water ride, an African safari ride, a runaway-train coaster, and the futuristic world of Pandora.

5 Disney Springs. A dining, shopping and entertainment extravaganza, the Springs is celebrity-chef restaurant central, along with live music, a multilevel bowling alley, and enough shops to satisfy almost any desire.

6 Disney's BoardWalk. A wide boardwalk, reminiscent of turn-of-the-century Atlantic City leads past a vast dance hall, dueling-piano bar, a craft brewery, fine restaurants, and a sports fan's utopia where multiple screens show multiple games.

7 Blizzard Beach. Water thrills range from steep flume rides to tubing expeditions in the midst of a park that you'd swear is a slowly melting ski resort. There's plenty for little ones, too.

8 Typhoon Lagoon. Sandy beaches, oceanlike waves, and a themed water coaster invite castaways to enjoy a day of fun and relaxation. Take the kids on Bay Slides and the family fun raft ride Miss Adventure Falls.

2

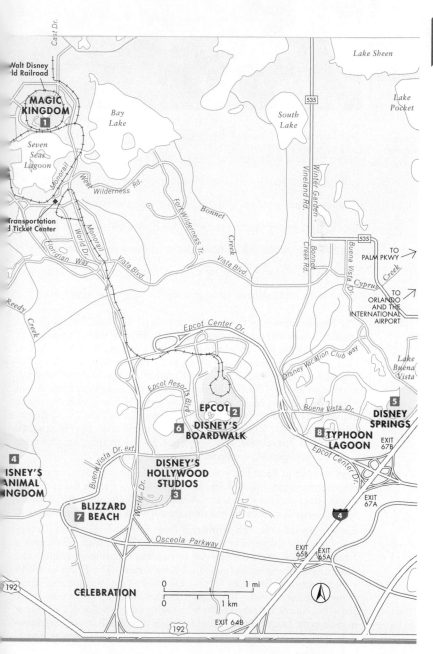

Lake Sheen

Lake Pocket

South Lake

535

Cast Dr.

Walt Disney World Railroad

MAGIC KINGDOM 1

Bay Lake

Seven Seas Lagoon

West Wilderness Rd.

Transportation and Ticket Center

Monorail

Floridian Way

World Dr.

Vista Blvd.

Fort Wilderness Tr.

Bonnet Creek

Vista Blvd.

Winter Garden - Vineland Rd.

Bonnet Creek Rd.

535

Buena Vista Dr.

Cyprus Creek

TO PALM PKWY

TO ORLANDO AND THE INTERNATIONAL AIRPORT

Epcot Center Dr.

Epcot Resorts Blvd.

Disney Vacation Club Way

Lake Buena Vista

EPCOT 2

DISNEY'S BOARDWALK 6

Buena Vista Dr.

DISNEY SPRINGS 5

TYPHOON LAGOON 8

EXIT 67B

DISNEY'S HOLLYWOOD STUDIOS 3

Buena Vista Dr. ext.

World Dr.

Epcot Center Dr.

EXIT 67A

4

DISNEY'S ANIMAL KINGDOM 4

BLIZZARD BEACH 7

Reedy Creek

Osceola Parkway

EXIT 65B

EXIT 65A

192

CELEBRATION

0   1 mi

0   1 km

EXIT 64B

192

Updated by Jennifer Greenhill-Taylor

Mickey Mouse. Tinker Bell. Cinderella. What would childhood be like without the magic of Disney? When kids and adults want to go to *the* theme park, they're heading to Disney. Here you're walking amid people from around the world and meeting characters like Snow White and Donald Duck while rides whirl nonstop and the irrepressible "it's a small world" tune and lyrics run through your head. You can't help but believe dreams really do come true here.

The **Magic Kingdom** is the heart and soul of the Walt Disney World empire. It was the first Disney outpost in Florida when it opened in 1971, and it's the park that launched Disney's presence in France, Japan, Hong Kong, and Shanghai. For a landmark that wields such worldwide influence, the 142-acre Magic Kingdom may seem small—indeed, Epcot is more than double the size of the Magic Kingdom, and Animal Kingdom is almost triple the size when including the park's expansive animal habitats. But looks can be deceiving. Packed into six different "lands" are nearly 50 major crowd-pleasers, and that's not counting all the ancillary attractions: shops, eateries, live entertainment, character meet-and-greet spots, fireworks shows, and parades.

Nowhere but at **Epcot** can you explore and experience the native food, entertainment, culture, and arts and crafts of countries in Europe, Asia, North Africa, and the Americas. What's more, employees at the World Showcase pavilions actually hail from the countries the pavilions represent.

Epcot, originally the "Experimental Prototype Community of Tomorrow," was the inspiration for Walt Disney World. Walt envisioned a future in which nations coexisted in peace and harmony, reaping the miraculous harvest of technological achievement. The Epcot of today is both more and less than his original dream. Less, because the World Showcase presents views of its countries that are, as an Epcot guide once put it, "as Americans perceive them"—highly idealized. But this is a minor quibble in the face of the major achievement: Epcot is that rare paradox—a successful educational theme park that excels at entertainment, too.

Disney's Hollywood Studios was designed to be a trip back to Tinseltown's golden age, but the park is now looking to the future, and the focus has shifted to spaceships and *Star Wars*.

The result is a theme park that blends movie nostalgia with breathtaking rides and *Star Wars* themes. The park's old-time Hollywood atmosphere begins with a rosy-hued view of the moviemaking business of the 1930s and '40s, amid sleek art-moderne buildings in pastel colors, funky diners, and kitschy decorations. Toy Story Land, expected in summer 2018, is where familiar childhood toys come to life. And, behind the construction fences, in a galaxy far, far away, *Star Wars* dreams are becoming reality.

Thanks to a rich library of film scores, the park is permeated with music, all familiar, all evoking the magic of the movies, including *Star Wars*, and all constantly streaming from the camouflaged loudspeakers at a volume just right for humming along.

Disney's Animal Kingdom explores the stories of all animals—real, imaginary, and extinct. Enter through the Oasis, where you hear exotic background music and find yourself surrounded by gentle waterfalls and gardens alive with exotic birds, reptiles, and mammals.

At 403 acres and several times the size of the Magic Kingdom, Animal Kingdom is the largest in area of all Disney theme parks. Animal habitats take up much of that acreage. Creatures here thrive in careful re-creations of landscapes from Asia and Africa. Throughout the park, you'll also learn about conservation in a low-key way.

Amid all the nature are thrill rides, a 3-D show (housed in the "root system" of the iconic Tree of Life), two first-rate musicals, and character meet and greets. Cast members are as likely to hail from Kenya or South Africa as they are from Kentucky or South Carolina. It's all part of the charm. Pandora—The World of Avatar, based on the movie *Avatar*, opened in 2017, a fitting addition, since the film's theme of living in harmony with nature reflects the park's eco-philosophy.

Typhoon Lagoon and **Blizzard Beach** are two of the world's best water parks. What sets them apart? It's the same thing that differentiates all Disney parks—the detailed themes. Whether you're cast away on a balmy island at Typhoon Lagoon or washed up on a ski-resort-turned-seaside-playground at Blizzard Beach, the landscaping and clever architecture will add to the fun of flume and raft rides, wave pools, and splash areas. Another plus: the vegetation has matured enough to create shade. The Disney water parks give you that lost-in-paradise feeling on top of all those high-speed, wedgie-inducing waterslides. They're so popular that crowds often reach overflow capacity in summer. If you're going to Disney for four days or more between April and October, add the Water Park Fun & More option to your Magic Your Way ticket.

PLANNING

ADMISSION

At the gate, the per-person, per-day price for Magic Kingdom guests is $107 for adults (ages 10 and older) and $101 for children (ages 3–9), depending on the season. Peak prices are considerably higher. At Disney's other three parks, Epcot, Hollywood Studios, and Animal Kingdom, the per-person, per-day price is $99 for adults (ages 10 and older) and $93 for children (ages 3–9). You can buy tickets at the Ticket and Transportation Center (TTC) in the Magic Kingdom, from booths at other park entrances, in all on-site resorts if you're a guest, at the Disney store in the airport, and at various other sites around Orlando. You can also buy them in advance online—the best way to save time and money.

If you opt for a multiday ticket, you'll be issued a nontransferable pass that uses your fingerprint for ID. Hold your pass up to the reader, just like people with single-day tickets, and also press your finger on the reader. If you have a MagicBand wristband it serves as park ticket, attraction Fastpass+ ticket, and even hotel room key.

OPERATING HOURS

Walt Disney World operates 365 days a year. Opening and closing times vary by park and by season, with the longest hours during prime summer months and year-end holidays. The parking lots open at least an hour before the parks do.

In general, openings hover around 9 am, though certain attractions might not start up till 10 or 11. Closings range between 5 and 8 pm in the off-season and between 8 and 10, 11, or even midnight in high season. Disney Springs and BoardWalk shops stay open as late as midnight.

EXTRA MAGIC HOURS

The Extra Magic Hours program gives Disney resort guests free early and late-night admission to certain parks on specified days—check ahead (*www.disneyworld.disney.go.com/calendars*) for information about each park's "magic hours" days to plan your early- and late-visit strategies.

PARKING AND IN-PARK TRANSPORT

Parking at Disney parks is free to resort guests; all others pay $20 for cars and $22 for RVs and campers. Parking is free for everyone at Typhoon Lagoon, Blizzard Beach, Downtown Disney, ESPN Wide World of Sports, and the BoardWalk. Trams take you between the theme-park lots (*note your parking location!*) and turnstiles. Disney's buses, boats, and monorails whisk you from resort to park and park to park. If you're staying on Disney property, you can use this system exclusively. Either take a Disney bus or drive to Typhoon Lagoon and Blizzard Beach. Once inside the water parks, you can walk, swim, slide, or chill out. Allow up to an hour for travel between parks and hotels on Disney transportation.

Disney *Magic Your Way* Price Chart

TICKET OPTIONS (PRICES ARE BEFORE SALES TAX)								
TICKET	**1-DAY**	**2-DAY**	**3-DAY**	**4-DAY**	**5-DAY**	**6-DAY**	**7-DAY**	**10-DAY**
BASE TICKET								
Ages 10–up	$102–$129	$209	$305	$380	$395	$405	$415	$445
Ages 3–9	$96–$123	$197	$287	$360	$375	$385	$395	$425

Base Ticket admits guest to one of the four major theme parks per day's use. A 1-day admission to the Magic Kingdom is more expensive than other parks.
Park choices are: Magic Kingdom, Epcot, Disney's Hollywood Studios, Disney's Animal Kingdom.
8- and 9-day tickets are also available.
Prices per ticket are $21.30 less when purchased in advanced.

ADD: Park Hopper	$62	$65	$65	$75	$75	$75	$75	$75

Park Hopper option entitles guest to visit more than one theme park per day's use. Park choices are any combination of Magic Kingdom, Epcot, Disney's Hollywood Studios, Disney's Animal Kingdom.

ADD: Park Hopper Plus	$90 2 visits	$90 2 visits	$90 3 visits	$90 4 visits	$100 5 visits	$100 6 visits	$100 7 visits	$100 10 visits

Park Hopper Plus option entitles guest to visit a choice of entertainment and recreation venues. Choices are Blizzard Beach, Typhoon Lagoon, Disney's Oak Trail golf course, Fantasia Gardens, Winter Summerland, and Wide World of Sports, in addition to the four theme parks.

MINOR PARKS AND ATTRACTIONS		
TICKET	**AGES 10–UP**	**AGES 3–9**
Typhoon Lagoon or Blizzard Beach 1-Day 1-Park	$65	$59
Disney's Oak Trail Golf Course 1-Day	$41.54	$22.37
Disney's ESPN Wide World of Sports	$19.70	$14.38
Disney's Fantasia Gardens or Winter Summerland	$14.91	$12.78

*All prices are subject to Florida sales tax

Get wet on the 12-story Summit Plummet at Disney's Blizzard Beach.

FASTPASS+

Fastpass+ helps you avoid lines, and it's included in regular park admission. Using the new My Disney Experience app or Fastpass+ kiosks in each park, you can select up to three attractions at one time; each appointment will give you a one-hour window within which you can experience each attraction. The Fastpass+ appointments are loaded directly to your plastic theme-park ticket or your MagicBand. It's best to make appointments only for the most popular attractions and to stick with the standby queue for attractions that aren't in such demand. Strategy is everything.

Guests can get Fastpass+ reservations for some designated character greetings, parades, and shows. These "experience" Fastpass+ reservations count just the same as those for the rides. You get three to start with (in a single park) and can add as many more as you have time for (and these can be in a different park if you have the Park Hopper option). Best Fastpass+ practices are explained by the program. It will direct you to the attractions where Fastpass+ is most helpful. If these attractions don't meet your family's specific needs—your kids are too young to ride coasters, for example—the program will also help you customize your Fastpass+ selections.

DISNEY STRATEGIES

Keep in mind these essential strategies, tried and tested by generations of Disney fans.

Buy tickets before leaving home. It saves money and gives you time to look into all the ticket options. It also offers an opportunity for you to consider vacation packages and meal plans and to register with the My Disney Experience program and mobile app for vacation planning.

Make dining reservations before leaving home. If you don't, you might find yourself eating fast food (again) or leaving Disney for dinner. On-site restaurants, especially those featuring character appearances, book up months ahead, and you can reserve 180 days before you arrive.

Arrive at least 30 minutes before the parks open. We know, it's your vacation and you want to sleep in. But you probably want to make the most of your time and money, too. Plan to be up by 7:30 am to get the most out of your park visits. After transit time, it'll take you 15–20 minutes to park, get to the gates, and pick up your park guide maps and *Times Guide*.

See top attractions in the morning. And we mean *first thing*. Decide in advance on your can't-miss attractions, find their locations, and hotfoot it to them before 10 am.

Use Fastpass+. The system is free, easy, more streamlined than ever with the new Fastpass+ online prebooking system, and it's your ticket to the top attractions with little or no waiting in line. Even if you wait to book once you're in the park, you can now schedule up to three Fastpass+ events at one time. Your attraction appointments are loaded onto your MagicBand or card, whichever you choose to use.

Use Baby Swap. Disney has a theme-park "rider switch" policy that works like this: one parent waits with the baby or toddler while the other parent rides the attraction. When the ride ends, they switch places with minimal wait.

Build in rest time. Start early and then leave the parks around 2 or 3 pm, thus avoiding the hottest and often most crowded period. After a couple of hours' rest at your hotel, head back for a nighttime spectacle or to ride a big-ticket ride (lines often are shorter around closing time).

Create an itinerary, but leave room for spontaneity. Don't try to plot your trip hour by hour. If you're staying at a Disney resort, find out which parks have Extra Magic Hours on which days.

Eat at off-hours. To avoid the mealtime rush hours, have a quick, light breakfast at 7 or 8 am, lunch at 11, and dinner at 5 or 6.

OTHER DISNEY SERVICES

If you can shell out $360–$500 an hour (with a six-hour minimum), you can take a customized **VIP Tour** with guides who help you park hop and get good seats at parades and shows. These tours don't help you skip lines, but they make navigating easy. Groups can have up to 10 people; book up to three months ahead.

FAMILY **WDW Tours.** Reserve with WDW Tours up to 180 days in advance for behind-the-scenes tours. Participant age requirements vary, so be sure to check before you book. ⊠ *Walt Disney World* ☎ *407/939–8687* ⊕ *www.disneyworld.com.*

Character meals. Mickey, Belle, and other characters sign autographs and pose for photos. Book through Disney's dining reservations line up to 180 days out; these hugging-and-feeding frenzies are wildly popular.

DISNEY CONTACTS

Cruise Line: ☎ *800/370–0097* ⊕ *www.disneycruise.com*

Dining Reservations: ☎ *407/939–3463*

Extra Magic Hours: ⊕ *www.disneyworld.disney.go.com/calendars*

Fairy-Tale Weddings: ☎ *321/939–4610* ⊕ *www.disneyweddings.disney. go.com*

Golf Reservations: ☎ *407/939–4653*

Guest Info: ☎ *407/824–4321*

VIP Tours: ☎ *407/560–4033*

WDW Travel Company: ☎ *407/828–8101*

Web: ⊕ *www.disneyworld.disney.go.com*

THE MAGIC KINGDOM

Whether you arrive at the Magic Kingdom via monorail, boat, or bus, it's hard to escape that surge of excitement or suppress that smile upon sighting the towers of Cinderella Castle or the spires of Space Mountain. So what if it's a cliché by now? There's magic beyond the turnstiles, and you aren't going to miss one memorable moment.

Most visitors have some idea of what they'd like to see and do during their day in the Magic Kingdom. Popular attractions like Space Mountain and Splash Mountain are on the lists of any thrill seeker, and Fantasyland is Destination One for parents of small children and seekers of moderate thrills like the Seven Dwarfs Mine Train. Visitors who steer away from wilder rides are first in line at the Jungle Cruise or Pirates of the Caribbean in Adventureland.

It's great to have a strategy for seeing the park's attractions, grabbing a bite to eat, or scouring the shops for souvenir gold. But don't forget that Disney Imagineers—the creative pros behind every themed land and attraction—are famous for their attention to detail. Your experience will be richer if you take time to notice the extra touches—from the architecture to the music and the costumes. The same genius is evident even in the landscape, from the tropical setting of Adventureland to the red-stone slopes of Frontierland's Big Thunder Mountain Railroad.

Wherever you go, watch for hidden Mickeys—silhouettes and abstract images of Mickey Mouse—tucked by Imagineers into every corner of the Kingdom. For instance, at the Haunted Mansion, look for him in the place settings in the banquet scene.

Much of the Magic Kingdom's pixie dust is spread by the people who work here, the costumed cast members who do their part to create fond memories for each guest who crosses their path. Maybe the grim ghoul who greets you solemnly at the Haunted Mansion will cause you to break down and giggle. Or the sunny shop assistant will help your

TOP ATTRACTIONS

FOR AGES SEVEN AND UP

Big Thunder Mountain Railroad. An Old West–theme, classic coaster that's not too scary; it's just a really good, bumpy, swervy thrill.

Buzz Lightyear's Space Ranger Spin. A shoot-'em-up ride where space-ranger wannabes compete for the highest score.

Haunted Mansion. With its razzle-dazzle special effects, this classic is always a frightful hoot.

Pirates of the Caribbean. Don't miss this family cruise through pirate territory, especially if you're a fan of the movies.

Seven Dwarfs Mine Train. Train cars sway gently to and fro during the rollicking, musical ride through a mine full of glittery gems.

Space Mountain. The Magic Kingdom's scariest ride zips you along the tracks in near-total darkness except for the stars.

FOR AGES SIX AND UNDER

Dumbo the Flying Elephant. The elephant ears get them every time, and the ride offers double the number of pachyderm vehicles as it did originally.

Enchanted Tales with Belle. Young girls and boys, and some parents, too, clamor to play characters from "Beauty and the Beast" in this well-done interactive story adventure.

The Magic Carpets of Aladdin. On this must-do for preschoolers, you can make your carpet go up and down to avoid occasional water spurts as mischievous camels spit at you.

The Many Adventures of Winnie the Pooh. Hang on to your honey pot as you get whisked along on a windy-day adventure with Pooh, Tigger, Eeyore, and friends.

Under the Sea: Journey of the Little Mermaid. Wander past waterfalls and tide pools into the cave beneath Prince Eric's Castle for some interactive fun and a clamshell ride through Ariel's story.

daughter find the perfect sparkly shoes to match her princess dress. You get the feeling that everyone's in on the fun; actually, you wonder if they ever go home!

MAGIC KINGDOM PLANNER
GETTING ORIENTED

The park is laid out on a north–south axis, with Cinderella Castle at the center and the various lands surrounding it in a broad circle.

As you pass underneath the railroad tracks, symbolically leaving behind the world of reality and entering a world of fantasy, you'll immediately notice the charming buildings lining Town Square and Main Street, U.S.A., which runs due north and ends at the Hub (also called Central Plaza), in front of Cinderella Castle. If you're lost or have questions, cast members are available at almost every turn to help you.

PARK AMENITIES

Baby Care: The quiet baby-care center is next to the Crystal Palace between Main Street and Adventureland. Rocking chairs and low lighting make nursing comfortable, though it can get crowded. Toddler-size toilets are a hit with tots. There are also changing tables, formula, baby food, pacifiers, diapers, and children's pain relievers. Most park restrooms also have changing tables.

Cameras: The camera center at Town Square Theater (formerly Exposition Hall), opposite City Hall, sells batteries, digital memory cards, and film. If a Disney photographer took your picture in the park, you can buy digital copies here, or use the $169 Memory Maker option to view and download all PhotoPass images. This area is a Mickey Mouse meet-and-greet spot and features a Fastpass+ ticket to meet Mickey.

First Aid: The first-aid center, staffed by registered nurses, is beside the Crystal Palace. More than a dozen automated external defibrillators are across the park.

Guest Relations: To the left in Town Square as you face Main Street, **City Hall** houses Guest Relations (aka Guest Services), the Magic Kingdom's principal information center (☎ 407/824–4521). Here you can search for misplaced belongings or companions, ask questions of staffers, and pick up a guide map and a *Times Guide* with schedules of events and character-greeting information. ■ **TIP→ If you're trying for a last-minute lunch or dinner reservation, you may be able to book it at City Hall.**

Lockers: Lockers ($7 or $9 plus $5 deposit) are in an arcade under the Main Street railroad station. If you're park hopping, use your locker receipt to get a free locker at the next park.

Lost People and Things: Instruct your kids to talk to anyone with a Disney name tag if they lose you. **City Hall** also has a Lost and Found and a computerized message center, where you can leave notes for your companions in the Magic Kingdom and other parks.

Main Lost and Found. After a day, found items are taken to the Lost and Found office at the Ticket and Transportation Center. On Disney property, follow signs to Magic Kingdom and, at the toll plaza entrance, tell an attendant you are going to Lost and Found so you aren't charged for Magic Kingdom parking. The attendant will direct you to Lost and Found parking at the Transportation and Ticket Center location. There is no address that works with your GPS. ⊠ *Ticket and Transportation Center [TTC], Magic Kingdom* ☎ *407/824–4245* ⊕ *www.disneyworld.com.*

Package Pick-Up: Have large purchases sent to Package Pick-Up at the Chamber of Commerce next to City Hall, so you won't have to carry them around. Allow three hours for the delivery. You also can have packages delivered to your Disney hotel if you are a resort guest.

Services for People with Disabilities: The Magic Kingdom gets decent marks from visitors with disabilities. Level entrances and ramps provide wheelchair access. Frontierland is the only area of the park, aside from Main Street, that has sidewalk curbs; there are ramps in several locations.

Pick up a *Guide for Guests with Disabilities* at Guest Relations, or download it from the Disney website. It gives mobility details and notes where you can use handheld-captioning, assisted-listening, video-captioning, and other devices (which are available for free but require a deposit). The guide also indicates which attractions have sign-language interpretation and when, which attractions don't permit service animals, and locations of designated "break" areas for animals.

Braille maps of the park can be found near guest relations locations. You can rent wheelchairs only at the park's entrance before passing under the train station for $12 daily, $10 a day for multiday rental. Electronic convenience vehicles (ECV) are $50 per day plus a refundable $20 security deposit. ■ TIP→ Neither wheelchairs nor ECVs can be booked ahead, so arrive early to rent them—ECV availability is limited.

Stroller Rentals: The Stroller Shop is near the entrance on the east side of Main Street. Single strollers are $15 daily, $13 for multiday rental; doubles are $31 daily, $27 for multiday rental.

Wait-time Updates: At the end of Main Street, on the left as you face Cinderella Castle, just before the Hub, is the **Tip Board**, a large board with constantly updated information about attractions' wait times.

PARK TOURS

Book any park tours ahead of your visit by calling ☎ 407/939–8687.

Magic Kingdom guided tours. Several Disney-run Magic Kingdom guided tours are available. Ask about discounts when booking, and arrive 15 minutes ahead of time to check in. Park admission is required in addition to the tour fee unless otherwise noted. ⊠ *Magic Kingdom* ☎ *407/939–8687.*

Family Magic Tour. It's a two-hour "surprise" scavenger hunt in which your guide encourages you to find things that have disappeared. Disney officials don't want to reveal the tour's components—after all, it's the Family "Magic" Tour—but they will say that a special character-greeting session awaits you at the end of the adventure. Tours leave the Chamber of Commerce adjacent to City Hall in Town Square daily ($39 for adults and children 3 and up). ⊠ *Main Street, U.S.A., Magic Kingdom* ☎ *407/939–8687.*

Keys to the Kingdom Tour. The five-hour tour gives you a feel for the Magic Kingdom's layout and what goes on behind the scenes. The walking tour, which costs $99, includes lunch. Park admission must be purchased separately. No one younger than 16 is allowed. Tours leave from the Chamber of Commerce adjacent to City Hall in Town Square several times daily. Included are visits to "backstage" zones: the parade staging area, the wardrobe area, and other locations in the web of tunnels beneath the Magic Kingdom. ⊠ *Main Street, U.S.A., Magic Kingdom* ☎ *407/939–8687.*

Magic Behind Our Steam Trains. This tour, which gives you an inside look at the daily operation of the WDW railroad, became so popular that it was lengthened from two to three hours and is offered on six days. Tours begin at the front-entrance turnstile at 7:30 am Monday through Saturday. Visitors 10 years old and up may participate. The cost is $54 per person, plus park admission. ⊠ *Magic Kingdom* ☎ *407/939–8687.*

Walt Disney: Marceline to Magic Kingdom Tour. Walt Disney spent much of his early childhood in Marceline, Missouri, and this insider's walking tour offers insight into the boy who became the man behind the Disney kingdom. It also offers a peek at the design and operation of attractions. Open to ages 12 and up, tours ($49) leave from the Main Street Chamber of Commerce, next to City Hall, daily at 8 am. ⊠ *Main Street, U.S.A., Magic Kingdom* ☎407/939–8687.

VISITING TIPS

Use insect repellent. Take advantage of the Disney-provided repellent at locations throughout the park, especially in the warm months.

Take advantage of parades. Ride a star attraction during a parade, when lines ease considerably. (But be careful not to get stuck on the wrong side of the parade route when it starts, or you may never get across.)

Pick up a map. You'll find them at City Hall, near the park's Town Square entrance; also get a *Times Guide,* which lists showtimes, character-greeting times, and hours for attractions and restaurants.

Book character meals early. Main Street, U.S.A.'s The Crystal Palace, A Buffet with Character has breakfast, lunch, and dinner with Winnie the Pooh, Tigger, and friends. All three meals at the Fairy Tale Dining experience in Cinderella Castle are extremely popular—so much so that you should reserve your spot six months out. The same advice goes for booking the full-service dinner at Be Our Guest Restaurant in the Beast's Castle in Fantasyland.

EXPLORING THE MAGIC KINGDOM

MAIN STREET, U.S.A.

With its pastel Victorian-style buildings, antique automobiles ahoohga-oohga-ing, sparkling sidewalks, and an atmosphere of what one writer has called "almost hysterical joy," Main Street is more than a mere conduit to the other enchantments of the Magic Kingdom. It's where the spell is first cast.

You emerge from beneath the Walt Disney World Railroad Station into a realization of one of the most tenacious American dreams. The perfect street in the perfect small town in a perfect moment of time is burnished to jewel-like quality, thanks to a four-fifths-scale reduction, nightly cleanings with high-pressure hoses, and constant repainting. And it's a very sunny world, thanks to an outpouring of welcoming entertainment: live bands, barbershop quartets, and background music from Disney films and American musicals played over loudspeakers. Horse-drawn trolleys and omnibuses with their horns tooting chug along the street. Vendors in Victorian costumes sell balloons and popcorn. And Cinderella's famous castle floats enchantingly in the distance where Main Street disappears.

Although attractions with a capital A are minimal on Main Street, there are plenty of inducements—namely, shops and eateries—to while away your time and part you from your money. The largest of these, the Emporium, is often the last stop for souvenir hunters at day's end. At the Main Street Bakery, you can find your favorite Starbucks latte and a sandwich or baked treats like cupcakes and brownies. If you can't resist an interactive challenge while making your way through the park, head first to the Firehouse, next to City Hall, to join the legendary wizard Merlin in the Sorcerers of the Magic Kingdom role-playing game. For

2

no extra charge, you can take ownership of special cards with "magic spells" that help you search for symbols and bring down Disney villains like Yzma and Kronk from the Disney film *The Emperor's New Groove*. Don't worry—you'll have time between fireball battles and cyclone spells to ride Space Mountain.

The Harmony Barber Shop lets you step back in time for a haircut ($18 for children 12 and under, $19 for anyone older). Babies or tots get free Mickey Ears, a souvenir lock of hair, and a certificate if it's their first haircut ever, but you pay $25 for the experience. At the Town Square Theater Mickey Mouse meets you for photos and autographs. And you can pick up a Fastpass+ appointment for such meet and greets. While you're here, stock up on batteries and memory cards or disposable cameras.

Walt Disney World Railroad. If you click through the turnstile just before 9 am with young children in tow, wait at the entrance before crossing beneath the station. In a few moments, you'll hear a whistle in the distance and see the day's first steam-driven train arrive. For a great overview of the whole Magic Kingdom, step right up to the elevated platform above the Magic Kingdom's entrance for a ride into living history. All the locomotives date from 1928, the same year Mickey Mouse was created.

Disney scouts tracked down these vintage carriers in Mexico (where they transported sugarcane in the Yucatán), brought them back, and overhauled them. They're splendid, with striped awnings, brightly painted benches, authoritative "choo-choo" sounds, and hissing plumes of steam.

The 1½-mile track runs along the perimeter of the Magic Kingdom, with much of the trip through the woods, and stops in Frontierland and Fantasyland. The four trains run at five-to-seven-minute intervals. **For people with disabilities:** You can remain in a standard wheelchair or transfer to one if you're in an ECV. Equipped for handheld-captioning. ■TIP➔ The ride is a good introduction to the layout of the park; it's also great as relief for tired feet. You can't load bulky strollers—like those Disney rents. Go midafternoon, when there's no line, or early, before 9 am, to enjoy a leisurely circuit of the Kingdom while you plan your itinerary. ⊠ *Magic Kingdom* ⌖ *Duration: 21 mins. or less depending where you disembark. Crowds: Moderate. Audience: All ages.*

ADVENTURELAND

From the scrubbed brick, manicured lawns, and meticulously pruned trees of the Central Plaza, an artfully dilapidated wooden bridge leads to the jungles of Adventureland. Here, South African cape honeysuckle droops, Brazilian bougainvillea drapes, Mexican flame vines cling, spider plants clone, and three varieties of palm trees sway. The bright, all-American sing-along tunes that fill the air along Main Street and Central Plaza are replaced by the recorded repetitions of trumpeting elephants, pounding drums, and squawking parrots. The architecture is a mishmash of the best of Thailand, the Middle East, the Caribbean, Africa, and Polynesia, arranged in an inspired disorder that recalls comic-book fantasies of far-off places.

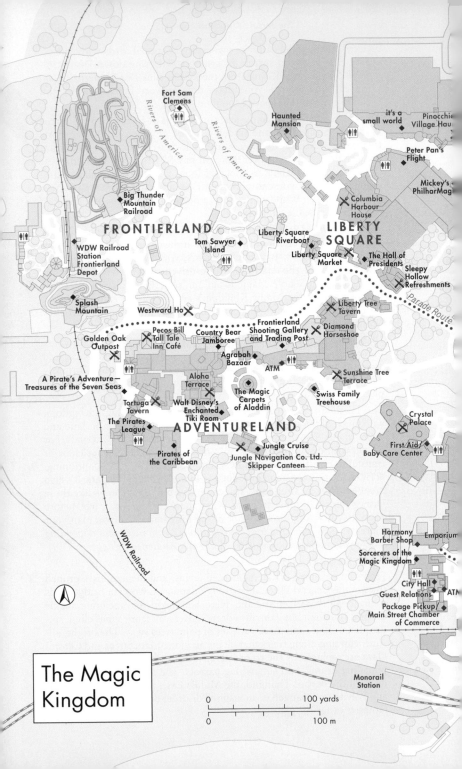

The Magic Kingdom

Fort Sam Clemens

Rivers of America

Rivers of America

Haunted Mansion

it's a small world

Pinocchio Village Hau

Peter Pan's Flight

Mickey's PhilharMag

Big Thunder Mountain Railroad

FRONTIERLAND

Columbia Harbour House

LIBERTY SQUARE

Tom Sawyer Island

Liberty Square Riverboat

Liberty Square Market

The Hall of Presidents

WDW Railroad Station Frontierland Depot

Sleepy Hollow Refreshments

Parade Route

Splash Mountain

Westward Ho

Liberty Tree Tavern

Pecos Bill Tall Tale Inn Café

Country Bear Jamboree

Frontierland Shooting Gallery and Trading Post

Diamond Horseshoe

Golden Oak Outpost

Agrabah Bazaar

ATM

Sunshine Tree Terrace

A Pirate's Adventure—Treasures of the Seven Seas

Aloha Terrace

The Magic Carpets of Aladdin

Swiss Family Treehouse

Crystal Palace

Tortuga Tavern

Walt Disney's Enchanted Tiki Room

First Aid/ Baby Care Center

The Pirates League

ADVENTURELAND

Pirates of the Caribbean

Jungle Cruise

Jungle Navigation Co. Ltd. Skipper Canteen

Harmony Barber Shop

Emporium

Sorcerers of the Magic Kingdom

WDW Railroad

City Hall

Guest Relations

ATM

Package Pickup/ Main Street Chamber of Commerce

Monorail Station

0   100 yards

0   100 m

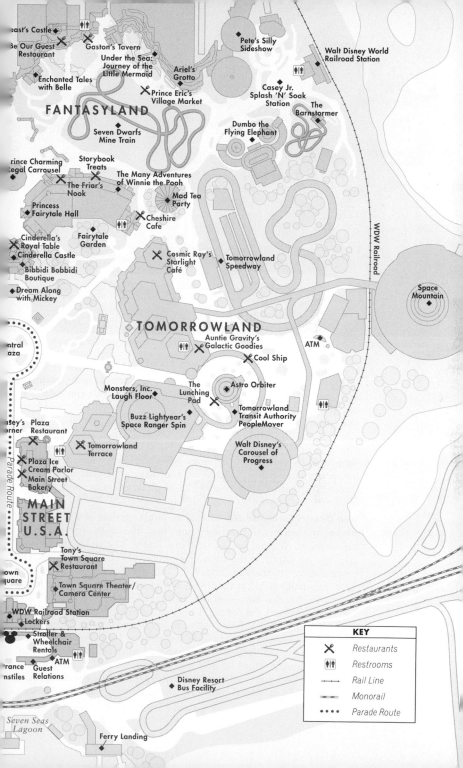

east's Castle
Be Our Guest Restaurant
Gaston's Tavern
Pete's Silly Sideshow
Walt Disney World Railroad Station
Under the Sea: Journey of the Little Mermaid
Ariel's Grotto
Enchanted Tales with Belle
Prince Eric's Village Market
Casey Jr. Splash 'N' Soak Station
The Barnstormer

FANTASYLAND

Dumbo the Flying Elephant

Seven Dwarfs Mine Train

rince Charming Regal Carrousel
Storybook Treats
The Friar's Nook
The Many Adventures of Winnie the Pooh
Mad Tea Party

Princess Fairytale Hall
Cheshire Cafe

Cinderella's Royal Table
Fairytale Garden
Cosmic Ray's Starlight Café
Tomorrowland Speedway

Cinderella Castle

Bibbidi Bobbidi Boutique

Space Mountain

Dream Along with Mickey

TOMORROWLAND

ntral Plaza

Auntie Gravity's Galactic Goodies
ATM
Cool Ship

sey's orner
Plaza Restaurant
Monsters, Inc. Laugh Floor
The Lunching Pad
Astro Orbiter
Tomorrowland Transit Authority PeopleMover

Buzz Lightyear's Space Ranger Spin

Tomorrowland Terrace
Walt Disney's Carousel of Progress

Plaza Ice Cream Parlor
Main Street Bakery

MAIN STREET U.S.A.

Tony's Town Square Restaurant

own quare

Town Square Theater/ Camera Center

WDW Railroad Station
Lockers

Stroller & Wheelchair Rentals

rance nstiles
ATM
Guest Relations

Disney Resort Bus Facility

Seven Seas Lagoon

Ferry Landing

Adventureland Adventure Number 1: Gliding through the muggy, steamy Caribbean world of pirates. Yo ho ho!

Once contained within the Pirates of the Caribbean attraction, Captain Jack Sparrow and the crew of the Black Pearl are brazenly recruiting new hearties at the Pirates League, adjacent to the ride entrance. You can get pirate and mermaid makeovers (for lots of doubloons) here. On a nearby stage furnished with pirate booty, the captain instructs scurvy dog recruits on brandishing a sword at Captain Jack Sparrow's Pirate Tutorial (several shows a day). And that's not all! At A Pirate's Adventure: Treasures of the Seven Seas, park guests embark on an interactive quest with a pirate map and talisman to complete "raids" through Adventureland as they fight off pirate enemies along the way. Shiver me timbers—it's a pirate's life for ye!

Walt Disney's Enchanted Tiki Room. The latest version of Disney's first Audio-Animatronics attraction brings back the original show, *Tropical Serenade*. Winged hosts Jose, Fritz, Pierre, Michael, and the boys take you on a tour of the attraction while cracking lots of jokes. The original ditty "In the Tiki, Tiki, Tiki, Tiki, Tiki Room" is second only to "it's a small world" as the Disney song you most love to hate. Many people do hate this attraction, finding the talking birds obnoxious and the music too loud and peppy. But you can also hear old-timers singing along to "Let's All Sing Like the Birdies Sing," tweet, tweet tweet, tweet, tweet. Plus, it's a haven of cool in the summer heat. **For people with disabilities:** Accessible for those in standard wheelchairs; equipped for handheld-captioning, audio description, and assisted-listening devices. ■ **TIP→** Go when you need to sit down with a/c. ⊠ *Adventureland, Magic Kingdom* ☞ *Duration: 12 mins. Crowds: Moderate. Audience: All Ages.*

2

Jungle Cruise. Cruise through three continents and along four rivers: the Congo, the Nile, the Mekong, and the Amazon. The canopied launches are loaded, the safari-suited guides make a point of checking their pistols, and the *Irrawady Irma* or *Mongala Millie* is off for another "perilous" journey. The guide's shtick is surprisingly funny in a wry and cornball way, provided he or she has mastered the art of enunciation. Along the way, you'll encounter Disney's famed Audio-Animatronics creatures of the African veld: bathing elephants, slinky pythons, an irritated rhinoceros, a tribe of hungry headhunters, and a bunch of hyperactive hippos (good thing the guide's got a pop pistol). Then there's Old Smiley, the crocodile, who's always waiting for a handout—or, as the guide quips, "a foot out."

The animals are early-generation and crude by Disney standards—anyone who's seen the real thing at the Animal Kingdom or even a good zoo won't be impressed. Unless you're an old-school Disney fan, the Jungle Cruise isn't really worth a Fastpass+. **For people with disabilities:** Several boats have lifts that allow wheelchair access; equipped for assisted-listening. Sign language is provided some days. ■TIP➜ Go during the afternoon parade, but not after dark—you miss too much. ⊠ *Adventureland, Magic Kingdom* ☞ *Duration: 10 mins. Crowds: Heavy. Audience: All ages.*

The Magic Carpets of Aladdin. Brightening the lush Adventureland landscape is this jewel-toned ride around a giant genie's bottle. You can control your own four-passenger, state-of-the-art carpet with a front-seat lever that moves it up and down and a rear-seat button that pitches it forward or backward. Part of the fun is dodging the right-on aim of a water-spewing "camel." The ride is short but a big hit with kids, who are also dazzled by the colorful gems implanted in the surrounding pavement. Parents must ride with toddlers. **For people with disabilities:** There's ramp access for guests in wheelchairs. If you're in an ECV, you must transfer to a standard wheelchair. ■TIP➜ Fastpass+ is available here but you may not need one, as lines move fairly quickly. ⊠ *Adventureland, Magic Kingdom* ☞ *Duration: 3 mins. Crowds: Heavy. Audience: All ages.*

FAMILY **Pirates of the Caribbean.** This is one of the few rides in the world that inspired a film (*Haunted Mansion* with Eddie Murphy was another) rather than the other way around.

The gracious arched entrance soon gives way to a dusty dungeon, redolent of dampness and of a spooky, scary past. Lanterns flicker as your boat sails, and a ghostly voice intones, "Dead men tell no tales." Next, a deserted beach, strewn with shovels, a skeleton, and a disintegrating map indicating buried treasure prefaces this story of greed, lust, and destruction. You'll pass right through a water-mist screen featuring the maniacal mug of Davy Jones, complete with squirming tentacle beard and barnacle-encrusted hat. Emerging from a pitch-black tunnel after a mild, tummy-tickling drop, you're caught in the line of fire as a pirate ship cannon blasts away at a stone fortress. Look for Captain Barbossa, evil nemesis of Captain Jack Sparrow. Audio-Animatronics pirates hoist the Jolly Roger while brave soldiers scurry to defend the fort—to no avail.

Adventureland Adventure Number 2: Being shipwrecked with the Swiss Family Robinson and exploring their tree house.

Politically correct nerves may twinge as the women of the town are rounded up and auctioned, but the wenches rule in another scene, where they chase roguish rapscallions with glee. The wild antics of the pirates—Captain Jack Sparrow pops up in several situations—result in a conflagration; the town goes up in flames, and all go to their just reward amid a catchy chorus of "A Pirate's Life for Me." **For people with disabilities:** Boarding requires transferring from a standard wheelchair to the ride vehicle; the very small flume drop may make the attraction inappropriate for those with limited upper-body strength or those wearing neck or back braces. Equipped for audio-description and handheld-captioning devices. ■TIP➜ A Fastpass+ is available but not always necessary. It's best to ride in the heat of the afternoon, and lines move steadily. ⊠ *Adventureland, Magic Kingdom* ☞ *Duration: 12 mins. Crowds: Moderate. Audience: All but very young kids.*

Swiss Family Treehouse. Inspired by the classic novel by Johann Wyss about the adventures of the Robinson family, who were shipwrecked en route to America, the tree house shows what you can do with a big faux tree and a lot of imagination. Disney detail abounds: the kitchen sink is a giant clamshell; the boys' room, strewn with clothing, has two hammocks instead of beds; and an ingenious system of rain barrels and bamboo pipes provides running water in every room.

As you clamber around the narrow wooden steps and rope bridges that connect the rooms in this split-level dwelling, take a look at the Spanish moss. It's real, but the tree itself—some 90 feet in diameter, with more than 1,000 branches—was constructed by the props department. The 300,000 leaves are vinyl. Toddlers unsteady on their feet may have trouble with the stairs. **For people with disabilities:** With its 100 steps and lack of narration, this attraction gets low ratings among those with mobility and visual impairments. ■**TIP→** If you're with children 4 to 12 who like to explore, plan to climb while you're already in Adventureland. ⊠ *Adventureland, Magic Kingdom* ⌖ *Duration: Up to you. Crowds: Light to moderate. Audience: All ages.*

NEED A
BREAK

If you're looking for real refreshment and an energy boost, stop by **Aloha Isle**, where you'll find some of the tastiest and most healthful goodies. Try the fresh pineapple spears, or sip the popular Frozen Dole Whip or just some fruit juice, while you relax on one of the benches scattered around Adventureland.

FRONTIERLAND

Frontierland evokes the American frontier and is planted with mesquite, twisted Peruvian pepper trees, slash pines, and cacti. The period seems to be the latter half of the 19th century, and the West is being won by Disney cast members dressed in checked shirts, leather vests, cowboy hats, and brightly colored neckerchiefs. Banjo and fiddle music twangs from tree to tree, and every once in a while a line dance flash mob will erupt in front of the Country Bear Jamboree. (Beware of hovering seagulls that migrate to the parks during cooler months—they've been known to snatch snacks.)

The screams that drown out the string music aren't the result of a horse throwing a cowboy. They come from two of the Magic Kingdom's more thrilling rides: Splash Mountain, an elaborate flume ride, and Big Thunder Mountain Railroad, a roller coaster. The Walt Disney World Railroad tunnels past a colorful scene in Splash Mountain and drops you off between it and Thunder Mountain.

Fodor's Choice
★

Big Thunder Mountain Railroad. Set in gold-rush days, this thrilling roller coaster simulates a runaway train. It's a bumpy ride with several good drops (pregnant women and guests wearing back, neck, or leg braces should avoid this one). There are moments when you feel like you're going to fly right off the tracks. Overall it's more fun than scary, and you'll see kids as young as 7 lining up to ride. The train rushes and rattles past 20 Audio-Animatronics figures—mostly critters—as well as $300,000 worth of genuine antique mining equipment, tumbleweeds, a derelict mining town, hot springs, and a flash flood.

The 197-foot mountain landscape is based on the windswept scenery of Arizona's Monument Valley, and thanks to 650 tons of steel, 4,675 tons of concrete, and 16,000 gallons of paint, it replicates the area's gorges, tunnels, caverns, and dry river beds. **For people with disabilities:** You must be able to step into the ride vehicle and walk short distances. Service animals aren't permitted. ■**TIP→** Use Fastpass+ unless you go first thing in the morning or during a parade. The ride is most exciting at night, when you can't anticipate the curves and the track's rattling really sounds as if something's about to give. ⊠ *Frontierland, Magic Kingdom* ⌖ *Duration: 4 mins. Crowds: Absolutely. Audience: Not small kids.*

Country Bear Jamboree. Wisecracking, cornpone, lovelorn Audio-Animatronics bears joke, sing, and play country music and 1950s rock and roll in this stage show. Even timid youngsters love them. The emcee, the massive but debonair Henry, leads the stellar cast of Grizzly Hall, which includes the robust Trixie, who laments love lost while perching on a swing suspended from the ceiling; Bubbles, Bunny, and Beulah, harmonizing on "All the Guys That Turn Me on Turn Me Down"; and Big Al, the off-key cult figure who has inspired his own shopping kiosk. **For people with disabilities:** Wheelchair accessible; reflective captioning provided; equipped for assisted-listening devices. If you lip-read, ask to sit up front. ■TIP→ Visit before 11 am, during the afternoon parade, or late in the day. Stand to the far left in the anteroom for the front rows and to the far right for the last row, where small kids can perch atop seats to see better. ⊠ *Frontierland, Magic Kingdom* ⏱ *Duration: 17 mins. Crowds: Moderate. Audience: All ages.*

Fodor's Choice
★

Splash Mountain. One of the most popular thrill rides after Space Mountain, this log-flume water ride was based on animated sequences in Disney's 1946 film *Song of the South*. Here the Audio-Animatronics creations of Brer Rabbit, Brer Bear, Brer Fox, and a menagerie of other Brer beasts frolic in bright, cartoonlike settings. Settle into the eight-person hollowed-out logs, and the fun begins.

As the boat carries you up the mountain, Brer Rabbit's silhouette hops merrily ahead to the tune of the ride's theme song, "Time to Be Moving Along." Every time some critter makes a grab for the bunny, your log boat drops out of reach. But Brer Fox has been studying his book *How to Catch a Rabbit*, and our lop-eared friend looks as if he's destined for the pot. Things don't look so good for the flumers, either. You get one heart-stopping pause at the top of the mountain—just long enough to grab the safety bar—and then the boat plummets about five stories at a 45-degree angle into a large, wet briar patch. It's enough to reach speeds of 40 mph—and makes you feel weightless. Clench your teeth and smile: as you begin to drop, a flashbulb pops. Another photographic memento for sale as you "Zip-a-Dee-Doo-Dah" your way to the next ride.

You may get wet, so plan accordingly. If you need to use Baby Swap you can take the young ones to a play area in a cave under the attraction; riders must be at least 40 inches tall. Do not ride if you're pregnant or have heart, back, or neck problems. **For people with disabilities:** You must be able to step into the ride vehicle and walk short distances. Service animals aren't permitted. ■TIP→ Plan to use Fastpass+ or ride when the park opens, during meal or parade times. ⊠ *Frontierland, Magic Kingdom* ⏱ *Duration: 11 mins. Crowds: Yes! Audience: Not small kids.*

Tom Sawyer Island. Tom Sawyer Island is a playground of hills, trees, rocks, and shrubs. Most attractions are on the main island, where your raft docks. The Mystery Mine is like a secret passageway to exploration. Children love Injun Joe's Cave, where there are lots of columns and crevices from which to jump out and startle siblings. As you explore the shoreline on the dirt paths, watch out for the barrel bridge—the whole contraption bounces at every step.

Coasting down Splash Mountain in Frontierland will put some zip in your doo-dah and some water on your clothes.

On the other island is Fort Langhorn, a log fortress from which you can fire air guns with great booms and cracks at the passing *Liberty Belle* riverboat. **For people with disabilities:** With its stairs, bridges, inclines, and narrow caves, this attraction isn't negotiable by those using a wheelchair. ■**TIP➜ Get away from the crowds here. Watch toddlers closely, as it's easy to lose track of them.** ✉ *Frontierland, Magic Kingdom* ☞ *Duration: Up to you. Crowds: Light. Audience: Kids and tweens.*

LIBERTY SQUARE

The rough-and-tumble Western frontier gently folds into Colonial America as Liberty Square picks up where Frontierland leaves off. The weathered siding gives way to solid brick and neat clapboard. The mesquite and cactus are replaced by stately oaks and masses of azaleas. The theme is Colonial history, which is portrayed here as solid Yankee. The buildings, topped with weather vanes and exuding prosperity, are pure New England.

A replica of the Liberty Bell, crack and all, seems an appropriate prop to separate Liberty Square from Frontierland. There's even a Liberty Tree, a more than 150-year-old live oak, transported here from elsewhere on Disney property. Just as the Sons of Liberty hung lanterns on trees as a signal of solidarity after the Boston Tea Party, the Liberty Tree's branches are decorated with 13 lanterns representing the 13 original colonies. Around the square are tree-shaded tables for an alfresco lunch and plenty of carts and fast-food eateries to supply the goods.

NEED A
BREAK

Sleepy Hollow offers quick pick-me-ups in the form of funnel cakes, soft-serve ice cream, espresso drinks, and waffle sandwiches.

The Hall of Presidents. With the latest in Disney Audio-Animatronics (this attraction introduced the technology in 1971, and underwent a total high-tech transformation in 2017) this show, housed in a redbrick building inspired by Philadelphia's Independence Hall, tells a moving story of the bond between the presidents and "We, the People." Producers reshot the accompanying film in high-definition video and added more than 130 images culled from the National Archives, Library of Congress, and other collections. A digital soundtrack, LED lighting, and a dramatic narration further enhance the experience. The film covers more than two centuries of U.S. history and emphasizes anecdotes about presidents who've reached out to people in times of strife. Both George Washington and Abraham Lincoln grab a bit of the spotlight, the latter by delivering his famous Gettysburg Address.

DID YOU KNOW?

It's hard to keep the Haunted Mansion's 200-odd trunks, chairs, harps, dress forms, statues, rugs, and knickknacks appropriately dusty. Disney buys its dust in five-pound bags and scatters it with a gadget resembling a fertilizer spreader. Word is, enough dust has been dumped since the park's 1971 opening to completely bury the mansion. Where does it all go? Perhaps the voice is right in saying that something will follow you home.

The best part of the show is a roll call of all 44 U.S. presidents. (Fun fact: President Trump is officially the 45th president because Grover Cleveland is counted twice due to his having served nonconsecutive terms.) President Trump recites his oath of office. Each chief executive responds with a nod, and those who are seated rise (except for wheelchair-bound Franklin Delano Roosevelt, of course). The robots nod and whisper to each other as the roll call proceeds. Anyone interested in presidential artifacts will enjoy the wait in the lobby area, where First Ladies' dresses, presidential portraits, and even George Washington's dental instruments are on display. **For people with disabilities:** Wheelchair accessible; enter through a door on the right. Reflective captioning available; equipped for assisted-listening devices. ■ **TIP→ Visit anytime.** ⊠ *Liberty Sq., Magic Kingdom ⏰ Duration: 22 mins. Crowds: Moderate to heavy. Audience: Not small kids.*

Fodor's Choice
★

Haunted Mansion. The special effects here are a howl. You're greeted at the creaking iron gates of this Gothic mansion by a lugubrious attendant, who has one of the few jobs at Disney for which smiling is frowned upon, and ushered into a spooky picture gallery. A disembodied voice echoes from the walls: "Welcome, foolish mortals, to the Haunted Mansion. I am your ghost host." An audio system with 30-plus surround-sound speakers ups the ghost-host fright factor. A scream shivers down, the room begins to "stretch," and you're off into one of Disney's classic attractions. Don't rush out of this room when other visitors depart; linger for some ghoulish bonus whispers.

Liberty Square's Haunted Mansion by day—pretty scary or just pretty? You decide.

Consisting mainly of a slow-moving ride in a cocoonlike "doom buggy," the Haunted Mansion is really scary only for younger children, and that's mostly because of the darkness. Everyone else will laugh while they gawk at the special effects. Watch the ghostly ballroom dancers, Madame Leota's talking head in the crystal ball, and ghostly footprints that move along a staircase. In the "bride in the attic" scene, keep an eye on the portraits. Just when you think the Imagineers have exhausted their bag of ectoplasmic tricks, you discover that your doom buggy has gained an extra passenger. This is a high-capacity, fast-loading ride, and lines usually move steadily. **For people with disabilities:** Those in wheelchairs must transfer to the "doom buggies" and take one or more steps; however, if you can walk up to 200 feet, you'll enjoy the preshow as well as the ride's sensations and eerie sounds. Equipped for handheld-captioning and audio-description devices. ■**TIP➜ When you reach a fork in the queue before entering the mansion, go left through the cemetery for interactive graveyard fun. The Musical Crypt and Secret Library help you forget you're in line. Nighttime adds an extra fright factor.** ✉ *Liberty Sq., Magic Kingdom* ☞ *Duration: 8 mins. Crowds: Heavy. Audience: Not small kids.*

Liberty Square Riverboat. An old-fashioned steamboat, the *Liberty Belle* is authentic, from its calliope whistle and the gingerbread trim on its three decks to the boilers that produce the steam that drives the big rear paddle wheel. The boat misses authenticity on only one count: there's no mustachioed captain needed to guide it during the ride around the Rivers of America. That task is performed by an underwater rail. The 1½-mile cruise is slow and not exactly thrilling, but there are lovely

Continued on page 74

A MAN, A MOUSE, A LEGACY

By Jennie Hess

Walt Disney once said, "I only hope that we never lose sight of one thing—that it was all started by a mouse." His legendary mouse, Mickey, took the world by storm in 1928 in the theatrical debut of the animated short film *Steamboat Willie*. Today, Walt is Mickey, Mickey is Walt, and their legacy is legendary.

Above: Walt Disney; below: Mickey from *Fantasia*, 1940; right: *Pinocchio*, 1940

There's a tale still told (and disputed) that Walt imagined Mickey while on a train from New York to California, after a disastrous meeting where he lost the rights to a character called Oswald the Lucky Rabbit. Walt's friend and colleague, gifted Dutch cartoonist Ub Iwerks, first drew Mickey, but it was Walt who gave him a voice and personality.

He planned to name the mouse Mortimer, but his wife, Lilian, insisted the name didn't fit the cheerful little rodent.

The man behind the mouse, Walter Elias Disney, was born December 5, 1901, in Chicago. His early Midwestern years were spent nurturing his love of drawing. After driving an ambulance for the Red Cross in France during World War I, Walt returned to the States and worked for an ad company, where he met Ub.

Though Mickey appeared in the silent short *Plane Crazy* in May of 1928, the amiable mouse didn't really take a bow until the November debut of *Steamboat Willie*. Walt's use of synchronized sound made all the difference. By 1937, Walt and company had released their first animated feature-length film, *Snow White and the Seven Dwarfs*.

The many films that followed formed the creative and financial bedrock for a legacy of one theme park after another. But perhaps the greatest legacy of Walt and his mouse is that they both make memories for generation upon generation.

Shirley Temple presents Disney with one big and seven dwarf-size Oscars for *Snow White*, 1939; right: *Snow White*; *Steamboat Willie* poster, 1928

A Mouse Is Born

1920s–30s

Walt and his brother, Roy, establish a Hollywood studio in 1923. Animated shorts *Plane Crazy* and *Steamboat Willie*, starring both Mickey and Minnie, are released in 1928. Thereafter, Walt and his artists create dozens of Mickey shorts like 1930's *The Chain Gang*, when an orange pup named Pluto first appears.

Two years later, good-natured Goofy debuts as an audience extra in *Mickey's Revue*. His spasmodic laugh earns him a series of his own animated short films. Hot-tempered Donald Duck and his loyal girl-friend, Daisy, follow.

In 1937, America's first full-length animated feature, *Snow White and the Seven Dwarfs*, becomes the highest-grossing feature of its time. *Gone with the Wind* doesn't blow by that record until 1939, the same year that Disney's groundbreaking feature earns a special Academy Award: one full-size Oscar and seven dwarf Oscars presented by Shirley Temple.

■ **Visit:** Walt Disney: One Man's Dream; The Magic of Disney Animation

Goofy

Characters Come to Life

1940s–50s

Fans of all ages flock to see successive hits, from *Pinocchio* and *Fantasia* (both 1940) to *Dumbo* (1941) and *Bambi* (1942). Though *Fantasia* is panned by some, it earns Academy Awards kudos for innovating in the area of visualized music—specifically, animation set to music by composers such as Bach, Tchaikovsky, and Beethoven and recorded under the direction of conductor Leopold Stokowski.

During World War II, the Disney studio springs to patriotic action with a series of military training and propaganda films. After the war, the animation wizards cast a spell over the

Left: *Dumbo* and *Lady and the Tramp*; right: entrance to Sleeping Beauty's Enchanted Castle, Disneyland, late 1960s

country with *Cinderella* (1950), *Alice in Wonderland* (1951), *Peter Pan* (1953), *Lady and the Tramp* (1955), *Sleeping Beauty* (1959), and others.

Walt's love for nature leads him to produce 13 True-Life Adventure films, eight of which win Oscars. Walt also brings his first live-action adventure film, *Treasure Island*, to the screen. He and his brother, Roy, begin dreaming up a new adventure altogether—Disneyland.

The first Disney theme park opens on July 17, 1955, in Anaheim, California. Many attractions and rides have Disney film themes. Drawing on his lifelong train infatuation, Walt encircles the park with the Disneyland Railroad.

- **Visit:** Cinderella Castle
- **Ride:** Prince Charming Regal Carrousel, Peter Pan's Flight, Dumbo the Flying Elephant, and Walt Disney World Railroad
- **See:** Mickey's PhilharMagic

Cinderella Castle today

1960s–70s

A Magical New Frontier

In the early 1960s, Walt purchases 27,500 Orlando acres—an area twice the size of Manhattan. Sadly, he dies (December 1966) before Walt Disney World opens.

On October 1, 1971, the Magic Kingdom gates swing open, and a sleek monorail glides to the Contemporary and the Polynesian resort hotels. In November, a 640-acre western-style camping resort, Fort Wilderness, opens.

- **Visit:** Magic Kingdom
- **Ride:** The Monorail

TIMELINE

Tokyo Disneyland
opens

Disneyland Paris
opens

1990

2000

Above: Disney Paris; Mickey hat; right: EPCOT's iconic
Spaceship Earth

1980s–90s

A Worldlier Walt

Prior to his death, Walt begins work on what he hopes will be an ideal city. He names the project Experimental Prototype Community of Tomorrow. After the Magic Kingdom opens, Disney executives use some of Walt's ideas to create EPCOT Center. What opens in 1982 is the second Florida theme park—celebrating the world's cultures, the past, and the future—rather than an experimental community.

The 1980s are banner years for Disney Parks and Resorts. In 1983, the company's first international park—Tokyo Disneyland—opens. In 1989, Florida's third park, Disney-MGM Studios (later Disney's Hollywood Studios) premiers with celebrity fanfare. Not far from it, a new nightlife district, Pleasure Island, pumps up the volume, and Typhoon Lagoon crashes onto the scene with 6-foot waves and thrill-slide appeal.

The decade that follows is no less ambitious. In 1992 Euro Disney Resort (now Disneyland Paris) becomes the Mouse's second international destination; the first Disney cruise ships are launched from Port Canaveral, Florida; and the fourth Florida park, Disney's Animal Kingdom, earns raves for its authentic habitats. The icing on the Magic Kingdom's 20th anniversary cake? The animation studio is once again making big-screen hits with *Beauty and the Beast* (1991), *Aladdin* (1992), and *The Lion King* (1994)

■ **Visit:** Spaceship Earth at EPCOT; Beauty and the Beast—Live on Stage at the Studios; Kilimanjaro Safaris at Animal Kingdom; Typhoon Lagoon

Aladdin

FINDING MICKEY

A Hidden Mickey at Epcot

Hidden Mickeys began as an inside joke among Disney Imagineers, the creative folks behind the theme parks. When finishing an attraction, they'd slip a Mickey into the motif to see who might notice. You can get a list of Hidden Mickeys at any Guest Relations location, at ⊕www.allears.net, or at ⊕www.hiddenmickeys. org. Here are just a few to get you started, though:

Big Thunder Mountain Railroad (Magic Kingdom). As your train nears the station, look to your right for three rusty gears on the ground.

DINOSAUR (Animal Kingdom). Stare at the bark of the painted tree in the far left background of the wall mural at the entrance.

Haunted Mansion (Magic Kingdom). As you move through the ballroom, notice the Mouse-eared place setting on the table.

Spaceship Earth (Epcot). Mickey smiles down from a constellation behind the loading area.

Twilight Zone Tower of Terror (Hollywood Studios). In the boiler room, look for a water stain on the wall after the queue splits.

Finding Nemo's, Dory and Nemo

New Millennium

To Infinity and Beyond!

The new millennium sends the Mouse into overdrive. Hong Kong Disneyland opens (2005), as do several World attractions, among them one with a *Toy Story* theme, and two with a *Nemo* theme. Disney World also adds to its accommodations, bringing the total to 30,000 rooms, 3,200 Disney Vacation Club villas, and 800 campsites. New eateries like the Trattoria al Forno at Disney's Boardwalk open, as do luxurious on-Disney property resorts including Four Seasons Resort Orlando.

Looking ahead, it seems as if pixie dust will permeate the World for years to come. The Magic Kingdom's Fantasyland is complete with everyone's newest favorite ride, the Seven Dwarfs Mine Train family coaster. Disney Cruise Line now sails with four ships including the newer *Disney Fantasy* and *Disney Dream.* The multimillion-dollar makeover of Downtown Disney to Disney Springs has brought new shops, restaurants, and entertainment, and parking. In 2017, Pandora–The World of Avatar opened to acclaim. A new Toy Story Land opened in 2018, and Star Wars: Galaxy Edge opens in 2019.

Toy Story's Buzz Lightyear

views of Tom Sawyer Island and surrounding attractions. Children like exploring the boat. Lines move quickly. **For people with disabilities:** Wheelchair accessible; enter through exit on right or left. ■**TIP→ Come when you need a break from the crowds. Check Times Guide—the river-boat is open seasonally.** ⊠ *Liberty Sq., Magic Kingdom* ☞ *Duration: 15 mins. Crowds: Light to moderate. Audience: All ages.*

FANTASYLAND

Walt Disney called this "a timeless land of enchantment," and Fantasyland does conjure pixie dust. Perhaps that's because the fanciful gingerbread houses, gleaming gold turrets, and, of course, the rides are based on Disney-animated movies.

Many of these rides, which could ostensibly be classified as rides for children, are packed with enough delightful detail to engage the adults who accompany them. Fantasyland has always been the most heavily trafficked area in the park, and its rides and shows are almost always crowded.

The good news for anyone who hasn't visited in a few years is that Fantasyland underwent the largest expansion in the park's history in 2012 to expand the number of attractions and experiences. Dumbo the Flying Elephant doubled in size, flying above circus-themed grounds that also include the Great Goofini coaster, starring Goofy as stuntman. There's also a Walt Disney World Railroad station in Fantasyland. And a circus-themed Casey Jr. Splash 'N' Soak Station provides water-play respite for kids. Ariel of *The Little Mermaid* invites you to her own state-of-the-art attraction, Under the Sea: Journey of the Little Mermaid. Disney princesses welcome you for a photo op in the glittering Princess Fairytale Hall. You can be part of the show when you join Belle, Lumiere, and Madame Wardrobe of *Beauty and the Beast* at the Enchanted Tales with Belle attraction for a story performance. Meanwhile, Beast may be brooding in his castle, where the Be Our Guest dining room beckons to lunch and dinner guests. The musical Seven Dwarfs Mine Train family coaster completes the expansion.

You can enter Fantasyland on foot from Liberty Square, Tomorrowland, or via the Walt Disney World Railroad, but the classic introduction is through Cinderella Castle. As you exit the castle's archway, look left to discover a charming and often overlooked touch: Cinderella Fountain, a lovely brass casting of the castle's namesake, who's dressed in her peasant togs and surrounded by her beloved mice and bird friends.

From the southern end of Liberty Square, head toward the park hub and stop at the Disney PhotoPass picture spot for one of the park's best, unobstructed ground-level views of Cinderella Castle. It's a great spot for that family photo.

Ariel's Grotto. Every mermaid princess should have a giant seashell throne, and that's where Ariel fans can meet the fashionably finned, redheaded beauty. Built into the rock work of Prince Eric's castle, the grotto provides shade for those waiting in the queue and a more secluded experience for families who want to photograph or video-tape the royal meet-up. ■**TIP→ Mermaid fans will be happy to know Fastpass+ is available. It's a natural to visit with young children before**

DID YOU KNOW?

The quintessential Disney icon, Cinderella Castle, was inspired by the palace built by the mad Bavarian king Ludwig II at Neuschwanstein. At 180 feet, it's 100 feet taller than Disneyland's Sleeping Beauty Castle.

or after visiting Under the Sea: Journey of the Little Mermaid. ⊠ *Fantasyland, Magic Kingdom* ☞ *Duration: About 2 mins. Crowds: Yes. Audience: Young kids.*

The Barnstormer. This coaster stars the Great Goofini, stunt master— a perfect fit for Fantasyland's Storybook Circus area. The twisting, turning roller coaster "flight" takes you high above the circus fun. It's perfect for young children's first thrill ride if they are 35 inches or taller. Circus props and themed posters tell Goofini's tale with references to some of the short films of Goofy's heyday. **For people with disabilities:** You must be able to walk a few steps from your wheelchair to board the ride. Service animals are not permitted. ■**TIP➔ Book a Fastpass+ or, first thing in the morning, take the Walt Disney World Railroad to Fantasyland and hop in line before the crowds arrive.** ⊠ *Fantasyland, Magic Kingdom* ☞ *Duration: 1 min. Crowds: Heavy. Audience: All but smallest kids. Height requirement: 35 inches.*

Casey Jr. Splash 'N' Soak Station. The Casey Jr. circus train has just pulled into town, and train cars full of faux circus animals are taking a break in this circus-themed play area across from Dumbo the Flying Elephant. The critters may not be real, but they sure do put out a lot of water as children run hooting and squealing past spitting camels, spraying elephants, and other water hazards. **For people with disabilities:** Wheelchair accessible. ■**TIP➔ While the kids cool off and burn energy, parents can take a break and grab a hot dog or soft pretzel from nearby carts. Pack towels and fresh clothing for cooler days.** ⊠ *Fantasyland, Magic Kingdom* ☞ *Duration: As long as you like. Crowds: Moderate to heavy. Audience: Young kids.*

Cinderella Castle. Although similar to Disneyland's Sleeping Beauty Castle, at 189 feet this iconic castle is more than 100 feet taller; and with its elongated towers and lacy fretwork, it's more graceful. Don't miss the elaborate mosaics on the walls of the archway as you rush toward Fantasyland from the Hub. The five panels, measuring some 15 feet high and 10 feet wide were created from a million bits of multicolored Italian glass, silver, and 14-karat gold by mosaicist Hanns-Joachim Scharff. The mosaics tell the story of the little cinder girl as she goes from pumpkin to prince to happily ever after.

The fantasy castle has absolutely real foundations, made of solid steel beams, fiberglass, and 500 gallons of paint. Instead of dungeons, there are service tunnels for the Magic Kingdom's less-than-magical quotidian operations, such as Makeup and Costuming. These are the same tunnels that honeycomb the ground under much of the park.

Within the castle's archway is the **Bibbidi Bobbidi Boutique**, where the "royal treatment" transforms little girls age three and older into princesses or divas. Hair and makeup are by a Fairy Godmother-in-training. The valiant Knight Package offers a heroic makeover that includes hairstyle, sword, and shield. If you have reservations to dine at **Cinderella's Royal Table,** you enter the castle by way of an ascending spiral staircase. You are attended by costumed waiters and joined by Cinderella and other princesses in one of Disney's most popular character-dining experiences. **For people with disabilities:** For those with limited mobility, elevator

See Lumiere chat with Belle at Enchanted Tales with Belle in Fantasyland.

access to the dining experience is provided. ■**TIP→ Call or book online 180 days ahead, if possible, to reserve the character breakfast, lunch, or dinner known as Fairytale Dining.** ⊠ *Fantasyland, Magic Kingdom.*

Dumbo the Flying Elephant. Based on the movie about the gigantic-eared baby elephant who learns he can fly, the ride consists of flying pachyderms, each packing a couple of kids and a parent. A joystick controls your Dumbo's up-and-down movement. A popular feature for parents and children: the Big Top "play while you wait" indoor area chock full of climbing equipment for kids of most ages. As you enter the colorful circus tent, a Disney "ringmaster" hands you a pager that buzzes when it's your turn to join the ride queue. Parents can supervise tots in a small circus ring of play equipment while older kids burn up energy on multilevel climbers like the "Thrilling Tower of Flames." Adults enjoy the bench seating. **For people with disabilities:** If using a wheelchair, prepare to transfer to a ride vehicle. ■**TIP→ Get a Fastpass+ if you're in a hurry; otherwise, let the kids enjoy the play area before riding.** ⊠ *Fantasyland, Magic Kingdom* ⌇ *Duration: 2 mins. Crowds: Heavy. Audience: Young kids.*

Fodor's Choice ★ **Enchanted Tales with Belle.** Stroll the path through an artfully planted woodland and meadow to a rustic French cabin complete with waterwheel, where Belle's father, Maurice, tinkers with his inventions. The small homestead oozes Belle's provincial life, with a giant pot hanging in the fireplace and books stacked on a simple wooden chair. Inside her father's workshop, amid blueprints and tools, a giant gold-framed mirror hangs. A costumed cast member welcomes your group to the workshop (*Bonjour!*) and implores everyone to chant, "Take me back to the day Belle and Beast fell in love!" *Voilà!* The mirror becomes an animated screen straight from the Disney film *Beauty and the Beast* before transforming into a portal that leads to an elegant room of Beast's Castle. Inside, an Animatronic Madame Armoire encourages guests to grab props and play character roles from the "tale as old as time." Then it's on to the library, where a spot-on Animatronic Lumiere holds court from the mantle. Families grab a cushy bench as a coiffed actress playing Belle joins guests to act out a scene from the enchanted tale. You'll dance around the room to "Be Our Guest," and you may shed a tear as the interactive story unfolds. This live performance gets to the heart of Disney storytelling, and every participant poses for photos with Belle before a very happy ending. **For people with disabilities:** Wheelchair accessible; equipped for handheld captioning and assisted listening. ■TIP➔ **You can book a Fastpass+ or visit while waiting for your Under the Sea: Journey of the Little Mermaid or other nearby Fastpass+ appointments.** ⊠ *Fantasyland, Magic Kingdom* ☞ *Duration: 15 mins. Crowds: Yes. Audience: All ages; perfect for families.*

it's a small world. Visiting Walt Disney World and not stopping for this tribute to terminal cuteness—why, the idea is practically un-American. The attraction is essentially a boat ride through several candy-colored lands, each representing a continent and each crammed with musical moppets, all madly singing. Disney raided the remains of the 1964–65 New York World's Fair for sets, and then appropriated the theme song of international brotherhood and friendship for its own. Some claim that it's the "revenge of the Audio-Animatrons," as 450 simplistic dolls differentiated mostly by their national dress—Dutch babies in clogs, Spanish flamenco dancers, sari-wrapped Indians waving temple bells, Swiss yodelers, Japanese kite fliers, Middle East snake charmers, and young French cancan dancers, to name just a few—parade past, smiling away and wagging their heads in time to the song. Now all together: "It's a world of laughter, a world of tears. It's a world of hope and a world of fears." Warning: the song will not leave your head for days. Take enchanted tots through again if the line is short.

For people with disabilities: You can board with your standard wheelchair through the designated entrance; if you use a scooter, transfer to one of the attraction's standard chairs available at the ride entrance. Equipped for handheld-captioning and audio-description devices. ■TIP➔ **Fastpass+ is available, but lines usually move quickly for those in the stand-by queue.** ⊠ *Fantasyland, Magic Kingdom* ☞ *Duration: 11 mins. Crowds: Heavy. Audience: All ages.*

Mad Tea Party. This whirling carnival staple is for the vertigo addict looking for a fix. The Disney version is based on its own 1951 film *Alice in Wonderland*, in which the Mad Hatter hosts a tea party for his un-birthday. You hop into oversize, pastel-colored teacups and whirl around a giant platter. Add your own spin to the teacup's orbit with the help of the steering wheel in the center. Check out the soused mouse that pops out of the teapot centerpiece. **For people with disabilities:** If using a wheelchair, enter through the exit on right, then transfer to a ride vehicle. ■TIP➔ **Fastpass+ is available but not recommended unless you can't resist a good fast**

spin. Lines move slowly. ⊠ *Fantasyland, Magic Kingdom* ⟳ *Duration: 2 mins. Crowds: Moderate. Audience: Small kids.*

Fodor's Choice
★
The Many Adventures of Winnie the Pooh. The famous honey lover and his exploits in the Hundred Acre Wood are the theme for this ride. You can read posted passages from A.A. Milne's stories as you wait in line. Once you board your "Hunny Pot," Pooh and his friends wish you a "happy windsday." Pooh flies through the air, held aloft by his balloon, in his perennial search for "hunny," and you bounce along with Tigger, ride with the Heffalumps and Woozles, and experience a cloudburst. This ride replaced Mr. Toad's Wild Ride; look for the painting of Mr. Toad handing the deed to Owl. **For people with disabilities:** If using a scooter, see a cast member about transferring to a standard wheelchair for the ride. Equipped for handheld-captioning and audio-description devices. ■ **TIP→** Use a Fastpass+ if crowds are heavy. ⊠ *Fantasyland, Magic Kingdom* ⟳ *Duration: 3 mins. Crowds: Heavy. Audience: Small kids.*

Mickey's PhilharMagic. Mickey Mouse may be the headliner here, but it's Donald Duck's misadventures—reminiscent of Mickey's as the sorcerer's apprentice in *Fantasia*—that set the comic pace in this 3-D animated film. As you settle into your seat, the on-screen action takes you behind the curtains at a grand concert hall where Donald and Mickey are preparing for a musical performance. But when Donald misuses Mickey's sorcerer's hat, he finds himself on a whirlwind journey that includes a magic carpet ride and an electrifying dip under the sea. And you go along for the ride. On the way you meet Ariel, Simba, Aladdin, Jasmine, Peter Pan, Tinker Bell, and others.

The film startles with its special-effects technology—you'll smell a fresh-baked apple pie, feel the rush of air as champagne corks pop, and get lost in the action on the 150-foot-wide screen. The 3-D film marks the first time that classic Disney characters appear in a computer-generated animation attraction. Some of the effects can startle small children, and some of the darker scenes are a bit muddy through the recycled 3-D glasses. **For people with disabilities:** There's a special viewing area for guests in wheelchairs. Reflective captioning is provided; equipped for assisted-listening and audio-description devices. ■ **TIP→** Fastpass+ is offered, but it's a big theater, so waits aren't long. ⊠ *Fantasyland, Magic Kingdom* ⟳ *Duration: 12 mins. Crowds: Heavy. Audience: All ages.*

Peter Pan's Flight. This sweet indoor ride was inspired by Sir James M. Barrie's 1904 novel about the boy who wouldn't grow up, which Disney animated in 1953. Aboard two-person magic sailing ships with brightly striped sails, you soar into the skies above London en route to Neverland. Along the way you can see Wendy, Michael, and John get sprinkled with pixie dust while Nana barks below, wave to the Lost Boys, spot the evil Captain Hook, and cheer for the ticktocking, clock-swallowing crocodile who breakfasted on Hook's hand.

Children—especially preschoolers—love this ride. Adults enjoy the dreamy views of London by moonlight. The downsides are the ride's brevity and its low-tech look. **For people with disabilities:** You must transfer from your wheelchair to the ride vehicle. Service animals aren't permitted. Equipped for handheld-captioning and audio-description devices. ■**TIP→** Use Fastpass+ here or ride early, late, or during the parade. ⊠ *Fantasyland, Magic Kingdom* ☞ *Duration: 2 1/2 mins. Crowds: Heavy. Audience: Small kids.*

Pete's Silly Sideshow. No other Disney character meet-and-greet location is quite as much fun as Pete's Silly Sideshow, named after the Mickey Mouse archenemy created in 1925. But you won't meet Strongman Pete under this big top, although he does make a poster appearance; instead, you'll grip and grin with Goofy, Minnie Mouse, Donald Duck, and his sweetheart, Daisy. Each character poses for photos and signs autographs against a sideshow backdrop: the Great Goofini, "Broken Bone Record Holder," in his stunt garb; the Astounding Donaldo dressed as a snake charmer; Minnie Magnifique, pretty in pink feathers, and her "pirouetting Parisian poodles," and Madame Daisy Fortuna with crystal ball as "seer of all fate and destinies." Two queues move guests along fairly quickly, and elaborate themed backdrops offer extra-fun photo ops. ■**TIP→** Line up your Fastpass+ for Enchanted Tales with Belle or Under the Sea: Journey of the Little Mermaid, then head back to the Storybook Circus area to meet these characters and ride Dumbo the Flying Elephant. ⊠ *Fantasyland, Magic Kingdom* ☞ *Duration: About 1–2 mins. per character meet and greet. Crowds: Yes, but double queue makes wait shorter. Audience: Young kids.*

Prince Charming Regal Carrousel. This ride is great for families and for romantics, young and old. Seventy-two of the 90 dashing wooden steeds date from the original carousel built in 1917 by the Philadelphia Toboggan Company; additional mounts were made of fiberglass. All are meticulously painted, and each one is completely different. One wears a collar of bright yellow roses; another, a quiver of Native American arrows. Eighteen panels beneath the wooden canopy depict scenes from Disney's 1950 film *Cinderella*. As the ride spins, the mirrors sparkle, the fairy lights glitter, and the band organ plays favorite Disney movie tunes. **For people with disabilities:** If using a wheelchair, or if you have a service animal, check with a host for boarding information. ■**TIP→** Lines move quickly. Come while waiting for your Peter Pan's Flight Fastpass+ reservation. ⊠ *Fantasyland, Magic Kingdom* ☞ *Duration: 2 mins. Crowds: Moderate to heavy. Audience: Families.*

Fodor's Choice ★ **Seven Dwarfs Mine Train.** Quick! Can you name all Seven Dwarfs in seven seconds? Sleepy, Doc, Grumpy, Bashful, Sneezy, Happy, and Dopey. Snow White's hardworking pals display impressive Audio-Animatronics flair as they mine a mountain full of glittering gems and "Heigh-ho" their way into theme-park fans' hearts at the Seven Dwarfs Mine Train. Set amid a steep Enchanted Forest landscaped with red poppies, cedars, and birch trees, the attraction is a visual feast of LED-illuminated gems, playful woodland creatures, and beloved characters from Walt Disney's 1937 animated film classic, *Snow White and the Seven Dwarfs*. A rough-hewn entrance to the mine leads to a covered queue designed to keep riders occupied as they wend their way toward the train load area. Fun interactive diversions include animated "floating" gems that you can catch and match in a touch-screen jewel-washing trough. The musical family coaster serves up thrills, but no stomach-churning plunges, with cars that twist, climb, drop rapidly, and rock gently when slowing down for riders to enjoy the artfully crafted scene of the dwarfs at work in the mine. As the train rounds its final curve, you'll see Snow White dancing with her diminutive pals in the storybook cottage as the Wicked Queen, disguised as an old hag, lurks outside. The ride is not appropriate if you're pregnant or have heart, back, or neck problems. **For people with disabilities:** You must transfer from wheelchair to ride vehicle. ■**TIP➜** Book your Fastpass+ at the closest park kiosk if you didn't reserve it at the My Disney Experience website or mobile app. If circumstances deposit you in the stand-by queue, enjoy the clever hands-on activities along the way. ⊠ *Fantasyland, Magic Kingdom* ☞ *Duration: 2.5 mins. Crowds: Heavy. Audience: All ages. Height requirement: 38 inches.*

Under the Sea: Journey of the Little Mermaid. The shipwreck theming, craggy grotto rock work, waterfalls, lagoons, and magical landscape of this attraction draw you into Ariel's world long before you board a giant clamshell for a journey under the sea. As you wend your way through the long queue, you'll see starfish embedded in rocks, a sandy beach, palm trees, sea-grape plants, and other authentic seaside touches. Once inside the cavern beneath Prince Eric's Castle, you can join in an interactive game that plays out around every corner starring Scuttle the seagull and his animated crab pals. Through a cave portal, you'll enter the castle's stone hallways, where you hop aboard a clamshell ride vehicle and, thanks to cold air and light effects, feel the sensation of descending under the sea. You'll float past animated and Audio-Animatronic scenes from *The Little Mermaid* film, including a Broadway-style "Under the Sea" number with Sebastian conducting the undersea orchestra. There are fish conga lines and ominous scenes starring villainess Ursula but, of course, a fairy-tale ending is in store featuring Menken-Ashman showstopper "Kiss the Girl." Most children love this ride, but some tots are afraid in the dark Ursula scene. **For people with disabilities:** Guests in scooters must transfer to a standard wheelchair to ride; equipped for handheld captioning and audio description. ■**TIP➜** You can get a Fastpass+, but you'll miss the fun of the interactive stand-by queue. ⊠ *Fantasyland, Magic Kingdom* ☞ *Duration: 7 mins. Crowds: Absolutely! Audience: All ages.*

TOMORROWLAND

The "future that never was" spins boldly into view as you enter Tomorrowland, where Disney Imagineers paint the landscape with whirling spaceships, flashy neon lights, and gleaming robots. This is the future as envisioned by sci-fi writers and moviemakers in the 1920s and '30s, when space flight, laser beams, and home computers were fiction, not fact. Retro Jetsonesque styling lends the area lasting chic.

Gamers who want a break from the crowds can find their favorite video challenges in the arcade attached to Space Mountain. SEGA race car, NASCAR, and Fast and Furious Super Bikes games draw tweens and teens; Lil' Hoops give young kids a manageable basketball challenge. Though Tomorrowland Transit Authority (TTA) PeopleMover isn't a big-ticket ride, it's a great way to check out the landscape from above as it zooms in and out of Space Mountain and curves around the entire land.

Astro Orbiter. This gleaming superstructure of revolving planets has come to symbolize Tomorrowland as much as Dumbo represents Fantasyland. Passenger vehicles, on arms projecting from a central column, sail past whirling planets; you control your car's altitude but not the velocity. The line is directly across from the entrance to the TTA PeopleMover. **For people with disabilities:** You must be able to walk several steps and transfer to the vehicle. ■**TIP➡** The line moves slowly; come while waiting for a Space Mountain Fastpass+ appointment or if there's a short line. Skip on your first visit if time is limited. ⊠ *Tomorrowland, Magic Kingdom* ⏱ *Duration: 2 mins. Crowds: Moderate to heavy. Audience: All ages.*

Fodor's Choice
★
Buzz Lightyear's Space Ranger Spin. Based on the wildly popular *Toy Story*, this ride gives you a toy's perspective as it pits you and Buzz Lightyear against the evil Emperor Zurg. You're seated in a fast-moving two-passenger Star Cruiser vehicle with an infrared laser gun and a centrally located lever for spinning your ship to get a good vantage point. Throughout the ride you shoot at targets to help macho space toy, Buzz, defeat the emperor and save the universe. You have to hit the targets marked with a "Z" to score, and the rider with the most points wins. To infinity and beyond! **For people with disabilities:** To board you must transfer to a standard wheelchair. Equipped for audio-description and handheld-captioning devices. ■**TIP➡** Use Fastpass+ or go during a parade. If you're with kids, time the wait and—if it's only 15 or 20 minutes—ride twice so they can have a practice run. ⊠ *Tomorrowland, Magic Kingdom* ⏱ *Duration: 5 mins. Crowds: Heavy. Audience: All ages–truly.*

Monsters, Inc. Laugh Floor. The joke's on everyone at this interactive attraction starring Mike Wazowski, the one-eyed hero from Disney-Pixar's hit film *Monsters, Inc.* In the 400-seat theater, you can interact with an animated Mike and his sidekicks in the real-time, unscripted way that the character Crush from *Finding Nemo* performs at Epcot in Turtle Talk with Crush at The Seas with Nemo & Friends. Here the premise is that Mike realizes laughter can be harnessed as a power source, and Mike's new comedy club is expected to generate power for the future. The more the audience yuks it up, the greater the power produced. You can text-message jokes from cell phones to the show's producer; they might even be used in the show. **For people with disabilities:** Wheelchair accessible. Sign language is available some days. Equipped for assisted-listening and video-captioning devices. ■**TIP➡** Skip the Fastpass+ for this show; come when you're waiting for your Buzz Lightyear or Space Mountain Fastpass+ appointment. ⊠ *Tomorrowland, Magic Kingdom* ⏱ *Duration: 15 mins. Crowds: Heavy. Audience: All ages.*

Fodor's Choice
★
Space Mountain. The needlelike spires and gleaming, white, concrete cone of this 180-foot-high attraction are almost as much a Magic Kingdom landmark as Cinderella Castle. Inside is what is one of the world's most imaginative roller coasters, one that had a real astronaut, Gordon Cooper, for a creative consultant. Although there are no loop-the-loops or high-speed curves, the thrills are many as you take a trip into the depths of outer space—in the dark.

In Tomorrowland, interplanetary travel is within your reach on the Astro Orbiter.

You can pass the wait time playing big-screen interactive space games in the long, dark queue area. As you walk to the loading area, you'll pass whirling planets and hear the screams and shrieks of the riders, pumping you up for your own launch. Once you blast off, the ride lasts only two minutes and 38 seconds, with a top speed of 28 mph, but the devious twists and invisible drops in the dark make it seem twice as long. You can hear the screams from other cars, but you don't know where they are, adding an additional fright factor. Stow personal belongings securely. Not appropriate for pregnant women or guests wearing back, neck, or leg braces. **For people with disabilities:** You must be able to step into the ride vehicle and walk short distances. Guests in wheelchairs should see a cast member for boarding options. Service animals aren't permitted. ■**TIP➜ The wait can be long. Get a Fastpass+, or come early, late, or during a parade.** ✉ *Tomorrowland, Magic Kingdom* ☞ *Duration: 2 1/2 mins. Crowds: You bet! Audience: Not young kids. Height requirement: 44 inches.*

Tomorrowland Speedway. This is one of those rides that incite instant addiction in children and immediate regret in their parents. The reasons for the former are evident: the brightly colored Mark VII model cars that swerve around the four 2,260-foot tracks with much *vroom-vroom-vrooming.* Like real sports cars, the vehicles are equipped with rack-and-pinion steering and disc brakes; unlike the real thing, these run on a track. But the track is so twisty that it's hard to keep the car on a straight course. Expect to spend a lot of time waiting your turn on the track and returning your vehicle after your lap. All this for a ride that achieves a top speed of 7 mph.

MAGIC KINGDOM KIDS TOUR

The Magic Kingdom is alive with thrilling distractions for young children, so let them take the lead now and then. Toddlers may want to jump from their strollers and dance along to the barbershop quartet on Main Street. Children who love to explore will have a ball scrambling around Frontierland and hopping a raft to Tom Sawyer's playground.

STOP AND SMELL THE ROSES

Head down Main Street, U.S.A., and, if you're lucky, the park's **Dapper Dan's barbershop quartet** will be harmonizing sweet tunes and tossing out one-liners from a small alcove along the street (check the park's *Times Guide* for performances). Young children are thrilled with the music and colorful costumes of these talented singers.

As you continue on, veer right toward the rose garden for a scenic picture spot where you can snap one of the prettiest shots in the park: the kids by the garden amid Mickey and Minnie topiaries, with Cinderella Castle in the background.

Fantasyland is dead ahead, and after you've soared on **Dumbo the Flying Elephant** and nabbed a Fastpass+ for Under the Sea: Journey of the Little Mermaid or the Seven Dwarfs Mine Train family coaster, head straight to Enchanted Tales with Belle where the kids get to participate. Then try to catch a character performance in front of **Cinderella Castle** or during one of the daily parades or street parties.

PUT THE ZIP IN YOUR DOO-DAH

With little ones in tow, when it's time for food, fast is best. **Cosmic Ray's Starlight Café** is a high-energy quick stop with multiple choices for the entire family. Kids can head straight to the dance floor where Audio-Animatronics entertainer Sonny Eclipse keeps the tunes coming. After refueling, board the **Walt Disney World Railroad** at Main Street, U.S.A., Fantasyland, or Frontierland. While in Frontierland, too-short-to-ride kids can burn energy in the cavelike play area beneath **Splash Mountain** while parents take turns riding. The short raft trip to **Tom Sawyer Island** is worth it for kids who like exploring. Not far from the Country Bear Jamboree, sure shots can take aim at Western-style targets in the often-missed **Frontierland Shootin' Arcade**—at about $1 per 35 shots, it's a blast for any aspiring sheriff.

BECOME THE CHARACTER

Get the makeover of a lifetime ($55–$195) at **Bibbidi Bobbidi Boutique,** in Cinderella Castle. Hair, nails, makeup—even a sprinkling of pixie dust—it's all here. At the **Pirates League** in Adventureland by Pirates of the Caribbean, a scurvy sea-dog makeover ($29.95–$45) lets the inner buccaneer emerge. Don't want to be a pirate? Try the mermaid makeover ($35–$75).

Afterward, be sure to catch a character meet and greet (see *Times Guide* for schedule) so the little rascals get all the hugs, autographs, photos, and magical memories they deserve.

2

For people with disabilities: To drive the cars, you must be able to steer, press the gas pedal, and transfer into the low car seat. ■TIP→ **Don't waste a Fastpass+ on this one; skip on a first-time visit unless you'll break your child's heart.** ⊠ *Tomorrowland, Magic Kingdom* ☞ *Duration: 5 mins. Crowds: Moderate. Audience: Young kids and tweens. Height requirements: With an adult must be at least 32 inches; those who wish to drive must reach 54 inches.*

Tomorrowland Transit Authority PeopleMover. A reincarnation of what Disney old-timers may remember as the WEDway PeopleMover, the TTA PeopleMover gives you a nice, leisurely ride with great views of Tomorrowland, circling the Astro-Orbiter and gliding through the middle of Space Mountain. Disney's version of future mass transit is smooth and noiseless, thanks to an electromagnetic linear induction motor that has no moving parts, uses little power, and emits no pollutants. **For people with disabilities:** You must be able to walk several steps and step on and off a moving ramp to transfer to a ride vehicle. Equipped for handheld-captioning and audio-description devices. ■TIP→ **Come to view Tomorrowland, to preview Space Mountain, if you have young children, or if you need a relaxing ride.** ⊠ *Tomorrowland, Magic Kingdom* ☞ *Duration: 10 mins. Crowds: Light. Audience: All ages.*

Walt Disney's Carousel of Progress. Originally seen at New York's 1964–65 World's Fair, this revolving theater traces the impact of technological progress on the daily lives of Americans from the turn of the 20th century into the near future. Representing each decade, an Audio-Animatronics family sings the praises of modern-day gadgets that technology has wrought. **For people with disabilities:** Wheelchair accessible; equipped for assisted-listening, handheld-captioning, audio-description, and video-captioning devices. ■TIP→ **Skip on a first-time visit unless you adore nostalgia. May close early or entirely in low season.** ⊠ *Tomorrowland, Magic Kingdom* ☞ *Duration: 20 mins. Crowds: Moderate. Audience: All ages.*

MAGIC KINGDOM SPECTACLES

Once Upon a Time. Before the popular fireworks show most evenings, and some nights twice, Cinderella Castle lights up to tell a story to park guests with the help of cutting-edge projector technology that wraps colorful images around the castle in sequences enhanced by music. For 14 minutes, the castle is a magical canvas that transforms into scenes from favorite Disney animated films, *Alice in Wonderland, Frozen, Peter Pan,* and more. **For people with disabilities:** Ask any cast member along Main Street for the best wheelchair viewing location; several areas are set aside. ■TIP→ **Try for a better view and some breathing room away from the crowds by migrating to one of the walkways that lead from the castle hub to Tomorrowland or Adventureland.** ⊠ *Central Plaza, Magic Kingdom* ☞ *Duration: 10 mins. Crowds: Heavy. Audience: All ages.*

Fodor's Choice
★

Disney Festival of Fantasy Parade. Who'd want to miss a parade that delivers in 12 entertainment-packed minutes a lineup of Disney characters and royalty, a Steampunk-inspired, fire-breathing dragon, elaborate towering floats, and handsome pairs of dancers twirling to some of

Princesses Anna and Elsa are featured in Disney's Festival of Fantasy Parade.

Disney's best tunes? This daily 3 pm parade celebrates Walt's legacy with vignettes featuring the glamour, drama, and fun of classic films like *Sleeping Beauty, Beauty and the Beast,* and *Peter Pan* while also catering to fans of contemporary box-office hits like *Brave* and *Frozen.* The colorful pageant of nine floats outperforms its predecessors with übercreative costuming, inventive float technology, a cast of nearly 100 gung-ho performers, and a musical score that invites singing along with familiar medleys. From the 50-foot-long topiary garden float of Disney royal couples led by dancers in ball gowns with iridescent feathers to the 32-foot-tall Airship float finale with Mickey and Minnie, the parade energizes spectators as it rolls past. A Lost Boy from *Peter Pan* may grab your hand and kiss it. A stilt-walker might lean into your camera for a snapshot. You'll hear viewers gasp or shout when the towering 53-foot-long, green-eyed Maleficent Dragon, created with help from Tony-award-winning designer Michael Curry, rears its head and spews flames. **For people with disabilities:** There are viewing areas for guests in wheelchairs along the route; ask any cast member for guidance. A sign-language schedule is available at Guest Relations. ■**TIP→** The parade runs from Frontierland to Town Square. Check your guide map for the complete route. Disney distributes a limited number of Fastpass+ reservations, but book as far ahead as possible. Otherwise, find shade beneath a Frontierland porch at least an hour before showtime. If you've seen the parade, this is a good time to head for popular rides while crowds gather along the route. ⊠ *Magic Kingdom* ↻ *Duration: 12 mins. Crowds: Heavy. Audience: All ages.*

Mickey's Royal Friendship Faire. The Cinderella Castle forecourt provides the perfect location for several daily performances of this Disney character celebration of friendship starring Mickey Mouse, Minnie Mouse, Donald Duck, Daisy Duck, Goofy, and their friends. As the spectacle begins, the Duck and Mouse families along with pal Goofy bounce through the castle doors and announce they've invited new friends from afar to come to the fair: Tiana and friends from the Land of the Bewitching Bayous arrive with Goofy, to a Dixieland beat; Donald brings a troupe of rowdy Vikings, while Daisy's pals Rapunzel and Flynn encourage them to sing instead of carouse; the final newcomers are the popular *Frozen* characters Elsa, Anna, and Olaf the snowman. For the finale everyone takes the stage for a waltz. If you want to sit (and don't mind an obstructed view), arrive 30 to 40 minutes before showtime to get a seat on a bench. ■**TIP→ If you have children, plan to stand or sit on the pavement near the stage for an unobstructed view.** ⊠ *Central Plaza, Magic Kingdom* ↻ *Duration: 20 mins. Crowds: Heavy. Audience: All ages.*

Fodor's Choice
★

Happily Ever After. When the lights dim on Main Street and familiar film tunes fill the air, you know the fireworks extravaganza is about to begin. In Happily Ever After, which replaced Wishes in 2017, popular Disney animated films are explored using song, fireworks, projections, and lasers. Cinderella Castle is transformed with spectacular projection technology for each musical segment of this 18-minute visual treat, from the title tune through familiar songs from nearly 20 Disney films. Snippets of the animated films appear on the castle's parapets and spires, and for some segments, the castle itself appears to become animated. Check the *Times Guide* for performance time, which varies seasonally. ■**TIP→ You can book a Fastpass+ ahead of your visit for best viewing. The castle forecourt and surrounding bridges offer great views; or find a place near the front of the park for a quick postshow exit.** ⊠ *Central Plaza, Magic Kingdom* ↻ *Duration: 12 mins. Crowds: Heavy. Audience: All ages.*

EPCOT

Walt Disney said that Epcot would "take its cue from the new ideas and new technologies that are now emerging from the creative centers of American industry." He wrote that Epcot—never completed, always improving—"will never cease to be a living blueprint of the future, a showcase to the world for the ingenuity of American free enterprise." That statement has never been more true than now, as so much in Epcot is undergoing big changes. Several attractions have closed, and Disney officials have announced new, and often more kid-friendly, attractions to be open by 2021.

The permanent settlement that Disney envisioned wasn't to be. Epcot opened in 1982—16 years after his death—as a showcase, ostensibly, for the concepts that would be incorporated into the real-life Epcots of the future. (Disney's vision *has* taken an altered shape in the self-contained city of Celebration, an urban-planner's dream opened in 1996 on Disney property near Kissimmee.)

Epcot, the theme park, has two key areas: Future World, where many changes are taking place during the next couple of years. Most pavilions are collaborations between Walt Disney Imagineering and U.S. corporations and are designed to demonstrate technological advances through innovative shows and attractions; and the World Showcase, where shops, restaurants, attractions, and live entertainment create microcosms of 11 countries from four continents.

For years, Epcot was considered the more staid park, a place geared toward adults. But after its 10th anniversary, Epcot began to evolve

TOP ATTRACTIONS

Frozen Ever After. *Frozen* fans line up in droves to hop in a longboat and join Elsa and Anna in this chilly adventure based on the film.

IllumiNations. This amazing musical laser-fountains-and-fireworks show is Disney nighttime entertainment at its best.

Mission: SPACE. Blast off on a simulated ride to Mars, if you can handle the turbulence.

Soarin'. Everyone's hands-down favorite: feel the breeze as you hang glide over spectacular global scenery.

Test Track. Design your concept car, then rev up to 60 mph on a hairpin turn in this wild ride on a Chevrolet proving ground.

Phineas and Ferb: Agent P's World Showcase Adventure. With starting points in several locations, this interactive adventure leads kids through all the international pavilions using clues on their own smartphone.

into a livelier, more child-friendly park, with such wow attractions as Future World's Test Track, Mission: SPACE, and Soarin'.

There's something for everyone here. The World Showcase appeals to younger children with the Kidcot Fun Stop craft stations and the Norway pavilion's Frozen Ever After ride. Soarin', in the Land Pavilion, is a family favorite. And the Seas with Nemo & Friends—with one of the world's largest saltwater aquariums and a Nemo-themed ride—is a must-see for all. Adrenaline junkie? Don't miss Test Track presented by Chevrolet, where you can design your own custom concept car, then put it through its high-speed paces.

Wear comfortable shoes—there's *a lot* of territory to cover here. Arrive early, and try to stay all day, squeezing in extras like Bruce's Shark World and a relaxing meal. If you enter through International Gateway before 11 am, cast members will direct you to Future World, which usually opens two hours before World Showcase, or you can indulge in a latte and éclair at the France bakery, the sole quick-service eatery open early in World Showcase.

ORIENTATION AND PLANNING
GETTING ORIENTED

Epcot is composed of two areas: Future World and the World Showcase. The inner core of Future World's pavilions has the Spaceship Earth geosphere and a plaza anchored by the computer-animated Fountain of Nations. Innoventions, popular for its hands-on, high-tech exhibits and immersion entertainment is much reduced, as part of the evolution at Epcot. Some pavilions have closed or seen their content reduced, and Disney officials announced in 2017 that some new attractions were coming to Epcot in time for Walt Disney World's 50th anniversary in 2021. One of them is a Guardians of the Galaxy attraction in place of Ellen's Energy Adventure, which closed in 2017.

Six pavilions compose Future World's outer ring. Each of the east pavilions has a ride and the occasional postride showcase; a visit rarely takes more than 30 minutes. The blockbuster exhibits on the west side contain rides and interactive displays; each exhibit can take up to 90 minutes for the complete experience.

World Showcase pavilions are on the promenade that circles the World Showcase Lagoon. Each houses architectural examples of a country, with shops, restaurants, and friendly international staffers; some have films or displays. Mexico offers a tame ride. Live entertainment is scheduled at several pavilions. Disney's monorail and buses drop you off at the main entrance in front of Future World. But if you're staying at one of the Epcot resorts (the BoardWalk, Yacht Club, Beach Club, Dolphin, or Swan), you can use the International Gateway entrance between World Showcase's France and U.K. pavilions.

PARK AMENITIES

Baby Care: The baby-care center at Odyssey Center in Future World has rocking chairs and low lighting. The center sells formula, baby food, pacifiers, and disposable diapers. Changing tables are available here, as well as in all women's and some men's restrooms.

Cameras: Disposable cameras and memory cards are widely available, and you can use the Disney PhotoPass Service to gather memories throughout the park. Other photo services are available at the Imagination! pavilion.

First Aid: Staffed by registered nurses, first aid is in the Odyssey Center. More than a dozen automated external defibrillators are located across the park.

Guest Relations: The two locations where you can pick up schedules and maps are to the right of the ticket windows at the park entrance and to the left of Spaceship Earth inside the park. You can also get maps at the park's International Gateway entrance and most shops. Guest Relations will also assist with dining reservations, ticket upgrades, and services for guests with disabilities.

Lockers: Lockers ($7 and $9, with $5 refundable deposit) are at the International Gateway and to the west of Spaceship Earth. Coin-operated lockers also are at the bus information center by the bus parking lot.

Lost People and Things: Instruct children to speak to someone with a Disney name tag if you become separated. If you have lost an item, check the park's Guest Relations office.

Epcot Lost and Found. Located in the Guest Relations lobby east of Spaceship Earth. ⊠ *Future World, Epcot* ☎ *407/560–7500.*

Main Lost and Found Office. After one day, all articles are sent here and can be retrieved between 9 am and 7 pm daily. ⊠ *Transportation and Ticket Center [TTC], Magic Kingdom* ☎ *407/824–4245.*

Package Pick-Up: Ask shop clerks to forward large purchases to Package Pick-Up at the Gift Stop in the Entrance Plaza and at the World Traveler at International Gateway. Allow three hours for delivery. You also can have packages sent to your Disney hotel.

Services for People with Disabilities: Accessibility standards are high. Many attractions and most restaurants and shops are fully wheelchair accessible. There are large Braille park maps at Guest Relations in Future

World and International Gateway as well as to the left of the walkway from Future World to the World Showcase Plaza.

At Guest Relations there's a schedule for sign-language presentations at some of the park attractions; you can also pick up special devices for hearing- and sight-impaired visitors.

At World Showcase most people stroll around the promenade, but there are also Friendship boats, which require visitors using oversized wheelchairs or scooters to transfer to Disney chairs.

You can rent wheelchairs at the gift stop outside the main entrance, at the Stroller & Wheelchair Rental Shop to the left of Spaceship Earth, or at the International Gateway. A limited number of electronic convenience vehicles (ECV) are available only at the Stroller & Wheelchair Rental.

Wheelchairs are $12 daily, $10 for multiday rental. ECVs are $50 per day plus a refundable $20 security deposit. Arrive early, because neither conveyance can be reserved. Several Orlando-area companies also rent and deliver ECVs.

Stroller Rentals: You can rent strollers on the east side of the Entrance Plaza and at the International Gateway. Singles are $15 daily, $13 for multiday rental; doubles cost $31 daily, $27 for multiple days. Even preschoolers will be glad for a stroller in this large park.

PARK TOURS

Epcot Seas Adventures—DiveQuest. The three-hour Epcot DiveQuest ($179, park admission not required or included) begins with a guide collecting you at Guest Services outside the entrance. You spend 40 minutes in the 5.7-million-gallon saltwater aquarium under the supervision of a master diver. Family and friends with Epcot admission can view your dive through the huge windows that line the aquarium. The tour takes place Tuesday through Saturday in the afternoon. Guests ages 10 and up must have open-water adult scuba certification; children 10 to 12 must dive with a parent or legal guardian. Diving equipment is supplied. ✉ *Epcot* ☎ *407/939–8687* 🖥 *$175.*

Epcot Seas Adventures—Aqua Tour. For this tour ($145, no park admission required or included) you wear a flotation device and snorkel gear, and you remain on the water's surface. Anyone age 8 and older can join the tour (those under 12 must be with a parent or legal guardian). Tours are limited to 12 guests, meet Tuesday through Saturday, and run about 2½ hours, with 30 minutes in the water. ✉ *Epcot.*

Gardens of the World Tour. Plant lovers of all levels will enjoy this three-hour tour ($85, plus park admission) with a Disney Horticulturist to see the World Showcase's wide range of exotic plantings and to learn about the role landscaping plays in Disney parks and resorts. Tours run on select days during the Epcot International Flower and Garden Festival from early to mid-March through late May or during the Epcot International Food and Wine Festival in the fall. For ages 12 and up. ✉ *Epcot* ☎ *407/939–8687* 🖥 *$64.*

UnDISCOVERed Future World. This tour ($69, plus park admission) leaves at 8:30 am Monday through Friday from a meeting spot between

EPCOT BY BOAT

Epcot is a big place at 305 acres; a local joke suggests that the acronym actually stands for "Every Person Comes Out Tired." But still, the most efficient way to get around is to walk.

To vary things, you can cruise across the lagoon in an air-conditioned, 65-foot water taxi. Also called Friendship Boats, they depart every 12 minutes from four World Showcase Plaza docks spaced around the lagoon.

The boat closer to Mexico zips to a dock by the Germany pavilion; the one closer to Canada heads to Morocco. You may have to stand in line to board, however.

Fountain View and Club Cool. The four-hour behind-the-scenes walk for guests 16 and older covers Future World pavilions and some VIP lounges and backstage areas, including the VIP lounge at Mission: SPACE. ✉ *Epcot* ☎ *407/939–8687* 💲 *$64.*

VISITING TIPS

Take your time. Epcot is so vast and varied that you really need two days to explore. With just one day, you'll have to be highly selective.

Go early in the week. Magic Kingdom tends to be busiest in the early days of the week.

Plan for the special events. If you like a good festival, visit during the International Flower and Garden Festival (early March through mid-May) or the International Food and Wine Festival (September through mid-November).

Ride the popular rides early. Once through the turnstiles at either the main Future World entrance or the back World Showcase entrance, make a beeline for the popular Mission: SPACE and Test Track (for fast-paced thrills) or Frozen Ever After and Soarin' (for family fun). Or get a Fastpass+ and return later.

EXPLORING EPCOT

FUTURE WORLD

Future World's inner core is composed of the iconic Spaceship Earth geosphere and, beyond it, a plaza anchored by the awe-inspiring computer-animated Fountain of Nations, which shoots water 150 feet skyward.

Several pavilions compose Future World's outer ring. On the east side, they are Mission: SPACE and Test Track. Disney pulled the plug on Ellen's Energy Adventure in 2017, announcing the opening of a Guardians of the Galaxy ride in its place, but not until 2021. On the west side are the Seas with Nemo & Friends, The Land, and Imagination! These blockbuster exhibits contain both rides and interactive displays; you could spend at least 1½ hours at each of these pavilions, but there aren't enough hours in the day, so prioritize.

2

■TIP→ Before setting out, look into the Disney PhotoPass at the Camera Center in the Entrance Plaza. It tracks photos of your group shot by Disney photographers, which you can view and purchase later at the center or online.

SPACESHIP EARTH

Balanced like a giant golf ball waiting for some celestial being to tee off, the multifaceted silver geosphere of Spaceship Earth is to Epcot what Cinderella Castle is to the Magic Kingdom. As much a landmark as an icon, it can be seen on a clear day from an airplane flying down either coast of Florida.

Spaceship Earth ride. Inside the giant geosphere you are transported past a series of tableaux that explore human progress and the continuing search for better forms of communication. Oscar-winner Dame Judi Dench narrates the journey that begins in the darkest tunnels of time, proceeds through history, and ends poised on the edge of the future. Revered author Ray Bradbury helped design the iconic ball, and wrote the original story. Ten-time Emmy winner Bruce Broughton composed the musical score.

Audio-Animatronics figures present Cro-Magnon man daubing mystic paintings on cave walls, Egyptian scribes scratching hieroglyphics on papyrus, Roman centurions building roads, Islamic scholars mapping the heavens, and 11th- and 12th-century Benedictine monks hand-copying manuscripts. As you move into the Renaissance, there's Michelangelo and Gutenberg, and, in rapid succession, the telegraph, radio, television, and computer come into being. A family views the moon landing on TV, and soon the personal computer is born.

As your ride vehicle swings backward and descends slowly, touch screens ask how you envision your own future, then play back an animated, *Jetsons*-esque scenario based on the answers. Siemens, which presents the attraction, created a fun-packed postshow with high-demand interactive games. As you enter the postshow, watch the giant digital map screen to see your photo taken during the ride and posted in your hometown location. **For people with disabilities:** You must be able to transfer to a standard wheelchair, then walk four steps to the ride vehicle. Guests with service animals should check with an attraction host for boarding information. The ride is equipped for handheld-captioning and audio-description devices available at Guest Relations.
■TIP→ Ride while waiting for a Mission: SPACE or Soarin' Fastpass+ appointment. Lines are longest in the morning and shortest just before closing. ⊠ *Future World, Spaceship Earth, Epcot* ⟲ *Duration: 15 mins. Crowds: Moderate to heavy. Audience: All ages.*

INNOVENTIONS

This walk-through attraction contains interactive exhibits that entertain kids (some are especially designed for preschoolers) and adults as they investigate the innovations now improving the world around us.

With soft drinks going for more than $2 per cup at park concessions, **Club Cool** is the place to visit when you're thirsty and in the mood to be adventurous. Here Coca-Cola's bold red-and-white colors guide you to a room full of soda machines and logo merchandise. You can sample

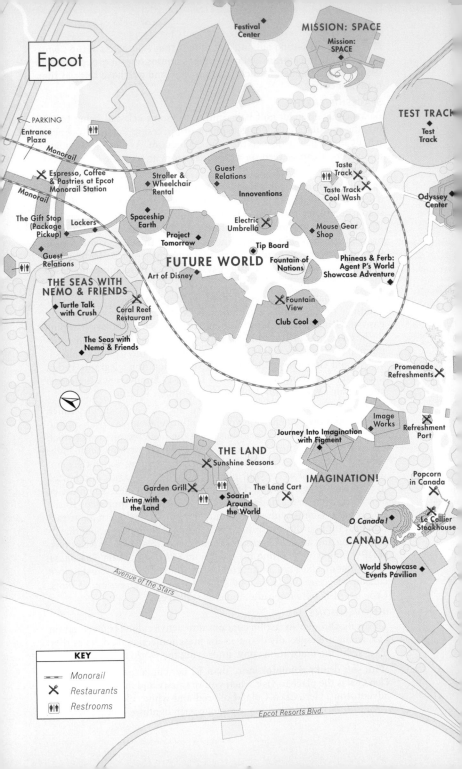

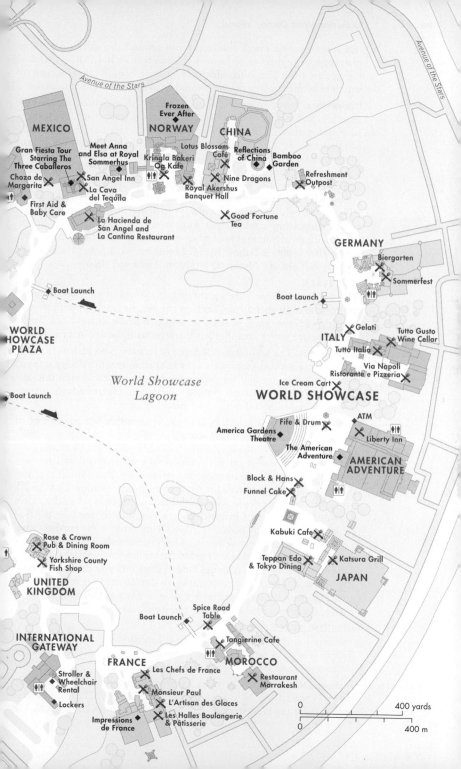

Avenue of the Stars

Avenue of the Stars

MEXICO

Gran Fiesta Tour Starring The Three Caballeros

Meet Anna and Elsa at Royal Sommerhus

Choza de Margarita

San Angel Inn

La Cava del Tequila

First Aid & Baby Care

La Hacienda de San Angel and La Cantina Restaurant

NORWAY

Frozen Ever After

Kringla Bakeri Og Kafe

Lotus Blossom Café

Royal Akershus Banquet Hall

CHINA

Reflections of China

Nine Dragons

Bamboo Garden

Refreshment Outpost

Good Fortune Tea

GERMANY

Biergarten

Sommerfest

Boat Launch

Boat Launch

WORLD SHOWCASE PLAZA

Gelati

ITALY

Tutto Italia

Tutto Gusto Wine Cellar

Via Napoli Ristorante e Pizzeria

Ice Cream Cart

WORLD SHOWCASE

Boat Launch

World Showcase Lagoon

Fife & Drum

ATM

America Gardens Theatre

The American Adventure

Liberty Inn

AMERICAN ADVENTURE

Block & Hans

Funnel Cake

Kabuki Cafe

Rose & Crown Pub & Dining Room

Yorkshire County Fish Shop

Teppan Edo & Tokyo Dining

Katsura Grill

UNITED KINGDOM

JAPAN

Boat Launch

Spice Road Table

INTERNATIONAL GATEWAY

Tangierine Cafe

Stroller & Wheelchair Rental

FRANCE

Les Chefs de France

MOROCCO

Restaurant Marrakesh

Lockers

Monsieur Paul

L'Artisan des Glaces

Impressions de France

Les Halles Boulangerie & Pâtisserie

0   400 yards

0   400 m

(for free) the cola king's products from around the world, including mainstays Vegitabeta from Japan and Beverly from Italy. Other refreshing sips are from Thailand, Africa, Brazil, and Peru. It's entertaining to watch kids' faces when their taste buds react to an unfamiliar flavor.

Innoventions. Innoventions was once loaded with activities designed to entertain and inspire kids and adults and was a great place for families to play together. Many of the innovative activities have been closed, but two remain: Colortopia, presented by Glidden, which offers color mixing-and-matching games, as well as a creative experience where you can wield your own "magical paintbrush," and The SpectacuLAB, presented by Murata, where basic scientific principles are explored. **For people with disabilities:** This attraction is completely wheelchair accessible—some exhibits inside this always-evolving attraction may require transferring from a wheelchair. Guests with service animals should check with an attractions host when entering. ■ **TIP→ Come before 11 am or after 2 pm.** ⊠ *Future World, Innoventions, Epcot* ☞ *Duration: Up to you. Crowds: Moderate to heavy. Audience: All ages.*

TEST TRACK

This pavilion is shaped like a giant disk. As you wait to enter the building for the high-speed ride, cars on the return track whiz past you. Outside kids can get a soaking or a frozen drink in the Cool Wash, an interactive water area that lets them pretend they're in a car wash.

Fodor's Choice
★

Test Track ride. The white-knuckle finale of this fan favorite is as thrilling as ever. Create a custom concept vehicle at an interactive design station, and then buckle up in a six-person SimCar to put the design through its paces in a neon-splashed, futuristic setting that surrounds the attraction's original hills and mountain switchbacks.

The High-Speed Test is last: your vehicle bursts through an opening in the Test Track building to negotiate a steeply banked loop at a speed of nearly 60 mph. At the special effects–laden postshow, you can check out how your custom car performed and create your own car commercial. The speeds and some jarring effects may prove unsettling. The ride isn't suitable for pregnant women or guests wearing back, neck, or leg braces. **For people with disabilities:** Visitors in wheelchairs are provided a special area in which to practice transferring into the ride vehicle before actually boarding. One TV monitor in the preshow area is closed-captioned. Service animals aren't permitted onboard. ■ **TIP→ If you use a Fastpass+, you won't get to customize your vehicle—it will be a predesigned version. A Single Rider queue lets you skip a long wait. The ride won't function on wet tracks, so don't head here after a downpour.** ⊠ *Future World, Test Track, Epcot* ☞ *Duration: 5 mins. Crowds: Heavy. Audience: Not small kids. Height requirement: 40 inches.*

MISSION: SPACE

The exterior of this pavilion has a sleek, futuristic look with a planetary theme. When the weather is warm enough, kids like to hop around in the fountain out front.

Fodor's Choice
★

Mission: SPACE. It took five years for Disney Imagineers, with the help of 25 experts from NASA, to design Mission: SPACE, the first ride ever to take people "straight up" in a simulated rocket launch. The

2

story transports you and co-riders to the year 2036 and the International Space Training Center, where you are about to embark on your first launch. Before you board the four-person rocket capsule, you're assigned to a position: commander, navigator, pilot, or engineer. And at this point you're warned several times about the intensity of the ride and the risks for people with health concerns. Pregnant women and anyone with heart, back, neck, balance, blood-pressure, or motion-sickness problems shouldn't ride.

■TIP➔ **Many people exit this ride feeling nauseated and disoriented from the high-speed spinning, which is what makes you feel as if you're rocketing into space. These effects are often cumulative, so stick with one go-round.**

> ## MISSION: SPACE CAUTION
>
> Parents should exercise caution when deciding whether to let children ride Mission: SPACE. Even if your child meets the height requirement, she may not be old enough to enjoy the ride. In the capsule, you're instructed to keep your head back against the seat and to look straight ahead for the duration of the ride. (Closing your eyes or not looking straight ahead can bring on motion sickness.) Your role as a "crew member" also means you're supposed to hold on to a joystick and push buttons at certain times. All these instructions can confuse younger kids and get in the way of their enjoyment of the ride.

For those who can handle the intense spinning, the sensation of liftoff is a turbulent, heart-pounding experience that flattens you against your seat. Once you break into outer space, you'll even feel weightless. After landing, you exit your capsule into the Advanced Training Lab, where you can play some very entertaining space-related games. **For people with disabilities:** This ride requires a transfer from wheelchair to seat. Service animals aren't permitted to board. Video-captioning devices can be used on the ride; assisted-listening devices can be used in the postshow Training Lab. ■TIP➔ **Arrive before 10 am or use Fastpass+ during peak season. Don't ride on a full stomach.** ✉ *Future World, Mission: SPACE, Epcot* ⏱ *Duration: 4 mins. Crowds: You bet! Audience: Not small kids. Height requirement: 44 inches.*

THE SEAS WITH NEMO & FRIENDS

This pavilion has always been a draw with its 5.7-million-gallon aquarium filled with 65 species of sea life, including sharks, but it was reworked to capitalize on the popularity of the Disney-Pixar film *Finding Nemo.*

The Seas with Nemo & Friends. Hop into a "clamobile" and take a ride under the sea to look for Nemo, who has wandered off from Mr. Ray's class field trip. This ride adds clever fun to the aquarium attraction—an astonishing animation-projection effect makes it appear as if Nemo and his pals are swimming among the marine life of the actual Seas aquarium. As your ride progresses, Dory, Nemo's spacey sidekick, helps Bruce, Squirt, and other pals find him. After the ride, walk around the tank to Bruce's Shark World for some fun photo ops and shark facts, discover how dolphins communicate, and visit an endangered Florida

DID YOU KNOW?

Disney's original conception for the Epcot Center—as sort of a futuristic master-planned community—didn't quite pan out in the park but instead took form in the town of Celebration, near Kissimmee.

EPCOT FAMILY TOUR

A trip to Italy is on hold, but Mom knows she can find a taste of Venice in the World Showcase. Dad, the *Popular Mechanics* devotee, can't wait to check out Test Track. Each can have a great day—in his or her own way.

STRATEGIZE

Devise a plan before pushing through the Epcot turnstiles. Everyone will probably want to take off at Soarin' in The Land for the one-ride-fits-all thrill of simulated hang gliding (there are even special safety restraints for little ones). If your kids are too small for the height restrictions at Test Track, let Dad shift into overdrive while the rest of you play Innoventions games. Meet up with Dad at the Imagination! pavilion to ride along with Figment, the purple dragon, or head back to the Land for a Sunshine Seasons treat. Don't miss an under-the-sea ride at the Seas with Nemo & Friends before meeting the coolest dude of all at Turtle Talk with Crush.

GET YOUR WORLD SHOWCASE PASSPORTS

On the way into the World Showcase, let the kids get their own passports, complete with stickers, at any merchandise location. As you visit each country, they can get their passports stamped—not only a fun lesson in geography but a great keepsake. Before you cross the Future World border, stop and let young kids play in the dancing fountains if they're operating—it'll be one of their happiest memories. Bring a towel and a change of clothing, and you'll be happy, too.

FOR THE LITTLE ONES (AND MOM)

Younger children can be creative at Kidcot Fun Stops, where a Disney cast member gets them started on a craft activity, such as coloring a Carnivale-style mask on a stick. At each of 11 Fun Stops, the kids can add something to the mask, such as a Viking ship at Norway after the Frozen Ever After ride. Children love Mexico because they can ride the boats at Gran Fiesta Tour starring the Three Caballeros. Now it's your turn, Mom. Italy is right around the corner, and the kids can watch a juggler or comedy troupe in the courtyard while you sip some wine at Enoteca Castello or go shopping.

LIVE PERFORMANCES

The Beatles, the Rolling Stones, Elton John, and more: hear top hits by iconic British musicians when the tribute band British Revolution amps up the fun outside the United Kingdom showcase five days each week. Grab a bench or dance to favorite tunes. Young children are thrilled to explore hedge mazes that surround the gazebo stage.

Live entertainment is one of Epcot's strong suits—best shows for younger kids are the Jeweled Dragon Acrobats at China, Mariachi Cobre musicians at Mexico, Sergio the clown and juggler at Italy, and the JAMMitors percussion group at Future World East and West (check the daily *Times Guide*).

manatee rehabilitation center. **For people with disabilities:** Guests in standard wheelchairs can wheel onto an accessible "clamshell" vehicle; those in ECVs must transfer to a standard wheelchair or the ride vehicle. Equipped for audio-description and handheld-captioning devices. ■TIP➔ **Visit early or book a Fastpass+.** ⊠ *Future World, The Seas with Nemo & Friends, Epcot* ☞ *Duration: Up to you. Crowds: Moderate to heavy. Audience: All ages.*

Turtle Talk with Crush. Head for the Sea Base area to line up for this real-time animated show starring Crush, the ancient sea turtle from *Finding Nemo.* Crush chats and jokes with kids so convincingly that young children, eyes wide as sand dollars, have walked up and touched the screen where Crush "swims." It's in a small theater and there's often a wait, but it's a hit with young children as well as their parents. **For people with disabilities:** The theater is wheelchair accessible, and assisted-listening devices can be used. ■TIP➔ **Check the Times Guide for show schedule; use a Fastpass+ or come early and prepare to be amazed.** ⊠ *Future World, The Seas with Nemo & Friends, Epcot* ☞ *Duration: 15 mins. Crowds: Moderate to heavy. Audience: Small kids, but great for all ages.*

THE LAND

Shaped like an intergalactic greenhouse, the enormous, skylighted Land pavilion dedicates six acres and a host of attractions to everyone's favorite topic: food. You can easily spend two hours exploring here, more if you take one of the guided greenhouse tours available throughout the day.

■ NEED A BREAK

Talk about a self-contained ecosystem: The Land Pavilion grows its own produce, including tomatoes and cucumbers, some of which show up on the menu at the healthful **Sunshine Seasons** food court. Much of the fare is cooked on a 48-inch Mongolian grill. The eatery offers oak-grilled salmon, spicy stir-fries, and fish tacos. A sandwich shop delivers oak-grilled veggie sandwiches on fresh breads, and yummy turkey on ciabatta with chipotle mayonnaise. The salad shop wows with roasted beets and goat cheese over mixed greens, or a "power salad" of chicken, quinoa, and almonds—among other options. Wood-fired grills and rotisseries sizzle with chicken, pork, and salmon, and the bakery's pastries are sure bets. To avoid crowds, eat at nonpeak times—after 2 for lunch and before 5 or after 7 for dinner.

Living with the Land. A canopied boat cruises through three artificial biomes—rain forest, desert, and prairie ecological communities—and into an experimental live greenhouse that demonstrates how food sources may be grown in the future, not only on the planet but also in outer space. Shrimp, tilapia, eels, catfish, and alligators are raised in controlled aquacells, and tomatoes, peppers, squash, and other fruits and vegetables thrive in the Desert Farm area via drip irrigation that delivers just the right amount of water and nutrients to their roots. Gardeners are usually interested in the section on integrated pest management, which relies on "good" insects like ladybugs to control more harmful predators.

2

See Mickey Mouse–shaped fruits and vegetables (there may be pumpkins, cucumbers, or watermelons) nurtured with the help of molds created by the Land's science team; scientists also have grown a "tomato tree"—the first of its kind in the United States—that has yielded thousands of tomatoes from a single vine. Many of the growing areas are actual experiments-in-progress, in which Disney and the U.S. Department of Agriculture have joined forces to produce, say, a sweeter pineapple or a faster-growing pepper. The plants (including the tomato tree's golf-ball-size tomatoes) and fish that grow in the greenhouse are regularly harvested for use in The Land's restaurants. **For people with disabilities:** Those using an oversize wheelchair or ECV must transfer to a standard wheelchair. Equipped for handheld-captioning and audio-description devices. ■ **TIP→ The line moves fairly quickly, but you might want a Fastpass+ appointment on a crowded park day.** ⊠ *Future World, The Land, Epcot* ☞ *Duration: 14 mins. Crowds: Moderate. Audience: All ages.*

Fodor's Choice ★ **Soarin' Around the World.** If you've ever wondered what it's like to fly, or at least hang glide, this attraction is your chance to enjoy the sensation without actually taking the plunge. It uses motion-based technology to literally lift you in your seat 40 feet into the air within a giant projection-screen dome.

As you soar above the wonders of the world, from the sharp peaks of the Alps, to the Great Wall of China, to Sydney Harbor in Australia, and the spires of Neuschwanstein Castle in Bavaria, you feel the wind and dodge the spray of leaping whales.

The flight is so mild (and the view so thrilling) that even very timid children love it. **For people with disabilities:** Those with mobility impairments must transfer from their wheelchairs to the ride system. Equipped for video-captioning devices. Service animals aren't permitted on the ride. ■ **TIP→ Book your Fastpass+ early or plan to wait an hour or longer in the standby queue.** ⊠ *Future World, The Land, Epcot* ☞ *Duration: 5 mins. Crowds: heavy. Audience: All who meet the height requirement. Height requirement: 40 inches.*

IMAGINATION!

The focus is on the fun that can be had when you turn your imagination loose. The fanciful leaping fountains outside the pavilion make the point, as do the Journey into Imagination with Figment ride, and Image Works, a sort of interactive fun house devoted to music and art.

Journey into Imagination with Figment. Figment, a fun-loving dragon, takes you on a sensory adventure designed to engage your imagination through sound, illusion, gravity, dimension, and color. After the ride—which could use some updating—you can check out Image Works, where several interactive displays allow you to further stretch your imagination. Although this ride is geared to smaller kids, be sure to prepare yours for a brief period of darkness.

For people with disabilities: Ride and Image Works are wheelchair accessible. Equipped for handheld-captioning and audio-description devices. ■ **TIP→ Skip the Fastpass+ and ride only if lines are short so you'll have plenty of time for preferred attractions on your list.** ⊠ *Future*

World, Imagination!, Epcot ⌖ Duration: 8 mins. Crowds: Light. Audience: Small kids.

WORLD SHOWCASE

Nowhere but at Epcot can you explore nearly a dozen countries in one day. As you stroll the 1.3 miles around the 40-acre World Showcase Lagoon, you circumnavigate the globe-according-to-Disney by

WATER PLAY

Preschoolers love to play in the interactive fountains in front of Mission: SPACE and in the walkways between Future World and the World Showcase. Bring swimsuits and a towel!

experiencing native food, entertainment, culture, and arts and crafts at pavilions representing countries in Europe, Asia, North Africa, and the Americas. Pavilion employees are from the countries they represent—Disney hires them as part of its international college program.

By far the most popular attraction among youngsters is the Frozen Ever After ride in the Norway pavilion. You'll see solid film attractions at the Canada, China, and France pavilions (where a Ratatouille ride is slated for 2021); several art exhibitions; and the chance to try your foreign language skills with the staff. Each pavilion also has a designated Kidcot Fun Stop, open daily from 11 or noon until about 8 or 9, where youngsters can try a cultural crafts project. Live entertainment is an integral part of the experience, and you'll enjoy watching the incredibly talented Jeweled Dragon Acrobats in China and the Matsuriza Taiko drummers in Japan or laughing along with the mime and juggler in the Italy courtyard.

Dining is another favorite pastime at Epcot, and the World Showcase offers tempting tastes of the authentic cuisines of the countries here.

For People with Disabilities. Attractions at Mexico, American Adventure, France, China, and Canada are all wheelchair accessible, as are the plaza areas where shows are presented. Mexico's Gran Fiesta Tour boat ride also is wheelchair accessible; personal-translator units amplify sound tracks. Most of the live entertainment around the World Showcase features strong aural as well as visual elements.

EN ROUTE A World Showcase Passport ($12) is a wonderful way to keep a kid interested in this more adult area of Epcot. The passports, available at vendor carts, come with stickers and a badge, and children can have them stamped at each pavilion. The World Showcase is also a great place to look for unusual gifts—you might pick up a Oaxacan wood carving in Mexico, a tea set in China, or a kimonoed doll in Japan.

CANADA

"Oh, it's just our Canadian outdoors," said a typically modest native guide upon being asked about the model for the striking rocky chasm and tumbling waterfall that represent just one of the pavilion's high points. The beautiful formal gardens do have an antecedent: Butchart Gardens, in Victoria, British Columbia. And so does the Hôtel du Canada, a French Gothic mansion with spires, turrets, and a mansard roof; anyone who's ever stayed at Québec's Château Frontenac or Ottawa's Château Laurier will recognize the imposing style favored by architects of Canadian railroad hotels.

Like the size of the Rocky Mountains, the scale of the structures seems immense; unlike the real thing, it's managed with a trick called forced perspective, which exaggerates the smallness of the distant parts to make the entire thing look gigantic.

You can browse shops that sell maple syrup; Canadian sports jerseys; and plush huggable bears, beavers, and huskies. Le Cellier Steakhouse is a great place for a relaxing lunch or dinner; due to its increasing popularity, you should book reservations far ahead.

O Canada! That's just what you'll say after seeing this CircleVision film's stunning opening shot—footage of the Royal Canadian Mounted Police surrounding you as they circle the screen. From there, you whoosh over waterfalls, venture through Montréal and Toronto, sneak up on bears and bison, mush behind a husky-pulled dogsled, and land pluck in the middle of a hockey game. The only downside: this is a standing-only theater, strollers aren't permitted, and toddlers and small children can't see unless they're held aloft. **For people with disabilities :** Wheelchair and ECV accessible; reflective captioning and equipped for assisted-listening and audio-description devices. ■TIP→ **Stop in on your stroll around World Showcase Promenade.** ⊠ *World Showcase, Canada, Epcot* ⟳ *Duration: 14 mins. Crowds: Moderate to heavy. Audience: All ages.*

UNITED KINGDOM

The United Kingdom rambles between the elegant mansions lining a London square to the bustling, half-timber shops of a village High Street to thatched-roof cottages from the countryside. (The thatch is made of plastic broom bristles due to local fire regulations.) And, of course, there's a pair of iconic red phone booths.

The pavilion has no single major attraction. Instead, you wander through shops selling tea, Welsh handicrafts, Scottish tweed, and English lavender fragrance by Taylor of London. There's a store with Beatles T-shirts, CDs, and memorabilia. Next door is the Historic Research Center, where you can research your family name and purchase printed, hand-painted, or embroidered versions of your family coat of arms.

Outside, the strolling World Showcase Players coax audience members to participate in lowbrow versions of Shakespeare. There's also a lovely garden and park with benches in the back that's easy to miss—relax and kick back to the tunes of the British Revolution, a band known for its on-target Beatles and other Brit-band performances. Kids love to run through the hedge maze as their parents travel back in time to "Yesterday." Check the *Times Guide* and arrive 30 minutes early for a bench or 15 minutes early for a curb. Restrooms are near the red phone booths.

NEED A BREAK

Revive yourself with a pint of the best at the **Rose & Crown**, a pub where you'll jostle for space any evening the pianist is in the house. The dining room serves hearty fare for lunch and dinner (reservations often required). The outdoor terrace is one of the best spots for watching IllumiNations. Arrive at least an hour or so in advance for a seat. If you're in a hurry, grab fish-and-chips to go from Yorkshire County Fish Shop, then nab a lagoon-side table.

2

FRANCE

You don't need the scaled-down model of the Eiffel Tower to tell you that you've arrived in France, specifically Paris. There's the poignant accordion music wafting out of concealed speakers, the trim sycamores pruned in the French style to develop signature knots at the end of each branch, and the delicious aromas surrounding Les Halles Boulangerie & Pâtisserie bakeshop. This is the Paris of dreams, a Paris of the years just before World War I, when solid mansard-roof mansions were crowned with iron filigree, when the least brick was drenched in romanticism. Another dream is coming to the France Pavilion, with the announcement in August 2017 that a ride based on the film *Ratatouille* is slated to open in 2021.

Here's a replica of the original Les Halles—the iron-and-glass barrel-roof market that no longer exists in the City of Light; there's an arching footbridge; and all around, of course, there are shops. You can inspect Parisian impressionist artwork at Galerie des Halles; sample perfume at the Guerlain shop; and acquire a Julia Child cookbook or bottle of Pouilly-Fuisse at Les Vins de France. If you plan to dine at Les Chefs de France, make a reservation for a late lunch or dinner; the second-floor Monsieur Paul (dinner only) is a gourmet treat.

**NEED A
BREAK**

It's worth it to brave the lines at **Les Halles Boulangerie & Pâtisserie**, a large Parisian-style counter-service café. Have wine with a cheese plate, quiche, or sandwich on crusty French bread. Or go for a creamy café au lait and a napoleon. The new **L'Artisan des Glaces** ice cream–and-sorbet shop is praiseworthy for its ultracreamy treats that include an ice cream "martini" with Grand Marnier and flavor-customized ice-cream sandwiches made with brioche or French *macaron*.

Impressions de France. The intimate Palais du Cinema, inspired by the royal theater at Fontainebleau, screens this homage to the glories of the country. Shown on five screens spanning 200 degrees, in an air-conditioned, sit-down theater, the film takes you to vineyards at harvest time, Paris on Bastille Day, the Alps, Versailles, Normandy's Mont-Saint-Michel, and the stunning châteaux of the Loire Valley. The music sweeps you away with familiar segments from Offenbach, Debussy, and Saint-Saëns, all woven together by longtime Disney musician Buddy Baker. **For people with disabilities :** Wheelchair and ECV accessible; reflective captioning and equipped for assisted-listening and audio-description devices. ■ TIP→ Visit anytime during your stroll around the World Showcase; theater seats are comfy and a great way to rest weary legs. ⊠ *World Showcase, France, Epcot* ☞ *Duration: 20 mins. Crowds: Moderate. Audience: All ages.*

MOROCCO

Walk through the pointed arches of the Bab Boujouloud Gate and you're transported to this strikingly beautiful North African country. The arches are ornamented with wood carvings and encrusted with mosaics made of 9 tons of handmade, hand-cut tiles; 19 native artisans were sent to Epcot to install them and to create the dusty stucco walls that seem to have withstood centuries of sandstorms. Look closely and you'll see that every tile has a small crack or other imperfection, and no tile depicts a living creature—in deference to the Islamic belief that only Allah creates perfection and life.

PHOTO TIP

You'll get a great shot of Spaceship Earth across the lagoon by framing it in the torii gate.

Koutoubia Minaret, a replica of the prayer tower in Marrakesh, acts as Morocco's landmark. Winding alleyways—each corner bursting with carpets, brasses, leatherwork, and other wares—lead to a tiled fountain and lush gardens. A highlight is Restaurant Marrakesh. Enjoy couscous and roast lamb while a belly dancer performs traditional dances. One of the hottest fast-food spots in Epcot is Tangierine Café, with tasty Mediterranean specialties like pita-pocket lamb and chicken sliders, killer baklava, and share-worthy vegetable platters with hummus, tabbouleh, falafel, lentils, and couscous. Spice Road Table is the ideal lagoon-side spot for tapas and the best sangria in Orlando. All eateries are open for lunch and dinner. Restrooms on the France side of the pavilion offer quick access.

JAPAN
A brilliant vermilion torii gate, based on Hiroshima Bay's much-photographed Itsukushima Shrine, frames the World Showcase Lagoon and stands as an emblem of Disney's serene version of Japan.

Disney horticulturists deserve a hand for authenticity: 90% of the plants they used are native to Japan. Rocks, pebbled streams, pools, and pruned trees and shrubs complete the meticulous picture. At sunset, or during a rainy dusk, the twisted branches of the corkscrew willows frame a perfect Japanese view of the five-story winged pagoda that is the heart of the pavilion. Based on the 8th-century Horyuji Temple in Nara, the brilliant blue pagoda has five levels, symbolizing the five elements of Buddhist belief—earth, water, fire, wind, and sky.

The peace is occasionally interrupted by performances on drums and gongs. Mitsukoshi, an immense retail firm known as Japan's Sears Roebuck, carries everything from T-shirts to kimonos and rows of Japanese dolls. For lunch and dinner, you'll be entertained by the culinary feats of chefs at Teppan Edo (which carries on the chop-toss-applaud antics of the original Teppanyaki Dining Room). Tokyo Dining focuses on presentation of traditional ingredients and cuisine from Japan, including sushi. At the pavilion's rear is a sake tasting bar that you'll miss if you don't look for it.

AMERICAN ADVENTURE
In a Disney version of Philadelphia's Independence Hall, the Imagineers prove that their kind of fantasy can beat reality hands down. The 110,000 bricks, made by hand from soft, pink Georgia clay, sheathe the familiar structure, which acts as a beacon for those across Epcot's lagoon. The pavilion includes an all-American fast-food restaurant, a shop, lovely rose gardens, and an outdoor theater. Restrooms are tucked away along the far left side of the restaurant, and a roomier restroom accommodation also is open by the gift shop.

Morocco's open-air market is like something out of an Indiana Jones movie. It's a maze of shops selling straw bags, colorful carpets, leather goods, and, of course, ceramics.

NEED A BREAK

What else would you order at the counter-service **Liberty Inn** but burgers, apple pie, and other all-American fare? On a summer evening this is the place to get an ice-cream sundae before IllumiNations starts. On a chilly winter day, the hot cocoa is a hit. At the **Fife & Drum** along the promenade, you can pair a beer with a turkey leg for a satisfying snack.

Fodor's Choice ★

The American Adventure. The pavilion's key attraction is this 100-yard dash through history, and you'll be primed for the lesson after reaching the main entry hall and hearing the stirring a cappella Voices of Liberty. Inside the theater, the main event begins to the accompaniment of "The Golden Dream," performed by the Philadelphia Orchestra. This show combines evocative sets, a rear-projection screen (72 feet wide), enormous movable stages, and 35 Audio-Animatronics players.

Beginning with the arrival of the Pilgrims at Plymouth Rock and their grueling first winter, Benjamin Franklin and a wry, pipe-smoking Mark Twain narrate the episodes, both praiseworthy and shameful, that have shaped the American spirit. Each speech and scene seems polished like a little jewel. You feel the cold at Valley Forge. You're moved by Nez Percé Chief Joseph's forced abdication of Native American ancestral lands, by Frederick Douglass's reminder of the miseries of slavery, and by women's rights campaigner Susan B. Anthony's speech. You laugh with Will Rogers's aphorisms and learn about the pain of the Great Depression through an affecting radio broadcast by Franklin Delano Roosevelt. **For people with disabilities :** Wheelchair and ECV accessible; reflective captioning and equipped for assisted-listening and audio-description devices. ■**TIP→** Check your Times Guide and arrive 10 minutes before the Voices of Liberty are slated to perform, then head inside to enjoy the a cappella tunes. ⊠ *World Showcase, American Adventure, Epcot* ☞ *Duration: 30 mins. Crowds: Heavy. Audience: All ages.*

America Gardens Theatre. On the edge of the lagoon, directly opposite Disney's magnificent bit of colonial fakery, is this open-air, partially tree-shaded venue for concerts and shows. Most performances are hot tickets with themes tied to Epcot events, such as "Garden Rocks" concerts with pop legends during the March through May Epcot International Flower and Garden Festival and Eat to the Beat concerts during the late-September through mid-November Epcot International Food and Wine Festival. This is also the setting for the annual yuletide Candlelight Processional—a not-to-be-missed event if you're at WDW during the holidays. The Candlelight Dinner Package (available through Disney's dining reservations hotline) includes lunch or dinner in a select World Showcase restaurant and preferred seating for the moving performance. Roomy restrooms are behind the Kidcot Fun Stop. ■ **TIP→ Arrive more than an hour ahead of time for holiday and celebrity performances.** ⊠ *World Showcase, American Adventure, Epcot* ☞ *Duration: Performances vary. Crowds: Vary. Audience: Varies.*

ITALY

Architectural reproductions of Venice's Piazza San Marco and the Doge's Palace are accurate right down to the gold leaf on the ringlets of the angel perched 100 feet atop the Campanile; the seawall stained with age, with barbershop-stripe poles to which two gondolas are tethered; and the Romanesque columns, Byzantine mosaics, Gothic arches, and stone walls that have all been carefully antiqued. Mediterranean plants such as grapevines, kumquat, and olive trees add verisimilitude. Shops sell Venetian beads and glasswork, leather purses, perfumes, olive oils, pastas, and Perugina cookies and chocolate kisses.

At Tutto Italia Ristorante, the cuisine—wines, handmade mozzarella, and fresh bread—is from several regions of Italy. Limited outdoor dining beneath umbrellas is lovely. The hot ticket is on the edge of the piazza: Via Napoli is a casual 300-seat pizzeria with wood-burning ovens and an airy, noisy dining room. Chefs use Caputo flour, San Marzano tomatoes, and fresh, handmade mozzarella to craft some of the best margherita pizza outside Naples! The Tutto Gusto Wine Cellar is a cool escape for a glass of prosecco and a small plate.

Sergio, a clown–juggler brings crowds to the piazza several times each day. This is a great spot for viewing IllumiNations if you're in the vicinity.

NEED A BREAK

✕ **Sommerfest.** Bratwurst and cold beer from the Sommerfest counter at the entrance of the Biergarten restaurant make a perfect quick and hearty lunch, while the apple strudel and Black Forest cake are ever-popular sweets. There's not much seating, so you may have to eat on the run. ⊠ *World Showcase, Germany, Epcot.*

2

GERMANY

Germany, a make-believe village that distills the best folk architecture from all over that country, is so jovial that you practically expect the Seven Dwarfs to come "heigh-ho"-ing out to meet you. If you time it right, you will spot Snow White as she poses for photos and signs autographs. The fairy tale continues as a specially designed glockenspiel on the clock tower chimes on the hour. You'll also hear musical toots and tweets from cuckoo clocks, folk tunes from the spinning dolls sold at Der Teddybär, and the satisfied sighs of hungry visitors chowing down on hearty German cooking.

The Biergarten's wonderful buffet serves several sausage varieties, as well as sauerkraut, spaetzle, and roasted potatoes, rotisserie chicken, and German breads, all accompanied by yodelers, dancers, and other lederhosen-clad musicians who perform a year-round Oktoberfest show. There are shops aplenty, including Die Weihnachts Ecke (the Christmas Corner), which sells nutcrackers and other Christmas ornaments. It's hard to resist watching the miniature trains that choo-choo along a garden track dotted with tiny villages. Restrooms are just steps away.

NEED A BREAK

✕ **Refreshment Coolpost.** The Refreshment Coolpost, between Germany and China, isn't one of the 11 World Showcase pavilions, but kids love to test their drumming skills on the large authentic drums that invite players to improvise their own African folklore performances. Village Traders sells African handicrafts and—you guessed it—souvenirs relating to *The Lion King.* Buy an ice cream or frozen yogurt at the Coolpost, and enjoy the break at a table by the lagoon. ✉ *World Showcase, Epcot.*

CHINA

A shimmering red-and-gold, three-tier replica of Beijing's Temple of Heaven towers over a serene Chinese garden, an art gallery displaying treasures from the People's Republic, a spacious emporium devoted to Chinese goods, and two restaurants. The gardens—planted with a native Chinese tallow tree, water lilies, bamboo, and a 100-year-old weeping mulberry tree—are tranquil.

Piped-in traditional Chinese music flows gently over the peaceful hush of the gardens, which come alive with applause and cheers when the remarkable Jeweled Dragon Acrobats tumble into a roped-off area for their breathtaking act. At China's popular Nine Dragons Restaurant try the shrimp and chicken egg rolls or the peppery shrimp with spinach noodles; there are also several chicken and stir-fry favorites.

NEED A BREAK

✕ **Lotus Blossom Café.** The open-air Lotus Blossom Café offers some authentic Chinese fare: pot stickers, soups, and egg rolls. Entrées include orange chicken with steamed rice, vegetable curry, and a beef noodle soup bowl. ✉ *World Showcase, China, Epcot.*

Reflections of China. Think of the Temple of Heaven as an especially fitting theater for a movie in which sensational panoramas of the land and people are dramatically portrayed on a 360-degree CircleVision screen. Highlights include striking footage of Hong Kong, Shanghai, and Macao. This may be the best of the World Showcase films—the only drawbacks are that strollers aren't permitted and the theater has no chairs; lean rails are provided. ■**TIP→** **Come anytime and, before the show, visit the Tomb Warriors gallery, where you can see replicas of the terra-cotta soldiers unearthed by farmers in Xi'an, China, in 1974.** ⊠ *World Showcase, China, Epcot* ⟲ *Duration: 14 mins. Crowds: Moderate. Audience: All Ages.*

NORWAY

Although most visitors to the Norway Pavilion are on their way to the Frozen Ever After ride, there's plenty to look at while you wait in line. Among the rough-hewn timbers and sharply pitched roofs here— softened and brightened by bloom-stuffed window boxes and figured shutters—are lots of smiling young Norwegians, all eager to speak English and show off their country. The pavilion complex contains a 14th-century, fortresslike castle that mimics Oslo's Akershus, cobbled streets, rocky waterfalls, and a stave church modeled after one built in 1250, with wood dragons glaring from the eaves. The church houses an exhibit called "To the Ends of the Earth," which uses vintage artifacts to tell the story of two early-20th-century polar expeditions. It all puts you in the mood for the pavilion's shops, which sell *Frozen* souvenirs, spears, shields, and other Viking necessities perfect for next Halloween.

At Akershus Royal Banquet Hall, Princess Storybook Dining is a big deal. Visit the Norwegian *koldtbord* (buffet) for smoked salmon, fruit, and pastries, followed by a family-style hot breakfast of eggs, meats, and other treats served at the table. For lunch and dinner, you'll find traditional treats like chilled shrimp, salads, meats, and cheeses. Hot entrées served à la carte might include oven-roasted chicken breast, venison stew, or the traditional Scandinavian meatball dish called *kjottkake*. Family-style dessert is a treat with three of the chef's sweet specialties.

■**TIP→** **The restaurant is the only one in the park where you can dine with Disney princesses, who may include Aurora, Belle, or Snow White. You can reserve up to 180 days in advance, and we recommend booking as early as possible. Nevertheless, you can always check at Guest Relations for seats left by cancellations.**

NEED A BREAK

✕**Kringla Bakeri Og Kafe.** You can order smoked salmon, sandwiches, and a vegetable torte, as well as wine, beer, and the potent Viking coffee at Kringla Bakeri Og Kafe. Sweet pretzels, pastries, and cookies satisfy sugar cravings. ⊠ *World Showcase, Norway, Epcot.*

Fodor's Choice ★

Frozen Ever After. In Norway's dandy boat-ride homage to the popular *Frozen* film, which replaced the Maelstrom ride in 2016, you pile into a 16-passenger, dragon-headed longboat for a dark-ride voyage around Arendelle. The familiar form of Olaf welcomes you as you enter the frozen willow forest and head to Queen Elsa's ice palace, meeting up with Anna and many familiar *Frozen* characters along the way, and hearing the popular songs from the film. The animated figures are amazing, featuring Disney's first all-electric Audio-Animatronics, allowing much more fluid and graceful movement, and utilizing projection-mapped

Frozen Ever After has become a favorite ride at Epcot.

faces, which make the figures look exactly like their animated counterparts. For fans who miss the Maelstrom ride, keep a sharp eye open for Easter eggs that remain, particularly in the castle finale. **For people with disabilities:** You must step down into and up out of a boat to ride. Equipped with reflective captioning and for assisted-listening, audio-description, or handheld-captioning devices. ■**TIP➜** Grab a Fastpass+ appointment if the queue is long, so you can return after lunch or dinner. ⊠ *World Showcase, Norway, Epcot* ☞ *Duration: 10 mins. Crowds: Moderate to heavy. Audience: All ages.*

MEXICO

Housed in a spectacular Mayan pyramid surrounded by dense tropical plantings and brilliant blossoms, Mexico welcomes you onto a "moonlit" plaza that contains the Gran Fiesta Tour boat ride; an exhibit of pre-Columbian art; a very popular restaurant; and, of course, shopping kiosks where you can unload many, many pesos.

Modeled on the market in the town of Taxco, Plaza de los Amigos is well named: there are lots of friendly people—the women dressed in peasant blouses and bright skirts, the men in white shirts and dashing sashes—all eager to sell you trinkets from a cluster of canopied carts. The perimeter is rimmed with stores with tile roofs, wrought-iron balconies, and flower-filled window boxes. What to buy? Sombreros, baskets, pottery, jewelry, and maracas.

One of the pavilion's key attractions is the San Angel Inn, featuring traditional Mexican cuisine and wine and beer, and overlooking the faux-moonlit waterway traversed by Gran Fiesta Tour boats. The pavilion's La Cava del Tequila bar serves up tequila flights, exotic blended

The Temple of Quetzalcoatl (ket-zal-co-WAH-tal) at Teotihuacán (tay-o-tee-wah-CON), just outside Mexico City, is the model for the pyramid at the Mexico pavilion.

margaritas, and light snacks like guacamole with corn chips. The casual, outdoor La Cantina de San Angel is a 150-seat quick-service eatery adjacent to La Hacienda de San Angel, a 250-seat table-service restaurant with waterside view. You won't want to miss trying Mexican treats like the Queso Fundido, melted cheese with poblano peppers, chorizo, and tortillas, or La Hacienda mixed grill served with beans and fresh salsa.

FAMILY **Gran Fiesta Tour Starring the Three Caballeros.** In this attraction—which shines with the polish of enhanced facades, sound system, and boat-ride props—Donald teams with old pals José Carioca (the parrot) and Panchito (the Mexican charro rooster) from the 1944 Disney film *The Three Caballeros*. The Gran Fiesta Tour film sweeps you along for an animated jaunt as the caballeros are reunited for a grand performance in Mexico City. Donald manages to disappear for his own tour of the country, leaving José and Panchito to search for their missing comrade. **For people with disabilities:** The boat is accessible to guests using wheelchairs, but those using ECVs or oversize chairs must transfer to a Disney model. Equipped for handheld-captioning and audio-description devices. ■TIP➔ It's worth a visit if lines aren't long, especially if you have small children, who usually enjoy the novelty of a boat ride. ⊠ *World Showcase, Mexico, Epcot* ☞ *Duration: 9 mins. Crowds: Moderate. Audience: All ages.*

EPCOT SPECTACLE

Fodor's Choice
★

IllumiNations: Reflections of Earth. This marvelous nighttime spectacular takes place over the World Showcase Lagoon every night before closing. The show's Earth Globe—a gigantic, spherical, video-display system rotating on a 350-ton floating island—is three stories tall with 180,000 light-emitting diodes and projects images celebrating the diversity and unified spirit of humankind. The globe opens like a lotus flower in the grand finale, revealing a huge torch that rises 40 feet into the air as additional flames spread light across the lagoon. Nearly 2,800 fireworks shells paint colorful displays across the night sky. The best viewing spots are in front of the Italy pavilion, on the bridge between France and the United Kingdom, on the promenade in front of Canada, at the World Showcase Plaza, and at La Hacienda de San Angel and La Cantina de San Angel in Mexico. **For people with disabilities:** During the show, certain areas along the lagoon's edge at Showcase Plaza, Canada, and Germany are reserved for guests using wheelchairs. ■**TIP**➔ Limited Fastpass+ reservations are offered; otherwise, find your place 45 minutes in advance. ✉ *World Showcase, Epcot* ☞ *Duration: 12 mins. Crowds: Heavy. Audience: All ages.*

DISNEY'S HOLLYWOOD STUDIOS

The first thing you notice when you pass through the Hollywood Studios turnstiles is the laid-back California attitude. Palm-lined Hollywood Boulevard oozes old-time glamour. The second thing you notice is that nostalgia for the past glories of Hollywood film is giving way to nostalgia for its depiction of the future. As the focus shifts to *Star Wars* and the new land called Star Wars: Galaxy's Edge approaches its opening in 2019, more and more attractions around the park are being shuttered to make way for shows that focus on that famous galaxy far, far away. In addition, the popularity of the *Toy Story* film series brought another big change. Toy Story Land is opening in the summer of 2018, taking visitors into Andy's backyard, and bringing Woody, Buzz, and a host of familiar characters to life.

When the park opened in May 1989, its name was Disney–MGM Studios. Disney changed the name in 2008 to broaden its appeal. Another name change in the near future is not outside the realm of possibility. But no matter the name, the inspiration springs from the same place: America's love affair with the movies.

Although the park was built with real film and television production in mind, that has mostly halted. But there are still attractions that showcase how filmmakers practice their craft. If you're wowed by action-film stunts, you can learn the tricks of the trade at the Indiana Jones Epic Stunt Spectacular!, then you can take a close look at the legend himself,

TOP ATTRACTIONS

AGES EIGHT AND UP

Indiana Jones Epic Stunt Spectacular! The show's cast reenacts *Raiders of the Lost Ark* scenes with panache.

Walt Disney Presents. It's always fun to immerse yourself in Disney's world of animation.

Rock 'n' Roller Coaster Starring Aerosmith. Blast off to rockin' tunes on a high-speed, hard-core coaster.

Slinky Dog Dash. In the spirit of the Seven Dwarfs Mine Train, this new family coaster offers some speed and thrills but no real scares.

Star Tours—The Adventures Continue. Prepare for a high-speed chase on this updated simulator thrill ride through multiple scenarios in the *Star Wars* galaxy.

Toy Story Midway Mania! 3-D glasses? Check. Spring-action shooter? Check. Ride and shoot your way through the midway with Buzz, Woody, and others.

Twilight Zone Tower of Terror. The TV classic theming of this free-fall "elevator" screamer is meticulous.

AGES SEVEN AND UNDER

For the First Time in Forever: A "Frozen" Sing-Along Celebration. Every audience member can "Let It Go" and sing along to the popular tunes from Disney's blockbuster film *Frozen*.

Beauty and the Beast—Live on Stage! Memorable music, talented performers, dancing kitchen objects, and a fairy-tale ending make this a must-see show.

Disney Junior—Live on Stage! The preschool crowd can't get enough of the characters here from Disney Channel shows like *Jake and the Never Land Pirates, Mickey Mouse Clubhouse, Doc McStuffins,* and *Sofia the First.*

Voyage of the Little Mermaid. Live performers, puppets, and song let youngsters hang out with their favorite mermaid.

Muppet*Vision 3-D. Children (and most adults) shriek with laughter during this 3-D movie.

at Walt Disney Presents, where sketches, artwork, and early animation join previews of what's coming next.

Several of the popular attractions have closed down, and you'll find a substantial amount of construction fencing. But big-hit attractions such as Toy Story Midway Mania! and the 3-D Star Wars–themed simulator ride, Star Tours—The Adventures Continue, along with The Twilight Zone Tower of Terror and Rock 'n' Roller Coaster starring Aerosmith keep the crowds happy.

ORIENTATION AND PLANNING

GETTING ORIENTED

The park is divided into sightseeing clusters. **Hollywood Boulevard** is the main artery to the heart of the park and is where you find the glistening replica of Graumann's Chinese Theater.

Encircling it are **Sunset Boulevard,** the **Animation Courtyard, Mickey Avenue, Pixar Place, Commissary Lane, the Streets of America area,** and **Echo Lake.**

The entire park is 135 acres, and has fewer than 20 attractions (compared with Magic Kingdom's 40-plus). It's small enough to cover in a day and even repeat a favorite ride or two.

If you're staying at one of the Epcot resorts (BoardWalk, Yacht or Beach Club, Swan, or Dolphin), getting to the Entrance Plaza on a motor launch is part of the fun. Disney resort buses also drop you at the entrance.

If you're staying off-property and driving, your parking ticket will remain valid for parking at another Disney park later in the day—provided, of course, you have the stamina.

PARK AMENITIES

Baby Care: The small baby-care center next to Guest Relations has nursing and changing facilities. Formula, baby food, pacifiers, and disposable diapers are for sale next door at Movieland and at Oscar's Super Service. There are also diaper-changing areas in all women's rooms and some men's rooms.

Cameras: At the Darkroom (or next door at Cover Story) on Hollywood Boulevard, you can buy memory cards and disposable cameras. And if a Disney photographer takes your picture in the park, you can pick up a Disney PhotoPass from him or her that lets you see the pictures online. Photo CD packages are $169.95 and $199.95, and you can purchase prints ($16.95 for an 8-inch-by-10-inch photo; other sizes available).

First Aid: The station is in the Entrance Plaza adjoining Guest Relations.

Guest Relations: You'll find it just inside the turnstiles on the left side of the Entrance Plaza. A Fastpass+ kiosk is at the corner of Hollywood and Sunset boulevards.

Lockers: You can rent lockers at the Crossroads of the World kiosk in the center of the Entrance Plaza. The cost is $7 or $9 with a $5 refundable key deposit. The lockers themselves are at Oscar's Super Service.

Lost People and Things: Instruct your kids to go to a Disney staffer with a name tag if they can't find you. If you lose them, ask any cast member for assistance; logbooks of lost children's names are kept at Guest Relations, which also has a computerized message center where you can leave notes for companions.

Disney's Hollywood Studios Lost and Found. Report lost or found articles at Guest Relations. ⊠ *Hollywood Blvd., Disney's Hollywood Studios* ☎ *407/560–4666.*

Main Lost and Found. Seek out articles lost for more than one day here. ⊠ *Transportation and Ticket Center [TTC], Magic Kingdom* ☎ *407/824–4245.*

Package Pick-Up: You can ask shop clerks to forward purchases to your hotel if you're staying on Disney property or to Package Pick-Up next to Oscar's Super Service in the Entrance Plaza, so you won't have to carry them around. Allow three hours for delivery.

Services for People with Disabilities: The Studios' restaurants, shops, theaters, and attractions are wheelchair accessible, although there are boarding restrictions on some rides. Some theater-type attractions,

DINNER AND A SHOW

Call or check ahead to visit on a day when you can see the after-dark *Fantasmic!* show, with its 30 powerful minutes of Disney characters, special effects, fireworks, flames, fountains, and even animation sequences projected onto water screens. If you're not crazy about the idea of arriving at the huge Hollywood Hills Amphitheater more than an hour ahead of showtime for a good seat, it's worth booking a *Fantasmic!* lunch or dinner package.

You get a prix-fixe meal at buffet-style Hollywood & Vine or a full table-service dinner at Hollywood Brown Derby or Mama Melrose's, along with a preferred-entry pass to the VIP seating area at the *Fantasmic!* show. Each dinner includes appetizer, entrée, dessert (the Brown Derby's grapefruit cake is a sweet-tart wonder), and a nonalcoholic beverage.

There's a small catch (well, actually, there are three):

If you choose to book dinner, allow plenty of time between your dining time and your arrival for showtime. (Disney recommends that you show up at the theater 30 or more minutes ahead of time to choose your seat).

The dinner package is offered only for the first show on peak nights when *Fantasmic!* is performed twice.

If it rains, *Fantasmic!* might be canceled. You still get dinner, but you lose out on seeing the show with preferred seating.

The cost is $44 to $63 for adults, $18 to $33 for children. It's best to reserve the package 180 days or at least several months in advance. You'll have to provide a credit-card number and, if you cancel 48 hours or less before the show, your card will be charged $10 per person.

including Muppet*Vision 3-D, have reflective captioning, and most other attractions are equipped for assisted-listening and video- or handheld-captioning devices. There are large Braille park maps near the Guest Relations lobby and near the Tip Board at Hollywood and Sunset. Note that restaurants don't have Braille menus.

You can pick up Braille guides ($25 same-day refundable deposit) and assisted-listening devices (also $25 deposit) and check on sign-language interpretation schedules at Guest Relations. Although interpreters appear only two days each week, you can request them (at least 14 days in advance) on other days by calling ☎ *407/560-2547* or TTY ☎ *407/827–5141.*

Oscar's Super Service, to the right in the Entrance Plaza, rents wheelchairs ($12 daily, $10 multiday) and electronic convenience vehicles (ECVs; $50 per day plus a refundable $20 security deposit). Reservations aren't an option, so arrive early, especially to snag an ECV.

Stroller Rentals: Oscar's Super Service rents strollers. Single strollers are $15 daily, $13 for more than one day; doubles are $31 daily, $27 multiday.

VISITING TIPS

Visit early in the week. That's when most other people are at Magic Kingdom and Animal Kingdom.

Keep your eyes open. Look for attractions displaying short wait times to visit between Fastpass+ appointments.

Arrive early for Fantasmic! Be at the Fantasmic! amphitheater at least an hour before showtime if you didn't book the lunch or dinner package.

Grab a bite. Need a burst of energy? On-the-run hunger pangs? Try Fairfax Fare on Sunset. Alternatively, Hollywood Scoops ice cream next door is the place to be on a hot day.

EXPLORING DISNEY'S HOLLYWOOD STUDIOS

HOLLYWOOD BOULEVARD

With its palm trees, pastel buildings, and flashy neon, Hollywood Boulevard paints a rosy picture of midcentury Tinseltown. There's a sense of having walked right onto a movie set of old, with art deco storefronts and roving starlets and nefarious agents—actually costumed actors known as the Citizens of Hollywood. Throughout the park, characters from Disney movies new and old—from *Mickey Mouse* to *Toy Story* friends—pose for photos and sign autographs.

A new ride called Mickey and Minnie's Runaway Railway is being developed in the space formerly occupied by the Great Movie Ride with an opening planned for 2019.

SUNSET BOULEVARD

This avenue honors Hollywood with facades derived from the Carthay Circle, the Beverly Wilshire Theatre, and other City of Angels landmarks.

Beauty and the Beast—Live on Stage! This popular stage show takes place at the Theater of the Stars, a re-creation of the famed Hollywood Bowl. The actors playing a luminous Belle and delightfully vain Gaston sing with passion with a lively cast of characters and dancers. The enchanted prince (Beast) and household characters (Mrs. Potts, Chip, Lumiere, and Cogsworth) deftly navigate the stage despite their bulky costumes. Even some set pieces sway along during the charming "Be Our Guest" number. There's high drama during the mob scene and a sweet ending when ballroom dancers in frothy pink and purple waltz along with the fairy-tale couple.

As you arrive or depart, check out handprints and footprints set in concrete of the TV personalities who've visited Disney's Hollywood Studios. **For people with disabilities:** Wheelchair and ECV accessible and equipped for handheld captioning, audio description, and assisted listening. Sign language twice a week. ■TIP➜ Book a Fastpass+ or line up at least 30 minutes prior to showtime. Performance times vary, so check the Times Guide. ⊠ *Sunset Blvd., Disney's Hollywood Studios* ✆ *Duration: 30 mins. Crowds: Moderate to heavy. Audience: All ages.*

Fodor's Choice ★ **Rock 'n' Roller Coaster Starring Aerosmith.** Although this is an indoor roller coaster like Magic Kingdom's Space Mountain, the similarity ends there. With its high-speed launch (0 to 60 in 2.8 seconds), multiple inversions, and loud rock music, it generates delighted screams from coaster junkies, though it's smooth enough and short enough that even the coaster-phobic have been known to enjoy it. The vehicles look like limos, and the track resembles the neck of an electric guitar that's been twisted. Hard-driving rock tunes by Aerosmith blast from vehicle speakers to accentuate the flips and turns.

Pregnant women and guests with heart, back, or neck problems or motion sickness should skip this one. **For people with disabilities:** Guests using wheelchairs must transfer to a ride vehicle. Service animals aren't allowed. ■TIP➡ **Ride when the park opens and try to book a Fastpass+ to go again, especially if visiting with tweens or teens. Another way to avoid a wait—split up and try the Single Rider Queue.** ⊠ *Sunset Blvd., Disney's Hollywood Studios* ⌇ *Duration: 1 min., 22 secs. Crowds: Huge. Audience: All but young kids. Height requirement: 48 inches.*

Fodor'sChoice ★ **The Twilight Zone Tower of Terror.** After you enter the dimly lighted lobby of the deserted Hollywood Tower Hotel and then the dust-covered library, a lightning bolt zaps a TV to life. Rod Serling recounts the story of the hotel's demise and invites you to enter the Twilight Zone. On to the boiler room, where you board a giant elevator ride. The fifth dimension awaits, where you travel forward past scenes from the popular TV series. Suddenly, the creaking vehicle plunges into a terrifying, 130-foot free fall and then, before you can catch your breath, shoots quickly up, down, up, and down all over again. No use trying to guess how many stomach-churning ups and downs are in store—Disney's ride engineers have programmed random drop variations into the attraction for a different thrill every time.

Those who are pregnant or have heart, back, or neck problems shouldn't ride. **For people with disabilities:** You must have full upper-body strength and be able to transfer to a ride seat. Equipped for video captioning. Service animals can't ride. ■TIP➡ **Get a Fastpass+ reservation. Otherwise, come early or wait until evening, when crowds thin and it's spookier.** ⊠ *Sunset Blvd., Disney's Hollywood Studios* ⌇ *Duration: 10 mins. Crowds: You bet! Audience: All but young kids. Height requirement: 40 inches.*

ANIMATION COURTYARD

As you exit Sunset Boulevard, veer right through the high-arched gateway to the Animation Courtyard. Straight ahead are *Disney Junior— Live on Stage!*, Star Wars Launch Bay, and *Voyage of the Little Mermaid*.

Disney Junior—Live on Stage! This is one of Walt Disney World's best shows for tots and preschoolers. A cast of Disney Channel characters joins the show's perky host, Casey, on a larger-than-life storybook stage. Puppets of Mickey Mouse, Goofy, and friends team up on the Mickey Mouse Clubhouse set to prep for Minnie's surprise birthday bash. In another skit, characters from Jake and the Never Land Pirates devise a clever way to thwart Captain Hook and defend their treasure chest. A third show segment features princess-in-training Sofia the First and Doc McStuffins. Sofia enlists sorcerer Mr. Cedric to cast a spell and make her father's royal ball a success. Meanwhile, Lambie's dance moves cause a

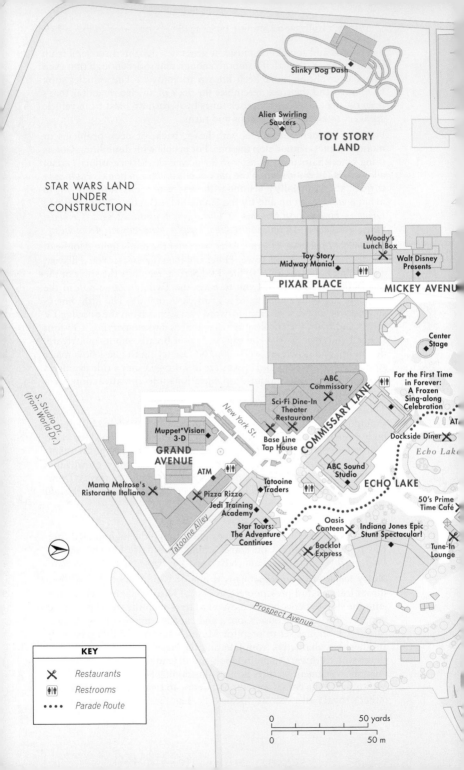

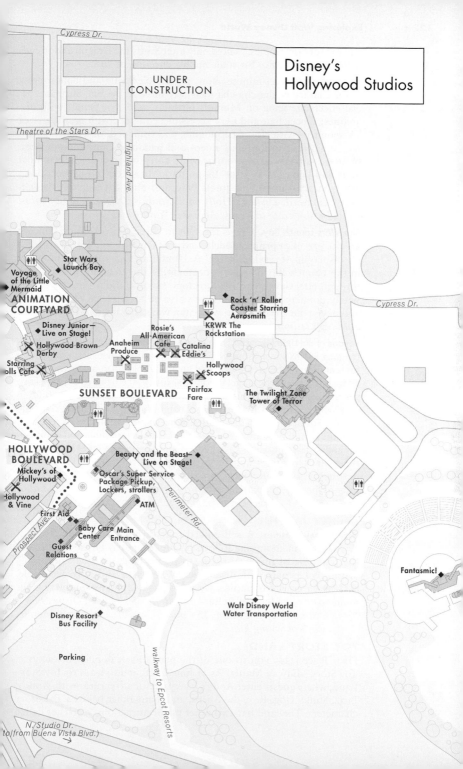

Disney's Hollywood Studios

Cypress Dr.

UNDER CONSTRUCTION

Theatre of the Stars Dr.

Highland Ave.

Cypress Dr.

Star Wars Launch Bay

Voyage of the Little Mermaid

ANIMATION COURTYARD

Rock 'n' Roller Coaster Starring Aerosmith

KRWR The Rockstation

Disney Junior— Live on Stage!

Rosie's All-American Cafe

Catalina Eddie's

Anaheim Produce

Hollywood Brown Derby

Starring Rolls Cafe

Hollywood Scoops

SUNSET BOULEVARD

Fairfax Fare

The Twilight Zone Tower of Terror

HOLLYWOOD BOULEVARD

Beauty and the Beast— Live on Stage!

Mickey's of Hollywood

Oscar's Super Service Package Pickup, Lockers, strollers

Hollywood & Vine

ATM

First Aid

Baby Care Center

Main Entrance

Prospect Ave.

Perimeter Rd.

Guest Relations

Fantasmic!

Walt Disney World Water Transportation

Disney Resort Bus Facility

Parking

walkway to Epcot Resorts

N. Studio Dr.
to/from Buena Vista Blvd.)
→

bad case of "the rippies," cured only after Stuffy the Dragon and friends gather in Doc's office for some bubbly cheering-up fun.

Throughout the 24-minute show, preschoolers sing and dance along as the characters cha-cha-cha their way through the fun. Surprise special effects are icing on Minnie's birthday cake. **For people with disabilities:** Wheelchair and ECV accessible, equipped with preshow-area TV monitors with closed captioning, and equipped for assisted-listening, audio-description, and video- and handheld-captioning devices. ■**TIP**➜ Fastpass+ is offered; or come early, when your child is most alert and lines are shorter. Be prepared to sit on the carpet. Don't miss character meet and greets before or after the show. ⊠ *Animation Courtyard, Disney's Hollywood Studios* ᔕ *Duration: 24 mins. Crowds: Moderate to heavy. Audience: Young kids.*

Star Wars Launch Bay. This is the spot to check out costumes, concept art work, replica props, models, and artifacts from the *Star Wars* films on display in several galleries. A 10-minute film runs continuously in the Launch Bay Theater, documenting the creation of *Star Wars* through interviews with the directors, writers, and producers of this wildly popular film series. There's also an area where you can meet and have your photo taken with Star Wars characters. ⊠ *Hollywood Studios, Kissimmee.*

Voyage of the Little Mermaid. You join Ariel, Sebastian, and the underwater gang in this stage show, which condenses the movie into a marathon presentation of the greatest hits. In an admirable effort at verisimilitude, a fine mist sprays the stage; if you're sitting in the front rows, expect to get spritzed. Although this show is suitable for all ages, smaller children might be frightened by the dark theater and the evil, larger-than-life Ursula. **For people with disabilities:** Wheelchair accessible, has reflective captioning and preshow-area TVs with closed captioning, and equipped for audio-description and assisted-listening devices. ■**TIP**➜ If you're not riding Rock 'n' Roller Coaster or Tower of Terror, come first thing and put Fastpass+ to good use. Or wait until the stroller brigade's exodus later in the day. ⊠ *Animation Courtyard, Disney's Hollywood Studios* ᔕ *Duration: 15 mins. Crowds: Heavy. Audience: All ages.*

MICKEY AVENUE

Walt Disney Presents. A self-guided tour through a treasure trove of Walt Disney memorabilia follows his life from early boyhood, through the founding of his first studio, to Disneyland, and then to Disney World. **For people with disabilities:** Wheelchair and ECV accessible. ■**TIP**➜ Come while waiting for a Fastpass+ appointment at a high-demand ride like Rock 'n' Roller Coaster. ⊠ *Mickey Ave., Disney's Hollywood Studios* ᔕ *Duration: 15+ mins. Crowds: Light to moderate. Audience: Not young kids.*

TOY STORY LAND

Pixar Place leads you to one of the park's most popular attractions, Toy Story Midway Mania! As of June 2018, it also leads to Toy Story Land, where guests enter Andy's backyard for adventures with Woody, Buzz, Slinky Dog, Rex, the Aliens, and many other beloved *Toy Story* characters. The land has two other major attractions: a coaster called

Slinky Dog Dash and a dizzying ride called Alien Swirling Saucers, which is reminiscent of the Mad Hatter's Teacups at the Magic Kingdom. Woody's Lunch Box is your spot to grab a quick-service meal.

Alien Swirling Saucers. Based on the toys Andy got from the Pizza Planet claw machine in the first *Toy Story* movie, this swirling teacup-style ride puts you on a rocket being chased by aliens in flying saucers, who are trying to grab the rocket with The Claw. ⊠ *Disney's Hollywood Studios.*

Slinky Dog Dash. This family-friendly ride is the centerpiece of Toy Story Land, and is meant to be a roller coaster built by Andy using his Mega Coaster Play Kit. The bright-red track surrounds a primary colored building-block city with towers featuring Toy Story icons such as Cowgirl Jessie and Rex the dinosaur. The coaster vehicles are Slinky Dogs, whose slinky springs surround the cars. ⊠ *Disney's Hollywood Studios.*

Fodor's Choice   **Toy Story Midway Mania!** Great toys like Mr. Potato Head, Woody, and
★   Buzz Lightyear from Disney's hit film *Toy Story* never lose their relevance. The action here involves these beloved characters and takes place inside the toy box of Andy, the boy whose toys come to life when he's gone. Step right up and grab a pair of 3-D glasses before boarding your jazzed-up carnival tram. Soon you're whirling onto the midway where you can use your spring-action shooter to launch darts at balloons, toss rings at aliens, and splatter eggs at barnyard targets.

You'll rack up points for targets hit and see your tally at ride's end. Try to hone a rat-a-tat shooting system to increase your score. Don't let Rex's fear of failure slow you down—shoot for the stars and you'll deserve a salute from the Green Army Men. **For people with disabilities:** Guests using ECVs must transfer to a standard wheelchair. Equipped for video-captioning and audio-description devices. Check with a host about boarding with a service animal. ■TIP→ It's so addictive, you might want to come first thing, ride, and get a Fastpass+ for another go. ⊠ *Pixar Pl., Disney's Hollywood Studios* ☞ *Duration: 7 mins. Crowds: Heavy. Audience: All ages.*

GRAND AVENUE

Formerly Streets of America, this area of the park has changed most in the past year, with many of the familiar facades fallen to the bulldozer, replaced by construction fences behind which grows the magic of Toy Story Land. But Miss Piggy, Kermit, and their Muppet pals are still entertaining their fans at the theater on Grand Avenue.

Muppet*Vision 3-D. You don't have to be a Miss Piggyphile to get a kick out of this combination 3-D movie and musical revue. All the Muppet characters make appearances, including Miss Piggy in roles that include the Statue of Liberty. In the waiting area, movie posters advertise the world's most glamorous porker in *Star Chores* and *To Have and Have More,* and Kermit the Frog in an Arnold Schwarzenegger parody, *Kürmit the Amphibian,* who's "so mean, he's green." Special effects are built into the walls and ceilings of the theater; the 3-D effects are coordinated with other sensory stimulation. **For people with disabilities:** Wheelchair accessible; has reflective captioning and preshow-area TVs with closed captioning; and equipped for assisted-listening, video-captioning, and audio-description devices. ■TIP→ Get your Fastpass+ or arrive 10 minutes early. And don't worry—there are no bad seats. ⊠ *Streets of America, Disney's Hollywood Studios* ☞ *Duration: 25 mins. Crowds: Moderate to heavy. Audience: All ages.*

ECHO LAKE

In the center of an idealized slice of Southern California is a cool, blue lake—an oasis fringed with trees, benches, and things like pink-and-aqua, chrome-trimmed restaurants with sassy waitresses and black-and-white TVs at the tables; the shipshape Min & Bill's Dockside Diner; and Tatooine Traders, where kids can build their own light sabers and browse a trove of *Star Wars*–inspired goods. You'll also find two of the park's longest-running attractions, the Indiana Jones Epic Stunt Spectacular! and Star Tours—The Adventures Continue, where a 3-D attraction transformation jazzes up the galaxy.

Fodor's Choice ★ **Indiana Jones Epic Stunt Spectacular!** The rousing theme music from the Indiana Jones movies heralds action delivered by veteran stunt coordinator Glenn Randall, whose credits include *Raiders of the Lost Ark, E.T.,* and *Jewel of the Nile*. Presented in a 2,200-seat amphitheater, the show starts with a series of near-death encounters in an ancient Mayan temple. Indy slides down a rope from the ceiling, dodges spears, avoids getting chopped by booby-trapped idols, and snags a forbidden gemstone, setting off a gigantic boulder that threatens to flatten him.

Next comes the Cairo street scene, circa 1940, where lucky audience members are chosen to perform as extras. When the nasty Ninja-Nazi stuntmen come out, you start to think that it's probably better to be in the audience.

Eventually Indy returns with his redoubtable girlfriend, Marian Ravenwood, portrayed by a Karen Allen look-alike. She's kidnapped and tossed into a truck while Indy fights his way free with bullwhip and gun, and bad guys tumble from every corner and cornice.

The actors do a commendable job of explaining their stunts, and you'll learn how cameras are camouflaged for trick shots. Only one stunt remains a secret: how do Indy and Marian escape the grand finale explosion? That's what keeps 'em coming back. **For people with disabilities:** Wheelchair accessible. Equipped for assisted-listening, audio-description, and handheld-captioning devices. There's sign language interpretation twice weekly. ■TIP➔ Don't waste your Fastpass+ here; there's plenty of room. Come at night to see the idols' eyes glow. ⊠ *Echo Lake, Disney's Hollywood Studios* ☞ *Duration: 30 mins. Crowds: Moderate to heavy. Audience: All but very young kids.*

Fodor's Choice ★ **Star Tours: The Adventures Continue.** *Star Wars* fans, wield those light sabers! This fan favorite multiplies the thrills with more than 50 ride scenarios powered up by Dolby 3-D video combined with motion-simulator technology. Here's the basic storyline: C-3PO and R2-D2, at the helm of a misappropriated spaceship, must navigate the galaxy with a rebel spy on board (it could be you!) while Imperial forces try to thwart the journey.

Each ride is different: you'll encounter multiple thrills from the *Star Wars* universe including the lush Wookiee planet Kashyyyk and the

HOLLYWOOD STUDIOS KIDS TOUR

Young children always get a kick out of Hollywood Boulevard's wacky street performers and the park's energetic stage shows.

The minute you enter, head straight to Toy Story Midway Mania! and get in line (unless you made a Fastpass+ reservation). Everyone loves this busy ride—even young children who have to learn how to operate their spring-action shooters to rack up midway points. If you can ride *and* come back for your Fastpass+ reservation, you'll be your kids' hero.

Combine lunch with more playtime at the Disney Junior Play 'n Dine at Hollywood & Vine family buffet, where characters from Disney Junior: Live on Stage! mix and mingle with the children. Don't forget your camera and the kids' autograph books!

SEE THE CHARACTERS COME TO LIFE

Shows and attractions based on Disney films and TV series really grab young children. Check your *Times Guide* for performances of Beauty and the Beast: Live on Stage and Disney Junior: Live on Stage! After tots and preschoolers have danced along at the Disney Junior show, they can meet the characters in the Animation Courtyard, then catch a Beauty and the Beast performance or watch Ariel "under the sea" in *Voyage of the Little Mermaid.*

Check other character greeting locations and times—the Green Army Men from *Toy Story* put the kids through their marching paces on Pixar Place; Mickey Mouse or *The Incredibles* stars might turn up at the Magic of Disney Animation. Make time to meet Phineas and Ferb near Mama Melrose's Ristorante Italiano. Then watch Kermit display his wry wit and Miss Piggy steal the show at Muppet*Vision 3-D. It's not easy being green. ...

GRAB THE SPOTLIGHT

Jedi wannabes can suit up to clash with the Dark Force at Jedi Training Academy, which is scheduled throughout the day. At the ABC Sound Studio near Star Tours, children ages 4–12 should sign up early in the day for a chance to grab a light saber and let the Force be with them. During each 20-minute show, crowds gather and cheer the kids as they learn to "cut to the left shoulder, step back, and duck!" when clashing with a costumed Darth Vader. Needless to say, the Dark Force can't compete.

underwater world of Naboo. One flight propels you through a dangerous asteroid field before skimming the second Death Star construction zone. You may come face-to-menacing-mask with Darth Vader or meet favorite sage Yoda. Other characters sprinkled throughout the different films include Admiral Ackbar, Chewbacca, and Boba Fett. Your 40-passenger Starspeeder 1000 rockets through space with enough high-speed twists, turns, and nosedives to guarantee that the Force is, indeed, with you.

Those who are pregnant or have heart, back, neck, or motion-sickness issues shouldn't ride. Children less than 40 inches tall may not ride. **For people with disabilities:** Guests using wheelchairs must transfer to a ride seat. Equipped for handheld-captioning and video-captioning devices.

HOLLYWOOD STUDIOS GROWN-UP TOUR

At the Studios, the best of Disney animation—from *Toy Story* to *Beauty and the Beast*—is reborn as park attractions. The old small-screen favorite *The Twilight Zone* is taken to new heights, and Indiana Jones performs action-packed stunts to bring famous film moments to life.

FIND YOUR ADRENALINE RUSH

Two words—thrills and chills—define the top two attractions for older kids and adults. Head straight to Sunset Boulevard and grab the thrills at Rock 'n' Roller Coaster Starring Aerosmith, where multiple inversions, twists, and turns rock to the tune of "Dude (Looks Like a Lady)." Feel the chills at the Twilight Zone Tower of Terror, when something goes terribly wrong with your elevator car, and it veers off its ghostly course.

A quick walk to Echo Lake lands you in Wookiee territory, where you can climb aboard the Star Tours flight simulator for a wild flight to the Moon of Endor; 3-D upgrades and more than 50 different ride scenarios increase the thrill factor.

DISCOVER YOUR TALENT

Are you an actor, an artist, a singer, or a midway-game fanatic? If the Citizens of Hollywood Talent Agent doesn't get your number, you can try out your act at one of several park attractions.

At the Indiana Jones Epic Stunt Spectacular! 10 guests are chosen to perform as show extras (arrive early and get noticed). At Toy Story Midway Mania! join Woody and Buzz for a manic midway ride past moving targets that test your spring-action-shooter mettle.

TASTES OF THE PAST

Refuel at one of the park's many quick-service stands, let "Mom" serve you meat loaf and a peanut butter–and-jelly shake at the '50s Prime Time Café, or boost your image with a plush booth and a Cobb salad at the Hollywood Brown Derby.

Back at Echo Lake, the Tune-In Lounge is a great place to grab a mojito or margarita before heading to the nighttime extravaganza Fantasmic! That's a wrap.

Service animals aren't allowed. ■TIP➔ Lines swell when the Indiana Jones show lets out. Use a Fastpass+ or visit early or late. For the wildest ride, sit in the back. ✉ *Echo Lake, Disney's Hollywood Studios* ☞ *Duration: 6 mins. Crowds: Heavy. Audience: All but young kids.*

NEED A BREAK

Sweet tooth acting up? Funnel cakes and soft-serve ice cream are the ticket at the Oasis Canteen. If you're ready for a heartier bite, Sci-Fi Dine-In Theater Restaurant is the spot for a burger and fries while you sit in a car-shaped booth and watch old sci-fi movies. You can even buy a beer here.

HOLLYWOOD STUDIOS SPECTACLES

Disney Movie Magic. This 10-minute night-time projection show lights up the facade of the iconic Grauman's Chinese Theater and surrounding buildings with snippets from favorite films, including sword fights from *Pirates of the Caribbean*, heroic chase scenes from the Indiana

Jones films, chimney sweeps popping down chimney stacks from *Mary Poppins*, Groot and the gang from *Guardians of the Galaxy* and many more. ⊠ *Orlando.*

Fantasmic! The Studios' after-dark show wows huge audiences with its special effects and Disney characters. The omnipresent Mickey, in his sorcerer's apprentice costume, plays the embodiment of Good in the struggle against forces of Evil, personified by Disney villains such as Cruella DeVil, Scar, and Maleficent. Animated clips of these famous baddies, alternating with clips of Disney sweethearts, are projected onto screens made of water—high-tech fountains surging high in the air. The epic battle plays out amid water effects and flames, explosions, and fireworks worthy of a Hollywood shoot-'em-up. All this, plus the villainous action, is why small kids may find this show frightening.

Arrive early at the Hollywood Hills Amphitheater opposite the Twilight Zone Tower of Terror. Check ahead for information on show days and times. This show often runs twice nightly during peak season; fewer times during nonpeak periods. **For people with disabilities:** Wheelchair and ECV accessible. Equipped with reflective captioning and for assisted-listening, hand-held captioning, and audio-description devices. ■TIP→ Fastpass+ seating is available. If you didn't book it, arrive at least an hour early and sit toward the rear, near the entrance/exit. Or consider the lunch or dinner package, which includes a special block of seating for the show. If you sit in front rows, you will get wet. ⊠ *Sunset Blvd., Disney's Hollywood Studios* ☞ *Duration: 30 mins. Crowds: Heavy. Audience: Not small kids.*

For the First Time in Forever: A Frozen Sing-Along Celebration. Ever since the Disney film *Frozen* hit the jackpot, Disney's theme parks have been mining the blockbuster with character meet and greets, entertainment vignettes, a ride, and a half-hour show that's packing the house up to 10 times a day. The show's comical emcees are two costumed "Royal Historians" of Arendelle, who pepper the 30-minute show with witticisms as they narrate the *Frozen* story. Animated segments of the film accompany the narration on a giant screen as the story unfolds and the audience sings along to the film's play list. Live actors portray Anna, Elsa, and Kristoff convincingly as they interact with the "historians" and audience. Kids in the audience rock the Academy Award–winning "Let It Go" most enthusiastically and can't resist the sweetly melodic "Do You Want to Build a Snowman?" Song lyrics, including those for Olaf's whimsical anthem, "In Summer," as well as "For the First Time in Forever" and "Love Is an Open Door," are displayed for the audience on two additional video screens. **For people with disabilities:** Wheelchair accessible. ■TIP→ Fastpass+ is available and recommended. ⊠ *Disney's Hollywood Studios* ☞ *Duration: 30 mins. Crowds: Heavy. Audience: All ages.*

2

DISNEY'S ANIMAL KINGDOM

If you're thinking, "Oh, it's just another zoo, let's skip it," think again. Walt Disney World's fourth theme park, opened in 1998 and celebrating its 20th anniversary in 2018 takes its inspiration from humankind's enduring love for animals and the environment and pulls out all the stops. Your day will be packed with unusual animal encounters, enchanting entertainment, and themed rides, one of them out of this world, that'll leave you breathless.

A large chunk of the park is devoted to animal habitats, especially the forest and savanna of Africa's Kilimanjaro Safaris. Towering acacia trees and tall grasses sweep across the land where antelopes, giraffes, and wildebeests roam. A lion kopje, warthog burrows, a zebra habitat, and an elephant watering hole provide ample space for inhabitants.

About 94 acres contain foliage like hibiscus and mulberry, perfect for antelope and many other species. The largest groups of Nile hippos and African elephants in North America live along the winding waterway that leads to the savanna. The generously landscaped Pangani Forest Exploration Trail provides roaming grounds for troops of gorillas and authentic habitats for meerkats, birds, fish, and other creatures.

Beyond the park's Africa territory, similar large spaces are set aside for the homes of Asian animals like tigers and giant fruit bats, as well as for creatures such as Galápagos tortoises and a giant anteater.

Disney Imagineers didn't forget to include their trademark thrills, from the astonishing Avatar Flight of Passage in Pandora, to the Kali River Rapids ride in Asia to the fast-paced DINOSAUR journey in DinoLand U.S.A., and Expedition Everest, a "runaway" train ride on a faux rugged mountain complete with icy ledges, dark caves, and a yeti legend.

The latest land to open takes visitors totally off-planet to a world inspired by the film *Avatar*. Pandora—The World of Avatar is filled

TOP ATTRACTIONS

AFRICA

Festival of the Lion King. Singers and dancers dressed in fantastic costumes representing many wild animals perform uplifting dance and acrobatics numbers and interact with children in the audience.

Kilimanjaro Safaris. You're guaranteed to see dozens of wild animals, including giraffes, gazelles, hippos, rhinos, zebras, and elephants, living in authentic, re-created African habitats. If you're lucky, the lions and cheetahs will be stirring, too.

ASIA

Expedition Everest. This roller coaster is a spine-tingling trip into the snowy Himalayas to find the abominable snowman. It's best reserved for brave riders seven and up.

PANDORA–THE WORLD OF AVATAR

Avatar: Flight of Passage. Simply one of the most exciting theme park rides you'll experience.

DINOLAND U.S.A.

DINOSAUR! Extremely lifelike giant dinosaurs jump out as your vehicle swoops and dips. We recommend it for fearless kids eight and up.

Finding Nemo: The Musical Don't miss a performance of this outstanding musical starring the most charming, colorful characters ever to swim their way into your heart.

DISCOVERY ISLAND

Tree of Life: It's Tough to Be a Bug! This clever and very funny 3-D movie starring Flik from the Disney film *A Bug's Life* is full of surprises, including "shocking" special effects. Some young children are scared of the loud noises.

TOUR

Wild Africa Trek. The price tag is hefty, but this behind-the-scenes wild-animal adventure is a memory maker.

with breathtaking technology, astonishing alien beauty, and the park's biggest thrill attraction, Avatar Flight of Passage. The whole park is open at night since Pandora opened in 2017, to best view the lighted alien landscape.

The only downside to the Animal Kingdom layout is that walking paths and spaces can get very crowded and hot in the warmest months. Your best bet is to arrive very early and see the animals first before the heat makes them (and you) woozy.

Keep an eye peeled throughout the day for the spectacular appearance of a flock of macaws soaring overhead. The brightly colored birds—scarlet, hyacinth, blue, and gold and more—make periodic flights throughout the park.

ORIENTATION AND PLANNING
GETTING ORIENTED

Animal Kingdom's hub is the Tree of Life, in the middle of Discovery Island. The park's lands, each with a distinct personality, radiate from Discovery Island. To the southwest, lies Pandora–The World of Avatar, inspired by *Avatar* and its upcoming sequels. The area is best viewed after dark, when the alien landscape lights up, but the floating islands are spectacular at any time of day. North of the hub is Africa, where Kilimanjaro Safaris travel across extensive savanna. In the northeast corner is Rafiki's Planet Watch with conservation activities.

Asia, with thrills like Expedition Everest and Kali River Rapids, is east of the hub, and DinoLand U.S.A. brings *T. rex* and other prehistoric creatures to life in the park's southeast corner.

If you're staying on Disney property, you can take a Disney bus to the Entrance Plaza. If you drive, the $20 parking fee allows you to park at other Disney lots throughout the day.

Although this is technically Disney's largest theme park, most of the land is reserved for the animals. Pedestrian areas are actually quite compact, with relatively narrow passageways. The only way to get around is on foot or in a wheelchair or electronic convenience vehicle (ECV).

PARK AMENITIES

Baby Care: At Discovery Island you can stop in to nurse babies in the quiet baby-care center, which is equipped with rocking chairs and low lighting. There are changing tables, which are also available in restrooms (including some men's restrooms), and you can buy disposable diapers, formula, baby food, and pacifiers.

Cameras: You can buy film and digital memory cards at several shops throughout the park. If a Disney photographer takes your picture, sign up for a Disney PhotoPass—later, you can view and purchase the pictures online ($199 for full digital Memory Maker access) or at the park's photo center in the Oasis.

First Aid: The first-aid center, staffed by registered nurses, is in Discovery Island, and at least a dozen automated external defibrillators are in key park areas.

Mosquito Control: Disney offers complimentary insect repellent for guests throughout all its parks.

Guest Relations: This office will help with tickets at a window to the left just before you pass through the turnstile. Once you've entered, Guest Relations staffers in the Oasis can provide park maps, schedules, and answers to questions. They can also assist with dining reservations, ticket upgrades, and services for guests with disabilities.

Lockers: Lockers are in Guest Relations in the Oasis. Rental fees are $7 to $9 (depending on size) for a day plus a $5 key deposit.

Lost People and Things: Instruct your kids to speak to someone with a Disney name tag if you become separated. Lost children are taken to the baby-care center, where they can watch Disney movies, or to Guest Relations, whichever is closer. If you do lose your child, contact any cast member immediately and Disney security personnel will be notified.

Animal Kingdom Lost and Found. To retrieve lost articles on the same day, visit or call Lost and Found, which is in the lobby of Guest Relations, just inside the park. ⊠ *Oasis, Animal Kingdom* ☎ *407/938–2785.*

Main Lost and Found. If more than a day has passed since you've lost something, contact the Main Lost and Found office at the Magic Kingdom Transportation and Ticket Center. ☎ *407/824–4245.*

Package Pick-Up: You can have shop clerks forward purchases to Package Pick-Up near the Main Entrance in the Oasis, so that you won't have to carry them around all day. Allow three hours for the journey. If you're staying at a Disney hotel, you can also have packages delivered there.

Services for People with Disabilities: Guests using wheelchairs will have ready access to restaurants, shops, and most attractions—including the Finding Nemo: The Musical theater in DinoLand U.S.A. and the Tree of Life theater showing It's Tough to Be a Bug!(Theaters also are accessible to ECVs.) Some monitor-equipped attractions have reflective-captioning boxes.

Scripts and story lines for all attractions are available, and you can book sign-language interpreters with notice of two or more weeks. Large Braille park maps are by Guest Relations and near the Tip Board at the entrance to Discovery Island. Guest Relations is also where you can borrow assisted-listening, handheld-captioning, and video-captioning devices with a refundable deposit. Service animals are allowed in most, but not all, areas of the park.

You can rent wheelchairs ($12 daily, $10 for multiple days) and ECVs ($50 per day plus a refundable $20 security deposit) at Garden Gate Gifts in the Oasis. You can't, however, reserve these items, so arrive early to get one—particularly if you want an ECV.

Stroller Rentals: Garden Gate Gifts in the Oasis rents strollers. Singles are $15 daily, $13 multiday; doubles run $31 daily, $27 multiday.

TOURS

Backstage Tales. This tour ($90) takes an in-depth look at animal conservation, stopping at the state-of-the-art veterinary hospital and other behind-the-scenes areas. It's a great way to learn about animal behaviors and how handlers manage a diverse population of critters in captivity. The nearly four-hour tour includes a visit to the animal housing area and the animal nutrition center to see how animal handlers prepare and deliver more than four tons of food. Participants must be at least 12 years old. ⊠ *Animal Kingdom* ☎ *407/939–8687.*

Fodor's Choice ★ **Wild Africa Trek.** You will cover exciting ground on this three-hour, walking-riding adventure ($189 to $249 per person depending on season) into unexplored areas of the park. For a close-up view of the hippos, you'll wear a special vest with a harness that's tethered to a rail at the edge of a bluff. You'll cross a rope bridge above a pool of Nile crocodiles. Your exclusive open-air safari vehicle makes multiple stops for leisurely viewing of giraffes, wildebeests, cheetahs, and other creatures of the savanna. Burning all those calories pays off when breakfast or lunch treats are served (think prosciutto, salmon, Brie, fresh fruit) at the open-air Boma Landing on the edge of the savanna. The tour is good for anyone age 8 and older who's fit. Included in the admission price is a CD-photo souvenir of your trek. A portion of the tour price is donated to the Disney Worldwide Conservation Fund. ☎ *407/939–8687.*

VISITING TIPS

Try to visit during the week. Pedestrian areas are compact, and the park can feel uncomfortably packed on weekends.

Plan on a full day here. That way, while exploring Africa's Pangani Forest Exploration Trail, say, you can spend 10 minutes (rather than just two) watching vigilant meerkats stand sentry or tracking a mama gorilla as she cares for her youngster.

Arrive a half hour before the park opens. That way you'll see the animals at their friskiest (first thing in the morning or at night is the best time to do the safari ride) as you get a jump on the crowds.

Check the Tip Board. For updates on line lengths, particularly for Pandora's Avatar Flight of Passage, check the Tip Board, just after crossing the bridge into Discovery Island.

Eat here. Animal Kingdom has some of Disney World's best food, including Tiffins, which may be the best upscale restaurant anywhere in Walt Disney World.

Plan your meet-up. Good places to rendezvous include the outdoor Dawa Bar or Tamu Tamu Refreshments areas in Africa, in front of DinoLand U.S.A.'s Boneyard, or on one of the benches outside Expedition Everest in Asia.

EXPLORING ANIMAL KINGDOM

THE OASIS

This entrance makes you feel as if you've been plunked down in the middle of a rain forest. Cool mist, the aroma of flowers, playful animals, and colorful birds enliven a miniature landscape of streams and grottoes, waterfalls, and glades fringed with banana leaves and jacaranda. It's also where you can take care of essentials before entering. Here you'll find guide maps, stroller and wheelchair rentals, Guest Relations, and an ATM.

DISCOVERY ISLAND

The park hub and site of the Tree of Life, this island is encircled by Discovery River, which isn't an actual attraction but makes for attractive views from the bridge to Harambe and another between Asia and DinoLand U.S.A. The amphitheater on the east side of the river is home to the night-time attraction Rivers of Light. The island's whimsical architecture, with wood carvings from Bali, lends charm and a touch of fantasy. The Discovery Island Trails that lead to the Tree of Life provide habitats for African crested porcupines, lemurs, Galápagos tortoises, and other creatures you won't want to miss.

As you are walking through this area, watch for the awe-inspiring sight of a flock of multicolored macaws flying free over your head. They used to be part of the Flights of Wonder show in Asia, which closed at the end of 2017, but these lovely avians still soar six times a day.

You'll discover some great shops and good counter-service eateries here. Visitor services that aren't in the Oasis are here, on the border with Harambe, including the baby-care center and the first-aid center.

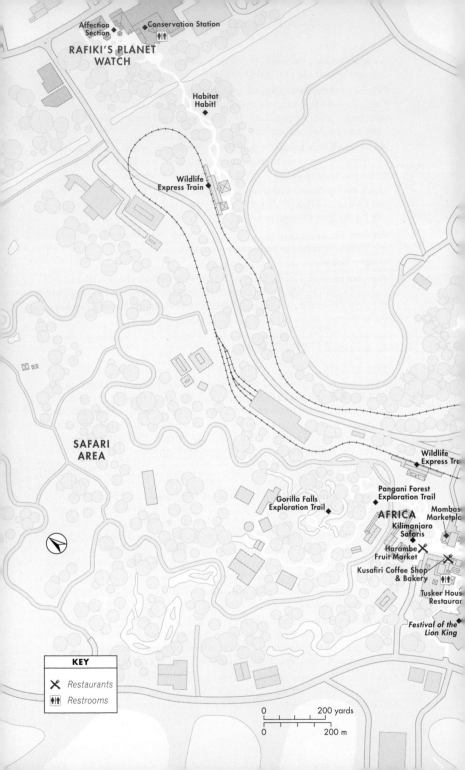

Disney's Animal Kingdom

ASIA

Expedition Everest–
Legend of the
Forbidden Mountain

Thirsty River Bar
and Trek Snacks

Serka Zong
Bazaar

Kali River
Rapids

Rivers of Light

Anandapur
Ice Cream Truck

Maharajah
Jungle Trek

Finding Nemo—
The Musical

Rivers of Light

Yak & Yeti
Quality Beverages

Dino Diner

Primeval
Whirl

Yak & Yeti
Local Food Cafe

Fossil Fun
Games

Chester Hester's
Dinosaur Treasures

Yak & Yeti
Restaurant

The Boneyard

TriceraTop
Spin

The Dino
Institute Shop

Warung

Adventurers
Outpost

Wilderness
Explorers

**DINOLAND
U.S.A.**

DinoSue

Caravan
Road

Mr Kamal's

Flame Tree
Barbecue

Eight Spoon
Café

Isle of Java

Trilo-Bites

Dino-Bite
Snacks

DINOSAUR

Tree of Life,
*It's Tough to
Be a Bug!*

Discovery Trading
Company

Restaurantosaurus

Harambe
Market

Awakenings

Dug & Russell's Wilderness
Explorer Club House

Wilderness
Explorers

Tamu Tamu
Refreshments

**DISCOVERY
ISLAND**

Mahindi

Discovery
Island
Trails

Terra
Treats

Winged
Encounters

Island
Mercantile

Garden
Gate Gifts

ATM

Dawa
Bar

Strollers &
Wheelchairs

First Aid/
Baby Care
Center

Creature
Comforts

Pizzafari

Tiffins

THE OASIS

Entrance

Nomad
Lounge

Lockers

Guest
Relations

Safari Bar

Rainforest
Café

**PANDORA-
THE WORLD OF AVATAR**

Wilderness
Explorers

Satu'li
Canteen

Valley of
Mo'ara

Na'vi River
Journey

Pongu Pongu

Avatar Flight
of Passage

Discovery River

The Tree of Life is the iconic centerpiece of Disney's Animal Kingdom.

Fodor's Choice
★

It's Tough to be a Bug! A monument to all of Earth's creatures, the park's centerpiece is an imposing 14 stories high and 50 feet wide at its base. Its 100,000-plus leaves are several shades of green fabric, each carefully placed for a realistic effect. Carved into its thick trunk, gnarled roots, and soaring branches—some of which are supported by joints that allow them to sway in a strong wind—are nearly 350 intricate animal forms that include a baboon, a whale, a horse, the mighty lion, and even an ankylosaurus. At night, the tree is lit up by projections onto the vast trunk and leaves. Outside, paths tunnel underneath the roots as the fauna-encrusted trunk towers overhead.

The path leads you inside the tree trunk, where you get a bug's-eye view of life. The witty 3-D film adventure *It's Tough to Be a Bug!* is modeled on the animated film *A Bug's Life* from Disney-Pixar . Special effects spray you with "poison," zap you with a swatter, and even poke you with a stinger—all in good fun.

Although the show has something for all ages, it's very loud. Some effects frighten young children. **For people with disabilities:** Wheelchair accessible, but, to fully experience all the special effects, guests using wheelchairs should transfer to a seat. Equipped with reflective captioning and for audio-description and assisted-listening devices. If you have a service animal, check with a host before entering the theater. ■TIP➔ **Fastpass+ is offered; enter across from the Disney Outfitters store via the Discovery Island Trails.** ⊠ *Discovery Island, Animal Kingdom* ☞ *Duration: 20 mins. Crowds: Moderate to heavy. Audience: All but young kids.*

2

DINOLAND U.S.A.

Just as it sounds, this is the place to come in contact with re-created prehistoric creatures, including the fear-inspiring carnotaurus and the gentle iguanodon. The landscaping includes live plants that have evolved over the last 65 million years. In collaboration with Chicago's Field Museum, Disney displays a complete, full-scale skeleton cast of Dino-Sue—also known as "Sue"—the 65-million-year-old *Tyrannosaurus rex* discovered near the Black Hills of South Dakota.

After admiring Sue, you can go on the thrilling DINOSAUR ride, play in the Boneyard, or take in the Finding Nemo: The Musical show at the Theater in the Wild. Kids will want to try the TriceraTop Spin and the Primeval Whirl family coaster, which has spinning "time machines." There's no need to dig for souvenirs at Chester and Hester's Dinosaur Treasures gift shop—all you need is your wallet.

Timing Tip: Because of the proximity of the two attractions, Finding Nemo: The Musical is a good place to take younger kids while older siblings do Expedition Everest.

NEED A BREAK

Famished but not much time for lunch? Make tracks for a counter-service burger and fries or a hearty salad at **Restaurantosaurus** and you'll be ready to take on *T. rex.*

The Boneyard. Youngsters can slide, dig, bounce, slither, and stomp around this archaeological dig site–cum–playground, the finest play area in any of the four Disney parks. In addition to a huge sand pit where children can dig for mammoth bones, there are twisting short and long slides, climbing nets, caves, a maze, and a jeep to climb on. Stomp on the dino footprints to make 'em roar. **For people with disabilities:** This fossil play maze is wheelchair accessible. ■**TIP**➔ Let the kids burn off energy here while waiting for a Fastpass+ appointment. Or head over late in the day when kids need to run free. ⌧ *DinoLand U.S.A., Animal Kingdom* ☞ *Duration: Up to you. Crowds: Moderate to heavy. Audience: Young kids.*

DINOSAUR. This wild adventure through time puts you face-to-face with huge dinosaurs that move and breathe with uncanny realism. When a carload of guests rouses a cantankerous carnotaurus from his Cretaceous slumber, it's showtime. You travel back 65 million years on a fast-paced, twisting adventure and try to save the last living iguanodon as a massive asteroid hurtles toward Earth. Exciting Audio-Animatronics and special effects bring to life dinosaurs like the raptor, pterodactyl, styracosaurus, alioramus, and compsognather. Be prepared for a short but jolting drop toward the end of the ride.

Guests who are pregnant or have back, neck, or heart problems should avoid this very bumpy ride. The jostling and realistic carnivores may frighten young children. **For people with disabilities:** You must transfer from your wheelchair to board this ride. Equipped for video-captioning and assisted-listening devices. No service animals. ■**TIP**➔ Come first thing in the morning or at the end of the day, or use Fastpass+. ⌧ *DinoLand U.S.A., Animal Kingdom* ☞ *Duration: Under 4 mins. Crowds: Heavy. Audience: All but young kids. Height requirement: 40 inches.*

Fodor's Choice **Finding Nemo–The Musical.** The performance of this fish tale is so cre-
★ ative and fun that many have likened it to a first-rate Broadway show.
Indeed, Disney Imagineers collaborated with several Broadway talents
to produce it. Original songs by Tony Award–winning *Avenue Q* co-
composer-creator Robert Lopez and a-cappella musical *Along the Way*
co-creator Kristen Anderson-Lopez add depth and energy. Michael
Curry, who co-designed the character puppets of Broadway's *The Lion
King,* also created this show's eye-popping puppetry.

Multigenerational humor, special effects, and larger-than-life puppets
acted by gifted performers, dancers, and acrobats all bring you into
Nemo's world. The sweet story remains the same as in the movie—
Nemo and his father, Marlin, go on separate journeys that teach them
how to understand each other. Zany Dory, with her memory lapses,
Crush the sea turtle dude, tap-dancing sharks, and others give memorable supporting-role turns. **For people with disabilities:** Wheelchair
accessible. Equipped with reflective captioning and for audio-description and assisted-listening devices. Check with Guest Relations for
sign-language schedule. ■TIP➡ Arrange a Fastpass+ or arrive 30 to 40
minutes before showtime. Bring little kids here while older tweens and
teens ride Expedition Everest. ⊠ *DinoLand U.S.A., Animal Kingdom*
☞ *Duration: 40 mins. Crowds: Heavy. Audience: All ages.*

Fossil Fun Games. A carnival-style midway in the middle of DinoLand
U.S.A., this fun fair draws crowds with games like Whack a Packy-
cephalosaur and the basketball-inspired Bronto-Score. The prehistoric
fun comes at a price, however, and stone currency is not accepted. Prizes
are mostly of the plush-character variety—you might win your sweetheart a stuffed Nala. **For people with disabilities:** Wheelchair accessible.
■TIP➡ It costs $4 a game, or $10 for three games. Vouchers can be
purchased at the souvenir stand. ⊠ *DinoLand U.S.A., Animal Kingdom*
☞ *Duration: Up to you. Crowds: Light. Audience: All ages.*

Primeval Whirl. In a free-spinning, four-passenger vehicle, you head on
a brief journey back in time on this outdoor open-air coaster, twisting,
turning, and even venturing into the jaws of a dinosaur "skeleton."
Crazy cartoon dinosaurs in shades of turquoise, orange, yellow, and
purple pop up along the track bearing signs that warn "The End Is
Near." More signs alert you to incoming "Meteors!" and suggest that
you "Head for the Hills!"—coaster hills, that is. Halfway through the
ride, your car seems to spin out of control and you take the next drop
backward. The more weight in the vehicle, the more you spin.

Pregnant women or guests with back, neck, or heart problems should
skip this one. **For people with disabilities:** Guests using wheelchairs
must transfer to the ride vehicle. No service animals. ■TIP➡ Fastpass+
is recommended. Kids might want to ride twice if the wait isn't long.
⊠ *DinoLand U.S.A., Animal Kingdom* ☞ *Duration: 2½ mins. Crowds:
Heavy. Audience: All but young kids. Height requirement: 48 inches.*

TriceraTop Spin. TriceraTop Spin is designed for playful little dinophiles
who ought to get a kick out of whirling around this ride's giant spinning
toy top and dodging incoming comets in their dino mobiles. "Pop!"
goes the top and out comes a grinning dinosaur as four passengers

On Asia's Expedition Everest, you'll chug, twist, turn, and plunge up, through, and down Mt. Everest on nearly a mile of track. Oh, yeah, and beware of the yeti!

in each vehicle fly in a circle and maneuver up and down. **For people with disabilities:** Wheelchair accessible, but guests using ECVs must transfer to standard wheelchairs. ■**TIP**➔ Ride early or take little ones while older kids are riding DINOSAUR or Primeval Whirl. ⊠ *DinoLand U.S.A., Animal Kingdom* ☞ *Duration: 2 mins. Crowds: Heavy. Audience: Young kids.*

ASIA

Meant to resemble an Asian village, this land is full of remarkable rain-forest scenery and ruins. Groupings of trees grow from a crumbling shrine populated by roaming tigers, and massive towers—representing Thailand and Nepal—are the habitat for gibbons, whose hooting fills the air.

Fodor's Choice
★

Expedition Everest—Legend of the Forbidden Mountain. A fierce yeti guards the route to Mt. Everest. Of course, you're willing to risk running across the big guy in your roller-coaster quest to reach the summit. So, you board an "aging," seemingly innocuous, 34-passenger, steam-engine train into the mountains. You roll past bamboo forests, waterfalls, and glacier fields as you climb higher through snowcapped peaks. Suddenly the train becomes a runaway, barreling forward then backward around icy ledges and through dark snowy caverns.

Nearly a mile of twists and turns cut through the dark mountain, and at one point your train plunges a harrowing 80 feet. Will you find the yeti? Buildings along the queue look like Himalayan mountain dwellings and teem with things like prayer flags, totems, and other artifacts from Tibet, Nepal, and the entire region.

Since the coaster is supposed to be less intense than, say, Space Mountain, brave children who meet the 44-inch minimum-height requirement can ride. Pregnant women or guests with back, neck, or heart problems shouldn't ride. **For people with disabilities:** You must transfer from your wheelchair to a ride vehicle; ask a cast member about the Transfer Practice Vehicle. No service animals. ■TIP➜ Unless you prefer to see the animals first, rush here as soon as the park opens and the wait isn't too long. Otherwise, grab a Fast Past+ or choose the Single Rider Queue. ⊠ *Asia, Animal Kingdom* ⏰ *Duration: 2½ mins. Crowds: Huge. Audience: All but young kids. Height requirement: 44 inches.*

Kali River Rapids. Asia's thrilling water adventure ride mixes the fun of a rafting experience with a solemn message to save pristine lands and animal habitats that are threatened by development. Aboard a round raft that seats 12, you run the Chakranadi River. After passing through a huge bamboo tunnel filled with jasmine-scented mist, your raft climbs 40 feet upriver, lurches and spins through sharp twists and turns, and then approaches an immense waterfall, which curtains a giant carved tiger face. Past rain forests and temple ruins, you find yourself face-to-face with the denuded slope of a logged-out woodland burning out of control. There are many more thrills, but why spill the beans?

You will get wet and you may get soaked. Unless you want to wring out your clothing in the nearest restroom afterward, bring a poncho. Better yet, bring a change of clothing in a plastic bag. The ride-height minimum is 38 inches. If you are pregnant or have heart, back, neck, or motion-sickness problems, sit this one out. **For people with disabilities:** Guests using wheelchairs must transfer to a ride raft. No service animals. ■TIP➜ Use Fastpass+ to avoid a long wait. ⊠ *Asia, Animal Kingdom* ⏰ *Duration: 7 mins. Crowds: Heavy. Audience: All but young kids.*

Maharajah Jungle Trek. Get an up-close view of some unusual animals along this trail, including giant fruit bats that hang to munch fruit from wires and fly very close to the open and glass-protected viewing areas and Bengal tigers in front of a maharajah's palace ruins. The tigers have their own view (with no accessibility, of course) of Asian deer and black buck, an antelope species. At the end of the trek, you walk through an aviary with a lotus pool. Disney interpreters, many from Asian countries, are on hand to answer questions. **For people with disabilities:** Wheelchair accessible; equipped for audio-description devices. Guests with service animals should check with a host before entering the aviary. ■TIP➜ Come anytime. Crowds stay fairly light, as people are constantly on the move. ⊠ *Asia, Animal Kingdom* ⏰ *Duration: Up to you. Crowds: Light. Audience: All ages.*

PANDORA—THE WORLD OF AVATAR

As you cross the bridge from the hub into Pandora, you sense an immediate change, in landscape, in lighting fixtures, in tone. The details are important, and they leave no doubt you are entering another world. Disney Imagineers worked for years along with *Avatar* film creator James Cameron and his Lightstorm Entertainment, to create the inventive, sometimes surreal, landscape of Pandora. The experience is set far in the future, generations beyond the war between the Na'vi and humans

Pandora–The World of Avatar is the newest addition to Animal Kingdom.

depicted in the film. Instead Alpha Centauri Expeditions (ACE) are bringing humans back to the planet. The emphasis now is on cooperation between human and Na'vi to ensure the environment is protected. In the daytime, you'll be awe-struck by the gravity defying floating islands and the lush plants, both earthlike and unearthly, that envelop the land. At night, when the bioluminescence cranks up, you feel slightly off balance, as if you were truly on an alien world, seeing alien things for the first time. That feeling only grows with a trip along the Na'vi River, or, deeper into the jungle where the Avatar Flight of Passage puts you atop a banshee for a stomach-lurching journey. But don't make the mistake of rushing to the thrill ride and missing all the beauty along the way. Be sure to stop by Satu'li Canteen to refuel with a delicious and healthy bowl of grains or noodles topped with grilled meats and a variety of vegetables, or Pongu Pongu, where drinks have been known to glow in the dark.

Fodor's Choice ★ **Avatar Flight of Passage.** Disney's latest, and most technically advanced, thrill ride puts you atop a dragonlike mountain banshee for the ride of your life. After a trek deep into the jungles of Pandora, you enter a room where scientists are pairing up banshees and visitors. On instruction, you board a vehicle resembling a motorcycle that faces a blank wall. After hopping on, you don special 3-D goggles, and the room springs to life, and you are one with your banshee. You feel it come to life beneath you, as Pandora comes to life before your eyes. The banshee's wing muscles pump as you hurtle down cliff faces and soar above the floating islands familiar from the film. The visuals are breathtaking, with dense jungles, seascapes, vast waterfalls, and alien plant life passing rapidly before your eyes, but even more astonishing are the subtle smells and temperature changes that accompany different landscapes, immersing you totally in the experience. ✉ *Pandora, Animal Kingdom.*

Fodor's Choice **Na'vi River Journey.** To enter this gentle river ride, you must first wander
★ through the inventive landscape of Pandora, designed by Disney Imagineers to include many tropical and subtropical plants found in Florida, enhancing them with creatively imagined alien plants, many of which light up at night. After entering the cavern and boarding a reed raft, you drift slowly past a bioluminescent rain forest, with an even more diverse range of flora and fauna, or a combination of both. The object of your quest is to find the Na'vi Shaman of Songs, the life force of Pandora, but you'll be so caught up in the stunning details of the landscape that you'll be surprised when the Audio-Animatronic Shaman shows up. ✉ *Pandora, Animal Kingdom.*

AFRICA

The largest of the lands is an area of forests and grasslands, predominantly an enclave for wildlife from the continent. Harambe, on the northern bank of Discovery River, is Africa's starting point. Inspired by several East African villages, this Disney town has so much detail that it's mind-boggling to try to soak it all up. Signs on the apparently peeling stucco walls are faded, as if bleached by the sun, and everything has a hot, dusty look. For souvenirs with Disney and African themes, browse through the Mombasa Marketplace and Ziwani Traders.

NEED A BREAK The tantalizing aroma of fresh-baked cinnamon buns leads to the **Kusafiri Coffee Shop & Bakery**, where, after just one look, you may give in to the urge. These buns are worth the banknotes, and they pair well with a cappuccino or espresso. Kids may opt for a giant cookie and milk.

Fodor's Choice *Festival of the Lion King.* If you think you've seen enough *Lion King* to last
★ a lifetime, you're wrong, unless you've seen this show. Disney presents a delightful tribal celebration of song, dance, and acrobatics that uses huge moving stages and floats. The show's singers are first-rate; lithe dancers wearing exotic animal-theme costumes portray creatures in the wild. Timon, Pumba, and other *Lion King* stars have key roles. The show is presented in the Harambe Theater in the park's Africa area. **For people with disabilities:** Wheelchair and ECV accessible; equipped for assisted-listening and handheld-captioning devices; sign-language interpretation is sometimes offered. ■TIP➔ Fastpass+ is offered. Without one, arrive 30–40 minutes before showtime. If you have a child who might want to get on stage, try to sit up front to increase his or her chance of getting chosen. ✉ *Africa, Animal Kingdom* ⏱ *Duration: 30 mins. Crowds: Moderate to heavy. Audience: All ages.*

Fodor's Choice **Kilimanjaro Safaris.** A giant Imagineered baobab tree is the starting point
★ for exploring this animal sanctuary. Although re-creating an African safari in the United States isn't a new idea, this safari takes great pains to create an authentic environment, allowing you to observe rhinos, hippos, antelopes, wildebeests, giraffes, zebras, cheetahs, elephants, lions, and the like as if you were seeing them at home. Illustrated game-spotting guides are available above the seats in the open-air safari vehicles,

ANIMAL KINGDOM GROWN-UP TOUR

Several thrill rides, a hilarious 3-D-and-special-effects-laden film, and two Broadway-style shows with animal and conservation themes can fill a memorable day.

ADVENTURE SEEKERS WANTED

The park's most popular thrill ride is **Avatar Flight of Passage** in Pandora, which puts you aboard a mountain banshee for a heart-stopping 3-D experience that takes you soaring above floating islands and plummeting down cliffs.

Next, make a beeline for Asia and **Expedition Everest.** If there's a wait for the attraction's high-speed train ride, the queue snakes through authentic rammed-earth and stacked-stone buildings of a Himalayan village. While in Asia, pile into a **Kali River Rapids** raft for a whitewater ride on the park's Chakranadi River (take off your shoes so they don't get wet).

Time-travel back to **DinoLand U.S.A.** for a DINOSAUR journey through a primeval forest and white-knuckle encounters with carnivorous creatures like the razor-toothed carnotaurus and other menacing creatures of prehistoric doom.

If it's a cool day, the park's animals should be active, so head to Africa. Your **Kilimanjaro Safaris** open-air journey is a bumpy 20-minute quest for exotic-animal sightings, and you won't be disappointed. Adventurous guests with dollars to spare should sign up for the park's Wild Africa Trek, one of Disney's most thrilling guided tours.

EAT, SHOP, LAUGH

Dining can be an adventure, too, at **Tusker House Restaurant** in Africa, where a colorful buffet of vegetables and carved meats is enhanced with African-inspired chutneys, hummus, spiced tandoori tofu, and couscous salad.

If you want to end your visit with a fine-dining experience, visit **Tiffins**, on Discovery Island at the bridge to Pandora. The cuisine (it deserves the term) is inspired by adventure travel, the globetrotting menu is served with style, and it may very well be the best restaurant in all of Walt Disney World.

Burn the calories during a shopping excursion to **Mombasa Marketplace,** where you can buy a bottle of South African wine or pick up hand-painted dishes from Zimbabwe. Onward to Discovery Island for a stroll along Discovery Island Trails into the Tree of Life show It's Tough to Be a Bug! Expect to laugh a lot.

DISCOVER ANIMAL ATTRACTION

Along the **Pangani Forest Exploration Trail,** you can view families of mountain gorillas through a glassed-in area or from a bridge as these magnificent primates move among the rocks and lush greenery.

Even though you feel safe from Bengal tigers on the **Maharajah Jungle Trek,** several raised viewing spots offer clear views with no glass or fence to mar your photos. Habitat backdrops like the Maharajah palace ruins create scenic props.

If you can squeeze in only one live show, choose to take in the beautiful dance moves of "animal" performers at **Festival of the Lion King.**

2

and as you lurch and bump over some 110 acres of savanna, forest, rivers, and rocky hills, you'll see most of the Harambe Reserve's 34 species of animals—sometimes so close you feel that you could reach out and touch them. It's easy to suspend disbelief here because the landscape and habitats are so effectively modeled and replenished by Disney horticulturists. Keep an eye out for animal babies here and on the postsafari Pangani Forest Exploration Trail; the park's breeding programs have been extremely successful, with new additions including elephants, rhinos, okapi, giraffes, and several gorillas. It's a completely different experience at night, and the animals are often much more lively and interesting, so this experience definitely deserves a revisit. If you have to choose, the nighttime experience is probably superior.

Parents should hang on tightly to their small tykes. The ride is very bumpy and should be avoided by expectant guests or those with heart, back, or neck problems. **For people with disabilities:** Wheelchair accessible, but ECV users must transfer to standard wheelchairs. Equipped for assisted-listening and video-captioning devices. Guests with service animals should check with a host for boarding information. ■TIP➔ During the hottest months, come first thing in the morning when animals are most active, using Fastpass+ if necessary. Otherwise come at day's end when it cools down a bit or at night. For best photo ops, ask to be seated in the very last row of seats (you may have to wait for the next vehicle) where you can pivot for an unobstructed view of the animals you just passed. ⊠ *Africa, Animal Kingdom* ☞ *Duration: 18 mins. Crowds: Moderate to heavy. Audience: All ages.*

Pangani Forest Exploration Trail. Calling this a nature walk doesn't really do it justice. A path winds through dense foliage, alongside streams, and past waterfalls. En route there are viewing points where you can watch a beautiful rare okapi (a member of the giraffe family) munching the vegetation, a family and a separate bachelor group of lowland gorillas, hippos (which you usually can see underwater), comical meerkats (a kind of mongoose), exotic birds, and a bizarre colony of hairless mole rats. Native African interpreters are at many viewing points to answer questions. **For people with disabilities:** Wheelchair accessible and equipped for audio-description devices. Guests with service animals should check with a host before entering. ■TIP➔ Come while awaiting a Kilimanjaro Safaris Fastpass+ appointment or just after you exit your safari vehicle; avoid coming at the hottest time of day, when the gorillas like to nap. ⊠ *Africa, Animal Kingdom* ☞ *Duration: Up to You. Crowds: Moderate to Heavy. Audience: All Ages.*

RAFIKI'S PLANET WATCH

While in the Harambe, Africa, section, board the 250-passenger rustic Wildlife Express steam train for a ride to a unique center of eco-awareness named for the wise baboon from *The Lion King*. Young children especially enjoy the chance to explore these three animal-friendly areas.

Affection Section. In this petting zoo, children and adults can pet and even borrow brushes to groom goats, sheep, donkeys, and other domesticated creatures. **For people with disabilities:** Guests must transfer from ECVs to standard wheelchairs. No service animals are allowed in this

A silverback gorilla at Gorilla Falls Exploration Trail

area. ■**TIP→** If you visit at the right time, you might see pigs demonstrate how they've learned to paint with their snouts. ⊠ *Rafiki's Planet Watch, Animal Kingdom* ☞ *Duration: Up to you. Crowds: Light to moderate. Audience: All ages, mostly children.*

Conservation Station. This is a great place to meet some of the park's animal handlers and to gather round for a critter encounter. You'll learn about the park's veterinary care, ongoing research, and food preparation for hundreds of animal inhabitants. Interactive exhibits are simple fun for younger children and have messages about worldwide efforts to protect endangered species and their habitats. Here, you also can find out how to connect with conservation efforts in your own community. **For people with disabilities:** Guest may remain in wheelchairs or ECVs. ■**TIP→** This is a great place to begin a family conservation project. ⊠ *Rafiki's Planet Watch, Animal Kingdom* ☞ *Duration: Up to you. Crowds: Light to moderate. Audience: All ages.*

Habitat Habit! On this educational wildlife trail that focuses heavily on animal conservation efforts, you get a close-up look at cotton-top tamarins (small white-headed monkeys) and their entertaining antics while you learn how to live with all of the Earth's animals. The South American primates are named for their flowing white mane of hair. **For people with disabilities:** Wheelchair accessible. ■**TIP→** Ask questions; the animal-care cast members enjoy telling you about these cute critters. ⊠ *Rafiki's Planet Watch, Animal Kingdom* ☞ *Duration: Up to you. Crowds: Light to moderate. Audience: All ages.*

ANIMAL KINGDOM SPECTACLE

Tree of Life Awakenings. The iconic tree has developed a night-time persona now that the park stays open after dark. As night falls, fireflies begin to flicker among the leaves of the tree. The tiny lights expand, and through the magic of high-tech projections, the animals carved into the trunk—from dinosaurs to gorillas to tropical birds to a deer—begin to awaken in a swirl of color, until the whole tree is alive with light. The experience repeats every 10 minutes from dark until park closing time. ⊠ *Discovery Island, Animal Kingdom.*

Rivers of Light. As dusk falls, radiance lights up the waterfront Discovery River amphitheater in a tranquil 15-minute performance that combines video, live performances, projections, floats, and an original musical score. Lanterns transform into animal spirit forms—the Elephant, the Tiger, the Turtle, and the Owl. The projections move across jungles, oceans, savannas, and mountains, using curtains of mist as screens. ⊠ *Discovery River, Animal Kingdom.*

2

DISNEY SPRINGS

East of Epcot and close to Interstate 4 along a large lake, is a vast shopping, dining, and entertainment complex that was built to serve both locals and park guests.

It is comprised of four areas: the Marketplace, West Side, The Landing, and Town Center. To anchor the development, Disney Imagineers have created a beautiful network of clear, turquoise waterways that replicate the look of Florida's natural springs. Several multi-story garages provide free parking right next door. You can rent lockers, strollers, or wheelchairs, and there are two Guest Relations centers.

The main draw to Disney Springs is the vast array of shops and restaurants rather than attractions, but there are a few other things to do besides eat and shop. Most recently, Cirque du Soleil's La Nouba closed, but a replacement will open in its place in 2019. DisneyQuest, the elaborate arcade, has also closed and will be replaced by a new NBA Experience. In the meantime, a new Star Wars attraction has already opened. You can also attend a movie or bowl.

EXPLORING

Marketplace. In the Marketplace, the easternmost Disney Springs area, you can meander along winding sidewalks and explore hidden alcoves. Children love to splash in fountains that spring from the pavement and ride the miniature train and old-time carousel ($3). Toy stores entice with creation-stations and too many treasures to comprehend. There are plenty of spots to grab a bite, sip a cappuccino, or enjoy an ice cream along the lakefront, while watching the volcano atop the Rainforest Cafe erupt. Most Marketplace shops, boutiques, and eateries begin opening at 9:30 am and stay open through 11 pm to midnight. ⊠ *Disney Springs*.

FAMILY **The Landing.** A family-oriented dining and entertainment district, this part of Disney Springs has nearly a dozen eateries, some run by celebrity chefs such as Morimoto, Art Smith, and Rick Bayless. The restaurants all offer indoor and patio dining, and some, such as Raglan Road, also offer entertainment, in this case music and traditional Irish step-dance performances every night and during weekend brunch. Paradiso 37 also welcomes diners indoors and alfresco. The Boathouse features attractive waterfront dining, with views of the water taxis delivering folks across the lake, and the tiny, colorful boat-cars tootling up and down the ramp. Paddlefish, a three-story eatery inspired by a Mississippi paddle steamer, serves seafood, and the view from the top-floor lounge includes the erupting volcano at Rainforest Cafe across the water. ⊠ *Disney Springs.*

NBA Experience. In a building inspired by the soaring architecture of NBA arenas around the country, this state-of-the-art attraction will include interactive games and competitions, immersive experiences, a retail store, and an adjacent restaurant. ⊠ *West Side, Disney Springs.*

Star Wars™: Secrets of the Empire by ILMxLAB and The VOID. New to Disney Springs in December 2017, this multisensory, untethered hyper-reality adventure is a collaboration between ILMxLAB and The VOID. You can move around while wearing virtual reality headgear that meshes the real world with the virtual one through 3-D imagery and sound, letting you interact with popular *Star Wars* characters—as well as each other. Guests under 16 must have a parent or guardian present. ⊠ *West Side, Disney Springs* ⊕ *www.thevoid.com* 🖃 *$29.95.*

The Town Center. The Town Center is the shopping mecca of Disney Springs, with dozens of upscale and chain shops such as Zara and Uniqlo selling everything from clothing to jewelry to perfume. In between shopping sprees, have a bite at The Polite Pig, a locally owned eatery that serves fast-casual farm-to-table fare. Or, if a Mexican snack is what you want, try Rick Bayless's Frontera Cocina to-go window. Or, take the kids to the dinosaur-themed T-Rex for a dining experience they won't forget. ⊠ *Town Center, Disney Springs.*

West Side. Big changes are still underway at the West Side. The main attractions are the House of Blues music hall, the former home of Cirque du Soleil's La Nouba, and Splitsville Luxury Lanes, a modern take on the American classic bowling alley, with 30 bowling lanes on two floors, weekend DJs, and upscale eats like fillet sliders and sushi at indoor and outdoor tables. DisneyQuest, the long-time virtual reality indoor attraction, was bulldozed in 2017 to make way for The NBA Experience, a basketball-focused attraction expected to open in summer 2019, Cirque du Soleil's La Nouba show, resident of the big white tent for two decades, gave its final performance at the end of 2017, and the new show, an original creation by Cirque du Soleil that will pay homage to Disney's rich history of animation has been announced, but with no definite opening date. You can take a ride in the Aéro30 helium balloon tethered here ($20 ages 10 and up, $15 ages 3–9), shop in boutiques, or dine in such restaurants as Planet Hollywood Observatory or Bongo's Cuban Cafe, or hop on the water taxi at the dock and head across the lagoon to the Marketplace. Shops open at 9:30 or 10:30 am, and closing time is between 11 pm and 2 am. ⊠ *Disney Springs.*

DISNEY'S BOARDWALK

This charming, quarter-mile long promenade, minutes from the International Gate at Epcot, is rich with architecture and signage recalling the turn-of-the-20th-century esplanades all along the Atlantic seaboard. Boats chug across Crescent Lake toward Hollywood Studios or Epcot, lights outline the buildings, bicycle surreys with a fringe on top pedal along the waterfront, making this a delightful place for dining, meandering, or watching Epcot fireworks.

Disney's BoardWalk is a popular dining and entertainment area on Bay Lake. Anchored by Disney's BoardWalk Inn, it's within walking distance to Disney's Yacht Club and Beach Club resorts, as well as the Walt Disney World Dolphin and Swan Resorts and all their dining options. Boat shuttles take guests directly to either Disney's Hollywood Studios or Epcot, but the World Showcase entrance to Epcot is only a 10- or 15-minute walk from the BoardWalk. It's a less convenient and much longer bus trip to the Magic Kingdom or Animal Kingdom.

The BoardWalk is lined with nightspots, stores, and restaurants on either side of the hotel. Dining options include Big River Grill, a casual brew pub that's family-friendly, and Flying Fish, a more upscale steak and seafood restaurant. The ESPN Club is a sprawling, casual sports bar. At night, if you aren't watching a game on the big screens at the ESPN Club, you can go to the singalong piano bar Jellyrolls or the Atlantic Dance Hall for music and dancing. All ages are allowed into the ESPN Club, but both Jellyrolls and Atlantic Dance Hall are for adults 21 and older. There are several other more casual dining spots, including a funnel cake cart, a pizzeria that serves slices, a bakery that also has a limited sandwich selection, and an outlet for the New York City–based ice cream shop Ample Hills Creamery. The BoardWalk also has a handful of shops selling typical Disney souvenirs like pins and hats.

TYPHOON LAGOON

The beauty of Disney's water parks is that you can make the experience fit your mood. Like crowds? Head for the lounge chairs along the Surf Pool at Typhoon Lagoon or Melt-Away Bay at Blizzard Beach. Prefer peace? Walk past lush foliage along each park's circular path until you spot a secluded lean-to or tree-shaded patch of sand.

According to Disney legend, Typhoon Lagoon was created when the lush Placid Palms Resort was struck by a cataclysmic storm. It left a different world in its wake: surfboard-sundered trees, once-upright palms imitating the Leaning Tower of Pisa, and a lagoon cut off from the sea, trapping thousands of tropical fish. Nothing, however, topped the fate of *Miss Tilly*, a shrimp boat from "Safen Sound, Florida," which was hurled high in the air and became impaled on Mt. Mayday, a magical volcano that periodically tries to dislodge *Miss Tilly* with huge geysers.

Ordinary folks, the legend continues, would have been crushed by such devastation. But the resourceful residents of Placid Palms were made of hardier stuff—and from the wreckage they created 56-acre Typhoon Lagoon, the self-proclaimed "world's ultimate water park."

ORIENTATION AND PLANNING
GETTING ORIENTED
The layout is so simple. The wave and swimming lagoon is at the park's center. Note that the waves are born in the Mt. Mayday side and break on the beaches closest to the entrance. Any attraction requiring a gravitational plunge starts around the summit of Mt. Mayday. The cleverly named Miss Adventure Falls and Ketchakiddee Creek flank the lagoon, to Mt. Mayday's right and left, respectively, as you enter. The Crush 'n' Gusher water coaster is due right of Singapore Sal's.

You can take WDW bus transportation or drive to Typhoon Lagoon. There's no parking charge. Once inside, your options are to walk, swim, or slide.

WDW Information. Call WDW Information or check ⊕ *www.disney-world.com*'s park calendars for days of operation. ⊠ *1534 Blizzard Beach Dr., Blizzard Beach* ☎ *407/824–4321.*

WHAT TO EXPECT

You can speed down waterslides with names like Crush 'n' Gusher and Humunga Kowabunga or bump through rapids and falls at Mt. Mayday or join a treasure hunt at Miss Adventure Falls. You can also bob along in 5-foot waves in a surf pool the size of two football fields or, for a mellow break, float in inner tubes along the 2,100-foot Castaway Creek. Rubberneck as fellow human cannonballs are ejected from the Storm Slides, or hunker down in a hammock or lounge chair and read a book. Ketchakiddee Creek, for young children, replicates adult rides on a smaller scale. It's Disney's version of a day at the beach—complete with friendly Disney lifeguards. Most people agree that kids under seven and older adults prefer Typhoon Lagoon. Bigger kids and teens like Blizzard Beach.

During the off-season between October and April, Typhoon Lagoon closes for several weeks for routine maintenance and refurbishment.

PARKS AMENITIES

Dining: Picnicking is permitted, but coolers too large for one person to carry, glass containers, and alcoholic beverages not bought in the park are forbidden. There are tables at Getaway Glen, Typhoon Tilly's, and at pavilions across the park. You can always fork out $40 to $60 a day, depending on the season, for a reserved umbrella from Getaway Glen. Arrive early, though, and you can stake out a great spot for free. Park eateries and food stands have salads, burgers, pizza, and other treats, with a sweet emphasis on ice cream.

Dressing Rooms and Lockers: There are thatched-roof dressing rooms and lockers to the right on your way into the park. It costs $10 a day to rent a small locker and $15 for a large one; there's also a $5 deposit. There are restrooms in every nook and cranny. Most have showers and are much less crowded than the dressing rooms. If you forgot your towel, rent ($2) or buy one at Singapore Sal's.

First Aid: The small first-aid stand, run by a registered nurse, is on your left as you enter the park.

Guest Services: The staff at Typhoon Lagoon's Guest Services window outside the entrance turnstiles, to your left, can answer many questions. ■ TIP➜ A chalkboard inside gives water temperature and surfing information.

Lost People and Things: Ask about your misplaced people and things at the Guest Services window near the entrance turnstiles. Lost children are taken to an area by the Tip Board near the front of the park, where Disney cast members entertain them with games.

Private Patios: The park has a dozen premium, roped-off Beachcomber Shacks (patios, really) that groups of as many as six can rent. They generally offer shade and sun as well as plush loungers and other chairs, a table with an umbrella, and an ice chest with two bottles of water per guest (up to six). Each guest also gets two beach towels and a refillable soft-drink mug. The whole group gets a locker to share and an attendant to take and deliver food orders (cost of meals not included). The patios cost about $325 during peak season (usually March through late August), between $160 and $240 the rest of the year. Reserve (☎ 407/939–8687) well in advance or arrive very early to book one at High 'N Dry. In summer, any patio that isn't prebooked sells out within a half hour of the park opening.

Services for People with Disabilities: The paths connecting the different areas are wheelchair accessible, but most of the waterslides are not. There is, however, an elevator that takes you to the loading zone of the Crush 'n' Gusher water coaster. If you transfer from your chair to a raft or inner tube, you can float in Typhoon Lagoon Surf Pool or Castaway Creek.

Wheelchairs are available at the entrance turnstile area and are free with ID. You can trade a land-based wheelchair for chairs that go into the water by asking a lifeguard.

Supplies: You can get inner tubes at Castaway Creek and inner tubes, rafts, or slide mats at the rides. Borrow life vests at **High 'N Dry.** Near the main entrance is **Singapore Sal's,** where you can pick up free life jackets, buy sundries, and rent (or buy) towels and lockers.

VISITING TIPS

In summer, come first thing in the morning (early birds can ride several times before the lines get long), late in the afternoon when park hours run later, or when the weather clears after a thundershower (rainstorms drive away crowds). Afternoons are also good in cooler weather, as the water is a bit warmer. To make a whole day of it, avoid weekends, when locals and visitors pack in.

Women and girls should wear one-piece swimsuits unless they want to find their tops somewhere around their ears at the bottom of the waterslide.

Invest in sunscreen and water shoes. Plan to slather sunscreen on several times throughout the day. An inexpensive pair of water shoes will save tootsies from hot sand and walkways and from restroom floors.

Arrive 30 minutes before opening, so you can park, buy tickets, rent towels, and snag inner tubes before the crowds descend, and, trust us, it gets very crowded.

EXPLORING TYPHOON LAGOON

Bay Slides. Kids scramble up several steps tucked between faux-rock formations, where a lifeguard sits to supervise their slide into Blustery Bay. The incline is small, but the thrill is great for young kids, who whoosh into the bay (sometimes into the arms of waiting parents). These two scaled-down versions of the Storm Slides are geared to kids shorter than 60 inches. ■TIP➜ Kids really burn up energy going up the steps and down the slides repeatedly. Parents should be prepared for their wanting to ride over and over again. ⊠ *Typhoon Lagoon* ☞ *Duration: Up to you. Crowds: Light to moderate. Audience: Small kids.*

Castaway Creek. This circular, 15-foot-wide, 3-foot-deep, 2,000-foot-long waterway is chill. Snag an inner tube and float along a creek that winds through the park and around the Surf Pool and beaches. You pass through a rain forest that showers you with spray, you slide through caves and grottoes, you float by overhanging trees and flowering bushes, and you get dumped on at the Water Works with "broken" pipes. The current flows a gentle 2½ feet per second. Along the way there are five landing areas where you can hop in and out. **For people with disabilities:** Guests using wheelchairs must transfer to an inner tube. ■TIP➔ A full circuit takes about 20 minutes, longer if you stop at one of the five lifeguard-manned launches. ⊠ *Typhoon Lagoon* ⊂ *Duration: Up to 20 mins. Crowds: Vary by season. Audience: All ages.*

Fodor's Choice ★ **Crush 'n' Gusher.** If flume rides, storm slides, and tube races aren't wild enough for your inner thrill-seeker, get ready to defy gravity on Disney's multipassenger water coaster. Designed to propel you uphill and down along a series of flumes, caverns, and spillways, this ride should satisfy the most enthusiastic daredevil. Keeping with park lore, Crush 'n' Gusher flows through what appears to be a rusted-out tropical fruit factory, weaving in and out of the wreckage and debris that once transported fruit through the plant's wash facilities. Three fruit spillways are aptly named Banana Blaster, Coconut Crusher, and Pineapple Plunger. Guests shouldn't ride if they are pregnant or have heart, back, or neck problems. **For people with disabilities:** An elevator takes guests using wheelchairs to the loading area; there's a short distance between this area and the ride. ■TIP➔ Ride first thing in the morning before lines get too long. And don't forget to say cheese for the cameras! ⊠ *Typhoon Lagoon* ⊂ *Duration: 1 min. Crowds: Moderate to heavy. Audience: Not small kids. Height requirement: 48 inches.*

Gangplank Falls. Families who climb Mt. Mayday for this ride are in for an adventure—more of an adventure than they might expect. Upon takeoff, a 6½-foot-long inflated raft plunges down the slide with impressive speed. It even gets bumpy at times along the 300-foot river. Not too scary for the tykes, and yet not a bore for parents, Gangplank Falls is great family fun! Those who are pregnant or have heart, back, or neck problems should sit this one out. ■TIP➔ The inner tubes are heavy, so be sure to have at least two willing carriers. Also be prepared to ride with two to four riders (five if some are smaller kids). ⊠ *Typhoon Lagoon* ⊂ *Duration: 1 min. Crowds: Vary by season. Audience: Not small kids.*

Humunga Kowabunga. There's little time to scream, but you'll hear just such vociferous reactions as the survivors emerge from the catch pool. The basic questions are: want to get scared out of your wits in four seconds flat—and did you like it enough to go back for more? The three side-by-side Humunga Kowabunga speed slides deserve acclaim among thrill lovers, as they drop 214 feet downhill at a 60-degree angle in seconds. Oh yes, and then you go through a cave. In the dark. The average speed is 30 mph; however, you can really fly if you lie flat on your back, cross your ankles, wrap your arms around your chest, and arch your back. One caveat: the ride lasts only a few seconds—too short for us—and lines are often too long to requeue for another

2

plunge. This ride isn't appropriate for guests who are pregnant or who have heart, back, or neck problems. ■TIP➔ Race against your friends or family; there are three slides at the top. ⊠ *Typhoon Lagoon* ↻ *Duration: 4 secs. Crowds: Heavy. Audience: Not small kids. Height requirement: 48 inches.*

Keelhaul Falls. Do you need to chill out after the high-velocity Humunga Kowabunga? Then venture up to Keelhaul Falls, a laid-back trip down the left side of Mt. Mayday. Just kick back and relax as your blue tube cruises down the 400-foot slide and splashes into the pool below. Keelhaul feels a little slow if you ride it right after Mayday Falls, so thrill seekers may be disappointed. Yet its winding path and scenic descent make for a satisfying ride. This ride isn't appropriate for guests who are pregnant or who have heart, back, or neck problems. ■TIP➔ Ride before or after Mayday Falls. ⊠ *Typhoon Lagoon* ↻ *Duration: 1 min. Crowds: Vary by season. Audience: Not young kids.*

PARK VIEWS

Mt. Mayday. What goes down can also go up—and up and up. Climbing Mt. Mayday "[is] like climbing Mt. Everest," wailed one teenager about a climb that seems a lot steeper than an 85-foot peak should be. Nevertheless, it's Mt. Everest with hibiscus flowers, a rope bridge, and stepping-stones set in plunging waters. The view encompasses the entire park. Lovers of white-water rafting should head to Mayday Falls, Keelhaul Falls, and Gangplank Falls at Mt. Mayday. These rides in oversize inner tubes plunge down the mountain's left side. They have caves, waterfalls, and intricate rock work. ⊠ *Typhoon Lagoon.*

Ketchakiddee Creek. Typhoon Lagoon's play area for young children has slides, mini rapids, faux sand castles, squirting whales and seals, bouncing barrels, waterfalls, sprinklers, and all the other ingredients of a splash fiesta. The bubbling sand ponds, where youngsters can sit in what seems like an enormous whirlpool bath, are special favorites. Little ones also love the tiny-scale tube ride. Small water cannons let kids engage in water-spray wars. Families can camp beneath lots of shady lean-tos when not in the water. **For people with disabilities:** Accessible for people using water-appropriate wheelchairs. ■TIP➔ Parents can take turns watching the kiddies here and riding the thrill slides. ⊠ *Typhoon Lagoon* ↻ *Duration: Up to you. Crowds: Light. Audience: Small kids. Height requirement: Adults must be accompanied by a child under 48 inches and vice versa.*

Mayday Falls. This 460-foot slide in bright-yellow inner tubes is the longest and bumpiest of the three falls. It's a long trek up to Mayday Falls—even higher than Keelhaul—but the increased speed and longer descent are well worth the climb. It's a relatively straight slide over the falls into a catchment, but it's not as thrilling as the up-and-down water jets on the Crush 'n' Gusher. This ride isn't appropriate for guests who are pregnant or who have heart, back, or neck problems. ■TIP➔ While you're in the neighborhood, ride Keelhaul Falls, too. ⊠ *Typhoon Lagoon* ↻ *Duration: 1 min. Crowds: Vary by season. Audience: Not young kids.*

From the wreckage—like that shown here—in the wake of a storm, Placid Palms Resort residents created 56-acre Typhoon Lagoon. Or so the story goes ...

Fodor's Choice
★

Storm Slides. Each of these three body slides is about 300 feet long and snakes in and out of rock formations, through caves and tunnels, and under waterfalls, but each has a slightly different view and offers a twist. The one in the middle has the longest tunnel; the others feature secrets you'll have to discover for yourself. Brace for splashdown on all three slides! Maximum speed is about 20 mph, and the trip takes about 20 seconds. These slides are not appropriate for guests who are pregnant or who have heart, back, or neck problems. ■TIP➜ Try each of the three slides for different twists. ⊠ *Typhoon Lagoon* ☞ *Duration: 15–20 secs. Crowds: Moderate to heavy. Audience: Not young kids.*

Fodor's Choice
★

Typhoon Lagoon Surf Pool. This is the heart of the park, a swimming area that spreads out over 2½ acres and contains almost 3 million gallons of clear, chlorinated water. It's scalloped by coves, bays, and inlets, all edged with white-sand beaches—spread over a base of white concrete, as bodysurfers soon discover when they try to slide into shore. Ouch! The waves are the draw. Twelve huge water-collection chambers hidden in Mt. Mayday dump their load into trapdoors with a resounding whoosh to create waves large enough for Typhoon Lagoon to host amateur and professional surfing championships.

A piercing double hoot from *Miss Tilly* (the boat that legend says was deposited on Mt. Mayday's highest peak during a storm) signals the start and finish of wave action: about every 2 hours, for 1½ hours, 5-to-6-foot waves issue forth every 90 seconds; the last half hour is devoted to moderate bobbing waves. Even during the big-wave periods, however, the waters in Blustery Bay and Whitecap Cove are protected. Surfers who don't want to risk a fickle ocean can surf here on certain days before the park opens. Instruction and a soft-sided surfboard are included in the $165 cost, and the surfing experience (ages eight and older) lasts for 2½ hours. Reserve your waves by calling *407/939–7529*. **For people with disabilities:** Accessible for people using water-appropriate wheelchairs. ■TIP➔ See the chalkboard at beach's edge for the day's wave schedule if you want to time your bodysurfing. ✉ *Typhoon Lagoon* ☞ *Duration: Up to you. Crowds: Heavy. Audience: All ages.*

NEED A
BREAK

Leaning Palms, to your left as you enter the park, has burgers, pizzas, turkey sandwiches, salads, beer, and, of course, ice cream and frozen yogurt. **Let's Go Slurpin'** is a beach shack on the edge of Typhoon Lagoon that dispenses frozen margaritas as well as wine and beer. **Typhoon Tilly's,** on the right just past Miss Adventure Falls, serves sandwiches, salads, and snacks of all kinds and pours mostly sugary, nonalcoholic grog—though you can grab a Davy Jones "lager."

BLIZZARD BEACH

With its oxymoronic name, Blizzard Beach promises the seemingly impossible—a seaside playground with an alpine theme. As with its older cousin, Typhoon Lagoon, Disney Imagineers have created a legend to explain the park's origin.

The story goes that after a freak winter storm dropped snow over the western side of Walt Disney World, entrepreneurs created Florida's first downhill ski resort. Saunalike temperatures soon returned. But as the 66-acre resort's operators were ready to close up shop, they spotted a playful alligator sliding down the 120-foot-tall "liquid ice" slopes. The realization that the melting snow had created the world's tallest, fastest, and most exhilarating water-filled ski and toboggan runs gave birth to the ski resort–water park.

From its imposing ski-jump tower to its 1,200-foot series of rushing waterfalls, Blizzard Beach delivers cool fun even in the hot summertime. Where else can you wear your swimsuit on the slopes?

ORIENTATION AND PLANNING
GETTING ORIENTED

The park layout makes it fairly simple to navigate. Once you enter and rent a locker, you'll cross a small bridge over Cross Country Creek before choosing a spot to park your towels and cooler. To the left is the Melt-Away Bay wave pool. Dead ahead you can see Mt. Gushmore, a chairlift to the top, and the park's many slopes and slides.

If thrills are your game, come early and line up for Summit Plummet, Slush Gusher, and Downhill Double Dipper before wait times go from light to moderate (or heavy). Anytime is a good time for a dip in Melt-Away Bay or a tube trip around Cross Country Creek. Parents with young children should claim their spot early at Tike's Peak, to the park's right even before you cross the bridge.

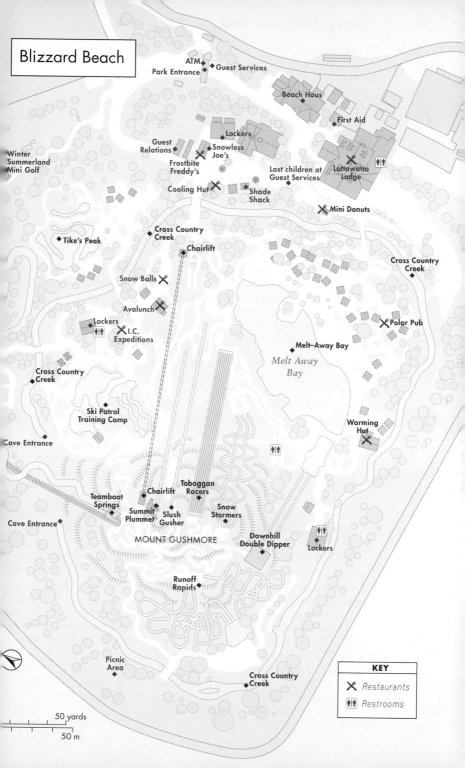

Blizzard Beach

ATM
Park Entrance
Guest Services
Beach Haus
First Aid
Guest Relations
Lockers
Snowless Joe's
Frostbite Freddy's
Lost children at Guest Services
Lottawatta Lodge
Winter Summerland Mini Golf
Cooling Hut
Shade Shack
Mini Donuts
Cross Country Creek
Tike's Peak
Chairlift
Cross Country Creek
Snow Balls
Avalunch
Lockers
I.C. Expeditions
Polar Pub
Melt-Away Bay
Melt Away Bay
Cross Country Creek
Ski Patrol Training Camp
Warming Hut
Cave Entrance
Teamboat Springs
Chairlift
Toboggan Racers
Cave Entrance
Summit Plummet
Slush Gusher
Snow Stormers
MOUNT GUSHMORE
Downhill Double Dipper
Lockers
Runoff Rapids
Picnic Area
Cross Country Creek

KEY

✕ *Restaurants*
🚻 *Restrooms*

50 yards
50 m

You can take WDW bus transportation or drive to Blizzard Beach. There's no charge for parking. Once inside, your options are to walk, swim, or slide.

WHAT TO EXPECT

Disney Imagineers have gone all out here to create the paradox of a ski resort in the midst of a tropical lagoon. Lots of verbal puns and sight gags play with the snow-in-Florida motif. The centerpiece is Mt. Gushmore, with its 120-foot-high Summit Plummet. Attractions have names like Teamboat Springs, a white-water raft ride. Themed speed slides include Toboggan Racers, Slush Gusher, and Snow Stormers. Between Mt. Gushmore's base and its summit, swim-skiers can also ride a chairlift converted from ski-resort to beach-resort use—with multihued umbrellas and snow skis on their undersides. Older kids and devoted waterslide enthusiasts generally prefer Blizzard Beach to other water parks.

PARKS AMENITIES

Dining: You can't bring oversize coolers, glass containers, or your own alcoholic beverages into the park. Picnicking is welcome, however, and there are several pleasant pavilions and other spots, most notably the terrace outside Lottawatta Lodge. This is also where you can reserve your own picnic spot ($40–$60 for a day), which includes chairs (two of them loungers), an umbrella and small table, and four beach towels. Arrive early enough, and you'll snag your ideal spot in the park for free. You can get burgers, hot dogs, and salads at Lottawatta Lodge or other eateries and food stands. You could go for the usual snacks—snowballs or ice cream. But a truly sublime nibble is the melt-in-your-mouth mini-doughnut from the Mini Donuts stand across from Lottawatta Lodge.

Dressing Rooms and Lockers: Dressing rooms, showers, and restrooms are in the village area, just inside the main entrance. There are other restrooms in Lottawatta Lodge, at the Ski Patrol Training Camp, and just past the Melt-Away Bay beach area. Lockers are near the entrance, next to Snowless Joe's Rentals, and near Tike's Peak (the children's area and the most convenient if you have little swim-skiers in tow). It costs $8 to rent a small locker and $10 for a large one, and there's a $5 deposit. Note that there are only small lockers at Tike's Peak. The towels for rent ($2) at Snowless Joe's are tiny. If you forgot yours, you're better off buying a proper one at the Beach Haus.

First Aid: The first-aid stand, overseen by a registered nurse, is in the village, between Lottawatta Lodge and the Beach Haus.

Guest Services: Disney staffers at Blizzard Beach's Guest Services window, to the left of the ticket booth as you enter the park, can answer most of your questions. Get free life vests or rent towels and lockers at **Snowless Joe's**. Inner tubes, rafts, and slide mats are provided at the rides. Buy beach gear or rent towels or lockers at **Beach Haus. Shade Shack** is the place for a new pair of sunglasses.

Lost People and Things: Instruct youngsters to let a lifeguard know if they get lost. The lost-children station is beneath a large beach umbrella near the front of the park. And don't worry about the kids—a Disney cast member will keep them busy with activities.

2

Private Patios: The park has 14 Polar Patios to rent to groups of as many as six people. For $325 a day in peak season (usually March through late August) and between $160 and $240 other times of year, you get plush loungers, chairs, a table with umbrella, refillable beverage mugs, an ice chest with two water bottles per person, a group locker, and an attendant who will take your orders for and deliver lunch and snacks (food costs extra). It's best to book a patio far ahead of time (407/939–8687). If you arrive early enough, there might be an open patio; check at the Shade Shack.

SERVICES FOR PEOPLE WITH DISABILITIES
Most of Blizzard Beach's paths are flat and level. If you can transfer from your chair a short distance, you can also access all the waterslides except Summit Plummet. Or settle into a large inner tube and float in Cross Country Creek.

A limited number of wheelchairs—some suitable for the water—are available near the park entrance and are free if you leave an ID.

EXPLORING BLIZZARD BEACH

Chairlift. No subtropical skiing paradise would be complete without a chairlift, and this one is an attractive alternative to trekking to the top of Mt. Gushmore over and over again. The two-minute chairlift ascent is a great opportunity to scout out other slides and to enjoy the "ski beach" scenery. **For people with disabilities:** Guests using wheelchairs must transfer to a ride seat and subsequent attractions. A companion will have to meet you with the wheelchair at the base of Mt. Gushmore. ■TIP➜ If the wait is too long or you have children under 32 inches tall, hiking up is good exercise. ⊠ *Blizzard Beach* ☞ *Duration: 2 mins. Crowds: Light to Moderate. Audience: Not young kids. Height requirement: 32 inches.*

Cross Country Creek. Just grab an inner tube, hop on, and circle the entire park during a leisurely 25-minute float on this 3,000-foot-long creek. Along the way, you'll get doused with frigid water in an ice cave—wonderful on a steamy Florida day. Tubes are provided at seven launch sites, but they're not required. Kids soon discover that the fastest and most enjoyable way to get around the park is to glide with the current and hop off at whichever landing they wish. **For people with disabilities:** Guests using wheelchairs must transfer to inner tubes. ■TIP➜ There are landings near most thrill rides, and moving through the park this way is oodles more fun than walking. ⊠ *Blizzard Beach* ☞ *Duration: 25 mins. Crowds: Vary by season. Audience: All ages.*

Fodor's Choice
★
Downhill Double Dipper. If you're on your way to Snow Stormers or Toboggan Racers on the purple slopes, you may notice a cool-looking slide on the left. This is the Downhill Double Dipper, and it's well worth the stop. The best thing about this slide is that you are timed from blastoff to finish line! Competition may get heated as kids (48 inches or taller) vie for the glory of fastest speed slider, but even the least competitive will enjoy tearing down Mt. Gushmore in their racing tubes. Expectant mothers shouldn't ride, nor should guests with heart conditions or neck or back problems. **For people with disabilities:** Guests

using wheelchairs must transfer to the tube-launch site. ■**TIP→ Ride early; this popular purple-slope attraction gets crowded after lunch. (And, oh yeah—our fastest time was 5.89 seconds—can you beat that?)** ⊠ *Blizzard Beach* ☞ *Duration: Under 10 secs. Crowds: Heavy. Audience: Not young kids. Height requirement: 48 inches.*

Melt-Away Bay. The park's main pool is a 1-acre oasis that's constantly fed by "melting snow" waterfalls. The man-made waves are positively oceanlike. If you're not a strong swimmer, stay away from the far end of the pool, where the waves originate. You can get temporarily stuck in a pocket even if your head is still above water. If you prefer to stay beached, there are plenty of recliner chairs spread out around the bay. This is where moms and dads often relax and watch their kids swim in the lifeguard-protected waters. **For people with disabilities:** Guests using water-appropriate wheelchairs can enjoy shallow waters here. ■**TIP→ Get an inner tube if you plan to venture to deeper waters, and arrive early if you want to find a shady spot (there are limited giant umbrellas).** ⊠ *Blizzard Beach* ☞ *Duration: Up to you. Crowds: Vary by season. Audience: All ages.*

Runoff Rapids. It's easy to overlook this three-track flume ride hidden on the far red slope of Mt. Gushmore. Yet if you have the courage to carry your tube all the way up to the top, you'll eventually come upon three twisting, turning 600-foot-long flumes—even one that's in the dark (keep in mind the tunnel slide is for single riders only, while the open slides are for one- or two-passenger tubes). Once you're in, it's way more fun than scary. Still, guests who are pregnant or who have heart, neck, or back problems should skip it. **For people with disabilities:** Guests using wheelchairs must transfer to inner tubes. ■**TIP→ It's worth riding both an open slide and the tunnel slide, but remember that the tunnel slide is only for single riders.** ⊠ *Blizzard Beach* ☞ *Duration: 35 secs. Crowds: Light to moderate. Audience: Not young kids.*

Ski Patrol Training Camp. Preteens might want to spend most of their time on the T-bar drop, Cool Runners slides, and Snow Falls downhill body slide. In addition, there's a chance to take on the Thin Ice Training Course, a wide-open area where kids can jump from one slippery mogul to the next. The moguls really look more like bobbing baby icebergs, and kids don't mind when they miss a berg and plop into the pool. **For people with disabilities:** Guests using water-appropriate wheelchairs can enjoy wading areas here. ■**TIP→ The optimum time to come is early in the day or after a thunderstorm, when crowds thin out. That said, lines are often short at the zipline drop and the iceberg obstacle course.** ⊠ *Blizzard Beach* ☞ *Duration: Up to you. Crowds: Light to moderate. Audience: Tweens.*

Fodor's Choice ★ **Slush Gusher.** This speed slide, which drops through a snow-banked mountain gully next door to Summit Plummet on the green slopes, isn't quite as intimidating, but it's a real thriller nonetheless. Instead of one scream-inducing steep drop, the Slush Gusher features a fast, hilly descent to the base of Mt. Gushmore. Although the Slush Gusher will not disappoint thrill seekers, it is perfect for those who want some adventure but tremble at the sight of Summit Plummet. For guests who are pregnant or who have heart, back, or neck problems, this ride is not recommended. **For people with disabilities:** Guests using wheelchairs must transfer to the slide. ■ TIP➜ The earlier you ride, the better. On crowded days waits can last up to 90 minutes. ⊠ *Blizzard Beach* ☞ *Duration: 15 secs. Crowds: You bet! Audience: Not young kids. Height requirement: 48 inches.*

NEED A BREAK

Lottawatta Lodge—a North American ski lodge with a Caribbean accent—is the park's main emporium of fast food. Lines are long at peak feeding times. The **Warming Hut,** which is open seasonally, offers salads, sandwiches, and ice cream. Specialty hot dogs, and salads are on the menu at **Avalunch. Frostbite Freddy's** and **Polar Pub,** on the main beach, both sell frozen drinks and spirits.

Snow Stormers. No water park would be complete without a meandering waterslide, and Blizzard Beach has one. Here three flumes, each 350 feet long, descend from the top of Mt. Gushmore along a switchback course of ski-type slalom gates on the purple slopes. Snow Stormers offers an exciting change of pace from the straight-down slides of the green slopes, and riders are in for a grand total of eight hairpin turns before finally splashing into the pool at the bottom. This ride isn't appropriate for guests who are pregnant or who have heart, neck, or back problems. **For people with disabilities:** Guests using wheelchairs must transfer to a toboggan-style slide mat with handles. ■ TIP➜ This is a belly-down ride. Hold on tight! ⊠ *Blizzard Beach* ☞ *Duration: 20 secs. Crowds: Moderate to Heavy. Audience: All Ages.*

Fodor's Choice
★

Summit Plummet. This is Mt. Gushmore's big gun, one of the world's tallest, fastest free-fall speed slides. From Summit Plummet's "ski jump" tower at the very top of the green slopes, it's a wild 55-mph, 12-story plunge straight down, then into a tunnel before a white-water splash landing at the end of the 360-foot-long run. It looks almost like a straight vertical drop, and you can't help but feel like a movie stunt double as you take the plunge. If you're watching from the beach below, you can't hear the yells of the participants, but you can bet many of them are screaming their heads off. The ride is not for guests who are pregnant or who have heart, back, or neck problems. ■ TIP➜ Make this one of your first stops. The line will only get longer as the day goes on. (Summer afternoon waits can be up to two hours.) ⊠ *Blizzard Beach* ☞ *Duration: 10 crazy secs. Crowds: Absolutely. Audience: Not young kids. Height requirement: 48 inches.*

Teamboat Springs. Six-passenger rafts zip along green slopes in one of the world's longest family white-water raft rides. Since its original construction, it has doubled its speed of departure onto its twisting, 1,200-foot channel of rushing water, which ends with a refreshing waterfall dousing. This ride is a good place for kids too big for Tike's Peak to test more grown-up waters. Those who are pregnant or have heart, neck, or back problems should avoid this one. **For people with disabilities:** Guests using wheelchairs must transfer to the ride. ■ TIP➜ This is an excellent ride for the whole family: there are no age or height requirements (other than "No Infants"), tubes seat four to six people, and lines generally move quickly. ⊠ *Blizzard Beach* ☞ *Duration: 1½ mins. Crowds: Moderate. Audience: Families.*

Fodor'sChoice **Tike's Peak.** Disney never leaves the little ones out of the fun, and this
★ junior-size version of Blizzard Beach, set slightly apart from the rest of the park, has scaled-down elements of Mt. Gushmore, with sand, slides (including one with tubes), faux snow drifts, and igloolike tunnels. Parents can find sun or shade beneath lean-tos while watching over the little ones. Several lifeguards are on hand, but parents should still watch their youngsters at all times. **For people with disabilities:** Guests using water-appropriate wheelchairs can enjoy the wading areas. ■**TIP→ Stake out lounge chairs early, especially for a shady spot. If your tykes don't swim well, get them fitted with a free life vest, and pull your chair up to the water's edge.** ⊠ *Blizzard Beach* ☞ *Duration: Up to you. Crowds: Vary by season. Audience: Small kids. Height requirement: Children shorter than 48 inches must be accompanied by adults.*

Toboggan Racers. Grab your mat, wait for the signal, and go. You and eight other racers whiz simultaneously down the watery trail on the purple slopes toward the finish line at the base of the mountain. The racing aspect and dips along the 250-foot-long slope make the ride fun, but it lacks the speed of single-rider green-slope rides like Slush Gusher. For a ride combining speed and friendly competition, check out the Downhill Double Dipper. Expectant mothers shouldn't ride, nor should guests with heart, neck, or back problems. **For people with disabilities:** Guests using wheelchairs must transfer to slide mats. ■**TIP→ It's more fun when you race family members or friends—up to eight people can ride at the same time.** ⊠ *Blizzard Beach* ☞ *Duration: 10 secs. Crowds: Moderate to heavy. Audience: Not young kids.*

EXPLORING
UNIVERSAL ORLANDO

WELCOME TO UNIVERSAL ORLANDO

TOP REASONS TO GO

★ **The Variety:** Universal Orlando is an ever-evolving universe centered around the film-focused Universal Studios and fantasy-driven Islands of Adventure (IOA) theme parks; the clubs and restaurants of the CityWalk entertainment complex; several on-site resort hotels, and the new-in-2017 Volcano Bay water theme park.

★ **Theme-Park Powerhouse:** Neither SeaWorld nor any of Disney's four theme parks can match the collective energy at Universal Studios and Islands of Adventure. Wild rides, clever shows, constantly updated attractions, and an edgy attitude all push the envelope here.

★ **Party Central:** Throughout the year, Universal hosts festive parkwide events such as A Celebration of Harry Potter (January), Mardi Gras (February–April), summertime's Rock the Universe Christian-music celebration, Halloween Horror Nights, and holiday events including Grinchmas, Macy's Holiday Parades, and Christmas celebrations at the Wizarding Worlds of Harry Potter.

Although the resort is constantly expanding with land purchases and new hotels, the core of the Universal Orlando Resort is tucked into a corner created by the intersection of Interstate 4 and Kirkman Road (Highway 435), midway between Downtown Orlando and the Walt Disney World Resort. Here you'll be about 15 minutes from each and just 10 minutes from SeaWorld.

1 **Universal Studios Florida.** This theme park is the centerpiece of Universal Orlando, a creative and quirky tribute to Hollywood past, present, and future. Overall, the collection of wild rides, quiet retreats, live shows, street characters, and clever movies (both 3-D and 4-D) are as entertaining as the motion pictures they celebrate. Another plus is that they're always adding something new. *Always.*

2 **Islands of Adventure.** Certainly the most significant addition to any Orlando theme park came when Islands of Adventure introduced an entire land dedicated to Harry Potter, which, in turn, sparked a substantial surge in attendance (and inspired an equally inventive Harry Potter land at neighboring Universal Studios). Also here are Spider-Man, the Hulk, velociraptors, the Cat in the Hat, and dozens of other characters that give guests every reason to head to the islands.

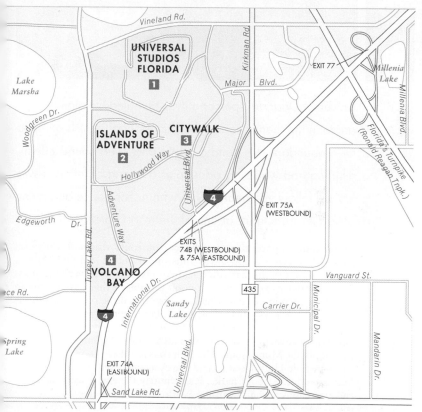

3 CityWalk. Even when the parks are closed (*especially* when the parks are closed), locals and visitors come to this sprawling entertainment and retail complex to watch movies, dine at theme restaurants, shop for everything from cigars to surf wear to tattoos, and stay up late at nightclubs that mimic party time in the French Quarter, Jamaica, and the coolest clubs of New York City.

4 Volcano Bay. After closing its distant Wet 'n Wild water park, Universal premiered this sprawling South Seas–style "water theme park" in 2017, making a big splash indeed. The flood of high-energy aquatic thrills are balanced by quiet areas with shaded cabanas and white-sand beaches.

Updated
by Gary
McKechnie

Universal Orlando's personality is revealed the moment you arrive in the theme parks where music, cartoonish architecture, abundant eye candy, subtle and overt sound effects, whirling and whizzing rides, plus a throng of fellow travelers will follow you nearly everywhere. For peace and quiet, seek out a sanctuary at one of the resort hotels.

At a breathless pace, there's a chance you *could* visit both Universal parks (Universal Studios and Islands of Adventure *aka* "IOA") in a single day, but to do that you'll have to invest in a Universal Express Pass. Without it, you'll spend a good portion of that day waiting in line at the premium attractions. So allow two days, or perhaps three; a day for each park plus a "pick-up" day to return to your favorite attractions—or skip them both in favor of a leisurely day at Volcano Bay. Which attractions are the main attractions? At Universal Studios, Revenge of the Mummy and The Simpsons are always popular; at IOA, the Incredible Hulk Coaster and the Amazing Adventures of Spider-Man are a hit. At both parks, it's definitely the entire scope of shops and attractions at the Wizarding Worlds of Harry Potter.

Universal Studios appeals primarily to those who like loud, fast, high-energy attractions—generally teens and adults. Covering 444 acres, it's a rambling montage of sets, shops, and soundstages housing themed attractions, and reproductions of New York, San Francisco, London, and the fictional town of Springfield.

When Islands of Adventure first opened in 1999, it took attractions to a new level. Each section—from Marvel Super Hero Island to Toon Lagoon to Seuss Landing and the Lost Continent—was impressive enough to suggest they had out-Disneyed Disney. And when the 20-acre Wizarding World of Harry Potter—Hogsmeade opened in 2010, IOA received well-deserved worldwide attention. Universal Studios made another huge leap forward with the 2014 unveiling of a full-scale version of Diagon Alley, complete with Gringotts Bank and a magical train that departs for IOA from Platform 9¾. Stay tuned: These lands are so popular there are always plans for expansions.

PLANNING

GETTING HERE AND AROUND

East on Interstate 4 (from WDW and Tampa), exit at Universal Boulevard (75A); take a left into Universal Orlando, and follow the signs. Heading west on Interstate 4 (from Downtown or Daytona), exit at Universal Boulevard (74B), turn right, and follow Hollywood Way.

Both Universal Studios and IOA require a lot of walking—a whole lot of serious walking. Start off by using the parking area's moving walkways as much as possible. Arrive early at either park, and you may be able to complete a single lap that will get you to the main attractions.

OPERATING HOURS

Universal Studios and IOA are open 365 days a year, with opening/closing times typically from 9 am to 7 pm but changing throughout the year (and sometimes varying by the week). Check online for the most accurate hours of each park and CityWalk. Some Universal resort hotel guests receive early admission (see below).

PARKING

Universal's two garages total 3.4 million square feet, so after you park *note your parking space.* The cost is a steep $20 for cars and motorcycles (free after 6 pm), $22 for RVs and buses, and $30 for "prime" parking, which puts you on a lower level closer to the entrance. Although moving walkways get you partway, you could walk up to a half mile to reach the gates, which explains why some guests opt for valet parking ($20 for up to two hours, $40 for more than two hours), which literally puts them at the entrance to CityWalk and near the turnstiles of the parks.

ADMISSION

The at-the-gate, per-person, per-day single-park rate for either Universal Studios Florida or IOA changes throughout the year in what they call "value," "anytime," or "mixed" seasons. The least expensive one-day admissions is $110 for an adult (i.e., anyone over 9 years old). Less expensive are multiday passes that are available in an equally diverse range of prices and combinations. To save time (and money), order online or call ahead.

EXPRESS PASSES

Another ticket option that comes with a widely varied price range is the Universal Express Pass that takes you to the front of most lines and can save you a lot of time. The price ranges from around $60 off-season to around $130 for one park in peak and holiday seasons. Keep in mind, the pass is for one use only at each attraction, and only at attractions that accept the pass. A more expensive "unlimited" pass that takes you to the head of the line again and again and again ranges from around $80 to $150 for a single park. For a pass that works at both parks, add about $20 to $30 to the standard or unlimited option. Note: If you're a guest at one of Universal's premium hotels (Royal Pacific, Hard Rock, Portofino Bay), this perk is free; your room key serves as an unlimited Express Pass from the day you check in to the day you check out.

Universal Orlando Ticket Price Chart

TICKET OPTIONS				
TICKET	1-DAY	2-DAY	3-DAY	4-DAY
BASE TICKET				
Ages 10–up	$115	$204.99	$224.99	$234.99
Ages 3–9	$110	$194.99	$214.99	$224.99
Base Ticket admits guest to one park per day, either Universal Studios or Islands of Adventure.				
PARK-TO-PARK				
Ages 10–up	$170	$264.99	$284.99	$299.99
Ages 3–9	$165	$254.99	$274.99	$289.99
Park-to-Park Ticket allows guest to go back and forth between Universal Studios and Islands of Adventure; 7-day ticket available.				
ADD: Quick Service Dining Plan	$23.99			
Blue Man Group	From $60			
City Walk Party Pass	$11.99			
City Walk Party Pass with a Movie	$15.00			
CityWalk Party Pass gives guest one-night access to CityWalk clubs and venues (some of which require you to be at least 21). CityWalk Party Pass and Movie adds to that a free movie at the AMC Universal Cineplex 20.				
ADD: Volcano Bay to Universal Orlando Part-to-Park Ticket (2-day)	$319.99 for adults, $309.99 for kids.			
One-day Volcano Bay Ticket	$80 for adults, $75 for kids.			
ADD: Universal Express Pass	Prices vary greatly by options and season; check website for details.			
Gives guest access to much shorter lines at Universal Studios and Islands of Adventure rides. (Note that this pass is included in the room rate at Universal Resort hotels.)				
All prices are subject to Florida sales tax				

Universal Orlando.

UNIVERSAL DINING PLAN

You can save up to 30% by paying in advance for a Quick Service meal which includes one meal, one snack, and a nonalcoholic beverage ($23 adults, $15 kids). There are more than 100 locations where you can use the plan in the parks and at CityWalk, from full- service to quick-dining options. Some of the more popular choices are Mel's Drive-In, Louie's Italian, Beverly Hills Boulangerie, and the Classic Monsters Café at Universal Studios and the Comic Strip Café, Croissant Moon, the Burger Digs, and Café 4 at Islands of Adventure.

UNIVERSAL TIPS AND ADVICE

Arrive early. Note what time the park opens and arrive an hour earlier than that. Seriously. Better to be first through the gates and share the park with hundreds of people instead of thousands. You'll also spend less time going through security, which eats up time as everyone funnels in from the parking garages.

Visit on a weekday. Crowds are lighter, especially fall through spring, when kids are in school and locals are at work.

Don't forget anything in your car. Universal's parking areas are at least a half mile from park entrances, and a round-trip hike will eat up valuable time. If you can afford it, consider valet parking. It costs $40 for longer than two hours before 6 pm (that's twice as much as regular parking), but it puts you much closer to Universal's park entrances and just steps from CityWalk.

Know the restrictions. A few things aren't allowed in the parks: alcohol and glass containers, hard-sided coolers, soft-sided coolers larger than 8½ inches wide by 6 inches high by 6 inches deep, and any bags or coolers with wheels. But if your flight's leaving later, you can check your luggage at the parks (unless you just leave them in your car).

Order in advance. Among the things that can take far too long when you arrive is standing in line at a kiosk to buy tickets or standing in line at Will Call to pick up tickets. If possible, take time to check out the many ticket options online (including Universal Express Passes), make your selection, print your tickets, and then arrive ready to go. If you purchase tickets through the Universal app, the scan code is your admission ticket. If you've printed out your tickets on regular paper, you can swap that out for regular tickets when you arrive. But do that at Guest Services once you've entered the park since it's far less crowded than Guest Services outside the turnstiles.

Food for thought. Meals and snacks are relatively pricey, and unless you shell out a lot of cash for a souvenir cup, there are no free refills on drinks. If you're on a budget, consider ordering drinks without ice (asking for a separate cup of ice on the side), packing snacks to eat along the way, and limiting yourself to a single meal in the park. You can always eat at a nearby restaurant outside the park.

Look into the Express Pass. Jumping to the front of the line with this pass may well be worth the extra cost on busy days—unless you stay at the Portofino Bay, Hard Rock, or Royal Pacific hotel, in which case unlimited front-of-line access is one of the perks.

Download the app. The Universal Orlando mobile app includes maps, wait times, and information on hours, dining, shopping, clubs, events, shows and attractions.

Ride solo. If you don't mind the possibility that your group will be split up, some Universal attractions have a single-rider line that moves much faster than regular lines.

Get expert advice. The folks at Guest Services (aka Guest Relations) have great insight. The reps can even create a custom itinerary free of charge.

Check out Child Swap. At certain Universal attractions, one parent can enter the attraction, take a spin, and then return to take care of the baby while the other parent rides without having to wait in line again.

FOR PEOPLE WITH DISABILITIES

The *Studio Guide for Guests with Disabilities* (aka *Rider's Guide*) details attractions with special entrances and viewing areas, interpreters, Braille scripts, and assistance devices. In general, if you can transfer from your wheelchair unassisted or with the help of a friend, you can ride many attractions. Some rides have carts that accommodate manual wheelchairs, though not motorized wheelchairs or electronic convenience vehicles (ECVs).

CONTACTS

Universal Orlando Resort ☎ *407/363–8000* ⊕ *www.universalorlando.com*

Universal (Loews Resorts) Room Reservations ☎ *877/819–7884*

3

UNIVERSAL STUDIOS

Updated
by Gary
Mckechnie

Inspired by the California original and opened in Orlando in 1990 (when the city assumed it would become "Hollywood East"), Universal Studios was meant to celebrate the movies. Like the back lot sets at a film studio, the park is a jumble of areas and attractions that can make navigating a challenge, but the payoff is the opportunity to immerse yourself in this highly creative take on motion picture magic.

The first area past the entrance is Production Central, where large soundstages house attractions based on TV programs and films like *Shrek, Despicable Me,* and *The Transformers.* Because it's right near the entrance, it can be the park's most crowded area.

Past Production Central is New York. Nearly every studio has its own Big Apple sets, and Universal is no exception. A cleverly constructed collection of sparkling public buildings, well-worn neighborhoods, and back alleys is the next-best thing to Manhattan itself (but not even NYC has Revenge of the Mummy or a Jimmy Fallon virtual reality ride).

Subtle changes in architecture and design tell you you're entering San Francisco, home of the new-in-2018 attraction Fast & Furious: Supercharged. A nice place to pause for a bite, the area offers places for burgers, pastries, and candy, as well as table-service meals at the waterfront Lombard's Seafood Grille.

You'll next reach the land adored by wizards and muggles alike: the Wizarding World of Harry Potter: Diagon Alley. What the books describe and what filmmakers created, Universal has replicated in great detail, immersing you in this fantastic world.

Just ahead, World Expo features a single attraction—MEN IN BLACK: Alien Attack, a futuristic experience that's the polar opposite of neighboring Springfield: Home of the Simpsons, which is perhaps the park's most visually dynamic area. Its next door neighbor, Woody

TOP ATTRACTIONS

AGES SEVEN AND UP

Harry Potter and the Escape from Gringotts. Getting into the vault at Gringotts Bank can be a challenge, but it's also a first-class adventure thanks to technology similar to that of The Transformers and IOA's Spider-Man and Harry Potter and the Forbidden Journey.

Hollywood Rip Ride Rockit. On this superwild coaster, you select the soundtrack.

MEN IN BLACK: Alien Attack. The "world's first ride-through video game" gives you a chance to compete for points by plugging away at an endless swarm of aliens.

Revenge of the Mummy. It's a jarring, rocketing indoor coaster that takes you past scary mummies and billowing balls of fire (really).

Shrek 4-D. The 3-D film with sensory effects picks up where the original film left off—and adds some creepy extras in the process.

The Simpsons Ride. It puts you in the heart of Springfield on a wild-and-crazy virtual reality experience.

Transformers: The Ride 3-D. Universal Studios' version of IOA's fantastic Spider-Man experience, but this one features a rough-and-tumble encounter with the mechanical stars of the film franchise.

Universal Orlando's Horror Make-Up Show. Often gross but always entertaining, the monster makeup demonstration merges the best of stand-up comedy with creepy effects.

AGES SIX AND UNDER

Animal Actors on Location! It's a perfect family show starring a menagerie of animals whose unusually high IQs are surpassed only by their cuteness and cuddle-ability.

Curious George Goes to Town. The celebrated simian visits the Man with the Yellow Hat in a small-scale water park.

A Day in the Park with Barney. Young children love the big purple dinosaur and the chance to sing along with Barney and co-star Baby Bop.

Woodpecker's KidZone, offers colorful attractions designed for toddlers and the under-10 crowd with diversions that include a junior-size roller coaster, a mini–water park, and a chance to meet E.T. and Barney the dinosaur.

Although the quiet parks, themed restaurants, and facades of flashy Rodeo Drive are truly an attraction in themselves, Hollywood has a few standout attractions, including Universal Orlando's Horror Make Up Show. By the time you've circled the park, you really will feel that Universal has put you in the movies.

ORIENTATION AND PLANNING

GETTING ORIENTED

On a map, the park appears neatly divided into eight areas positioned around a huge lagoon. There's Production Central, which covers the entire left side of the Plaza of the Stars; followed by New York, with rides along with various street performances; San Francisco and the new-in-2018 Fast and Furious: Supercharged; next are the streets of

Save the planet from interstellar invaders in World Expo's interactive MEN IN BLACK: Alien Attack. Zap aliens in city streets and compete with other guests to score points.

London that lead to the Wizarding World of Harry Potter: Diagon Alley; the futuristic World Expo; Homer and Bart's hometown of Springfield; then Woody Woodpecker's KidZone; and, finally, Hollywood.

What's tricky is that—because it's designed like a series of movie sets with side streets, city blocks, and alleyways—there's no straightforward way to tackle the park. You'll probably make some detours and do some backtracking. To save time and shoe leather, ask theme park hosts for itinerary suggestions and time-saving tips. Here are a few of our own suggestions.

TOURING TIPS

We highly recommend you purchase your tickets online because it gives you plenty of time to consider your many options and includes a discount. If you're confused by the array of options, call Universal for advice as you consider your purchase. Entering Universal Studios can be overwhelming as you and thousands of others flood through the turnstiles at once. Pick up a map in the entryway to CityWalk or by the park turnstiles and spend a few minutes reviewing it. Map out a route, find show schedules, and select restaurants. If a host is nearby, ask for insider advice on what to see first.

The "right" way. Upon entering, avoid the temptation to go straight toward the towering soundstages and loop the park clockwise. Instead consider heading right—bypassing shops, restaurants, and some crowds to primary attractions like the Horror Make-Up Show, The Simpsons Ride, and MEN IN BLACK: Alien Attack.

Photo ops. Universal Studios posts signs that indicate photo spots and show how best to frame your shot.

Rendezvous. Good meeting spots include the Hello Kitty shop near the entrance; Mel's Drive-In, which is roughly in the center of the park at the top of the lagoon; or by the purple triple-decker Knight Bus in the Wizarding World of Harry Potter.

PARK AMENITIES

Baby Care: There are diaper-changing stations in many of the men's and women's restrooms, and a nursing station offers comfort and privacy at the park's first-aid station near the entrance. Baby supplies (diapers, food, wipes, and so on) are available at larger stores; ask for them at the counter, though, as they're not displayed on shelves.

Photos: Just inside the main entrance, On Location was primarily a camera and film shop before cameras and film were condensed into smartphones. Nowadays the shelves are stocked with gifts, souvenirs, and drinks while a staff assists guests with souvenir photos taken by Universal's squad of photographers.

First Aid: There are two first-aid centers: one just inside the turnstiles, to the right near the Studio Audience Center, and another around the corner from Louie's Italian Restaurant in New York.

Guest Services: You can get strategic advice *before* visiting the park by calling Guest Services at *407/224–4233*.

Lockers: Daily rates for lockers near the park entrance are $10 for a small unit and $12 for a larger one. There are free lockers near the entrances of some high-speed attractions (such as MEN IN BLACK: Alien Attack and Revenge of the Mummy), where you can stash your stuff before your ride. Those lockers are available to you for up to 90 minutes.

Lost People and Things: If you plan to split up, be sure everyone knows where and when to reconnect. Staffers take lost children to Guest Services near the main entrance. This is also where you might find lost personal items.

Services for People with Disabilities: Universal has made it as easy as possible for guests with disabilities to enjoy the park. It starts when you arrive in the parking garage, where you can rent wheelchairs or ECVs before making the long trek to the park entrance (though there's also chair rentals at the entrance), and extends to guidebooks with icons indicating which shows feature sign-language interpreters.

Guest Services (near the entrance just outside and inside the park) is the place to pick up assisted-listening and other devices, such as clickers that trigger closed-captioning. Other services include special viewing areas for people in wheelchairs, automatic doors, well-equipped restrooms, and walking areas for service animals. Be sure to pick up the *Studio Guide for Guests with Disabilities* (aka *Rider's Guide*), which is full of details on equipment and other services.

Accessibility information is posted at each attraction. Note that although ride lines can accommodate standard wheelchairs, often you'll be ushered into a waiting area while the rest of your party goes through the line. Many shows have seating to accommodate manual wheelchairs, but, in general, you'll have to transfer from your chair to ride vehicles.

For hearing-impaired guests, captioning, assistive listening, and/or ASL interpreters are available at Despicable Me, Shrek, MEN IN BLACK: Alien Attack, Transformers: The Ride 3-D, Animal Actors, and A Day in the Park with Barney.

Stroller Rentals: Just inside the main entrance, there are strollers for $15 (single) and $25 (double) a day. You can also rent small kiddie cars ($18) or large ones ($28) by the day.

Wheelchair Rentals: You can rent manual wheelchairs ($12 per day) at the parking garages and inside the main entrance. Because there are limited quantities of electronic convenience vehicles (ECVs, available in the park for $50), reserve one in advance. A photo ID and a $50 deposit on a credit card are required for wheelchairs. ECVs with a sunshade canopy are $70 per day.

Where to Snack: Surpassing the number of rides are the number of restaurants—some of which are on the cost-saving Universal Dining Plan (check online or when purchasing the plan). You can satisfy your appetite at **Mel's Drive-In**, a *Happy Days*–era soda shop–burger joint; **Louie's Italian Restaurant** (pizza, spaghetti, salads); and the **Classic Monsters Café** (pizzas, hot dogs, pasta, salads, rotisserie chicken). There's also **Beverly Hills Boulangerie** for breakfast croissants and pastries, and full-service restaurants including **Finnegan's Bar and Grill** (Irish pub) and **Lombard's Seafood Grille** (seafood).

Among the self-serve restaurants are **Richter's Burger Co.** (burgers, salads), **Schwab's Pharmacy** for ice cream, and the **Kid Zone Pizza Company** for pizza, chicken tenders, and other kid-geared dishes. At Diagon Alley, the Leaky Cauldron serves British pub fare, including cottage pie, bangers and mash, fish-and-chips, and cool, smooth mugs of Butterbeer. Near The Simpsons Ride, a strip called Fast Food Boulevard includes several Springfield-inspired eateries, including **Krusty Burger** (hamburgers, hot dogs), **Cletus' Chicken Shack** (chicken sandwiches, platters), the **Frying Dutchman** (fried seafood), **Luigi's Pizza, Lard Lad Donuts** (pastries, sweets), **Bumblebee Man's Taco Truck** (Mexican), and **Lisa's Teahouse of Terror** (salads, wraps, sandwiches). Want a cold one? Drop by **Moe's Tavern** for a Duff's beer or a Flaming Moe.

TOURS

VIP Tours. Universal has several VIP tours that are worthwhile if you're in a hurry, if crowds are heavy, if you're with a large group—and if you have the money to burn. The tours include extras like front-of-the-line access (that is, the right to jump to the head of the line). You can also arrange for extras like priority restaurant seating, bilingual guides, gift bags, refreshments at check-in, wheelchairs, strollers, and valet parking. You'll need to arrange the tour at least 48 hours in advance by calling ahead or setting it up online. Prices cited here do not include sales tax or, more important, park admission; and tour prices vary by season, so consider these just estimated costs.

Nonexclusive one-day tours (i.e., you'll tour with other park guests) cost $189 to $429 per person for one park (five hours) and visit a minimum of eight major attractions. The cost goes up to $199 to $449 per person for a two-park, seven-hour tour. Then there are exclusive tours for your group only. If you're traveling with up to 10 people, consider splitting the cost of an eight-hour tour customized to your interests, which includes a sit-down breakfast, lunch, and dinner at the park of your choice. The private VIP tour for one park ranges from $2,999 to $3,899 plus tax for a group of five, with an extra $325 to $425 for each additional person. An eight-hour, two-park exclusive price is $3,099 to $3,999 for five people ($350 to $450 extra for each additional person). ⊠ Orlando ☎ 866/346–9350 ⊕ www.universalorlando.com.

EXPLORING UNIVERSAL STUDIOS

PRODUCTION CENTRAL

Expect plenty of loud, flashy, rollicking rides that appeal to tweens, teens, and adults. Clear the turnstiles and go straight. You can use the Universal Express Pass at all attractions.

Despicable Me: Minion Mayhem. Even if you've never seen the hit animated film, it doesn't take long to fall for Gru, the Scourge of Humanity, in this wild virtual reality chase through the movie. Two extremely funny (and cute) preshow rooms—Gru's living room and laboratory—set the stage for the 3-D ride. With help from his adopted daughters Margo, Edith, and Agnes (and ever-so-anxious minions), Gru reviews everyone to make sure they're ready to become minions. Next, sporting your "minion goggles" (aka 3-D glasses) you are transformed into minions for the rollicking ride itself, which is filled with close calls and colorful characters as you pursue the ever-elusive prize: the girls' gift for their dad on the one-year anniversary of their adoption. To celebrate, the ride exits into a minion disco (of course). The 3-D experience, with preshows, lasts about 20 minutes. Not recommended for expectant mothers or anyone with motion sickness or back, neck, or heart problems. **For people with disabilities:** Closed-captioned devices are available; wheelchair guests may remain in their chairs. ■ TIP→ Go for the stationary seats if you think you'll suffer from motion sickness. ⊠ Production Central, Universal Studios ⊕ www.universalorlando. com ↻ Duration: 5 mins. Crowds: Heavy. Audience: All ages. Height requirement: 40 inches.

Fodor's Choice ★ **Hollywood Rip Ride Rockit.** Looking like an endless strand of spaghetti, this half-mile-plus coaster loops, twists, dives, and winds above and through Production Central. After you're locked into your seat, you'll select your personal soundtrack (choose from heavy metal, techno, country, rap, and pop) to accompany the video (starring you) that's shot as you scream your way along. And you will scream! It all starts as you're hauled nearly *17 stories straight up* before you drop nearly *17 stories straight down* before being lifted again into a towering loop and released into what seems like a never-ending series of twists, curves, sideways slings, and snap rolls at speeds up to 65 mph. By the time you return to the station, you might be woozy and a little spent—but you might spend a little more: the video with the soundtrack you selected is available for purchase. Off-season the line never seems too bad. In season consider using a Universal Express Pass. The ride isn't suitable for expectant mothers; anyone with neck, back, or heart problems; or people

DID YOU KNOW?

On Production Central's Hollywood Rip Ride Rockit, you choose the soundtrack for your roller-coaster ride from songs within several genres of music. After the whole experience, you can buy a video of your ride with the music you selected.

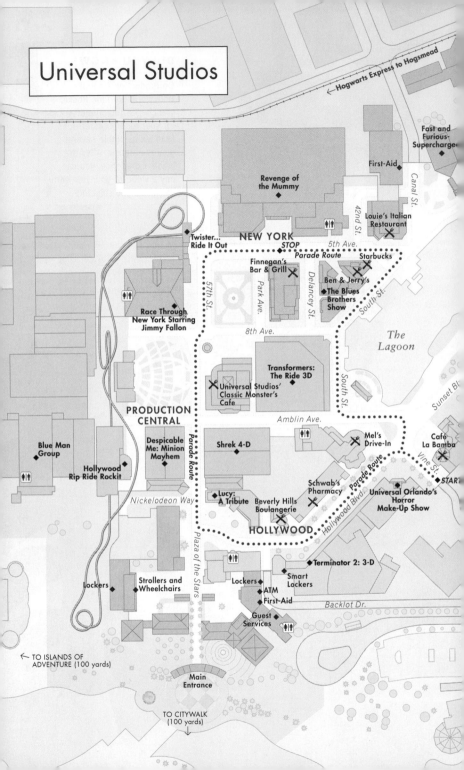

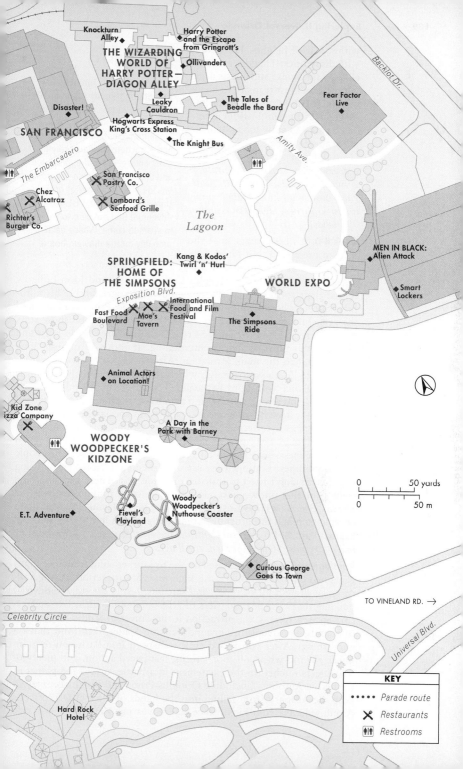

with a fear of heights. **For people with disabilities:** This does include closed-captioning, and guests using wheelchairs must transfer to a ride vehicle. ■TIP➜ **Come early or late or choose the single-rider line—and be sure to stow loose items in the available lockers.** ✉ *Production Central, Universal Studios* ⊕ *www.universalorlando.com* ☞ *Duration: 2 mins. Crowds: You Bet! Audience: Not small kids. Height minimum: 51 inches. Height maximum: 79 inches.*

Shrek 4-D. It's been years since the hit film premiered, but *Shrek* fans still line up at this animated 3-D

saga. Mike Myers, Eddie Murphy, Cameron Diaz, and John Lithgow reprise their vocal roles as the swamp-dwelling ogre, Shrek; his faithful chatterbox companion, Donkey; Shrek's bride, Princess Fiona; and the vengeful Lord Farquaad (or rather his ghost). The preshow stars the Gingerbread Man, Magic Mirror, and the Three Little Pigs; and although this intro is slightly entertaining, at about 15 minutes long it's longer than the main attraction. Afterward you're given OgreVision (aka 3-D) glasses through which to view Shrek as he attempts to rescue Fiona from Lord Farquaad. The adventure includes a battle between fire-breathing dragons and a pretty scary plunge down a virtual 1,000-foot waterfall—all made more intense by special theater seats and surprising sensory effects (mainly blasts of air and sprinkles of water) that create the "4-D" part. The ride can be unsettling for those with motion sickness—but fun as all get-out for everyone else. **For people with disabilities:** Equipped for assisted-listening devices. Those using wheelchairs don't need to transfer to a ride seat. There are, however, eight seats that allow guests with disabilities to fully experience the sensory effects. ■TIP➜ **Despite a capacity for 300, you may wait up to an hour to reach the preshow. Come early or late in the day. Accepts Express Pass.** ✉ *Production Central, Universal Studios* ☞ *Duration: 12 mins. Crowds: Heavy. Audience: All ages.*

Transformers: The Ride 3-D. Based on the toy-turned–film franchise that's generated billions of dollars, this high-intensity attraction has the ability to generate a lot of thrills and screams. Inside the stark industrial building that's the headquarters of NEST (Nonbiological Extraterrestrial Species Treaty), the attraction is the Universal Studios equivalent of Islands of Adventure's groundbreaking Spider-Man (and that's a good thing). After you board your transport, in a flash you're in an illusory world where 60-foot screens, fast-paced action, and plenty of 3-D effects ratchet up the excitement in a battle to save the planet as the heroic Autobots (including Optimus Prime and Bumblebee) try to keep the Allspark from falling into the hands of the evil Decepticons (Confused? Ask your kids). Since you're wearing 3-D glasses, you ride through the attraction getting spun, twirled, splashed, dropped, and faced with some tremendously realistic intergalactic encounters that rock and roll you through the Transformers' world. Very loud and very wild. The height minimum is 40 inches, and this ride isn't suitable for expectant mothers; anyone with neck, back, or heart problems; or people with a fear of heights. **For people with disabilities:** Guests using wheelchairs must transfer to a ride vehicle. ■ **TIP→ Come early or late, use Universal Express, or choose the single-rider line.** ⊠ *Production Central, Universal Studios* ⊕ *www.universalorlando.com* ⨈ *Duration: 5 mins. Crowds: You bet! Audience: Not small kids.*

NEED A BREAK

In the heart of Production Central, the self-serve **Classic Monsters Cafe** resembles a mad scientist's lab. It offers wood-fired-oven pizzas, pastas, chef salads, four-cheese ravioli, and rotisserie chicken. Inside the restaurant, actual props and costumes from vintage Universal horror films provide great photo ops.

NEW YORK

Universal has gone all out to re-create New York's skyscrapers, commercial districts, ethnic neighborhoods, and back alleys—right down to the cracked concrete. Hidden within these structures are restaurants, arcades, gift shops, and key attractions. And although they're from Chicago, the Blues Brothers drive from the Second City to New York City in their Bluesmobile for free performances at 70 Delancey. Here you can use Universal Express Pass at Revenge of the Mummy and Race Through New York Starring Jimmy Fallon.

Fodor's Choice
★

Race Through New York Starring Jimmy Fallon. Walking through the queue area of this new-in-2017 attraction is like walking through the history of *The Tonight Show*, with showcases featuring memorabilia that pays tribute to more than a half century of hosts who have put their stamp on the most famous program in late night: Steve Allen, Jack Paar, Johnny Carson, Jay Leno, Conan O'Brien, and taking the reins in 2014, Jimmy Fallon. Fond memories of the past pave the way to a rocketing road trip that begins only after a serenade by the Ragtime Gals, a visit by Hashtag the Panda, and a preshow area where, for the first time anywhere (more than likely) safety instructions are offered in a freestyle rap performed by Tariq "Black Thought" Trotter of The Roots. After the doors open, you'll find a seat before a towering screen that really comes to life when you fasten your seat belt, put on your 3-D glasses, and find yourself on the set of the show getting ready to race Jimmy through the halls of 30 Rock, down Broadway, through the streets of New York—and beyond. You follow in your own "car" beside Jimmy as you whip past taxis, pedestrians, and local landmarks, before heading into space to land on the moon. **For people with disabilities:** Guests using wheelchairs must transfer to a ride vehicle. ■ **TIP→ Cut down on wait times: head for the single-rider line. Otherwise, use Express Pass or come early or late. Free lockers are available for loose items. Use them.** ⊠ *New York, Universal Studios* ⊕ *www.universalorlando.com* ⨈ *Duration: 7 mins. Crowds: Heavy. Audience: Not young kids (under 7). Height requirement: 40 inches.*

Revenge of the Mummy. Action, adventure, and horror are in abundance in this $40-million spine-tingling thrill ride that combines roller-coaster technology, pyrotechnics, and some super-scary skeletal warriors. The entrance is set up like the tomb of a pharaoh, which means you'll walk through winding catacombs in the near-dark passing Egyptian artifacts and archaeological scenes before reaching your vehicle. After boarding the multipassenger coaster car and zipping into the heart of a haunted labyrinth, "dead" ahead you're given the chance to sell your soul for safety and riches. Whether you take the deal or not, a guardian mummy thinks it's high time to send you hurtling through underground passageways and Egyptian burial chambers, where you must escape a beetle-infested burial chamber, zip backward through fog, and then race full-tilt into the mummified mouth of Imhotep. Take note: you feel the 1.5 g-forces when flying uphill, and much of the ride takes place in the dark, which adds to its unforgettable intensity. Needless to say, this isn't a good choice for expectant mothers or anyone with neck, back, or heart problems. **For people with disabilities:** Guests using wheelchairs must transfer to a ride vehicle. ■**TIP→** Cut down on wait times: head for the single-rider line. Otherwise use Express Pass or come early or late. Free lockers are available for loose items. Use them. ✉ *New York, Universal Studios* ⊕ *www.universalorlando.com* ☞ *Duration: 3 mins. Crowds: Heavy. Audience: Not small kids. Height requirement: 48 inches.*

SAN FRANCISCO
This area celebrates the West Coast with the wharves and warehouses of San Francisco's Embarcadero and Fisherman's Wharf districts.

NEED A BREAK

Richter's Burger Co. (across from Fast & Furious: Supercharged) lets you drop in and dress up your own burger or grilled-chicken sandwich. It's pretty quick, pretty convenient, and there are seats inside and out.

Fast & Furious: Supercharged. Fast & Furious: Supercharged was set to open here in 2018 to replace Disaster! ✉ *Universal Studios* ⊕ *www. universalorlando.com.*

SPRINGFIELD: HOME OF THE SIMPSONS
One of television's longest-running shows inspired one of the park's most enjoyable lands; a strangely surreal yet familiar small town filled with landmarks you'd recognize, from Moe's Tavern to the towering Lard Lad of doughnut fame. The two primary attractions—The Simpsons Ride and Kang & Kodos' Twirl 'n' Hurl—offer fast admission with Universal Express Pass.

Kang & Kodos' Twirl 'n' Hurl. Inspired by the intergalactic creatures that make an occasional appearance in Springfield, here's a new spin on an old favorite. About a dozen flying saucers encircle a towering statue of Kang (or Kodos), the one-eyed, fang-toothed, octopus-tentacled alien. Once you've climbed into your saucer the ride begins when, as at Seuss Landing's One Fish, Two Fish, Red Fish, Blue Fish, the spinning ride takes flight and whirls you and your co-pilot around Kang (or Kodos). Kids who love the opportunity to take the controls raise and lower the craft in hopes of avoiding the jets of water shot from surrounding

One of the most popular areas of Universal Studios (after The Wizarding World of Harry Potter) is Springfield: Home of the Simpsons.

poles. A pleasing, fun, low-thrill attraction that kids enjoy. ⊠ *Springfield: Home of the Simpsons, Universal Studios* ⊕ *www.universalorlando.com* ☞ *Duration: 3 mins. Crowds: Light to medium. Audience: Small kids and up.*

Fodor's Choice ★ **The Simpsons Ride.** As you enter this ride through Krusty the Clown's gaping mouth, and then receive a video greeting by citizens of Springfield, police chief Clancy Wiggum reminds you that if you must get sick, do it in your hat—and thus the tone is set for your arrival in one of television's most popular animated communities. The preshow explains that Krusty has expanded his empire to include a theme park, which his disgruntled former sidekick, Sideshow Bob, plans to sabotage. After a fairly tame start, your virtual car soars through virtual Springfield, plunging toward familiar businesses and buildings, and narrowly escaping disaster as Sideshow Bob tears up the tracks and sends you racing through wild scenes in a variety of locations such as Disney, SeaWorld—and hell. Several times you're saved by the split-second timing of an unexpected hero. If you have even a scintilla of motion sickness, this one will throw you for a colorful, cartoonish loop. Guests who are pregnant or who have heart, back, or neck problems shouldn't ride. **For people with disabilities:** Guests in wheelchairs must transfer to a ride vehicle. ■**TIP**➔ Use Express Pass. ⊠ *Springfield: Home of the Simpsons, Universal Studios* ⊕ *www.universalorlando.com* ☞ *Duration: 6 mins. Crowds: Heavy. Audience: Not small kids. Height requirement: Must be at least 40 inches to ride; adults must accompany kids between 40 and 48 inches.*

WORLD EXPO

At the far end of the park is a futuristic set of buildings containing one of Universal Studios' most popular attractions, MEN IN BLACK: Alien Attack.

MEN IN BLACK: Alien Attack. The preshow of "the world's first ride-through video game" provides the storyline: To earn membership in MIB you must round up aliens that escaped when their shuttle crashed on Earth. On board your vehicle with a few others, you enter the back-streets of a city where aliens pop out from windows, trash cans, and doorways. Fire at them with that laser gun mounted to your futuristic car, and since there's no limit to the number of shots you can take, blast away. Even though the gun's red laser dot is just a pinpoint, an onboard scoreboard helps you keep track of what you've hit. Aliens fire back at you, and if they score a hit it'll cause your car to spin out of control. Depending on the collective score, your ride will wrap up with one of 35 endings, ranging from a hero's welcome to a loser's farewell. All in all, it's pretty exciting. The spinning nature of the cars may cause dizziness, so use caution if you're prone to motion sickness. Don't ride if you have heart, back, or neck problems. **For people with disabilities:** Equipped for assisted-listening devices. Guests using wheelchairs must transfer to a ride vehicle. ■**TIP➜** In summer, waits may reach up to an hour. Come first thing or save time by splitting up and using the shorter single-riders line or by using Express Pass. ⊠ *World Expo, Universal Studios* ⊕ *www.universalorlando.com* ☞ *Duration: 4½ mins. Crowds: Heavy. Audience: Not small kids. Height requirement: 42 inches to ride without an adult.*

THE WIZARDING WORLD OF HARRY POTTER: DIAGON ALLEY

Don't think the facade of London row homes is all there is to see here. On the contrary, as in the Harry Potter movies, the good stuff remains hidden to mere mortals. When you spy an opening through a broken brick wall and step into Diagon Alley, the world changes as you see what an incredible blueprint J.K. Rowling created through her words. You can literally spend hours in this one district looking at the complete range of Potter-centric places: Universal Studios' version of Ollivanders wand shop; Weasleys' Wizard Wheezes (magical jokes and novelty items); the Magical Menagerie (all creatures furry, feathered, or scaly); Madam Malkin's Robes for All Occasions (wizard wear); Wiseacre's Wizarding Equipment; and Quality Quidditch Supplies. For practitioners of the Dark Arts, venture down Knockturn Alley and step inside Borgin and Burkes. For an appetizing break, stop at the Leaky Cauldron, the land's signature restaurant, or cool off at Florean Fortescue's Ice-Cream Parlour.

And when you're ready to head to the village of Hogsmeade (conveniently located at the neighboring Islands of Adventure), make sure you have a park-to-park pass before stepping aboard the wonderful, magical Hogwarts Express—now departing to Islands of Adventure from Platform 9¾.

A fire-breathing dragon is a ceterpiece to The Wizarding World of Harry Potter: Diagon Alley.

Fodor's Choice
★   **Harry Potter and the Escape from Gringotts.** How do you know you've reached Gringotts Bank? Aside from a massive dragon perched on top of the building is the statue of a Gringotts goblin standing atop a towering stack of gold coins. Those two features alone will tell you that what lies ahead will be highly themed—and highly entertaining. The queue to the ride is an essential part of the attraction itself: you'll walk through the bank where a multitude of goblins are each working at their desks, diligently and wordlessly ... eerie. Soon you're in a ride vehicle, and after it departs the station it's only a matter of moments before Bellatrix Lestrange notices your presence and then does everything in her supernatural power to prevent you from traveling any farther. So from here on out, your vehicle will come face to 3-D face with a towering security detail that destroys the tracks and sends you deeper into the bank's recesses. Be warned that your first encounter with the one who shall not be named (aka Lord Voldemort) isn't your last. After he presents you with a fiery souvenir, he and Bellatrix return again—but they're no match for the scaly superhero who comes to your rescue. If you've ridden Universal's Spider-Man or The Transformers, you'll recognize the technology that blends virtual reality, 3-D effects, 4-D sensations, and gargantuan movie screens featuring scenes synchronized with the motion of your vehicle. Thankfully this attraction tones down much of the volume and excess motion that pushes the envelope on the others, so it's enjoyable for everyone. **For people with disabilities:** Guests using wheelchairs must transfer to a ride vehicle. ■**TIP→** Be patient; Express Passes aren't accepted, but the single-rider line moves fairly briskly. ⊠ *The Wizarding World of Harry Potter, Diagon Alley,*

Universal Studios ⊕ *www.universalorlando.com* ☞ *Duration: 5 mins. (ride) Crowds: Yes! Audience: Everyone but small kids. Height requirement: 42 inches minimum.*

Hogwart's Express—King's Cross Station. When Universal announced the Studios' Diagon Alley would connect to IOA's Hogsmeade via a train ride, many fans assumed an open-air train ride through the park's backstage area. But many people aren't nearly as creative as the geniuses at Universal. To reach Hogsmeade, you walk through an exact recreation of a London rail station where a magical effect takes you to Platform 9¾. Even as the train pulls in, you're already being transported into another world. Settle into the compartment with other guests, and soon the ride is an attraction in itself. Chuffing out of the station, outside your window an owl follows you out of London, music plays, and you get the sense you're traveling hundreds of miles across the English countryside. Adding to the magic, silhouettes of Harry, Ron, and Hermione appear in the corridor outside your window, with their narration adding to the drama of the trio's attempt to banish Dementors (and attempt to corral a loose box of chocolate frogs). By the time Hagrid appears and you arrive in Hogsmeade, you really feel as if ... *you've arrived in Hogsmeade.* ⊠ *Universal Studios* ⊕ *www.universalorlando.com.*

WOODY WOODPECKER'S KIDZONE

With its colorful compilation of rides, shows, and play areas, this entire section caters to preschoolers. It's a pint-size Promised Land, where kids can try out a roller coaster and get sprayed, splashed, and soaked in a water-park area. Surprisingly this is also a great place for parents, since it gives them a needed break after nearly circling the park. All shows and attractions except Curious George and Fievel accept Universal Express Pass.

Animal Actors on Location! Animal shows are usually fun—and this one is better than most thanks to an arkful of live animal stars. The tricks (or *behaviors*) they perform are mostly audience-participation segments, which makes it entertaining for young and old alike. Birds, cats, pigs, parrots, otters, ducks, dogs, hawks, and a skunk have been trained to portray a range of thespian actions that are woven into a series of vignettes, from a clever parrot that has a knack for plucking cash from the outstretched hand of an audience member to a dog that is a convincing actor in a staged melodrama. Although the line-up of animals and the scenes they perform may vary, the show's fast pacing and variety make it seem that you're watching several shows in one. Enjoy it! These are some of the cutest actors ever to hit the stage. **For people with disabilities:** The theater is equipped for assisted-listening devices and is wheelchair accessible. Some shows include a sign language interpreter. ■TIP➜ There's plenty of seating but come early for a good seat, or use Express Pass to get you in ahead of the crowd. ⊠ *Woody Woodpecker's KidZone, Universal Studios* ⊕ *www.universalorlando.com* ☞ *Duration: 20 mins. Crowds: Moderate to heavy. Audience: All ages.*

Curious George Goes to Town. The celebrated simian visits the Man with the Yellow Hat in a no-line, no-waiting, small-scale water park. The main town square has brightly colored building facades, and the plaza is an interactive aqua playground that adults avoid but kids are drawn to like fish to water. Yes, there's water, water everywhere, especially atop the clock tower, which periodically dumps a mighty 500 gallons down a roof and straight onto a screaming herd of preschoolers. Kids love the levers, valves, pumps, and hoses that gush at the rate of 200 gallons per minute, letting them get sprayed, spritzed, splashed, and splattered. At the head of the square, footprints lead to a dry play area, with a rope climb and a ball cage where youngsters can frolic among thousands of foam balls. You can get into the act, sit it out on nearby benches, or take a few minutes to buy souvenir towels to dry off your waterlogged kids. **For people with disabilities:** Most of this attraction is barrier-free. ■TIP➔ Crowds are heavy midmorning: come in late afternoon or early evening—especially in the summertime. Kids will get drenched; so stash a bathing suit or change of clothing in a nearby locker. ⊠ *Woody Woodpecker's KidZone, Universal Studios* ⊕ *www. universalorlando.com* ⟳ *Duration: Up to you. Crowds: Moderate to heavy. Audience: Small kids.*

A Day in the Park with Barney. If your kids can't get enough of the big purple dinosaur, here he is again! A fairly long preshow features a goofy, kid-friendly emcee before you and your preschoolers enter a pleasant theater-in-the-round filled with brilliantly colored trees, clouds, and stars. Within minutes, the kids will cheer like baby boomers at a McCartney concert as their beloved TV playmate and Baby Bop dance and sing though clap-along, sing-along monster classics including "Mr. Knickerbocker," "If You're Happy and You Know It," and (of course) "I Love You." Following the very pleasing and thoughtful show and a chance to meet Barney up close, you exit to an elaborate play area with hands-on activities—a water harp, wood-pipe xylophone, and musical rocks—that propel the already excited kids to even greater heights. **For people with disabilities:** The theater is equipped for assisted-listening devices and is wheelchair accessible. ■TIP➔ Arrive 10–15 minutes early for a good seat—up close and in the center. Express Passes may be used here. ⊠ *Woody Woodpecker's KidZone, Universal Studios* ⊕ *www. universalorlando.com* ⟳ *Duration: 20 mins. Crowds: Light. Audience: Small kids.*

E.T. Adventure. This well-meaning, circa 1990, ride is looking (and even smelling) a little tired, although you may still get a kick out of the take on Steven Spielberg's *E.T.* Once Spielberg himself advises you that it's your mission to help E.T. return to his planet, you board a bicycle mounted on a movable platform and fly 3 million light years from Earth, past a squadron of policemen and FBI agents to reach E.T.'s home. Here colorful characters climb on vines, play xylophones, and swing on branches in what looks like an alien Burning Man festival. Listen very closely for the payoff: having given your name to a host at the start of the ride, E.T. is supposed to bid you a personalized good-bye. This ride isn't suitable for guests with heart, back, neck, or motion-sickness problems. **For people with**

UNIVERSAL STUDIOS GROWN-UP TOUR

At Universal Studios, Hollywood is just a short walk from New York City; San Francisco is a stone's throw from the fictional Middle America of Springfield. The genius here is in the details, so take your time and notice the secondhand items in the windows of New York shops, for instance, or the cable-car tracks running through San Francisco.

SOUTH SIDE

Upon entering, don't head straight into Production Central; instead, turn right—onto Rodeo Drive. In a few steps you're in the heart of **Hollywood.** If you're tempted to stop for a soda at Schwab's or burger at Mel's, try to schedule your meal in time to catch Universal Orlando's Horror Make-Up Show just down the street. As you continue past the lovely Garden of Allah bungalows (that look as if they were actually moved from Tinseltown), you'll see the entrance to Woody Woodpecker's KidZone, which most adults will be happy to skip.

After this, it's Springfield: Home of the Simpsons. Although **The Simpsons Ride** is a thrill, so is the amazing pop art that sets the stage for it. The facade is decorated like a carnival, with games of chance bordering the towering face of Krusty the Clown. Watch for the kiosk that sells Squishees ("America's favorite icy goo"), and take your time

along Fast Food Boulevard where you'll have plenty of food ops—and photo ops—including Lard Lad (of donut fame), Moe's Tavern, and Bumblebee Man's taco truck. Really.

NORTH SIDE

The facade of this Wizarding World looks like a fashionable London district, but be sure to look for a broken brick wall that masks the entrance to **Diagon Alley,** a complete re-creation of Harry Potter's world.

Cobblestone streets, redbrick buildings, and a waterfront inspired by Fisherman's Wharf create **San Francisco**, which is home to the new-in-2018 attraction Fast & Furious: Supercharged.

With narrow alleys, fire escapes, a Chinese laundry, pawnshops, secondhand stores, offices, Italian restaurants, and an Irish pub, **New York** captures the character of nearly every borough. Round a corner and you'll even see the Guggenheim Museum. It's an amazing assemblage of styles, with clever signage, props, effects (and attractions like Revenge of the Mummy and Race Through New York Starring Jimmy Fallon).

Completing the circle you'll arrive in **Production Central,** where several blocks of soundstages present attractions that bring movies and television to life.

disabilities: Guests with mobility issues must be in a standard-size wheelchair or transfer to a ride vehicle. Service animals aren't permitted. There's some sudden tilting and accelerating, but those for whom these movements are a concern can ride in E.T.'s orbs (spaceships) instead of the flying bicycles. ■TIP→ **Use Universal Express Pass or come early.** ✉ *Woody Woodpecker's KidZone, Universal Studios* ⊕ *www.universalorlando.com* ☞ *Duration: 5 mins. Crowds: Moderate to heavy. Audience: All ages. Height requirement: 34 inches.*

Fievel's Playland. Based on the Spielberg animated film *An American Tail*, this playground features larger-than-life props and sets designed to make everyone feel mouse-size. An ingenious collection of massive boots, cans, and other ordinary objects disguise tunnel slides, water play areas, ball crawls, and a gigantic net-climb equipped with tubes, ladders, and rope bridges. A harmonica slide plays music when you slide along the openings, and a 200-foot waterslide gives kids (and a parent if so desired) a chance to swoop down in Fievel's signature sardine can. It should keep the kids entertained for hours. The downside? You might have to build one of these for your backyard when you get home. **For people with disabilities:** Unfortunately, this ride isn't fully accessible to people using wheelchairs, although an elevator can transport wheelchairs to the top of the waterslide. ■TIP➜ On hot days, come after supper to avoid waits for the waterslide. Kids will get drenched; stash a bathing suit or change of clothing in a nearby locker. ⊠ *Woody Woodpecker's KidZone, Universal Studios* ⊕ *www.universalorlando. com* ⌁ *Duration: Up to you. Crowds: Light to moderate. Audience: Small kids.*

Woody Woodpecker's Nuthouse Coaster. Unlike the maniacal coasters that put you through zero-g rolls and inversions, this is a low-speed, mild-thrill version (top speed 22 mph) that makes it a safe bet for younger kids (who must be at least 36 inches tall) and action-phobic adults. It races (a relative term) through a structure that looks like a gadget-filled factory; the cars are shipping crates—some labeled "mixed nuts," others "salted nuts," and some tagged "certifiably nuts." Children generally love this low-level introduction to thrill rides (which is duplicated at Flight of the Hippogriff at the Wizarding World of Harry Potter). **For people with disabilities:** Guests using wheelchairs must transfer to a ride vehicle. ■TIP➜ Use Express Pass and/or come at park closing, when most little ones have gone home. ⊠ *Woody Woodpecker's KidZone, Universal Studios* ⊕ *www.universalorlando.com* ⌁ *Duration: 1½ mins. Crowds: Moderate to heavy. Audience: Small kids.*

HOLLYWOOD

The quintessential tribute to the golden age of the silver screen, this area to the right of the park entrance celebrates icons like the Brown Derby, Schwab's Pharmacy, and art deco Hollywood.

Fodor's Choice ★ **Universal Orlando's Horror Make-Up Show.** This funny, highly entertaining show begins in an intriguingly creepy preshow area where masks, props, and rubber skeletons from classic and contemporary horror films and tributes to great makeup artists like Lon Chaney, Rick Baker, and Jack Pierce make a great backdrop for a horrifying family photo. Once inside the theater, your host brings out a special-effects expert who describes and shares some secrets about what goes into (and oozes out of) creepy movie effects (e.g., corn syrup and food coloring make for a dandy blood substitute). Despite the potentially frightening topic, most of the audience gets a kick out of the whole show, because the subject is handled with an extraordinary amount of dead-on humor. Older children, in particular, eat up the blood-and-guts stories. One-liners delivered with comedy-club timing, audience participation, knives, guns, loose limbs—all this goes into creating a flat-out fantastic show that entertains everyone. **For people with disabilities:** The theater is wheelchair accessible. Good scripts and good shtick mean that those with visual impairments can enjoy the show. ■**TIP**→ If busy, use Express Pass or come in the afternoon or evening. Arrive about 15 minutes before showtime (doors close immediately after show starts). ⊠ *Hollywood, Universal Studios* ⊕ *www.universalorlando.com* ⌁ *Duration: 25 mins. Crowds: Light. Audience: Not small kids.*

NEED A BREAK

In the heart of Hollywood, **Schwab's Pharmacy** is a re-creation of the legendary drugstore where—studio publicists claim—Lana Turner was discovered. What you'll discover is a quick stop where you can order soda-fountain treats as well as hand-carved turkey and ham sandwiches. The catch? It may be closed off-season.

3

ISLANDS OF ADVENTURE

More so than just about any other theme park, Islands of Adventure has gone all out to create settings and attractions that transport you from reality into the surreal. What's more, no one island here has much in common with any other, so in a way, a visit here is almost like a visit to half a dozen different parks.

IOA's unique nature is first revealed when you arrive at the Port of Entry and are greeted by a kaleidoscope of sights and a cacophony of sounds. It's all designed to put you in the frame of mind for adventure.

When you reach the central lagoon, your clockwise journey commences with Marvel Super Hero Island and its tightly packed concentration of roller coasters and thrill rides. Of special note is the astonishingly high-tech and dazzling Amazing Adventures of Spider-Man. Although you'll get your recommended daily allowance of thrills on this one island alone, you've only just begun.

Stepping into Toon Lagoon is like stepping into the pages of a comic book; which is the exact opposite feeling you'll get at neighboring Skull Island, where you'll find the high-intensity attraction Skull Island: Reign of Kong. The prehistoric battles here set the tone for several attractions in the upcoming island, Jurassic Park, where you'll come face-to-face with dozens of dinosaurs.

You move from the world of science fiction into the world of magic when you segue into the Wizarding World of Harry Potter: Hogsmeade. For the first time anywhere, you—and not just a few fortunate actors— can wander through the magnificently fictional, yet now very realistic, realm of the young wizard and his Hogwarts classmates and tutors. Beyond belief.

But that's not the end of it. In the Lost Continent the mood is that of a Renaissance fair, where crafters work inside colorful tents. It's as pronounced an atmosphere as that of the final island, Seuss Landing,

TOP ATTRACTIONS

AGES SEVEN AND UP

Amazing Adventures of Spider-Man. Get ready to fight bad guys and marvel at the engineering and technological wizardry on this dazzling attraction.

Dudley Do-Right's Ripsaw Falls. Even if its namesake is a mystery to anyone born after the 1960s, everyone loves the super splash-down at the end of this log-flume ride dedicated to the exploits of the animated Canadian Mountie.

Harry Potter and the Forbidden Journey. This ride brings J.K. Rowling's books to life on a wild, virtual reality adventure through Hogwarts and beyond with Harry, Hermione, and Ron.

Incredible Hulk Coaster. This super-scary coaster blasts you skyward before sending you on seven inversions. It's hard to walk straight after this one.

Skull Island: Reign of Kong. The sole attraction on Skull Island is a super-thrilling tram ride through a prehistoric world created through extraordinary theming, exciting motion pictures, and amazing robotics.

AGES SIX AND UNDER

The Cat in the Hat. It's like entering a Dr. Seuss book: all you have to do is sit on a moving couch and see what it's like when the Cat in the Hat drops by to babysit.

Flight of the Hippogriff. Some of the younger Hogwarts "students" will enjoy this low-key coaster in Harry Potter's world.

Popeye & Bluto's Bilge-Rat Barges. This tumultuous (but safe) raft ride lets younger kids experience a big-deal ride that's not too scary—just wild and wet.

which presents the incredible, topsy-turvy world of Dr. Seuss. It's a riot of colors and shapes and fantastic wildlife that pay tribute to the good doctor's vivid imagination.

ORIENTATION AND PLANNING

GETTING ORIENTED

Getting your bearings at IOA is far easier than at its sister park, Universal Studios. Brochures in a multitude of languages are in a rack a few steps beyond the turnstiles; a quick look inside and a foldout map will acquaint you with the park's simple layout (it's a circle). Ahead by the lagoon, boards are posted with up-to-the-minute ride and show information—including the length of lines at the major attractions.

After you pass through the turnstiles, you enter the Port of Entry plaza, a bazaar that brings together bits and pieces of architecture, landscaping, music, and wares from many lands—Dutch windmills, Indonesian pedicabs, African masks, restrooms marked "Loo's Landing," and Egyptian figurines that adorn a massive archway inscribed with the notice "The Adventure Begins." From here, themed islands—arranged around a large lagoon—are connected by walkways that make navigation easy. When you've done the full circuit, you'll recall the fantastic range of sights, sounds, and experiences and realize there can be truth in advertising. This park really *is* an adventure.

TOURING TIPS

Hosts. Just about any employee is a host, whether they're at a kiosk or attraction or turnstile. Ask them about their favorite experiences—and for suggestions for saving time.

Photo Ops. Islands of Adventure posts signs that indicate picture spots and show how best to frame your shot.

Retreat. Explore little-used sidewalks and quiet alcoves and you'll find sanctuaries to counter IOA's manic energy.

Split the difference. If the park's open late, consider splitting the day in half. See part of it in the morning, head off-site to a restaurant for lunch (your parking ticket is good all day) then head to your hotel for a swim or a nap (or both). Return in the cooler, less crowded evening.

PARK AMENITIES

Baby Care: There are diaper-changing stations in many of the men's and women's restrooms at IOA, as well as a nursing station for comfort and privacy at the first-aid station near the entrance. Baby supplies (diapers, food, wipes, and so on) are available at larger stores; ask for those items at the counter, though, as they aren't out on the shelves.

Cameras: Just inside the park, on your right after the turnstiles, is DeFoto's which, like its counterpart at Universal Studios, was primarily a camera and film shop before cameras and film were condensed into smartphones. Nowadays the shelves are stocked with gifts, souvenirs, and drinks, and the staff helps guests with souvenir photos taken by Universal's squad of photographers.

First Aid: There are two health-services/first-aid centers: one at the front entrance inside Guest Services, and another near Sindbad's Village in the Lost Continent. Just look for the Red Cross symbol on the building across from Oasis Coolers (or ask a park host).

Lockers: There are $10-a-day lockers across from Guest Services at the entrance; for $12 a day you can rent a family-size model. You have unlimited access to both types throughout the day—although it's a hike back to retrieve things. Scattered strategically throughout the park—notably at the Incredible Hulk Coaster and Forbidden Journey—are so-called Smart Lockers that are free while you ride (usually up to 75 minutes). Fee lockers, which are available near other attractions like Jurassic Park River Adventure, cost a few dollars per hour and are a useful place to stash backpacks and cameras while you're being drenched on a watery ride or going through the spin cycle on a twisty one.

Lost People and Things: If you've misplaced something, head to Guest Services in the Port of Entry. This is also where park staffers take lost children.

Services for People with Disabilities: Islands of Adventure has made an all-out effort to make the premises accessible for people with disabilities. Most attractions and all restaurants are wheelchair accessible, and all employees attend workshops on how to meet the needs of guests with disabilities. You may occasionally spot staffers using wheelchairs; many employees have had basic sign-language training. There's also a counter in Guest Services where you can pick up assisted-listening and other devices.

You can rent manual wheelchairs ($12 per day) and electronic convenience vehicles (ECVs; $50 per day, $70 for a model with a sun canopy) at the Port of Entry to the left after you enter the turnstiles. A photo ID and a $50 deposit on a credit card are required. Because it's a long way between the parking garages and the park entrance, you may want to rent a push wheelchair at the garages and then upgrade to an ECV when you reach the park entrance. Quantities of the latter are limited, so reserve in advance.

Even when the crowds are heavy, the park's avenues are wide enough to maneuver a wheelchair. Hosts and hostesses will direct you to a special attraction entrance or a special show seating area. Icons on the guide maps indicate which of the shows include an interpreter.

Assisted-listening devices are available for Cat in the Hat, Sindbad, Spider-Man, Incredible Hulk, Doctor Doom, Jurassic Park, and Poseidon's Fury.

Stroller Rentals: You can rent strollers ($15 per day for singles, $25 for doubles) at the Port of Entry to your left after the turnstiles. You can also rent kiddie cars—small ones for $18, and large ones for $28.

Where to Snack: If you decide to pay in advance, you can save a bit of money with Quick Service meals that include, for adults, one meal, two snacks, and a nonalcoholic beverage ($23). The kids' version ($15) includes one kids meal, one snack, and a nonalcoholic beverage. There are many options at Islands of Adventure including the Comic Strip Café (Asian, Italian, American, and fish), Burger Digs (hamburgers, chicken sandwiches, chicken fingers, milk shakes), Café 4 (pizzas, subs, and salads), and Croissant Moon (deli sandwiches, panini, and pastries).

In the Wizarding World of Harry Potter, the signature dining experience is **Three Broomsticks,** where you can order the "Feast for Four" that includes a combination of rotisserie smoked chicken, spareribs, corn on the cob, and roasted potatoes. Other popular options include **Circus McGurkus Cafe Stoo-pendous** (chicken, pasta, pizza, burgers, salads) in Seuss Landing and, in Toon Lagoon, **Blondie's** (jumbo deli sandwiches). **Pizza Predattoria** and **Thunder Falls Terrace** (rotisserie chicken and ribs) are in Jurassic Park, and near the Port of Entry is the comparably more upscale **Confisco Grille,** with its steaks, salads, sandwiches, soups, pasta, and neat little pub. At IOA, the ultimate dining experience is the Lost Continent's **Mythos Restaurant.** Although its Continental dishes change seasonally, the warm, gooey, chocolate-banana cake is a constant.

EXPLORING ISLANDS OF ADVENTURE

MARVEL SUPER HERO ISLAND

The facades on Stanley Boulevard (named for Marvel's famed editor and co-creator Stan Lee) put you smack in the middle of an alternatively pleasant and apocalyptic comic-book world—complete with heroes, villains, and cartoony colors and flourishes. Although the spiky, horrific towers of Doctor Doom's Fearfall and the vivid green of the Hulk's coaster are focal points, the Amazing Adventures of Spider-Man is the must-see attraction. At various times Doctor Doom, Spider-Man, and the Incredible Hulk are available for photos, and sidewalk artists are on hand to paint your face like your favorite hero (or villain). All rides here accept Universal Express Pass.

Amazing Adventures of Spider-Man. One of Universal's most popular attractions, the experience combines moving vehicles, 3-D film with the highest-definition resolution available, simulator technology, and special effects. What does that mean? It means that after donning 3-D glasses, you drive through the streets of New York in a special car that will pitch and roll as you get swept into weird all-encompassing cartoon battle. How weird? When Spider-Man lands on your car, you feel the bump; when Electro runs overhead, you hear his steps. You feel the sizzle of electricity, the frigid spray of water from Hydro Man, and the heat from a flaming pumpkin tossed by the Hobgoblin. No matter how many times you visit, you cringe when Doc Ock breaks through a brick wall, raises your car to the top of a skyscraper, and then releases it for a 400-foot free fall. The bizarre angles and perspectives really do make you feel as if you're swinging from a web. *Do not miss this one.* Youngsters accustomed to action TV shows should be fine, but timid kids won't. Not recommended if you're pregnant or have heart, back, or neck problems. **For people with disabilities:** Equipped for assisted-listening devices. Guests using wheelchairs must transfer to a ride vehicle. ■TIP➔ Come early or at dusk—or most definitely head to the single-rider line. Be sure to check out the wanted posters of Spider-Man villains on the walls. ⊠ *Marvel Super Hero Island, Islands of Adventure* ⊕ *www.universalorlando.com* ☞ *Duration: 4½ mins. Crowds: Absolutely. Audience: All but small kids. Height requirement: 40 inches minimum; between 40 and 48 inches must be accompanied by an adult.*

Doctor Doom's Fearfall. Although the 200-foot-tall towers look really scary, the ride itself is just *kind* of scary (but still pretty cool). Several sets of four chairs wrap around the tower, and you and three fellow guests are seated and strapped in just out of the sight of other riders before the disembodied voice of Dr. Doom tells you the contraption is designed to extract fear he'll collect to use and rule the world. Without warning, all the chairs are rocketed to the peak, which jump-starts a surge of adrenaline as it rises, falls, rises and falls again in a very brief, but quite thrilling, experience. Often it's easy enough to have a second go as you can actually step off and get right back into line again. Guests who are pregnant or have heart, back, neck, or motion-sickness problems should sit this one out. **For people with disabilities:** Guests using wheelchairs must transfer to a ride vehicle. ■TIP➔ Line moves fairly fast, though it's crowded early in the day; come late or use Express Pass. ⊠ *Marvel Super Hero Island, Islands of Adventure* ☞ *Duration: 1 min. Crowds: Light to moderate. Audience: All but small kids. Height requirement: 52 inches.*

Incredible Hulk Coaster. Just seeing this attraction from the sidewalk is a thrill: its cars shoot out from a 150-foot catapult that propels them from 0 to 40 mph in less than *two seconds*. If this piques your interest, get in line where the wait for the prized front-row seats is the

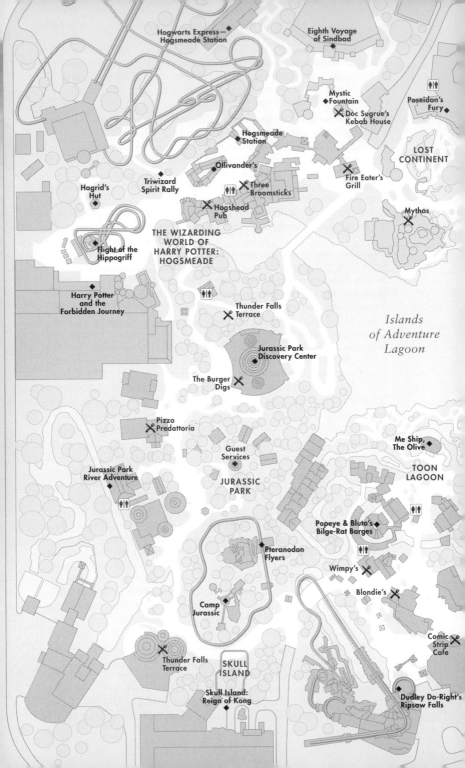

Hogwarts Express—
Hogsmeade Station

Eighth Voyage
of Sindbad

Mystic
Fountain

Doc Sugrue's
Kebab House

Poseidon's
Fury

LOST
CONTINENT

Hogsmeade
Station

Ollivander's

Fire Eater's
Grill

Mythos

Hagrid's
Hut

Triwizard
Spirit Rally

Three
Broomsticks

Hogshead
Pub

THE WIZARDING
WORLD OF
HARRY POTTER:
HOGSMEADE

Flight of the
Hippogriff

Harry Potter
and the
Forbidden Journey

Thunder Falls
Terrace

Islands
of Adventure
Lagoon

Jurassic Park
Discovery Center

The Burger
Digs

Pizza
Predattoria

Me Ship,
The Olive

Guest
Services

TOON
LAGOON

Jurassic Park
River Adventure

JURASSIC
PARK

Popeye & Bluto's
Bilge-Rat Barges

Pteranodon
Flyers

Wimpy's

Blondie's

Camp
Jurassic

Thunder Falls
Terrace

SKULL
ISLAND

Comic
Strip
Cafe

Skull Island:
Reign of Kong

Dudley Do-Right's
Ripsaw Falls

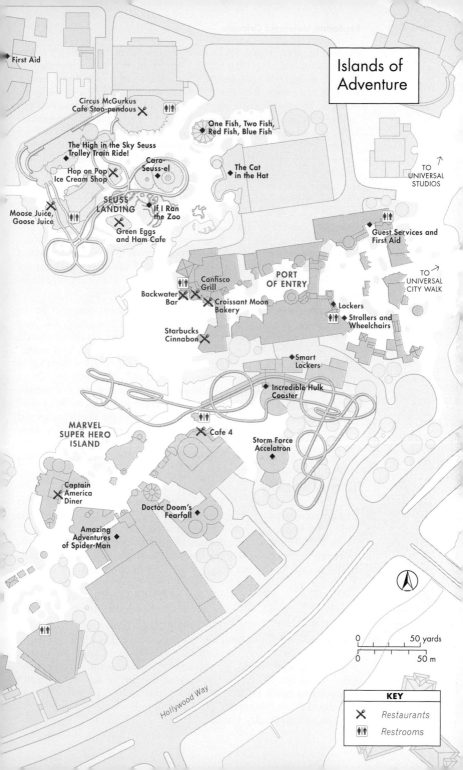

Islands of Adventure

First Aid

Circus McGurkus
Cafe Stoo-pendous

One Fish, Two Fish,
Red Fish, Blue Fish

The High in the Sky Seuss
Trolley Train Ride!

Caro-
Seuss-el

The Cat
in the Hat

Hop on Pop
Ice Cream Shop

TO
UNIVERSAL
STUDIOS

SEUSS
LANDING

Moose Juice,
Goose Juice

If I Ran
the Zoo

Guest Services and
First Aid

Green Eggs
and Ham Cafe

Canfisco
Grill

PORT
OF ENTRY

TO
UNIVERSAL
CITY WALK

Backwater
Bar

Croissant Moon
Bakery

Lockers

Strollers and
Wheelchairs

Starbucks
Cinnabon

Smart
Lockers

Incredible Hulk
Coaster

MARVEL
SUPER HERO
ISLAND

Cafe 4

Storm Force
Accelatron

Captain
America
Diner

Doctor Doom's
Fearfall

Amazing
Adventures
of Spider-Man

0   50 yards

0   50 m

Hollywood Way

KEY

✕ *Restaurants*

🚻 *Restrooms*

longest; however, every seat lets you experience flesh-pressing g-forces that match those of an F-16 fighter. When you're launched into the ride (and we mean launched), you're whipped into an upside-down, zero-g position more than 10 stories up before being zipped into a dive at some 60 mph. You then race along the track before spinning through seven rollovers and making a plunge into two deep, foggy subterranean enclosures. Just when you think it's over—it's not. This coaster seems to keep rolling along well after you've exhausted your supply of screams and shrieks. Powerful. In 2017, the attraction underwent some fine-tuning with an upgraded track and new neon-trimmed train cars that made the ride itself quieter—which seems to amplify the sound effects and screams. Pregnant women and people with neck, back, heart problems, or motion-sickness issues shouldn't ride. **For people with disabilities:** Guests using wheelchairs must transfer to a ride vehicle. ■**TIP**➜ **Come here first (effects are best in the morning and up front). Use Express Pass. Loose articles are not permitted, so stow things in a convenient locker.** ✉ *Marvel Super Hero Island, Islands of Adventure* ☞ *Duration: 2¼ mins. Crowds: Yes! Audience: All but small kids. Height requirement: 54 inches.*

Storm Force Accelatron. On this whirling ride, X-Men character Storm harnesses the weather to battle Magneto by having people like you board Power Orbs. Yes, the story line is that the containers convert human energy into electrical forces through the power of "cyclospin." Strip away the veneer, however, and what you've got seems like a faster version of Disney World's twirling teacups. Still, it's a high-adrenaline ride that's not for anyone who suffers from motion sickness. It's also not suitable for guests who are pregnant or who have heart, back, or neck problems. **For people with disabilities:** Guests using wheelchairs must transfer to a ride vehicle. ■**TIP**➜ **Ride whenever—except right after eating. Use Express Pass when needed.** ✉ *Marvel Super Hero Island, Islands of Adventure* ☞ *Duration: 2 mins. Crowds: Light. Audience: All but small kids.*

TOON LAGOON

The main street, Comic Strip Lane, makes use of cartoon characters that are recognizable to anyone—anyone born before 1940, that is. Pert little Betty Boop, gangly Olive Oyl, muscle-bound Popeye, Krazy Kat, Mark Trail, Flash Gordon, Pogo, and Alley Oop are all here, as are the relatively more contemporary Dudley Do-Right, Rocky, Bullwinkle, Beetle Bailey, Cathy, and Hagar the Horrible. With its colorful backdrops, chirpy music, hidden alcoves, squirting fountains, and highly animated scenery, Toon Town is a natural for younger kids (even if they don't know who these characters are). All attractions here accept Universal Express Pass except Me Ship, The Olive.

Dudley Do-Right's Ripsaw Falls. In the 1960s, Dudley Do-Right was recognized as the well-intentioned (but considerably dim) Canadian Mountie who somehow managed to always save the damsel and "get his man" (that is, foil the villain). But you don't need to be familiar with this character to enjoy this "waterlogged" attraction. The twisting, up-and-down flume ride through the Canadian Rockies begins with your mission to help Dudley rescue Nell, his belle, from the evil, conniving

3

Snidely Whiplash. Tucked inside a hollow log, you'll drift gently down the stream before dropping through the rooftop of a ramshackle dynamite shack. After an explosive dive into a 400,000-gallon lagoon, you're not just damp—you're soaked. If the weather is cold or you absolutely must stay dry, pick up a poncho at Gasoline Alley, opposite the ride entrance, and store other items in a locker. This isn't suitable for guests who are pregnant, experience motion sickness, or have heart, back, or neck problems. **For people with disabilities:** Guests using wheelchairs must transfer to a ride vehicle. ■**TIP**➡ Use Express Pass, and come in late afternoon, when you're hot as can be, or at day's end, when you're ready to head back to your car. Expect to get completely soaked. ✉ *Toon Lagoon, Islands of Adventure* ☞ *Duration: 5½ mins. Crowds: Heavy in summer. Audience: All but small kids. Height requirement: 44 inches minimum; under 48 inches must ride with an adult.*

NEED A BREAK

Blondie's is home of the Dagwood—the jumbo club sandwich that's sold in sections (much too large for any one person to tackle). The eatery also sells cookies and Nathan's hot dogs (Chicago, chili, Reuben, slaw) as well as turkey, roast beef, and tuna sandwiches.

Me Ship, The Olive. Disguised as a teetering-tottering ship, this is actually a fantastic three-story playground. From bow to stern, there are dozens of participatory activities to keep kids busy as they climb around this jungle gym moored on the edge of Toon Lagoon. Toddlers enjoy crawling in Swee' Pea's Playpen, and with high-powered squirt guns, older children and their parents can take aim at unsuspecting riders twisting through the rapids over at Popeye & Bluto's Bilge-Rat Barges ride. The most excited participants are small kids who can't get enough of the whistles, bells, tunnels, and ladders. Check out the view of the park from the top of the ship. **For people with disabilities:** The playground area is wheelchair accessible. ■**TIP**➡ Come in the morning or around dinnertime. ✉ *Toon Lagoon, Islands of Adventure* ☞ *Duration: Up to you. Crowds: Heavy. Audience: Small kids.*

Popeye & Bluto's Bilge-Rat Barges. As with every ride at IOA, there's a story line here, but the real attraction is boarding the wide circular raft with 11 other passengers and then getting soaked, splashed, sprayed, or deluged as the watercraft bounces and bobs down and around the twisting stream. The degree of wetness varies, since the direction your raft spins may or may not place you beneath torrents of water flooding from a shoreline water tower or streaming from water guns fired with enthusiasm by guests at an adjacent play area. Pregnant women and guests with heart, back, neck, or motion-sickness problems should skip this one. **For people with disabilities:** Guests using wheelchairs must transfer to a ride vehicle. ■**TIP**➡ Come first thing in the morning or an hour before closing. Use Express Pass, and stow your items in a locker if needed, since you will likely get completely soaked. ✉ *Toon Lagoon, Islands of Adventure* ☞ *Duration: 5 mins. Crowds: Heavy. Audience: All but small kids. Height requirement: 42 inches minimum; 42 to 48 inches must be accompanied by an adult.*

SKULL ISLAND

If you've ever seen the 1933 classic *King Kong*, you may recall that for its time (and ours) it was an intensely thrilling presentation of special effects and incredible characters. The same is true of this present-day incarnation, which recreates the mood and settings found in the original. Tucked in an area between Toon Lagoon and Jurassic Park, Skull Island presents a singular attraction—and what an attraction it is: an ongoing battle between King Kong and a host of oversized adversaries. Parents should note that this is the only attraction where there's a warning that the *preshow* area may be too intense for kids.

Skull Island: Reign of Kong. As you follow a winding path that leads into the heart of a towering mountain, the mood surrounding this attraction grows more ominous. Navigating darkened corridors that are inhabited by "scare actors" (hence the warning that kids may find the preshow too intense, you pass a proliferation of skulls and then meet an old crone who hints that something unsettling lies ahead—and you'll find that out when you and your fellow travelers enter a primeval world where things get very scary, very quickly. To the eerie chants of "Kong! Kong! Kong!" your guided tram drives through a towering set of doors where the skeletal remains of a great ape greet you. Put on your 3-D glasses and soon other amazing sights will be presented—namely Peg, a steely-nerved scientist whose exploits are the centerpiece of the attraction. Swarms of bats are followed by swarms of pteranodons that lift her up and away, and now it's up to you to come to her rescue. Although Peg works to save herself, she lands in the middle of swamp infested with scorpions and slimy snakelike creatures. As she blasts them with a machine gun, you feel the splash of their guts before the tram speeds to the next scene where velociraptors try taking a bite out of your tram. Those agile, snapping dinosaurs are soon overshadowed by a Tyrannosaurus rex, who is soon overshadowed by your hero: King Kong. With the action taking place on both sides of the tram, you're in the middle of a high-energy, over-the-top battle royale that's thrilling from start to finish. Hint: After riding it once, go back again and wait for a seat on the opposite side to catch scenes you may have missed (they're just as exciting). Pregnant women and guests with heart, back, neck, or motion-sickness problems should skip this one. **For people with disabilities:** Guests using wheelchairs must transfer to a ride vehicle. ■TIP➔ The preshow is part of the fun, so go even if the line is long. But not too long. Otherwise, use the Express Pass. ✉ *Skull Island, Islands of Adventure* ⊕ *universalorlando.com* ↻ *Duration: 5 mins. Crowds: Often heavy. Audience: All but small kids. Height requirement: 36 inches minimum. May be too intense for preteens. Use Universal Express.*

JURASSIC PARK

Pass through the towering gates of Jurassic Park and the music becomes slightly ominous, the vegetation tropical and junglelike. All of this, plus the high-tension wires and warning signs, does a great job of re-creating the Jurassic Park of Steven Spielberg's blockbuster movie (and its sequels). The half-fun, half-frightening Jurassic Park River Adventure (the only attraction here that uses Universal Express Pass) is the stand-out, bringing to life key segments of the movie's climax.

In the Jurassic Park Discovery Center, your kids might just learn something about dinosaurs that they didn't already know.

Camp Jurassic. Remember when you were content with just a swing set and monkey bars? Well, such toys have been replaced by themed play areas like this. Though the prehistoric camp is primarily for kids, some adults join in, racing along footpaths through the forests, slithering down slides, clambering over swinging bridges and across streams, scrambling up net climbs and rock formations, and exploring mysterious caves full of faux lava. Watch for the dinosaur footprints; when you jump on them, a dinosaur roars somewhere (different footprints are associated with different roars). Also look out for the watery crossfire nearby—or join in the shooting yourself. **For people with disabilities:** Much of this attraction is wheelchair accessible (its upper levels probably aren't). ■**TIP**→ Great anytime. ⊠ *Jurassic Park, Islands of Adventure* ☞ *Duration: Up to you. Crowds: Light to moderate. Audience: All ages.*

Jurassic Park Discovery Center. Since it sits to the side of the walkway and doesn't reveal much from the outside, this attraction is often overlooked but may be worth a visit if you have kids who have a passion for dinosaurs. There are demonstration areas where a realistic raptor is being hatched, and where you can see what you'd look like (or sound like) if you were a dino. In the Beasaur area ("Be-a-Saur"), you get a dinosaur's view of the world. There are numerous hands-on exhibits and a dinosaur trivia game, although the museumlike feel seems a little off-kilter at an amusement park. Burger Digs, the casual restaurant upstairs, is a nice place to take an air-conditioned break, and tables on the balcony overlook the lagoon. Step outside and a wide promenade affords a lovely perspective of the entire park. **For people with disabilities:**

The attraction is fully wheelchair accessible. ✉ *Jurassic Park, Islands of Adventure* ⊕ *www.universalorlando.com* ☞ *Duration: Up to you. Crowds: Light. Audience: All but small kids.*

Jurassic Park River Adventure. Your excursion begins as a peaceful raft cruise on a mysterious river past friendly, vegetarian dinosaurs. Naturally, something has to go awry, and a wrong turn is all that it takes to float you into the Raptor Containment Area. Drifting into a research lab, you'll see that it's been overrun by spitting dinosaurs and razor-clawed raptors—and this is when things get plenty scary: straight ahead is a towering, roaring T. rex ready to use his sharp claws and teeth the size of hams to guard the getaway route. Just when you think you're about to become a Cretaceous period entrée, your raft slips down a tremendously steep 85-foot plunge that will start you screaming. Smile! This is when the souvenir photos are shot. Thanks to high-capacity rafts, the line moves fairly quickly. Not suitable for guests who are pregnant or who have heart, back, or neck problems. **For people with disabilities:** Guests using wheelchairs must transfer to a ride vehicle; assisted-listening devices are available. ■TIP➜ Come early in the morning and/or use Express Pass. ✉ *Jurassic Park, Islands of Adventure* ☞ *Duration: 6 mins. Crowds: Heavy. Audience: All but small kids. Height requirement: 42 inches.*

■ **NEED A BREAK** | **Thunder Falls Terrace** is open for lunch and dinner. Beneath towering ceilings in a spacious setting, one side is entirely glass, which makes it a great place to view the plunge at the adjacent Jurassic Park River Adventure. On a nice day, consider sitting outdoors next to the thundering waterfall and dine on barbecue ribs, wraps, chicken, turkey legs, soup, and salads. If Thunder Falls is too crowded, a short distance away are **Burger Digs** and **Pizza Predattoria**.

Pteranodon Flyers. These prehistoric bird-style gondolas are eye-catching and may tempt you to stand in line for a lift. The catch is that this is a very slow, very low-capacity ride that can eat up a lot of your park time. Do it only if (1) your child asks, (2) you want a prehistoric-bird's-eye view of the Jurassic Park compound, or (3) you've been to the park a dozen times and this is the last ride to conquer. **For people with disabilities:** Guests using wheelchairs must transfer to a ride vehicle. ■TIP➜ Crowds are usually perpetual, and since the ride loads slowly, waits can be quite a while. Skip this on your first visit. ✉ *Jurassic Park, Islands of Adventure* ⊕ *www.universalorlando.com* ☞ *Duration: 2 mins. Crowds: Heavy. Audience: All ages. Height requirement: Between 36 and 56 inches tall; taller adults must be accompanied by a child who meets these height requirements.*

THE WIZARDING WORLD OF HARRY POTTER: HOGSMEADE

In mid-2010 Islands of Adventure fulfilled the fantasy of Harry Potter devotees when it unveiled the biggest theme-park addition since the arrival of Disney's Animal Kingdom in 1998. At the highly publicized premiere, even the actors from the Potter film franchise were amazed. Having performed their roles largely before a green screen,

Hogsmeade Village

Hogsmeade is the village that's the home of Hogwarts, the alma mater of Harry, Ron, and Hermione. You may also find it's a perfect representation of the imaginary land you visualize when engrossed in the pages of your favorite Harry Potter books. In the village you can run errands, pick up sundries, and pretend you're really in Harry Potter's world. Send a postcard or letter stamped with a novelty (and very real cancellation mark) at Owl Post before selecting (or being selected by) a magic wand at Ollivanders. If you can't get into Ollivanders due to the line, kiosks and small shops sell an impressive variety of wands—some that are even interactive and come with a chart informing young wizards how to move the wand to trigger flowing water, turn on lights, start a sign swinging, and so on at areas throughout Hogsmeade. Pick up some practical jokes (shrunken heads, extendable ears, screaming yo-yos) at Zonko's, and sample strange sweets at Honeydukes. But the best place to shop for Potterabilia is Dervish and Banges, where there are Hogwarts school uniforms, robes, scarves, T-shirts, and broomsticks—including the legendary Nimbus 2000. Highly recommended is savoring your time here, stopping at the signature restaurant, Three Broomsticks, which serves traditional British fare as well as an assortment of kids' meals, and the Hog's Head Pub, where you can down a pint of Butterbeer (tastes like cream soda, butterscotch, and shortbread cookies) or pumpkin juice (pumpkin, apple cider, and spices). To explore even more of Harry's favorite haunts, board the train to Universal Studios' Diagon Alley. Much more than a train ride, it's an exciting prequel to an equally enjoyable Potter-themed experience.

they had never seen anything like this. Neither have you. It's fantastic and unbelievable. The movie-magic-perfect re-creations of mythical locales such as Hogwarts and Hogsmeade Village are here, while playing supporting roles are a handful of candy shops, souvenir stores, and restaurants expertly and exquisitely themed to make you believe you've actually arrived in the incredible fantasy world of J.K. Rowling. Wands, candy, novelties, and more are unique to this magical land. Expect to be impressed—and to wait in line unless you can use your Universal Express Pass. And if you have a two-park pass, you can board the Hogwarts Express for a delightful train journey to Diagon Alley at Universal Studios.

Flight of the Hippogriff. This kid-friendly coaster is a simple way to introduce your children to the pleasures of g-forces and vertigo. The queue takes you past Hagrid's hut and then on board for a "training flight" above the grounds of Hogwarts Castle. On the brief journey, there are some nice little twists and dips that'll give them a pint-size dose of adrenaline—just enough to please parents as well as the kids themselves. That said, this ride isn't appropriate for people with heart, back, or neck problems or who are prone to motion sickness. **For people with disabilities:** Guests using wheelchairs must transfer to a ride vehicle. ■ TIP→ Use Express Pass. ⊠ *The Wizarding World of Harry Potter,*

Islands of Adventure ⊕ *www.universalorlando.com* ☞ *Duration: 1 min. Crowds: Moderate. Audience: Small kids. Height requirement: 36 inches.*

Fodor's Choice
★
Harry Potter and the Forbidden Journey. Of all of Universal's rides, this is the one that *really* puts you in the movies. In the queue you enter the hallowed halls of Hogwarts, where you are introduced to the founders of the school and the story of the journey. Inside the academy, you'll see the sights you know from the books and films: Headmaster Dumbledore's office, Defence Against the Dark Arts classroom, Gryffindor common room, Room of Requirement, and the greenhouse. You'll also encounter the Sorting Hat, the One-Eyed Witch statue, as well as several talking portraits. Keep in mind, so far all of this has just been the pre-show. Before you reach the actual ride, heroes Harry, Ron, and Hermione arrive and try to persuade you to skip a lecture and follow them on a soaring journey—and so you go. Thanks to a combination of live-action, robotic technology and innovative filmmaking, your broomstick flight brings you face-to-face with a flying dragon and the Whomping Willow before being propelled into the heart of a Quidditch match. You also zip through a dozen scenes and encounter supporting characters Albus Dumbledore, Rubeus Hagrid, Draco Malfoy, and members of the Weasley family. All in all, a fantastic attraction—especially for fans of the series who may feel like they've been written into the script of a Harry Potter blockbuster. Not suitable for those with neck, back, or heart problems. If you're pregnant or suffer from motion sickness, take a pass. **For people with disabilities:** Guests using wheelchairs must transfer to a ride vehicle. ■ **TIP➜ Be patient; Express Pass isn't an option here, so relax and enjoy your tour of the school before boarding the ride.** ✉ *The Wizarding World of Harry Potter, Islands of Adventure* ⊕ *www.universalorlando.com* ☞ *Duration: 50–60 mins. Crowds: Yes! Audience: All but small kids. Height requirement: 48 inches minimum, 6 feet 3 inches maximum. Weight requirement: less than 250 pounds.*

Hogwart's Express—Hogsmeade Station. If you're traveling on the Hogwarts Express for the first time, the trip will keep you under a magical spell so that when you arrive at King's Cross Station at Universal Studios (at Platform 9¾ no less), you're still in a wizarding state of mind. After you've settled into the compartment, you can look out your window and see the village of Hogsmeade and towering Hogwarts Castle from your window. But it's when the train leaves the station that the visual effects really kick in. Hagrid waves goodbye, centaurs gallop beside you, and the Weasley brothers fly by on their broomsticks. The journey lasts about four minutes as Hogwarts gradually disappears in the distance and you travel briskly across the rainy British countryside, truly believing you're actually leaving a land known only to wizards. But wait. When you roll past the streets of London you'll discover the fantasy will continue. When the train stops you're only steps away from the magic of Diagon Alley. ✉ *Wizarding World of Harry Potter, Islands of Adventure* ⊕ *www.universalorlando.com.*

ISLANDS OF ADVENTURE FAMILY TOUR

As you go through IOA, try to pretend that you are not so much a park guest as you are a fledgling explorer and amateur sociologist (sometimes just watching people having fun *is* the fun). Imagine that you're taking in an entirely new world, rather than merely visiting a theme park.

In **Marvel Super Hero Island**, most guests race into the Hulk roller coaster and Spider-Man attractions. Instead, spend some time on the bridge or along the waterfront, where you can watch the the frequent launching of the Hulk coaster and perhaps meet some of Marvel's superheroes.

In **Jurassic Park**'s Camp Jurassic is a series of paths that loop through a prehistoric playground. So why not get lost for a while?

Take time to explore the hallowed halls of Hogwarts and surrounding Hogsmeade village at the **Wizarding World of Harry Potter.** The **Lost Continent,** with its tents and crafters and colorful bangles, is yet another place to stop and take things in.

Toon Lagoon, the less intense alternative to Super Hero Island provides plenty of places to explore, including a marked path that lets you follow the trail of Billy (of *Family Circus* comic fame), who's wandered off on his own. At **Seuss Landing** find a quiet place to sit and spend some time just watching children (and adults). The closest thing here to a fountain of youth is spinning on a carousel, riding on a Seussian trolley, and meeting the fabled Cat in the Hat.

LOST CONTINENT

Just beyond a wooden bridge, huge mythical birds guard the entrance to a land where trees are hung with weathered metal lanterns, and booming thunder mixes with chimes and vaguely Celtic melodies. Farther along the path, the scene looks similar to a Renaissance fair. Seers and fortune-tellers practice their trade in tents, and in a huge theater Sindbad leaps and bounces all over Arabia. This stunt show and Poseidon let you bypass lines using Universal Express Pass.

Eighth Voyage of Sindbad. The story line of this live stunt show is simple: Sindbad and his sidekick Kabob arrive in search of treasure, get distracted by the beautiful Princess Amoura, and are threatened by the evil sorceress Miseria. That's all you really need to know, and it's enough to get the good guy kicking off 25 nonstop minutes of punching, climbing, diving, and leaping his way through the performance. Kids are pleased with the action, and women are pleased with Sindbad. One downside is that it's sometimes hard to understand the stuntmen who (1) aren't exactly actors and (2) lip-sync to a script that's not always as funny as the writers intended. Still you'll probably be satisfied by the water explosions, flames, and pyrotechnics that end with a daring, flaming high dive. Also, the 1,700-seat theater is a nice place to sit a spell and replenish your energy. **For people with disabilities:** The theater is wheelchair accessible and is equipped for assisted-listening devices. Some shows have sign language interpreters. ■TIP➔ Find seats about

15 minutes before showtime. Don't sit too far up front—the experience is better a few rows back. ⊠ *Lost Continent, Islands of Adventure* ⊕ *www.universalorlando.com* ☞ *Duration: 25 mins. Crowds: Light. Audience: All but small kids.*

Poseidon's Fury. This walk-through attraction begins only after a long walk through cool ruins guarded by the Colossus of Rhodes before a young archaeologist arrives to take you on a trek to find Poseidon's trident. Each chamber you enter looks interesting, and there's a story told in each one, but actually very little happens in most of them. Most of the time your group is simply walking through the ruins until the attraction attempts to ratchet up the entertainment for the final scene. That comes after you've walked through a water vortex and entered the final hall where, on a 180-degree movie screen, actors playing Poseidon and his archenemy appear. As they shout at each other, a memorable fire- and waterworks extravaganza erupts all around you as massive waves crash and scorching fireballs fly. This finale is loud, powerful, and hyperactive. Is it worth the investment of time? Meh. Give it a whirl if you've done everything else. **For people with disabilities:** The theater is equipped for assisted-listening devices and is wheelchair accessible. ■TIP➔ Stay left against the wall as you enter, and position yourself opposite the central podium. In each succeeding section of the presentation, get into the very first row, particularly if you aren't tall. ⊠ *Lost Continent, Islands of Adventure* ☞ *Duration: 20 mins. Crowds: Heavy. Audience: All but small kids.*

SEUSS LANDING

This 10-acre tribute to Dr. Seuss puts you in the midst of his classic children's books. This means spending quality time with the Cat, Things 1 and 2, Horton, the Lorax, and the Grinch. From topiary sculptures to lurching lampposts to curvy fences (there was never a straight line in any of the books) to buildings that glow in lavenders, pinks, peaches, and oranges, everything seems surreal. It's a wonderful place to wrap up a day. Even the Cat would approve. All rides here except If I Ran the Zoo accept Universal Express Pass.

Caro-Seuss-el. Ordinary horse-centric merry-go-rounds seem so passé compared with the menagerie on this one: the cowfish from *McElligot's Pool*, the elephant birds from *Horton Hatches the Egg*, and the Birthday Katroo from *Happy Birthday to You!* It's an entire ark of imaginary and interactive animals—indeed, the animals' eyes blink, and their tails wag. It may be a cliché, but there's a good chance you'll feel like a kid again when you hop aboard one of these fantastic creatures. You'll love it. **For people with disabilities:** Modified mounts let guests using wheelchairs ride without having to transfer to a ride vehicle. ■TIP➔ Use Express Pass, and/or make this a special end to your day. Lines move pretty well, so don't be intimidated. ⊠ *Seuss Landing, Islands of Adventure* ⊕ *www.visitorlando.com* ☞ *Duration: 2 mins. Crowds: Moderate. Audience: All ages. Height requirement: Children under 48 inches must be accompanied by an adult.*

The Cat in the Hat. Enter the pages of this classic book and you'll encounter a crazy cat ready to wreak havoc while your mom is out. As you

The Cat in the Hat, Circus McGurkus, and fish both red and blue are among the attractions geared to the under-7 set at Seuss Landing.

sit on a couch that spins, whirls, and rocks its way through the house, you'll roll past 18 scenes, 30 characters, and 130 effects that will keep you on the edge of your seat. You're never alone. The mischievous cat appears balanced on a ball; hoists china on his umbrella; introduces Thing 1 and his wild sibling, Thing 2; and flies kites in the house while the voice of reason, the fish in the teapot, sounds the warning about the impending return of the family matriarch. As the tension builds, so does the fun—and kids love pointing out scenes from the book. This isn't the right ride for anyone who's pregnant; prone to motion sickness; or suffers from heart, neck, or back problems. **For people with disabilities:** The ride accommodates guests using wheelchairs and is equipped for assisted-listening devices. ■**TIP→** Use Express Pass and/or come early or late. ⊠ *Seuss Landing, Islands of Adventure* ⊕ *www.universalorlando.com* ☞ *Duration: 4½ mins. Crowds: Heavy. Audience: All ages. Height requirement: Under 48 inches must be accompanied by an adult.*

The High in the Sky Seuss Trolley Train Ride! Colorful and quirky miniature Seussian trains on separate tracks embark on a slow and pleasing tour that provides an aerial view of the area, with Seusslike narration along the way. You'll roll right through the Circus McGurkus Café Stoo-pendous and along the shores of the lagoon, where you can see the Sneetches as they enjoy the beaches. Kids love trains, and with its cartoonish design they'll love this train even more. A treat for kids (and grown-ups, too!). **For people with disabilities:** Guests using wheelchairs must transfer to a ride vehicle. ■**TIP→** Kids love trains, so plan to get in line, especially if you have young ones. Express Pass is available here. ⊠ *Seuss Landing, Islands of Adventure* ⊕ *www.universalorlando.com*

☞ *Duration: 3 mins. Crowds: Heavy. Audience: Small kids. Height requirement: 34 to 48 inches must be accompanied by an adult.*

If I Ran the Zoo. In this interactive Seussian maze, kids can leave the adults behind and have fun at their level. As they explore the playground, they'll come face-to-face with several of Dr. Seuss's fantasy creatures as they climb, jump, and crawl around them and then push buttons to animate strange and wonderful animals. Park designers have learned that kids' basic needs include eating, sleeping, and getting splashed, so they've thoughtfully added some interactive fountains as well. **For people with disabilities:** The area is wheelchair accessible. ■ **TIP→** If you can talk your kids into waiting, come at the end of your visit. ✉ *Seuss Landing, Islands of Adventure* ⊕ *www.universalorlando.com* ☞ *Duration: Up to you. Crowds: Moderate. Audience: Small kids.*

One Fish, Two Fish, Red Fish, Blue Fish. Dr. Seuss put elephants in trees and green eggs and ham on trains, so it doesn't seem far-fetched that fish can circle "squirting posts" to a Jamaican beat. After a rather lengthy wait for what will seem like a very short experience, you climb into your fish, and as it spins around a center pole, you (or your child) control its up-and-down motion. The key is to follow the lyrics of the special song—if you go down when the song tells you to go up, you may be drenched courtesy of the aforementioned squirting post. Then again, if the guests ahead of you miss their cue, the water's still spraying—and will likely splash you, too. Mighty silly, mighty fun. **For people with disabilities:** Modified mounts let guests using wheelchairs ride without having to transfer to a ride vehicle. ■ **TIP→** Use Express Pass and/or come early or late. Consider skipping it on your first visit. ✉ *Seuss Landing, Islands of Adventure* ⊕ *www.universalorlando.com* ☞ *Duration: 2+ mins. Crowds: Heavy. Audience: Small kids. Height requirement: Under 48 inches must be accompanied by an adult.*

VOLCANO BAY

It may come as a surprise that when you're at Volcano Bay, you're not at a water park. You're at a 25-acre *water theme park*. The distinction is clear when you arrive at the entrance and see detailed South Pacific theming woven into every attraction, every cabana, every locker, every restaurant, and every white-sand beach. It doesn't take much imagination to feel as if you really are on a South Seas island, miles from civilization but somehow surrounded by more than 30 unique experiences. Some guests drop by for a few hours after visiting Universal Studios or Islands of Adventure, but with the park's multidirectional wave pool, sandy beaches, winding river, multirider raft rides, body slides, and other aquatic attractions, you can definitely make a full day of it if you have the extra time to spend.

ORIENTATION AND PLANNING
GETTING ORIENTED

Building on the foundation created by Wet 'n Wild, America's first full-scale water park and, until late 2016, one of Universal's satellite parks, Volcano Bay has given some of the "wettest and wildest" attractions a new twist, adding several other innovative designs and presenting them here in an incredibly well-detailed South Seas setting. But it's not just the attractions that are colorful, lively, and exciting—it's the entire park. You might experience moments of sensory overload from the visuals alone: the towering volcano and the light and water shows within, the multicolored slides and chutes, the torrents of whitewater, and the

TOP ATTRACTIONS

AGES SEVEN AND UP

Ko'okiri Body Plunge. When a trapdoor is sprung, so begins a 12-story plunge from the top of the volcano into the pool below.

Kala & Tai Nui Serpentine Body Slides. Packed with a lot of twists, these twin drops inside the volcano send you through winding, serpentine tubes before you make a splashdown.

TeAwa the Fearless River. More lively than your old run-of-the-mill streams, this not-so-lazy river's swift current and circuitous course takes you past attractions and through the volcano, making it worth some tube time.

Ohyah and Ohno Drop Slides. Riding either of these sloshing tubes is a thrill that reaches its peak when you come to the end of the line. From here, it's a 4 (or 6)-foot fall into a deep pool.

AGES SIX AND UNDER

Runamukka Reef and Tot Tiki Reef The side-by-side play areas are filled with activities and water toys specifically designed for children under 48 inches.

endless parade of people. But don't be overwhelmed. Just take your time, find a spot to settle down, and explore the park at your own pace.

Before you begin, you may detect one noticeable drawback: No parking. Getting to Volcano Bay requires waiting for a shuttle bus to take you to the entrance—but you'll still have to pay $20 to park at the main Universal garages if you aren't a resort guest. That plus the fact you may be carrying a beach bag filled with stuff and sitting on a bus in your bathing suit (and perhaps returning wearing a wet bathing suit and carrying a beach bag filled with stuff) can be a glitch. But once you arrive and pass the turnstiles, that tends to fade away as you turn your attention to the park and the best way to see it.

One way you'll see it is with a wristband. If you anticipated a day when you can lose track of technology, this is not that day. Every guest is given a waterproof "TapuTapu" wristband that can be paired with an account they create online, so meals and merchandise can be charged with a wave of their hand. Even if they opt out of tying it into a personal account, the wristband is still needed to reserve a place in a "virtual line" on most rides. You go to the attraction, pass the wristband by a scanner, and you're shown the estimated waiting time, with the wristband buzzing when it's time for you to return. So although you may be tied into technology, you'll avoid long waits in line.

Once you get settled in and find yourself lazing in a beach chair or reading a book in the shade of your private cabana, the day is yours. Make it as relaxing or exhilarating as you desire.

TOURING TIPS

Tap In. Volcano Bay prides itself on the technology tied to its TapuTapu wearable, waterproof wristband, a device that can assist in multiple ways including the aforementioned ability to save your place in a virtual line. In addition, its TapTu Play feature lets you try experiences throughout the park, such as shooting jets of water at guests floating down the Kopiko Wai Winding River, illuminating images in the volcano's hidden caves, or making whales spurt water at the Tot Tiki Reef. If you're comfortable with the thought of syncing your device to a credit card, use TapTu Pay to purchase meals and merchandise throughout the entire park. Link your entire party's tickets to your account and everyone can use the feature on their own wristbands, unlinking it when you leave the park.

Wanna Cabana? On the sands of Waturi Beach, there are hundreds of free beach chairs along with dozens of "premium seats"—a pair of padded loungers with an adjustable shade canopy, a built-in storage lockbox, and the services of an area attendant, who'll see to your food and drink orders (those start at $30 per day). The most luxurious offerings are private one- and two-story cabanas for between six and 16 guests. Each features padded lounge chairs, bottled water stored in a small refrigerator, complimentary fruit and snack baskets, towels and lockers, and concierge service that brings meals right to your door. There are cabanas throughout the park, with prices varying by season, from around $160 to $300 a day.

Stick Close. If you're a guest at the neighboring Cabana Bay Beach Resort, you can avoid the shuttle bus and extra parking fee by taking a walkway from the hotel to the Volcano Bay entrance. Next to Cabana Bay, the Sapphire Falls resort is also within walking distance; you just need to walk to Cabana Bay to reach the walkway (about 15 to 20 minutes). If you're staying at a premium resort (Hard Rock, Royal Pacific, Portofino Bay), shuttle buses depart directly from the hotels to Volcano Bay.

Tickets to Ride. Like you, every other guest is anxious to get inside, claim their spot, and start their day. So, as at the other theme parks, it's recommended you purchase your tickets in advance (online, at your Universal hotel, or when buying tickets for other Universal parks or activities) so you can start your day as soon as possible.

Early to Rise. By arriving early, you'll have a better choice of the better beach locations and get a lead on reaching the most popular rides and attractions. But don't worry if you're a little late. In that case, just head to the back of the park, where there's plenty more room. In fact, there are water slides, lockers, restaurants, and refreshment kiosks in every part of the park.

Leisure Time. After you've reserved your place in a virtual line, how do you spend that wait time? Volcano Bay suggests several ways, including drifting along the Kopiko Wai Winding River, hanging out on Waturi Beach, taking time to grab a bite, or simply hanging out on your beach chair or cabana. You can also visit other attractions and watch for "Ride Now" signs, jumping into those attractions without losing your place in the virtual line.

Food for Thought. Peak dining times are between noon and 2 pm. Arrive an hour earlier or later, and chances are you'll avoid the long lunch lines.

Liquid Sunshine. In the summer season especially, thunderstorms roll in from the coast—but usually don't last too long. While others pack up their things and go, duck out of the rain and into a gift shop or restaurant until the sun comes out.

Rendezvous. The park is surrounded by winding walkways and sidewalks that branch off toward attractions. Before you get lost, agree on a meet-up point like the visually memorable Dancing Dragons or Kunuku Boat Bars or, even simpler, Guest Services near the entrance to the park.

PARK AMENITIES

Baby Care: A nursing station is available near the entrance, by First Aid.

Photo ops. Volcano Bay is nothing if not a visual wonder, which is one reason there are interactive photo kiosks throughout the park. Take a souvenir picture through your TapTu Snap/My Universal Photo Access feature and those pictures, which automatically link to your account, can be viewed, shared, and purchased later at the Waturi Marketplace.

First Aid: If you require care, tell a host or lifeguard. For more serious issues, you'll find First Aid near the entrance.

Lockers: Three different sizes of lockers are available throughout the park and can be linked up to four TapuTapu wristbands so the entire family has access. Your wristband will also unlock the locker. Without the link, lockers can be paid through cash or credit card.

Lost People and Things: Missing someone? Missing something? The first place to look is Guest Services near the entrance.

Services for People with Disabilities: There are no specific services for guests with disabilities.

Stroller Rentals: There are no stroller rentals in the park, but you're welcome to bring your own.

Wheelchair Rentals: Due to the nature of the park, there are no wheelchair rentals here.

Where to Snack: The range of dining options is impressive, with kiosks and sit-down restaurants flavored with South Pacific-inspired dishes from mahimahi sandwiches to tropical salads to chocolate pineapple upside down cake.

EXPLORING

Hammerhead Beach. If you arrive too late to find a prime spot on Waturi Beach, this smaller, secluded beach near the back of the park may be the perfect substitute. Less crowded, it's between the entrance to TeAwa the Fearless River and the Maku and Puihi Round Raft Rides. ⊠ *Volcano Bay* ⊕ *www.universalorlando.com.*

Honu of Honu Ika Moana. This attraction comes stamped with the postscript "Turtle and Whale," which simply means that when you reach the top you'll find two tubes (the other being the "Ika Moana" of Honu Ika Moana). Similar to other rides where you slip into an inner tube and then ride through a slick channel, the difference here is that you join three others in a four-person raft. Although the speed isn't as fast as single-rider attractions, the sensations are just as enjoyable as the raft sloshes and sweeps around huge walls and rounded corners, into tubes

Universal Orlando's new water park, Volcano Bay, opened in 2017.

and then out again to flop into the final pool. ⊠ *Volcano Bay* ⊕ *www. universalorlando.com* ☞ *Height requirement: 48 inches.*

Ika Moana of Honu Ika Moana. The counterpart to the Honu four-passenger raft is a few feet away in this five-passenger raft. The ride is slow, sloshy, and easy to handle, even when the raft glides around turns and passes over geysers that erupt like a whale's spout. Accepts Universal Express Pass. Wheelchair guests must transfer to raft. ⊠ *Volcano Bay* ⊕ *www.universalorlando.com* ☞ *Minimum Height requirement: 42 inches; under 48 inches a supervising companion should ride along.*

Kala & Tai Nui Serpentine Body Slides. A warning sign that this is a "freefall slide that starts when a trap door is removed" could be a warning to some, an invitation to others. If you're among the latter, then step into the volcano that's the centerpiece of the park and begin your ascent. Scaling what seems like endless stairwells, you'll be sprinkled with water dripping from intertwined blue and green tubes twisting overhead. These are Kala and Tai Nui, which are soon to be your ride home. As you climb higher and higher, occasionally you'll catch a wonderful aerial view of the park (as well as neighboring I–4), a view that reveals just how far you've come—and just how far you'll fall. When you enter your tube, cross your arms, cross your feet, and then just wait for gravity to do its stuff. When the door drops, so do you, shooting down the slick, splashing tube as it sends you into high, banking corners and spinning around for nearly 25 seconds in a thrilling race (with the person in the opposite tube) to a splashdown finish. ⊠ *Volcano Bay* ⊕ *www.universalorlando.com* ☞ *Height requirement: 48 inches.*

Ko'okiri Body Plunge. The towering, steaming volcano commands attention from every part of the park. What commands the most attention from within the volcano itself is this simple, yet extraordinarily effective, experience. It's based on the simple concept that a body remains at rest until acted upon by another force. You step onto a seemingly solid floor that supports your body weight; the "other force" is when the door disappears. That's when the reaction is your body falling through the void and into a 12-story drop that has you flying on a dizzying descent that rockets you right into the splashdown pool. Rinse and repeat. ⊠ *Universal Orlando Resort* ⊕ *www.universalorlando.com* ☞ *Height requirement: 48 inches.*

Kopiko Wai Winding River. Encircling a substantial portion of the park and winding through the lush foliage, this lazy river lets you go with the flow as you drift on an inner tube past tropical surroundings and, occasionally, are sprayed by streams of water triggered by guests along the banks. When you enter Stargazer's Cavern inside the volcano, the scenery changes again—this time to a brilliant night sky. There are several entrance and exit points along the way (some entrances are wheelchair accessible) as well as lifeguards keeping an eye on things. ⊠ *Volcano Bay* ⊕ *www.universalorlando.com* ☞ *Height requirement: Under 48 inches must wear a life vest.*

Krakatau Aqua Coaster. A sign that reads "Greater than any man-made thrill" greets you at this attraction. But is it really greater? You'll find out after you slip into a four-person canoe that speeds down a toboggan-style run, whips around corners, shoots you through dark, enclosed tubes, and then drops you down steep falls again and again and over and over until you're alternately screaming and laughing. A quick 60 seconds later, you plunge toward the finish through a shimmering waterfall. So, yeah, it's pretty great. Accepts Universal Express Pass. Wheelchair guests must transfer to "canoe." ⊠ *Volcano Bay* ⊕ *www. universalorlando.com* ☞ *Minimum Height requirement: 42 inches; under 48 inches a supervising companion should ride along.*

Maku of Maku Puihi Round Raft Rides. It will take several flights of stairs to reach the starting point of this ride, one that pairs you up with as many as five others on a rafting adventure. After settling in, a little push is all it takes to have gravity take over and water wash you into a humongous enclosed tube for a short stretch before you are spat out into the daylight and into a massive basin where your forward motion sends you up toward the rim (but not over it). From here, you wash back down again and slide into another tube before the cycle repeats, taking you through another tube followed by a circular tour of another basin before finally flowing into a calm pool. Universal Express Pass accepted. ⊠ *Volcano Bay* ⊕ *www.universalorlando.com* ☞ *Height requirement: 42 inches; under 48 inches should have a supervising companion.*

Ohno of Ohyah & Ohno Drop Slides. At some point you'll realize that the most thrilling rides at Volcano Bay are ones that involve climbing several flights of stairs. Height is what makes those attractions work, and this is one of them. On your way to the top, you cross a deep chasm and walk across rope bridges before finding yourself at the entrance to the

Ohno tube (Ohyah is right over there). Like its counterpart, you'll slip and slide through a serpentine run until the tube runs out and you're flying out on a 6-foot drop into the waters at the base of Krakatau. Universal Express Pass accepted. ⊠ *Volcano Bay* ⊕ *www.universalorlando. com* ☞ *Height requirement: 48 inches.*

Ohyah of Ohyah & Ohno Drop Slides. You don't need a mat; you don't need a raft; you just need *you* to enjoy the first of two side-by-side body slides that snake around corners and shoot into straightaways on a fast-paced slide to the finish. On this side of the ride, the finish comes with a 4-foot drop into a swirling pool. Oh yeah! Universal Express Pass accepted. ⊠ *Volcano Bay* ⊕ *www.universalorlando.com* ☞ *Height requirement: 48 inches.*

Puihi of Maku Puihi Round Raft Rides. Like its neighbor Maku, this multiperson rafting ride follows a similar journey but one that includes a few different twists and turns—primarily one that includes a moment of zero-gravity hang time as you spring out of an immense funnel. The twists keep coming as you cling to the raft handles as you rock and roll to a spectacular splash finish. Universal Express Pass accepted. ⊠ *Volcano Bay* ⊕ *www.universalorlando.com* ☞ *Height requirement: 42 inches; under 48 inches should have a supervising companion..*

Puka Uli Lagoon. A relaxing place for families, this small leisure pool is relatively secluded from the park's most active areas (albeit beside the splashdown pool of the Ohyah and Ohno slides) and includes elements that kids will appreciate—namely jets of water they can spray and tropical bongo drums they can beat. Wheelchair guests can transfer into pool. ⊠ *Volcano Bay* ⊕ *www.universalorlando.com* ☞ *Height requirement: Life vest required for under 48 inches.*

Punga Racers. For some friendly family competition, grab a mat and pick a lane. There are four tracks on this attraction, and once you have your mat you'll launch yourself into a tube that twists and turns and then changes to an open-air slide just to keep things interesting. By the time you reach the end of the watery race, who's the winner? The first racer to cross the line receives a celebratory spray of water. Universal Express Pass accepted. ⊠ *Volcano Bay* ⊕ *www.universalorlando.com* ☞ *Minimum Height: 42 inches; under 48 inches with a supervising companion.*

The Reef. This intimate leisure pool has one of the best views in the park, at the base of Krakatau and beside the clear acrylic tube that carries those who've braved the Ko'okiri Body Plunge. You'll often see people lined up along the tube, watching as guests drop out of sight at the top of the mountain and reappear seconds later as they flash past on their way to a splashy finish. With its own waterfall, this is a nice spot to find a little peace and quiet that's still close to many of the park's main attractions. Guests can transfer from wheelchair. ⊠ *Volcano Bay* ⊕ *www.universalorlando.com* ☞ *Height requirement: Under 48 inches must wear life vest.*

Runamukka Reef. Designed for kids, this colorful, creative aquatic playground gives them plenty to discover through a wide range of toys and activities that'll keep them busy and entertained. There are shallow wading areas, low-pitched slides (that probably seem stupendously huge from their perspective), spray guns, bubbling geysers, and dump cups. Wheelchair guests can transfer into water. ⊠ *Volcano Bay* ⊕ *www.universalorlando.com* ☞ *Height requirement: Under 48 inches require life vests.*

Taniwha Tubes. Two slides are better than one, but this attraction doubles that with four slides that mimic the snaking trunks and twisting roots of puka trees. The tubes alternate in color (green and blue) and they alternate in experiences from channels that are completely enclosed for the entire run to tracks that are enclosed until they suddenly reveal the open air and use your speed to send you up on a high-banked turn. So take it for a spin. Or two. Or four. Universal Express Pass accepted. ⊠ *Volcano Bay* ⊕ *www.universalorlando.com* ☞ *Height requirement: 42 inches; under 48 inches with supervising companion.*

TeAwa the Fearless River. This is definitely not your typical gentle river. The water's fairly shallow in this waterway, but since it flows at a pretty good clip the strong current means life vests are required (and that's on top of the inner tube you're on top of). There are several things to like about this ride, and one of those is its duration. Unlike other rides that are as short as 10 seconds, it takes a good six minutes to completely experience this river ride. In addition, the river flows past various areas of the park, passing beneath bridges and rides and by restaurants from Hammerhead Beach through the volcano and into the Rainforest Village, all of which reveal a new perspective on the village of Volcano Bay. Wheelchair guests can transfer into water. ⊠ *Volcano Bay* ⊕ *www.universalorlando.com* ☞ *Height requirement: 42 inches; under 48 inches with a supervising companion.*

Tot Tiki Reef. Directly across from Runamukka Reef is this shallow-water play area with kid-sized slides, spraying fountains, singing whales, and a miniature water volcano. Guests can transfer from wheelchairs. ⊠ *Volcano Bay* ⊕ *www.universalorlando.com.*

Waturi Beach. In the shadow of Krakatau, the volcano that looms over the park, is this wide beach where chairs are stretched out by the hundreds. Arrive early to claim the best spot, or upgrade by renting a premium seat that includes a sun canopy. Depending on your mood, you can park yourself in a chair and do absolutely nothing, or venture into the water where every so often a set of waves washes across the bay. So the choice is yours: swim and splash, or rest and relax. Or maybe a little of both. Guests can transfer into water from wheelchair. ⊠ *Volcano Bay* ⊕ *www.universalorlando.com* ☞ *Height requirement: Under 48 inches require a life vest.*

CITYWALK

With an attitude that's distinctly non-Disney, Universal has created nightlife for adults who want to party. The epicenter is CityWalk, a 30-acre entertainment-and-retail complex at the hub of promenades that lead to both Universal parks.

When it comes to retail, much of the merchandise includes things you can find elsewhere—and most likely for less. But when you're swept up in the energy of CityWalk and dazzled by the degree of window-shopping (not to mention the fact that you're on vacation and you're more inclined to spend), chances are you'll want to drop into stores selling everything from surf wear and cigars to tattoos and timepieces.

In addition to stores, the open and airy gathering place includes an over-the-top discotheque, a theater for the fabulous and extremely popular Blue Man Group, and a huge hall where karaoke's king. There's a New Orleans bar, a Jamaican reggae lounge, a casual Key West hangout, and the family-friendly Hollywood Drive-In Golf, a pair of fun-filled 1950s sci-fi movie–themed miniature golf courses. On weeknights you find families and conventioneers; weekends a decidedly younger crowd parties until the wee hours. If you arrive before 6 pm be prepared to pay $20 for parking; after 6 the parking fee drops to nothing. Now the money you save can be invested in a Party Pass, the one-price-all-clubs admission that starts at $11.99. You can upgrade to a Party Pass-and-a-Movie for $15, a Party Pass-and-a-Meal for $21, a Movie-and-a-Meal for $21.95, or a Meal-and-a-Mini-Golf Deal for $23.95.

At AMC Universal Cineplex, with its 20 screens (including IMAX), there's certain to be something you like—including nightly midnight movies. Call for showtimes or other information. ☎ *407/354–3374 (showtimes only), 407/363–8000 (Universal Orlando main line)* ⊕ *www.universalorlando.com.*

EXPLORING ORLANDO AND ENVIRONS

WELCOME TO
ORLANDO AND ENVIRONS

TOP REASONS
TO GO

★ **Liberal Arts:** Orlando's theaters host symphony orchestras, Broadway road shows, and local thespians of all types. Jazz, blues, world music, and rock are all part of the music scene. Area museums showcase folk art, Tiffany glass, and 14th- through 20th-century European and American paintings.

★ **The Sciences:** The revamped Orlando Science Center has many worthwhile exhibits. At WonderWorks, simula-tors let you survive an earthquake or pilot a jet. Skeletons: Museum of Osteology chills and delights kids with displays of 500 real animal skeletons.

★ **Cultivated Spaces:** Gardens devoted to his-torical blooms, camellias, azaleas, and roses are among the more refined outdoor offerings.

★ **Wild Places:** Experience Gatorland or see rescued raptors at the Audubon Center for Birds of Prey. Fish, boat, or swim in Wekiwa Springs State Park or Ocala National Forest.

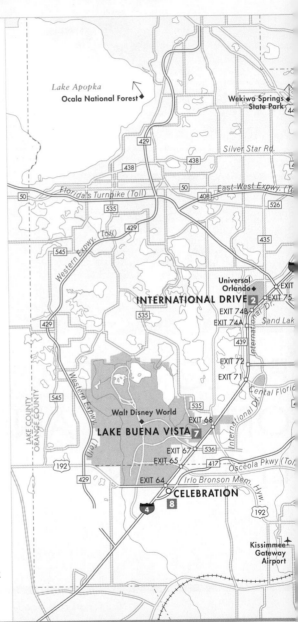

4

1 Central Orlando. Orlando has a thriving Downtown and bustling residential neighborhoods.

2 International Drive. Called "I-Drive," this conduit is lined with hotels, chain restaurants, and attractions.

3 South Orlando. South Orlando is the dynamic home of Lake Nona, the fastest-growing community in Florida.

4 Sand Lake Road. The eastern side bisects I-Drive; the west has been dubbed "Restaurant Row."

5 Winter Park. Winter Park left its bedroom-community beginnings a long time ago and now attracts tourists, wealthy shoppers, and a hip dining crowd.

6 Kissimmee. Kissimmee offers chain restaurants, cheap motels, and traffic, but the sprawl hides an attractive and historic downtown.

7 Lake Buena Vista. Immediately adjacent to Disney, Lake Buena Vista has a host of chain restaurants as well as a few hotels.

8 Celebration. Walt Disney's original residential concept for Epcot has emerged farther south with a small-town-feeling center.

Updated by
Joseph Hayes

Most Orlando locals look at the theme parks as they would a unruly neighbors: they're big and loud, but they keep a nice lawn (and they secretly love them). Central Florida's many theme parks can become overpowering for even the most enthusiastic visitor, and that's when an excursion into the "other" Orlando—the one the locals know and love—is in order.

Orlando is a diverse town. The Downtown area, though small, is dynamic, thanks to an ever-changing skyline of high-rises, sports venues, museums, restaurants, nightspots, a history museum, and several annual cultural events—including film festivals and the popular Orlando International Fringe Theater Festival. Downtown also has a central green, Lake Eola Park, which offers a respite from otherwise frantic touring. Neighborhoods such as Thornton Park (great for dining), hipster Audubon Park, and upscale suburban town Winter Park are fun to wander. Not too far to the north, you can come in contact with natural Florida in Maitland and Wekiwa Springs—its manatees, gators, and crystal clear waters in spring-fed lakes.

Closer to the theme-park action, International Drive, the hub of resort and conference hotels, offers big restaurants and even bigger outlet-mall bargains. Sand Lake Road, between the two, is Orlando's Restaurant Row, with plenty of exciting dining prospects.

If museums are your thing, charming Winter Park has the Charles Hosmer Morse Museum of American Art with its huge collection of Tiffany glass. While in Winter Park, you can indulge in some high-end shopping and dining on Park Avenue or take a leisurely boat tour of the lakefront homes. But don't forget the city-owned cultural hot spots of museums, theaters, and galleries right in Orlando.

Got kids to educate and entertain? Check out WonderWorks or the Orlando Science Center, where you can view live gators and turtles, or visit I-Drive 360 and its seaquarium, wax museum, and towering viewing wheel. Even more live gators (some as long as 14 feet) can be viewed or fed (or even eaten) at Gatorland, just south of Orlando.

Kissimmee is a 19th-century cattle town south of Orlando that proudly hangs on to its roots with a twice-yearly rodeo where real cowboys ride bulls and rope cattle. The town sits on Lake Tohopekaliga, a favorite spot for airboat rides or fishing trips.

There are ample opportunities for day trips in the immediate area. Mount Dora offers antiquers endless opportunities and surprisingly sophisticated dining; Sanford, easily reachable via the SunRail commuter train, is becoming a hip dining area; and LEGOLAND, an hour south of Orlando, offers a "we can do it" alternative to the Big Three theme parks. If the outdoors is your thing, you can swim or canoe at Wekiwa Springs State Park or one of the area's many other sparkling springs, where the water remains a refreshing 72°F no matter how hot the day. Alternatively, you can hike, horseback ride, canoe, and camp in the Ocala National Forest.

ORLANDO AND ENVIRONS PLANNER

GETTING HERE AND AROUND

Orlando is spread out and filled with lakes, making straight-line surface travel almost impossible. During rush hour, car traffic crawls along the often-crowded Interstate 4 (particularly now that the multibillion-dollar upgrade, expected to end in 2021, has begun, relocating and closing key exits and entrances), which runs to both coasts. If you're heading east, you can also take Route 528 (aka the Beachline), a toll road that heads directly for Cape Canaveral and points along the Space Coast. The Central Florida GreeneWay avoids major highway traffic between Sanford and Lake Mary to the north and Celebration to the south and is a pleasant, albeit expensive, way to approach Disney.

If you avoid rush-hour traffic, traveling to points of interest shouldn't take too much time out of your vacation. Winter Park is no more than 20 minutes from Downtown; International Drive and the theme parks are about 30 minutes away in heavier traffic. Orlando International Airport is only 9 miles south of Downtown, but it will take about 30 minutes via a circuitous network of highways (Interstate 4 west to Florida's Turnpike south to Route 528 east).

LYNX Bus service takes visitors from the main Downtown depot to theme parks, outlet shopping, and even the airport for a fraction of taxi fare. And like most urban areas, Uber and Lyft are ubiquitous, even within the theme parks (and much cheaper than regular taxis).

Contacts LYNX Bus. ⊠ *455 N. Garland Ave., Downtown Orlando* ☎ *407/841–5969* ⊕ *www.golynx.com.*

TOURS
KISSIMMEE
FAMILY **Historic Downtown Kissimmee.** Established well over a century ago, Kissimmee has a story rooted in the founding of the state. It was an important air base during World War II (even a POW camp), and was vital in

the development of the Orlando cattle and orange industries as ranches and a railroad hub. The visitors bureau sponsors chili cook-offs and a Tuesday evening farmers' market. You can learn more on the self-guided audio tour or free map tour available at the Main Street Welcome Station or downloadable from the Experience Kissimmee website. ⊠ *215 Celebration Pl., Kissimmee* ☎ *407/569–4800* ⊕ *www.experiencekissimmee.com/visitor-information.*

FAMILY
Fodor's Choice
★

Kissimmee Swamp Tours. The 60- or 90-minute cruises in high-powered airboats take you through the marshes and swamps of Lake Kissimmee—home to hundreds of species of birds and other critters. ⊠ *4500 Joe Overstreet Rd., Lake Kissimmee, Kenansville* ☎ *407/436–1059* ⊕ *www.kissimmeeswamptours.com* 🎫 *$49–$64.*

WINTER PARK

FAMILY
Scenic Boat Tour. Head east from Park Avenue and, at the end of Morse Boulevard, you'll find the launching point for this tour, a Winter Park tradition since 1938. The one-hour cruise takes in 12 miles of waterways, including three lakes and narrow, oak- and cypress-shaded canals built in the 1800s as a transportation system for the logging industry. A well-schooled skipper shares stories about the moguls who built their mansions along the shore and points out wildlife and remnants of natural Florida still surrounding the expensive houses. Cash or check only is accepted. ⊠ *312 E. Morse Blvd., Winter Park* ☎ *407/644–4056* ⊕ *www.scenicboattours.com* 🎫 *$14.*

VISITOR INFORMATION

Contacts City of Winter Park. ⊠ *151 W. Lyman Ave., Winter Park* ☎ *407/644–8281* ⊕ *winterpark.org.* **Experience Kissimmee.** ⊠ *215 Celebration Pl., Suite 200, Kissimmee* ☎ *407/742–8200* ⊕ *www.experiencekissimmee.com.* **Orlando Visitors Bureau.** ⊠ *8102 International Dr.* ☎ *407/363–5872, 800/972–3304* ⊕ *www.visitorlando.com.*

CENTRAL ORLANDO

A thriving metropolis made of brick-streeted neighborhoods, urban sprawl, quiet lakeside parks and, oh yes, the biggest theme parks in the world and lots of them.

FAMILY
Crayola Experience. One of the company's four "experiences" in the country, Crayola offers a 70,000-square-foot haven of color at the Florida Mall. An overwhelming 25 interactive stations extend throughout the two-floor center, including painting and modeling stations, where tykes can create animals out of clay and melted crayons. Don't miss the younger set's favorite: You Design, a virtual studio for coloring and digitally accessorizing a car or fashion wardrobe before watching the personal design make its debut on a large projected screen. Also be sure to make it a priority to check out the Crayon Factory, where live demonstrations show the crayon creation process from wax to wrapper. ⊠ *The Florida Mall, 8001 Orange Blossom Trail, Central Orlando* ☎ *407/825–9234* ⊕ *www.crayolaexperience.com* 🎫 *$22.99.*

Central Orlando

0   1/2 mi

0   1/2 km

Orlando
Executive
Airport

TO
ORLANDO
INT'L AIRPORT
via Route 436
(Semoran Blvd.)

Bennet Rd.

General Rees Av.

Winter Park Rd.

Maguire Blvd.

Corrine Dr.

Lake
Sue

Lake
Rowena

Primrose Dr.

Washington St.

South St.

Bumby Av.

Hampton Av.

Ferncreek Av.

Central Blvd.

Virginia Dr.

Mills Av.

Colonial Dr.

Mills Av.

Livingston St.

Robinson St.

Summerlin Av.

Broadway Av.

Marks St.

Orange Av.

Magnolia Av.

Garland Av.

Orange Av.

Hughey Av.

Farramore Av.

Lake
Ivanhoe

Lake
Concord

Lakeview St.

Edgewater Dr.

Princeton St.

Orange Blossom Terr.

Spring
Lake

Rock
Lake

Washington St.

Central Blvd.

Church St.

South St.

Orange Blossom Terr.

Tampa Av.

Lake
Lorna
Doone

Colonial Dr.

Old Winter Garden Rd.

Lake
Sylvan

John Young Pkwy.

Mercey Dr.

TO
WINTER
PARK

EXIT 85

EXIT 84

EXIT 83A

Lake
Underhill

438

441
92

441
92

92
441

441
92

438

423

50

50

50

527

527

17
92

408

438

CLOSE UP

Central Florida Art

There are a surprising number of world-class art museums in Central Florida—from Orlando and Winter Park to St. Petersburg and Sarasota; from sublime stained glass to surrealist paintings and folk art to circus folk.

Mennello Museum of American Folk Art, Central Orlando. The Mennello holds the nation's most extensive permanent collection of Earl Cunningham paintings, as well as pieces by many other "outsider" artists. Works by Wyeth, Cassatt, Eastman, and others have made their Central Florida debuts here.

Orlando Museum of Art, Orlando. Contemporary, mid-18th- and 19th-century American art and one of the largest collections of ancient artifacts of the Americas in the South. The museum's collection of Chihuly glass is among the finest in the country.

Charles Hosmer Morse Museum of American Art, Winter Park. Known as the "Tiffany museum," the expanded galleries contain the largest and most comprehensive collection of art by Louis Comfort Tiffany, including stained-glass windows and lamps, blown-glass vases, and gem-studded jewelry.

Snap! Orlando. Artistic, thoughtful, and at times challenging, the two galleries operated by local photographer Patrick Kahn highlight the value of the still frame, with exhibits from internationally known artists and talented newcomers to the camera.

Modernism Museum, Mount Dora. A refined and dazzling private collection of American and international works from modernist artists features the work of George Nakashima and Wendell Castle, as well as that of the more radical group Memphis, including pieces collected by musician David Bowie.

Fodor's Choice ★ **Harry P. Leu Gardens.** A few miles outside Downtown—on the former lakefront estate of a citrus entrepreneur—is this 50-acre garden. Among the highlights are a collection of historical blooms (many varieties of which were established before 1900), ancient oaks, a 50-foot floral clock, and one of the largest camellia collections in eastern North America (in bloom November–March). Mary Jane's Rose Garden, named after Leu's wife, is filled with more than 1,000 bushes; it's the largest formal rose garden south of Atlanta. The simple 19th-century Leu House Museum, once the Leu family home, preserves the furnishings and appointments of a well-to-do, turn-of-the-20th-century Florida family. Admission is free on the first Monday of the month from January through September. ✉ 1920 N. Forest Ave., Audubon Park ☎ 407/246–2620 ⊕ www.leugardens.org 💲 $10.

FAMILY **Lake Eola Park.** This beautifully landscaped 43-acre park is the verdant heart of Downtown Orlando, its mile-long walking path a gathering place for families, health enthusiasts out for a run, and culture mavens exploring area offerings. The well-lighted playground is alive with children; and ducks, swans, and native Florida birds call the lake home. A popular and expanded farmers' market takes up residence on Sunday morning and afternoon. The lakeside Walt Disney Amphitheater is a dramatic site for concerts, ethnic festivals, and spectacular Fourth of July fireworks. Don't resist the park's biggest draw: a ride in a swan-shaped pedal boat. Up to five adults can fit comfortably in each. (Children under 16 must be accompanied by an adult.) The Relax Grill, by the swan-boat launch, is a great place for a snack. The park is surrounded by great Downtown and Thornton Park restaurants and lounges. The ever-expanding skyline rings the lake with modern high-rises, making the peace of the park even more welcome. The landmark fountain features an LED-light-and-music show on summer evenings at 9:30. ⊠ *195 N. Rosalind Ave., Downtown Orlando ⊹ Center of Downtown Orlando* ☎ *407/246–4485 park, 407/246–4485* ⊕ *www.cityoforlando.net/parks/lake-eola-park* ⊠ *Swan boat rental $15 per ½ hr.*

Fodor's Choice ★ **Mennello Museum of American Folk Art.** One of the few museums in the United States devoted to folk art has intimate galleries, some with lovely lakefront views. Look for the nation's most extensive permanent collection of Earl Cunningham paintings as well as works by many other self-taught artists. There's a wonderful video about Cunningham and his "curio shop" in St. Augustine, Florida. Temporary exhibitions have included the works of Wyeth, Cassatt, and Michael Eastman. At the museum shop you can purchase folk-art books, toys, and unusual gifts. The Marilyn L. Mennello Sculpture Garden is always open to the public. Oversized outdoor sculptures include works by Alice Aycock and Barbara Sorensen, shown alongside the 350-year-old live oak tree called "The Mayor." The Mennello is the site of the annual Orlando Folk Festival, held the second weekend of February. ⊠ *900 E. Princeton St., Lake Ivanhoe* ☎ *407/246–4278* ⊕ *www.mennellomuseum.org* ⊠ *$5* ⊘ *Closed Mon.*

FAMILY **Orlando Museum of Art.** Part of the City of Orlando's collection of arts venues, the Museum of Art sits in the Loch Haven Park complex. It exhibits contemporary, mid-18th- and 19th-century American art and an important collection of ancient artifacts of the Americas. In addition to American art created before 1945, and an extensive photography collection, exhibits of African textiles and graphic art from such artists as Andy Warhol and Jasper Johns add to the diversity of its displays. The museum's collection of Chihuly glass, obtained during an exclusive exhibition in 2004, is among the finest in the country. A live music and art social mixer, called 1st Thursdays, runs 6 to 9 pm. ⊠ *2416 N. Mills Ave.* ☎ *407/896–4231* ⊕ *omart.org* ⊠ *$15* ⊘ *Closed Mon.*

FAMILY **Fodor's Choice** ★ **Orlando Science Center.** A new and very popular Kids Town and a new gift shop were opened in 2016, part of an ongoing $30 million renovation of the museum, which opened in 1997. With exhibits about the human body, mechanics, computers, math, nature, the solar system, and optics, the science center has something for every child's inner geek. Traveling shows include an astronaut experience, the science of human anatomy, and the annual interactive technology expo called Otricon.

The four-story internal atrium is home to live gators and turtles and is a great spot for simply gazing at what Old Florida once looked like. The 300-seat Dr. Phillips CineDome, a movie theater with a giant eight-story

The 300-seat Dr. Phillips CineDome, a movie theater with an eight-story screen at the Orlando Science Center, offers large-format iWERKS films.

screen, offers large-format iWERKS films and planetarium programs. The Crosby Observatory and Florida's largest publicly accessible refractor telescope are here, as are several smaller telescopes.

Adults like the science center, too, thanks to events like the annual Science of Wine and Cosmic Golf Challenge; evenings of stargazing in the Crosby Observatory; and the very popular First Wednesdays wine-and-music gatherings. ⊠ *777 E. Princeton St., Lake Ivanhoe* ☎ *407/514–2000* ⊕ *www.osc.org* ⌨ *$20.95; parking $5* ☉ *Closed Wed. (except for First Wednesday evenings).*

FAMILY **Orange County Regional History Center.** Exhibits here take you on a journey back in time to discover how Florida's Paleo-Indians hunted and fished the land, what the Sunshine State was like when the Spaniards first arrived, and how life in Florida was different when citrus was king. Exhibitions cover the history of citrus-growing in Central Florida, samples of the work of the famed Highwaymen painters, and the advancement of the theme parks. Traveling exhibits bring modern technology and art to the museum. Free audio tours are available. ⊠ *65 E. Central Blvd., Downtown Orlando* ☎ *407/836–8500, 800/965–2030* ⊕ *www.thehistorycenter.org* ⌨ *$8.*

SNAP! Orlando Founded by international photographer Patrick Kahn, SNAP! is the leading repository of contemporary images in Orlando. Between the two locations in Downtown Orlando and hipster Colonialtown, the galleries have shown cutting-edge photos from artists such as Shawn Theodore, Roger Ballen, and musician Moby, along with world premiere exhibitions, emerging graffiti artists, and even jewelry makers. The other location is at 1013 E. Colonial Dr., 407/286–2185 (closed

Thurs.–Sat.). ⊠ *420 E. Church St., Downtown Orlando* ☎ *407/286–2185* ⊕ *snaporlando.com* ⊗ *Closed Sun.*

INTERNATIONAL DRIVE

FAMILY **Aquatica.** SeaWorld's water park offers a variety of both single-rider and family raft rides, fast and slow rivers, the enclosed body slide Dolphin Plunge, two massive wave pools and an extensive kids area. With 84,000 square feet of beaches and lagoons, pools and river rafting rides on 59 acres, Aquatica measures up comparably to Disney water parks and Universal's new Volcano Bay water theme park. And with more than 40 water slides, from the gentle Kata's Kookaburra Cove to the freefall experience of Ihu's Breakaway Falls, Aquatica holds its own in water thrills. Kids are attracted to Walkabout Waters, a 60-foot-tall water-soaking jungle gym, where they can climb, slide, and get soaked. The new Ray Rush family raft ride offers multiple high-speed paths through enclosed tubes and transparent spheres. Teens and adults flock to the Dolphin Plunge, where two side-by-side transparent tubes allow you to join a pod of black-and-white dolphins underwater. Various mascot animals entertain throughout the park. Orcas, dolphins, and two entertaining sea lions, Clyde and Seamore, conduct comedy routines daily. There are height requirements of at least 42 inches for some rides, and all visitors need to know how to swim. ⊠ *5800 Water Play Way, International Drive* ☎ *407/545–5500* ⊕ *aquaticabyseaworld. com/en/orlando* ⊠ *$59.99* ⊗ *Closed some days Jan.–Feb.*

The Coca-Cola Orlando Eye. The 400-foot-tall Orlando Eye offers an almost unobstructed view of theme parks, lush green landscape, and the soaring buildings of the City Beautiful from the tallest observation wheel on the East Coast. Only 15 minutes from Walt Disney World and Universal Studios Orlando, the massive Ferris wheel anchors I-Drive 360 and its attractions, including Madame Tussaud's and the Skeletons: Museum of Osteology exhibit. The wheel's 30 high-tech capsules complete a rotation every 30 minutes. Apple iPad Air tablets on board help to locate points of interest throughout the trip, including the nearby theme parks, scenic landscapes, and even the Atlantic coast. Visibility on clear days can be more than 50 miles, reaching all the way east to Cape Canaveral. Rent a private capsule for up to 15 people, with champagne, for a sky-high experience. ⊠ *I-Drive 360, 8401 International Dr., International Drive* ☎ *407/270–8644* ⊕ *i-drive360.com* ⊠ *$27.50.*

FAMILY **Discovery Cove.** The only theme park in Orlando that may be called "exclusive," Discovery Cove offers you an uncrowded, daylong experience of animal encounters with dolphins, otters, sharks, and rays, as well as opportunities for relaxing swims and resort-style amenities. Lockers, wet suits, parking, breakfast, lunch, drinks, and snacks are all included in entry. Right next door to SeaWorld, the park has tropical landscaping, white-sand beaches, waterfalls, and vast freshwater lagoons to tempt waterbabies. The Explorer's Aviary houses hundreds of tropical birds. People come for the Atlantic bottlenose dolphin swimming experiences (which are included with park admission but which have been criticized by some animal rights activists), and you can snorkel

The views from the Coca Cola Orlando Eye can extend to more than 50 miles on a clear day.

with tropical fish and rays at the Grand Reef, hand-feed exotic birds, or just float on the Wind Away lazy river. Add-on experiences, such as using a diving helmet in the Grand Reef, or swimming with sharks, are available for an additional cost, and they often sell out. Prices vary wildly depending on day and package options (there are many). Visitors to Discovery Cove get unlimited admission to SeaWorld and Aquatica for 14 consecutive days around the reservation date. ⊠ *6000 Discovery Cove Way, International Drive* ☎ *407/513–4600* ⊕ *discoverycove.com* ⊠ *From $230; package options can add up to another $185.*

FAMILY **Fun Spot America.** Virtual reality met real excitement when Fun Spot added a VR system to its Freedom Flyer coaster, adding a high-tech element to a park known for wooden roller coasters, go-karts, and twirling teacups. You can see the neon-lit rides from miles away as you approach International Drive. Four go-kart tracks offer a variety of driving experiences. Though drivers must be at least 10 years old and meet height requirements, parents can drive younger children in two-seater cars on several of the tracks, including the Conquest Track. Nineteen rides range from the dizzying Paratrooper to an old-fashioned Revolver Ferris Wheel to the twirling toddler Teacups. Fun Spot features Central Florida's only wooden roller coaster as well as the Freedom Flyer steel suspension family coaster, a kiddie coaster, and SkyCoaster—part skydive, part hang-glide. There's also an arcade. The park's newest addition is the Gator Spot, in partnership with the iconic Gatorland and starring several live alligators and other Florida wildlife; it's a throwback to the old days of Orlando roadside attractions. ⊠ *5700 Fun Spot Way, International Drive* ✛ *From Exit 75A, turn left onto International Dr.,*

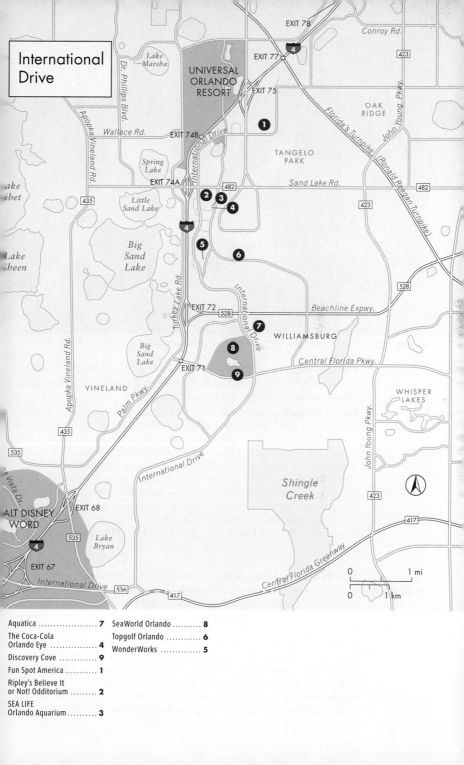

International Drive

EXIT 78

Conroy Rd.

EXIT 77

423

Lake Marsha

UNIVERSAL ORLANDO RESORT

EXIT 75

OAK RIDGE

John Young Pkwy.

Florida's Turnpike (Ronald Reagan Turnpike)

Dr. Phillips Blvd.

Wallace Rd.

EXIT 74B

1

Apopka Vineland Rd.

International Drive

TANGELO PARK

Spring Lake

EXIT 74A

482

Sand Lake Rd.

482

Lake Tibet

435

Little Sand Lake

2 **3**

4

423

Lake Sheen

Big Sand Lake

5

6

528

Turkey Lake Rd.

International Drive

Beachline Expwy.

EXIT 72

528

7

WILLIAMSBURG

Big Sand Lake

8

Central Florida Pkwy.

WHISPER LAKES

EXIT 71

9

VINELAND

Palm Pkwy.

International Drive

435

John Young Pkwy.

535

International Drive

Shingle Creek

423

Buena Vista Dr.

WALT DISNEY WORLD

EXIT 68

417

EXIT 67

535

Lake Bryan

Central Florida Greenway

International Drive

536

417

0 — 1 mi

0 — 1 km

The clear tunnel at Shark Encounter in SeaWorld takes you underwater and underneath the sharks.

then left on Fun Spot Way ☎ *407/363–3867* ⊕ *www.funspotattractions. com* ✉ *$44.95 for all rides (online discounts available) or pay per ride; admission for nonriders free; arcade extra.*

Ripley's Believe It or Not! Odditorium A 10-foot-square section of the Berlin Wall. A pain and torture chamber. Two African fertility statues that women swear have helped them conceive. These and almost 200 other oddities (shrunken heads included) speak for themselves in this museum-cum-attraction in the heart of tourist territory on International Drive. The building itself is designed to appear as if it's sliding into one of Florida's notorious sinkholes. Give yourself an hour or two to soak up the weirdness, but remember: this is a looking, not touching, experience; it might drive antsy youngsters—and their parents—crazy. ■ TIP➜ **Buy tickets online ahead of time, and you can get discounts.** ⊠ *I-Drive 360, 8201 International Dr., International Drive* ☎ *407/351–5803* ⊕ *www.ripleysorlando.com* ✉ *$19.99; parking free.*

FAMILY
Fodor's Choice
★

SEA LIFE Orlando Aquarium. In the shadow of the Orlando Eye and within the I-Drive 360 entertainment complex stands a kaleidoscope of underwater colors, where you can see some 5,000 sea creatures and explore various habitats. Plan to spend the better part of an afternoon exploring the attraction, as all ages delight at the close encounters with the aquarium's sharks, green sea turtles, and jellyfish. With an emphasis on education and conservation, exhibits are playful and informative, with fun features that include a 360-degree ocean tunnel and a children's soft play area. Combo tickets are available for SEA LIFE, the Orlando Eye, and Madame Tussauds. ⊠ *I-Drive 360, 8449 International Dr., International Drive* ☎ *866/622–0607* ⊕ *www2.visitsealife.com/orlando* ✉ *$25.*

4

SeaWorld Orlando. The oldest operating, biggest, and perhaps most controversial marine mammal park in the country, SeaWorld has been anchoring the Orlando Disney-alternative theme park business since 1964. Much has been made of the company's handling of animals, and they've been in "rebuild and repair" mode for several years after attendance and stock prices plummeted. But rumors of a sale haven't kept the park from introducing new, water-themed attractions: the birth of two walrus calves, Ginger and Aku, garnered a lot of attention, as did the virtual reality–augmented Kraken Unleashed coaster, and the world's tallest river raft drop, the Infinity Falls River Rapids. Coaster rides and literal spills are the order of the day, with more swirling, looping, and very wet coasters than just about anywhere. The 400-foot Sky Tower offers a bird's-eye view of the park, while the Mako and Manta coasters skim tantalizingly close to the water; SeaWorld proclaims Mako as Orlando's tallest, fastest, and longest roller coaster. Kraken Unleashed soars to 150 feet while riders dangle their feet from the floorless track and experience a virtual reality, headset-driven, sea-floor experience. The continuing animal attractions focus more on education than performance, but dolphin and orca stadium shows are still a big draw. You can visit the ice-filled home of Puck the penguin in Antarctica: Empire of the Penguin, while Clyde and Seamore's Sea Lion High brings out playful sea lions, walruses, and otters. Shark Encounter leads parkgoers through one of the world's largest underwater viewing tunnels to be surrounded by sharks, while the Stingray Lagoon offers hands-on encounters with stingrays and mantas. Much heralded by the park, marine animal rehab is the focus of the Manatee Rehabilitation Area, where visitors can see an up-close view of rescue operations; Pelican Preserve with bird rescue; and Pacific Point Preserve, which focuses on rehabilitating injured sea lions. ✉ *7007 SeaWorld Dr., International Drive* ☎ *407/545–5550* ⊕ *seaworld.com* ⊞ *$79.99, $20 parking.*

FAMILY **Topgolf Orlando.** A high-tech combination of bowling, golf simulators, and video games, Topgolf lets duffers hit electronic golf balls in climate-controlled, outdoor hitting bays surrounded by giant video screens. The mammoth complex offers kids golf lessons and something for non-golfers as well, with full bars featuring craft beer and cocktails, bar snacks, burgers, and desserts. ✉ *9295 Universal Blvd., International Drive* ☎ *407/218–7714* ⊕ *topgolf.com* ⊞ *From $30 per hour for up to six players.*

FAMILY **WonderWorks.** The building seems to be sinking into the ground—at a precarious angle and upside down. Many people stop to take pictures in front of the topsy-turvy facade, complete with upended palm trees and broken skyward-facing sidewalks. Inside, the upside-down theme continues only as far as the lobby. After that, it's a playground of 100 interactive experiences—some incorporating virtual reality, others educational (similar to those at a science museum), and still others pure entertainment. You can experience an earthquake or a hurricane, land a space shuttle using simulator controls, make giant bubbles in the Bubble Lab, play laser tag in the enormous laser-tag arena and arcade, design and ride your own roller coaster, lie on a bed of real nails, and play baseball with a virtual Major League batter. An Outta Control Magic

Comedy Dinner Show is held here nightly. ✉ *9067 International Dr., International Drive* ☎ *407/351–8800* ⊕ *www.wonderworksonline.com/orlando* ✐ *$29.99; Outta Control Magic Comedy Dinner Show extra (online discounts available); parking $4–$10.*

SOUTH ORLANDO

South Orlando is home to expansive resort hotels, chain restaurants, the headwaters of the Everglades, and not much more.

SAND LAKE ROAD

The eastern side of Sand Lake bisects tourist-heavy International Drive as one of the busiest intersections in town; the west side has been dubbed "Restaurant Row" for its abundance of eateries.

WINTER PARK

6 miles northeast of Orlando, 20 miles northeast of WDW.

This peaceful, upscale community may be just outside the hustle and bustle of Orlando, but it feels like a different country. The town's name reflects its early role as a warm-weather haven for those escaping the frigid blasts of Northeast winters. From the late 1880s until the early 1930s, wealthy industrialists and their families would travel to Florida by rail on vacation, and many stayed, establishing grand homes and cultural institutions. The lovely town retains its charm with brick-paved streets, historic buildings, and well-maintained lakes and parkland. Even the town's bucolic 9-hole golf course (open to the public) is on the National Register of Historic Places.

On Park Avenue you can spend a few hours sightseeing, shopping, or both. The street is lined with small boutiques and fine restaurants and bookended by world-class museums: the Charles Hosmer Morse Museum of American Art, with the world's largest collection of artwork by Louis Comfort Tiffany; and the Cornell Fine Arts Museum, on the campus of Rollins College (the oldest college in Florida).

To reach Winter Park from Downtown Orlando, take Interstate 4 for four miles to Exit 87, and head east on Fairbanks Avenue for three miles to Park Avenue. LYNX Bus Nos. 102 and 443 run from the main depot to Winter Park.

Albin Polasek Museum and Sculpture Gardens. Stroll along on a guided tour through gardens showcasing the graceful sculptures created by internationally known Czech sculptor Albin Polasek (1879–1965). The late artist's home, studio, galleries, and private chapel are centered on 3 acres of exquisitely tended lawns, colorful flower beds, and tropical foliage on the edge of Lake Osceola. Paths and walkways lead past classical life-size, figurative sculptures and whimsical mythological pieces. Inside the museum are works by Hawthorne, Chase, and Mucha. The Capen House, a historic 1885 building, has been moved to the grounds to be

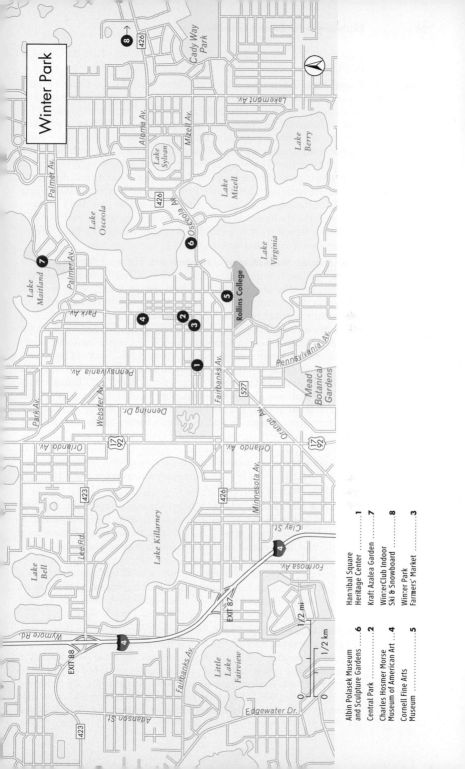

Winter Park

Cady Way Park

Lakemont Av.

Aloma Av.

Mizel Av.

Lake Sylvan

Lake Berry

Palmer Av.

Lake Osceola

426

Osceola Av.

Lake Mizell

Palmer Av.

Lake Maitland

Park Av.

Lake Virginia

Rollins College

Pennsylvania Av.

Fairbanks Av.

527

Orange Av.

Mead Botanical Gardens

Park Av.

Webster Av.

Denning Dr.

Pennsylvania Av.

Orlando Av.

17 92

Orlando Av.

17 92

Minnesota Av.

Lake Killarney

423

Lee Rd.

Clay St.

426

EXIT 87

Formosa Av.

Lake Bell

Wymore Rd.

EXIT 88

Fairbanks Av.

Adanson St.

Little Lake Fairview

Edgewater Dr.

423

1/2 mi

0   1/2 km

used for public events. ✉ *633 Osceola Ave., Winter Park* ☎ *407/647–6294* ⊕ *www.polasek.org* 🎫 *$10* ⊘ *Closed Mon.*

Fodor's Choice ★ **Central Park.** Given to the City of Winter Park by the Genius family (benefactors of the Morse Museum), this 11-acre green spot has manicured lawns, specimen plantings, a beautiful rose garden available for private functions, a fountain, and a gazebo. If you take a seat and listen as the Amtrak passenger train rolls by the west end of the park, it's not hard to imagine how Winter Park looked and sounded in the late 19th century. The SunRail commuter train stops right within the park, giving great car-free access to Downtown Orlando and during the packed art festivals. The Winter Park Farmers' Market draws people to the southwest corner on Saturday morning. If you don't want to browse in the shops across the street, a walk through the park beneath the moss-covered trees is a delightful alternative. ✉ *251 Park Ave. S, Winter Park* ⊕ *cityofwinterpark.org.*

Fodor's Choice ★ **Charles Hosmer Morse Museum of American Art.** The world's most comprehensive and important collection of work by Louis Comfort Tiffany—including immense stained-glass windows, lamps, watercolors, and desk sets—is in this museum, which also contains American decorative art and paintings from the mid-19th to the early 20th century. Among the draws is the 1,082-square-foot Tiffany Chapel, originally built for the 1893 World's Fair in Chicago. It took craftsmen two and a half years to painstakingly reassemble the chapel here. Many of the works were rescued from Tiffany's Long Island estate, Laurelton Hall, after a 1957 fire destroyed much of the property. The 12,000-square-foot Laurelton Hall wing allows for much more of the estate's collection to be displayed at one time. Exhibits in the wing include architectural and decorative elements from Laurelton's dining room, living room, and Fountain Court reception hall. There's also a re-creation of the striking Daffodil Terrace, so named for the glass daffodils that serve as the capitals for the terrace's marble columns. ✉ *445 N. Park Ave., Winter Park* ☎ *407/645–5311* ⊕ *www.morsemuseum.org* 🎫 *$6; free Nov.–Apr., Fri. 4–8* ⊘ *Closed Mon.*

Cornell Fine Arts Museum. On the Rollins College campus, this museum houses Florida's oldest art collection (its first paintings acquired in 1896)—one with more than 5,000 works, from Italian Renaissance to 19th- and 20th-century American and European paintings. Special exhibitions feature everything from Native American artifacts to Soviet propaganda posters. Outside the museum, a small but charming garden overlooks Lake Virginia. The museum is free to visit; free guided tours Sat. and Sun. at 1 pm. ✉ *Rollins College, 1000 Holt Ave., Winter Park* ☎ *407/646–2526* ⊕ *www.rollins.edu/cfam* 🎫 *Free* ⊘ *Mon.*

FAMILY **Hannibal Square Heritage Center.** Almost crowded out by the glitz of new shops, restaurants, and art galleries is the original, once-thriving town of Hannibal Square, one of the oldest African-American communities in the country and home to Pullman porter families to this day. The Heritage Center hosts a permanent photographs and oral-history collection of the significant West Winter Park area. It's a touching and important memorial to a neighborhood that influenced American history. ✉ *642*

The Charles Hosmer Morse Museum of American Art is also known as the Tiffany Museum because of its extensive collection of art by Louis Comfort Tiffany.

W. New England Ave., Winter Park ☎ *407/539–2680* ⊕ *www.hannibalsquareheritagecenter.org* ✉ *Free.*

FAMILY **Kraft Azalea Garden.** Enormous cypress trees shade this 5-acre public park on the shores of Lake Maitland, hidden within an upscale neighborhood, which is alive with heady color from January through March. The thousands of blooming azaleas (hence the name) make a perfect backdrop for romantic strolls, and sunset weddings are common at the park's Exedra monument overlooking the lake. ✉ *1365 Alabama Dr., Winter Park* ☎ *407/599–3334* ⊕ *www.cityofwinterpark.org.*

FAMILY **WinterClub Indoor Ski & Snowboard.** Snow enthusiasts can opt for the truly unique experience of skiing and snowboarding in shorts and a T-shirt at Orlando's WinterClub Indoor Ski & Snowboard, proving that heading south doesn't necessarily cancel out winter sports. The region's first indoor ski center welcomes participants at all levels to come practice and play on these high-tech "endless slopes." WinterClub's interactive Ski Simulator fuses high-definition, large video wall ski runs with a unique chassis that allows skiers to experience the same g-force effects as they would skiing in real life. ✉ *2950 Aloma Ave., Winter Park* ☎ *407/618–1123* ⊕ *www.winterclubski.com* ✉ *From $49.*

FAMILY **Winter Park Farmers' Market.** It's worth getting up early on a Saturday morning and ambling through the local farmers' market (there are actually a couple of local farmers to make the name legit). A favorite for food, flowers, and fellowship since 1979, the market takes over a historical train station and its outside spaces every week, where upward of 85 vendors hawk everything from fresh vegetables to handmade croissants to local honey and dried fruit. Eggs from Lake Meadow Naturals share

Kissimmee's Lake Tohopekaliga (affectionately known as Lake Toho) is famous with fishers the world over. It's also great for wildlife spotting—an especially exhilarating experience when done from an airboat.

space with Luna moth and swallowtail chrysalises from the "Butterfly Man" and chopped pineapple at the Indian River fruit stand. A quick coffee and croissant are a good start to a day of Park Avenue shopping. Park on nearby streets and the public lots on New York Avenue and Morse Boulevard, and Lyman and New England avenues. ✉ *200 W. New England Ave., Winter Park* ☎ *407/599–3397* ◷ *Closed Sun.–Fri.*

KISSIMMEE

18 miles south of Orlando, 10 miles southeast of Walt Disney World (WDW).

Although Kissimmee is primarily known as the gateway to Disney (technically, the vast Disney property of theme parks and resorts lies in both Osceola and Orange counties), its non-WDW attractions just might tickle your fancy. They range from throwbacks to old-time Florida to dinner shows for you and 2,000 of your closest friends. Orlando used to be prime cattle country, and the best sampling of what life was like is here during the Silver Springs Rodeo in February and June.

With at least 100,000 acres of freshwater lakes, the Kissimmee area brings anglers and boaters to national fishing tournaments and speedboat races. A 50-mile-long series of lakes, the Kissimmee Waterway, connects Lake Tohopekaliga—a Native American name that means "Sleeping Tiger"—with huge Lake Okeechobee in South Florida, and from there, to both the Atlantic Ocean and the Gulf of Mexico.

From Downtown Orlando it's easy to reach Kissimmee's main road, U.S. 192, from Interstate 4, Exit 64, just past the last Disney exit.

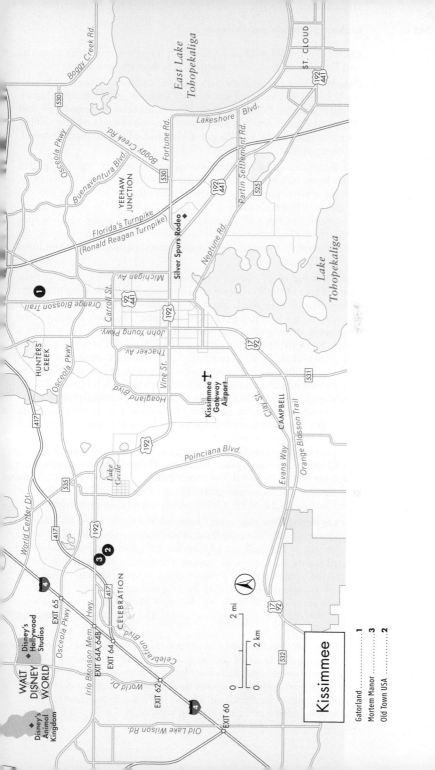

Kissimmee

Osceola Parkway (Toll Road 522) heads directly from Disney property, and Florida's turnpike runs north–south through Kissimmee.

FAMILY   **Gatorland.** This campy attraction near the Orlando–Kissimmee border on U.S. 441 has endured since 1949 without much change, despite competition from the major parks. Over the years, the theme park and registered conservancy has gone through some changes while retaining its gator-rasslin' spirit. Kids get a kick out of this unmanufactured, old-timey thrill ride.

The Gator Gulley Splash Park is complete with giant "egrets" spilling water from their beaks, dueling water guns mounted atop giant gators, and other water-park splash areas. There's also a small petting zoo and an aviary. A free train ride is a high point, taking you through an alligator breeding marsh and a natural swamp setting where you can spot gators, birds, and turtles. A three-story observation tower overlooks the breeding marsh, swamped with gator grunts, especially come sundown during mating season.

For a glimpse of 37 giant, rare, and deadly crocodiles, check out the Jungle Crocs of the World exhibit. To see eager gators leaping out of the water to catch their food, come on cool days for the Gator Jumparoo Show (summer heat just puts them to sleep). The most thrilling is the first one in the morning, when the gators are hungriest. There's also a Gator Wrestlin' Show, and although there's no doubt who's going to win the match, it's still fun to see the handlers take on those tough guys with the beady eyes. In the educational Upclose Encounters show, the show's host handles a variety of snakes. Recent park additions include Panther Springs, featuring brother-and-sister endangered panthers, and the wheelchair-accessible Screamin' Gator Zip Line (additional cost). The park's newest offering is the Stompin' Gator Off-Road Adventure, a cross between a pontoon boat and an off-road monster truck that tours untamed Florida. This is a genuine experience, and you leave knowing the difference between a gator and a croc. ■ **TIP➔ Discount coupons are available online.** ⊠ *14501 S. Orange Blossom Trail, between Orlando and Kissimmee, Kissimmee* ☎ *407/855–5496, 800/393–5297* ⊕ *www. gatorland.com* ⊠ *$29.99; $36.99 all extras; $10 off-road tours.*

FAMILY   **Mortem Manor.** This year-round haunted attraction turns the haunted house on its head. The two-floor, actor- and animatronic- filled house frankly scares the heck out of visitors, with dark tableaux and unexpected frights. For those with unshakable stamina, the Last Ride "burial simulator" reduces the experience down to several sound-filled minutes in an actual coffin; it may be of questionable taste, but visitors seem to enjoy it. ⊠ *5770 W. Irlo Bronson Memorial Hwy., Kissimmee* ☎ *407/507–0051* ⊕ *mortemmanor.com* ⊠ *$15; $5 Last Ride Simulator* ☉ *Closed Mon.–Tues.*

FAMILY   **Old Town USA.** A collection of shops and themed restaurants, Old Town was literally the heart of tourist Kissimmee before Disney moved in. With a new owner and the rickety-but-fun amusement park rides gone (Fun Spot next door takes up the slack), the 1950s theme is continued by magic shows in the Great Magic Hall, a haunted funeral parlor attraction, video game and shooting arcades, a laser-tag hall, go-karts

Go gator! After a visit to authentic, rustic Kissimmee's Gatorland, you'll truly know the difference between a gator and a croc (and you'll see both).

and bumper cars, and long-standing weekly classic car shows. Shopping has become the realm of "As Seen on TV" stores and flea market staples, and dining takes the form of generic Chinese and food court staples. ⊠ *5770 W. Irlo Bronson Memorial Hwy., Kissimmee* ☎ *407/396–4888* ⊕ *www.myoldtownusa.com* ✉ *Free.*

SPORTS AND THE OUTDOORS

RODEOS

FAMILY **Silver Spurs Rodeo.** A throwback to the days when cattle and horses ruled Central Orlando, Silver Spurs claims to be the largest rodeo east of the Mississippi. Started in 1949, the twice-yearly show brings contestants from across the country to compete in bull riding, saddle bronc riding, and barrel racing for $100,000 in prize money. Rodeos fill Kissimmee with cowboys during the third weekend in February and first week of June (the summer rodeo is free). ⊠ *1875 Silver Spur Lane, Kissimmee* ☎ *321/697–3495* ⊕ *www.silverspursrodeo.com* ✉ *$20.*

LAKE BUENA VISTA

The city immediately west of Walt Disney World rings the Disney theme parks with additional lodging options, chain restaurants, and heavy traffic.

CELEBRATION

Walt Disney's original residential concept for Epcot has emerged farther south with designer homes, beautiful lakeside diversions, and a small-town-feeling center. If you are familiar with Seaside and some of the planned towns on the Panhandle, this area will look familiar. There's also a hotel and several restaurants here, so some guests visiting Walt Disney World base themselves here.

EXCURSIONS FROM ORLANDO

Escape from the lights of the big city usually means heading north, west, or south, with visits to Mt. Dora, Sanford, Maitland, Wekiwa Springs, and the building-block joys of LEGOLAND.

4

MAITLAND

10 miles northeast of Orlando, 25 miles northeast of Walt Disney World.

An Orlando suburb with an interesting mix, Maitland is home to both the Florida Save the Manatee Society and one of Central Florida's larger office parks. A number of spectacular homes grace the shores of this town's various lakes, and there's a bird sanctuary and an art center.

GETTING HERE AND AROUND
Take Interstate 4 Exit 90A, then Maitland Boulevard east, and turn right (south) on Maitland Avenue.

EXPLORING

FAMILY **Audubon Center for Birds of Prey.** More than 20 bird species, including hawks, eagles, owls, falcons, and vultures, make their home at this wildlife rehabilitation center on Lake Sybelia. You can take a self-guided conservation tour with interactive exhibits and walkways through the wetlands, or you can call ahead for a private tour ($100), which includes up-close interaction with different birds in the center. There's an earnestness to this working facility, which takes in more than 800 injured wild birds of prey each year. Fewer than half the birds can return to the wild; some permanently injured birds continue to live at the center and can be seen in the aviaries along the pathways and sitting on outdoor perches. From U.S. 17–92, turn west on Lake Avenue, then north on East Street. ⊠ *1101 Audubon Way, Maitland* ☎ *407/644–0190* ⊕ *fl.audubon.org/audubon-center-birds-prey* ☐ *$8* ☉ *Closed Mon.*

FAMILY **Enzian Theatre.** The nonprofit "club" called The Enzian is a cinematic
Fodor'sChoice treasure: first-run, quirky independent films shown in an intimate the-
★ ater, where locally sourced food is served right to your table (yes, there are tables). Home to the acclaimed Florida Film Festival, Jewish, South Asian, and Reel Short Teen film fests—and the very popular outdoor Eden Bar—the theater has plans for future expansion from one to three screens. ⊠ *1300 South Orlando Ave., Maitland* ☎ *407/629–0054* ⊕ *enzian.org* ☐ *$11.*

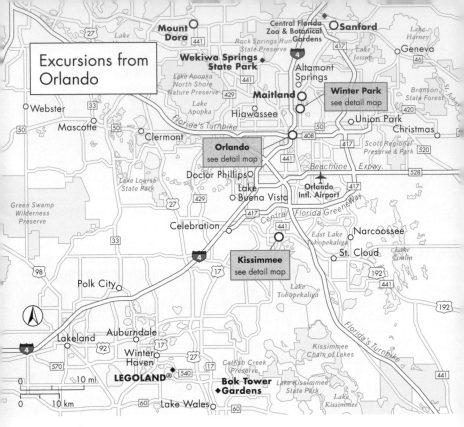

Excursions from Orlando

FAMILY **Maitland Arts Center.** Hidden down a tree-lined side street is this collection of 23 buildings in the Mayan Revival style—with Mesoamerican motifs—that contain an art gallery and artists' studios. Recognized by Florida as a historic site and on the National Register of Historic Places, the center was founded as an art colony in 1937 by American artist and architect André Smith (1880–1959), and it continues his tradition of art instruction and contains a major collection of his works. The center is part of the Art & History Museums Maitland, including the Maitland Historical Museum, the Carpentry Shop Museum, and the quirky Telephone Museum. ⊠ *231 W. Packwood Ave., Maitland* ☎ *407/539–2181* ⊕ *www.artandhistory.org* ⊠ *$9.*

FAMILY **Zora Neale Hurston National Museum of Fine Arts.** This museum is in Eatonville, just a few minutes west of Maitland, the first African-American town to be incorporated after the Civil War. It showcases works by artists of African descent during five six-week-long exhibits each year, with one reserved for up-and-comers. The museum is named after former resident Zora Neale Hurston (1891–1960), a writer, folklorist, and anthropologist best known for her novel *Their Eyes Were Watching God.* This is the home of Zora Fest, a street festival and cultural arts and music event celebrating Hurston's life, which is held each year in late

January. ✉ *227 E. Kennedy Blvd., Eatonville* ☎ *407/647–3307* ⊕ *www. zoranealehurstonmuseum.com* ✉ *Donations accepted.*

WHERE TO EAT

$

AMERICAN

FAMILY

✕ **Kappy's Subs.** Call it a sub shop, a hot dog stand, or a drive-in, Kappy's has been serving all-beef New York hot dogs for more than 50 years—and it looks the part. Behind the scenes, the cooking inside the vintage-Valentine stainless-steel diner car is surprisingly fulfilling, with a giant selection of grilled sandwiches, cheesesteaks, and hot dogs, many made with local ingredients. **Known for:** vintage-diner atmosphere; hot dogs and Philly cheesesteaks; outdoor and car seating. $ *Average main: $8* ✉ *501 N. Orlando Ave., Maitland* ☎ *407/647–9099.*

WEKIWA SPRINGS STATE PARK

13 miles northwest of Orlando, 28 miles north of Walt Disney World.

FAMILY

Fodor's Choice

★

Wekiwa Springs State Park. *Wekiva* is a Creek Indian word meaning "flowing water"; *wekiwa* means "spring of water." The river, springs, and surrounding 6,400-acre Wekiwa Springs State Park are well suited to camping, hiking, picnicking, swimming, canoeing, and fishing. The area is also full of Florida wildlife: otters, raccoons, alligators, bobcats, deer, turtles, and birds.

Canoe trips can range from a simple hour-long paddle around the lagoon to observe a colony of water turtles to a full-day excursion through the less congested parts of the river, which haven't changed much since the area was inhabited by the Timacuan Indians. You can rent canoes in the town of Apopka, near the park's southern entrance.

The park has 60 campsites: some are "canoe sites" that you can reach only via the river, and others are "trail sites," meaning you must hike a good bit of the park's 13½-mile trail to reach them. Most, however, are for the less hardy—you can drive right up to them. Sites have electric and water hookups.

To get here, take Interstate 4 Exit 94 (Longwood) and turn left on Route 434. Go 1¼ miles to Wekiwa Springs Road; turn right and go 4½ miles to the entrance, on the right. ✉ *1800 Wekiva Circle, Apopka* ☎ *407/884–2008, 407/884–2009* ⊕ *www.floridastateparks.org/park/ wekiwa-springs* ✉ *$2 per pedestrian or bicycle; $6 per vehicle.*

SANFORD

30 miles northeast of Orlando, 45 miles northeast of Walt Disney World.

At one time Sanford was the heart of Central Florida—a vital vacation spot and transportation hub on the St. Johns River. But that was before vacationers focused on Orlando and Walt Disney World. In recent years, Sanford has been focusing on its downtown area, increasing the size of its airport (Orlando–Sanford International), which is favored by flights from the United Kingdom, and gaining new trendy restaurants. The Sanford stop on the SunRail commuter train has become popular with day-trippers.

Wildlife-rich Wekiwa Springs State Park is a great place to camp, hike, picnic, canoe, fish, swim, or snorkel.

GETTING HERE AND AROUND

From Orlando International Airport or Downtown Orlando, Interstate 4 to exit 104; follow U.S. 17–92 to West 1st Street.

EXPLORING

FAMILY **Central Florida Zoo and Botanical Gardens.** Sanford has had a zoo since 1923, and although there's nothing here to rival San Diego or New York, there's a certain charm about the place. In addition to 400-plus animals, including giraffes (you can feed them), cheetahs, monkeys, and crocodiles, there's the Zoom Air Adventure Park, with rope bridges and a zipline through the treetops, and the Wharton-Smith Tropical Splash Ground, a mini water playground. The new Florida black-bear habitat and Florida Trek are very popular. The steam-powered 1/5-scale train that puffs around the zoo is as fun for adults as it is for kids. ✉ *3755 N.W. U.S. 17–92, Sanford* ✛ *Take I-4 to Exit 104 and turn left on U.S. 17–92; the zoo is on the right.* ☎ *407/323–4450* ⊕ *www.centralflorida-zoo.org* ✉ *$19.50; Zoom Air and train extra charge.*

MOUNT DORA

35 miles northwest of Orlando, 50 miles north of WDW.

The unspoiled Lake Harris chain surrounds remote Mount Dora, an artsy valley community with a slow-and-easy pace, a rich history, New England–style charm, and excellent antiquing. Although the town's population is only about 12,000, there's plenty of excitement here, especially in fall and winter. The first weekend in February is the annual Mount Dora Art Festival, which opens Central Florida's spring art-fair season. Attracting more than 250,000 people over a three-day period, it's one of the region's major outdoor events.

During the year there's also the annual Taste in Mount Dora event (April), a sailing regatta (April), a bicycle festival (October), a crafts fair (October), and many other happenings. Mount Dora draws large crowds during monthly antiques fairs (third weekend, except December) and thrice-yearly antiques "extravaganzas" (third weekends of January, February, and November) at popular Renninger's Twin Markets, an antiques center plus farmers' and flea markets. The revived Royal Palm Railroad Experience and Polar Express Christmas train runs between the cities of Mount Dora, Tavares, and Eustis.

4

GETTING HERE AND AROUND

Take U.S. 441 (Orange Blossom Trail in Orlando) north or take Interstate 4 to Exit 92, then Route 436 west to U.S. 441, and follow the signs.

VISITOR INFORMATION

Contacts Mount Dora Chamber of Commerce. ✉ *341 Alexander St., at 3rd Ave., Mount Dora* ☎ *352/383–2165* ⊕ *www.mountdora.com.*

EXPLORING

Lakeside Inn. Listed on the National Register of Historic Places, this country inn, built in 1883, overlooks 4,500-acre Lake Dora and is the oldest continuously operating hotel in the State of Florida. A stroll around the grounds, and the sight of seaplanes disembarking guests, makes you feel as if you've stepped out of the pages of *The Great Gatsby.* You can book cruises and seaplane tours that leave from the inn's large dock. ✉ *100 N. Alexander St., Mount Dora* ☎ *352/383–4101* ⊕ *www.lakeside-inn.com.*

FAMILY
Fodor's Choice
★

Modernism Museum. A refined and dazzling private collection of American and international works from mid-20th-century modernist artists features the work of George Nakashima and Wendell Castle, as well as those of the more radical group Memphis; included as well are pieces collected by musician David Bowie. The museum shares resources and a gift shop with the 1921 restaurant across the street; special dining and exhibition events are held throughout the year. ✉ *145 E. 4th Ave., Mount Dora* ☎ *352/385–0034* ⊕ *www.modernismmuseum.org/* 🖃 *$8* ⊙ *Closed Mon.*

FAMILY
Mount Dora Center for the Arts. Local and national artists are highlighted in this lovely art center that grew out of the annual arts festival. The center is a focal point for the community, serving as headquarters of the arts festival, a gallery, a gift shop, and a place to take art lessons. ✉ *138 E. 5th Ave., Mount Dora* ☎ *352/383–0880* ⊕ *www.mountdora-centerforthearts.org.*

WHERE TO EAT

$$$$
AMERICAN
Fodor's Choice
★

✕ **1921 by Norman Van Aken.** Van Aken, the James Beard Award–winning "Father of New Florida Cuisine," took a risk by opening an ambitious restaurant in a quiet Florida town, but it seems to have paid off. Food that could easily be served in Miami, Chicago, or New York finds its way to tables in this converted tearoom, offering locally sourced

Legoland Florida is a kid-friendly attraction a little more than an hour from Orlando.

ingredients and eye-rollingly good dinner and brunch. **Known for:** new interpretations of Florida cuisine from award-winning chef; locally sourced seafood and chicken; in-house pastry chef. $ *Average main: $32* ✉ *142 E. 4th Ave., Mount Dora* ☎ *352/385–1921* ⊕ *1921nva.com* ⊗ *Closed Mon.*

LEGOLAND

50 miles southwest of Orlando.

From 1936 to 2009, the sleepy town of Winter Haven was home to the Sunshine State's first theme park, Cypress Gardens. Today, the spot holds the world's largest LEGOLAND, 150 acres of buildings built using nearly 56 million LEGOs.

GETTING HERE AND AROUND

Two new hotels, the 152-room LEGOLAND Hotel and the seaside-themed Beach Retreat, have opened here, offering building-block accented accommodations right by the parks, so if this theme park is an important destination, you can save yourself more than an hour of commute time by spending a night or two here. For day-trippers who don't have a rental car, round-trip transportation from Orlando Premium Outlets, on Vineland Avenue, leaves at 9 am and costs $5.

About 54 miles and an hour from Downtown Orlando, LEGOLAND is reached by Interstate 4 West to Exit 48; U.S. 17 to FL540/Cypress Blvd.

EXPLORING

FAMILY
Fodor's Choice
★

LEGOLAND Florida. In addition to its 1:20-scale LEGO miniature reproductions of U.S. cities, the park features more than 50 rides, shows, and attractions throughout 10 different zones, as well as the marvelous botanical gardens from the original park. The World of Chima presented by Cartoon Network invites guests into a fantastical world of animal tribal habitats anchored by an interactive water ride, the Quest for CHI. In Chima's Speedorz Arena, participants compete to win a supply of the mystical CHI energy source. A 4-D movie and Chima-character meet and greets round out the experience.

The Danish toy company's philosophy is to help children "play well." And play they do, as LEGOLAND attractions are very hands-on. Kids can hoist themselves to the top of a tower, power a fire truck, or navigate a LEGO robot. Sights include huge LEGO dragons, wizards, knights, pirates, castles, roller coasters, racetracks, villages, and cities.

The cityscapes in Miniland USA fascinate children and adults, who delight in discovering what's possible when you have enough bricks. Miniland opens with Kennedy Space Center, where a six-foot shuttle waits on the launch pad. Miami Beach features bikini-clad bathers and art deco hotels; St. Augustine and its ancient fort play into LEGO's pirate theme; Key West's Mallory Square is accurate right down to the trained cats leaping through rings of fire. The rest of the United States is not ignored: New York City, Las Vegas, San Francisco, and Washington, D.C., appear in intricate detail. Visitors spend hours looking for amusing details hidden in each city, like New York's purse snatcher.

Among other highlights are Ninjago, where kids battle computer-generated bad guys; LEGO Kingdoms, whose castle towers over a jousting area and a roller coaster where knights, damsels, dragons, and ogres are found; Land of Adventure, where you can explore hidden tombs and hunt for treasure; and the Imagination Zone, showcasing LEGO Mindstorms robots, where a giant head of Albert Einstein invites kids to explore and invent. Things get wild in LEGO Technic, the most active of the park's zones, where Test Track, Aquazone Wave Racers, and Technicycle let the family expend some energy. And the live Pirates' Cove show, where seafaring sailors wearing LEGO suits defend a huge ship from attacking pirates on water skis.

LEGOLAND Water Park features a wave pool; Build-a-Raft, where families construct a LEGO vessel and float down a lazy river; a 375-foot pair of intertwined waterslides that plunge riders into a pool; and a DUPLO toddler water play area. Not to be forgotten, Cypress Gardens, at the heart of the park, preserves one of Florida's treasures. Families can wander the lush, tropical foliage and gasp at one of the world's largest banyan trees. Two on-site hotels offer LEGO-themed accommodations and park packages. ⊠ *1 LEGOLAND Way, Winter Haven* ☎ *877/350–5346* ⊕ *www.legoland.com* ✉ *$94; parking $15; water park $20 additional* ⊙ *Closed Tues. and Wed. during Jan. and Feb.*

BOK TOWER GARDENS

57 miles southwest of Orlando, 42 miles southwest of WDW.

GETTING HERE AND AROUND

Interstate 4 West to Exit 55; U.S. 27 South to Burns Ave. in Lake Wales; follow Tower Blvd. to Gardens.

EXPLORING

FAMILY Fodor's Choice ★ **Bok Tower Gardens.** You'll see citrus groves as you ride south along U.S. 27 to the small town of Lake Wales and the Bok Tower Gardens. This appealing sanctuary of plants, flowers, trees, and wildlife has been something of a local secret for years. Shady paths meander through pine forests with silvery moats, mockingbirds and swans, blooming thickets, and hidden sundials. The majestic, 200-foot Bok Tower is constructed of coquina—from seashells—and pink, white, and gray marble. The tower houses a carillon with 60 bronze bells that ring out each day at 1 and 3 pm during 30-minute recitals that might include early-American folk songs, Appalachian tunes, Irish ballads, or Latin hymns. The bells are also featured in recordings every half hour after 10 am, and sometimes even moonlight recitals.

The landscape was designed in 1928 by Frederick Law Olmsted Jr., son of the planner of New York's Central Park. The grounds include the 20-room, Mediterranean-style Pinewood Estate, built in 1930 and open for self-guided touring. From January through April, guides lead you on a 60-minute tour of the gardens (included in the admission price); tours of the inside of the tower are a benefit of membership.

✉ *1151 Tower Blvd., Lake Wales* ☎ *863/676–1408* 🌐 *boktowergardens.org* 🎟 *From $14* 🕑 *Hours and access to Pinewood Estate vary seasonally.*

WHERE TO EAT

$ SEAFOOD FAMILY 🍴 **Crazy Fish Bar and Grill.** You can enjoy outdoor patio dining at this popular seafood shack in Lake Wales, which was visited in 2016 by Emeril Lagasse for his show "Emeril's Florida." Fresh Florida shrimp, blue crab, and catfish in season are all on the menu. **Known for:** fresh Florida seafood; very casual atmosphere; appearance on Emeril's Florida TV show. [$] *Average main: $12* ✉ *802 Henry St., Lake Wales* ☎ *863/676–6361* 🌐 *www.crazyfishlakewales.com* 🕑 *Closed Sun. No lunch Mon.*

WHERE TO EAT

CHARACTER MEALS

Character meals are larger-than-life experiences that might be the high point of your child's visit to Walt Disney World or Universal. Mickey, Minnie, and more come alive and welcome your kids as if they were old friends.

These meals, ranging from Alice in Wonderland–themed tea parties to Mickey Mouse–hosted barbecues (and everything in between) are unique, one-on-one opportunities where characters pose for pictures and engage with the little ones. Kids adore hugging or getting an autograph from their favorites; even tots who may be shy at first will usually warm up to their most-loved character.

TOP PICKS FOR BREAKFAST
WALT DISNEY WORLD

Princess Storybook Dining at Akershus Royal Banquet Hall, Epcot. Belle, Jasmine, Snow White, the *Little Mermaid*'s Ariel and many more princesses could appear at this medieval castle–styled Norwegian building.

Chef Mickey's Fun Time Buffet, Disney's Contemporary Resort. This breakfast combines space-age Disney styling with Mickey Mouse, Donald, and the gang, plus the ever-popular Mickey-shaped waffles.

'Ohana's Best Friends Breakfast with Lilo & Stitch, Disney's Polynesian Resort. The intergalactic Stitch and his human friend, Lilo, join your family in a tropical setting for this very popular breakfast. Every 30 minutes, Mickey and Pluto join in while kids parade around the restaurant with maracas and wide grins.

UNIVERSAL
Superstar Character Breakfast, Universal Studios. SpongeBob SquarePants, Gru from *Despicable Me,* and E.B. from *Hop* are among the superstars who may stop by to say hi at Café La Bamba every morning.

TOP PICKS FOR LUNCH
WALT DISNEY WORLD
The Crystal Palace Character Meal, Magic Kingdom. A lovely Victorian setting is the perfect place for the old-fashioned and lovable Winnie the Pooh and friends to greet your kids. This is the only meal at which you'll find characters from the Hundred Acre Wood.

Disney Junior Play n' Dine, Disney's Hollywood Studios. The Hollywood & Vine Restaurant brings Disney Channel stars to life. Handy Manny and Special Agent Oso, as well as June from Disney's *Little Einsteins* march around the room, singing and dancing to the delight of their energetic fans.

My Disney Girl's Perfectly Princess Tea Party, Disney's Grand Floridian Resort. Girls ages 3 to 11 enjoy the princess experience here. Dressing up is encouraged, and lunch, featuring tea and sandwiches, is served on china plates. Princess Aurora (Sleeping Beauty herself) will make an appearance. Little ones receive a special Disney Girl Princess doll, jewelry, a ribbon tiara, and a photo scrapbook page.

TOP PICKS FOR DINNER
WALT DISNEY WORLD
Mickey's Backyard BBQ, Fort Wilderness Resort. This dinner show has everything from dancing and foot-stomping country music with Cowboy Mickey Mouse, to finger-food goodies like hot dogs and smoked ribs.

Cinderella's Happily Ever After Dinner, Disney's Grand Floridian Resort. A dinner buffet of worldly cuisine is complete with Cinderella, Prince Charming, and their family (including the wicked steps) making the rounds.

UNIVERSAL
The Kitchen, Hard Rock Hotel at Universal Orlando. Scooby Doo and others appear on Saturday nights. The special Kids' Crib area supplies crayons and cartoon videos, allowing parents to have a break while everyone enjoys their meals.

Trattoria Del Porto, Loews Portofino Bay Hotel. Delectable Italian cuisine will please parents, while Bart Simpson and Scooby Doo may be on hand to distract the kids on Friday nights between 5:30 and 10 pm, which coincides with Pasta Cucina Kitchen, an all-you-can-eat experience where guests create their own pastas.

EPCOT INTERNATIONAL FOOD AND WINE FESTIVAL

For an ever-expanding length of autumn weeks, Epcot hosts the Epcot International Food and Wine Festival, attracting folks more interested in a fine phyllo than a photo op with Cinderella.

(Above) A wine-and-cheese tasting at the Epcot International Food and Wine Festival. (Bottom right) Diners at Epcot's Teppan Edo. (Top right) Marinated strawberries with basil served at the Argentina kiosk.

The festival, which in 2017 ran for a record 75 days, is essentially a compendium of food- and beverage-related offerings, some free with the price of Epcot admission, others costing anywhere from a $3.75 piece of cake to several hundred dollars for extravagant wine dinners. Mixology or cheese seminars compete with cookbook signings by famous chefs, and tapas-size portions of foods served from about 30 internationally-themed stalls encircle the World Lagoon. Throughout the event, Disney and guest chefs host brunches, lunches, and wine-pairing dinners at Epcot and in hotels, some posh, others festive, and yet more T-shirt-and-shorts-friendly. The headliners change annually but might include names like Chef Masaharu Morimoto, Rick Bayless, or the cast of ABC's *The Chew*. The festival's food and beverage lineup changes every year, too, so for more information and to make reservations (during festival season only, generally midsummer through early November), call *407/939–3378* or visit *www.disneyworld.com/foodandwine*.

GARDEN OF EATING

Epcot has expanded the offerings at its annual Flower & Garden Festival, which runs for a staggering 90 days in 2018. The springtime celebration of all things green and floral features more than a dozen outdoor kitchens whose dishes are inspired by produce and fresh foods from around the world, and are served throughout the World Showcase—with paired beverages, of course.

SHOPPING FOR A SNACK

The heart of the Food and Wine Festival—and the most approachable event for hungry tourists on a budget—takes place around Epcot's World Showcase. Ordinarily a miniature world of 11 pavilions themed around one country apiece, the area takes on new life when as many as 36 "international marketplaces" take up residence.

Most of the marketplaces, from Brazil to South Korea, offer a taste of one country, selling approximately three appetizer-size food items and a few beverages that pair well—nearly all for $3.25 to $10 apiece. Indisputably popular creations like the cheddar soup ladled out endlessly at Canada are keepers; regulars might revolt if those were absent at any time. Still, a majority of the menu will change from year to year. Attendees might taste Brazilian crispy pork belly with black beans (paired with Xingu Black beer), Beijing roasted duck bao with hoisin sauce (with vodka "Kung Fu Punch") or chicken with red-eye gravy and griddled corn cakes (with a Florida Orange Groves mango wine).

At a few marketplaces, a certain item is featured instead of a locale. The Desserts and Champagne booth, for instance, pours a bounty of bubbly and special sweets. A craft beer marketplace puts out several regional brews along with complementary snacks like spicy pimento cheese with crackers. And the all-American Craft Beers market often specializes in fare U.S. citizens can be proud of, such as the Zesty Cheeseburger Handwich and Cigar City Brewing's Invasion Pale Ale from Tampa.

Lines tend to get very long, especially on weekends, when locals pour in for their regular fix of foreign fare, so consider timing your tour during the day or on a weekday evening, when most spots have shorter waits. And keep an eye on the budget: those little dishes can add up quickly.

FESTIVAL OF THE SENSES

Several evenings throughout the festival, food and wine enthusiasts clad in cocktail attire saunter into the gala called Party for the Senses. Billed as a "grand tasting," the upscale bash starts booking in July and sells out within days. In a dramatically decorated, high-ceilinged room, 10 to 15 chefs from around the country host as many as 50 food stations, serving a hearty appetizer-size portion of one passionately prepared dish. Some are Disney chefs eager to show their talents, and others are known nationally. Big names such as François Payard, Allen Susser, and Walter Staib have participated. Reserved seating for all guests is now offered, a welcome reprise from the "stand and carry" model. Live entertainment such as acrobats and vocalists gives attendees something to watch while taking a break between bites. Seats in the Wine View Lounge include early entrance and private transport.

Updated by
Joseph Hayes

The dining scene in Orlando was at one time epitomized by a plethora of fast-food fare, but there's been such an explosion of artisanal and locally sourced restaurants over the past five years that there are now seven local chefs and nine international celebrity chefs with James Beard Award nominations around the city. Some of the best restaurants in town can be found in resort hotels and theme-park complexes such as Disney Springs, but if you have the time, explore the local treasures beyond the resorts.

The signs of Orlando's dining progress is most evident in the last place one would look: Disney's fast-food outlets. Every eatery on Disney property offers a tempting vegetarian option, and kiddie meals come with healthful sides and drinks unless you specifically request otherwise. Chefs at Disney's table-service restaurants consult face-to-face with guests about food allergies.

Around town, locals flock to the Ravenous Pig, the Rusty Spoon, Artisan's Table, and other gastropubs where the menu changes regularly; Luma on Park, a suave home of thoughtfully created cutting-edge meals; and any number of dining establishments competing to serve the very finest steak. Orlando's culinary blossoming began in 1995, when Disney's signature California Grill debuted, featuring farm-to-table cuisine and wonderful wines by the glass. Soon after, celebrity chefs started opening up shop. And in 2013, Disney completely revamped California Grill so it's a trendsetter once again.

Orlando's destination restaurants can be found in the theme parks, as well as in the outlying towns. Sand Lake Road is now known as Restaurant Row for its eclectic collection of worthwhile tables. Here you'll find fashionable outlets for sushi and seafood, Italian and chops, Hawaiian fusion and upscale Lebanese. Heading into the residential areas, the neighborhoods of Winter Park (actually its own city), Thornton Park, and Downtown Orlando are prime locales for chow. Scattered throughout Central Florida, low-key ethnic restaurants specialize in the fare of Turkey, India, Peru, Thailand, Vietnam—you name it. Prices in these family-owned finds are usually delightfully low.

DINING PLANNER

WHERE SHOULD WE EAT?

With thousands of eateries competing for your attention, it may seem like a daunting question. But fret not—our expert writers and editors have done most of the legwork. The selections here represent the best this city has to offer—from hamburger joints to fine dining. Search "Best Bets" for top recommendations by price, cuisine, and experience. Or find a review quickly in the listings, organized alphabetically within theme park or neighborhood. Dive in and enjoy!

CONSIDERATIONS FOR DIFFERENT TYPES OF TRAVELERS

FAMILIES WITH YOUNG KIDS

If you're traveling with small children, you really should include a character meal. Walt Disney World offers breakfast, lunch, and dinner with characters at each of its four parks and some of its resorts. Some are buffets; others are family-style or à la carte. Regardless of the format, Mickey, Donald, Goofy, Chip 'n' Dale, Cinderella, and other favorites show up to sign autographs and pose for snapshots.

At Universal, character meals move around. Cafe La Bamba might feature characters from *Hop* and *Despicable Me*. Universal's hotels also have character dinners, including the Simpsons, on select nights.

When possible, reserve your spot far in advance.

■TIP➔ If your young children are theme-park newbies, have your character meal near the end of a visit, so they'll be used to seeing the large and sometimes frightening figures.

Except for two, the ultraformal Victoria & Albert's and Christini's, most restaurants in and near the theme parks welcome children. Crayons, games, and kiddic menus are standard.

FAMILIES WITH TWEENS

Tweens are impressed by highly themed concepts. Consider the 50's Prime Time Café in Disney's Hollywood Studios, a kitschy 1950s-themed space where "Mom," the waitress, may make parents finish their vegetables. At the Sci-Fi Dine-In Theater nearby, guests eat in top-down convertible cars that face a big screen airing '50s and '60s sci-fi and monster trailers; there are even tasty vegetarian offerings.

Universal's Islands of Adventure also has themed eateries based on superheroes or other classic characters. The Three Broomsticks replicates a Hogsmeade tavern, while Leaky Cauldron resembles a British pub. Both are boons for Harry Potter fans.

FAMILIES WITH TEENS

CityWalk is filled with high-energy themed eateries that teens love. In fact, local high schoolers tend to congregate in the CityWalk common areas on weekend evenings. The lively Hard Rock Cafe is a consistent favorite.

At Disney's Boardwalk, the ESPN Club is a great choice for teen sports fans. Even its bathrooms are equipped with video monitors, so you don't have to miss a second of a great game.

COUPLES

Truly, you'd be hard-pressed to find more romantic restaurants than the ones on Disney property. Jiko, at the Animal Kingdom Lodge, pairs superb African-accented cuisine with an exceptional South African wine list and dramatic decor. If you really want to go all out, there's absolutely nothing like Victoria & Albert's, in the Grand Floridian. Treat yourself to a gourmet, seven-course prix-fixe meal to live harp music.

Outside the theme parks, Norman's, at the Ritz-Carlton, has a sophisticated dining room and impressive New World cuisine.

SINGLES OR GROUPS OF FRIENDS

Singles often dine at the bars of upscale-casual favorites, including Seasons 52, Prato, and at Downtown Orlando's Ceviche. Groups enjoy the festive antics of International Drive's Taverna Opa, where visitors often find themselves dancing around the dining room.

LARGE GROUPS

Restaurants in theme-park hotels, in nearby convention hotels, on Sand Lake Road, and on International Drive have private party rooms for large groups more often than not. For an alternative, consider dinner shows. The food is plentiful and the entertainment keeps younger family members engaged. The luaus at Disney and Universal hotels are good for all ages, as is the wonderfully hokey Hoop-Dee-Doo Musical Revue at Disney's Fort Wilderness Resort.

Many off-park venues also offer themed dining with shows. The concepts range from medieval jousting on horseback to pirates to comedic murder mysteries.

MEAL PLANS

Disney Magic Your Way Plus Dining Plan allows you one table-service meal, one counter-service meal, and one snack per day of your trip at more than 100 theme-park and resort restaurants, provided you stay in a Disney hotel. You'll also receive a refillable drink mug for use at your hotel's fast fooderies. For more money, you can upgrade the plan to include more; to save, you can downgrade to a counter-service-only plan. Used wisely, a Disney dining plan is a steal, but be careful to buy only the number of meals you'll want to eat. Moderate eaters can end up turning away appetizers and desserts to which they're entitled. Plan ahead, and use "extra" meals to your advantage by swapping two table-service meals for a Disney dinner show, say, or an evening at a high-end restaurant like California Grill.

Universal Dining Plan offers sit-down and quick-service meal plans at participating walk-up eateries inside Universal Studios and Islands of Adventure, plus a snack and soft drink. Daily prices are $52 and $18 (both parks) and must be purchased with a resort stay. A quick-service-only arrangement, with one meal a day, is $29 and $23. All-you-can-drink soft drinks are $15 daily for all.

WHAT IT COSTS				
	$	$$	$$$	$$$$
AT DINNER	under $15	$15–$21	$22–$30	over $30

Prices are per person for a median main course, at dinner, excluding tip and tax of 6.5%.

RESERVATIONS

Reservations are strongly recommended throughout the theme parks. Indeed, make reservations for Disney restaurants and character meals at both Universal and Disney at least 90 (and up to 180) days out. And be sure to ask about the cancellation policy—at all table service Disney restaurants, for instance, you will be charged $10 per guest if you don't give 24 hours' notice.

For restaurant reservations within Walt Disney World, call 407/939-3463 (*WDW–DINE*) or book online at *www.disneyworld.com/dining*. You can also get plenty of information on the website, including the meal periods served, price range, and specialties of all Disney eateries. Menus for all restaurants are posted online and tend to be up to date. For Universal Orlando reservations, call 407/224-9255 (theme parks and CityWalk) or 407/503-3463 (hotels). Learn about the complex's 50-plus restaurants at *www.universalorlando.com/dining*.

In our reviews, reservations are mentioned only when they're essential or not accepted. Unless otherwise noted, the restaurants listed are open daily for lunch and dinner.

TIPPING AND TAXES

In most restaurants, tip the waiter 15%–20% of the food and beverage charges before tax. Tip at least $1 per drink at the bar, and $2 for valet parking.

WHAT TO WEAR

Because tourism is king around Orlando, casual dress is the rule. Flip-flops and cutoffs are acceptable in just about all fast-food and midprice restaurants. Although it's best to dress up for the ritzier restaurants, don't be shocked to find diners beside you in Levi's and polo shirts. Men need jackets only in the most exclusive establishments; however, such establishments are strict about enforcing dress code. If you plan to eat at a nicer place, check on dress codes so you aren't caught unprepared and turned away at the door.

ABOUT OUR PRICE CATEGORIES AND MAPS

Prices in the restaurant reviews are the average cost of a main course at dinner or, if dinner is not served, at lunch; taxes and service charges are generally included.

Throughout the chapter, you'll see mapping symbols and coordinates (3:F2) at the end of each review. Maps are within the chapter. The first number after the ⊕ symbol indicates the map number. After that is the property's coordinate on the map grid.

WALT DISNEY WORLD

MAGIC KINGDOM

Dining options in the Magic Kingdom are mainly counter service, with a few delightful exceptions, and every land has its share of fast-food places selling burgers, hot dogs, grilled-chicken sandwiches, and salads. Each has a different regular and children's menu. The walkways are peppered with carts dispensing smoked turkey legs, popcorn, ice-cream bars, lemonade, bottled water, and soda. The Magic Kingdom's almost no-liquor policy (wine and beer is offered only during dinner at Be Our Guest) fits the theme park most suited for little kids. The spirits ban does not extend to the rest of Walt Disney World.

$$$$
FRENCH
Fodor's Choice
★

✕ **Be Our Guest.** This massive restaurant offers a *Beauty and the Beast* theme, French flair, and the Magic Kingdom's first wine and beer served at dinner; breakfast and lunch remain a fast-casual affair. Prix-fixe menus are served for breakfast, lunch, and dinner in one of three rooms: a gilded ballroom, whose ceiling sports cherubs with the faces of Imagineers' children; the tattered West Wing, with a slashed painting that changes from prince to beast during faux storms; and the Rose Gallery. **Known for:** the best French dip sandwich in town; dessert platter; artwork that changes by the hour. $ *Average main: $55* ⊠ *Fantasyland, Magic Kingdom* ✢ *North end of Fantasyland* ☎ *407/939–3463* ⊕ *disneyworld.disney.go.com/dining* ✢ *1:B1.*

$$$$
AMERICAN

✕ **Cinderella's Royal Table.** Cinderella and other Disney princesses appear at this eatery in the castle's old mead hall, offering prix-fixe Fairyland dining as only Disney can supply. The Fairytale Breakfast offers all-you-can-eat options such as beef tenderloin and eggs and caramel apple–stuffed French toast. **Known for:** breakfasts from oatmeal to shrimp and grits; character appearances and autograph signings; distinctive medieval castle decor. $ *Average main: $59* ⊠ *Cinderella Castle, Magic Kingdom* ☎ *407/939–3463* ⊕ *disneyworld.disney.go.com/dining* ✢ *1:B1.*

$$$$
AMERICAN
FAMILY

✕ **The Crystal Palace.** A lovely Victorian setting is the perfect place for the old-fashioned and lovable Winnie the Pooh and friends to greet your kids via A Buffet with Character, offered here three meals a day. This is the only restaurant where you can find characters from the Hundred Acre Wood. **Known for:** character dining with Disney favorites; all-you-can-eat buffet; shrimp, meat-carving, and dessert stations. $ *Average main: $45* ⊠ *Main Street, U.S.A., Magic Kingdom* ☎ *307/939–3463* ⊕ *www.disneyworld.com* ✢ *1:B1.*

$$$$
AMERICAN
Fodor's Choice
★

✕ **Liberty Tree Tavern.** Now serving beer and wine, this formerly "dry" tavern holds a prime spot on the parade route, so you can catch a good meal while you wait. Each of the six dining rooms commemorates a historical U.S. figure, like Betsy Ross or Benjamin Franklin. **Known for:** Patriot's Platter of roast turkey, sliced pot roast, and carved pork roast; multiroom, authentic-looking colonial decor; Samuel Adams Boston Lager and wine. $ *Average main: $35* ⊠ *Liberty Square, Magic Kingdom* ☎ *407/939–3463* ⊕ *disneyworld.disney.go.com/dining* ✢ *1:B1.*

$$$ ╳ **Tony's Town Square Restaurant.** Inspired by the animated classic *Lady*
ITALIAN *and the Tramp,* Tony's offers everything from spaghetti with meat-
FAMILY balls to braised short ribs with mascarpone polenta to garlicky shrimp
scampi with linguini. Wine and beer are available, including Italian
Birra Moretti lager. **Known for:** Lady and the Tramp references; wine-
and-beer menu; braised short ribs with polenta. Ⓢ *Average main: $27*
⊠ *Main Street, U.S.A., Magic Kingdom* ☎ *407/939–3463* ⊕ *www.dis-
neyworld.disney.go.com/dining* ✛ *1:B1.*

MAGIC KINGDOM RESORT AREA

$$$$ ╳ **Artist Point.** If you're not a guest at the Wilderness Lodge, a meal
AMERICAN here is worth it just to see the giant totem poles and huge rock fire-
Fodor's Choice place in the lobby of the hotel; it's also one of the best, and most
★ overlooked, of the Disney restaurants. The specialty at this restaurant,
which focuses on foods of the American Northwest, is cedar-plank
salmon, served with seasonal items like sweet potato mash, house-
smoked bacon, and apple cider gastrique (it's worth its price tag).
Known for: seasonal cedar-plank wild-caught salmon; house-made
and house-smoked venison; 32-ounce aged bone-in rib eye for two.
Ⓢ *Average main: $39* ⊠ *Wilderness Lodge, 901 Timberline Dr., Magic
Kingdom Resort Area* ☎ *407/939–3463* ⊕ *www.disneyworld.disney.
go.com/dining* ◔ *No lunch* ✛ *1:C1.*

$$$$ ╳ **California Grill.** The view from the surrounding Disney parks from this
AMERICAN 15th-floor restaurant—the World's signature dining establishment since
Fodor's Choice 1995—is as stunning as the food, especially after dark, when you can
★ watch the nightly Magic Kingdom fireworks from an outdoor viewing
area. The space has stylish midcentury modern furnishings and chande-
liers, while the exhibition kitchen is so well equipped that it has a cast-
iron flat grill designed specifically for cooking fish. **Known for:** stunning
views of the parks and fireworks; wild game charcuterie and fresh sushi;
Sunday brunch. Ⓢ *Average main: $47* ⊠ *Contemporary Resort, 4600
N. World Dr., Magic Kingdom Resort Area* ☎ *407/939–3463* ⊕ *disney-
world.disney.go.com/dining* ◔ *No lunch* ✛ *1:B1.*

$$$$ ╳ **Chef Mickey's.** The fact that the Disney monorail zooms overhead
AMERICAN right through the Contemporary hotel, and that Mickey, Minnie, or
FAMILY Goofy hang around for breakfast and dinner, would be enough to make
it popular, but the food at Chef Mickey's is surprisingly good. After a
renovation in 2017, Chef Mickey's is shiny and bright, still offering
a breakfast buffet that includes French toast, mountains of specialty
pancakes, and even a breakfast pizza. **Known for:** character meals and
Storybook Moments; family fare buffet and lots of it; specialty cocktails
for the grown-ups. Ⓢ *Average main: $47* ⊠ *Contemporary Resort, 4600
N. World Dr., Magic Kingdom Resort Area* ☎ *407/939–3463* ⊕ *disney-
world.disney.go.com/dining* ◔ *No lunch* ✛ *1:B1.*

$$$$ ╳ **Citricos.** With an ambitious menu that's fundamentally American with
ECLECTIC influences of Tuscan, Provençal, and Spanish-Mediterranean cuisine,
this Grand Floridian restaurant is one of the resort's best dollar-to-din-
ing options. Standout entrées include oak-grilled yellowtail tuna with
cannellini ragu, and the red wine–braised beef short ribs with hand-
harvested mushrooms. **Known for:** superb cheese-course selections;

5

oak-grilled meats; casually elegant atmosphere. Ⓢ *Average main: $47* ✉ *Grand Floridian Resort & Spa, 4401 Floridian Way, Magic Kingdom Resort Area* ☎ *407/939–3463* ⊕ *www.disneyworld.disney.go.com/dining* ◔ *No lunch* ✛ *1:B1.*

$$$$ ✕**Garden View Tea Room.** Disney's Perfectly Princess Tea Party is after-
BRITISH noon tea at its grandest as children ages 3 to 9 enjoy the royal treatment with Mom (or Dad). Dressing up is encouraged, and an early
lunch, featuring tea and sandwiches, is served on china plates (apple
juice, peanut butter, and ham-and-cheese sandwiches for the little
darlings; cheeses and finger sandwiches for adults). **Known for:** highly
elegant afternoon tea for young princesses and princes and refined
adults; character appearances; house-made scones, sandwiches, and
sweets. Ⓢ *Average main: $150* ✉ *Grand Floridian Resort & Spa, 4401
Floridian Way, Magic Kingdom Resort Area* ☎ *407/939–3463* ⊕ *www.
disneyworld.com* ✛ *1:B1.*

$$$$ ✕**Mickey's Backyard BBQ.** The Hootin' Tootin Hoedown at Mickey's
BARBECUE Backyard BBQ is a dinner show in an open-air pavilion that has every-
FAMILY thing from dancing and foot-stomping country music to finger-food
Fodor's Choice goodies like hot dogs and smoked ribs. Plus Cowboy Mickey and his
★ friends make appearances several times a night. **Known for:** Cowboy
Mickey and friends make appearances; barbecued pork ribs, burg-
ers, hot dogs; sangria, beer and wine for adults. Ⓢ *Average main: $62*
✉ *Campsites at Disney's Fort Wilderness Resort, 4510 Fort Wilderness
Trail, Magic Kingdom Resort Area* ☎ *407/939–3463* ⊕ *www.disney-
world.com* ◔ *No lunch* ✛ *1:C1.*

$$$$ ✕**Narcoossee's.** The dining room, with Victorian-style columns, high
SEAFOOD ceilings, and hardwood floors, makes a great place not only to enjoy
"coastal cuisine"—especially steaks and seafood—but to gaze out at the
nightly fireworks over the Seven Seas Lagoon; an announcement is made
when fireworks commence and music is piped in. The menu changes
regularly. **Known for:** intimate and well-stocked bar; seafood flown in
daily; black Angus steaks. Ⓢ *Average main: $54* ✉ *Grand Floridian,
4401 Floridian Way, Magic Kingdom Resort Area* ☎ *407/939–3463*
⊕ *www.disneyworld.disney.go.com/dining* ◔ *No lunch* ✛ *1:B1.*

$$$$ ✕**1900 Park Fare.** Disney characters delight guests throughout the day
AMERICAN at this sprawling, though dainty, lobby restaurant. Mary Poppins and
friends join guests during the Supercalifragilistic Breakfast, posing for pics
while cheerful tunes are played on an antique organ called Big Bertha.
Known for: Florida strawberry soup; character dining buffets throughout
the day; Wonderland Tea Party. Ⓢ *Average main: $45* ✉ *Grand Florid-
ian Resort & Spa, 4401 Floridian Way, Magic Kingdom Resort Area*
☎ *407/939–3463* ⊕ *www.disneyworld.com* ◔ *No lunch* ✛ *1:B1.*

$$$$ ✕**'Ohana.** This Polynesian-themed restaurant offers two thoroughly
SOUTH PACIFIC entertaining, though incredibly different, experiences. Early in the day,
FAMILY the Best Friends Breakfast with Lilo & Stitch is destination-worthy.
Known for: storytelling, shows and games between courses; chicken,
seafood and steak skewers; fun family atmosphere; full bar for adults.
Ⓢ *Average main: $46* ✉ *Polynesian Village Resort, 1600 Seven Seas Dr.,
Magic Kingdom Resort Area* ☎ *407/939–3463* ⊕ *www.disneyworld.
com/dining* ◔ *No lunch* ✛ *1:B2.*

$$$$ MODERN AMERICAN Fodor's Choice ★

🍴 **Victoria & Albert's.** At this ultraposh Disney restaurant, a well-polished service team will anticipate your every need, providing one of the plushest fine-dining experiences in Florida; the setting is so sophisticated that children under 10 aren't on the guest list. Several options for meals and seating are available, from the seven- and 10-course main dining room or the 10-course intimate Queen Victoria's Room, to the over-the-top Chef's Table, which is actually in the restaurant's kitchen. **Known for:** highest-priced restaurant at WDW; enormous and expensive wine list; exclusive additions like Osetra caviar and Miyazaki beef. [$] *Average main: $200* ✉ *Grand Floridian, 4401 Floridian Way, Magic Kingdom Resort Area* ☎ *407/939–3862* 🌐 *www.victoria-alberts.com* 🕒 *No lunch* 👔 *Jacket required* ✣ *1:B1.*

EPCOT

5

Epcot's World Showcase offers some of the finest dining in Orlando. Every pavilion has at least one and often two or even three eateries. Where there's a choice, it's between a relatively expensive full-service restaurant and a more affordable, ethnic fast-food spot, plus carts and shops selling snacks ranging from French pastries to Japanese ices—whatever's appropriate to the pavilion.

$$$$ SCANDINAVIAN FAMILY

🍴 **Akershus Royal Banquet Hall.** This restaurant has character buffets at all three meals, with an array of Disney princesses, including Ariel, Belle, Jasmine, Snow White, Aurora, Mary Poppins, and even an occasional cameo appearance by Cinderella. The breakfast menu is American, but lunch and dinner find an ever-changing assortment of Norwegian specialties, which may be foreign to children. **Known for:** an expansive buffet of Nordic specialties; Scandinavian appeal; scallops, mussels, and shrimp casserole. [$] *Average main: $50* ✉ *Norway Pavilion, World Showcase, Epcot* ☎ *407/939–3463* 🌐 *disneyworld.disney.go.com/dining* ✣ *1:D4.*

$$$$ GERMAN

🍴 **Biergarten Restaurant.** Oktoberfest runs 365 days a year here, where cheerful crowds and an oompah band set the stage for a buffet of German specialties. The menu and level of frivolity are the same at lunch and dinner. **Known for:** bratwurst, sausages, and other German specialties; lively oompa band music; buffet-style servings, including dessert bar. [$] *Average main: $47* ✉ *Germany Pavilion, World Showcase, Epcot* ☎ *407/939–3463* 🌐 *disneyworld.disney.go.com/dining* ✣ *1:D4.*

$$$$ AMERICAN

🍴 **Garden Grill.** Family-style dinner fare is served here as the restaurant revolves, giving you an ever-changing backstage view of the Living with the Land boat ride. Offering quantity over quality, the restaurant serves all-you-can-eat meals with visits from Chip 'n' Dale, Pluto, and occasionally Mickey. **Known for:** character dining; unusual revolving restaurant within the Land pavillion; family-style servings with beer and wine available. [$] *Average main: $45* ✉ *The Land Pavilion, Epcot* ☎ *407/939–3463* 🌐 *www.disneyworld.disney.go.com/dining* 🕒 *No lunch* ✣ *1:D4.*

$$$$ CANADIAN

🍴 **Le Cellier Steakhouse.** This popular, charming eatery with stone arches and dark woods transports diners to a well-heeled setting similar to a cozy Canadian château, offering a menu heavy on meat and a good

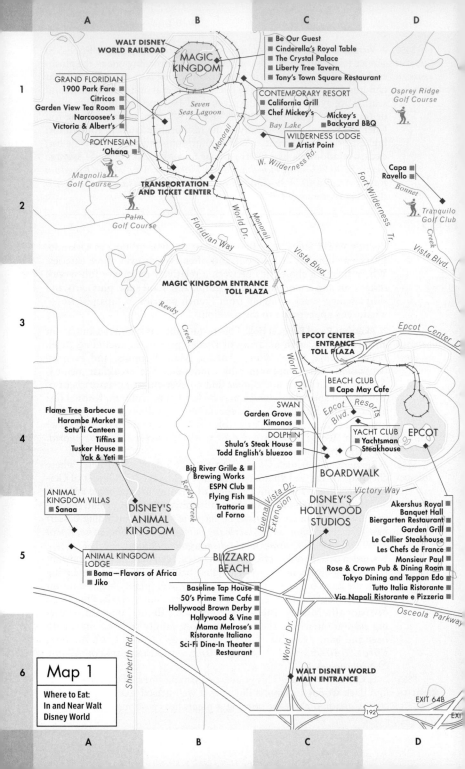

WALT DISNEY WORLD RAILROAD

MAGIC KINGDOM

■ Be Our Guest
■ Cinderella's Royal Table
■ The Crystal Palace
■ Liberty Tree Tavern
■ Tony's Town Square Restaurant

GRAND FLORIDIAN
■ 1900 Park Fare
■ Citricos
■ Garden View Tea Room
■ Narcoosee's
■ Victoria & Albert's

Osprey Ridge Golf Course

CONTEMPORARY RESORT
■ California Grill
■ Chef Mickey's

POLYNESIAN
■ 'Ohana

Seven Seas Lagoon

Bay Lake

■ Mickey's Backyard BBQ

WILDERNESS LODGE
■ Artist Point

W. Wilderness Rd.

Magnolia Golf Course

TRANSPORTATION AND TICKET CENTER

Capa ■■
Ravello ■■

Bonnet

Fort Wilderness Tr.

Tranquilo Golf Club

Palm Golf Course

Floridian Way

World Dr.

Monorail

Vista Blvd.

Vista Blvd.

MAGIC KINGDOM ENTRANCE TOLL PLAZA

Reedy Creek

Epcot Center Dr.

EPCOT CENTER ENTRANCE TOLL PLAZA

World Dr.

BEACH CLUB
■ Cape May Cafe

Flame Tree Barbecue ■
Harambe Market ■
Satu'li Canteen ■
Tiffins ■
Tusker House ■
Yak & Yeti ■

SWAN
Garden Grove ■
Kimonos ■

Epcot Resorts Blvd.

YACHT CLUB
■ Yachtsman Steakhouse

EPCOT

DOLPHIN
■ Shula's Steak House
■ Todd English's bluezoo

Big River Grille & ■
Brewing Works
ESPN Club ■
Flying Fish ■
Trattoria al Forno ■

BOARDWALK

Victory Way

ANIMAL KINGDOM VILLAS
■ Sanaa

DISNEY'S ANIMAL KINGDOM

Reedy Creek

Buena Vista Dr. Extension

DISNEY'S HOLLYWOOD STUDIOS

Akershus Royal ■
Banquet Hall
Biergarten Restaurant ■
Garden Grill ■
Le Cellier Steakhouse ■
Les Chefs de France ■
Monsieur Paul ■
Rose & Crown Pub & Dining Room ■
Tokyo Dining and Teppan Edo ■
Tutto Italia Ristorante ■
Via Napoli Ristorante e Pizzeria ■

ANIMAL KINGDOM LODGE
■ Boma—Flavors of Africa
■ Jiko

BLIZZARD BEACH

Baseline Tap House ■
50's Prime Time Café ■
Hollywood Brown Derby ■
Hollywood & Vine ■
Mama Melrose's ■
Ristorante Italiano
Sci-Fi Dine-In Theater ■
Restaurant

Osceola Parkway

World Dr.

Map 1

Where to Eat:
In and Near Walt
Disney World

WALT DISNEY WORLD MAIN ENTRANCE

Sherberth Rd.

EXIT 64B

EXI

192

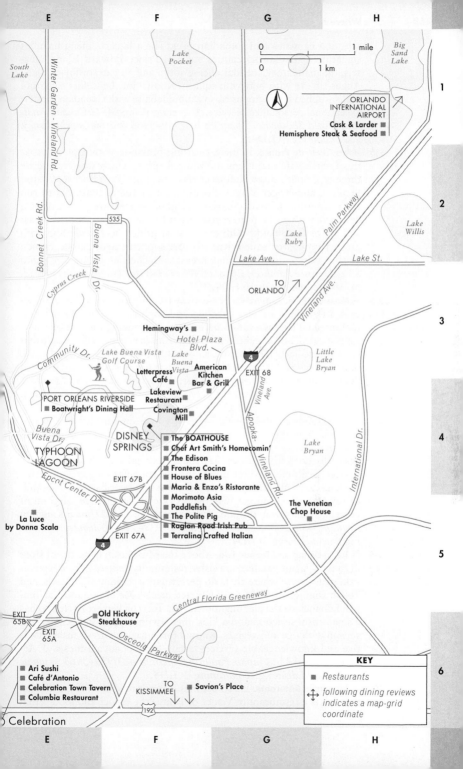

E   **F**   **G**   **H**

South Lake

Lake Pocket

Big Sand Lake

0 _____ 1 mile
0 _____ 1 km

1

ORLANDO INTERNATIONAL AIRPORT
Cask & Larder ■
Hemisphere Steak & Seafood ■

Winter Garden - Vineland Rd.

Bonnet Creek Rd.

535

Buena Vista Dr.

Cyprus Creek

2

Lake Ruby

Palm Parkway

Lake Willis

Lake Ave.

Lake St.

Vineland Ave.

TO ORLANDO

3

Hemingway's ■

Hotel Plaza Blvd.

Community Dr.

Lake Buena Vista Golf Course

Lake Buena Vista

Letterpress Café ■

American Kitchen Bar & Grill ■

4

EXIT 68

Little Lake Bryan

PORT ORLEANS RIVERSIDE
■ Boatwright's Dining Hall

Lakeview Restaurant ■

Covington Mill ■

Buena Vista Dr.

DISNEY SPRINGS

TYPHOON LAGOON

Epcot Center Dr.

EXIT 67B

■ The BOATHOUSE
■ Chef Art Smith's Homecomin'
■ The Edison
■ Frontera Cocina
■ House of Blues
■ Maria & Enzo's Ristorante
■ Morimoto Asia
■ Paddlefish
■ The Polite Pig
■ Raglan Road Irish Pub
■ Terralina Crafted Italian

Apopka-

Vineland Rd.

Lake Bryan

The Venetian Chop House ■

International Dr.

4

La Luce by Donna Scala ■

4

EXIT 67A

5

EXIT 65B

EXIT 65A

Old Hickory Steakhouse ■

Central Florida Greeneway

Osceola Parkway

6

■ Ari Sushi
■ Café d'Antonio
■ Celebration Town Tavern
■ Columbia Restaurant

TO KISSIMMEE

Savion's Place ■

192

Celebration

KEY

■ *Restaurants*

↔ *following dining reviews indicates a map-grid coordinate*

E   **F**   **G**   **H**

selection of wines and Canadian beer. The à la carte menu includes signature Canadian specialties such as Prince Edward Island mussels, the mandatory cheddar cheese soup, and an extraordinary Black Angus rib eye with butternut squash. **Known for:** Le Cellier signature coffee-rubbed black Angus rib eye; bouillabaise with Canadian lobster; exceptional personalized service. [$] *Average main: $45* ✉ *Canada Pavilion, World Showcase, Epcot* ☎ *407/939–3463* 🌐 *disneyworld.disney.go.com/dining* ✣ *1:D4.*

$$$ FRENCH 🍴 **Les Chefs de France.** A busy, bustling brasserie with a plush look, this French café maintains its original spirit, which was created by three of France's most famous chefs at the time: Paul Bocuse, Gaston Lenôtre, and Roger Vergé—Bocuse's son, Jerome, continues to run the restaurant. Classic escargots, a good starter, are prepared in a casserole with garlic butter; you might follow up with roasted breast and leg of duck confit with cherries, or grilled beef tenderloin with green peppercorn sauce. **Known for:** sophisticated, classic French cuisine; salmon in white wine; breast with cherries. [$] *Average main: $30* ✉ *France Pavilion, Epcot* ☎ *407/939–3463* 🌐 *www.disneyworld.disney.go.com/dining* ✣ *1:D4.*

$$$$ FRENCH Fodor's Choice ★ 🍴 **Monsieur Paul.** A mere staircase away from Epcot's busy World Showcase, Monsieur Paul is a subdued and sophisticated fine French restaurant. Make a reservation here if you are looking for an expensive, sophisticated, and delightful diversion from the theme park's bustle that is not particularly kid-friendly. **Known for:** the service is so good you'll think you're at a Michelin-starred restaurant; magret de canard (roasted duck breast); an extensive wine list. [$] *Average main: $42* ✉ *France Pavilion, World Showcase, Epcot* ☎ *407/939–3463* 🌐 *disneyworld.disney.go.com/dining* ✣ *1:D4.*

$$$ BRITISH FAMILY 🍴 **Rose & Crown Pub & Dining Room.** If you're an Anglophile and you love a beer so thick you could stand a spoon up in your mug, this is the place to soak up both the suds and British street culture and get the best fish-and-chips in town. Try the traditional English fare—cottage or shepherd's pie, and, at times, the ever-popular bangers-and-mash (sausage over mashed potatoes). **Known for:** beer-battered fish-and-chips; Angus beef burger with Welsh rarebit sauce; wide selection of beers and ciders from the pub. [$] *Average main: $24* ✉ *United Kingdom Pavilion, World Showcase, Epcot* ☎ *407/939–3463* 🌐 *disneyworld.disney.go.com/dining* ✣ *1:D4.*

$$$ JAPANESE FAMILY 🍴 **Tokyo Dining and Teppan Edo.** Above the Mitsukoshi department store in Epcot's Japan pavilion are sister restaurants Teppan Edo, a teppanyaki steak house where chefs do performance cooking at 20 grills, and Tokyo Dining, for sushi and preplated meals . Menu standouts at Teppan Edo include the filet mignon and the Tori chicken breast. It also has a small sushi selection and a kids' menu with Teppan-style chicken or shrimp with rice and veggies. **Known for:** amazingly fresh sushi; attentive and knowledgeable service; family-fun teppanyaki meals. [$] *Average main: $25* ✉ *Japan Pavilion, Epcot* ☎ *407/939–3463* 🌐 *www.disneyworld.disney.go.com/dining* ✣ *1:D4.*

$$$ ITALIAN 🍴 **Tutto Italia Ristorante.** It's sometimes difficult to shake off the illusion that this is a restaurant in Venice or Rome; the service and food is that

good. Offerings include polenta with braised short ribs and meatballs, grilled salmon with shaved fennel salad, and rosemary chicken. **Known for:** generous antipasto platter; Italian polenta with short ribs; casual but attentive service. $ *Average main: $28* ✉ *Italy Pavilion, Epcot* ☎ *407/939–3463* ⊕ *www.disneyworld.disney.go.com/dining* ✛ *1:D4.*

$$$
PIZZA
FAMILY

✕ **Via Napoli Ristorante e Pizzeria.** Loud, mad, bustling, and chaotic, this casual, family-friendly restaurant in the Italy Pavilion features a menu of authentic, thin-crust Neapolitan-style pizzas from massive ovens named after Italian volcanoes that's supplemented by a large menu of southern Italian favorites. Pizzas come topped with pepperoni, mushrooms, or eggplant, artichokes, cotto ham, cheese, and even prosciutto and melon. **Known for:** pizzas from wood-fired ovens; spaghetti with veal meatballs; generous kid portions. $ *Average main: $30* ✉ *Italy Pavilion, World Showcase, Epcot* ☎ *407/939–3463* ⊕ *disneyworld.disney. go.com/dining* ✛ *1:D4.*

EPCOT RESORT AREA

$$
AMERICAN
FAMILY

✕ **Big River Grille & Brewing Works.** Strange but good brews, like Rocket Red Ale, Southern Flyer Light Lager, Steamboat Pale Ale, and Gadzooks Pilsner, abound here at Walt Disney World's only microbrewery. You can dine inside among the giant stainless-steel brewing tanks or sip your suds outside on the lake-view patio. **Known for:** massive burgers; Disney's only microbrewery; ribs, steaks, and flame-grilled meatloaf. $ *Average main: $19* ✉ *BoardWalk Inn, 2101 Epcot Resorts Blvd., Epcot Resort Area* ☎ *407/560–0253* ⊕ *www.bigrivergrille.com* ✛ *1:C4.*

$$$$
SEAFOOD
FAMILY

✕ **Cape May Cafe.** With the feel of a New England seafood house—the type your grandma might enjoy—this bustling spot in the Beach Club Resort features popular buffet meals. For breakfast, Goofy and other cast classics visit tables while families help themselves to American classics from waffles to sausage links from the buffet. **Known for:** character breakfast; seafood buffet; casual atmosphere in an out-of-the-way setting. $ *Average main: $48* ✉ *Beach Club Resort, 1800 Epcot Resorts Blvd., Epcot Resort Area* ☎ *407/939–3463* ⊕ *www.disneyworld.com/ dining* ☾ *No lunch* ✛ *1:C4.*

$$
AMERICAN

✕ **ESPN Club.** Not only can you watch every possible televised sporting event on a big-screen TV here (the restaurant has about 100 monitors), but you can also periodically see ESPN programs being taped in the club itself while enjoying typical sports-bar food and beer. Food ranges from a variety of half-pound burgers, made with Angus chuck (and one topped with peanut butter and jelly), to Philly cheesesteaks and *char siu* sliders. **Known for:** gigantic space that still fills up on game days; pub food: nachos, chicken and waffles, big burgers; wine and regional beers. $ *Average main: $17* ✉ *Disney's Boardwalk, 2101 Epcot Resorts Blvd., Epcot Resort Area* ☎ *407/939–3463* ⊕ *disney-world.disney.go.com/dining* ✛ *1:C4.*

$$$$
SEAFOOD
Fodor'sChoice
★

✕ **Flying Fish.** Completely renovated in 2016, Flying Fish maintains its place as one of Disney World's finest restaurants, with a menu heavy on the freshest seasonal seafood as well as steaks. The menu includes such options as wild Alaskan King salmon, Wagyu beef, and even exotic fare like bison and Hokkaido scallops; special chef's table menus are available by reservation. **Known for:** sophisticated dining on the Disney Boardwalk; fresh daily local and international seafood; AbracadaBAR cocktail lounge next door. [$] *Average main: $48* ✉ *Disney's Boardwalk, 2101 Epcot Resorts Blvd., Epcot Resort Area* ☎ *407/939–2359* 🌐 *disneyworld.disney.go.com/dining* ⏲ *No lunch* ✥ *1:C4.*

$$$$ AMERICAN FAMILY 🍴 **Garden Grove.** With twinkling lights hung amid the branches of its oversized 25-foot signature tree, this restaurant, designed to resemble New York's Central Park, specializes in character meals. At dinner nightly, guests dine on classic American fare like prime rib while Goofy and his buddies make their rounds. **Known for:** character meals; cedar plank–blackened salmon; seafood buffet. [$] *Average main: $34* ✉ *Walt Disney World Swan, 1200 Epcot Resorts Blvd., Epcot Resort Area* ☎ *407/934–1618* 🌐 *www.swandolphinrestaurants.com* ✥ *1:C4.*

$$$ JAPANESE 🍴 **Kimonos.** Knife-wielding sushi chefs prepare world-class sushi and sashimi but also other Japanese treats like soups and salads at this sleek hotel sushi bar, where bamboo-style floor tiles and dark teakwood furnishings create an inviting environment. Popular rolls include the Dragon Roll (giant shrimp and tuna), Banzai Roll (spicy tuna, avocado, and eel), and the Bagel Roll (smoked salmon, cream cheese, and cucumber). **Known for:** open until midnight; nightly karaoke; extensive sushi menu. [$] *Average main: $24* ✉ *Walt Disney World Swan, 1200 Epcot Resorts Blvd., Epcot Resort Area* ☎ *407/934–1609* 🌐 *www.swandolphinrestaurants.com/kimonos* ⏲ *No lunch* ✥ *1:C4.*

$$$$ STEAKHOUSE 🍴 **Shula's Steak House.** The hardwood floors, dark-wood paneling, and pictures of former Miami Dolphins coach Don Shula make this restaurant resemble an annex of the NFL Hall of Fame. Among the best selections are the porterhouse, lamb chops, and prime rib. **Known for:** steak, steak, steak; extensive whiskey menu; 48-ounce porterhouse. [$] *Average main: $79* ✉ *Walt Disney World Dolphin, 1500 Epcot Resorts Blvd., Epcot Resort Area* ☎ *407/934–1362* 🌐 *www.swandolphinrestaurants.com/shulas* ⏲ *No lunch* ✥ *1:C4.*

$$$$ SEAFOOD 🍴 **Todd English's bluezoo.** Celebrity chef Todd English designed the menu for this upscale seafood eatery, known perhaps more for style than substance. The sleek, modern restaurant resembles an underwater dining hall, with blue walls and carpeting, aluminum fish along the wall behind the bar, and bubblelike lighting fixtures. **Known for:** variety of seafood; celebrity chef dining; two hours of complimentary child care while dining. [$] *Average main: $44* ✉ *Walt Disney World Dolphin Hotel, 1500 Epcot Resorts Blvd., Epcot Resort Area* ☎ *407/934–1111* 🌐 *www.thebluezoo.com* ⏲ *No lunch* ✥ *1:C4.*

$$$ ITALIAN FAMILY 🍴 **Trattoria al Forno.** Themed as an old-time Italian home along a boardwalk, this Disney resort restaurant melds new and old, from the homey decor with contemporary touches to the menu, where Italian-American dishes are refreshed for today's tastes. Share a pizza topped with fennel sausage, salame piccante, and house-made pickles. **Known for:** large portions; whole roasted fish; house-made desserts and gelato. [$] *Average main: $27* ✉ *BoardWalk Inn, 2101 Epcot Resorts Blvd., Epcot Resort Area* ☎ *407/939–3463* 🌐 *www.disneyworld.com* ⏲ *No lunch.* ✥ *1:C4.*

$$$$ STEAKHOUSE 🍴 **Yachtsman Steakhouse.** Aged beef, the attraction at this New England–themed casual steak house in the upscale Yacht and Beach Club, can

be seen mellowing in the glassed-in butcher shop near the entryway. The chefs are proud of their beef in this woodsy, family-friendly spot, and the quality seems to prove it. **Known for:** an ambitious assortment of steaks from Kansas City to Wagyu; artisan-selected cheese plates; house-made charcuterie. [$] *Average main: $45* ✉ *Yacht and Beach Club, 1700 Epcot Resorts Blvd., Epcot Resort Area* ☎ *407/939–3463* 🌐 *www.disneyworld.disney.go.com/dining* 🕓 *No lunch* ⊕ *1:C4.*

DISNEY'S HOLLYWOOD STUDIOS

Many areas in Hollywood Studios are being revamped, replaced, or renamed. Even the themes are changing from classic movie cities (San Francisco, New York) to the new, fantastic worlds of *Star Wars* and *Toy Story.* Some well-regarded restaurants do remain such as the Brown Derby and Mama Melrose's Ristorante, but precursory website visits and phone calls are a must to make sure the place you're looking for is still open. **■ TIP→ Dinner packages that include the Fantasmic! after-dark show can be booked by phone or online, in person at a Disney hotel, or at the park's Guest Relations (aka Guest Services).**

$$$ AMERICAN
🍴 **Baseline Tap House.** Part of the new Grand Avenue area of Hollywood Studios, Base Line Tap House (re)creates a downtown Los Angeles corner pub, serving California wines and craft beers. Charcuterie boards featuring California cheeses, and Bavarian pretzels with fondue, are snackable highlights. **Known for:** urban Los Angeles feel; casual snacks; California beers, ciders, and wines. [$] *Average main: $25* ✉ *Grand Ave., Disney's Hollywood Studios* ☎ *407/939–3463* 🌐 *disneyworld.disney.go.com/dining* ⊕ *1:C5.*

$$ AMERICAN FAMILY
🍴 **50's Prime Time Café.** If you grew up in middle America in the 1950s—or if you're just a fan of classic TV shows like *I Love Lucy* and *The Donna Reed Show*—you'll appreciate the vintage atmosphere and all-American classic menu at this diner-style restaurant. Clips of old TV shows will welcome you as you feast on meat loaf, pot roast, or fried chicken, all served on a Formica tabletop. **Known for:** showing clips of classic TV shows during dinner; "Mom" wandering around tables telling kids to eat their veggies; golden-fried chicken, pot roast, and meat loaf sampler. [$] *Average main: $18* ✉ *Echo Lake, Disney's Hollywood Studios* ☎ *407/939–3463* 🌐 *disneyworld.disney.go.com/dining* ⊕ *1:C5.*

$$$$ AMERICAN FAMILY
🍴 **Hollywood & Vine.** Disney Channel stars come to life at this restaurant through its Disney Junior Play 'n Dine meals for breakfast and lunch. Handy Manny and Agent Oso, along with friends of *Sofia the First* and *Doc McStuffins*, are among the cheerful characters marching around the room, singing and dancing to the delight of energetic fans. **Known for:** character breakfasts; meat, shrimp, and salad buffets; VIP dining package for Fantasmic! nighttime show. [$] *Average main: $35* ✉ *Echo Lake, Disney's Hollywood Studios* ☎ *407/939–3463* 🌐 *www.disneyworld.com* ⊕ *1:C5.*

$$$$ AMERICAN
🍴 **Hollywood Brown Derby.** At this reproduction of the famous 1940s Hollywood favorite, the walls are lined with caricatures of older movie stars. The specialty is a Cobb salad, which was invented by Brown Derby founder Robert Cobb and still tossed table-side. **Known for:**

old-Hollywood atmosphere; the Cobb Salad; duck two ways. [$] *Average main: $40* ✉ *Hollywood Blvd., Disney's Hollywood Studios* ☎ *407/939–3463* 🌐 *disneyworld.disney.go.com/dining* ⊕ *1:C5.*

$$$ ITALIAN FAMILY 🍴 **Mama Melrose's Ristorante Italiano.** To replace the energy you've no doubt depleted by miles of theme-park walking, you can load up on carbs at this casual Italian restaurant that looks like a classic San Francisco Italian eatery. Good main courses include spaghetti with meatballs, and wood-grilled chicken in a four-cheese sauce with pasta and vegetables. **Known for:** old-fashioned-Italian-restaurant atmosphere; Fantasmic! dining package; authentic San Francisco seafood cioppino. [$] *Average main: $25* ✉ *Grand Ave., Disney's Hollywood Studios* ☎ *407/939–3463* 🌐 *www.disneyworld.disney.go.com/dining* ⊕ *1:C5.*

$$$ AMERICAN 🍴 **Sci-Fi Dine-In Theater Restaurant.** If you don't mind zombies leering at you while you eat, then head to this enclosed faux drive-in, where you can eat in a booth that looks like a candy-colored 1950s convertible while watching clips from classics like *Attack of the Fifty-Foot Woman* and *Teenagers from Outer Space*. The menu includes choices like steak and garlic mashed potatoes, an Angus or veggie burger, shrimp with whole-grain pasta, and a huge Reuben sandwich with fries or cucumber salad. End with a hot-fudge sundae. **Known for:** menu of American classics like steak and Reuben sandwich; build-your-own Angus burger; wine, sangria, and fun cocktails. [$] *Average main: $25* ✉ *Commissary La., Disney's Hollywood Studios* ☎ *407/939–3463* 🌐 *disneyworld.disney.go.com/dining* ⊕ *1:C5.*

DISNEY'S ANIMAL KINGDOM

Disney's Animal Kingdom is not usually thought of as a food destination, but, like much of Disney, new attractions (and dining options) are on the horizon, and one of the best restaurants on Disney's property, Tiffins, resides here. In the meantime, Disney's highly themed zoo offers variety, including an African-themed buffet, a Chinese restaurant with table service, and surprises like a tea stand, a fruit market, and, at times, picnic lunches packaged to go.

$ FAST FOOD FAMILY 🍴 **Flame Tree Barbecue.** This quick-service eatery is one of the relatively undiscovered gems of Disney's culinary offerings; there's nothing fancy here, but you can dig into ribs, chicken, and pulled-pork sandwiches. For something with a lower calorie count, try the smoked turkey sandwich served with cranberry mayo or a great barbecued chicken served with baked beans and coleslaw. **Known for:** reasonably priced barbecue in an Animal Kingdom setting; ribs, chicken, and pulled-pork sampler; variety of beer and wine. [$] *Average main: $12* ✉ *Discovery Island, Animal Kingdom* 🌐 *disneyworld.disney.go.com/dining* ⊕ *1:A4.*

$ AFRICAN FAMILY Fodor's Choice ★ 🍴 **Harambe Market.** Carved into the walkway leading to the Wildlife Express train, this four-station food mart offers tikka masala chicken at Kitamu Grill, African spice–rubbed chicken at Chef Mwanga's, specialty meats at Famous Sausages, and fruit juices, beer, and sangria at Wanjoni Refreshments. **Known for:** shaded, family-sized, outdoor-market seating; African-inspired chicken, sausage, and ribs; appealing kids meals.

$ *Average main: $12* ✉ *Africa Walt Disney World, Animal Kingdom* ☎ *407/939–5277* ⊕ *disneyworld.disney.go.com/dining* ✛ *1:A4.*

$$ ✕ **Satu'li Canteen.** Situated in the heart of the new Pandora land of Animal Kingdom, Satu'li walks a line between fast-casual and fine dining with counter (or phone app-ready) ordering and surprisingly sophisticated, internationally inspired dishes with a healthy flair. The menu caters to grain bowl and bao sandwich aficionados with fresh-cooked ingredients and kids meals that are actually healthy. **Known for:** grain bowls, bao buns, and curry-pod sandwiches; fresh cooked, high-quality chicken, beef, and tofu; phone app ordering eliminates waiting. $ *Average main: $12* ✉ *Pandora—The World of Avatar, Animal Kingdom* ☎ *407/939–1947* ⊕ *disneyworld.disney.go.com/dining* ✛ *1:A4.*

INTERNATIONAL
FAMILY
Fodor's Choice
★

$$$$ ✕ **Tiffins.** Inspired by the worldwide journeys of Disney Imagineers, Tiffins is the theme parks' newest upscale sit-down restaurant and possibly the best eatery on Disney property, serving a wide-ranging international menu that changes constantly. Superb cross-cultural food is served in an inventive space with enough unique decor to fill a museum. **Known for:** superbly cooked, changing menu with Asian, Latin, and African flavors; elaborate decor; kids meals that aren't dumbed down. $ *Average main: $41* ✉ *Discovery Island, Animal Kingdom* ☎ *407/939–1947* ⊕ *disneyworld.disney.go.com/dining* ✛ *1:A4.*

INTERNATIONAL
FAMILY
Fodor's Choice
★

$$$$ ✕ **Tusker House.** This good-value restaurant offers all-buffet dining three meals a day, and a Donald's safari-themed character crew complements the African-esque decor and menu. Tusker House offers healthier fare like curry chicken, *peri-peri* (African hot pepper) marinated salmon, strip loin rubbed with *berbere* (an African spice mix), and saffron-infused root vegetables, along with the standard kids' fare. **Known for:** great food with reasonable prices; character appearances; wide-ranging buffet choices. $ *Average main: $42* ✉ *Africa, Animal Kingdom* ☎ *407/939–3463* ⊕ *www.disneyworld.disney.go.com/dining* ✛ *1:A4.*

AFRICAN
FAMILY
Fodor's Choice
★

$$$ ✕ **Yak & Yeti.** This large, pan-Asian restaurant offers sit-down service in a two-story, 250-seat venue in the Asia section, offering everything from a variety of noodles to curries to Korean barbecued ribs. The decor is pleasantly faux-Asian, with cracked plaster walls, wood carvings, and tile mosaic tabletops. **Known for:** large menu with Indian, Japanese, Chinese, and Korean influences; welcoming lounge for escaping the weather; shareable dim sum and appetizer baskets. $ *Average main: $22* ✉ *Asia, Animal Kingdom* ☎ *407/939–3463* ⊕ *disneyworld.disney. go.com/dining* ✛ *1:A4.*

ASIAN

5

ANIMAL KINGDOM RESORT AREA

$$$$ ✕ **Boma—Flavors of Africa.** Boma takes Western-style ingredients and prepares them with an African twist—then invites guests to walk through an African marketplace–style dining room to help themselves at counters piled high with flavor from an upscale buffet like no other. The dozen or so serving stations have entrées such as roasted pork, Durban-style chicken, spice-crusted beef, and fish served with tamarind

AFRICAN
FAMILY
Fodor's Choice
★

and other robust sauces; intriguing salads; and some of the best hummus this side of the Atlantic. **Known for:** superb food that appeals to the timid and adventurous alike; African flavors and dishes; endless buffet with wonderful service that appeals to kids. $ *Average main: $43* ⊠ *Animal Kingdom Lodge, 2901 Osceola Pkwy., Animal Kingdom Resort Area* ☎ *407/939–3463* ⊕ *disneyworld.disney.go.com/dining* ⊗ *No lunch* ✣ *1:A5.*

$$$$ ✕ **Jiko.** The name of this restaurant means "the cooking place" in Swa-
AFRICAN hili, and it is certainly that, offering a menu that is more African-inspired
Fodor's Choice than purely African as well as a strong selection of South African wines.
★ The dining area surrounds two big, wood-burning ovens and a grill area where you can watch cooks in North African–style caps working on your meal. **Known for:** African cuisine with an American flair and Indonesian accents; sophisticated surroundings and decor; Wagyu beef and Moroccan lamb. $ *Average main: $45* ⊠ *Animal Kingdom Lodge, 2901 Osceola Pkwy., Animal Kingdom Resort Area* ☎ *407/939–3463* ⊕ *disneyworld.disney.go.com/dining* ⊗ *No lunch* ✣ *1:A5.*

$$$ ✕ **Sanaa.** Most of the flavors are from India, yet Sanaa is really a cel-
AFRICAN ebration of the Spice Islands—locales off the coast of Africa that for cen-
FAMILY turies hosted traders from the world's corners. Exotic yet approachable
Fodor's Choice lunches and dinners make it a true find on the outer edges of the Disney
★ empire; views of zebras and giraffes on the savannah right out the picture windows are another draw. **Known for:** surprising combinations of African and Indian flavors; Indian style bread service; Goan seafood curry. $ *Average main: $26* ⊠ *Animal Kingdom Villas—Kidani Village, 3701 W. Osceola Pkwy., Animal Kingdom Resort Area* ☎ *407/989–3463* ⊕ *www.disneyworld.disney.go.com/dining* ✣ *1:A5.*

DISNEY SPRINGS

The phoenix of the former Downtown Disney/Pleasure Island complex has risen as Disney Springs, a shopping and dining extravaganza that features upscale shopping (from Disney-centric boutiques to Uniqlo's only Florida outlet), surprisingly tranquil walking paths, and some of Orlando's best—and celebrity chef-filled—dining.

$$$$ ✕ **The BOATHOUSE.** Contemporary and upscale, The BOATHOUSE sits
SEAFOOD directly on the Disney Springs waterfront, offering a menu of primarily fresh seafood and views of the restaurant's main attraction, so-called Amphicar tours. Boats that look like vintage, retrofitted vehicles offer the chance for a one-of-a-kind tour of Disney Springs as each vessel's four wheels submerge underwater, and a propeller jet glides riders throughout the lake. **Known for:** fresh seafood; lobster bake for two with whole Maine lobster and clams; "Amphicars" for rent. $ *Average main: $35* ⊠ *Disney Springs, The Landing, Disney Springs* ☎ *407/939–2628* ⊕ *disneyworld.disney.go.com/dining* ⊟ *No credit cards* ✣ *1:F4.*

$$$ ✕ **Chef Art Smith's Homecomin'.** Southern cookin' superstar Art Smith
AMERICAN brings his country concoctions to Disney Springs in this sprawlin' ode
FAMILY to fried chicken and comfort food. The portions are enormous and the flavors are bold. **Known for:** celebrity chef Art Smith's comfort food; "famous" fried chicken; signature cocktails and hummingbird cake.

$ *Average main: $28* ✉ *Disney Springs, The Landing, Disney Springs* ☎ *407/560–0100* ⊕ *www.homecominkitchen.com/* ⊹ *1:F4.*

$$$ ✕ **The Edison.** A massive brick structure that, according to Disney lore,
ITALIAN was the original power plant for the town of Disney Springs, now houses The Edison, an entertainment arena where food and drink mingle with circus entertainment and cabaret. The "industrial Gothic" decor, featuring a massive clock in the main lobby and a working steam engine lends itself to drama. **Known for:** sophisticated bar food like lamb balls and candied bacon; speakeasy late-night entertainment; steampunk industrial atmosphere in a "power plant" setting. $ *Average main: $25* ✉ *Disney Springs, The Landing, Disney Springs* ☎ *407/939–6244* ⊕ *www.theedisonfla.com/* ⊹ *1:F4.*

$$ ✕ **Frontera Cocina.** Under the watchful eye of celebrity chef Rick Bay-
MEXICAN less, Frontera brings a sophisticated yet casual approach to classic
FAMILY Mexican food. Diners experience genuine dishes from Oaxaca and Mexico City like house-made guacamole, short-rib tacos, and exquisite pan-roasted Florida shrimp. **Known for:** hand-crafted tortillas and guacamole; vegetarian options like zucchini enchiladas and mushroom tortas; fun and flavorful kids' meals. $ *Average main: $20* ✉ *Disney Springs, Town Center, Disney Springs* ☎ *407/560–0100* ⊕ *www.fronteracocina.com/* ⊹ *1:F4.*

$$ ✕ **House of Blues.** You're unlikely to like this place unless you enjoy
AMERICAN listening to high-decibel music during your meal. But if you do, this
FAMILY is a great spot to chow down from an eclectic menu that offers everything from ribs to shrimp and grits to a tasty chicken Caesar salad. **Known for:** high-end burgers and New Orleans fare; Sunday gospel brunch; loud background music at all times. $ *Average main: $21* ✉ *Disney Springs, West Side, 1490 E. Buena Vista Dr., Disney Springs* ☎ *407/934–2583* ⊕ *www.houseofblues.com* ⊹ *1:F4.*

$$$ ✕ **Maria & Enzo's Ristorante.** Built on the bones of the former Adventurer's
ITALIAN Club, this complex of three restaurants—Maria & Enzo's, Enzo's Hide-
FAMILY away Tunnel Bar and Restaurant, and Pizza Ponte—form a haven of
Fodor's Choice authentic Italian cuisine served up by two internationally known chefs.
★ The Disney "story" tells of an immigrant Italian couple who convert the Disney Springs Air Terminal into a fine dining restaurant, a pizzeria and bakery, and a belowground "speakeasy." The reality is, Maria & Enzo's offers fine Southern Italian cuisine in a sophisticated setting. **Known for:** authentic Roman and Southern Italian cuisine; some of the best steaks in Orlando; whimsical and detail-rich atmospheres. $ *Average main: $25* ✉ *Disney Springs, The Landing, Disney Springs* ☎ *407/560–8466* ⊕ *www.patinagroup.com/maria-enzos/* ⊹ *1:F4.*

$$$$ ✕ **Morimoto Asia.** Created by the Iron Chef himself, Masaharu Morim-
ASIAN FUSION oto, this is Morimoto's first restaurant that moves outside the sushi realm. The pan-Asian menu includes interesting variations on Chinese duck, Korean noodles, Singaporean laksa, and more. **Known for:** high-end sushi and pan-Asian cuisine; late-night hours until 1 am on weekends; best views of the Disney Springs lagoon from the upstairs patio. $ *Average main: $35* ✉ *Disney Springs, The Landing, Lake Buena Vista* ☎ *407/939–6686* ⊕ *www.patinagroup.com/morimoto-asia* ⊹ *1:F4.*

5

$$$$ SEAFOOD 🍴 **Paddlefish.** Housed in a paddleboat on Lake Buena Vista, Paddlefish (the once popular Fulton Crab House) is a sophisticated seafood destination with multiple outdoor dining areas. Same-day catch is presented in any number of ways, from raw bar delicacies to traditional Gulf-shore jambalaya or the Build-Your-Own Seafood Boil. **Known for:** freshest possible seafood from around the world; casual, late-night vibe from the rooftop lounge bar; raw bar and impeccably cooked dishes. [$] *Average main: $34* ✉ *Disney Springs, The Landing, Disney Springs* ☎ *407/939–2268* 🌐 *disneyworld.disney.go.com/dining* ✥ *1:F4.*

$$ AMERICAN FAMILY 🍴 **The Polite Pig.** The James Beard Award–nominated chef-owners of the critically acclaimed Ravenous Pig gastropub in Winter Park opened this sit-down restaurant to give visitors a taste of Orlando's finest. They do it by house-smoking ribs, brisket, and chicken, and offering locally made beer and cocktails on tap. **Known for:** locally sourced ingredients; ribs, brisket, and chicken smoked on premises; locally owned and operated by James Beard Award–nominated chefs. [$] *Average main: $18* ✉ *Disney Springs, Town Center, Disney Springs* ☎ *407/938–7444* 🌐 *politepig.com* ✥ *1:F4.*

$$$ IRISH FAMILY Fodor's Choice ★ 🍴 **Raglan Road Irish Pub.** If an authentic Irish pub—actually transported from the Old Country plank by plank—is your thing, Raglan Road is the place to go, for both superb traditional dishes and inventive twists. In addition to excellent fish-and-chips and shepherd's pie, the chefs twist Irish cuisine to include Gulf shrimp and risotto with buffalo mozzarella and fresh peas. **Known for:** first-rate dining and special chef-driven events; extensive beer and ale selections, including exclusive brews; nightly, sometimes hourly, entertainment. [$] *Average main: $25* ✉ *Disney Springs, The Landing, Disney Springs* ☎ *407/938–0300* 🌐 *www.raglanroadirishpub.com* ✥ *1:F4.*

$$$ ITALIAN 🍴 **Terralina Crafted Italian.** Under the guidance of James Beard Award winner and *Top Chef* master Tony Mantuano, Terralina (the former Portobello Country Italian Trattoria) brings back sophistication and Southern Italian cuisine to Disney Springs. Meticulously planned to look like a resort in Italy's Lake District, Terralina's open design and wood-fired grills provide a stylish atmosphere and some of the best recipes Mantuano can create, including wood-fired pizzas. **Known for:** antipasti tower starter; wood-fired pizzas, steaks, and seafood; stylish, Italian country atmosphere. [$] *Average main: $30* ✉ *Disney Springs, The Landing, Disney Springs* ☎ *407/939–6244* 🌐 *www.terralinacrafteditalian.com/* ✥ *1:F4.*

DISNEY SPRINGS RESORT AREA

$$$ CAJUN FAMILY 🍴 **Boatwright's Dining Hall.** A very impressive, handcrafted dining hall that looks like the internal workings of a wooden sailing ship—complete with an inverted hull on the ceiling and weathered shipbuilding tools—offers guests a menu of tasty Bayou dishes that ranges from Louisiana etouffee to crawfish bisque and andouille-stuffed catfish. Decadent desserts include the likes of St. Louis gooey butter cake and Bourbon Street pecan tarts. **Known for:** out of the way resort offering fine Louisiana cuisine; Cajun bayou catfish and jambalaya; seafood Charleston-style grits. [$] *Average main: $30* ✉ *Disney's Port Orleans Resort—Riverside,*

Disney Springs Resort Area ☎ *407/939–5277* 🌐 *disneyworld.disney.go.com/dining* ⏲ *No lunch* ✥ *1:E3.*

UNIVERSAL ORLANDO RESORT

With dozens of restaurants, including the world's largest Hard Rock Cafe, Universal Orlando is a mecca for those seeking a meal, plain or fancy. Islands of Adventure has from one to six eateries—not all of them strictly burger-and-fries affairs—in each of its lands. Universal Studios Florida has yet more places for lunch and dinner. And at CityWalk, a dining, retail, and entertainment complex that you have to pass as you leave the two theme parks, you'll find even more tempting eateries. CityWalk recently added several new eateries, including the highly themed Mexican concept Antojitos, the sushi-burger duo Cowfish, and a so-called artisan pizza place.

UNIVERSAL STUDIOS

While Universal Studios Florida is experiencing massive and continuous change, behind-the-scenes movie action is still the theme at Universal Studios Florida. Dining options are purposely cliché versions of restaurants you might see on the silver screen: an old-fashioned Italian joint, a '50s drive-in, an Irish pub, and a seafood house, for example. Be sure to snack on a sundae at a replica of Schwab's Pharmacy, where many starlets were "discovered." For Harry Potter fans, Leaky Cauldron is a must.

$$$ AMERICAN FAMILY

🍴 **Cafe La Bamba.** In the relaxed L.A. backdrop of the Hollywood Hotel, La Bamba is an unfussy sprawling spot that hosts Universal's Superstar Character Breakfast. The stars may vary, but *Hop* and *Despicable Me* faves tend to join Nickelodeon staples. **Known for:** character dining; Old Hollywood environment; pancakes, eggs, and fruit menu. [$] *Average main: $26* ✉ *Hollywood, 6000 Universal Blvd., Universal Studios* ☎ *407/224–9255* 🌐 *www.universalorlando.com* ✥ *2:D1.*

$$ IRISH

🍴 **Finnegan's Bar & Grill.** This Irish pub would look just right in Downtown Manhattan during the Ellis Island era. The menu offers classic Irish comfort food like shepherd's pie, corned beef and cabbage, bangers and mash, and fish-and-chips, plus Guinness on tap and a five-beer sampler. **Known for:** live music; classic Irish comfort food like shepherd's pie and beef stew; good place for a quick, filling sandwich. [$] *Average main: $16* ✉ *New York, Universal Studios* ☎ *407/363–8757* 🌐 *www.universalorlando.com* ✥ *2:D1.*

$ BRITISH FAMILY

🍴 **Leaky Cauldron.** British pub staples are fitting fare for Diagon Alley's restaurant. The drinks menu complements those hearty meals with kooky-sounding beverages from the Harry Potter books like Tongue-Tying Lemon Squash, Otter's Fizzy Orange Juice, and Fishy Green Ale (it's minty, with blueberry-flavored boba). **Known for:** quick-service; Potter-inspired meals; plowman's lunch of meats, cheeses, and salad; Butterbeer, of course. [$] *Average main: $14* ✉ *The Wizarding World of Harry Potter: Diagon Alley, Universal Studios* ☎ *407/224–9716* 🌐 *www.universalorlando.com* ✥ *2:D1.*

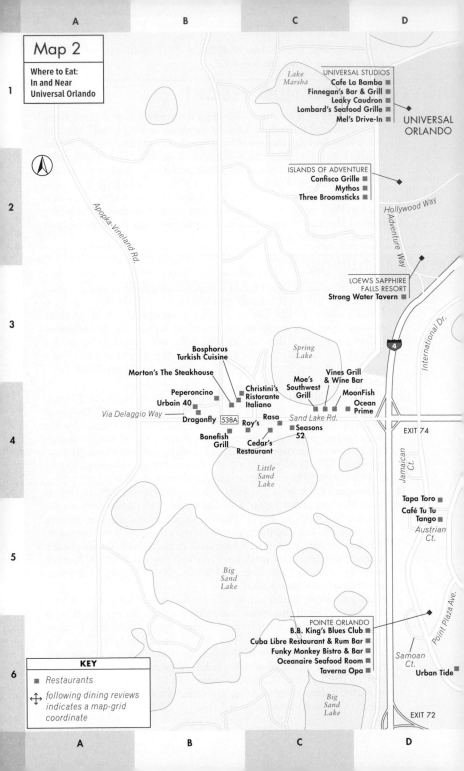

Map 2

**Where to Eat:
In and Near
Universal Orlando**

A   **B**   **C**   **D**

1

*Lake
Marsha*

UNIVERSAL STUDIOS
Cafe La Bamba ■
Finnegan's Bar & Grill ■
Leaky Cauldron ■
Lombard's Seafood Grille ■
Mel's Drive-In ■

♦ UNIVERSAL
ORLANDO

2

ISLANDS OF ADVENTURE
Confisco Grille ■
Mythos ■
Three Broomsticks ■ ——♦

Apopka-Vineland Rd.

Hollywood Way

Adventure Way

LOEWS SAPPHIRE
FALLS RESORT
Strong Water Tavern ■

International Dr.

3

*Spring
Lake*

〔4〕

**Bosphorus
Turkish Cuisine**

Morton's The Steakhouse

Peperoncino ■
Urbain 40 ■

**Christini's
Ristorante
Italiano** ■

**Moe's
Southwest
Grill** ■

**Vines Grill
& Wine Bar** ■

MoonFish ■
**Ocean
Prime** ■

Via Delaggio Way

Dragonfly ■ ⟨538A⟩ **Roy's** ■ **Rasa** ■

Sand Lake Rd.

EXIT 74

4

**Bonefish
Grill** ■

**Cedar's
Restaurant** ■

■ **Seasons
52**

*Little
Sand
Lake*

*Jamaican
Ct.*

Tapa Toro ■
**Café Tu Tu
Tango** ■
*Austrian
Ct.*

5

*Big
Sand
Lake*

Point Plaza Ave.

POINTE ORLANDO ——♦
B.B. King's Blues Club ■
Cuba Libre Restaurant & Rum Bar ■
Funky Monkey Bistro & Bar ■
Oceanaire Seafood Room ■
Taverna Opa ■

*Samoan
Ct.*

Urban Tide ■

6

KEY

■   *Restaurants*

⟨✛⟩   *following dining reviews
indicates a map-grid
coordinate*

*Big
Sand
Lake*

EXIT 72

A   **B**   **C**   **D**

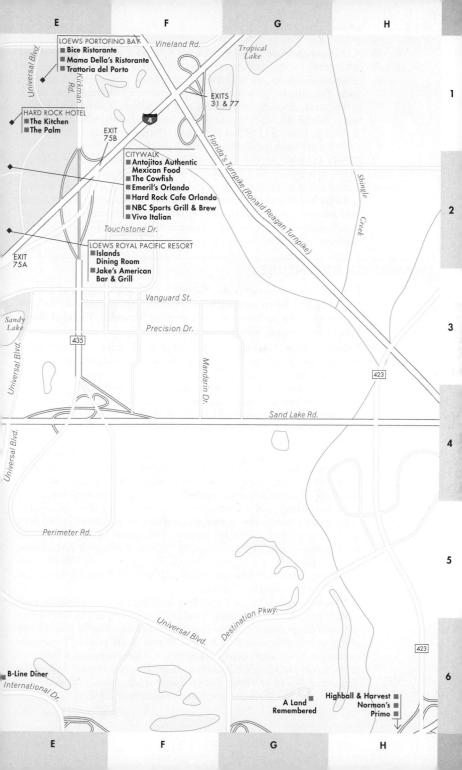

E **F** **G** **H**

LOEWS PORTOFINO BAY
■ Bice Ristorante
■ Mama Della's Ristorante
■ Trattoria del Porto

Vineland Rd.

Tropical Lake

Universal Blvd.

Kirkman Rd.

EXITS 31 & 77

1

HARD ROCK HOTEL
■ The Kitchen
■ The Palm

EXIT 75B

Shingle Creek

CITYWALK
■ Antojitos Authentic Mexican Food
■ The Cowfish
■ Emeril's Orlando
■ Hard Rock Cafe Orlando
■ NBC Sports Grill & Brew
■ Vivo Italian

Florida's Turnpike (Ronald Reagan Turnpike)

2

Touchstone Dr.

EXIT 75A

LOEWS ROYAL PACIFIC RESORT
■ Islands Dining Room
■ Jake's American Bar & Grill

Vanguard St.

Sandy Lake

Precision Dr.

3

435

Mandarin Dr.

423

Sand Lake Rd.

Universal Blvd.

4

Perimeter Rd.

5

Destination Pkwy.

Universal Blvd.

423

B-Line Diner

International Dr.

6

A Land Remembered

Highball & Harvest ■
Norman's ■
Primo ■

E **F** **G** **H**

$$ SEAFOOD FAMILY 🍴 **Lombard's Seafood Grille.** Fresh fried fish, fried shrimp, and assorted other takes on seafood are the specialty at this restaurant designed to resemble a Fisherman's Wharf warehouse from 19th-century San Francisco. You can also get a Boursin steak sandwich with fried onion strips, hamburgers, chicken sandwiches, and big salads. **Known for:** Fisherman's Wharf decor; fresh-catch fish basket; Lombard's lobster roll. [$] *Average main: $15* ✉ *San Francisco, Universal Studios* ☎ *407/224–6400* 🌐 *www.universalorlando.com* ✥ *2:D1.*

$ AMERICAN FAMILY 🍴 **Mel's Drive-In.** At the corner of Hollywood and Vine is a flashy 1950s-style eatery with a pink-and-white 1956 Ford Crown Victoria parked out in front. For burgers and fries, this is one of the best choices in the park, and it comes complete with a roving doo-wop group during peak seasons. **Known for:** drive-in styling; live entertainment; frosty milk shakes and grilled burgers. [$] *Average main: $11* ✉ *Hollywood, Universal Studios* ☎ *407/363–8766* 🌐 *www.universalorlando.com* ✥ *2:D1.*

ISLANDS OF ADVENTURE

Here the food always fits the "island," from green eggs and ham at Seuss Landing (open seasonally) to an otherworldly grotto in the Lost Continent to the barbecue fare on tap in the Wizarding World of Harry Potter's Hogsmeade Village.

$ AMERICAN 🍴 **Confisco Grille.** You could walk right past this full-service restaurant without noticing it, but if you want a good meal and sit-down service, don't pass by too quickly. The menu is American with international influences. **Known for:** Italian, Greek, Asian, and Mexican dishes; overlooked location means better chance of seating; Backwater Bar next door. [$] *Average main: $13* ✉ *Port of Entry, Islands of Adventure* ☎ *407/224–4404* 🌐 *www.universalorlando.com* ✥ *2:D2.*

$$ ECLECTIC Fodor's Choice ★ 🍴 **Mythos.** Built into a rock cliff, the menu at this enchanting eatery includes such mainstays as pad Thai and pan-seared salmon with lemon-basil butter and sandwiches like crab-cake sliders and roast beef panini with caramelized yellow onions, roasted red peppers, and pepperoncini. The building itself—which looks like a giant rock formation from the outside and a huge cave (albeit one with plush upholstered seating) from the inside—is enough to grab your attention, but so does the waterfront view of the big lagoon in the center of the theme park. **Known for:** spectacular decor; one of the best theme park restaurants; lamb burgers, crab cake sandwiches. [$] *Average main: $17* ✉ *The Lost Continent, Islands of Adventure* ☎ *407/224–4533* 🌐 *www.universalorlando.com* ⏲ *No dinner* ✥ *2:D2.*

$ BRITISH 🍴 **Three Broomsticks.** Harry Potter fans flock here to taste pumpkin juice (with hints of honey and vanilla) and Butterbeer (sort of like bubbly butterscotch cream soda, or maybe shortbread cookies). They're on the menu along with barbecue and traditional British foods at this Hogsmeade restaurant. **Known for:** quirky Harry Potter atmosphere; quick and courteous service; full English breakfast daily. [$] *Average main: $12* ✉ *The Wizarding World of Harry Potter: Hogsmeade, Islands of Adventure* ☎ *407/224–4233* 🌐 *www.universalorlando.com* ✥ *2:D2.*

CITYWALK

Restaurants, bars, clubs, shops, live entertainment, and movie theaters make Universal CityWalk an attraction on its own. The upbeat expanse serves as the entrance to both Universal Orlando theme parks—you can't reach the parks from the parking lot without walking through—and is an after-dark destination for tourists and locals alike.

$$
MEXICAN
FAMILY
✗ **Antojitos Authentic Mexican Food.** The massive and very noisy Antojitos brings the specialties of Mexican cantinas and food carts to CityWalk. The outside looks like it's been spray-painted with shocking pastels. **Known for:** noisy atmosphere; table-side guacamole; beer-braised goat stew. $ *Average main: $17* ⊠ *Universal CityWalk, 6000 Universal Blvd., CityWalk* ☎ *407/224–2807* ⊕ *www.universalorlando.com* ⊘ *No lunch* ✛ *2:E2.*

$$
BURGER
FAMILY
✗ **The Cowfish.** Burgers, sushi, and a combo the founders call "burgushi" bring Universal goers to this contemporary second-story restaurant. The setting is flashy, with colorful booths and playful decor touches complementing an array of video screens showing schools of fish swimming by, aquarium-style. **Known for:** unusual combinations of beef and fish sushi; signature "fusion" rolls; large burger menu. $ *Average main: $15* ⊠ *Universal CityWalk, 6000 Universal Blvd., CityWalk* ☎ *407/224–9255* ⊕ *www.thecowfish.com* ⊘ *No lunch* ✛ *2:E2.*

$$$$
CAJUN
Fodor's Choice
★
✗ **Emeril's Orlando.** The popular eatery is a culinary shrine to Emeril Lagasse, the famous TV chef who occasionally makes an appearance. Although the modern interior, with its 30-foot ceilings, blond woods, second-story wine loft, and lots of galvanized steel looks nothing like the French Quarter, the hardwood floors and linen tablecloths create an environment befitting the stellar nature of the cuisine. **Known for:** inventive and creative Louisiana cooking; signature dishes from celebrity chef Emeril; authentic New Orleans po-boy sandwiches. $ *Average main: $33* ⊠ *Universal CityWalk, 6000 Universal Blvd., CityWalk* ☎ *407/224–2424* ⊕ *www.emerils.com* ✛ *2:E2.*

$$$
AMERICAN
FAMILY
✗ **Hard Rock Cafe Orlando.** Built to resemble Rome's Colosseum yet surprisingly sophisticated inside, this 1,000-seat restaurant—the largest Hard Rock Cafe in the world–is huge, yet getting a seat at lunch or dinner can still require a long wait. The music is always loud and the walls are filled with rock memorabilia. **Known for:** largest Hard Rock in the world; on-site smoked barbecue; cowboy rib-eye steak. $ *Average main: $23* ⊠ *Universal CityWalk, 6050 Universal Blvd., CityWalk* ☎ *407/351–7625* ⊕ *www.hardrockcafe.com* ✛ *2:E2.*

$
AMERICAN
FAMILY
✗ **NBC Sports Grill & Brew.** Though it's not a working brewery (sorry to say, the giant beer tanks are just for show), the more than 100 beers in bottles and on tap should provide something for everyone. If not, they can be distracted by the more than 100 giant TV screens, which are everywhere. **Known for:** massive burgers; giant TV screens at every turn; more than 100 beers on tap and bottled. $ *Average main: $14* ⊠ *Universal CityWalk, CityWalk* ☎ *407/224–3663* ⊕ *universalorlando.com* ✛ *2:E2.*

$$$
ITALIAN
✗ **Vivo Italian.** House-made pasta and inventive cocktails are highlights at the ultrahip Vivo, which is styled after a trendy Roman nightclub. The waiters are attentive and the food is quietly impressive—the blazing

5

wood oven makes almost instantaneous pizzas. **Known for:** wood-fired pizza; fresh made pasta; Tuscan chicken and beef specialties. [$] *Average main: $22 ✉ Universal CityWalk, 6000 Universal Blvd., CityWalk ☎ 407/224-2691 🌐 www.universalorlando.com ✣ 2:E2.*

UNIVERSAL HOTELS

$$$$ ITALIAN 🍴 **Bice Ristorante.** Trendy, pricey Bice is the Orlando unit of an international upscale chain of Italian restaurants. Bice (pronounced "*BEACH*-ay") is an Italian nickname for Beatrice, as in Beatrice Ruggeri, who founded the original Milan location of this family restaurant in 1926. **Known for:** upscale Italian cuisine; house-made pasta; braised veal osso buco. [$] *Average main: $34 ✉ Loews Portofino Bay Hotel, 5601 Universal Blvd., Universal Orlando Resort ☎ 407/503–1415 🌐 www.orlando.bicegroup.com ⏲ No lunch ✣ 2:E1.*

$$$ ASIAN FUSION FAMILY 🍴 **Islands Dining Room.** An airy room with a tropical decor and menu items inspired by the Pacific Rim, Islands not only serves breakfast and dinner, it also has a play area that keeps tots entertained. On Monday, Wednesday, and Thursday nights, diners are treated to visits from assorted characters such as Scooby Doo and Shaggy—at no extra cost. **Known for:** character dining; breakfast buffet; extensive kids' menus. [$] *Average main: $22 ✉ Loews Royal Pacific Resort, 6300 Hollywood Way, Universal Orlando Resort ☎ 407/503–3463 🌐 www.loewshotels.com ⏲ No lunch ✣ 2:E2.*

$$$ AMERICAN FAMILY 🍴 **Jake's American Bar & Grill.** From noon through the evening, Jake's is more of a gastropub with an air-flight theme, but every morning the cozy space welcomes characters and the guests who adore them. Character breakfasts here are buffet-style, and the costumed entertainers might be from The Simpsons, Scooby-Doo, or Despicable Me. **Known for:** character breakfast; beer festival events; crawfish chowder. [$] *Average main: $27 ✉ Loews Royal Pacific Resort, 6300 Hollywood Way, Universal Orlando Resort ☎ 407/503–3463 🌐 www.universalorlando.com ✣ 2:E2.*

$$$$ MODERN AMERICAN FAMILY 🍴 **The Kitchen.** Contemporary yet comfy, this hotel restaurant tends to straddle various worlds. Its menu has comfort food with creative upscale twists. **Known for:** burgers and rotisserie chicken; special Kids' Crib area; visiting rock stars. [$] *Average main: $31 ✉ Hard Rock Hotel, 5800 Universal Blvd., Universal Orlando Resort ☎ 407/503–3463 🌐 www.hardrockhotelorlando.com ✣ 2:E1.*

$$$ ITALIAN 🍴 **Mama Della's Ristorante.** Like stepping into Mama Della's dining room, this playfully themed Italian restaurant happens to have excellent food. The premise is that you're eating at a home-turned-restaurant—there's an actual "Mama Della" who appears nightly—and that warmth enhances the experience (as does the serenade by an accordionist, guitar player, and vocalist). **Known for:** intimate New York/Neapolitan environment; better-than-usual Italian cuisine; house-made gnocchi. [$] *Average main: $30 ✉ Loews Portofino Bay Hotel, 5601 Universal Blvd., Universal Orlando Resort ☎ 407/503–3463 🌐 www.loewshotels.com ⏲ No lunch ✣ 2:E1.*

$$$$ STEAKHOUSE 🍴 **The Palm.** With its dark-wood interior and hundreds of framed celebrity caricatures, this pricey restaurant resembles its famed New York City namesake. For most diners the steaks are the star of the show. **Known for:** steak, steak, and steak; surprisingly superb seafood starters; Italian dishes from old family recipes. [$] *Average main: $42* ✉ *Hard Rock Hotel, 5800 Universal Blvd., Universal Orlando Resort* ☎ *407/503–7256* 🌐 *www.thepalm.com* 🕒 *No lunch* ✥ *2:E1.*

$$ CARIBBEAN Fodor's Choice ★ 🍴 **Strong Water Tavern.** Billed as a "hotel lounge," Strong Water breaks all the rules for hotel dining. The surrounds are comfortable, and the attentive staff serves some of the most memorable food in Orlando. **Known for:** Caribbean food and drink; surprisingly popular curried goat; extensive rum menu. [$] *Average main: $20* ✉ *Loews Sapphire Falls Resort at Universal Orlando, 6601 Adventure Way, West Orlando* ☎ *407/503–5000* 🌐 *loewshotels.com/sapphire-falls-resort/dining/lounges* ✥ *2:D2.*

$$$ ITALIAN FAMILY 🍴 **Trattoria del Porto.** Italian cuisine will please parents, while Bart Simpson or Scooby-Doo may be on hand to distract the kids, at this casual hotel restaurant with a dedicated children's play area. Characters appear on Friday nights between 6 and 10 pm, coinciding with "Pasta Cucina" ($26 adult, $12 child), an all-you-can-eat experience where guests create their own pasta dishes. **Known for:** family meals; in-house pastry chef; children's play area with cribs and high chairs. [$] *Average main: $26* ✉ *Loews Portofino Bay Hotel, 5601 Universal Blvd., Universal Orlando Resort* ☎ *407/503–3463* 🌐 *www.loewshotels.com/portofino-bay-hotel* ✥ *2:E1.*

5

CENTRAL ORLANDO

Central Orlando is quintessential urban Florida and offers much more than typical chain restaurants. Here you'll find a local, independent dining scene that's driven by award-winning and inventive chefs, creating a hot spot for creative cuisine.

$$ ITALIAN 🍴 **Armando's.** Armando Martorelli has opened many local restaurants in his career since coming from Italy to Florida, but his namesake eatery is the epitome of his craft. Like the Winter Park location, here you'll find a relaxed, molto-Italian atmosphere with a great neighborhood vibe that keeps people coming back for superb seafood and what is perhaps the area's best pizza. **Known for:** Neapolitan specialties; wood-fired oven pizza; extensive wine and cocktail list with a very popular bar area. [$] *Average main: $18* ✉ *2305 Edgewater Dr., College Park* ☎ *407/930–0333* 🌐 *armandosorlando.com* ✥ *3:C4.*

$ MEXICAN FUSION FAMILY Fodor's Choice ★ 🍴 **Black Rooster.** Nestled in the funky neighborhood of Mills 50, this small, casual taco place has everything from corn tortillas to guacamole that are made to order with every dish. Get the pulled roasted chicken tinga for sophisticated tastes, and the crispy fish for an unusual alternative to the Rooster's seared beef carne asada. **Known for:** inventive and flavorful tacos; chocolate chip spicy flan; made to order guacamole. [$] *Average main: $4* ✉ *1323 N Mills Ave., Central Orlando* ☎ *407/601–0994* 🌐 *www.blackroostertaqueria.com/* 🕒 *Closed Mon.* ✥ *3:E5.*

$$ AMERICAN 🍴 **Blue Jacket Grille.** A humble hideaway located near a strip mall, Blue Jacket draws the hipster crowd as well as the still-vibrant former navy

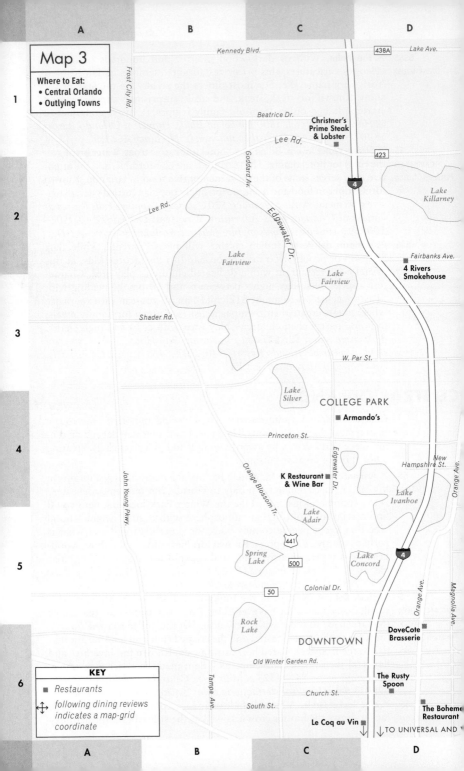

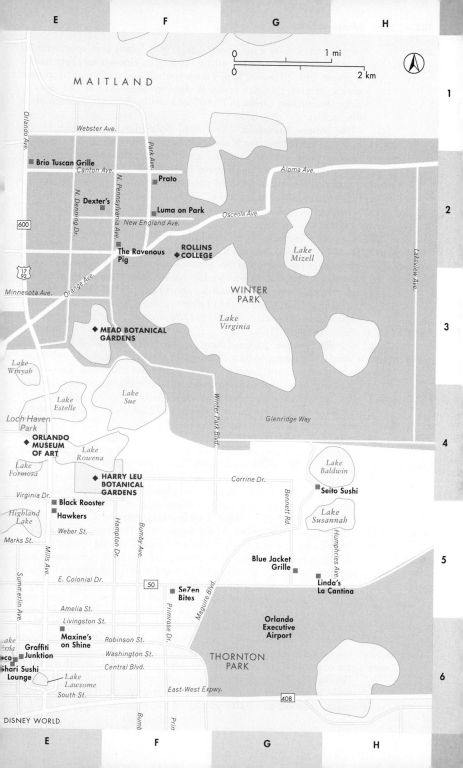

population. This is a (gourmet) burger and (craft) beer spot, with 20 brews on tap and another 40 by the bottle. **Known for:** very casual taproom with 20 brews; happy hour specials and trivia nights; chicken wings, burgers, and flatbreads. [$] *Average main: $15* ✉ *745 Bennett Rd., Downtown Orlando* ☎ *407/868–9006* 🌐 *www.facebook.com/bluejacketgrille/* ✥ *3:G5.*

$$$$ ECLECTIC 🍴 **The Boheme Restaurant.** The Grand Bohemian, a boutique, luxury hotel, is the setting for a sleek city-center restaurant. As a prelude to your main, try the calamari served with pumpkin-crab bisque or grilled Spanish octopus. **Known for:** upscale, chef-driven dining in a fashionable hotel; pre- and postdinner bar; elaborate Sunday jazz brunch. [$] *Average main: $34* ✉ *Grand Bohemian Hotel Orlando, 325 S. Orange Ave., Downtown Orlando* ☎ *407/313–9000* 🌐 *www.grandbohemianhotel.com* ✥ *3:D6.*

$$$ BRASSERIE Fodor's Choice ★ 🍴 **DoveCote Brasserie.** Chef Clay Miller brings big city sophistication to Downtown Orlando with a French-American fusion menu and craft cocktails. Everything that can be made in-house, such as pickles, condiments, and bread, are. **Known for:** handcrafted charcuterie and cocktails; lemon thyme chicken; braised short ribs with trumpet mushrooms. [$] *Average main: $24* ✉ *Bank of America Building, 390 N Orange Ave., Downtown Orlando* ☎ *407/930–1700* 🌐 *dovecoteorlando.com* 🕒 *No dinner Sun.* ✥ *3:D6.*

$ BURGER FAMILY 🍴 **Graffiti Junktion.** Astoundingly popular, Graffiti Junktion holds the casual burger/wrap/sandwich crowd in thrall. Noisy and visually loud, picnic benches and commissioned graffiti are the decor. **Known for:** late hours and noisy atmosphere; fresh-formed burgers with inventive toppings; hand-cut french fries. [$] *Average main: $12* ✉ *700 East Washington St., Downtown Orlando* ☎ *321/424–5800* 🌐 *graffitijunktion.com* ✥ *3:E6.*

$$ ASIAN FUSION Fodor's Choice ★ 🍴 **Hawkers.** Hipsters, families, and business groups dine side by side at this popular restaurant, a laid-back spot that specializes in Asian street food. Travel the continent with scratch-made specialties from all around Southeast Asia. **Known for:** typical dishes like roti canai, sesame noodles, and stir-fried udon; hip and casual atmosphere; extensive and exotic beer selections. [$] *Average main: $16* ✉ *1103 Mills Ave., Mills 50 District* ☎ *407/237–0606* 🌐 *eathawkers.com* ✥ *3:E5.*

$$$$ AMERICAN Fodor's Choice ★ 🍴 **K Restaurant & Wine Bar.** At the forefront of Orlando's local and sustainable dining scene, K is a hot spot for locals, serving upscale, eclectic American and Italian cuisine in an intimate setting. Besides happy-hour specials and dinner, K hosts wine tastings in the garden or on the patio and popular prix-fixe wine dinners. **Known for:** ever-changing seasonal menu; great local meeting spot away from Downtown Orlando; mac-and-cheese specials. [$] *Average main: $34* ✉ *1710 Edgewater Dr., College Park* ☎ *407/872–2332* 🌐 *www.krestaurant.net/* 🕒 *Sun.* ✥ *3:C4.*

$$$ STEAKHOUSE FAMILY 🍴 **Linda's La Cantina.** A favorite among locals since 1947, this down-home steak house serves good cuts of meat, cooked expertly and served at a reasonable price. Butchery is done on premises, and there are no TVs over the bar to distract from a pleasant conversation over a great steak. **Known for:** classic Orlando institution; hand-cut, house-aged steaks; seafood and pasta entrées. [$] *Average main: $26* ✉ *4721 E.*

Colonial Dr., Downtown Orlando ✣ Near Orlando Executive Airport ☎ 407/894–4491 🌐 lindaslacantinasteakhouse.com/ ⏲ No lunch. Closed Sun. and Mon. ✣ 3:G5.

$$ AMERICAN 🍴 **Maxine's on Shine.** A holdover to when neighborhood restaurants were actually in a neighborhood, Maxine's is casual, hip, local, and friendly. The menu ranges from sophisticated seafood to brisket burgers and Black Angus filet mignon. **Known for:** lively, neighborhood atmosphere; outdoor dining; seafood dishes from a veteran local chef. [$] *Average main: $16 ✉ 337 N. Shine, Downtown Orlando ☎ 407/674–6841 🌐 maxinesonshine.com ⏲ Closed Mon. ✣ 3:E6.*

$$$ AMERICAN Fodor's Choice ★ 🍴 **The Rusty Spoon.** Lovingly raised animals and locally grown produce are the menu foundation at this Downtown gastropub owned by chef Kathleen Blake, a four-time James Beard Award nominee. An ideal spot for a business lunch or dinner before a basketball game, theater, or concert, the wood-and-brick dining room is a comfortable backdrop to hearty, seasonal American meals with Italian and Southern elements. **Known for:** locally sourced and Florida-specific ingredients; "Lake Meadow" salad, with local greens and sautéed chicken livers; impressive service. [$] *Average main: $25 ✉ 55 W. Church St., Downtown Orlando ☎ 407/401–8811 🌐 www.therustyspoon.com ⏲ No lunch weekends ✣ 3:D6.*

$$ JAPANESE FUSION Fodor's Choice ★ 🍴 **Seito Sushi.** The epitome of modern Japanese cuisine, Seito offers crowd-pleasing traditional ramen bowls as well as unique, handcrafted sushi combinations. The sophisticated and fun bar specializes in cask whiskey and multiple exclusive sake brands. **Known for:** hand-pulled ramen noodles; exclusively crafted sushi; boneless, fried whole snapper for two. [$] *Average main: $18 ✉ 4898 New Broad St., Central Orlando ☎ 407/898–8801 🌐 seitosushi.com [M] Baldwin Park ✣ 3:G4.*

$$ AMERICAN FAMILY Fodor's Choice ★ 🍴 **Se7en Bites.** Trina Gregory-Propst and her team of bakers and cooks make the biggest and most satisfying breakfasts, lunches, and sweet treats in town. Try a scratch chicken pot pie with the most glorious crust, a mile-high meatloaf sandwich, or the "7th Trimester" of buttermilk garlic biscuit, over-medium egg. and smoked bacon, smothered in five-cheese mac-and-cheese. **Known for:** over the top Southern breakfast specials; funky Downtown location; featured on *Diners, Drive-ins, and Dives.* [$] *Average main: $15 ✉ 617 Primrose Dr., Central Orlando ☎ 407/302–0727 🌐 www.se7enbites.com ⏲ No dinner; closed Mon ✣ 3:F5.*

$$$ JAPANESE 🍴 **Shari Sushi Lounge.** Resplendent with metallic leather and chic white seats, this trendy eatery has more the atmosphere of a fast-lane singles bar than of an Asian oasis, but the dishes from the kitchen—fresh sushi and cooked Asian entrées—distinguish the place as a legit dining establishment. If you're here for the sushi, the place will not disappoint. **Known for:** young, dressed-up crowd; multicultural dishes like Korean tacos; extensive sushi menu. [$] *Average main: $24 ✉ 621 E. Central Blvd., Thornton Park ☎ 407/420–9420 🌐 www.sharisushilounge.com ⏲ No lunch ✣ 3:E6.*

$$$ SOUTHERN 🍴 **Soco.** Under the talented hands of executive chef Greg Richie, Southern staples get mighty fancy at Soco, as both the decor and the menu mesh classic and creative in a suave way. Vegetarians get one of the

5

best meatless entrées in town with the chicken-fried cauliflower steak, a massive dish finished with a rich tomato gravy. **Known for:** funky daily specials like TV Dinner Thursday; sophisticated bar; vegetarian options. [$] *Average main: $23* ✉ *629 E. Central Blvd., Thornton Park* ☎ *407/849–1800* 🌐 *www.socothorntonpark.com* 🕓 *No lunch.* ✥ *3:E6.*

INTERNATIONAL DRIVE

A number of restaurants are scattered among the hotels that line International Drive. Many are branches of chains, from fast-food spots to themed coffee shops and up, but the food here can be quite good. To get to the area, take Interstate 4 Exit 72 or 74A. Count on it taking up to half an hour from the Kissimmee area or from a WDW property.

$$ BARBECUE 🍴 **B.B. King's Blues Club.** This massive restaurant is dedicated to soul food, live blues, and the legacy of B.B. King. **Known for:** live bands and dancing; barbecued ribs, brisket, and shrimp and grits; messy and delicious burgers. [$] *Average main: $18* ✉ *Pointe Orlando, 9101 International Dr., International Drive* ☎ *407/370–4550* 🌐 *bbkings.com/orlando/* ✥ *2:D6.*

$$ AMERICAN FAMILY 🍴 **B-Line Diner.** As you might expect from its location in the Hyatt Regency, this slick modern diner is not exactly cheap, but the salads, sandwiches, and griddle foods are tops. The classic combo—a thick, juicy burger with fries and a milk shake—is done beautifully. **Known for:** 1950s dinner theme; 24-hour service with late-night specials; large dessert menu. [$] *Average main: $20* ✉ *Hyatt Regency Orlando, 9801 International Dr., International Drive* ☎ *407/284–1234* 🌐 *orlando.regency.hyatt.com* ✥ *2:D6.*

$$$ ECLECTIC 🍴 **Café Tu Tu Tango.** The food here is served tapas-style—everything is appetizer size but plentiful, and relatively inexpensive. The restaurant is designed to resemble an artist's loft; artists paint at easels while diners take a culinary trip around the world. **Known for:** small plates ideal for sharing; live entertainment; "Wine Down Wednesday" drink specials. [$] *Average main: $23* ✉ *8625 International Dr., International Drive* ☎ *407/248–2222* 🌐 *www.cafetututango.com* ✥ *2:D5.*

$$$ CUBAN 🍴 **Cuba Libre Restaurant & Rum Bar.** The dining rooms at this Cuban restaurant feel as if they're movie sets of Old Havana, with dramatic touches upstairs and down. Carved second-level balconies, "weathered" facades, and stained glass replicate the Cuban city. **Known for:** exotic Cuban village decor; extensive rum bar; seafood paella and Cuban sandwiches. [$] *Average main: $28* ✉ *Pointe Orlando, 9101 International Dr., International Drive* ☎ *407/226–1600* 🌐 *www.cubalibrerestaurant.com* 🕓 *No lunch.* ✥ *2:D6.*

$$$ ECLECTIC 🍴 **Funky Monkey Bistro & Bar.** Funky Monkey brings to the Convention Center area an enticing mix of creative American cuisine, sushi, interesting wines, and occasional entertainment—including Friday- and Saturday-night drag shows. Fried goat cheese, soy-ginger glazed pork tenderloin, and salmon lo mein are typical choices. **Known for:** crab cake sandwich; appetizer menu; Friday and Saturday night "Drag Diva" shows. [$] *Average main: $29* ✉ *Pointe Orlando, 9101 International Dr., International Drive* ☎ *407/418–9463* 🌐 *www.funkymonkeywine.com* 🕓 *No lunch Sun.* ✥ *2:D6.*

$$$$ ✕**Oceanaire Seafood Room.** Don't let the 1930s-era ocean-liner interior
SEAFOOD fool you: as theme restaurants go, this place is a good one, packing
everything from—depending on the season—Canadian walleye, Costa
Rican swordfish, or Ecuadorian mahimahi. The straightforward preparation here—grilled or broiled, brushed with lemon butter—is welcome.
Known for: exceptional seafood; large wine menu; "Grand Shellfish
Tower" raw bar offering. $ *Average main: $46* ✉ *Pointe Orlando,*
9101 International Dr., International Drive ☎ *407/363–4801* ⊕ *www.*
theoceanaire.com ◷ *No lunch* ⊹ *2:D6.*

$$$ ✕**Tapa Toro.** Chef Wendy Lopez serves authentic tapas and paella at
SPANISH this Spanish restaurant in the heart of the I-Drive 360 complex (look
for the giant revolving observation wheel). Tapas dishes include a
great gazpacho soup and fiery *patatas bravas* (home fries with a
spicy tomato sauce), and the kitchen does well with grilled meats like
lamb and rib eye. **Known for:** family-style tapas and entrées; several
varieties of paella; live entertainment. $ *Average main: $22* ✉ *8441*
International Dr., International Drive ☎ *407/226–2929* ⊕ *tapatoro.*
restaurant ⊹ *2:D5.*

$$$ ✕**Taverna Opa.** This high-energy Greek restaurant offers a fun evening
GREEK in a lively environment to supplement excellent Greek staples and a
FAMILY nice selection of *meze* (small plate) appetizers. Here the ouzo flows like
a mountain stream, the Greek (and global) music almost reaches the
level of a rock concert, and the roaming belly dancers actively encourage diners to join in. **Known for:** traditional Greek taverna food; live
entertainment; large selection of meze, with vegetarian options. $ *Aver-*
age main: $27 ✉ *Pointe Orlando, 9101 International Dr., International*
Drive ☎ *407/351–8660* ⊕ *www.opaorlando.com* ⊹ *2:D6.*

$$$ ✕**Urban Tide.** A wide-ranging menu of high-end coastal Florida cuisine
AMERICAN offers something for everyone, from extravagant steaks and seafood to
a surprisingly complete vegetarian larder. The food at this chef-run spot
is as appealing as the extensive wine list; it includes items like seafood
charcuterie, lobster sausage, and salmon pastrami. **Known for:** house-
made seafood charcuterie; locally sourced produce and meats; extensive
wine list. $ *Average main: $30* ✉ *Hyatt Regency Orlando, 9801 Inter-*
national Dr., International Drive ☎ *407/345–4570* ⊕ *orlando.regency.*
hyatt.com ⊹ *2:D6.*

SOUTH ORLANDO

$$$$ ✕**A Land Remembered.** Located in the golf clubhouse of the Rosen Shingle
STEAKHOUSE Creek resort, the name of this award-winning steak house comes from
the iconic novel about Florida by Patrick D. Smith. **Known for:** house-
aged steaks; resort atmosphere; Cataplana broiled seafood sampler.
$ *Average main: $58* ✉ *Rosen Shingle Creek, 9939 Universal Blvd.,*
South Orlando ☎ *407/996–9939* ⊕ *www.landrememberedrestaurant.*
com ◷ *No lunch* ⊹ *2:G6.*

$$$ ✕**Highball & Harvest.** Modern spins on locally sourced Southern staples
SOUTHERN is the crux of this sprawling restaurant, where scratch cooking by Ritz
chefs is the rule; produce is grown on the resort's own Whisper Creek
private farm. Cocktails are handcrafted; even the ice is shaved from

Popular Chain Restaurants

When all you want is a quick bite, consider these chain restaurants. They seem to crop up everywhere, and all have tables where you can sit for a few moments before heading back out to the shops and attractions.

Anthony's Coal-Fired Pizza: Thin-crust pizzas with generous toppings like arugula and pepperoni are baked—charred, really—in a coal-fired oven. The chicken wings are also popular in these bustling spaces near Restaurant Row and in Altamonte Springs. *www.anthonyscoalfiredpizza. com*

Bubbalou's Bodacious Bar-B-Que: A quintet of local smokers serves up mounds of Southern barbecue, from baby back ribs to pulled-pork sandwiches. The restaurant on Kirkman Road and Conroy-Windermere Road is minutes from Universal Orlando. *www.bubbalous.com*

Einstein Bros. Bagels: For a light breakfast or lunch, Einstein's satisfies with a menu of bagels, wraps, salads, and sandwiches. *www.einsteinbros. com*

First Watch: Breakfast classics like pancakes and waffles make First Watch a popular choice for locals, who line up on weekends for Key West "crepeggs" (a crepe filled with eggs that have been scrambled with turkey, avocado, bacon, tomatoes, and Monterey Jack cheese), and Floridian French toast with bananas, kiwi, and berries. *www.firstwatch.com*

Five Guys Burgers and Fries: This burger joint has a nearly cultlike

following for its freshly ground beef. Fifteen toppings are available for no charge, and the fries are freshly cut. *www.fiveguys.com*

4 Rivers Smokehouse: The king of local barbecue slow-smokes Texas-style brisket, serves mountains of St. Louis ribs, and acres of towering desserts. *www.4rsmokehouse.com*

Hawker's: Local Asian street food restaurant made good, expanding in recent years from one to five locations, three in the Orlando area. *www.eatathawkers.com*

Jimmy John's: Lunchtime lines are out the door at Orlando's many Jimmy John's, where the "world's greatest gourmet sandwiches" are essentially subs and clubs. *www.jimmyjohns.com*

Panera Bread: Fresh-baked pastries and bagels are the mainstays here, although you can grab a hearty and inexpensive meal like smoked-turkey panino on three-cheese bread or a bowl of soup served in a hollowed-out sourdough loaf. *www.panerabread. com*

Pei Wei Asian Diner: Bold flavors from all corners of Asia come together at these fast-casual restaurants, where a hearty noodle bowl, orange-peel beef, or sweet-and-sour tofu will come in at less than $10. *www.peiwei.com*

TooJay's Gourmet Deli: A New York deli it ain't, but the TooJay's chain offers a welcome pastrami fix for those with a yen for salty meat on crusty seeded rye. *www.toojays.com*

a block to order. **Known for:** hyperlocal produce from on-site farm; seasonal menus; handcrafted cocktails. $ *Average main: $25 ⊠ Ritz-Carlton Orlando Grande Lakes, 4012 Central Florida Pkwy., South Orlando* ☎ *407/393–4422* ⊕ *www.grandelakes.com* ✛ *2:H6.*

$$$$
FRENCH

✕ **Le Coq au Vin.** This traditional French restaurant, owned by Sandy and Reimund Pitz, is a hideaway located in a small nondescript house in South Orlando. In business since 1976, it seats 100 people in three quaint dining rooms. **Known for:** traditional high-style French cooking; steamed mussels and onion soup; exemplary service. $ *Average main: $32 ⊠ 4800 S. Orange Ave., South Orlando* ☎ *407/851–6980* ⊕ *www.lecoqauvinrestaurant.com* ☽ *No lunch. Closed Mon.* ✛ *3:D6.*

$$$$
ECLECTIC
Fodor's Choice
★

✕ **Norman's.** Legendary Florida chef Norman Van Aken brings impressive credentials to the restaurant that bears his name. Van Aken's culinary roots go back to the Florida Keys, where he's credited with creating "Floribbean" cuisine, part Key West and part Caribbean—although he now weaves in flavors from all continents. **Known for:** James Beard Award–winning chef; creative preparations with wide-ranging international influences; extensive wine list. $ *Average main: $49 ⊠ Ritz-Carlton Orlando Grande Lakes, 4000 Central Florida Pkwy., South Orlando* ☎ *407/393–4333* ⊕ *www.normans.com* ☽ *No lunch* ✛ *2:H6.*

$$$$
ITALIAN
Fodor's Choice
★

✕ **Primo.** Chef Melissa Kelly cloned her Italian-organic Maine restaurant in an upscale Orlando hotel and brought her farm-to-table sensibilities with her. Here the daily dinner menu pays tribute to Italian cuisine utilizing produce grown in the hotel's organic garden. **Known for:** constantly changing menu using locally sourced ingredients; interesting pizzas; house-made pastas. $ *Average main: $43 ⊠ JW Marriott Orlando Grande Lakes, 4040 Central Florida Pkwy., South Orlando* ☎ *407/393–4444* ⊕ *www.primorestaurant.com* ☽ *No lunch* ✛ *2:H6.*

SAND LAKE ROAD

This area, known as Restaurant Row, is the only place in town where locals dine beside convention goers and adventuresome theme-park visitors. From Interstate 4, take the Sand Lake Road exit, 74A.

$$
SEAFOOD

✕ **Bonefish Grill.** Fish dishes served in an upscale-casual setting distinguish Bonefish Grill from other area chains. Regulars rave about the Bang Bang Shrimp, a spicy appetizer of breaded and fried shrimp tossed in a tangy, spicy, mayonnaise-based sauce. **Known for:** seasonal fresh fish; happy hour and daily bar specials; pasta bowls and fish tacos. $ *Average main: $21 ⊠ Plaza Venezia, 7830 Sand Lake Rd., Sand Lake Rd. Area* ☎ *407/355–7707* ⊕ *www.bonefishgrill.com* ☽ *No lunch* ✛ *2:B4.*

$$$
TURKISH
FAMILY

✕ **Bosphorous Turkish Cuisine.** Exceptional Turkish cuisine served in a relaxing, indoor-outdoor setting is a welcome surprise among the big-budget chains on Sand Lake Road. Servers at this independently owned neighborhood favorite bring to the table piping-hot, oversize *lavas* (hollow bread) to dip in appetizers such as a hummus, *ezme* (a zesty, garlicky, chilled chopped salad), and baba ghanoush. **Known for:** Turkish appetizer plates; grilled sea bass; chicken and lamb shish kebab. $ *Average main: $26 ⊠ Marketplace at Dr. Phillips, 7600 Dr.*

5

Phillips Blvd., Suite 108, Sand Lake Rd. Area ☎ *407/352–6766* ⊕ *www. bosphorousrestaurant.com* ✚ *2:B4.*

$$$
MIDDLE EASTERN

✕ **Cedar's Restaurant.** This family-owned Lebanese eatery, set in a major upscale strip shopping center that's become part of Restaurant Row, serves Middle Eastern standards like shish kebab, baba ghanoush (an ultrasmoky variety that is the very best in town), and hummus as well as tasty daily specials. One of the most notable regular entrées is the *samak harra* (sautéed red snapper fillet topped with onions, tomatoes, and cilantro). **Known for:** authentic hummus and falafel; kafta kabab; rack of lamb. $ *Average main: $27* ⊠ *Plaza Venezia, 7732 W. Sand Lake Rd., Sand Lake Rd. Area* ☎ *407/351–6000* ⊕ *www.orlandocedars.com* ✚ *2:C4.*

$$$$
ITALIAN

✕ **Christini's Ristorante Italiano.** Business travelers love to spend money at Christini's, one of the city's fanciest places for Northern Italian cuisine. A throwback to elegant dining in the 1950s, the menu is filled with high-end versions of familiar dishes like chicken marsala and veal with lemon-wine sauce. **Known for:** Chris Christini, the charming owner for 45 years; upscale classic Italian cuisine; distinguished wine list. $ *Average main: $50* ⊠ *Marketplace at Dr. Phillips, 7600 Dr. Phillips Blvd., Sand Lake Rd. Area* ☎ *407/345–8770* ⊕ *www.christinis.com* ⊘ *No lunch* ✚ *2:B4.*

$$
MODERN ASIAN

✕ **Dragonfly.** Sleek and stylish, Dragonfly is a bit of everything the young and beautiful people want: a pretty space featuring sushi, colorful martinis, and modern, *izakaya*-style small plates, both creative and simple. Groups of dressed-up twenty- and thirtysomethings gather indoors and out to share plates of *robata*-cooked meats and vegetables, along with tempura, rolls, noodle dishes, and salads, all beautifully presented. **Known for:** modern takes on traditional Japanese fare; robata charcoal-grilled specialties; daily happy hour specials. $ *Average main: $15* ⊠ *Dellagio, 7972 Via Dellagio Way, Sand Lake Rd. Area* ☎ *407/370–3359* ⊕ *www.dragonflyorlando.com* ⊘ *No lunch* ✚ *2:B4.*

$
SOUTHWESTERN

✕ **Moe's Southwest Grill.** At this great fast-food alternative, meals cost well south of $10—and come with free chips and assorted salsas. It is an immensely casual joint but by no means a dive, with a youthful vibrancy (music blares over the sound system) that makes it a great place for a quick meal. **Known for:** fast-casual service; massive burritos; inexpensive menu items. $ *Average main: $6* ⊠ *Dolphin Plaza, 11062 International Dr., International Drive* ☎ *407/985–5808* ⊕ *www.moes.com* ✚ *2:C4.*

$$$$
SEAFOOD

✕ **MoonFish.** This splashy-looking restaurant caters to the convention crowd, with private rooms, polished service, and high prices—but the food is quite good. Ten to 15 fish varieties are flown in daily and prepared with a fusion of flavors from around the world. **Known for:** fresh fish; upscale atmosphere; Florida stone crab and lobster-encrusted trigger fish. $ *Average main: $35* ⊠ *The Fountains, 7525 W. Sand Lake Rd., Sand Lake Rd. Area* ☎ *407/363–7262* ⊕ *www.talkofthetownrestaurants.com* ⊘ *No lunch* ✚ *2:C4.*

$$$$
STEAKHOUSE

✕ **Morton's The Steakhouse.** This fine choice among Orlando's many steak houses looks like a sophisticated private club, and youngsters with mouse caps are not common at the nationwide chain's local outpost.

Center stage in the kitchen is a huge broiler, kept at 900°F to sear in the flavor of the porterhouses, sirloins, rib eyes, and other cuts of aged beef. **Known for:** house-aged steaks; seafood towers; mixed grill assortments with steak and lobster. $ *Average main: $46* ⊠ *Marketplace at Dr. Phillips, 7600 Dr. Phillips Blvd., Sand Lake Rd. Area* ☎ *407/248–3485* ⊕ *www.mortons.com* ⊘ *No lunch* ✛ *2:B4.*

$$$$
SEAFOOD

✕ **Ocean Prime.** From the Berries & Bubbles martinis (tart cocktails made with citrus and berry flavors and served bubbling and smoking, thanks to dry ice) that start off the meal, to the ultrarich chocolate peanut butter dessert draped in bittersweet chocolate ganache, Ocean Prime wows at every turn. This local outpost of an upscale chain holds its own with consistently good food, if uneven service. **Known for:** great lakeside view; inventive seafood selections; gluten-free menu. $ *Average main: $34* ⊠ *Rialto, 7339 W. Sand Lake Rd., Sand Lake Rd. Area* ☎ *407/781–4880* ⊕ *www.oceanprimeorlando.com* ⊘ *No lunch* ✛ *2:C4.*

$$$
ITALIAN
Fodor's Choice
★

✕ **Peperoncino.** You'll be transported to Calabria at this comfortable Italian restaurant. Divided into trattoria and pizzeria, chef-owners Barbara Alfano and Danilo Martorano put out a fresh menu of Italian specialties every evening. **Known for:** Southern Italian cuisine; duck breast and mushroom risotto; classic Italian pizza. $ *Average main: $25* ⊠ *Dellagio, 7988 Via Dellagio Way, Ste. 108, Sand Lake Rd. Area* ☎ *407/440–2856* ⊕ *www.peperoncinocucina.com* ✛ *2:B4.*

$$
SOUTH INDIAN
FAMILY

✕ **Rasa.** From the owners of nearby Saffron, Rasa brings Southern Indian street food to the next level. This cozy, sophisticated restaurant is not your standard "gravy curry" place, featuring marvelously diverse bites that include rice crepe dosa, inventive haka noodles, and an Indian thali lunch special that is the best deal in town. **Known for:** Southern Indian street food; authentic rice and noodle dishes; thali lunch special. $ *Average main: $18* ⊠ *Plaza Venezia, 7730 W. Sand Lake Rd., Sand Lake Rd. Area* ☎ *407/370–0909* ⊕ *www.eatatrasa.com* ✛ *2:C4.*

$$$$
HAWAIIAN

✕ **Roy's.** Chef Roy Yamaguchi has more or less perfected his own cuisine type, using European-style cooking techniques with Asian ingredients, primarily seafood, together with lots of imagination. The menu changes seasonally, but typical dishes include Hawaiian-style butterfish (black cod) with *furikake* rice, and hibachi-style grilled Atlantic salmon with Japanese citrus ponzu sauce. **Known for:** Hawaiian-inspired cuisine from celebrity chef Roy Yamaguchi; chef's tasting menu; hibachi salmon. $ *Average main: $34* ⊠ *Plaza Venezia, 7760 W. Sand Lake Rd., Sand Lake Rd. Area* ☎ *407/352–4844* ⊕ *www. roysrestaurant.com* ✛ *2:C4.*

$$$
AMERICAN
FAMILY

✕ **Seasons 52.** Parts of the menu change every week at this innovative restaurant that serves different foods at different times of year, depending on what's in season. It's hard to believe that a chain restaurant can continue to serve healthful yet hearty and very flavorful food, yet it does. **Known for:** waits for tables, even when you have a reservation; $5 plates and wines during the daily happy hour; flatbread starters that are big enough to share. $ *Average main: $21* ⊠ *Plaza Venezia, 7700 Sand Lake Rd., I–4 Exit 75A, Sand Lake Rd. Area* ☎ *407/354–5212* ⊕ *www.seasons52.com* ✛ *2:C4.*

5

$$$ ECLECTIC Fodor's Choice ★

🍴 **Urbain 40.** Headed by James Beard nominee Tim Keating, this American brasserie takes cues from classic French and Italian cuisine while adding a decidedly American spin. The simple elegant styling might recall a jazz club of the 1940s (hence the name) with live jazz piano during the evening, but people come for the food. **Known for:** inventive combinations of French, Italian, and Asian influences on American cuisine; perfectly prepared steak dishes; jazz lounge atmosphere during the evening. [$] *Average main: $30* ✉ *8000 Via Dellagio Way, Sand Lake Rd. Area* ☎ *407/872–2640* 🌐 *urbain40.com/* ⊕ *2:B4.*

$$$$ STEAKHOUSE

🍴 **Vines Grille & Wine Bar.** Live jazz and blues music fills the night at the bar section of this dramatically designed restaurant, but the food and drink in the snazzy main dining room are headliners in their own right. The kitchen bills itself as a steak house, but it really is far more than that. **Known for:** extensive wine selection and cocktails; prime steaks cooked on a wood-fired grill; live jazz performances. [$] *Average main: $62* ✉ *The Fountains, 7533 W. Sand Lake Rd., Sand Lake Rd. Area* ☎ *407/351–1227* 🌐 *www.seasons52.com* ⏲ *No lunch* ⊕ *2:C4.*

WINTER PARK

Winter Park has four restaurant hubs: Park Avenue, Orange Avenue, Hannibal Square, and Winter Park Village. To get into the area, follow Interstate 4 to Exit 87.

$$ ITALIAN

🍴 **Brio Tuscan Grille.** Head to this trendy restaurant for wood-grilled meats and fish, Italian classics like chicken Milanese, and plenty of pasta. Try the strip steak topped with Gorgonzola, or the mushroom ravioli with champagne brown butter sauce. [$] *Average main: $21* ✉ *480 N. Orlando Ave., Winter Park* ☎ *407/622–5611* 🌐 *www.brioitalian.com* ⊕ *3:E2.*

$$$$ STEAKHOUSE Fodor's Choice ★

🍴 **Christner's Prime Steak & Lobster.** Locals like this quiet, uncomplicated, family-run steak house, which delivers carefully prepared food and attentive service in a traditional setting of red leather and dark wood. When your steak arrives—still sizzling on a hot plate—the waiter asks you to cut into it and check that it was cooked as you ordered. **Known for:** simple, perfectly executed steaks; house-made desserts; extensive wine list. [$] *Average main: $45* ✉ *729 Lee Rd., Winter Park* ☎ *407/645–4443* 🌐 *www.christnersprimesteakandlobster.com* ⏲ *No lunch. Closed Sun.* ⊕ *3:C1.*

$$ ECLECTIC

🍴 **Dexter's.** A quartet of Central Florida restaurants, Dexter's is a low-key concept with a wildly creative menu, surprisingly low prices, a good wine list, and a faithful following among locals. Two of the best-selling entrées are the chicken tortilla pie—a stack of puffy, fried tortillas layered with chicken and cheese—and a pressed duck sandwich and a Brie sandwich. **Known for:** creative sandwiches; fresh local fish; live music several times a week. [$] *Average main: $16* ✉ *558 W. New England Ave., Winter Park* ☎ *407/629–1150* 🌐 *www.dexwine.com* ⊕ *3:E2.*

$
BARBECUE
FAMILY
Fodor's Choice
★

✕ **4 Rivers Smokehouse.** What started as a tiny business in a former tire repair shop has turned into a multistate dynasty. The popular 4 Rivers, now with 14 locations and more on the way, turns out slow-cooked barbecue standards like pulled pork and Texas-style brisket. **Known for:** slow-smoked ribs, brisket, and chicken; Sweet Shop bakeries; bacon-wrapped smoked jalapeños. $ *Average main: $13* ✉ *1600 W. Fairbanks Ave., Winter Park* ☎ *855/368–7748* ⊕ *4rsmokehouse.com* ☾ *Closed Sun.* ✛ *3:D2.*

$$$
MODERN
AMERICAN
Fodor's Choice
★

✕ **Luma on Park.** One of the Orlando area's best restaurants, Luma on Park is a popular spot for progressive American cuisine served in a fashionable setting, run by chef Brandon McGlammery. Every ingredient is carefully sourced from local producers when possible, and scratch preparation—from pastas to sausages to pickled rhubarb—is the mantra. **Known for:** North Carolina flounder and Snake River flank steak; extensive wine list; attention to detail. $ *Average main: $30* ✉ *290 S. Park Ave., Winter Park* ☎ *407/599–4111* ⊕ *www.luma-onpark.com* ✛ *3:F2.*

$$$
ITALIAN
Fodor's Choice
★

✕ **Prato.** Progressive Italian cuisine in a casual, bustling wood-and-brick setting immediately made Prato a local favorite. Every item from the pancetta to the amaretti is crafted from scratch. **Known for:** young, hip clientele; outdoor curbside dining; Neapolitan pizzas. $ *Average main: $23* ✉ *124 N. Park Ave., Winter Park* ☎ *407/262–0050* ⊕ *www.prato-wp.com* ☾ *No lunch Mon. and Tues.* ✛ *3:F2.*

$$$$
MODERN
AMERICAN
Fodor's Choice
★

✕ **The Ravenous Pig.** The first local restaurant to break into the "gastropub" category, the Pig is arguably Orlando's most popular foodie destination and has spawned several offshoots. Run by James Beard-nominees James and Julie Petrakis, this husband-and-wife chef team dispenses delicacies like pork porterhouse or the pub burger. **Known for:** merged with Cask & Larder brewery; open until midnight Thursday–Saturday; house-made charcuterie. $ *Average main: $31* ✉ *565 W. Fairbanks Ave., Winter Park* ☎ *407/628–2333* ⊕ *www.theravenouspig.com* ✛ *3:E3.*

KISSIMMEE

Kissimmee offers a huge number of dining choices, many of which are of the "burger barn" or dinner theater variety, but there are notable exceptions. Allow about 15 to 25 minutes to travel from WDW or about 35 minutes from International Drive.

$$$$
STEAKHOUSE

✕ **Old Hickory Steakhouse.** This upscale steak house in the Gaylord Palms resort is designed to look like rustic cabins in the Everglades. Beyond the playful facade is a polished restaurant with a classic steak-house menu of steaks and chops. **Known for:** particularly good steaks; free valet parking; consistently good service. $ *Average main: $47* ✉ *Gaylord Palms Resort, 6000 W. Osceola Pkwy., I–4 Exit 65, Kissimmee* ☎ *407/586–1600* ⊕ *www.gaylordpalms.com* ☾ *No lunch* ✛ *1:E6.*

$ CARIBBEAN FAMILY Fodor's Choice ★ 🍴 **Savion's Place.** A melding of island cuisine with American down-home dishes, Savion's independently owned atmosphere extends to the menu. Prince Edward Island mussels share space with lobster mac-and-cheese, while mushroom Marsala meatloaf can appear on the table with "Grandma's recipe" jambalaya. **Known for:** home cooking with a Haitian flair; seafood gumbo and jambalaya; patio dining. [$] *Average main: $12* ✉ *16 E Dakin Ave., Kissimmee* ☎ *407/572–8719* 🌐 *savionsplace.com/* ✣ *1:F6.*

LAKE BUENA VISTA

Lake Buena Vista, just to the east of Downtown Disney, is essentially a collection of midscale hotels, convention hotels, and chain restaurants catering to off-site visitors to Disney World.

$$$ AMERICAN 🍴 **American Kitchen Bar & Grill.** A focus on locally sourced ingredients from a network of Florida farmers makes this hotel restaurant particularly appetizing. Seating is at booths or communal tables, where guests dine on Southern specialties like the family-style South Carolina low country boil and Florida sweet corn soup or the free-range chicken, wild salmon, and local Wagyu beef. **Known for:** locally sourced ingredients from family farmers; free-range chicken; local Wagyu beef. [$] *Average main: $26* ✉ *B Resort & Spa, 1905 Hotel Plaza Blvd., Disney Springs Resort Area* ☎ *407/828–2828* 🌐 *bhotelsandresorts.com* ✣ *1:F4.*

$$$$ STEAKHOUSE Fodor's Choice ★ 🍴 **Capa.** Billed as a Spanish steak house, Capa is a concept cleverly executed in a chic, modern dining area. Clean lines are the palette for ancient-looking coins creatively arranged and a decor element of red ruffles reminiscent of a matador's red flag. **Known for:** superb steaks and seafood; grilled duck, lamb, and pork chops; enviable view of fireworks from the outdoor patio. [$] *Average main: $52* ✉ *Four Seasons Resort, 10100 Dream Tree Blvd., Lake Buena Vista* ☎ *407/313–7777* 🌐 *www.fourseasons.com/orlando/dining/* 🕒 *No lunch.* ✣ *1:D2.*

$$ AMERICAN FAMILY 🍴 **Covington Mill.** A polished space offering hearty buffet and à la carte breakfasts plus light lunches, Covington Mill turns into a kidfest on Sunday mornings. That's when Disney characters join the early risers, cheerfully signing autographs and posing for photographs. **Known for:** buffet breakfast; Disney character Sundays; create your own omelet option. [$] *Average main: $20* ✉ *Hilton Orlando Lake Buena Vista, 1751 Hotel Plaza Blvd., Disney Springs Resort Area* ☎ *407/827–4000* 🌐 *ww.hiltonorlandolakebuenavistahotel.com* 🕒 *No dinner* ✣ *1:F4.*

$$$$ SEAFOOD 🍴 **Hemingway's.** Business travelers and vacationers put on their khakis and sundresses to dine in this quiet seafood house loosely themed around Ernest Hemingway's travels. The Papa Doble cocktail, with rum and grapefruit juice, is reputedly Papa's own creation. **Known for:** tropical Key West atmosphere; scenic views of resort grounds; Duval Street shrimp scampi. [$] *Average main: $36* ✉ *Hyatt Regency Grand Cypress, 1 Grand Cypress Blvd., Lake Buena Vista* ☎ *407/239-3854* 🌐 *www.grandcypress.hyatt.com* 🕒 *No lunch* ✣ *1:F3.*

$$$ ITALIAN 🍴 **La Luce by Donna Scala.** Originated by the late California restaurateur and chef Donna Scala, La Luce brings Italian cuisine with a Napa Valley farm-fresh flair to this upscale Hilton at the edge of Walt Disney

World. Pastas are made fresh, steaks are handled with Italian care, and the cocktail bar is second to none. **Known for:** upscale and authentic Italian cuisine; "silk handkerchief" pasta; artwork created specially for the restaurant. [$] *Average main: $30* ✉ *Hilton Orlando Bonnet Creek, 14100 Bonnet Creek Resort La., Bonnet Creek* ☎ *407/597–3600* 🌐 *www.laluceorlando.com* 🕑 *No lunch* ✥ *1:E5.*

$$$ AMERICAN FAMILY 🍴 **Lakeview Restaurant.** Lake views for breakfast and dinner keep this hotel restaurant bustling twice a day. Yet the spot is at its peak on Tuesday, Thursday, and Saturday mornings when Disney characters come to visit. **Known for:** Disney character breakfast; lakefront view; almond-crusted chicken. [$] *Average main: $24* ✉ *Wyndham Lake Buena Vista Resort, 1850 Hotel Plaza Blvd., Disney Springs Resort Area* ☎ *407/828–4444* 🌐 *www.wyndhamlakebuenavista.com* 🕑 *No lunch* ✥ *1:F4.*

$ AMERICAN FAMILY 🍴 **Letterpress Cafe.** Southern-style cooking and Florida sourced ingredients spotlight the revamped menu at the former Watercress Cafe. High-end ingredients like Anson Mills grits, Angus beef, and locally baked bread elevate the Letterpress Cafe above the ordinary hotel restaurant. **Known for:** kettle soups; Florida fish; Southern-style cooking. [$] *Average main: $13* ✉ *Buena Vista Palace Hotel & Spa, 1900 E. Buena Vista Dr., Disney Springs Resort Area* ☎ *866/397–6516* 🌐 *www.buenavistapalace.com* ✥ *1:F4.*

$$$$ MODERN ITALIAN FAMILY 🍴 **Ravello.** Under the leadership of Neapolitan chef Fabrizio Schenardi, Ravello is a chic modern Italian restaurant after dark. Hand-tossed pizzas emerge from the oven—perhaps finished with house-made ricotta, arugula, and truffle oil. **Known for:** superbly executed cuisine of Naples; grilled lamb chops; Disney character breakfast. [$] *Average main: $32* ✉ *Four Seasons Orlando, 10100 Dream Tree Blvd., Lake Buena Vista* ☎ *407/313–6161* 🌐 *www.fourseasons.com/orlando* 🕑 *No lunch* ✥ *1:D2.*

$$$$ EUROPEAN 🍴 **The Venetian Chop House.** This fine-dining restaurant inside one of Lake Buena Vista's many convention hotels may have been designed as a place for execs on expense accounts to seal deals, but it has also become a haven for nontrendy locals seeking an old-fashioned romantic retreat. The architecture alone—it looks like Renaissance Venice—is enough to lure you. **Known for:** lobster bisque; Romantic Italian decor; black Angus beef. [$] *Average main: $40* ✉ *Caribe Royale, 8101 World Center Dr., Lake Buena Vista* ☎ *407/238–8060* 🌐 *www.thevenetianroom.com* 🕑 *No lunch. Closed Sun.* ☞ *Free parking with dinner reservation* ✥ *1:G5.*

CELEBRATION

The town's Market Street–area restaurants (predominately upscale) face a pastoral (though man-made) lake. To get here, take Interstate 4 to Exit 64 (192) and follow the "Celebration" signs.

$$$ JAPANESE FUSION FAMILY 🍴 **Ari Sushi.** This bright, modern Japanese restaurant serves Japanese and Korean dishes including fairly standard sushi rolls and an interesting range of hot dishes. Menu standouts include the beef bulgogi bowl (thin, marinated slices of beef or pork grilled on a barbecue) and kalbi (Korean barbecued short ribs). **Known for:** Japanese and Korean specialties; affordable lunch specials; Korean bento box combinations.

$ *Average main: $22* ✉ *671 Front St, Celebration* ☎ *407/566–1889* 🌐 *arisushi.net* ✣ *1:E6.*

$$ ITALIAN FAMILY 🍴 **Café d'Antonio.** The wood-burning oven and grill are worked pretty hard here, and the mountains of hardwood used in the open kitchen flavor the best of the menu—pizza, grilled fish and chicken, steaks and chops, and even the lasagna. A standout is the wood-fired veal chop stuffed with prosciutto, fontina, and spinach. **Known for:** fine Italian dining; wood-fired veal chop; mixed antipasto platter. $ *Average main: $21* ✉ *691 Front St., Celebration* ☎ *407/566–2233* 🌐 *www.antonio-sonline.com* ✣ *1:E6.*

$$$ SEAFOOD 🍴 **Celebration Town Tavern.** This New England–cuisine eatery, operated by a family with Boston roots, has a double personality. The interior is a brass, glass, and dark-wood-paneling kind of place, while the outside patio has table seating plus the Paddy O' Bar. **Known for:** 99-beer selection; fried Boston scrod; steak scampi. $ *Average main: $27* ✉ *721 Front St., Celebration* ☎ *407/566–2526* 🌐 *www.thecelebrationtown-tavern.com* ✣ *1:E6.*

$$$ LATIN AMERICAN Fodor's Choice ★ 🍴 **Columbia Restaurant.** Celebration's branch of this family-owned high-end chain might be better than the original in Tampa, which has been operating for a century now. Start with the garlic shrimp or the empanadas stuffed with beef, raisins, and olives. **Known for:** oldest continuous restaurant chain in Florida; upscale Cuban cuisine; paella à la Valenciana. $ *Average main: $29* ✉ *649 Front St., Celebration* ☎ *407/566–1505* 🌐 *www.columbiarestaurant.com* ✣ *1:E6.*

ORLANDO INTERNATIONAL AIRPORT

$$$$ AMERICAN 🍴 **Hemisphere Steak & Seafood.** The view competes with the food on the ninth floor of the Hyatt Regency Orlando International Airport hotel. Although Hemisphere overlooks major runways, you don't get any jet noise, just a nice air show. **Known for:** convenient airport location; sophisticated steak and seafood menu; relaxing lounge bar. $ *Average main: $32* ✉ *Hyatt Regency Orlando International Airport, 9300 Jeff Fuqua Blvd., Airport Area* ☎ *407/825–1234* 🌐 *orlandoairport.regency.hyatt.com* 🕒 *No lunch. Closed Sun* ✣ *1:H1.*

$$ SOUTHERN 🍴 **Cask & Larder.** People have been known to check their bags at the airport and then go back through security and change terminals just to eat at C&L. The draws at this locally owned restaurant are the gastropub-inspired menu and the microbrews. **Known for:** farm-to-terminal dining; breakfast starts at 5 am; organic, locally sourced ingredients. $ *Average main: $15* ✉ *Orlando International Airport, 9202 Jeff Fuqua Blvd., Southwest Terminal, Airport Area* ☎ *407/204–3296* 🌐 *www.caskandlarder.com* ✣ *1:H1.*

WHERE TO STAY

Updated
by Jennifer
Greenhill-Taylor

With tens of thousands of lodging choices available in the Orlando area, from tents to deluxe villas, there is no lack of variety in price or amenities. Actually, narrowing down the possibilities is part of the fun.

More than 60 million visitors come to the Orlando area each year, making it the most popular tourism destination on the planet. More upscale hotels are opening as visitors demand more luxurious surroundings, such as luxe linens, tasteful and refined decor, organic toiletries, or ergonomic chairs and work desks. But no matter what your budget or desires, lodging comes in such a wide range of prices, themes, color schemes, brands, and guest-room amenities, you will have no problem finding something that fits.

Resorts on and off Disney property combine function with fantasy, as befits visitor expectations. Characters in costume perform for the kids, pools are pirates' caves with waterfalls, and some, like the Gaylord Palms, go so far as to re-create Florida landmarks under a gargantuan glass roof, giving visitors the illusion of having visited more of the state than they expected.

International Drive's expanding attractions, including the Coca-Cola Orlando Eye, Madame Tussauds, and a widening array of eateries, are drawing more savvy conventioneers who bring their families along for the fun.

Many hotels have joined the trend toward green lodging, bringing recycling, water conservation, and other environmentally conscious practices to the table. Best of all, the sheer number and variety of hotel rooms means you can still find relative bargains throughout the Orlando area, even on Disney property, by researching your trip well, calling the lodgings directly, negotiating packages and prices, and shopping wisely.

LODGING PLANNER

WHERE SHOULD WE STAY?

When it comes to Orlando lodging, no matter who you are and where you decide to stay, you should book months in advance (at least six months for hotels at Disney). This is particularly important for travel when rates are lowest, specifically early January to mid-February, late April to mid-June, and mid-August to early December.

Your choices include resorts on Disney property (most owned and operated by Disney), those on Universal property, and those not in or affiliated with either park. Each type of property merits consideration.

HOTELS ON DISNEY AND UNIVERSAL PROPERTY

If you're interested solely in attractions at Disney or Universal, **in-park hotels are best**. For starters, they offer such convenient transportation options that you probably won't need a rental car—a huge cost savings.

Walt Disney World's massive campus is tied together by a dizzying array of complimentary monorails, buses, ferries, and water taxis. All get you anywhere on the property you want to go. Universal provides complimentary shuttles and water taxis between its two theme parks, the water park, and five (a sixth is scheduled to open in mid-2018, with two more to follow in 2019) on-site hotels, though most of the hotels and parks are within walking distance of one another.

Staying at a resort on Disney property, or at a Disney Good Neighbor hotel, brings a variety of benefits that other hotels don't offer—some designed to save money, some designed to save time. Among the perks: early park entry; extended park hours; and, if a round of golf is on the itinerary, guests receive reduced rates when playing at three Disney courses, along with priority tee times and complimentary transportation to and from the course.

HOTELS OFF THEME-PARK PROPERTY

If you plan to visit several parks or go sightseeing elsewhere in Central Florida, consider off-site hotels. Those closest to Disney are clustered in a few areas: along I-Drive; in the U.S. 192 area and Kissimmee; and in the Disney Springs–Lake Buena Vista Area, just off Interstate 4 Exit 68. I-Drive hotels such as the DoubleTree by Hilton at the Entrance to Universal Orlando and Hyatt Place Orlando/Universal are closest to Universal.

Nearly every hotel in these areas provides frequent (sometimes free) transportation to and from Disney or even Universal. In addition, there are some noteworthy and money-saving, if far-flung, options in the greater Orlando area. One suburban caveat: traffic on Interstate 4 in Orlando experiences typical freeway gridlock during morning (7–9) and evening (4–6) rush hours. Congestion is further complicated by the huge ongoing construction project on I-4, which affects nearly every exit and entrance throughout the tourist area.

■TIP→ Anyone can visit Disney hotels. To save money and still have on-site resort experiences, stay at a moderately priced hotel off-site and then visit the animals at the Animal Kingdom Lodge, say, or rent a boat at the Grand Floridian.

WHERE SHOULD WE STAY?

	VIBE	PROS	CONS
Disney	Thousands of rooms at every price; convenient to Disney parks; free transportation all over WDW complex.	Perks like early park entry, complimentary MagicBands or cards, and Magical Express, which lets you circumvent airport bag checks.	Without a rental car, you likely won't leave Disney. On-site buses, although free, can take a big bite of time out of your entertainment day; convenience comes at a price.
Universal	On-site hotels offer luxury, convenience, and value. There are less expensive options just outside the gates.	Central to Disney, Universal, SeaWorld, malls, and I–4; free water taxis to parks from on-site hotels.	Most on-site hotels are pricey; the Cabana Bay Beach Resort, however, is reasonable; expect heavy rush-hour traffic during drives to and from other parks.
I-Drive	A hotel, convention center, and activities bonanza. A trolley runs from one end to the other.	Outlet malls provide bargains; world-class restaurants; the Coca-Cola Orlando Eye lifts visitors up for a bird's-eye view; many hotels offer free park shuttles.	Transportation can be pricey, in cash and in time, as traffic is often heavy. After a rise in car burglaries and tourist-related crimes, the police presence was increased and area hotels and businesses beefed up security.
Kissimmee	It offers mom-and-pop motels and upscale choices, restaurants, and places to buy saltwater taffy.	It's just outside Disney, very close to Magic Kingdom. The town has Old Florida charm and the lodgings offer low prices.	Some of the older motels here are a little seedy. Petty crime in which tourists are victims is rare— but not unheard of.
Lake Buena Vista	Many hotel and restaurant chains here. Adjacent to WDW, which is where almost every guest in your hotel is headed.	Really close to WDW; plenty of dining and shopping options; easy access to I–4.	Heavy peak-hour traffic. As in all neighborhoods near Disney, a gallon of gas will cost 10%–15% more than elsewhere.
Central Orlando	Parts of town have the modern high-rises you'd expect. Other areas have oak tree–lined brick streets winding among small, cypress-ringed lakes.	Locally owned restaurants, trendy hotels, vibrant nightlife, and some quaint B&Bs. City buses serve the parks. There's good access to I–4.	You'll need to rent a car. And you will be part of the traffic headed to WDW. Expect the 25-mile drive to take at least 45 minutes.
Orlando International Airport	Mostly business and flight-crew hotels and car-rental outlets.	Great if you have an early flight or just want to shop in a mall. There's even a Hyatt on-site.	Watching planes, buses, taxis, and cars arrive and depart is all the entertainment you'll get.

CONSIDERATIONS FOR DIFFERENT TYPES OF TRAVELERS

Whether you stay on theme-park property or off, prioritize your needs. A great spa is wonderful, but if you're running around with three young kids, will you actually use it? Do you want luxury or rustic simplicity? A splurge or a supersaver?

In addition, weigh what you get for the money. Sure, you might spend more on a room at a Disney or Universal resort than at an off-site property. But if staying at a cheaper off-site hotel means renting a car or spending a lot of money and time on cab rides, you might not ultimately be saving that much. Conversely, if you're planning to split your time between, say, Disney, Universal, and SeaWorld, you probably won't make full use of all the Disney or Universal perks and might be better off shopping for a good-value, centrally located, off-site hotel with free theme-park shuttle service.

Finally, if you're traveling with children, be sure to mention their ages when you make reservations. Sometimes hotels have special features, such as rooms with bunk beds, just for families. Such things aren't necessarily offered up front, so be sure to ask.

■ TIP➔ Regardless of whether you stay at hotels near the theme parks or at on-site resorts, it can take between 20 minutes and an hour to get to and from park entrances.

FAMILIES WITH YOUNG KIDS

If this is a Disney trip, stick with Disney hotels or Hotel Plaza Boulevard properties: the transportation system makes it simple to scoot back for a nap or some downtime at the pool.

Many Disney properties are designed to appeal to kids, some with great children's facilities and programs. At the value-priced Art of Animation Resort, young kids love the familiarity of *Finding Nemo, Little Mermaid,* and *Cars* themes everywhere. The Polynesian Resort's Never Land Club has an enchanting Peter Pan–themed clubhouse and youngsters-only dinner show. Parents rave about the Sand Castle Club at the Yacht and Beach Club resorts. What's more, most of these clubs are open from late afternoon until midnight, so parents can slip out for a romantic meal while the kids play games, do art projects, and enjoy a snack or dinner.

■ TIP➔ Surprise kids with a wake-up call from Mickey while staying at a Disney resort.

If you do stay off-site, book a hotel geared to small children. The Holiday Inn Resort Orlando—Waterpark, in Lake Buena Vista, offers brightly colored suites with bunk beds. The resort has a huge waterpark, and tons of kids' activities, including 4-D movies and an arcade.

East of International Drive the connected JW Marriott and Ritz-Carlton Orlando, Grande Lakes resorts have rooms with adjoining kids' suites, complete with miniature furniture and toys. The Ritz also has a Kids Club with an engaging play area and daily scheduled activities.

Wherever you stay, inquire about child equipment. Most hotels—and certainly all owned by Disney—have amenities such as cribs. (Some hotels require you to reserve cribs in advance. Ask whether there will be an additional charge, and make sure the crib meets current child-safety standards.)

BABYSITTING IN ORLANDO

If you're staying in a room, suite, or condo and need to rent baby equipment, such as a stroller, bassinet, high chair, or even pool toys, call **Orlando Crib Rental** (407/433–7770 ⊕ www.orlandocribrental.com) for swift delivery and fair rates. You can order online. The company also provides some concierge services, such as grocery or baby-supply delivery.

If you want to plan an adults-only evening, consider the **Kid's Nite Out** (407/828–0920 or 800/696–8105 ⊕ www.kidsniteout.com) program, which works with hotels throughout Orlando. It provides in-room babysitting for children ages six weeks to 12 years. Fees start at $18 an hour for one child, and increase by $3 for each additional child. There's a four-hour minimum, plus a transportation fee of $10 for the sitter to travel to your hotel room. The service also rents baby equipment, such as strollers and jogging carriages, and will babysit your pet, too.

When you make a reservation, you must provide a credit-card number. There's a 24-hour cancellation policy; if you cancel with less than 24 hours' notice, your credit card is charged the four-hour minimum fee ($72 for one child, higher rates for multiple children booked). The service recommends booking from two weeks to 90 days in advance.

6

FAMILY WITH TWEENS

With tweens you don't really need a hotel that's super close to a theme park, so your selection is greater. Even properties that seem adult-oriented have offerings that tweens love. The "lazy-river" pools at hotels including the Omni Orlando Resort at ChampionsGate and the JW Marriott, for instance, are generally big hits.

Many hotels also have supervised camp-style programs, with trained counselors and fun, active, outdoorsy things to do. These are great for arrival and departure days, when you probably don't want to schlep to a park, but you also don't want to hear the dreaded "I'm so bored."

Standouts are at the Ritz-Carlton's Ritz Kids program, and in room camping and the Camp Hyatt program at the Hyatt Regency Grand Cypress, near Disney Springs. The latter is a top-class resort with sprawling grounds that abut Walt Disney World property, so it's perfect for families who want to be near the Mouse but prefer to take a break from Disney each night.

FAMILY WITH TEENS

A great hotel pool is a major boon for teens, who might not want to spend all their time in the theme parks. Stormalong Bay, the pool complex shared by the Yacht Club and Beach Club, has it all: a lazy river, waterslide, sandy-bottom pool, and elevated tanning deck. This location is also surrounded by the shops, restaurants, and leisure activities of Disney's BoardWalk, a great place for teens to explore on their own.

Teens are usually partial to Universal's thrills, so the 1950s beach-party themed Cabana Bay Beach Resort on Universal property is also an excellent choice. It has a swimming pool with a sandy beach and volleyball court; "dive-in" movies on select nights; and even a bowling alley. The rock-and-roll-themed Hard Rock Hotel is also a great Universal option, with underwater speakers piping rock and roll into the pool.

■ TIP→ **If at all possible, book more than one room. As they say, the family that sleeps together .. hates each other in the morning.** Teens are used to having their own space; crabby moods stemming from cramped conditions can put a damper on the vacation. When booking, request connecting rooms—with a door linking your room to that of your teen—as opposed to adjoining rooms, which means only that your rooms are next to each other.

If booking more than one room is too pricey, look into accommodations at all-suites hotels or family suites at off-site hotels. These larger quarters are often reasonably priced. Just be sure to check on the hotel's definition of *suite*. Sometimes it's merely an L-shaped room with a sitting area (i.e., there's no door separating you from your teen). The key question is, "Do your suites have two separate rooms with a door in between?"

SINGLES OR GROUPS OF FRIENDS

If you're traveling solo, you'll never feel lonely at a theme-park hotel. Consider one in Disney's BoardWalk area—perhaps the BoardWalk Inn and Villas, Disney's Yacht Club, or Disney's Beach Club. From here you're just steps from shopping, dining, and nightlife. Similarly, Universal hotels like the elegant Loews Portofino Bay Hotel are just a blink away from the shopping and the hopping nightlife of CityWalk. Plus, Portofino has a spa.

If theme parks aren't your only interest, you can get your wow factor by staying at a hotel like the Gaylord Palms Resort. The interior of this place is like a Hollywood spectacular movie—about Florida. Just walking around in the 4-acre atrium is an adventure, with indoor gardens evoking the Everglades and old St. Augustine. There's also a lot to do on-site, including dining, shopping, swimming, pampering yourself at the spa, or working out in the large fitness center.

COUPLES

Luxury properties such as the Ritz-Carlton Orlando, Grande Lakes or the Four Seasons spell romance. Ultraluxurious rooms, restaurants, and spa programs, plus championship golf courses, make these resorts among the best in the Orlando area. Another romantic option is Downtown's Grand Bohemian, with a rooftop pool, jazz in the Bösendorfer Lounge, and short-walk access to the Dr. Phillips Center for the Performing Arts and the Amway Center's NBA games and world-class concerts.

If you and your sweetie are Disneyphiles, Disney's five-star Grand Floridian absolutely drips with Victorian romance, and the Animal Kingdom Lodge offers the delights of sunsets over the savanna and giraffes and zebras munching leaves just below your balcony. The Port Orleans Resort–French Quarter, near Disney Springs, is a great, more affordable romantic choice for couples.

DISNEY AND UNIVERSAL RESORT PERKS

DISNEY PERKS

Extra Magic Hours. You get special early and late-night admission to certain Disney parks on specified days. Call ahead for details so you can plan your early- and late-visit strategies.

Free Parking. Parking is free for Disney hotel guests at Disney hotel and theme-park lots.

Magical Express. If you're staying at a select Disney hotel, this free airport service means you don't need to rent a car or think about finding a shuttle or taxi or worry about baggage handling.

At your hometown airport, you check your bags in and won't see them again till you get to your Disney hotel. At Orlando International Airport you're met by a Disney rep, who leads you to a coach that takes you to your hotel. Your luggage is delivered separately and usually arrives in your room an hour or two after you do. If your flight arrives before 5 am or after 10 pm, you will have to pick up your luggage and deliver it to the coach.

On departure, the process works in reverse (though only on some participating airlines, so check in advance). You get your boarding pass and check your bags at the hotel. At the airport you go directly to your gate, skipping check-in. You won't see your bags until you're in your hometown airport. Participating airlines include American, Delta, JetBlue, Southwest, and United.

Charging Privileges. You can charge most meals and purchases throughout Disney to your hotel room, using your MagicBands or cards.

Package Delivery. Anything you purchase at Disney—at a park, a hotel, or in Downtown Disney—can be delivered to the gift shop of your Disney hotel for free.

Priority Reservations. Disney hotel guests get priority reservations for rides in the parks, and at Disney restaurants, and choice tee times at Disney golf courses up to 30 days in advance, using MagicBands or cards and Fastpass+.

Guaranteed Entry. Disney theme parks sometimes reach capacity, but on-site guests can enter even when others would be turned away.

UNIVERSAL PERKS

Head-of-the-Line Access. Your hotel key (except at Cabana Bay, Loews Sapphire Falls, and Aventura Hotel) lets you go directly to the head of the line for most Universal Orlando attractions. Unlike Disney's Fastpass+ program, you don't need to use this at a specific time; it's always good. Hotel guests also get early admission to the often-crowded Harry Potter attractions.

Priority Seating. Many of Universal's restaurants offer priority seating to those staying at on-site hotels.

Charging Privileges. You can charge most meals and purchases throughout Universal to your hotel room.

Delivery Services. If you buy something in the theme parks, you can have it sent directly to your room, so you don't have to carry it around.

6

LARGE GROUPS

All-suites properties are the logical choice. If you're coming mainly for the theme parks, stay on Disney or Universal grounds, as the many perks—especially those involving transportation—definitely make life easier. Some Disney properties with suites include the cabins at Fort Wilderness Resort, the Beach Club Villas, the BoardWalk Inn and Villas, the Bay Lake Tower at the Contemporary Resort, the bungalows at the Polynesian Village Resort, the cabins at Wilderness Lodge, and the villas at Animal Kingdom. At the Universal properties, Cabana Bay has 1,800 rooms, half of them suites. But rest assured, area hotel reps are very familiar with group travel, and are happy to discuss options.

If you plan to spend time away from the parks or will be shuttling between Universal and Disney, consider reserving an apartment or condo. This works best for families who thrive on the chaos of communal living. (It also works better if you assign chores. This is a vacation for everyone, and it's just not fair if one or two people consistently do all the work.)

The only potential hang-up to the apartment-condo scenario is who gets the master suite. If it's a birthday, anniversary, or retirement event, the big room naturally goes to the guest(s) of honor. Otherwise, the decision isn't so straightforward. One solution: donate it to some of the kids. The suite will be plenty big for a slumber party, and you'll love the fact that their war-torn bathroom is blissfully out of sight.

If your family members tend to get in each other's hair, you're better off reserving a block of hotel rooms. Add a courtesy suite, and you have all the benefits of togetherness, plus a place to retreat to when you need it. Talk to a hotel agent to figure out how many people each room can accommodate comfortably, and how many rooms you'll need.

FACILITIES AND AMENITIES

All hotels and resorts in Central Florida have air-conditioning, and most have cable or satellite TV, coffeemakers, in-room irons, and ironing boards. Those in the moderate and expensive price ranges often have bathrobes and hair dryers. High-speed wireless access (Wi-Fi) is now common even at budget properties, but some hotels still charge a daily fee for Internet service. If being connected is important, it's best to ask. Most hotels, even the budget ones, have a pool, and many have fitness facilities and business centers. Be sure to ask whether the hotel charges a resort fee. Finding a week's worth of unexpected daily fees on your final bill can be a disconcerting surprise.

If a particular amenity is important to you, ask for it; many hotels will provide extras upon request. Double-check your bill at checkout, and if a charge seems unreasonable, this is the time to have it remedied. If you're traveling with pets, note the hotel's pet policies. Some hotels require substantial cleaning fees. A big note to smokers: most of the hotels and resorts in Central Florida are entirely smoke-free, meaning even smoking outdoors on hotel property is frowned upon or prohibited.

ROOM RATES

In the Orlando area there's an inverse relationship between temperature and room rates. The hot and humid weather in late summer and fall brings lower prices and possibly hurricanes. Conversely, the balmy days of late February, March, and April attract lots of visitors; hotel owners charge accordingly. One note about hurricane season—it officially begins in June, but a hurricane in Florida before August is rare. Rates are often low from early January to mid-February, from late April to mid-June, and from mid-August to the third week in November.

Always call several places—availability and special deals can drive room rates at a $$$$ hotel down into the $$ range—and don't forget to ask whether you're eligible for a discount. You can always save by preparing a few meals in a room, suite, or villa with a kitchenette or kitchen. Websites will often offer a better room rate; so compare the prices offered on the Web and through the hotel's local or toll-free number (if one is available). Always ask about special packages or corporate rates. Don't be shy. Polite assertiveness can save you money.

The Disney Dining Plan: On-site Walt Disney World Hotels don't offer meal plans in their rates, but you can choose a Disney Dining Plan. It can be added to any on-site package, and many families swear by it. The plan saves you from having to carry around cash and—at least on the surface—masks the sting of coughing up nine bucks for a cheeseburger. To see if a Disney Dining Plan is right for your family, go to *www.disneyworld.disney.go.com/dining* for more information.

RESERVATIONS

When booking by phone, expect a robot first, a sometimes protracted wait, then a real person who will be polite and helpful.

Walt Disney Travel Co. Packages can be arranged through the Walt Disney Travel Co. Guests can find planning tools on the website that allow them to customize vacation itineraries based on interests as well as age, height restrictions, and medical needs. ☎ *407/939–5277* ⊕ *www.disneyworld.com.*

WDW Central Reservations Office. You can book many accommodations—Disney-owned hotels and some non-Disney-owned hotels—through the WDW Central Reservations Office. The website allows you to compare prices at the various on-site resorts.

People with disabilities can also use this number, as the representatives are all knowledgeable about services available at resorts and parks for guests with disabilities. All representatives have TTY ability. The website is also a valuable source for specific needs. Go to Guest Services and search the word *Disabilities*. ☎ *407/939–7838* ⊕ *www.disneyworld.com.*

WHAT IT COSTS			
$	$$	$$$	$$$$
FOR TWO PEOPLE			
under $175	$175–$249	$250–$350	over $350

OUR REVIEWS

Prices: Prices in the hotel reviews are the lowest cost of a standard double room in high season, excluding taxes, service charges, resort fees, and meal plans (except at all-inclusives). Prices for rentals are the lowest per-night cost for a one-bedroom unit in high season. Note that taxes in Central Florida can be as high as 12.5%.

Maps: *Throughout the chapter, you'll see mapping symbols and coordinates (3:F2) after property names or reviews. Maps are within the chapter. The first number after the symbol indicates the map number. After that is the property's coordinate on the map grid.*

WALT DISNEY WORLD

Each Disney-owned is designed according to a theme (quaint New England, a Polynesian village, an African safari lodge, and so on), and each offers the same perks, including a free Magic Band, transportation from the airport and to the parks, the option to charge all your purchases to your room, and special guest-only park-visiting times.

MAGIC KINGDOM RESORT AREA

Take I–4 Exit 62, 64B, or 65.

The ritzy hotels near the Magic Kingdom all lie on the monorail route and are only minutes away from the park. Wilderness Lodge and Fort Wilderness Resort and Campground, with RV and tent sites, are a bit farther away from the Magic Kingdom, and access to the parks is by bus or boat.

$$$$
RESORT
FAMILY

The Cabins at Disney's Fort Wilderness Resort. The cabins in this 750-acre resort campground just a boat ride away from the Magic Kingdom don't exactly constitute roughing it, as they are compact, air-conditioned log homes that accommodate four grown-ups and two youngsters. **Pros:** lots of traditional camping activities and a real campground community feel; you can save money by cooking, but you don't have to, as there is a three-meals-a-day restaurant and nightly barbecue; nightly family-oriented entertainment options. **Cons:** shuttle to parks is free but slow; pricey for what is really just a mobile home encased in logs; it's a long hike to many of the campground entertainment and dining sites. $ *Rooms from: $435* ✉ *4510 N. Fort Wilderness Trail, Magic Kingdom Resort Area* ☎ *407/824–2900* ⊕ *www.disneyworld.disney.go.com/resorts* ⇌ *421 cabins* ⦶ No meals ✛ 1:C2.

$
RESORT
Fodor's Choice
★

The Campsites at Disney's Fort Wilderness Resort. One of the cheapest ways to stay on WDW property is in your own tent or RV, which can be set up in one of four different areas, from bargain-priced tent sites with water and electricity to deluxe RV sites equipped with electric, cable TV, Internet access, water and sewage hookups, outdoor charcoal grills, and picnic tables. **Pros:** Disney's most economical lodging; pets allowed; wide choice of recreation and entertainment options. **Cons:** amount of walking to reach the store, restaurants, etc., can be a bit much; shuttle rides to Disney parks take a long time; the mosquitoes can be irritating, except in winter. $ *Rooms from:*

$128 ✉ 4510 N. Fort Wilderness Trail, Magic Kingdom Resort Area ☎ 407/939–6244, 407/824–2742 🌐 www.disneyworld.disney.go.com/resorts 🛏 799 campsites 🍴 No meals ✥ 1:C2.

$$$$ RESORT 🏨 **Disney's Contemporary Resort.** You're paying for location at this sleek, modern, luxury resort next to the Magic Kingdom that despite being nearly 50 years old, still lives up to its name; park hopping is a breeze, as the monorail runs through the lobby. **Pros:** monorail access; Chef Mickey's, the epicenter of character-meal world; health and wellness suites. **Cons:** the mix of conventioneers and vacationers can make for chaos in the lobby; pricey; lobby eateries can be crowded and noisy. [$] *Rooms from: $534 ✉ 4600 N. World Dr., Magic Kingdom Resort Area ☎ 407/824–1000 🌐 www.disneyworld.com 🛏 950 rooms 🍴 No meals ✥ 1:B1.*

$$$$ RESORT Fodor's Choice ★ 🏨 **Disney's Grand Floridian Resort & Spa.** So close to the Magic Kingdom you can see the colors change on the Cinderella Castle, this red-roofed Victorian-style resort emulates the look of the great railroad resorts of the past with beautifully appointed rooms, rambling verandas, delicate, white-painted woodwork, and brick chimneys. **Pros:** one monorail stop from the Magic Kingdom; Victoria & Albert's offers an evening-long experience in fine dining; if you're a couple with no kids, this is definitely the most romantic on-property hotel. **Cons:** pricey; draws a large convention clientele; vacationing couples may be more comfortable than families with young children. [$] *Rooms from: $708 ✉ 4401 Floridian Way, Magic Kingdom Resort Area ☎ 407/824–3000 🌐 www.disneyworld.com 🛏 867 rooms 🍴 No meals ✥ 1:A1.*

6

$$$$ RESORT FAMILY 🏨 **Disney's Polynesian Village Resort.** This South Pacific–themed resort with its tropical backdrop of orchids, ferns, and palms, lies directly across the lagoon from the Magic Kingdom, on the monorail and water taxi routes, and has lots of kids activities, making it a good family choice. **Pros:** on the monorail line; great atmosphere; kids' activities. **Cons:** pricey; lots of loud children; Magic Kingdom ferry noise affects some bungalows. [$] *Rooms from: $703 ✉ 1600 Seven Seas Dr., Magic Kingdom Resort Area ☎ 407/824–2000 🌐 www.disneyworld.disney.go.com/resorts 🛏 504 rooms, 360 villas 🍴 No meals ✥ 1:B2.*

$ HOTEL FAMILY 🏨 **Shades of Green.** Operated by the U.S. Armed Forces Recreation Center, this resort is open only to active-duty and retired personnel from the armed forces, reserves, and National Guard, their families, and others connected with the military. **Pros:** large standard rooms; monorail a short walk away; Army–Air Force Exchange store discounts deeply for people with military IDs. **Cons:** prices vary based on rank; no MagicBands or Cards; can be very crowded during holidays. [$] *Rooms from: $115 ✉ 1905 W. Magnolia Palm Dr., Magic Kingdom Resort Area ☎ 407/824–3600, 888/593–2242 🌐 www.shadesofgreen.org 🛏 597 rooms 🍴 No meals ✥ 1:A2.*

$$$$ RESORT FAMILY 🏨 **Disney's Wilderness Lodge.** The architects designed this seven-story luxury resort to mimic the majestic turn-of-the-20th-century lodges of the American West. **Pros:** boarding point for romantic cruises or free water taxi to Magic Kingdom; elegant dining options; children's activity center. **Cons:** no direct bus to Magic Kingdom; no monorail access; noise from the antics at Whispering Canyon Cafe can be annoying.

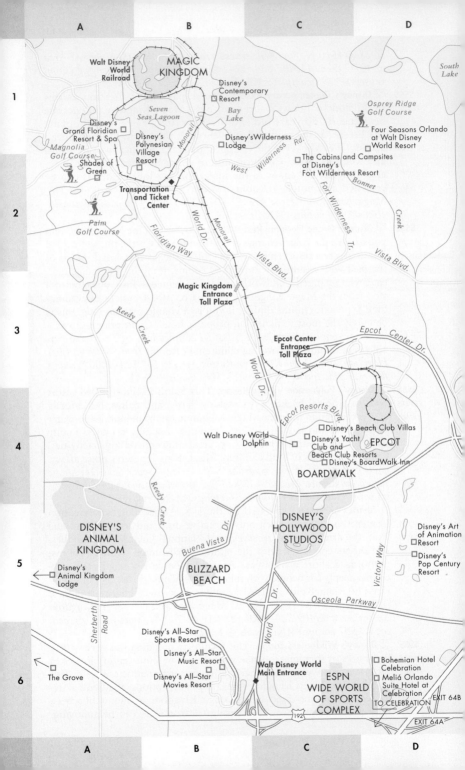

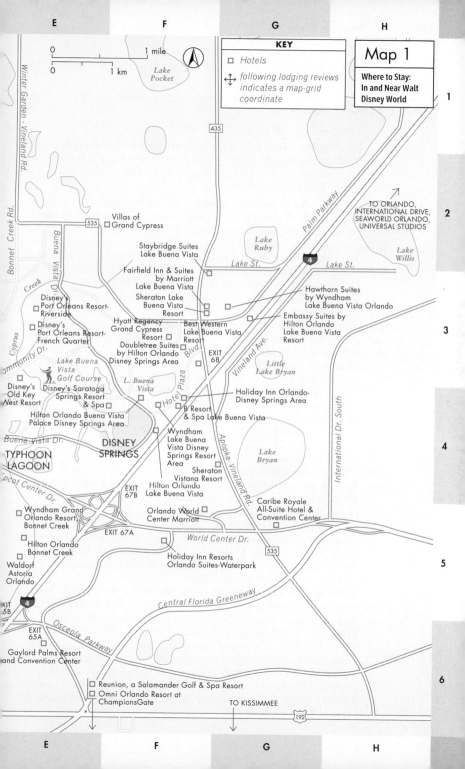

$Rooms from: $508 ⊠ 901 Timberline Dr., Magic Kingdom Resort Area ☎ 407/824–3200 ⊕ www.disneyworld.com ⬠ 841 rooms ⑩ No meals ✛ 1:B1.

EPCOT RESORT AREA

Take I–4 Exit 64B or 65.

From the Epcot resorts, you can walk or take a boat to the International Gateway entrance to Epcot, which deposits you right in the middle of the lands, or you can take the shuttle from your hotel or drive to the Future World (front) entrance.

$$
RESORT
FAMILY

Disney's Art of Animation Resort. This brightly colored, three-story resort is a kid's version of paradise: each of its four wings features images from *Finding Nemo, Cars, The Lion King,* or *The Little Mermaid,* and in-room linens and carpeting match the wing's theme. **Pros:** direct transportation to airport; free parking; images that kids adore. **Cons:** can be crowded; standard rooms fill up fast; the only on-site dining options are quick-service. $Rooms from: $195 ⊠ 1850 Animation Way, Epcot Resort Area ☎ 407/938–7000 ⊕ www.disneyworld.disney.go.com/resorts ⬠ 1,984 rooms ⑩ No meals ✛ 1:D5.

$$$$
RESORT
FAMILY

Disney's Beach Club Villas. Each villa in this pale-turquoise-and-white waterfront area next to the Yacht and Beach Club Resorts has a separate living room, kitchen, and one or two bedrooms, offering families some space, along with easy access to Disney's Boardwalk, Hollywood Studios, and Epcot. **Pros:** short walk or boat ride to the BoardWalk, Epcot, and Hollywood Studios; access to Stormalong Bay water park; in-suite kitchens let you save money on meals. **Cons:** boat traffic can be noisy; not close to Magic Kingdom or Animal Kingdom; pricey. $Rooms from: $950 ⊠ 1800 Epcot Resorts Blvd., Epcot Resort Area ☎ 407/934–8000 ⊕ www.disneyworld.disney.go.com/resorts ⬠ 576 units ⑩ No meals ✛ 1:C4.

$$$$
RESORT

Disney's BoardWalk Inn. Harking back to Atlantic City in its heyday, the striking red-and-white hotel has a wood-floored lobby filled with potted palms that looks over a classic waterfront promenade. **Pros:** casual, upscale atmosphere; lots of activities just outside the door; adjacent to Epcot and Hollywood Studios. **Cons:** pricey; long bus ride to Magic Kingdom; boat whistles can intrude if you have a waterfront room. $Rooms from: $619 ⊠ 2101 Epcot Resorts Blvd., Epcot Resort Area ☎ 407/939–5100 ⊕ www.disneyworld.disney.go.com/resorts ⬠ 372 rooms ⑩ No meals ✛ 1:C4.

$
RESORT
FAMILY

Disney's Pop Century Resort. Giant jukeboxes, 65-foot-tall bowling pins, an oversize Big Wheel and Rubik's Cube, and other pop-culture memorabilia are scattered throughout the grounds of this value resort. **Pros:** great room rates; coffeemakers in most rooms; proximity to Epcot, ESPN Wide World of Sports, and Disney's Hollywood Studios. **Cons:** having close to 3,000 rooms means big crowds at the front desk and in the food court; small rooms; lots of small kids around. $Rooms from: $153 ⊠ 1050 Century Dr., Epcot Resort Area ☎ 407/938–4000, 407/934–4639 ⊕ www.disneyworld.disney.go.com/resorts ⬠ 2,880 rooms ⑩ No meals ✛ 1:D5.

$$$$ RESORT FAMILY **Disney's Yacht Club and Beach Club Resorts.** These big Crescent Lake inns adjacent to Epcot and Hollywood Studios seem straight out of a Cape Cod summer, with their nautical decor, waterfront locale, light-filled rooms, rocking-chair porches, and family-friendly water-based activities. **Pros:** it's easy to walk or hop a ferry to Epcot or Hollywood Studios; gracious atmosphere; adjacent to Boardwalk entertainment and dining. **Cons:** distances within the resort can seem vast; remote from other parks; bus transportation is slow. [$] *Rooms from: $593 ✉ 1700 Epcot Resorts Blvd., Epcot Resort Area ☎ 407/934–8000 Beach Club, 407/934–7000 Yacht Club 🌐 www.disneyworld.disney.go.com/resorts 🛏 1,773 rooms 🍴 No meals ⊕ 1:C4.*

$$$$ RESORT **Four Seasons Orlando at Walt Disney World Resort.** The award-winning Four Seasons presides majestically over Disney's exclusive Golden Oak community, and its luxurious amenities and dedication to service are clear from the moment you step into the marble, flower-bedecked lobby and head for your room. **Pros:** free transportation to Disney parks; lots of on-site kids' entertainment; no resort fee; exclusive golf course for guests. **Cons:** pricey, but then, it is the Four Seasons; a long way from Universal or SeaWorld; remote from Disney parks. [$] *Rooms from: $769 ✉ 10100 Dream Tree Blvd., Epcot Resort Area ☎ 407/313–7777 🌐 www.fourseasons.com/orlando 🛏 444 rooms 🍴 No meals ⊕ 1:D2.*

$$$$ RESORT **Walt Disney World Dolphin.** A pair of 56-foot-tall sea creatures bookends this 25-story glass pyramid, a luxe resort designed, like the adjoining Swan (which is also on Disney property but not a Disney-owned resort), by world-renowned architect Michael Graves, and close enough to the parks that you can escape the midday heat for a dip in the pool. **Pros:** character meals available; access to all facilities at the Swan; free boat to BoardWalk, Epcot, and Hollywood Studios, buses to other parks. **Cons:** daily self-parking fee; a daily resort fee; no charging to room key at parks. [$] *Rooms from: $635 ✉ 1500 Epcot Resorts Blvd., Epcot Resort Area ☎ 407/934–4000, 800/227–1500 🌐 www.swandolphin.com 🛏 1,509 rooms 🍴 No meals ⊕ 1:C4.*

ANIMAL KINGDOM RESORT AREA

Take I–4 Exit 64B.

In the park's southwest corner, Disney's third resort area comprises a mix of high-end, moderate-range, and budget-price complexes.

$ RESORT FAMILY **Disney's All-Star Movies Resort.** Scenes and characters from favorite Disney movies dot the landscape of this large, value-priced, family resort: *101 Dalmatians* of all sizes scamper along railings; Mickey, in his *Sorcerer's Apprentice* robes, commands the waters at the *Fantasia* pool, and a larger-than-life Woody cavorts with his *Toy Story* pals. **Pros:** familiar characters and lots of activities to amuse kids; room rates among lowest at Disney; easy access to Animal Kingdom. **Cons:** at the opposite end of WDW from Magic Kingdom; rooms and decor need refreshing; few plugs for charging phones or tablets. [$] *Rooms from: $138 ✉ 1901 W. Buena Vista Dr., Animal Kingdom Resort Area ☎ 407/939–7000 🌐 www.disneyworld.disney.go.com/resorts/ 🛏 1,920 rooms 🍴 No meals ⊕ 1:B6.*

6

$ RESORT FAMILY

Disney's All-Star Music Resort. Music rules in this colorful, value-priced, family-centric resort that resembles a Florida beach hotel of the 1950s. **Pros:** good value for family holidays; music theme is carried throughout; two heated pools. **Cons:** suites have sleeper chair and sleeper ottoman; long way to Magic Kingdom; rooms and bathrooms are basic and small. [$] *Rooms from: $139* ✉ *1801 W. Buena Vista Dr., Animal Kingdom Resort Area* ☎ *407/939–6000* 🌐 *www.disneyworld.disney.go.com/resorts* 🛏 *1,704 rooms* 🍴 *No meals* ✥ *1:B6.*

$ RESORT FAMILY

Disney's All-Star Sports Resort. Stay here if you want the All-American, sports-mad, quintessential Disney-with-your-kids experience, or if you're a couple to whom all that pitter-pattering of little feet is a reasonable trade-off for a good deal on a room, albeit a small one. **Pros:** unbeatable price for a Disney property; kids love sports themes; close to Disney's ESPN Wide World of Sports Complex. **Cons:** no kids clubs or programs; distances between rooms and on-site amenities can seem vast; farthest resort from Magic Kingdom means you'll spend time on the bus. [$] *Rooms from: $139* ✉ *1701 W. Buena Vista Dr., Animal Kingdom Resort Area* ☎ *407/939–5000* 🌐 *www.disneyworld.disney.go.com/resorts* 🛏 *1,920 rooms* 🍴 *No meals* ✥ *1:B6.*

$$$$ RESORT FAMILY Fodor's Choice ★

Disney's Animal Kingdom Lodge. Entering the vast atrium lobby of this African-inspired lodge is like entering a cathedral with a roof formed of thatch instead of stone; giraffes, zebras, and other wildlife roam just outside the windows of the resort, designed to resemble a *kraal* (animal enclosure) in Africa. **Pros:** extraordinary wildlife and cultural experiences; excellent on-site restaurants; breakfast buffet in Boma is a bargain. **Cons:** shuttle to parks other than Animal Kingdom can take more than an hour; concierge-level rooms have $100-plus surcharge; long corridors. [$] *Rooms from: $436* ✉ *2901 Osceola Pkwy., Animal Kingdom Resort Area* ☎ *407/938–3000* 🌐 *www.disneyworld.disney.go.com/resorts* 🛏 *972 rooms, 499 villas* 🍴 *No meals* ✥ *1:A5.*

DISNEY SPRINGS RESORT AREA

Take I–4 Exit 64B or 68.

The Disney Springs–Lake Buena Vista resort area, east of Epcot, has a variety of inexpensive, midprice, and upscale hotels—some Disney owned, others not—all of which offer shuttles to the Disney parks.

$ RESORT FAMILY

B Resort & Spa Lake Buena Vista. The white-and-blue tower of the B Resort on Hotel Plaza Boulevard is just outside Disney Springs, and a stay there combines an excellent location with a reasonable price and whimsical design. **Pros:** walk to Disney Springs; kids' activities; park shuttles. **Cons:** resort fee; parking fee; need a car to get to Universal or Downtown Orlando. [$] *Rooms from: $159* ✉ *1905 Hotel Plaza Blvd., Disney Springs Resort Area* ☎ *407/828–2828* 🌐 *www.bhotelsandresorts.com/b-walt-disney-world* 🛏 *394 rooms* 🍴 *No meals* ✥ *1:F4.*

$ RESORT FAMILY Fodor's Choice ★

Best Western Lake Buena Vista Resort. Only a few minutes' walk from Disney Springs' wide range of shops and restaurants, this towering resort with its airy lobby offers luxury linens, flat-screen TVs, and, in many rooms, a bird's-eye view of the fireworks, all for a bargain price. **Pros:** a quick walk to shopping and restaurants; free transportation

Disney's Animal Kingdom Lodge

to parks, discount shops; kids eat free. **Cons:** inconvenient to Universal and Downtown Orlando; transportation to the parks can be slow and crowded; resort and parking fees. $ *Rooms from: $152* ✉ *2000 Hotel Plaza Blvd., Disney Springs Resort Area* ☎ *407/828–2424, 800/780–7234* ⊕ *www.lakebuenavistaresorthotel.com* ⬎ *325 rooms* ⦾ *No meals* ✛ *1:F3.*

$$$$
RESORT
FAMILY

⚎ **Disney's Old Key West Resort.** Villas and studios resembling early 20th-century Key West houses provide plenty of family space in this resort; a pleasant boat ride through tree-lined canals delivers you to Disney Springs and its nightlife. **Pros:** quiet and romantic; full kitchens in villas; laundry facilities. **Cons:** long walks between rooms and restaurants, recreation facilities, bus stops; bus service to parks can be frustrating; no elevators. $ *Rooms from: $526* ✉ *1510 N. Cove Rd., Disney Springs Resort Area* ☎ *407/827–7700* ⊕ *www.disneyworld.disney.go.com/ resorts* ⬎ *761 units* ⦾ *No meals* ✛ *1:E3.*

$$$
HOTEL

⚎ **Disney's Port Orleans Resort–French Quarter.** Big Easy–style row houses with wrought-iron balconies cluster around magnolia- and oak-shaded squares in this relatively quiet resort, which appeals to couples more than families, and offers direct boat transportation to Disney Springs. **Pros:** authentic—or as authentic as Disney can make it—fun, New Orleans–style; moderate price; lots of recreation options, including boat rentals and carriage rides. **Cons:** even though there are fewer kids here, public areas can still be quite noisy; shuttle service is slow; food court is the only on-site dining option. $ *Rooms from: $257* ✉ *2201 Orleans Dr., Disney Springs Resort Area* ☎ *407/934–5000* ⊕ *www.disneyworld. disney.go.com/resorts* ⬎ *1,008 rooms* ⦾ *No meals* ✛ *1:E3.*

$$ RESORT FAMILY 🏨 **Disney's Port Orleans Resort–Riverside.** Buildings in this family-friendly, moderately priced resort resemble Southern plantation–style mansions and rustic bayou dwellings all in a charming waterside setting. **Pros:** carriage rides through picturesque settings; river transportation to Disney Springs; lots of recreation options for kids. **Cons:** shuttle to parks can be slow; no shortage of noisy youngsters; the Old South vibe may not be everyone's cup of tea. [$] *Rooms from: $246* ✉ *1251 Riverside Dr., Disney Springs Resort Area* ☎ *407/934–6000* 🌐 *www.disneyworld.disney.go.com/resorts* 🛏 *2,048 rooms* 🍴 *No meals* ✥ *1:E3.*

$$$$ RESORT FAMILY 🏨 **Disney's Saratoga Springs Resort & Spa.** This sprawling property takes its inspiration from 19th-century horse-and-spa resorts in upstate New York, where hot springs and lakes ruled the landscape; studios have microwaves and refrigerators; multibedroom villas have full kitchens (Note: A few online grocery-delivery services deliver.). **Pros:** water taxis whisk you to Disney Springs; kitchens can shave down the food bill; abundance of rooms with whirlpool baths. **Cons:** it's a fair hike from some accommodations to the restaurant and other facilities; one bar-and-grill restaurant; bus transportation can be slow and crowded. [$] *Rooms from: $388* ✉ *1960 Broadway, Disney Springs Resort Area* ☎ *407/934–7639* 🌐 *www.disneyworld.disney.go.com/resorts* 🛏 *1,260 units* 🍴 *No meals* ✥ *1:F4.*

$$ HOTEL FAMILY 🏨 **DoubleTree Suites by Hilton Orlando Disney Springs Area.** Price and location make this all-suites, Hilton-owned hotel a good choice for families and business travelers, as there are amenities for both, and it's a quick, free bus ride to any of the Disney parks and within walkable distance to Disney Springs. **Pros:** within walking distance of Disney Springs; access to Disney golf courses; free shuttle to Disney attractions. **Cons:** daily fee for Wi-Fi; inconvenient to Universal and Downtown Orlando; daily fee for parking. [$] *Rooms from: $175* ✉ *2305 Hotel Plaza Blvd., Disney Springs Resort Area* ☎ *407/934–1000, 800/222–8733* 🌐 *www.doubletreeguestsuites.com* 🛏 *229 units* 🍴 *No meals* ✥ *1:F3.*

$$ RESORT FAMILY 🏨 **Hilton Orlando Buena Vista Palace Disney Springs Area.** This towering hotel is just yards from Disney Springs and caters to business and leisure guests, offering many on-site amenities and recreational options, in addition to free shuttles to Disney parks, character breakfasts, and access to Disney golf courses. **Pros:** good restaurants and bars on-site; kids' activities; across the street from Disney Springs. **Cons:** inconvenient to Universal and Downtown Orlando; steep daily resort fee for Wi-Fi and fitness center; parking fee. [$] *Rooms from: $209* ✉ *1900 E. Buena Vista Dr., Disney Springs Resort Area* ☎ *407/827–2727* 🌐 *www.buenavistapalace.com* 🛏 *1,012 rooms* 🍴 *No meals* ✥ *1:F4.*

$$$ HOTEL FAMILY 🏨 **Hilton Orlando Lake Buena Vista.** Disney character breakfasts and its Disney Springs location make this a family-friendly resort, which offers rooms with white duvet-style bedding, flat-screen TVs, great views, on-site eateries and two heated pools. **Pros:** character breakfasts; free transportation to Disney parks; connected to Disney Springs via a skybridge; access to advance tee times at Disney golf courses. **Cons:** pricey resort fee; parking fee; need a car to get to Universal and Downtown Orlando. [$] *Rooms from: $250* ✉ *1751 Hotel Plaza Blvd., Disney Springs Resort Area* ☎ *407/827–4000, 800/782–4414 reservations* 🌐 *www.hilton.com* 🛏 *814 rooms* 🍴 *No meals* ✥ *1:F4.*

$ HOTEL FAMILY **Holiday Inn Orlando–Disney Springs Area.** This hotel offers low-key elegance, bright rooms, and lots of free amenities for families; some rooms have balconies that offer views of Disney Springs and Epcot fireworks. **Pros:** no resort fee; walking distance to Disney Springs; free transportation to all Disney parks, free Wi-Fi. **Cons:** no free shuttle to Universal or SeaWorld; daily parking fee; need a car to get to Orlando. [$] *Rooms from: $149* ✉ *1805 Hotel Plaza Blvd., Disney Springs Resort Area* ☎ *407/828–8888, 888/465–4329* 🌐 *www.hiorlando.com* 🛏 *323 rooms* 🍴 *Breakfast* ✥ *1:F4.*

$$ RESORT FAMILY **Wyndham Lake Buena Vista Disney Springs Resort Area.** Any hotel within a skip and a hop of Disney Springs is a great draw, and one with a water-playground complex that can entice kids away from the Magic Kingdom during the midday heat is even better; deluxe bedding, large TVs, Disney fireworks views, and character breakfasts are the icing on the cake. **Pros:** good kids' programs; walk to Disney Springs; free shuttle to all Disney parks and attractions. **Cons:** daily resort fee; no shuttle to Universal and Downtown Orlando; daily parking fee. [$] *Rooms from: $224* ✉ *1850 Hotel Plaza Blvd., Disney Springs Resort Area* ☎ *407/828–4444* 🌐 *www.wyndhamlakebuenavista.com* 🛏 *619 rooms, 7 suites* 🍴 *No meals* ✥ *1:F4.*

6

LAKE BUENA VISTA

Hotels just beyond the Disney Springs Area tend to be less expensive than those right on Hotel Plaza Boulevard. If you're willing to take a 10-minute drive or shuttle ride, you might save as much as 35% off your room tab.

$ RESORT FAMILY **Caribe Royale All-Suite Hotel & Convention Center.** This big, all-suites pink palace, on 53 tropical acres just 10 minutes from Disney, melds luxurious decor; family-friendly ingredients like a children's recreation area with a big pool that has a 65-foot slide, interactive water-play area, cushy cabanas, a spa, and game rooms; and business-traveler amenities with an affordable price. **Pros:** family-friendly; award-winning restaurant; scheduled shuttle to Disney and to outlet mall. **Cons:** a hike to other shops and restaurants; no shuttle to Universal or SeaWorld; daily fee for Wi-Fi. [$] *Rooms from: $135* ✉ *8101 World Center Dr., Lake Buena Vista* ☎ *407/238–8000, 800/823–8300* 🌐 *www.thecaribehotelsorlando.com* 🛏 *1,218 suites, 120 villas* 🍴 *Breakfast* ✥ *1:G5.*

$$ HOTEL FAMILY **Embassy Suites by Hilton Orlando Lake Buena Vista Resort.** This Spanish-style all-suites hotel just off Interstate 4 near Disney Springs offers a central location for park hoppers with a car, in addition to roomy accommodations, with refrigerator and microwave, a heated pool with cabanas, tennis court, free breakfast, free evening cocktails, and kids activities. **Pros:** free shuttle to all Disney parks; free Wi-Fi; free breakfast and manager's reception. **Cons:** public areas can be noisy; no shuttle to other parks; long walk to shops and restaurants. [$] *Rooms from: $175* ✉ *8100 Lake St., Lake Buena Vista* ☎ *407/239–1144, 800/257–8483, 800/362–2779* 🌐 *www.embassysuites.com* 🛏 *334 suites* 🍴 *Breakfast* ✥ *1:G3.*

CLOSE UP

Top Spas

If you hit the ground running after arriving in Orlando, at some point you may need to shift your pace from "fast forward" to "pause." If so, head directly to one of Orlando's resort spas. The area has enough standout pampering palaces to indulge every theme park–weary parent, aching golfer, parched sunbather, and Disney princess.

Each of Orlando's resort spas is known for something special, whether it's the Balinese four-hand massage at the Mandara at Portofino Bay or customized therapies at the Waldorf. Several spas draw on Florida's citrus-producing region to offer refreshing orange, grapefruit, and lime therapies. And you can go global with massage techniques from Japan, Thailand, Polynesia, and Sweden.

Families who want to stay together can even spa together at treatment centers specializing in youth facials, massages, and manicure/pedicure (aka: mani-pedi) packages. The Ritz-Carlton Orlando treats kids like royalty with manicures, pedicures, and facials. Disney's Senses Spas at Saratoga Springs and the Grand Floridian offer Magical Manicures and Princess Pedicures.

Make your spa excursion special by planning enough time to use complimentary whirlpools, saunas, and steam rooms. Most spas offer free access to impressively equipped fitness centers and relaxation rooms stocked with herbal teas, fresh fruits, and other goodies. Book treatments early, and ask about gratuities—often 18% to 20%—which may or may not be included in your treatment or package.

TOP SPAS

Blue Harmony, Wyndham Grand Orlando Resort, Disney Springs Resort Area

Portofino Bay Mandara Spa, Portofino Bay Resort, Universal Orlando

Ritz-Carlton Spa, Grande Lakes Orlando, South Orlando

Senses Spa, Disney's Saratoga Springs Resort, Disney Springs Resort Area

Senses Spa, Grand Floridian Resort, Magic Kingdom Resort Area

The Spa at Hilton Orlando, International Drive, Orlando

$ HOTEL FAMILY 🏨 **Fairfield Inn & Suites by Marriott Lake Buena Vista.** Less than a mile from Disney Springs and within walking distance of a variety of restaurants and shops, this hotel, renovated in 2017, has in-room amenities and an attractive budget price. **Pros:** refrigerators and microwaves in every room; free shuttle to Disney; free parking. **Cons:** no real on-site restaurant; small pool; no room service. [$] *Rooms from: $112* ✉ *12191 S. Apopka Vineland Rd., Lake Buena Vista* ☎ *407/239–1115, 888/236–2427* 🌐 *www.marriott.com/mcofv* 🛏 *170 rooms* 🍴 *Breakfast* ✥ *1:F3.*

$ RESORT FAMILY 🏨 **Hawthorn Suites by Wyndham Lake Buena Vista Orlando.** A large, marble-columned lobby welcomes guests to this all-suites lodging less than a mile from Disney's door, and the amenities continue into the suites, most with a fully equipped kitchen, living room, and bedroom with multiple TVs. **Pros:** free hot breakfast, Wi-Fi, and parking; free shuttle to Disney and factory outlet mall; on public bus route. **Cons:** pool area can be noisy; no on-site restaurant; no free shuttle to Universal or SeaWorld. [$] *Rooms from: $144* ✉ *8303 Palm Pkwy., Lake Buena Vista* ☎ *407/597–5000, 866/756–3778* 🌐 *www.hawthornlakebuenavista.com* 🛏 *112 suites* 🍴 *Breakfast* ✥ *1:G3.*

$$ RESORT FAMILY 🏨 **Hilton Orlando Bonnet Creek.** The Hilton more than lives up to its next-door neighbor the Waldorf Astoria Orlando, with plenty of amenities, including a 3-acre lagoon pool with lazy river, rooms with deluxe bedding, flat-screen TVs, family-friendly activities, a golf course, and transportation to Disney parks. **Pros:** serene setting, just moments from Disney by shuttle; access to Waldorf Astoria Golf Club; next door to Waldorf and its amenities. **Cons:** nothing within walking distance, so car is helpful; daily parking fee; steep daily resort fee but it includes a free dinner. [$] *Rooms from: $213* ✉ *14100 Bonnet Creek Resort La., Bonnet Creek* ☎ *407/597–3600* 🌐 *www.hiltonbonnetcreek.com* 🛏 *1,009 rooms* 🍴 *No meals* ✥ *1:E5.*

$$ RESORT FAMILY Fodor's Choice ★ 🏨 **Hyatt Regency Grand Cypress Resort.** Sitting amid 1,500 palm-filled acres just outside Disney's gate, this huge luxury resort has a private lake with watercraft, four golf courses, and miles of trails. **Pros:** elaborate spa; lots of recreation options, including huge pool and equestrian center; good on-site restaurants; the resort's Grand Cypress Golf Club has four courses. **Cons:** need a car or taxi to get to Downtown Orlando or Universal; pricey daily resort and parking fees; lots of conventioneers. [$] *Rooms from: $247* ✉ *1 Grand Cypress Blvd., Lake Buena Vista* ☎ *407/239–1234, 800/233–1234* 🌐 *www.hyattgrandcypress.com* 🛏 *815 rooms* 🍴 *No meals* ✥ *1:F3.*

$ RESORT FAMILY 🏨 **Holiday Inn Resorts Orlando Suites—Waterpark.** The six-story resort, built around a colorful water park with slides, splash bucket, and climbing zones, is a jackpot for families looking for reasonably priced lodgings near Disney with suites and on-site activities to keep kids busy. **Pros:** extremely kid-friendly, even teens will have fun; Disney shuttles included in resort fee; mini golf course. **Cons:** daily resort fee of $30; way too frenetic for folks without kids; poolside rooms can be noisy. [$] *Rooms from: $138* ✉ *14500 Continental Gateway, Lake Buena Vista* ☎ *407/387–5437, 866/462–6425* 🌐 *www.nickhotel.com* 🛏 *777 rooms* 🍴 *No meals* ✥ *1:F5.*

$$ RESORT 🏨 **Orlando World Center Marriott.** This luxury golf resort is one of Orlando's largest, catering to conventions and families (because of its proximity to Disney); rooms have balconies, deluxe bedding, upscale bathrooms, flat-screen HDTVs, and, from the upper floors, spectacular views of Magic Kingdom and Epcot fireworks. **Pros:** full-service spa; wide variety of on-site eateries; Hawk's Landing Golf Course. **Cons:** daily fee for parking, daily resort fee for park shuttles and Internet; on-site restaurants have expense-account-size prices; nothing within walking distance. [$] *Rooms from: $249* ✉ *8701 World Center Dr., Lake Buena Vista* ☎ *407/239–4200, 800/621–0638* 🌐 *www.marriottworldcenter.com* 🛏 *2,009 rooms* 🍴 *No meals* ✥ *1:F5.*

$ RESORT FAMILY 🏨 **Sheraton Lake Buena Vista Resort.** This hotel, conveniently situated near the Disney Springs entrance to WDW, is a pool-centered oasis of cool; some guest rooms transform into family suites with separate bedroom and bunk beds. **Pros:** short walk to shops and restaurants;

6

Disney shuttle; on-site restaurants. **Cons:** on a busy commercial strip; relatively close to Disney Springs but a tad too far to walk in the summer heat (about 1 mile); resort fee and parking fee. [$] *Rooms from: $149* ✉ *12205 Apopka Vineland Rd., Lake Buena Vista* ☎ *407/239–0444, 800/423–3297* 🌐 *www.starwoodhotels.com* 🛏 *486 rooms* 🍴 *No meals* ✥ *1:F3.*

$ HOTEL FAMILY 🏨 **Staybridge Suites Lake Buena Vista.** Close to Disney, this pleasant all-suites hotel is perfect for a big family on a small budget who wants a home away from home; it's only a few miles along Palm Parkway from SeaWorld, Universal, and even the airport, so the frenzy of Interstate 4 can be avoided altogether. **Pros:** free scheduled shuttle service to WDW; free hot breakfast; free Wi-Fi and parking. **Cons:** no restaurant; no shuttles to Universal and SeaWorld; pool and dining areas can be crowded. [$] *Rooms from: $170* ✉ *8751 Suiteside Dr., Lake Buena Vista* ☎ *407/238–0777* 🌐 *www.sborlando.com/orlando-resorts.htm* 🛏 *150 rooms* 🍴 *Breakfast* ✥ *1:F3.*

$$$$ RESORT FAMILY 🏨 **Villas of Grand Cypress.** The views from the terraces of this 1,500-acre, award-winning golf resort's villas and suites take in the fairways of the Jack Nicklaus–designed North Course, waterways with migrating birds and lush tropical foliage. **Pros:** kids' activities at Hyatt Regency Grand Cypress next door; free transportation to all theme parks; in-room Wi-Fi; on-site Jack Nicklaus–designed courses. **Cons:** daily resort fee; far from Universal or SeaWorld; in a remote location. [$] *Rooms from: $336* ✉ *1 N. Jacaranda St., Lake Buena Vista* ☎ *407/239–4700, 800/835–7377* 🌐 *www.grandcypress.com* 🛏 *191 units* 🍴 *No meals* ✥ *1:F2.*

$$$$ RESORT Fodor's Choice ★ 🏨 **Waldorf Astoria Orlando.** Although it can't duplicate the famed original in New York City, this Waldorf echoes it with imagination and flair. **Pros:** lavish and luxurious hotel; free transportation to Disney parks; great spa and Rees Jones–designed golf course. **Cons:** pricey, but you knew that; if you can bear to leave your cabana, you'll need a car to see anything else in the area; steep daily resort fee. [$] *Rooms from: $489* ✉ *14200 Bonnet Creek Resort Ln., Bonnet Creek* ☎ *407/597–5500* 🌐 *www.waldorfastoriaorlando.com* 🛏 *328 rooms* 🍴 *No meals* ✥ *1:E5.*

$$$ RESORT FAMILY 🏨 **Wyndham Grand Orlando Resort, Bonnet Creek.** Despite being surrounded by Disney property, the lakeside locale of this family-friendly resort can feel remote, but generous accommodations, transportation to Disney parks, a full spa, access to Waldorf golf, and several pools offer diversions for everyone. **Pros:** practically in Mickey's lap; free shuttles to Disney parks; lots of activities. **Cons:** not convenient to Universal or Downtown Orlando; daily resort fee ; parking fee. [$] *Rooms from: $259* ✉ *14651 Chelonia Pkwy., Bonnet Creek* ☎ *407/390–2300* 🌐 *www.wyndhamgrandorlando.com* 🛏 *398 rooms* 🍴 *Breakfast* ✥ *1:E5.*

UNIVERSAL ORLANDO

Take I–4 Exit 74B or 75A.

Universal Orlando's three original on-site hotels were built in a little luxury enclave that has everything you need so you never have to leave Universal property. In minutes, you can walk from any hotel to

CityWalk, or take a ferry to the parks. Cabana Bay Beach Resort and Lowes Sapphire Falls are farther afield but are adjacent to the new Volcano Bay. More hotels are being built on the former site of Wet 'n Wild, but they are even farther from the parks.

A burgeoning hotel district across Kirkman Road and down to Sand Lake Road offers convenient accommodations and some even less expensive rates. Although these off-property hotels don't have the perks of the on-site places, you'll probably be smiling when you see your hotel bill.

$
HOTEL
FAMILY

Comfort Suites Universal Studios Area. If Universal's roller coasters and Harry Potter's Diagon Alley are your destinations, these homey accommodations just outside the park should fit the bill with rooms that offer a kitchenette with microwave, refrigerator, and coffeemaker; some even have dining tables. **Pros:** free hot breakfast; free Wi-Fi and free parking; free shuttle to Universal and SeaWorld. **Cons:** a bit of a hike to shops, restaurants; long way to Disney parks; no on-site full-service restaurant or room service. $ *Rooms from: $139* ⌂ *5617 Major Blvd., Universal Orlando Resort* ☎ *407/363–1967, 800/951–7829* ⊕ *www. choicehotels.com/florida/orlando/comfort-suites-hotels/fl616* ⟿ *150 suites* ⦿ *Breakfast* ✛ *2:D1.*

$
HOTEL
FAMILY

DoubleTree by Hilton at the Entrance to Universal Orlando. The name is a mouthful, but it's an accurate description for this value-priced hotel, which caters to business-trippers and pleasure seekers alike; it's so close to Universal that some of the tower rooms offer roller-coaster and Hogwarts views. **Pros:** three on-site restaurants; free Wi-Fi; free shuttle to Universal. **Cons:** fee for parking; on a fast-lane tourist strip; need a car to reach Disney and Downtown Orlando. $ *Rooms from: $149* ⌂ *5780 Major Blvd., Universal Orlando Resort* ☎ *407/351–1000, 800/327–2110* ⊕ *www.doubltreeorlando.com* ⟿ *742 rooms* ⦿ *No meals* ✛ *2:D1.*

$
HOTEL
FAMILY
Fodor's Choice
★

Drury Inn & Suites Orlando. This reasonably priced hotel, less than a mile from Universal, offers free Wi-Fi, free parking, free shuttle to Universal, free hot breakfast, free long-distance and local phone calls, and free hot food and cold beverages in the late afternoon. **Pros:** free everything; central location; reasonable price. **Cons:** if Disney is your destination, this might be a little far afield; next to two busy roadways; pool and gym are small. $ *Rooms from: $119* ⌂ *7301 W. Sand Lake Rd., at I–4, Universal Studios* ☎ *407/354–1101* ⊕ *www.druryhotels. com* ⟿ *238 rooms* ⦿ *Some meals* ✛ *2:C3.*

$$$
HOTEL

Hard Rock Hotel at Universal Orlando. Music rules in this mission-style building, from public areas decorated with rock memorabilia—Elvis's pajamas, Lady Gaga's latex gown, and Elton John's boots—to stylishly modern rooms, with deluxe bed linens, an entertainment center with flat-panel TV, and lots of accessible media device plugs. **Pros:** shuttle, water taxi, or short walk to Universal Parks and CityWalk; Universal Express Unlimited pass included; charge privileges extend to the other on-property Universal hotels. **Cons:** rooms and meals are pricey; fee for parking; loud rock music in public areas, even the pool. $ *Rooms from: $349* ⌂ *5800 Universal Blvd., CityWalk* ☎ *407/503–7625, 800/232–7827* ⊕ *www.hardrockhotelorlando.com* ⟿ *650 rooms* ⦿ *No meals* ✛ *2:D1.*

6

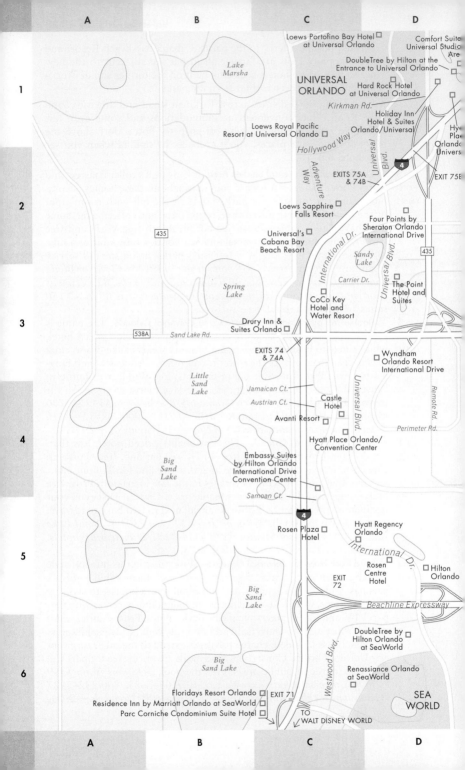

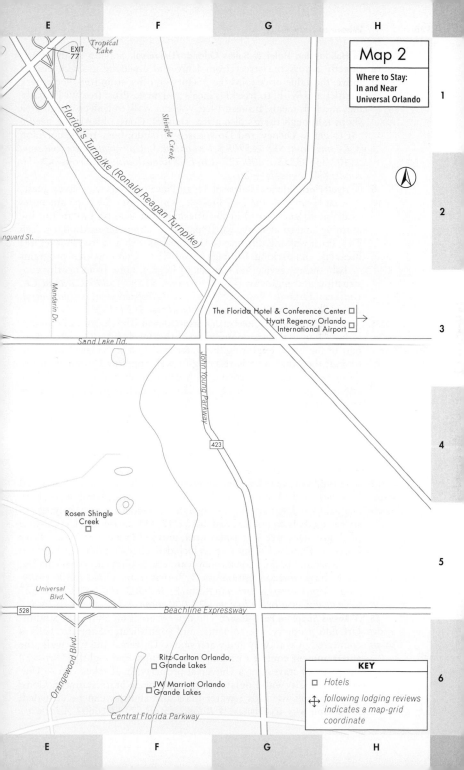

$ HOTEL FAMILY **Holiday Inn Hotel & Suites Orlando/Universal.** Staying at this hotel directly across the street from Universal could be a savvy budget move: the value price joins the freebies on offer, from free theme-park shuttles and Wi-Fi to free kids meals and more. **Pros:** free Wi-Fi, parking, and kids meals; no resort fee; you can walk to Universal and area shops (although there's also a free shuttle). **Cons:** older hotel; need a car to get to Disney and Downtown Orlando; busy traffic corridor. [$] *Rooms from: $88* ✉ *5905 S. Kirkman Rd., Universal Orlando Resort* ☎ *407/351–3333, 800/327–1364* 🌐 *www.hiuniversal.com* 🛏 *390 rooms* 🍴 *No meals* ✥ *2:D1.*

$ HOTEL **Hyatt Place Orlando/Universal.** Hyatt Place supports tech-savvy guests in what Hyatt calls the 24/7 lifestyle, which means the hotel amenities available to guests at 3 in the afternoon are also on tap at 3 in the morning, and rooms have work spaces and computer-ready, flat-screen TVs. **Pros:** walking distance to Universal as well as a free shuttle; free breakfast and parking; free high-speed Wi-Fi. **Cons:** no kids' programs or babysitting service; no shuttles to Disney; noise from nearby construction and highway. [$] *Rooms from: $159* ✉ *5895 Caravan Ct., Universal Orlando Resort* ☎ *407/351–0627* 🌐 *www.orlandouniversal.place.hyatt.com* 🛏 *151 rooms* 🍴 *Breakfast* ✥ *2:D1.*

$$$$ HOTEL Fodor's Choice ★ **Loews Portofino Bay Hotel at Universal Orlando.** The charm and romance of Portofino, Italy, are conjured up at this lovely luxury resort, where part of the fun is exploring the waterfront Italian "village" from end to end; the other part is relaxing in well-appointed rooms that are decorated in aqua and cream, with deluxe beds and flat-screen TVs, and three pools that offer aquatic fun or peaceful sunning. **Pros:** large spa; short walk or ferry ride to CityWalk, Universal; Universal Express Unlimited pass included. **Cons:** rooms and meals are pricey; daily fee for parking; not convenient to Disney parks. [$] *Rooms from: $359* ✉ *5601 Universal Blvd., Universal Orlando Resort* ☎ *407/503–1000, 800/232–7827* 🌐 *www.loewshotels.com/portofino-bay-hotel* 🛏 *750 rooms* 🍴 *No meals* ✥ *2:D1.*

$$$ RESORT FAMILY **Loews Royal Pacific Resort at Universal Orlando.** This Pacific Rim-themed hotel lies amid 53 serene acres of lush shrubs, soaring bamboo, orchids, and palms and features lots of amenities including a weekly Polynesian-style luau, daily character breakfasts, a 12,000-square-foot lagoon-style pool, an interactive water-play area, and kid-friendly activities. **Pros:** Universal Express Unlimited pass included; character dining; shuttle to CityWalk and parks. **Cons:** rooms can feel smallish; steep parking fee; can be busy with conventioneers. [$] *Rooms from: $304* ✉ *6300 Hollywood Way, Universal Orlando Resort* ☎ *407/503–3000, 800/232–7827* 🌐 *www.universalorlando.com* 🛏 *1,000 rooms* 🍴 *No meals* ✥ *2:C1.*

$$ RESORT FAMILY **Loews Sapphire Falls Resort.** The newest hotel on Universal Studios' Orlando property, the romantic and sophisticated Sapphire Falls is connected by walkway and water taxi to Universal and CityWalk, the entertainment complex of shops, restaurants, and nightlife. **Pros:** all the perks of staying at a Universal property; boat takes you to Universal and CityWalk; outstanding on-property bar/restaurant. **Cons:** few activities for kids ; water taxis and shuttles can be crowded; it's a long way to Disney. [$] *Rooms from: $214* ✉ *6601 Adventure*

Loews Portofino Bay Hotel at Universal Orlando

Way ☎ 888/430-4999 ⊕ *www.loewshotels.com/sapphire-falls-resort* ➷ *1,000 rooms* ⊙ *No meals* ✚ *2:C2.*

$ ⊞ **Universal's Cabana Bay Beach Resort.** Universal's Cabana Bay Beach
RESORT   Resort takes guests back in time to a 1950s Florida beach town with
FAMILY   a modern twist, and offers families a less expensive option to stay-
Fodor's Choice   ing on-site at Universal, with loads of benefits that include a 10-lane
★   bowling alley, a Jack LaLanne fitness studio, early park admission,
two pools, one with slide, lazy river, poolside activities, and complimentary shuttle buses to and from Universal parks and CityWalk and
to nearby SeaWorld and Aquatica. **Pros:** early access to Universal but
no Express pass; food court on property; two swimming pools. **Cons:**
parking fee; Disney is not close by; some rooms open onto outdoor
passageways. $ *Rooms from: $164* ⊠ *6550 Adventure Way, Universal
Orlando Resort* ☎ *407/503–4000* ⊕ *www.loewshotels.com/cabana-bay*
➷ *1,800 rooms* ⊙ *No meals* ✚ *2:C2.*

INTERNATIONAL DRIVE

Take I–4 Exit 72, 74A, or 75A.

The sprawl of hotels, time-shares, restaurants, malls, and dozens of
small attractions known as International Drive—I-Drive to locals—
makes a central base for visits to Walt Disney World, Universal, and
other Orlando attractions. Parallel to I–4, this four-lane boulevard
stretches from Universal in the north to Kissimmee in the south.

The I-Ride Trolley travels the length of I-Drive from Florida's Turnpike
to the outlet center on Vineland Avenue, stopping at Universal Orlando,

and SeaWorld. I-Ride is a more worthy transportation tool than you might think. Lots of hotels don't offer shuttle service to Disney, even for a fee, but you can take I-Ride to hotels that do offer a fee-based Disney shuttle, which, depending on the size of the family or group, can be cheaper than a cab.

$ RESORT FAMILY **Avanti Resort.** In the middle of all the activities on International Drive, this resort offers families a home away from home with plenty of amenities at a reasonable price; rooms and public areas are decorated in midcentury chic, and the large pool has a children's play area, a sandy beach with volleyball court, a shuffleboard court, and a bar and grill. **Pros:** scheduled shuttles to theme parks; complimentary cribs and high chairs; laundry facilities. **Cons:** daily resort fee, not exorbitant, covers Wi-Fi, parking, shuttles; elevators can be slow for those on top floors; theme-park shuttles can be slow and crowded. [$] *Rooms from: $105* ✉ *8738 International Dr., International Drive* ☎ *407/313–0100* 🌐 *www.avantiresort.com* 🛏 *652 rooms* 🍴 *No meals* ✥ *2:C4.*

$$$ HOTEL **Castle Hotel.** Amid International Drive's vibrant scene (you can almost reach out and touch the Coca-Cola Orlando Eye), the hotel offers a slightly kitschy sophistication, combining Alpine castle with Mardi Gras glitz. **Pros:** easy walk to I-Drive eateries and attractions; great views; sophisticated vibe. **Cons:** on a congested stretch of I-Drive; not close to Disney parks; self-parking fee. [$] *Rooms from: $339* ✉ *8629 International Dr., International Drive* ☎ *407/345–1511, 800/952–2785* 🌐 *www.castlehotelorlando.com* 🛏 *214 rooms* 🍴 *No meals* ✥ *2:C4.*

$ HOTEL FAMILY **CocoKey Hotel and Water Resort.** If swimming and sliding are among your family's top vacation desires, and your budget gets happy with value prices, this colorful resort with its on-property, 14-slide, three-pool water park could be the perfect destination. **Pros:** on-site water park; Wi-Fi, parking, and shuttle included in resort fee; value price. **Cons:** substantial daily resort fee; some rooms overlook noisy pools; water park closed some days in winter. [$] *Rooms from: $129* ✉ *7400 International Dr., International Drive* ☎ *407/351–2626* 🌐 *www.cocokeyorlando.com* 🛏 *391 rooms* 🍴 *No meals* ✥ *2:C3.*

$$ RESORT FAMILY **DoubleTree by Hilton Orlando at SeaWorld.** Combining low bungalow-style buildings and a 17-story tower, this Bali-inspired hotel creates a warm welcome and a comforting escape—lush linens, tranquil guest rooms, three pools, and tropical landscaping—from hectic I-Drive. **Pros:** on-site miniature golf; free shuttles to Universal, SeaWorld, and Aquatica; carpet-free rooms available for those with allergies. **Cons:** daily resort fee (includes Wi-Fi and parking); few shops and restaurants within walking distance; no shuttle to Disney World. [$] *Rooms from: $189* ✉ *10100 International Dr., International Drive* ☎ *407/352–1100, 800/327–0363* 🌐 *www.doubletreeorlandoseaworld.com* 🛏 *1,020 rooms* 🍴 *No meals* ✥ *2:D6.*

$$ HOTEL FAMILY **Embassy Suites by Hilton Orlando International Drive Convention Center.** An airy, eight-story atrium with palm trees and fountains lends an air of luxury to this moderately priced all-suites lodging, which offers free shuttles to all theme parks as well as free breakfast and late-afternoon drinks. **Pros:** easy walk to Convention Center, shopping, and dining; free shuttle to theme parks; free breakfast and afternoon cocktails.

Cons: on congested stretch of I-Drive; daily Wi-Fi charge in rooms; need a car to visit Disney. $ *Rooms from: $191* ⊠ *8978 International Dr., International Drive* ☎ *407/352–1400, 800/433–7275* ⊕ *www.embassysuitesorlando.com* ⊃ *244 suites* ⏐⊙⏐ *Breakfast* ✢ *2:C4.*

$$ ⚏ **Floridays Resort Orlando.** This pleasant, two- and three-bedroom condo resort—condos were upgraded in 2017—halfway between Universal Orlando and Disney World, has six six-story buildings, two pools, a game room, gym, business center, and café with room service. **Pros:** great, self-contained environment for a family vacation; shuttles to all theme parks; on the I-Ride trolley route. **Cons:** a car would be helpful, as it's too far to walk to almost anything meaningful; daily resort fee for Wi-Fi, parking, shuttles; remote location. $ *Rooms from: $240* ⊠ *12562 International Dr., Lake Buena Vista* ☎ *407/238–7700* ⊕ *www.floridaysresort.com* ⊃ *432 units* ⏐⊙⏐ *No meals* ✢ *2:C6.*
RESORT
FAMILY

$ ⚏ **Four Points by Sheraton Orlando International Drive.** With a hard-to-miss giant ball perched on top of its 20-story round tower, this hotel on the north end of International Drive is visible for blocks, and has a contemporary atmosphere, thanks to the clean, airy design of the lobby, and guest rooms that were totally refurbished (carpets, furniture, and appliances) in late 2017. **Pros:** convenient to Universal and SeaWorld; shuttle to Disney and Universal; free parking, Wi-Fi, and fitness center. **Cons:** located on a busy stretch of I-Drive; no on-site shop for essentials; pricey breakfast. $ *Rooms from: $119* ⊠ *5905 International Dr., International Drive* ☎ *407/351–2100, 800/327–1366* ⊕ *www.fourpoints.com* ⊃ *301 rooms* ⏐⊙⏐ *No meals* ✢ *2:D2.*
HOTEL
FAMILY

$$ ⚏ **Hilton Orlando.** Families visiting this award-winning hotel get two pools, a palm-fringed lazy river to relax in, a kids' club, basketball court, tennis court, full-service spa, and a shuttle to SeaWorld; conventioneers appreciate the vast meeting space, direct connection to the Convention Center, substantial restaurants and bars, work desks with Herman Miller chairs, and an on-site steak house. **Pros:** three pools; shuttle to SeaWorld; direct walkway to Convention Center. **Cons:** about 80% of guests are conventioneers; no free shuttle to Disney World or Universal; daily resort fee and parking fee. $ *Rooms from: $248* ⊠ *6001 Destination Pkwy., International Drive* ☎ *407/313–4300* ⊕ *www.thehiltonorlando.com* ⊃ *1,417 rooms* ⏐⊙⏐ *Breakfast* ✢ *2:D5.*
HOTEL
FAMILY

$$ ⚏ **Hyatt Place Orlando/Convention Center.** Youngish, high-tech-consuming business travelers and vacationing families find value here because of the location and amenities, such as 42-inch flat-panel HDTVs, work areas with computer access panel, wet bar with mini-refrigerator, and heated pool. **Pros:** free parking, Wi-Fi, and hot breakfast; convenient to Convention Center, shopping, restaurants, and nightlife; 24-7 fitness center. **Cons:** no kids' program or babysitting services; no theme-park shuttles; too far to walk to Convention Center. $ *Rooms from: $179* ⊠ *8741 International Dr., International Drive* ☎ *407/370–4720, 888/492–8847* ⊕ *www.hyatt.com* ⊃ *149 rooms* ⏐⊙⏐ *Breakfast* ✢ *2:D4.*
HOTEL

$$ ⚏ **Hyatt Regency Orlando.** This deluxe high-rise conference hotel on International Drive offers anything a resort customer could want, with richly appointed rooms, two pools with cabanas, a full-service spa and fitness center the size of your local Y, two large restaurants, and a 360-seat,
RESORT
FAMILY

6

glass-walled lounge overlooking the pool. **Pros:** good spa; walk to more shops and restaurants; on the I-Ride Trolley route. **Cons:** check-in can take a while if a convention is arriving; long walk from end to end; daily resort and parking fees. $ *Rooms from: $196* ⊠ *9801 International Dr., International Drive* ☎ *407/284–1234* ⊕ *www.orlando.regency.hyatt. com* ⤳ *1,639 rooms* ❍❘ *No meals* ✛ *2:C5.*

$ ⊡ **Parc Corniche Condominium Suite Hotel.** Set back from traffic on the
HOTEL south end of International Drive, this condo hotel offers a good deal
FAMILY for a family with suites that have separate bedrooms, flat-screen TVs, full kitchens with dishwasher, and bathrooms; the I-Ride Trolley passes the front door. **Pros:** free breakfast; well-equipped kitchens; free shuttle to Disney, Universal and SeaWorld. **Cons:** not much within walking distance; resort fee; heavy traffic on International Drive. $ *Rooms from: $142* ⊠ *6300 Parc Corniche Dr., International Drive* ☎ *407/239–7100, 800/446–2721* ⊕ *www.parccorniche.com* ⤳ *210 suites* ❍❘ *Breakfast* ✛ *2:C6.*

$ ⊡ **The Point Hotel and Suites.** In the center of the entertainment triangle
HOTEL bounded by I–4, Florida's Turnpike, and the Beachline Expressway,
FAMILY this all-suites resort is close to Universal, outlet shopping malls, I-Drive attractions, and the Convention Center, making it a good option for family vacations, romantic getaways, and business travel. **Pros:** central to I-Drive entertainment; Wi-Fi throughout the resort; shuttle to Disney and Universal theme parks. **Cons:** shuttle can be slow and crowded; daily resort fee; no ergonomic chair or separate work desk in room. $ *Rooms from: $110* ⊠ *7389 Universal Blvd., International Drive* ☎ *407/956–2000* ⊕ *www.thepointorlando.com* ⤳ *244 suites* ❍❘ *No meals* ✛ *2:D3.*

$$ ⊡ **Renaissance Orlando at SeaWorld.** With a 10-story atrium full of ponds,
HOTEL palm trees, and, ironically, a sushi bar, this SeaWorld neighbor offers
FAMILY tiny black-and-white Shamus instead of rubber duckies in the bath; rooms feature a king or two queen beds, sectional couches, flat-screen TVs, lush bedding, and ergonomic work areas. **Pros:** across from Sea-World; free shuttles to Universal, SeaWorld, and Aquatica; on the Lynx bus line to Disney World. **Cons:** can be a long walk to rooms; many conventioneers; steep resort and parking fees. $ *Rooms from: $249* ⊠ *6677 Sea Harbor Dr., International Drive* ☎ *407/351–5555, 800/468–3571* ⊕ *www.renaissanceseaworld.com* ⤳ *781 rooms* ❍❘ *No meals* ✛ *2:C6.*

$$$ ⊡ **Residence Inn by Marriott Orlando at SeaWorld.** From the welcoming
HOTEL lobby to the well-appointed suites (including dishwasher, microwave,
FAMILY pots, pans, dishes) and the parklike atmosphere around the pool, this
Fodor'sChoice hotel is a great choice if SeaWorld, Aquatica, I-Drive shopping, Univer-
★ sal, or the Convention Center are on your to-do list; a huge laundry is a boon for families. **Pros:** free shuttles to all theme parks; well-equipped kitchens; free breakfast, Wi-Fi, and parking. **Cons:** not much within walking distance; right next to busy Interstate 4; it's a long way to Disney. $ *Rooms from: $259* ⊠ *11000 Westwood Blvd., International Drive* ☎ *407/313–3600, 800/889–9728* ⊕ *www.residenceinnseaworld. com* ⤳ *350 suites* ❍❘ *Breakfast* ✛ *2:C6.*

$$$
RESORT
FAMILY

🖬 **Rosen Centre Hotel.** Directly across from the Orange County Convention Center, this 24-story resort attracts business customers but doesn't ignore families. **Pros:** free shuttles to Universal, SeaWorld, and Aquatica; preferred tee times at sister resort Rosen Shingle Creek Golf Club; five on-site restaurants. **Cons:** no free shuttle to Disney; need a car to get anywhere off I-Drive; lots of convention guests. $ *Rooms from: $278* ✉ *9840 International Dr., International Drive* ☎ *407/996–9840* ⊕ *www.rosencentre.com* ⚑. *Access to Rosen Shingle Creek course* ⥽ *1,334 rooms* ⦿ *No meals* ✛ *2:D5.*

$$$
HOTEL

🖬 **Rosen Plaza Hotel.** Close to the Convention Center, this 14-story hotel caters to its corporate clientele, but leisure travelers also like the prime location and long list of amenities, including a heated swimming pool, fitness center, babysitting services, and a vibrant nightclub that opens onto the pool. **Pros:** within walking distance of Pointe Orlando and other I-Drive restaurants and cinema; priority reservations at Shingle Creek Golf Course, the 18-hole golf course at nearby Rosen Shingle Creek; free shuttle to Universal. **Cons:** Convention Center traffic can be heavy; parking fee; not geared for families. $ *Rooms from: $253* ✉ *9700 International Dr., International Drive* ☎ *407/996–9700, 800/366–9700* ⊕ *www.rosenplaza.com* ⥽ *800 rooms* ⦿ *No meals* ✛ *2:C5.*

$$
RESORT
FAMILY

🖬 **Wyndham Orlando Resort International Drive.** Rebuilt and renovated in 2017 and located in the walkable neighborhood around Orlando's I-Drive 360 entertainment complex, this resort offers a central location for family theme-park visits and also has high-tech amenities for the business traveler. **Pros:** guests get a discount at the adjacent Coca-Cola Orlando Eye complex; within a safe walk of I-Drive restaurants and entertainment; free shuttle to Universal and SeaWorld. **Cons:** no elevators; Disney (about 30 minutes away) shuttle is pricey; daily resort fee. $ *Rooms from: $199* ✉ *8001 International Dr., International Drive* ☎ *407/351–2420, 800/996–3426* ⊕ *www.orlandowyndhamresort.com* ⥽ *613 rooms* ⦿ *No meals* ✛ *2:C3.*

CENTRAL ORLANDO

Take Exit 83B off I–4 westbound, Exit 84 off I–4 eastbound.

Central Orlando, north of Walt Disney World and the I-Drive area, is a thriving business district on weekdays and attracts a club and restaurant crowd on weekend nights.

$$
HOTEL

🖬 **Aloft Orlando Downtown.** In the heart of Orlando, steps from the arts center, sports arena and nightlife, this former utilities building has been transformed into a trendy urban hotel, with a busy bar, innovative rooms, and high-tech amenities. **Pros:** just steps to Downtown nightlife, arts, and sporting events; easy access to highways; trendy urban vibe. **Cons:** if Disney is your destination, it's a 45-minute hike down Interstate 4 to get there; only parking choice is valet or street parking; an urban vibe can be noisy. $ *Rooms from: $249* ✉ *500 S. Orange Ave., Downtown Orlando* ☎ *407/380–3500* ⊕ *www.aloftorlandodowntown.com* ⥽ *111 rooms* ⦿ *No meals* ✛ *3:B3.*

$
B&B/INN

🖬 **The Courtyard at Lake Lucerne.** Built more than a half century before Disney arrived, these four beautifully restored Victorian houses were

rescued and moved to this palm-lined courtyard that's within blocks of the city's arts and sports venues. **Pros:** great Victorian architecture; short walk to Downtown restaurants, the Amway Center, and performing arts center; free parking and Wi-Fi. **Cons:** far from theme parks and I-Drive; walking in some parts of Downtown at night can be a bit dicey; lots of weddings take place here, so noise could be an issue. $ *Rooms from: $140 ⊠ 211 N. Lucerne Circle E, Downtown Orlando* ☎ *407/648–5188* ⊕ *www.orlandohistoricinn.com* ⤳ *25 rooms* ❎ *Breakfast* ✛ *3:B3.*

$$ 🛏 **Embassy Suites by Hilton Orlando Downtown.** A short walk from a half-
HOTEL dozen cafés and restaurants, the Orange County History Center, and
FAMILY the performing arts center and sports venue, this hotel has numerous suites with views of nearby Lake Eola and its centerpiece fountain, swan boats, and jogging path. **Pros:** near Lake Eola and Downtown; free continental breakfast and afternoon beverages; free Wi-Fi. **Cons:** traffic can be heavy; on-street parking is hard to find, and there's a fee for on-site parking; Disney is at least 45 minutes away (an hour or more during rush hours). $ *Rooms from: $249 ⊠ 191 E. Pine St., Downtown Orlando* ☎ *407/841–1000, 800/609–3339* ⊕ *www.embassysuites.com* ⤳ *167 suites* ❎ *Breakfast* ✛ *3:B3.*

$$$ 🛏 **Grand Bohemian Hotel.** Located in the heart of Orlando, this Euro-
HOTEL pean-style property is Downtown's only Four Diamond luxury hotel; it's adjacent to the performing arts center, a block from the sports venue, and it showcases hundreds of pieces of art, along with a rare Imperial

Grand Bösendorfer piano, played by jazz pianists in the popular Bösendorfer Lounge. **Pros:** art gallery and sophisticated entertainment; free Wi-Fi; great restaurant; quiet, adult-friendly atmosphere. **Cons:** little to attract kids; meals are pricey; fees for parking, far from Disney and Universal. $ *Rooms from: $299* ✉ *325 S. Orange Ave., Downtown Orlando* ☎ *407/313–9000, 866/663–0024* ⊕ *www.grandbohemianhotel.com* ⇋ *212 rooms* ⦿ *No meals* ✛ *3:B3.*

SOUTH ORLANDO

$$$ ⛳ **JW Marriott Orlando Grande Lakes.** This lush resort, set in 500 acres
RESORT of natural beauty, offers amenities galore, including a European-style
FAMILY spa, a Greg Norman–designed golf course, a lazy river–style pool complex, and kids' programs; rooms have ergonomic workstations and flat-screen TVs, and the restaurants are supplied from the property's organic farm. **Pros:** pool is great for kids and adults; shares amenities with the Ritz Carlton, including huge spa; free shuttle to SeaWorld and Universal. **Cons:** steep daily resort fee for parking and in-room Wi-Fi; the resort is huge and spread out; need a car to reach Disney or shopping. $ *Rooms from: $309* ✉ *4040 Central Florida Pkwy., South Orlando* ☎ *407/206–2300, 800/576–5750* ⊕ *www.grandelakes.com* ⇋ *1,000 rooms* ⦿ *No meals* ✛ *2:F6.*

$$$$ ⛳ **Ritz-Carlton Orlando, Grande Lakes.** Orlando's only Ritz-Carlton is
RESORT a particularly extravagant link in the luxury chain: it shares a lush
FAMILY 500-acre campus with the JW Marriott, and offers exemplary service,
Fodor's Choice excellent restaurants, children's programs, a golf course, and 40-room
★ spa; suites have balconies, decadent white-marble baths, and deluxe bedding, and a Royal Suite satisfies even the most noble guest. **Pros:** truly luxurious; impeccable service; transportation to theme parks. **Cons:** remote from theme parks, attractions; lots of convention and meeting traffic; daily resort fee and parking fee. $ *Rooms from: $579* ✉ *4012 Central Florida Pkwy., South Orlando* ☎ *407/206–2400, 800/576–5760* ⊕ *www.ritzcarlton.com* ⇋ *582 rooms* ⦿ *Breakfast; Some meals* ✛ *2:F6.*

$$$ ⛳ **Rosen Shingle Creek.** Sitting amid 255 acres of subtropical landscape,
RESORT including a cypress-fringed creek and a championship golf course, this
FAMILY award-winning luxury resort offers a golf academy, fishing, nature
Fodor's Choice trails, four swimming pools, tennis, basketball, and volleyball courts,
★ and a huge spa to soothe those aching muscles. **Pros:** many dining choices on property; huge spa and fitness center; free shuttle to Universal, SeaWorld, Aquatica; award-winning golf course designed by Arnold Palmer Design Company. **Cons:** expansive grounds mean long walks between on-site amenities; no free shuttle to I-Drive or Disney; $18 daily parking fee. $ *Rooms from: $310* ✉ *9939 Universal Blvd., South Orlando* ☎ *407/996–9939, 866/996–6338 reservations* ⊕ *www.rosenshinglecreek.com* ⇋ *1,501 rooms* ⦿ *No meals* ✛ *2:E5.*

6

Ritz-Carlton Orlando, Grande Lakes

WINTER PARK

Take I–4 Exit 87 or 88.

Winter Park is a charming small town that's a 25- to 45-minute drive from the major attractions.

$$$$
HOTEL

The Alfond Inn. This serenely sophisticated building in the heart of Winter Park, just steps from the shops and restaurants of Park Avenue, combines an upscale hotel with an art gallery; owned by neighboring Rollins College, rooms are decorated in cool grays with touches of the iconic Winter Park peacock blue, and have work stations and flat-screen TVs. **Pros:** five-minute walk to Park Avenue for pleasant strolls and dining; restaurant on property; free Wi-Fi. **Cons:** at least an hour's drive to the theme parks; valet parking only at $18 a night; traffic passing on the brick streets can be a bit noisy at night. *Rooms from: $399 ⊠ 300 E. New England Ave., Winter Park ☎ 407/998–8090 ⊕ www.thealfondinn.com ☞ 112 rooms ⊙ No meals ✚ 3:B1.*

$
HOTEL

Park Plaza Hotel. Small and intimate, this beautifully updated 1922 establishment in tony Winter Park offers the charm of fern-bedecked wrought-iron balconies, along with free Wi-Fi and free breakfast in bed; the best accommodations are suites that open onto a flower-filled balcony over the street. **Pros:** valet parking; romantic atmosphere; view of Park Avenue shops and restaurants. **Cons:** railroad tracks are close, making for train noise at night; small rooms; a long way from theme parks. *Rooms from: $169 ⊠ 307 Park Ave. S, Winter Park ☎ 407/647–1072, 800/228–7220 ⊕ www.parkplazahotel.com ☞ 28 rooms ⊙ Breakfast ✚ 3:B1.*

KISSIMMEE

$$$ RESORT FAMILY

🏨 **Omni Orlando Resort at ChampionsGate.** This huge Mediterranean-style award-winning resort just six miles south of Disney, and within a 45-minute drive of LEGOLAND, includes a 1,200-acre golf club with two courses, a David Leadbetter academy, and multifield sports complex. **Pros:** Mokara spa; huge water park with lazy river and wave pool; five restaurants ranging from a casual café to upscale dining; two golf courses. **Cons:** remote location; daily resort fee for Internet, Disney shuttles, and gym; separate daily fee for parking. [$] *Rooms from: $289* ✉ *1500 Masters Blvd., South of Kissimmee, ChampionsGate* ☎ *407/390–6664, 800/843–6664* 🌐 *www.omniorlandoresort.com* 🛏 *862 units* 🍴 *No meals* ✥ *1:E6.*

$$ RESORT FAMILY

🏨 **Gaylord Palms Resort and Convention Center.** Built in the style of a grand turn-of-the-20th-century Florida resort, this huge building is meant to inspire awe, with an enormous glass-roofed atrium, and re-creations of Florida destination icons such as the Everglades, Key West, and old St. Augustine; there's also a water park and movie events. **Pros:** you could have a great vacation without ever leaving the grounds; free shuttle to Disney; excellent on-site dining. **Cons:** daily resort and parking fee; distant from Universal or Downtown Orlando; hotel is so big that you will get your exercise walking within the building. [$] *Rooms from: $239* ✉ *6000 W. Osceola Pkwy., Kissimmee* ☎ *407/586–0000* 🌐 *www.gaylordpalms.com* 🛏 *1,406 rooms* 🍴 *No meals* ✥ *1:E6.*

$$$ RESORT FAMILY

🏨 **The Grove.** New in 2017, this large property near the back gate of Disney offers upscale, modern decor in the suites and the lobby. **Pros:** spacious accommodations suitable for families and groups; choice of on-site eateries; rural location but five-minute drive to busy dining/shopping district on Hwy. 192. **Cons:** steep resort fee; long walk from some suites to lobby and amenities; 25-minute drive to Magic Kingdom. [$] *Rooms from: $320* ✉ *14501 Grove Resort Ave., Kissimmee* ☎ *407/545–7500, 844/203–0209* 🌐 *www.groveresortorlando.com* 🛏 *878 units* 🍴 *No meals* ✥ *1:A6.*

CELEBRATION

Celebration is immediately south of the Walt Disney World Resort, and while it's relatively close to the parks, the resorts in Lake Buena Vista, just west of Disney Springs, are closer to everything but Animal Kingdom.

$$$ HOTEL FAMILY

🏨 **Bohemian Hotel Celebration.** Like everything in the Disney-created town of Celebration, this boutique hotel in the middle of the charming village borrows from the best of the 19th, 20th, and 21st centuries. **Pros:** in the heart of Celebration village; rental bikes and golf carts make touring the village a breeze; free shuttle to Celebration Golf and Fitness Center. **Cons:** steep fee for parking; need a car (or ride share) to get anywhere other than Celebration; it's a long way to Universal. [$] *Rooms from: $314* ✉ *700 Bloom St., Celebration* ☎ *407/566–6000, 888/249–4007* 🌐 *www.celebrationhotel.com* 🛏 *124 rooms* 🍴 *No meals* ✥ *1:D6.*

$ HOTEL FAMILY

Meliá Orlando Suite Hotel at Celebration. Much like a European boutique hotel, the Meliá Orlando is very human in scale, minimalist in decor. **Pros:** shuttle to Celebration and Disney parks; spa privileges at Celebration Day Spa; free parking. **Cons:** busy U.S. 192 is close by; daily resort fee; need a car to visit Universal, SeaWorld, or Downtown Orlando. [$] *Rooms from: $98* ✉ *225 Celebration Pl., Celebration* ☎ *407/964-7000, 888/956-3542* 🌐 *www.melia.com* 🛏 *240 rooms* 🍴 *No meals* ✥ *1:D6.*

$$ RESORT FAMILY

Reunion a Salamander Golf & Spa Resort. Ten miles southwest of Disney and 45 minutes from LEGOLAND, this 2,300-acre resort with condo-style villas and estate-style houses contains three private golf courses—designed by Tom Watson, Arnold Palmer, and Jack Nicklaus—nine pools, a five-acre water park complex, a spa, and tennis courts. **Pros:** secluded, upscale atmosphere with golf galore; concierge grocery delivery; free Internet and parking. **Cons:** daily resort fee; about a 10-mile drive to Disney parks; no theme-park shuttles, so you'll need a car. [$] *Rooms from: $199* ✉ *7593 Gathering Dr., I–4 Exit 58, Reunion* ☎ *407/396-3200, 866/880-8563* 🌐 *www.reunionresort.com* ⛳ 🛏 *325 units* 🍴 *No meals* ✥ *1:E6.*

ORLANDO INTERNATIONAL AIRPORT

The area around the airport, especially the neighborhood just north of the Beachline Expressway, has a surfeit of hotels, mostly used by business travelers and airline staff. They're worth checking out if you have an early departure.

$ HOTEL FAMILY

The Florida Hotel & Conference Center. Five miles from the airport gates, this hotel is midway between Orlando International and I-Drive. **Pros:** in-room Wi-Fi; free parking; short drive to airport. **Cons:** neighborhood less than scenic; resort fee; Disney is 18 miles away, but there are no free shuttles. [$] *Rooms from: $169* ✉ *1500 Sand Lake Rd., Airport Area* ✥ *At S. Orange Blossom Trail* ☎ *407/859-1500, 800/588-4656* 🌐 *www.thefloridahotelorlando.com* 🛏 *511 rooms* 🍴 *No meals* ✥ *2:H3.*

$$$ HOTEL FAMILY

Hyatt Regency Orlando International Airport. If you have to catch an early-morning flight or have a long layover, this hotel inside the main terminal complex is a very convenient option; counting the time you spend waiting for the elevator, your room is a five-minute walk from the nearest ticket counter. **Pros:** despite being at the airport, rooms are quiet; people-watching from terminal-side balconies can be fun; terminal has 24-hour shopping and dining. **Cons:** nothing around but the airport; Downtown Orlando and theme parks at least 30 minutes away; daily fee for parking. [$] *Rooms from: $269* ✉ *9300 Jeff Fuqua Blvd., Airport Area* ☎ *407/825-1234, 800/233-1234* 🌐 *www.orlandoairport.hyatt.com* 🛏 *445 rooms* 🍴 *No meals* ✥ *2:H3.*

NIGHTLIFE

Updated by Gary McKechnie

As one of the world's leading tourist destinations, Orlando has to meet the challenge of offering entertainment to nearly 70 million visitors each year—and providing memorable experiences that will bring them back again and again.

The Walt Disney World Resort has created a wide array of after-dark options in recent years. The greatest collection is found at Disney Springs, an entertainment, dining, and retail complex with four sections: The Landing, Marketplace, West Side, and Town Center. Fifteen minutes away, Universal Orlando has a similar arrangement at CityWalk, their own entertainment, dining, and retail complex. And like Disney, they have assorted pubs, clubs, and shows in their theme parks and resort hotels. Outside the theme parks, too, you'll find a resurgence of nightlife, namely in Downtown Orlando, where a newly refurbished stage, Dr. Phillips Center for Performing Arts, welcomes A-list musicians, comedians, and touring shows, while Orange Avenue offers up an ever-evolving nightclub scene. Several blocks east, the trendy neighborhood of Thornton Park appeals primarily to young urbanites, while the nearby Bob Carr Performing Arts Center still hosts an impressive roster of stars and shows. The NBA's Orlando Magic play their home games at Downtown's Amway Center, but when they're away the venue's calendar is filled with top performers, special sporting events, and large scale productions such as Disney on Ice. Even smaller towns that surround Orlando each have their own selection of bars and nightclubs that are worth a visit.

WALT DISNEY WORLD

Just before Walt Disney selected Orlando as the site of what he called his Florida Project, he had very nearly settled on St. Louis as the follow-up to Disneyland park. But when St. Louis city officials asked which brewery would receive the Magic Kingdom's beer concession, Walt informed them the Magic Kingdom would be no place for beer, and the deal fell apart. Funnily enough, today you'll find almost as many watering holes as there are Disney characters. After beating your feet around a theme park all day, there are lounges, bars, speakeasies, pubs, sports bars, and microbreweries where you can settle down with a soothing libation. Your choice of nightlife can be found at various Disney shopping and entertainment complexes—from the casual down-by-the-shore BoardWalk to the much larger Disney Springs, which is comprised of the Marketplace, The Landing, Town Center, and the West Side, each with an impressive assortment of shopping and dining options.

MAGIC KINGDOM

FIREWORKS AND NIGHTTIME SHOWS

Both in the theme parks and around the hotel-side waterways, Walt Disney World offers up a wealth of fabulous sound-and-light shows after the sun goes down. WDW is one of the Earth's largest single consumers of fireworks—perhaps even rivaling mainland China. Traditionally, sensational short shows have been held at the Magic Kingdom at 10. Starting times may vary throughout the year, so just ask a Disney host or Guest Relations for the evening's schedule.

Fireworks are only part of the evening entertainment. Each park hosts shows staged with varying degrees of spectacle and style. For the widest variety, Epcot—with its showcase of international pavilions—is a good bet. Regular performers include Beatles tribute artists in the United Kingdom, mariachi bands in Mexico, taiko drummers in Japan, oompah bands in Germany, and acrobats in China. Street performances and assorted stage shows take place throughout the day in Canada, Italy, Norway, Morocco, France, and elsewhere around the world—all of which are included with admission.

Fodor's Choice ★ **Happily Ever After.** When the lights dim on Main Street and familiar film tunes fill the air, you know the fireworks extravaganza is about to begin. In Happily Ever After, which replaced Wishes in 2017, popular Disney animated films are explored using song, fireworks, projections, and lasers. Cinderella Castle is transformed with spectacular projection technology for each musical segment of this 18-minute visual treat, from the title tune through familiar songs from nearly 20 Disney films. Snippets of the animated films appear on the castle's parapets and spires, and for some segments, the castle itself appears to become animated. Check the *Times Guide* for performance time, which varies seasonally. ■**TIP→** You can book a Fastpass+ ahead of your visit for best viewing. The castle forecourt and surrounding bridges offer great views; or find a place near the front of the park for a quick postshow exit. ⊠ *Central Plaza, Magic Kingdom* ⟳ *Duration: 12 mins. Crowds: Heavy. Audience: All ages.*

EPCOT

BARS

La Cava del Tequila. Set inside the Mexico pavilion, this intimate bar serves more than 200 tequilas along with Mexican beers, wines, top-shelf cocktails, and a colorful array of margaritas. Try a tequila flight while snacking on tapas, chips, guacamole, and queso. ⊠ *World Showcase Mexico pavilion, Epcot* ⊕ *www.disneyworld.disney.go.com/dining/epcot/cava-del-tequila.*

Rose and Crown Pub. In this rollicking pub in the United Kingdom, patrons come to hear The Hat Lady, the resident piano player who knows every sing-along song ever written and possesses an impressive knack for improvising personalized tunes on the spot. On busy nights, people stand four-to-six-deep at the bar. The fish-and-chips are first-rate, as are the bangers and mash, cottage pie, and other dishes from across the pond. Grab a pint and let the fun begin! ⊠ *World Showcase United Kingdom pavilion, Epcot* ⊕ *www.disneyworld.disney.go.com/ dining/epcot/rose-and-crown-pub.*

Tutto Gusto. In Italy this cool and cozy wine cellar adjoining Tutto Italia is an ideal place to escape the crowds. You can order from among 200 varieties of wine, switch things up with a cold beer, and complement either with a small-plate selection of meats, cheeses, panini, pastas, and desserts. ⊠ *World Showcase Italy pavilion, Epcot* ⊕ *www.disneyworld. disney.go.com/dining/epcot/tutto-gusto-wine-cellar.*

FIREWORKS AND NIGHTTIME SHOWS

Fodor's Choice
★

IllumiNations: Reflections of Earth. This marvelous nighttime spectacular takes place over the World Showcase Lagoon every night before closing. The show's Earth Globe—a gigantic, spherical, video-display system rotating on a 350-ton floating island—is three stories tall with 180,000 light-emitting diodes and projects images celebrating the diversity and unified spirit of humankind. The globe opens like a lotus flower in the grand finale, revealing a huge torch that rises 40 feet into the air as additional flames spread light across the lagoon. Nearly 2,800 fireworks shells paint colorful displays across the night sky. The best viewing spots are in front of the Italy pavilion, on the bridge between France and the United Kingdom, on the promenade in front of Canada, at the World Showcase Plaza, and at La Hacienda de San Angel and La Cantina de San Angel in Mexico. **For people with disabilities:** During the show, certain areas along the lagoon's edge at Showcase Plaza, Canada, and Germany are reserved for guests using wheelchairs. ■TIP→ Limited Fastpass+ reservations are offered; otherwise, find your place 45 minutes in advance. ⊠ *World Showcase, Epcot* ⊙ *Duration: 12 mins. Crowds: Heavy. Audience: All ages.*

HOLLYWOOD STUDIOS

FIREWORKS AND NIGHTTIME SHOWS

Fantasmic! A must-see spectacular, this Hollywood Studios 25-minute special-effects blockbuster is held after dark in a packed 6,900-seat amphitheater (often with an additional 3,000 guests standing). Between music, lasers, and fireworks, Mickey Mouse emcees among an all-star cast of characters from new films and old to take on sinister villains in a fiery finish that dazzles audiences every night. ⊠ *Disney's Hollywood Studios, Lake Buena Vista* ⊕ *www.disneyworld.disney.go.com/ entertainment/hollywood-studios/fantasmic.*

ANIMAL KINGDOM

FIREWORKS AND NIGHTTIME SHOWS

Rivers of Light. As dusk falls, radiance lights up the waterfront Discovery River amphitheater in a tranquil 15-minute performance that combines video, live performances, projections, floats, and an original musical score. Lanterns transform into animal spirit forms—the Elephant, the Tiger, the Turtle, and the Owl. The projections move across jungles, oceans, savannas, and mountains, using curtains of mist as screens. ⊠ *Discovery River, Animal Kingdom.*

Tree of Life Awakenings. The iconic tree has developed a night-time persona now that the park stays open after dark. As night falls, fireflies begin to flicker among the leaves of the tree. The tiny lights expand, and through the magic of high-tech projections, the animals carved into the trunk—from dinosaurs to gorillas to tropical birds to a deer—begin to awaken in a swirl of color, until the whole tree is alive with light. The experience repeats every 10 minutes from dark until park closing time. ⊠ *Discovery Island, Animal Kingdom.*

DISNEY'S BOARDWALK

In the good ol' days, folks in New York and New Jersey escaped their city routines for breezy seaside boardwalks. That era is recreated on the shores of Crescent Lake at Disney's BoardWalk, just a short walk from Epcot. The quarter-mile promenade becomes a festive setting after sunset, where you can stroll past shops, bars, boutiques, nightlife, and street performances. And if you'd like to see the Epcot fireworks, you'll find a nice view from the bridge that connects the BoardWalk with the Yacht and Beach Club resorts just across the lake.

Atlantic Dance Hall. This high-energy dance club plays music from the '80s onward, with a huge screen showing videos requested by the crowd. The parquet dance floor is set off by furnishings of deep blue, maroon, and gold, and the ceiling glows with stars and twinkling lights. Signature cocktails are in demand, and you can sip a cognac or choose from a selection of popular beers to inspire your dance floor moves. ⊠ *BoardWalk, Epcot Resort Area* ☎ *407/939–2444* ⊕ *www.disneyworld.disney. go.com/entertainment/boardwalk/atlantic-dance-hall.*

Big River Grille & Brewing Works. Disney World's only brewpub welcomes families with intimate tables and a waterfront patio; either is a splendid place to sample craft brews and upscale American pub grub like barbecued ribs or blackened Creole salmon. You can order a sampler with five to seven three-ounce pours of whatever's on tap that day, usually including Red Rocket, Southern Flyer Light Lager, Gadzooks Pilsner, and Steamboat Pale Ale. ⊠ *BoardWalk, Epcot Resort Area* ☎ *407/560–0253* ⊕ *www.disneyworld.disney.go.com/dining/ boardwalk/big-river-grille-and-brewing-works.*

ESPN Club. The sports motif here is carried into every nook and cranny—the main dining area looks like an arena, with a basketball-court hardwood floor and a giant scoreboard that projects the day's big game. While you watch, you can munch on wings, nachos, and linebacker-size burgers. There are more than 100 TVs throughout the 13,000-square-foot hall (even in the restrooms) carrying satellite feeds of games from around the world, so you won't miss one action-packed minute. ■TIP→ The place is packed for big games, so plan to arrive early: Seats are first come, first served. ⊠ *BoardWalk, Epcot Resort Area* ☎ *407/939–1177* ⊕ *www. disneyworld.disney.go.com/dining/ boardwalk/espn-club.*

Jellyrolls. In this rockin', boisterous piano bar, comedians double as emcees as they play dueling grand pianos nonstop. Their speed and intricacy is impressive, as is the depth of their playlist. The steady stream of conventions at Disney makes this the place to catch CEOs doing the conga to Barry Manilow's "Copacabana" (if that's your idea

of a good time) and young Disney cast members checking in after they clock out. ⊠ *BoardWalk, Epcot Resort Area* ☎ *407/560–8770* ⊕ *www. disneyworld.disney.go.com/entertainment/boardwalk/jellyrolls* ⊠ *$12 cover* ☞ *Guests must be 21 and over.*

DISNEY SPRINGS

Walt Disney World is so much more than the Magic Kingdom and its theme-park siblings, Epcot, Disney's Hollywood Studios, and Disney's Animal Kingdom. Beyond the parks, there are enough diversions to keep you busy day and night. Divided into four areas (West Side, The Landing, Town Center, and the Marketplace), Disney Springs is the epicenter of evening entertainment. There are dozens of places for shopping, including the resort's largest Disneyana store, the World of Disney, as well as the LEGO Imagination Center, with its life-size LEGO people and animals, retail store, and play area. Then, of course, there's the nightlife.

WEST SIDE

West Side at Disney Springs is a hip outdoor complex for shopping, dining, and entertainment. Part of the Disney Springs complex, the West Side is anchored by the House of Blues, and a short walk away you'll find retro-cool bowling at Splitsville and trendy films shown at the Disney Springs 24. West Side is worth a visit for its waterside location, wide promenade, and diverse shopping and dining. Opening time is 11 am, closing time around 2 am; crowds vary with the season, but weeknights tend to be less busy. For entertainment times and more information, call ☎ *407/824–4500* or ☎ *407/824–2222.*

Bongos Cuban Café. Latin rhythms provide the beat at this restaurant and bar with a Havana theme owned by pop singer Gloria Estefan. Four bars are especially busy on weekends, when a Latin band kicks it up a notch with *muy caliente* music. Samba, tango, salsa, and merengue rhythms roll throughout the week. ⊠ *West Side, Disney Springs* ☎ *407/828–0999* ⊕ *www.bongoscubancafe.com.*

House of Blues. The restaurant serves up live blues performances and rib-sticking Mississippi Delta cooking all week long, and there's often a jam session on the front porch. The attached concert hall has showcased such artists as Aretha Franklin, David Byrne, Steve Miller, and Willie Nelson, but check the calendar in advance since large acts like these are rare. Come hungry (and with an admission ticket) for the popular Sunday Gospel Brunch, where there's always a show and all-you-can-eat Southern food. ⊠ *West Side, Disney Springs* ☎ *407/934–2583* ⊕ *www.disneyworld.disney.go.com/entertainment/disney-springs/house-of-blues-shows.*

DISNEY SPRINGS MARKETPLACE
Although the Marketplace offers little in the line of typical nightlife, there's hardly a more enjoyable place for families to spend a quiet evening window-shopping, enjoying ice cream at a courtyard café, or strolling among eclectic Disney stores. It's here that you can design your own Disney T-shirt or teddy bear, arrange for a princess-style makeover at the Bibbidi Bobbidi Boutique, and peruse a dozen themed showrooms in the largest Disney store of all: The World of Disney.

MAGIC KINGDOM RESORT AREA

With more than a dozen resort hotels on Walt Disney World property, the hotel-bar scene is understandably active. Depending on whether the resort is geared to business or romance, the lounges can be soothing or boisterous—or both. You do not have to be a resort guest to visit the bars and lounges, and a casual tour of them may well provide an evening's entertainment. To contact any of these hotel bars directly, you can call the Disney operator at ☎ *407/824–4500* or ☎ *407/824–2222.*

BARS
California Grill Lounge. This sophisticated lounge is a sublime place for predinner cocktails (with menu items from the adjacent California Grill restaurant available here as well), but what you'll really drink in is the beautiful view of the Magic Kingdom and the waters of Bay Lake and the Seven Seas Lagoon. ■ **TIP→ Time it right and enjoy an unparalleled view of the fireworks over Cinderella Castle.** ⊠ *Contemporary Resort, Magic Kingdom Resort Area* ⊕ *www.disneyworld.disney.go.com/dining/contemporary-resort/california-grill.*

Mizner's. A stylish, refined alcove named after Florida Renaissance architect Addison Mizner is tucked away at the far end of the Grand Floridian's second-floor lobby. It's a tasteful low-key getaway where you can unwind with a glass of champagne, a martini, or a Manhattan while listening to a live jazz band. The extensive drink menu includes multiple single-malt Scotch whiskies and after-dinner cognacs and ports. ⊠ *Grand Floridian Resort, Magic Kingdom Resort Area* ⊕ *www.disneyworld.disney.go.com/dining/grand-floridian-resort-and-spa/mizner-lounge.*

Narcoossee's. Inside the high-end restaurant is a bar that serves ordinary beer in expensive yard glasses, along with some exclusive and tasty cocktails. The porch-side views of the Seven Seas Lagoon, the nightly Electrical Water Pageant, and the Magic Kingdom fireworks are worth the premium you pay. ⊠ *Grand Floridian Resort, Magic Kingdom Resort Area* ⊕ *www.disneyworld.disney.go.com/dining/grand-floridian-resort-and-spa/narcoossees.*

Territory Lounge. The frontier theme here honors the Corps of Discovery (look overhead for a Lewis and Clark Expedition trail map). Between drinks, check out the surveying equipment, daguerreotypes, parka mittens, maps, and what the lounge claims is a pair of Teddy Roosevelt's boots. ⊠ *Wilderness Lodge, Magic Kingdom Resort Area* ⊕ *www.disneyworld.disney.go.com/dining/wilderness-lodge-resort/territory-lounge.*

DINNER SHOWS

Hoop-Dee-Doo Musical Revue. The longest-running show at Disney has hardly changed over the decades. The beloved Pioneer Hall Players—a group of Wild West singers, dancers, and comedians—perform romantic ballads, corny tunes, and slapstick. It's old-fashioned family fun you'll sing and clap along to while chowing down on barbecued ribs, fried chicken, corn on the cob, strawberry shortcake, and all the fixin's. Unlimited beverages include beer, wine, and sangria. ■ TIP→ Tickets are available up to 180 days in advance so plan as far ahead as possible. ⊠ *Fort Wilderness Resort, Magic Kingdom Resort Area* ☎ *407/939–3463* ⊕ *www.disneyworld.disney.go.com/dining/cabins-at-fort-wilderness-resort/hoop-dee-doo-musical-revue* 🍴 *$64–$72.*

Spirit of Aloha. This popular luau features an outdoor barbecue with colorful South Pacific–style entertainment. Fire jugglers and hula dancers capture the spirit of Tahiti, Samoa, Tonga, New Zealand, and Hawaii while regional dishes like Polynesian ribs and roasted chicken and pineapple-coconut guava cake transport your taste buds to the islands. ■ TIP→ Reservations can be made 180 days in advance. ⊠ *Polynesian Resort, Magic Kingdom Resort Area* ☎ *407/939–3463, 407/824–1593* ⊕ *www.disneyworld.disney.go.com/dining/polynesian-resort/disney-spirit-of-aloha-dinner-show* 🍴 *$66–$78.*

FIREWORKS AND NIGHTTIME SHOWS

Electrical Water Pageant. A long-running Disney tradition, this floating parade of illuminated sea creatures on the Seven Seas Lagoon and Bay Lake rolls past several Magic Kingdom–area resorts. Backed by an electronic score featuring Handel's *Water Music,* the low-key but always-pleasing show leads up to a stirring finale. Watch it from a resort bar like Narcoossee's, the campgrounds at Fort Wilderness, or the pier at the Grand Floridian. ⊕ *www.disneyworld.disney.go.com/entertainment/magic-kingdom/electrical-water-pageant.*

ANIMAL KINGDOM RESORT AREA

BARS

Victoria Falls. The exotic safari theme incorporates leather directors' chairs, native masks, and the gurgling of a stream that flows from the lobby and through the lounge to cascade over rockwork into a small pool at the Boma restaurant below. Before or after dinner, this is a great spot to watch a game, sip South African wines and beers, and enjoy a casual night out with friends and family. ■TIP➔ Arrive early and check out the zebras, giraffes, and other animals on the lodge's savanna. ⊠ *Animal Kingdom Lodge, Animal Kingdom Resort Area* ⊕ *www.disneyworld.disney.go.com/dining/animal-kingdom-lodge/victoria-falls-lounge.*

UNIVERSAL ORLANDO

With the wide range of nightlife you'll find at Universal, you may get the feeling that you're vacationing not in Orlando but in New York City. CityWalk's stores open by midmorning, and its restaurants come to life between lunchtime and late afternoon. Eateries that double as nightclubs (such as Pat O'Brien's, Bob Marley's, and the Red Coconut Club) start charging a cover before dusk and apply age restrictions (usually 21) around 9 pm. For details on a particular establishment, check with Guest Services (aka Guest Relations). A Party Pass ($11.90) is good for admission to the clubs of CityWalk, and Universal's hefty $20 parking fee is waived after 6 pm.

7

UNIVERSAL ORLANDO'S CITYWALK

Blue Man Group. At their own venue, the ever-innovative Blue Man Group continues to pound out new music, sketches, and audience interaction. Attempting to understand the apps on a GiPad (a gigantic iPad), they may appear clueless and perplexed about cutting-edge technology (which for them can be as basic as a can of paint), but they're always excited when they can drum out rhythms on lengths of PVC pipes and throw a rave party finale for all in attendance. The show is a surreal comic masterpiece. Three levels of admission (Poncho, Tier 1, and Tier 2) hint at how messy things can get when the Blue Men cut loose. ⊠ *CityWalk* ☎ *407/258–3626* ⊕ *www.universalorlando.com* ⊠ *$60–$110.*

Bob Marley—A Tribute to Freedom. Modeled after the King of Reggae's home in Kingston, Jamaica (even down to the air-conditioning window units), in a way this nightclub is also part museum, with more than 100 photographs and paintings showing pivotal moments in Marley's life. Though the place does serve Jamaican-influenced meals, most patrons are at the cozy bar or by the patio, where they can be jammin' to a (loud) live band that plays nightly. For a nice souvenir, pose by the wonderful Marley statue outside the club. Sunday is ladies' night from 9 pm until closing. ⊠ *CityWalk* ☎ *407/224–2692* ⊕ *www.universalorlando.com/web/en/us/things-to-do/dining/bob-marley-a-tribute-to-freedom/index.html.*

CityWalk's Rising Star. Here you and other hopeful (and hopeless) singers can really let loose in front of a live audience. Singers croon to recorded tracks on Sunday and Monday, but between Tuesday and Saturday you're accompanied by a live band complete with backup singers. A full bar is always on tap. Friday and Saturday are reserved for an over-21 crowd. ⊠ *6000 Universal Blvd., CityWalk* ☏ *407/224–2961* ⊕ *www. universalorlando.com/web/en/us/things-to-do/entertainment/rising-star-karaoke/index.html.*

the groove. In this cavernous multilevel hall, images flicker rapidly on several screens, with the lights, music, and mayhem appealing to a mostly under-30 crowd. Prepare for lots of fog, swirling lights, and sweaty bodies. The '70s-style Green Room is filled with beanbag chairs and everything you threw out when Duran Duran hit the charts. The Blue Room is sci-fi Jetson-y, and the Red Room is hot and romantic in a bordello sort of way. The music is equally diverse: Top 40, hip-hop, R&B, techno, and the occasional live band. ⊠ *6000 Universal Blvd., CityWalk* ☏ *407/224–2692* ⊕ *www.universalorlando.com/web/en/us/ things-to-do/entertainment/the-groove/index.html.*

Hard Rock Cafe. The Hard Rock Cafe here is the largest on earth, which means you can see plenty of memorabilia, including such Beatles rarities as John Lennon's famous New York City T-shirt, Paul's original lyrics for "Let It Be," and the doors from London's Abbey Road studios plus hundreds of other fascinating collectibles. And the food's great, too. Next door the Hard Rock Live concert hall (The Coliseum of Rock) hosts comedians, solo acts, and internationally recognized bands that make it one of the most popular venues at Universal. A few drawbacks: The seating's not the greatest, and if you arrive at the door carrying a large purse or bags, it won't be time to rock, it'll be time to walk—about a quarter-mile back to the parking garage to stow your stuff. For showtimes, call 407/351–5483. ⊠ *CityWalk* ⊕ *www.hardrocklive.com.*

Jimmy Buffett's Margaritaville. Buffett tunes fill the air at the restaurant here and at the Volcano, Land Shark, and 12 Volt bars. Inside there's a miniature Pan Am Clipper suspended from the ceiling, music videos projected onto sails, limbo and hula-hoop contests, a huge margarita blender that erupts "when the volcano blows," and live music nightly—everything that Parrotheads need to roost. Across the promenade, another full-size seaplane (emblazoned with "Jimmy Buffett, Captain") is the setting for the Lone Palm Airport, a pleasing and surprisingly popular outdoor waterfront bar. ⊠ *6000 Universal Studios Plaza, Suite 704, CityWalk* ☏ *407/224–2155* ⊕ *www.universalorlando.com/web/en/ us/things-to-do/dining/jimmy-buffetts-margaritaville/index.html.*

Pat O'Brien's. An exact reproduction of the legendary New Orleans original, this comes complete with flaming fountain and dueling pianists who are playing for highly entertained regulars and visitors—even on weekday afternoons. Outside, the cozy and welcoming Patio Bar has a wealth of tables and chairs, allowing you to do nothing but enjoy the outdoors and your potent, rum-based Hurricanes in Orlando's version of the Big Easy. ⊠ *6000 Universal Blvd., CityWalk* ☏ *407/224–2692* ⊕ *www.universalor-lando.com/web/en/us/things-to-do/dining/pat-o-briens/index.html.*

Red Coconut Club. Paying tribute to kitsch design of the 1950s, the interior here is part Vegas lounge, part Cuban club, and part Polynesian tiki bar. It's "where tropical meets trendy." There are three full bars on two levels, signature martinis, an extensive wine list, and VIP bottle service. Hang out in the lounge, on the balcony, or at the bar. On a budget? Take advantage of the daily happy hours and gourmet appetizer menu. A DJ (Sunday–Wednesday) or live music (Thursday–Saturday) pushes the energy with tunes ranging from Sinatra to rock. Thursday is ladies' night. ✉ *6000 Universal Blvd., CityWalk* ☎ *407/224–2425* ⊕ *www.universalorlando.com/web/en/us/things-to-do/entertainment/ red-coconut-club/index.html.*

ORLANDO

When Disney and Universal staked their claims on Orlando nightlife, there was an exodus from the city's Downtown clubs. But over the years, there has been a resurgence of after hours activities that attract a steady stream of club and concert goers. The Amway Center hosts the Orlando Magic, the Dr. Phillps Center for Performing Arts brings in leading musical artists and performers, and Downtown sees an ever-evolving and often changing lineup of nightclubs.

CENTRAL ORLANDO

The heart of Orlando nightlife spans several blocks from the intersection of Orange Avenue and Church Street. Bars, cantinas, lounges, dance clubs, movie theaters, a sports arena, and the performing arts center are all within this core area, creating an energetic blend of bourgeoisie and bohemian.

AERO. On a starry, starry night it's a treat to escape the crowded street-level clubs of Downtown to this rooftop nightclub on top of The Social. Surrounded by some of Orlando's tallest buildings, it exudes hip, trendy vibes that are just right for those looking to dance to a DJ outdoors. Ladies' nights, themed events, and even yoga classes are offered. ✉ *60 N. Orange Ave., Downtown Orlando* ☎ *407/274–8452* ⊕ *www.aeroorlando.com.*

Bull and Bush Pub. Here since 1987, this pub just a few miles east of Downtown has become a neighborhood institution. It's still one of the most atmospheric places in town, where you can get a hand-drawn pint, play a game of darts, and have a (still) smoky chat. The tap lineup covers 11 imported beers and ales and quadruples that number in bottled selections, while the kitchen prepares fish-and-chips, cottage pies, and Scotch eggs. Darts leagues and weekly pub quizzes make it feel like a piece of old London. ✉ *2408 E. Robinson St., Downtown Orlando* ☎ *407/896–7546* ⊕ *www.bullandbushorlando.com* ☾ *Closed Sun.*

Wall Street Plaza. Taking a cue from the once-popular (but now passé) Church Street Station, Wall Street Plaza created something different for Downtown partygoers: seven distinct, themed venues in one location. Choose the Wall Street Cantina for Mexican fare, the Hen House ("The World's Smallest Bardello") for craft beers and unique liquors, Hooch for an outdoor bar in steampunk style, the Shine dance club for its "moonshine warehouse" look, the Monkey Bar for a martini lounge, the outdoor WaiTiki Bar for tiki drinks, or Sideshow for a party scene. With a calendar packed with parties, this is considered Party Central for many in the Downtown crowd. ⊠ *19 N. Orange Ave., Downtown Orlando* ☎ *407/420–1515* ⊕ *www.wallstplaza.net.*

Wally's. If you're thirsting for an old-school bar with big pours, check out this Orlando icon. One of the city's oldest bars (circa 1954), the longtime local favorite is a hangout for a cross section of cultures and ages. Some would say it's a dive (which it is), but that doesn't matter to the students, bikers, lawyers, and barflies who land here to drink surrounded by the go-go-dancer wallpaper and '60s-era interior. Just grab a stool at the bar to take in the scene and down a cold one. ⊠ *1001 N. Mills Ave., Downtown Orlando* ☎ *407/896–6975* ⊕ *www.wallysonmills.com* ⊙ *Closed Sun.*

MUSIC CLUBS

Bösendorfer Lounge. One of only two Imperial Grand Bösendorfer pianos in the world takes center stage at what may be the classiest gathering spot in Orlando. The highly civilized (but not stuffy) lounge attracts a cross section of trendy Orlandoans, especially the after-work crowd, among whom conversation and camaraderie flow as smoothly as the champagne, beer, wine, and cocktails. And with its location across the street from the performing arts center, it's a draw pre-and postconcert. Art on the walls, comfortable couches, rich fabrics, sleek black marble, and seductive lighting invite you to stay a while. If music is what attracts you, call in advance for the schedule of jazz combos and solo pianists who perform in the lounge. Many are among the area's finest and most talented musicians. ⊠ *Grand Bohemian Hotel, 325 S. Orange Ave., Downtown Orlando* ☎ *407/313–9000* ⊕ *www.grandbohemianhotel.com.*

Fodor's Choice ★ **The Social.** Beloved by locals, The Social is a great place to see touring and area musicians. Up to seven nights a week, you can sip trademark martinis while listening to anything from indie rock to rockabilly to music mixed by DJs. Fans love the venue because the stage is low, the bands are close, and the enthusiasm is high. Several now-national acts got their start here, including Seven Mary Three (which released an album called "Orange Ave." in honor of the venue's location), Matchbox Twenty, and other groups that don't have numbers in their names. Hours vary, and there is usually a cover. ⊠ *54 N. Orange Ave., Downtown Orlando* ☎ *407/246–1419* ⊕ *www.thesocial.org.*

Tanqueray's. Of all the entertainment possibilities in Downtown Orlando, the most interesting one may be the hardest to find. Housed in a former bank vault, Tanqueray's is a belowground hideaway featuring live music nightly and a full bar, including craft beers and nightly drink specials. If you don't mind the smoky atmosphere, you can enjoy a variety of entertainment from one night to the next, including reggae, funk, and high-energy blues. No food is served here. ⊠ *100 S. Orange Ave., Downtown Orlando* ☎ *407/649–8540.*

NIGHTCLUBS

Chillers-Cahoots-Latitude. Known as Orlando's original party bar (it's been here since 1992), Chillers is a Key West–themed nightspot that features an entire wall of frozen daiquiri machines. More than just a place to sip on an adult version of a Slurpee, it's where a DJ spins dance music and hosts karaoke nights, where you'll find $1 drinks on Wednesdays, and sometimes two-for-one (or even three-for-one) drinks. Upstairs, Chillers' sister club, Cahoots, offers more than 100 craft beers and 40 bourbon whiskeys (with retro and modern arcade games as a chaser). Above that is Latitudes, a large rooftop bar with a tropical theme and Top 40 music. ⊠ *33 W. Church St., Downtown Orlando* ☎ *407/649–4270* ⊕ *www.churchstreetbars.com.*

Parliament House Resort. For those enamored of gay, lesbian, and high-camp entertainment, Parliament House is legendary and welcoming to every kind of audience. The 250-seat art deco performance space, which has been open since 1975, hosts live theater, musical acts, karaoke, cabaret, dance, and bawdy and hilarious drag shows. Le Club Disco and Dance bar, along with four other bars, draws thousands of partiers weekly. Unfortunately, Orange Blossom Trail remains a sketchy area, so wandering around the neighborhood isn't advised. ⊠ *410 N. Orange Blossom Trail, Downtown Orlando* ☎ *407/425–7571* ⊕ *www.parliamenthouse.com.*

THEATER

Bob Carr Theater. Formerly Orlando's performing arts center and the top venue for touring artists for nearly a century (in the mid-1950s, you could have seen Elvis Presley here), this venue became the Bob Carr Theater when the new Dr. Phillips Center claimed the title of Performing Arts Center in 2014. Now under the umbrella of the Dr. Phillips Center, the Bob Carr is still an impressive hall with wonderful acoustics. Nationally recognized musicians (rock, jazz, easy listening, classical), comedians, musicals, plays, and tribute acts still appear here. ⊠ *401 W. Livingston St., Downtown Orlando* ☎ *407/440–7900* ⊕ *www.drphillipscenter.org/explore/theaters-spaces/bob-carr-theater.*

Dr. Phillips Center for the Performing Arts. When this stunning, state-of-the-art venue opened in the heart of Downtown, it elevated the arts for Orlando. Encompassing the 2,700-seat Walt Disney Theater and the intimate 300-seat Jim and Alexis Pugh Theater, it's where major Broadway productions found a new home; where musicians such as Bob Dylan, Brian Wilson, and Elvis Costello have performed; and where opera, symphonies, ballet, and comedy shows fill the calendar year-round. Like a battery that's charged Downtown, Dr. Phillips has energized the area with new restaurants, galleries, and entertainment venues, attracting crowds who haven't ventured outside the theme parks since the heyday of Church Street decades ago. ⊠ *445 S. Magnolia Ave., Downtown Orlando* ☎ *844/513–2014* ⊕ *www.drphillipscenter.org.*

Mad Cow Theatre. Orlando's longest-standing professional theater company is where risks are taken. Regional premieres, new works, and thoughtful interpretations of classics such as *Death of a Salesman* make this a stage worth seeking. Local actors eager to show their talents line

Celebration at Night

Celebration. This community, where every blade of grass in every lawn seems perfect, is as picturesque as a movie set—although, to some critics, it would be one used in *The Stepford Wives*. But Celebration is a model of good American architecture and urban planning as well as a delightful place to spend a morning or afternoon.

Things appear nearly as faux as on Main Street, U.S.A., but as they unfold, you see signs of reality—and a pleasant one it is. Celebration is a real town, with its own hospital and school system. Houses and apartments spread out from the compact downtown area, full of restaurants, which wraps around the edge of a lake. Sidewalks are built for strolling,

restaurants have outdoor seating with lake views, and inviting shops beckon. After a walk around the lake, take youngsters over to the huge interactive fountain and have fun getting soaked.

The town has a year-round roster of special events and a noteworthy Sunday Farmers' Market. Starting the last Saturday in November and continuing through New Year's Eve, honest-to-goodness snow sprinkles softly down over Main Street every night on the hour from 6 to 9. ⊠ *Celebration ✛ 6 miles south of Epcot; take I–4 to Exit 64A and follow "Celebration" signs* ☎ *407/566–1200* ⊕ *www. celebrationfl.com.*

up to work here. ⊠ *54 W. Church St., Downtown Orlando* ☎ *407/297–8788* ⊕ *www.madcowtheatre.com.*

Orlando Shakespeare Theater. "Orlando Shakes" has four stages, where a typical season includes 11 plays covering classics (including Shakespeare, of course), contemporary, musicals, comedies, and family shows. The theater also hosts the very popular Orlando International Fringe Festival, the oldest in America. The season runs June through April, with the Fringe Festival in May. PlayFest! The Harriett Lake Festival of New Plays offers world-premiere and staged-reading opportunities for new playwrights. The theater is in Loch Haven Cultural Park, just a few minutes north of Downtown, where the Orlando Science Center and the Museum of Art also stand. ⊠ *812 E. Rollins St., Lake Ivanhoe* ☎ *407/447–1700* ⊕ *www.orlandoshakes.org.*

INTERNATIONAL DRIVE

BARS

B.B. King's Blues Club. The blues legend-turned-entrepreneur lent his name to a string of blues clubs across America, including this one in Orlando. Like the others, this club has music at its heart. There's a dance floor and stage for live performances by the B.B. King All-Star Band and touring musicians seven nights a week. The variety is impressive, with a wide range of tunes inspired by everyone from the King of Blues (B.B.) to the Queen of Motown (Aretha), and the Soul of Funk (take your pick). Since you can't really experience Delta blues without Delta dining, the club doubles as a restaurant with fried dill pickles, catfish bites, po' boys, ribs, and other comfort foods. Wash it all down with a drink from the full bar. ✉ *Pointe Orlando, 9101 International Dr., International Drive* ☏ *407/370–4550* ⊕ *www.bbkingclubs.com/orlando.*

NIGHTCLUB

ICEBAR. Thanks to the miracle of refrigeration, this is Orlando's coolest bar—literally and figuratively. Fifty tons of pure ice are kept at a constant 27°F and have been cut and sculpted by world-class carvers into a cozy (or as cozy as ice can be) sanctuary of tables, sofas, chairs, and a bar. The staff loans you a thermal cape and gloves (upgrade to a fur coat for extra $), and when you enter the frozen hall your drink is served in a glass made of crystal clear ice. There's no cover charge if you just want to hang out in the Fire Lounge or outdoor Polar Patio, but you will pay a cover to spend as much time as you can handle in the subfreezing ICEBAR. There's no beer or wine inside; it's simply too cold. ✉ *Pointe Orlando, 8967 International Dr., International Drive* ☏ *407/426–7555* ⊕ *www.icebarorlando.com.*

DINNER SHOWS

Dinner shows are an immensely popular form of nighttime entertainment around Orlando. For a single price, you get a theatrical production and a multicourse dinner. Performances run the gamut from jousting to jamboree tunes, and meals tend to be better than average; unlimited beer, wine, and soda are usually included, but mixed drinks (and often *any* drinks before dinner) cost extra. What the shows lack in substance and depth they make up for in grandeur and enthusiasm. The result is an evening of light entertainment, which youngsters in particular enjoy. Seatings are usually between 7 and 9:30, and there are usually one or two performances a night, with an extra show during peak periods. You might sit with strangers at tables for 10 or more, but that's part of the fun. Always reserve in advance, especially for weekend shows, and always ask about discounts, although you can often find online coupons (sometimes for half off) that you can print out yourself.

If you're in Orlando off-season, try to take in these dinner shows on a busy night—a show playing to a small audience can be uncomfortable. Don't let the big prices fool you—there's a flood of major discount (sometimes half-off) coupons papering International Drive restaurants, hotels, and at the Orlando/Orange County Convention & Visitors Bureau. Since performance schedules can vary depending on the tourist season, it's always smart to call in advance to verify show times. When buying tickets, ask if the cost includes a gratuity—servers anxious to pocket more cash may hit you up for an extra handout.

Fodor's Choice ★ **Sleuths Mystery Dinner Show.** If Sherlock Holmes has always intrigued you, head on over to this long-running show for a four-course meal served with a healthy dose of conspiracy. Sleuths is a hotbed of local acting talent, with 13 rotating whodunit performances staged throughout the year in three different theaters. The comedy-mystery show begins during your appetizer, and murder is the case by the time they clear your plates. You'll get to discuss clues and question still-living characters over dinner and solve the crime during dessert. Prizes go to top sleuths. Comedy and magic shows fill up the late-night lineup on weekends. ✉ *8267 International Dr., International Drive* ☎ *407/363–1985* ⊕ *www.sleuths.com* ◉ *$64.95.*

KISSIMMEE

DINNER SHOWS

Capone's Dinner and Show. This musical dramedy brings you back to gangland Chicago of the 1930s, when mobsters and their molls were the height of underworld society. You'll meet Al Capone and learn that you can become a member of the "family," but you've got to help take care of a rat in the organization. Flashy costumes and musical numbers are accompanied by an all-you-can-eat American and Italian buffet that includes beer, alcoholic mixed drinks, and cocktails for kids. Check the website for a 50% off coupon. ✉ *4740 W. Irlo Bronson Memorial Hwy., Kissimmee* ☎ *407/397–2378, 800/220–8428* ⊕ *www.alcapones. com* ◉ *$69.99; online discounts.*

FAMILY   **Medieval Times.** In a huge, ersatz-medieval manor you'll marvel at a tournament of sword fights, jousting matches, and other exciting games. More than a dozen charging horses and a cast of 75 knights, nobles, wizards, and maidens participate. Sound silly? It is. But it's also a true extravaganza. That the show takes precedence over the meat-and-potatoes fare is obvious: everyone sits facing forward at long, narrow banquet tables stepped auditorium-style above the tournament area. Kids love eating without forks; adults are swept away by the tremendous horse-riding artistry. Check the website and area attractions booklets for discounts. ✉ *4510 W. Vine St., Kissimmee* ☎ *407/396–1518, 888/935–6878* ⊕ *www.medievaltimes.com* ◉ *$62.95–$82.95.*

The Outta Control Magic Comedy Dinner Show. A preshow of sorts to the kid-friendly, hands-on science and activity center called Wonderworks, this dinner show is exactly as its name suggests: a magic show filled with jokes, gags, and tricks. The magicians' juvenile one-liners make this delightful for kids and pleasingly silly for adults, with audience participation playing a large role. A pizza/salad/soft drink buffet is open prior to the show. ✉ *Wonderworks, 9067 International Drive, International Drive* ☎ *407/351-8800* ⊕ *www.wonderworksonline.com/ orlando/the-experience/the-outta-control-magic-comedy-dinner-show* ◉ *$29.99; look for discounts online.*

SHOPPING

Updated by Gary McKechnie

From fairy-tale kingdoms to Old West–style trading posts to outlet malls, Walt Disney World and Orlando have a plethora of shopping opportunities that won't leave you disappointed. The colors are bright and energetic, the textures soft and cuddly, and the designs fresh and thoughtful.

Before you board any roller coaster or giggle at any show, you'll catch yourself window-shopping and delighting in the thought of making a purchase. With Orlando's rich source of retail offerings, it's no wonder some international travelers come just to shop, especially with some of America's largest outlet and upscale malls just a short drive away. Before you spend a dime, take this free advice: Competition is strong between theme parks, boutiques, flea markets, and shopping outlets, so work that in your favor. Be patient and you may find the same item offered at a lower price at the next stop on your shopping list.

WALT DISNEY WORLD

Even if you're not inclined to buy, the shops on Disney property are well worth a look. Across the board, they're open, inviting, cleverly themed, and often carry items exclusive to Disney. Of course, you could easily pick up $100 worth of goods before you've ventured even 10 feet into a store, but you're better off practicing some restraint. If you see something you like, think about it while you enjoy the rest of your day (you might see something even better in the next store). But if you find you're still thinking of that beautiful stuffed Cheshire Cat or Cinderella snow globe at the end of the day, you can always go back to get it. And if you stay on property at a Disney hotel, note this perk: You won't have to lug around shopping bags all day. Disney stores will deliver your merchandise to your room for free.

A few tips: Don't let the price tags scare you off. Small souvenirs (key chains, pens, small toys, etc.) can be found at nearly every store for just a few dollars—a great option when considering gifts for friends back home. Just be careful with souvenir-hungry kids since many attractions exit directly into gift shops. You can try to be the voice of reason and ask them to wait—or try a different approach: Give them a lump sum to spend during the day and let them choose (and live with) their purchases. To find the most current list of retail outlets searchable by name, by theme park, and by resort, visit ⊕ *www.disneyworld.disney.go.com/ shops.* If you return home and realize you've forgotten a critical souvenir, call WDW's Merchandise Mail Order service at ☎ *877/560–6477.*

MAGIC KINGDOM

Everywhere you turn in the Magic Kingdom there are shops and stalls urging you to take home a little piece of the magic.

MAIN STREET, U.S.A.

Crystal Arts. This shop dazzles with Arribas Brothers–engraved crystal pieces like a sparkling Cinderella coach or an iconic glass slipper in one of many sizes (though none will fit your foot!). ■TIP➔ Be sure to visit the glass studio and its 2,100°F furnaces in the back, where a glassblower explains the process while creating wineglasses and bowls. Fascinating! ⊠ *Main Street, U.S.A., Magic Kingdom* ⊕ *www. disneyworld.disney.go.com/shops/ magic-kingdom.*

The Emporium. This 17,000-square-foot department store (strategically placed right before the exit) is one of the largest souvenir shops in any of the parks. You'll find thousands of Disney character products, from Disney pins to plush toys. Princess items rock for little girls, the costume jewelry is an inexpensive souvenir, and there seem to be enough Mickey sweatshirts and T's to clothe everyone in the entire park. Ask cast members about deals or marked-down merchandise. Also available here are MagicBands, colorful wristbands that can be linked with your My Disney Experience app to enter the parks, buy food and merchandise, set up Fastpass+ access, and even unlock your Disney resort room. ⊠ *Main Street, U.S.A., Magic Kingdom* ⊕ *www.disneyworld.disney.go.com/shops/ magic-kingdom/emporium.*

Uptown Jewelers. This upscale boutique is a treasure chest of jewelry, figurines, art, and designer handbags and accessories. It's here you can buy Pandora's Disney Park Collection gems and charms and order canvases from a computerized kiosk. ⊠ *Main Street, U.S.A., Magic Kingdom* ⊕ *www.disneyworld.disney.go.com/shops/magic-kingdom/ uptown-jewelers.*

> **DRUMROLL, PLEASE …**
>
> Of more than 300 retail outlets at the Walt Disney World Resort, perhaps the best of all is the World of Disney in the Marketplace section of Disney Springs. You could actually skip many of the stores in the theme parks, since you'll find just about everything you want right here. And although it may be a cliché, there really *is* something for everyone, whether you're looking for something small and inexpensive like a $3 princess pen or a Disney collectible like an elegant Mickey timepiece or figurine.

8

ADVENTURELAND

Agrabah Bazaar. A Hollywood-fantasized version of an open-air Arabian market, this wildly colorful shop is the retail equivalent of a maharaja's treasure. Shelves are replete with Aladdin wear and Jasmine costumes, maracas and other inexpensive percussion instruments, gold- and silver-plated bangles, collectible pins, sunglasses, housewares, plush toys, and snappy safari hats. ⊠ *Adventureland, Magic Kingdom* ⊕ *www.disney-world.disney.go.com/shops/magic-kingdom/agrabah-bazaar.*

Plaza del Sol Caribe Bazaar. Just outside the Pirates of the Caribbean, you can stock up on pirate hats, swords, flintlocks, and hooks-for-hands. T-shirts, candy, and figurines are plentiful, but the ultimate scalawag topper is a Captain Jack Sparrow hat complete with braids. ⊠ *Adventureland, Magic Kingdom* ⊕ *www.disneyworld.disney.go.com/shops/magic-kingdom/plaza-del-sol-caribe-bazaar.*

FRONTIERLAND

Big Al's. This merchandise cart across the walkway from the Country Bear Jamboree has Davy Crockett coonskin caps, cowboy hats like Woody wears in *Toy Story*, personalized sheriff's badges, and other gear that draws oohs and aahs from aspiring cowboys and cowgirls. ⊠ *Frontierland, Magic Kingdom* ⊕ *www.disneyworld.disney.go.com/shops/magic-kingdom/big-als.*

LIBERTY SQUARE

Ye Olde Christmas Shoppe. You may think you've wandered into the North Pole at this quaint store, which sells character-themed stockings and ornaments, Mickey wedding top hats and Minnie bridal veils, plus art, housewares, and collectibles. ⊠ *Liberty Square, Magic Kingdom* ⊕ *www.disneyworld.disney.go.com/shops/magic-kingdom/ye-olde-christmas-shoppe.*

FANTASYLAND

Castle Couture. This shop on the corner near Cinderella Castle markets to little princesses with sparkly, shimmery dresses, bows, hats, and T-shirts as well as dolls, slippers, and jewelry. Taking the Fantasyland fantasy a step further is the Bibbidi Bobbidi Boutique next door, where little ones ages 3 to 12 can walk into a full-scale salon and, after being attended to by hair stylists and makeup artists, walk out as their favorite princess or knight. ⊠ *Fantasyland, Magic Kingdom* ⊕ *www.disneyworld.disney.go.com/shops/magic-kingdom/castle-couture.*

TOMORROWLAND

Mickey's Star Traders. One of the largest shops in the Magic Kingdom, Star Traders trades on the purchase of all things Disney. Toys, pins, T-shirts featuring favorite characters like Mickey, Stitch, and Mike from Monsters Inc. can be found here, as well as Goofy caps and oversized Mickey gloves. So much to see—so much to buy! ⊠ *Tomorrowland, Magic Kingdom* ⊕ *www.disneyworld.disney.go.com/shops/magic-kingdom/mickeys-star-traders.*

EPCOT

Fine goods and trinkets from all over the world, some handcrafted, are sold at the pavilions representing individual countries here. Check out the Japanese and Chinese kimonos, Moroccan fezzes, French wines, Norwegian sweaters, and Mexican wood carvings. A United Kingdom shop even helps you research your family coat of arms, which you can buy as a paper printout or dressed up with paint or embroidery.

FUTURE WORLD

Although there are quite a few pavilions, Future World shopping won't tempt you to spend much money unless you're heavily into Disney animation (which you'll find in the classic Disney paintings and limited edition prints at The Art of Disney). The biggest Disney World store inside any of the four theme parks, Mouse Gear, carries a little bit of everything.

WORLD SHOWCASE

Fodor's Choice
★

Each of the countries represented has at least one gift shop loaded with things reflective of the history and culture of that nation's homeland, and many of the items are authentic imported handicrafts.

If your shopping time is limited, check out the Port of Entry shop at the entrance to World Showcase.

CANADA

Northwest Mercantile. Along with an abundance of hockey-related merchandise and maple syrup, the shop offers a number of Canadian-centric items not otherwise available in the United States. You'll find plenty of teddy bears (and far more moose) on the shelves, as well as mugs and clothing celebrating Canadian brews. ⊠ *World Showcase, Canada Pavilion, Epcot* ⊕ *www.disneyworld.disney.go.com/shops/epcot.*

UNITED KINGDOM

Anglophiles will feel as if they've crossed the Atlantic upon entering the cobblestoned village at the United Kingdom, where an English pub sits on one side, and a collection of British, Irish, and Scottish shops beckons you on the other. The Toy Soldier carries popular British toys and memorabilia known by all Brits; the Sportsman Shoppe has books and team apparel from various UK football (aka: soccer) teams; and the Tea Caddy, which sells Twinings tea, teacups, teapots, and British sweets.

The Crown & Crest. This shop carries the widest range of items in the UK pavilion, from woolen sweaters from Scotland to Beatles-themed gifts and memorabilia. ⊠ *World Showcase, United Kingdom Pavilion, Epcot* ⊕ *www.disneyworld.disney.go.com/shops/epcot/the-crown-and-crest.*

Historic Research Center. The focus at this United Kingdom outpost in the Crown & Crest is tracking down your family name and coat of arms. Take home a printout of both for about $70. Drop the bigger bucks for a framed, embroidered, or hand-painted version. ⊠ *World Showcase, Epcot.*

FRANCE

La Signature. In the France pavilion, follow your nose for a sniff and a spritz of high-end French perfumes. Guerlain fragrances, cosmetics, and skin-care products like the Orchidée Impériale eye cream (most recently

8

selling for a whopping $200 apiece) draw fans from around the globe. ✉ *World Showcase, France Pavillion, Epcot* ⊕ *www.disneyworld.disney.go.com/shops/epcot/la-signature.*

MOROCCO

Tangier Traders. Morocco's open-air market is like something out of an Indiana Jones movie. It's a maze of shops selling straw bags and colorful carpets. It's also a great place to pick up something really different, like a Moroccan fez or belly-dancing gear, including a bright scarf, finger cymbals, and a CD with all the music you need to wow your audience. ✉ *World Showcase, Moroccan Pavilion, Epcot* ⊕ *www.disneyworld. disney.go.com/shops/epcot.*

JAPAN

Mitsukoshi Department Store. Hello Kitty, one of Japan's most popular toys, is on hand here, as are the Transformers and Godzilla. Dress up with a washable poly kimono or a more luxurious silk version, or check out the shimmering pearl jewelry. Other popular items include animé art, chopsticks, and Kit Kat bars in assorted flavors. You'll be tempted to take home some sweets after watching a Japanese Candy Art demonstration just outside the store (see *Times Guide* for demo schedule). ✉ *World Showcase, Japan Pavilion, Epcot* ⊕ *www.disneyworld.disney. go.com/shops/epcot/mitsukoshi-kiosk.*

ITALY

Il Bel Cristallo. Just like an elegant boutique in Milan, this shop sells chic Italian totes, designer handbags, clothing, collectibles, and fragrances by Fendi, Prada, and Bulgari. You'll also find porcelain, crystal, and Murano glass. ✉ *World Showcase, Italy Pavilion, Epcot* ⊕ *www.disneyworld.disney.go.com/shops/epcot/il-bel-cristallo.*

Tutto Gusto Wine Cellar. This café and wine bar in the Italy pavilion is an exclusive seller of some of the country's unique wines. ✉ *World Showcase, Italy Pavilion, Epcot* ⊕ *www.disneyworld.disney.go.com/dining/epcot/tutto-gusto-wine-cellar.*

GERMANY

Der Teddybår. Although you can buy wines and beer steins in the Germany pavilion, none give the warm, fuzzy feelings the teddy bears on display here do. Bears (or "bårs") share the boutique with Rapunzel and Snow White snow globes and plush toys, Minnie dolls and figurines, and German confections. ✉ *World Showcase, Germany Pavilion, Epcot* ⊕ *www.disneyworld.disney.go.com/shops/epcot/der-teddybar-toyshop.*

CHINA

House of Good Fortune. China's sprawling bazaar has a huge selection of tea sets ranging in style from traditional to contemporary, intricately embroidered robes, and fragranced candles that are sure to align your chi. Butterfly hair combs are beautiful, but the hottest items are little Buddha statues, available for less than $10. ✉ *World Showcase, China Pavilion, Epcot* ⊕ *www.disneyworld.disney.go.com/shops/epcot.*

NORWAY

Puffin's Roost. In Norway, Viking wannabes go crazy for the soft toy spears and shields. The plush seals are sweet for tots, and you can find Norwegian pewter, leather goods, and colorful woolen sweaters and knit caps, along with a wide variety of character goods from the hit movie *Frozen.*The shop's larger-than-life troll is always ready for a selfie. ⊠ *World Showcase, Norway Pavilion, Epcot* ⊕ *www.disney-world.disney.go.com/shops/epcot/puffins-roost.*

MEXICO

Plaza de Los Amigos. As you enter the Mexico pavilion and descend the staircase, stop in the village square here to browse the hand-painted wood carvings crafted by Zapotec Indians of Oaxaca in southern Mexico. Vendors' carts offer silver jewelry, leather goods, sombreros, piñatas, pottery, home decor, and more. Don't miss indoor shops including La Princesa de Cristal, which sells sparkling jewelry, etched glass, and Disney figurines cast in crystal, and La Tienda Encantada with fine jewelry, leather goods, and colorful accessories. Outside on the promenade is El Ranchito del Norte, a bazaar well stocked with similar items. ⊠ *World Showcase, Mexico Pavilion, Epcot* ⊕ *www.disneyworld. disney.go.com/shops/epcot/plaza-de-los-amigos.*

DISNEY'S HOLLYWOOD STUDIOS

HOLLYWOOD BOULEVARD

You can upgrade your look at Keystone Clothiers. Mickey's of Hollywood has something for everyone in the family.

Keystone Clothiers. This shop pops with stylish clothing and accessories for adults. Disney characters are emblazoned on T-shirts and button-up-shirts, ties, and accessories, while handbags and totes sport classic Mickey Mouse artwork. Colorful scarves with hidden Mickeys and other designs are popular buys. ⊠ *Hollywood Boulevard, Disney's Hollywood Studios* ⊕ *www.disneyworld.disney.go.com/shops/ hollywood-studios/keystone-clothiers.*

Mickey's of Hollywood. The largest store in Hollywood Studios is a mini-version of the Magic Kingdom's Emporium with toys, T-shirts, and doodads. Blue velvety *Sorcerer's Apprentice* hats have Mouse ears, plus a moon and stars that light up. You'll also find Minnie Mouse and Donald Duck character key chains and lots of Disney-character-embossed tech accessories, including the MagicBand, a wristband that links to your charge account so you can purchase meals, merchandise, and even Fastpasses. ⊠ *Hollywood Boulevard, Disney's Hollywood Studios* ⊕ *www.disneyworld.disney.go.com/shops/hollywood-studios/ mickeys-of-hollywood.*

Tower Hotel Gifts. After the screams and thrills of the Tower of Terror, what could be better than a mug from the hotel bar, the actual bell from the front desk, or a leather key fob from "your" room? In addition to leather handbags and bellboy hats, you can find some rather macabre takes on Disney characters that are exclusive to this shop. ⊠ *Sunset Boulevard, Disney's Hollywood Studios* ⊕ *www.disneyworld.disney. go.com/shops/hollywood-studios/tower-shop.*

ECHO LAKE

Two hyperpopular movie franchises—Star Wars and Indiana Jones—command attention in this section of the studios.

8

Indiana Jones Adventure Outpost. Almost as popular as the pirate hats in the Magic Kingdom are the Indiana Jones felt fedoras sold at this outpost near the stunt amphitheater. Small kids can get a complete Indy play set with fedora, machete, pistol, and gems for about $20. You can also find crystal skulls, plush exotic animals, polished rocks, and Raiders of the Lost Ark action figures. ⊠ *Echo Lake, Disney's Hollywood Studios.*

Tatooine Traders. The Star Wars theme is strong in this desert dome shop outside the Star Tours ride. Guests of all ages can build their own single or double light sabers complete with crystals, hilts, and blades. And what's a light saber without a droid to share it with? So build a droid as well. Collectible pins, books, action figures, art, clothing, and Vinylmation characters are also popular here. ⊠ *Echo Lake, Disney's Hollywood Studios* ⊕ *www.disneyworld.disney.go.com/shops/hollywood-studios/tatooine-traders.*

ANIMATION COURTYARD

In Character. Little girls love this open-air shop next to the Voyage of the Little Mermaid for the dolls, plush princess toys, and dress-up costumes. You can drop a small bundle on glass (plastic) slippers and a magical light-up wand or spring for the coveted Ariel mermaid costume gown. ⊠ *Animation Courtyard, Disney's Hollywood Studios* ⊕ *www.disneyworld.disney.go.com/shops/hollywood-studios/in-character-disneys-costume-shop.*

SUNSET BOULEVARD

Sunset Club Couture. It's the one shop you don't want to miss on Sunset Boulevard. Vintage-style T-shirts of Mickey, Pluto, Donald, and Grumpy are classy alternatives to standard-issue T's, and a white-sequined Mickey hat adds flair to any outfit. Women's fashion T's and costume bling draw lots of shoppers. Customized watches like those sold at the Magic Kingdom's Uptown Jewelers as well as purses and totes are sold here, too. ⊠ *Sunset Boulevard, Disney's Hollywood Studios.*

DISNEY'S ANIMAL KINGDOM

DISCOVERY ISLAND

Discovery Trading Company. This popular shop sells apparel and accessories, including Mickey ears with leopard spots and jewelry and pottery handcrafted by African artisans. There are also Disney-themed games such as dominos and Monopoly, plush dolls, mugs, and upscale clothing selections for men and women. ⊠ *Discovery Island, Animal Kingdom* ⊕ *www.disneyworld.disney.go.com/shops/animal-kingdom/discovery-trading-company.*

Island Mercantile. To the left as you enter Discovery Island from the Oasis, the Animal Kingdom's largest shop stocks clothing, cookware, photo frames, and logo souvenirs. Safari hats, caps, and straw hats—much of them designed with animal prints—range from $20 to $30, and you can buy a backpack or messenger bag. Load it with towels for when you emerge soaked from Kali River Rapids. Fans of *The Lion King* and *Pandora* will want to stop here for animal figurines and African percussion instruments. ⊠ *Discovery Island, Animal Kingdom* ⊕ *www. disneyworld.disney.go.com/shops/animal-kingdom/island-mercantile.*

DINOLAND U.S.A

Chester & Hester's Dinosaur Treasures. This colorful, cluttered souvenir shop (think: roadside America circa 1948) lures dinophiles with big displays of quite large and scary-looking, yet soft and huggable, T-rex, velociraptor, and other dinosaur figures (some you'll recognize from *Toy Story*). Beyond the prehistoric, the shop has retro candies, toys, and an attractive bin of rocks for collectors. ⊠ *DinoLand U.S.A., Animal Kingdom* ⊕ *www.disneyworld.disney.go.com/shops/animal-kingdom/ chester-and-hesters-dinosaur-treasures.*

ASIA

Yak & Yeti Bhaktapur Market. At this gem of a shop you'll find bejeweled sandals and thongs and gorgeous, colorful print scarves of silk, satin, or India chiffon. There's also a good chance you'll find something on the clearance shelves—anything from a calligraphy kit to a Buddha figurine. ⊠ *Asia, Animal Kingdom.*

AFRICA

Mombasa Marketplace and Ziwani Traders. In Harambe Village, this is a great stop for unusual items like hand-painted dishes from Zimbabwe and South African wines such as a Chakalaka red varietal by Spice Route Winery. Young kids like to play with the small, inexpensive figurines of giraffes, elephants, rhinos, and other critters they just saw on their Kilimanjaro Safaris ride. ⊠ *Africa, Animal Kingdom* ⊕ *www.disneyworld. disney.go.com/shops/animal-kingdom/mombasa-marketplace.*

PANDORA: THE WORLD OF AVATAR

Windtraders. Disney's futuristic hit inspired not only a new section of the park, but plenty of merchandise reflecting the culture and (super) nature of its world, Pandora. The store's design is as unusual as the merchandise, with Na'vi cultural artifacts, an Avatar Maker, and stations where you can create your own necklace (all of which can be taken back to Earth). Especially popular are tiny banshees that move their heads and flap their wings. ⊠ *Animal Kingdom, Animal Kingdom* ⊕ *www. disneyworld.disney.go.com/shops/animal-kingdom/windtraders.*

DISNEY SPRINGS

Fodor's Choice The latest name for a sprawling retail, dining, and entertainment complex,
★ Disney Springs is divided into four areas: the Marketplace, The Landing, Town Center, and West Side. Always active and popular (especially in the evenings), it's a great place to shop, dine, or catch a movie, without the admission fee of the theme parks. Explore dozens of stores, including the vast, hard-to-top World of Disney, the super-kid-friendly LEGO Imagination Center, and the überhip Tren-D clothing and accessory shop.

MARKETPLACE

A lakefront outdoor mall with meandering sidewalks, hidden alcoves, fountains for kids to splash around in, and absolutely fabulous toy stores, the Marketplace is a great place to spend a relaxing afternoon or active evening—especially if you're looking for a way to give the kids a break from standing in line. There are plenty of spots to grab a bite, rest your feet, or enjoy a cup of coffee while taking in the pleasant water views and the hustle and bustle of excited tourists. The Marketplace is generally open from 9:30 am to 11 pm. If you happen to run out of cash while you're shopping, you can apply for instant Disney credit at any register. How convenient.

Disney's Pin Traders. Many cast members and guests share (and wear) a common interest: pins that reflect favorite characters, special events, and all things Disney. Often affixed to lanyards, these Disney pins are a treasured part of the company's subculture, with owners buying and swapping pins the way kids used to trade baseball cards. This Marketplace shop is one of Disney's premier pin-trading destinations—and where you can find Mickey ears and MagicBands. ⊠ *Marketplace, Disney Springs* ⊕ *www. disneyworld.disney.go.com/shops/disney-springs/disneys-pin-traders.*

Disney's Design-a-Tee. Tucked next to the long-standing Art of Disney gallery, this shop wows creative types with touch-screen computer stations where you can select your shirt (color, size, style), then choose from among hundreds of Disney images (contemporary and vintage). Enhance your design by typing in your own words or selecting graphics to note a birthday, anniversary, first visit, or other special occasion. Although the shop also sells preprinted T-shirts, these personalized versions—which sell for about $30—can make a unique family-reunion keepsake. ⊠ *Marketplace, Disney Springs* ⊕ *www.disneyworld.disney. go.com/shops/disney-springs/disney-design-a-tee-by-hanes.*

The LEGO Store. When you spy a LEGO sea serpent in the lagoon, you know you're in the right place for a LEGO shopping spree. An impressive collection of large, elaborate sculptures and piles of colorful LEGO bricks welcome children, who head straight to hands-on play tables and begin work on toy castles, cars, and pirate ships. Check out the Pick-A-Brick Wall, where kids can create anything from a *Star Wars* spaceship to a miniature Sydney Opera House, and snap a photo with oversized character models like Woody and Buzz Lightyear. The discounted merchandise section is worth a look. ⊠ *Marketplace, Disney Springs* ⊕ *www.disneyworld.disney.go.com/shops/disney-springs/the-lego-store.*

LittleMissMatched. Girls and their moms are goofy for the candy-colored T-shirts, jammies, and duffels, at this Marketplace shop. Popular with tweens are the reversible swimwear, colorful fashion accessories, and mismatched socks (a pack of three pairs of knee-high socks are around $15). ∎TIP➔ Seasonal sales run periodically, and there's a good chance you can dress up with quirky flair for a bargain. ⊠ *Marketplace, Disney Springs* ⊕ *www.disneyworld.disney.go.com/shops/disney-springs/ littlemissmatched.*

Mickey's Pantry. If you're dying to get the recipe for a Disney dish you love, explore the cookbooks at Mickey's Pantry. It's hard to resist Mickey's own brand of kitchen items like oven mitts and chef's hats, while kids clamor for a bag of Mickey-shaped pasta. Look for cocoa, savory spices, gourmet teas, and seasonings from the Spice & Tea Exchange. ⊠ *Marketplace, Disney Springs* ⊕ *www.disneyworld.disney.go.com/ shops/disney-springs/mickeys-pantry.*

Once Upon A Toy. Classic board games and activity stations will keep you entertained in this well-stocked store. Themed toy rooms feature princess and fairy items or Star Wars stations where you can create your own light saber. There are lots of classic games redesigned with Disney themes, like the Haunted Mansion Game of Life. You can test-drive many of the toys, and at the Mr. Potato Head Creation Station, you can fill a box with assorted lips, noses, and even Mickey ears. ⊠ *Marketplace, Disney Springs ⊕ www.disneyworld.disney.go.com/ shops/disney-springs/once-upon-a-toy.*

Tren-D. This Marketplace boutique has *hip* and *eclectic* written all over it (hence the name). Chic sundresses with subtle Mickey-ear designs are perfect for an evening at the shops and clubs of Disney Springs. Designer items are from Billabong, Dooney & Bourke, Harveys (The Original Seatbeltbags), and Roxy, and many feature fairies and princesses. ⊠ *Marketplace, Disney Springs ⊕ www.disneyworld.disney. go.com/shops/disney-springs/trend.*

World of Disney. Beware of sensory overload at *the* world's largest Disney superstore—where approximately half a million items are featured in a dozen rooms that cover 50,000 square feet. Themed shopping areas like the princess room (hello, Cinderella dress or Ariel costume) help steer you to just the right toys, clothing, collectibles, candy, houseware, and pins. The Bibbidi Bobbidi Boutique, similar to the one at the Magic Kingdom, does princess makeovers. ⊠ *Marketplace, Disney Springs ⊕ www.disneyworld.disney.go.com/shops/ disney-springs/world-of-disney.*

THE LANDING
Largely populated by nautical-themed restaurants, The Landing has its share of cleverly appointed shops.

The Art of Shaving. Sure, shaving is a daily task for many men, but there's something wonderfully indulgent about really doing it right. For that, you need the high-end shaving creams, brushes, gels, after-shaves, moisturizers, and razors from this intriguing shop. For added indulgence, drop by the Barber Spa for a shave and a haircut. ⊠ *The Landing, Disney Springs ⊕ www.disneyworld.disney.go.com/shops/ disney-springs/art-of-shaving.*

Chapel Hats. Bride-and-groom ears are among the most recognizable fashion statements you'll see here, but they represent just a fraction of the inventory. Shelves are stacked with every shape and style: broad-brimmed sun hats, jaunty Panama hats, '60s-style porkpie hats, brightly colored fascinators, Indiana Jones–inspired fedoras, and a few dozen others to top off your trip. ⊠ *The Landing, 1642 E. Buena Vista Dr., Disney Springs ⊕ www.disneyworld.disney.go.com/shops/ disney-springs/chapel-hats.*

TOWN CENTER
The greatest concentration of shops at Disney Springs is in this area, where retailers including Anthropologie, Sephora, Kate Spade, ZARA, Tommy Bahama, Vera Bradley, and Lacoste are shoulder-to-shoulder along several blocks of buildings.

L'Occitane en Provence. Filled with fragrant beauty products, this French-inspired apothecary has everything you need to pamper yourself, from all-natural lotions, gels, creams, and oils to toners and serums to cleansers, moisturizers, and exfoliating scrubs. Shaving and grooming items for men are also well represented. Stop by and you can sample products, mix your own essential oils, and even get a complimentary minifacial or hand massage. ⊠ *Town Center, Disney Springs* ⊕ *www.disneyworld. disney.go.com/shops/disney-springs/loccitane-en-provence.*

WEST SIDE

The West Side is a wide promenade with an intriguing mix of shops, clubs, and restaurants. You'll also find a multiplex movie theater, a bowling alley, and the House of Blues, which has its own gift shop.

Orlando Harley-Davidson. America's largest motorcycle manufacturer has been going strong for more than a century, and the apparel has been nearly as popular. Harley enthusiasts of all ages can buy biker jackets, vests, T-shirts, patches, and other popular gear. Climb aboard an iconic hog for a photo op. ⊠ *West Side, Disney Springs* ⊕ *www.disneyworld. disney.go.com/shops/disney-springs/orlando-harley-davidson.*

Pelé Soccer. Soccer (or football, as the rest of the world knows it) has slowly but surely gained ground in the United States—especially during the World Cup. Teams from around the world are represented in a colorful array of club jerseys, and there's soccer gear and apparel for men, women, and children. ⊠ *West Side, 1502 E. Buena Vista Dr., Disney Springs* ⊕ *www.disneyworld.disney.go.com/shops/ disney-springs/pele-soccer.*

UNIVERSAL ORLANDO

Universal Orlando is the overarching title of three theme parks—Hollywood-inspired Universal Studios, fantasy-themed Islands of Adventure, and the new-in-2017 Volcano Bay water theme park. At both Universal Studios and Islands of Adventure, the merchandise is primarily themed to attractions based on films and television shows; nearly every themed ride channels you from the exit into a gift shop with related merchandise. But the range of retail items goes far beyond Universal's motion picture heritage. Even if you don't visit the parks, you'll find plenty of shopping opportunities at CityWalk, a retail-entertainment-dining complex at the hub leading to the theme parks.

UNIVERSAL STUDIOS FLORIDA

Massive soundstages, busy streets, and music flowing from every corner may be overwhelming when you first arrive, but you'll soon find shops, kiosks, and department stores sprinkled throughout the park. The largest concentration is near the park entrance around **Production Central** as well as in **Hollywood.** The Universal Studios Store—at the nexus of the two—offers one-stop shopping with items from the studio (and even some merchandise from Islands of Adventure's most popular attractions). By far the most active retail center is in the monstrously popular Wizarding World of Harry Potter: Diagon Alley.

Betty Boop Store—Hello Kitty. These side-by-side stores at the corner of Hollywood and Production Central are packed with souvenirs celebrating two of the most marketable icons in the merchandising world. Representing Old Hollywood is cartoonish flapper Betty Boop, whose image is affixed to mugs, apparel, gifts, jewelry, and other collectibles. Walk through the rainbow archway connecting the stores, and you'll find similar souvenirs celebrating internationally popular (and supercute) Hello Kitty. There's no shortage of choices, with specialty sections like the Hello Kitty Lounge (robes, slippers, toys and other items for a pajama party), the Sweet Yummy Shop's cupcakes, fudge, and candies, and Hello Kitty at the Movies, which places Kitty in some classic films. ⊠ *Hollywood, Universal Studios* ⊕ *www.universalorlando.com/web/en/ us/things-to-do/shopping/betty-boop-store-usf/index.html.*

Brown Derby. Felt fedoras, bush hats that seem straight from wardrobe for *Jurassic Park,* Cat in the Hat red-and-white stovepipes, Duff beer mug hats, baseball caps, and colorful cartoon-inspired toppers are among the many novelty chapeaux for sale at this Hollywood store. ⊠ *Hollywood, Universal Studios* ⊕ *www.universalorlando.com/web/en/ us/things-to-do/shopping/the-brown-derby-hat-shop/index.html.*

Kwik-E-Mart. This re-creation of the animated convenience store from the Simpsons is one of the park's most popular shopping stops. You'll find Kwik-E-Mart (Apu Nahasapeemapetilon, proprietor) caps and smocks, Duff Beer mugs, Lard Lad donuts, Marge-style blue bouffant wigs, and Homer T-shirts packaged in Duff Beer cans. In 2013, an assortment of Springfield-inspired locales appeared, making the shop and its surroundings one of the park's best photo ops. ⊠ *Springfield: Home of the Simpsons, Universal Studios* ⊕ *www.universalorlando.com/web/en/us/ things-to-do/shopping/kwik-e-mart/index.html.*

SpongeBob StorePants. With its cartoonish nautical theme (pink jellyfish overhead, a pineapple home in the middle of the store) this silly shop will have you stocking up on weird, fascinating SpongeBob merchandise from mugs to shorts to swimwear. ⊠ *Woody Woodpecker's KidZone, Universal Studios* ⊕ *www.universalorlando.com/web/en/us/things-to- do/shopping/spongebob-storepants/index.html.*

Super Silly Stuff. Talk about truth in advertising. This colorful gift shop tied to Despicable Me: Minion Mayhem is filled with what seems to be millions of cute minions (both one-eyed and two-eyed) on T-shirts, mugs, and stuffed dolls. Gru fans can also sport a black-and-gray scarf like the one worn by the supervillain—sold separately or silk-screened onto a T-shirt. ⊠ *Production Central, Universal Studios* ⊕ *www.universalorlando.com/web/en/us/things-to-do/shop- ping/super-silly-stuff/index.html.*

Universal Studios Store. Like the Magic Kingdom's Emporium, this sizable store is the last retail outlet guests see before exiting the park. Although it doesn't have all the merchandise sold in individual park gift shops, as the park's central shopping destination it does have most of it—and some of the best, including T-shirts, stuffed animals, hats, backpacks, gifts, mugs, and limited-edition Universal trading pins. A big plus is that even if you don't visit Islands of Adventure, you'll find

8

TOP ATTRACTIONS

The World of Disney. The perfect place for one-stop souvenir shopping in the Marketplace section of Disney Springs, of the dozens of stores in Disney, the massive World of Disney is easily the largest, best, and most well-stocked store on Disney property.

Epcot World Showcase. Trinkets from all over the world, some handcrafted and incredibly unique, are sold at the pavilions representing individual countries here. Check out the Japanese bonsai trees and Moroccan fez hats.

Main Street, U.S.A., Magic Kingdom. The Main Street buildings are adorable with their forced perspective architecture, pastel colors, and elaborately decorated facades. If you can resist temptation, pass them by in the morning in favor of reaching your favorite attractions, reserving an hour or so for a leisurely shopping trip on your way out of the park.

Mall at Millenia. Visiting this mall is like going to New York City for the afternoon. One look at the store names—Gucci, Dior, Chanel, Jimmy Choo, Cartier, Tiffany—and you'll think you've died and gone to retail heaven.

Park Avenue, Winter Park. The Central Florida equivalent of Palm Beach's Worth Avenue or Coral Gables' Miracle Mile, and just 45 minutes north of Orlando's attractions, Park Avenue is an idyllic setting for shopping. A lovely city park, redbrick streets, and sprawling oak trees accent several blocks of independent retail shops, restaurants, and sidewalk cafés.

popular merchandise sold primarily at the neighboring park. ⊠ *Production Central, Universal Studios* ⊕ *www.universalorlando.com/web/en/us/things-to-do/shopping/universal-studios-store-usf/index.html.*

Wizarding World of Harry Potter: Diagon Alley. J.K. Rowling's pages comes to life in this magical village, where a fire-breathing dragon atop Gringott's Bank towers over cobblestone streets lined with Harry Potter–themed shops. And more shops. Spend a few hours getting lost in Madame Malkin's Robes for All Occasions for cloaks, Ollivander's for a wand, Weasley's Wizard Wheezes for jokes and gags, Borgin and Burkes for dark arts objects and oddities, and Quality Quidditch Supplies for a broom or an elusive Golden Snitch. ⊠ *Wizarding World of Harry Potter: Diagon Alley, 6000 Universal Boulevard, Universal Studios* ⊕ *www.universalorlando.com/Theme-Parks/Universal-Studios-Florida/Wizarding-World-of-Harry-Potter-Diagon-Alley/Shopping.aspx.*

ISLANDS OF ADVENTURE

At Islands of Adventure (IOA) the merchandise varies in each section of the park. If you simply must have a Spider-Man T-shirt or Incredible Hulk coffee mug, for example, head to Marvel Super Hero Island.

The largest concentration of stores is near the gates at the **Port of Entry**. And, as at Universal Studios, a central emporium—the Trading Company—carries nearly every coveted collectible from nearly every park shop. Keep in mind that **Hogsmeade Village** in the Wizarding World of Harry Potter is the place for Potter-related memorabilia and wizard supplies, along with the train-connected Diagon Alley at Universal Studios (two-park ticket required).

TOP SOUVENIRS

Several stores carry superhero and film-themed souvenirs—from Spider-Man gear and Incredible Hulk fists at IOA to dinosaur-inspired apparel at Jurassic Park.

At Seuss Landing, Thing 1 and Thing 2 T-shirts are always a hit with couples and siblings. Or how about a couple of red-and-white-striped Cat in the Hat mugs?

Visit IOA's Wizarding World of Harry Potter: Hogsmeade, and you may find yourself heading home with a wand, omnioculars, a quaffle ball, Hogwarts robe, or Nimbus 2000 broomstick.

TOP SHOPS

Dinostore. Above a juvenile chorus of "I want this!" are adults counseling their kids on what they actually *need*. That can be a monumental task in this large store, which is packed with dino hats, shorts, necklaces, cards, mugs, squirt guns, figurines, and the clever T-rex T-shirt emblazoned with the helpful suggestion "Bite Me." Rest assured there are educational dino toys, too. ⊠ *Jurassic Park, Islands of Adventure* ⊕ *www.universalorlando.com/web/en/us/things-to-do/shopping/Dinostore/index.html.*

Islands of Adventure Trading Company. The rambling emporium inside the entrance/exit of IOA is the largest store in the park; filled with a little something of everything from everywhere, even some items from the attractions of Universal Studios. Here you'll find Kong, Spider-Man, superheroes, and *puh-lenty* of Potter products plastered on sandals, frames, mugs, cups, caps, and clothing. It's perhaps the park's best one-stop shopping experience. ⊠ *Port of Entry, Islands of Adventure* ⊕ *www.universalorlando.com/web/en/us/things-to-do/shopping/islands-of-adventure-trading-company/index.html.*

The Wizarding World of Harry Potter: Hogsmeade. After you board the Hogwarts Express and grab a pint of Butterbeer at The Three Broomsticks, head to the quirky wizarding shops here, including Filch's Emporium of Confiscated Goods (stocked with items taken from misbehaving Hogwarts students), Dervish and Banges (the main repository of Potterabilia with Hogwarts school uniforms, wands, broomsticks, sneakoscopes, spectrespecs, and omnioculars), and Honeydukes (for creative candies such as Fizzing Whizzbees, Chocolate Frogs, and Bertie Bott's Every Flavour Beans). ⊠ *Wizarding World of Harry Potter: Hogsmeade, Islands of Adventure* ⊕ *www.universalorlando.com/web/en/us/things-to-do/shopping/borgin-and-burkes/index.html.*

8

CITYWALK

This 30-acre entertainment and retail complex is at the hub of promenades that lead to Universal Studios and Islands of Adventure. Shops here sell fine jewelry, cool beachwear, fashionable clothing, and stylish accessories. The best stores are near the entrance/exit of the complex.

Fresh Produce. Featuring fashions that look right at home in sunny Florida, this boutique showcases comfortable and colorful swimwear, blouses, Capri slacks, dresses, footwear, beach gear, and accessories designed for coastal comfort. ✉ *City Walk* ☎ *407/363–9363* ⊕ *www.universalorlando.com/web/en/us/things-to-do/shopping/fresh-produce/index.html.*

Quiet Flight. Granted the closest beach is about 60 miles east, you can still get outfitted like a surfer at this shop, which sports an inventory featuring brand names such as Billabong, Quicksilver, Hurley, and Oakley. In addition to shorts and shirts, Quiet Flight also sells sandals, watches, sunglasses (Ray-Ban, Prada, and D&G among the featured names)—and surfboards! ✉ *City Walk* ☎ *407/224–2125* ⊕ *www.universalorlando.com/web/en/us/things-to-do/shopping/quiet-flight-surf-shop/index.html.*

ORLANDO

Visitors from as far away as Britain and Brazil often arrive in Orlando with empty suitcases for their purchases. Although shopping has all but disappeared from Downtown, the metro area is filled with options. There really is something for everyone—from high-end fashion to outlet-mall chic, from antique treasures to hand-hewn Florida finds.

The simultaneously glitzy and kitschy International Drive has more than 500 designer outlet stores and odd, off-brand electronics shops. The factory outlets on the north end of I-Drive once consisted of shops with merchandise piled on tables; today the shops here are equal to their higher-priced first-run cousins. The strip also has plenty of massive restaurants, movie theaters, and entire retail/entertainment/dining complexes.

CENTRAL ORLANDO

SHOPPING CENTERS

Florida Mall. With more than 250 stores and 1.7 million square feet of shopping, this mall is large enough to vacation in (even easier since there's a 511-room hotel attached). Its location between the airport and International Drive makes it an easy stop for incoming and departing tourists hunting for a bargain. Exclusive shops include American Girl, the Crayola Experiences, and M&M World. Anchor stores include Sears, JC Penney, Dillard's, and Macy's, and dining is equally impressive, with two dozen restaurants and eateries. Stroller and wheelchair rentals are available, as are concierge services and currency exchange. ✉ *8001 S. Orange Blossom Trail, South Orlando* ⊕ *www.simon.com/mall/the-florida-mall.*

Mall at Millenia. Located midway between the attractions and Downtown, this 1.2 million-square-foot giant is as upscale as Florida shopping gets. Anchor stores are Neiman Marcus, Bloomingdale's, and Macy's, but you'll also find 150 other retailers, including luxury brands Chanel, Louis Vuitton, Gucci, Prada, Bulgari, and Cartier. Other merchants include Kate Spade New York, Brooks Brothers, Sephora, and one of the finest (and busiest) Apple stores in America. Hungry? Dine at restaurants such as Capital Grill, P.F. Chang's China Bistro, and The Cheesecake Factory. There's also a full-service concierge and foreign currency exchange. ✉ *4200 Conroy Road* ☎ *407/363–3555* ⊕ *www.mallatmillenia.com.*

SPECIALTY SHOPS

Orlando Harley-Davidson. During Daytona Beach Bike Week in March and Biktober Fest in October, this is Hog Central. Anything Harley is available at the shop beside I-4 (just a few miles south of Downtown) from chrome pipes, leather clothing, and cycle GPS units to actual motorcycles to buy or rent—yes, rent. The calendar includes themed events with free food and live music. There are other locations in East Orlando and Kissimmee, as well as shops selling gear on International Drive, at Disney Springs, and at the airport. ✉ *3770 37th St., South Orlando* ☎ *407/423–0346* ⊕ *www.orlandoharley.com.*

Rock & Roll Heaven. Vinyl records are popular again, but according to R&R Heaven, they never left. Here since 1977, the shop has thousands upon thousands of LPs, 45s, CDs, and cassettes, in every conceivable (and a few unbelievable) music style, starting at as little as $1. The posters rock, too. ✉ *1814 N. Orange Ave., Lake Ivanhoe* ☎ *407/896–1952* ⊕ *www.rock-n-rollheaven.com.*

Washburn Imports. Here you'll find an eclectic mix of antiques, commissioned furniture, and one-of-a-kind home furnishings the owner has brought back from Indonesia, India, Thailand, Burma, Vietnam, and China. There's a second location in Sanford. After hours, the back room turns into the Imperial Wine Bar, a popular hipster haven of craft beers, boutique wines, and classic cocktails. ✉ *1800 N. Orange Ave., Lake Ivanhoe* ☎ *407/228–4403* ⊕ *www.washburnimports.com.*

INTERNATIONAL DRIVE

FACTORY OUTLETS

The International Drive area features many factory outlet stores, most on the northeast end just a mile or so from Universal Orlando. These outlets are clumped together in expansive malls or scattered along the drive, and much of the merchandise is ostensibly discounted 20%–75%. You can find just about anything, some of it top quality, but be advised: retailers have learned that they can fool shoppers into believing they must be getting a deal because they're at a stripped-down outlet store. Actually, prices may be the same as or higher than those at other locations.

Orlando International Premium Outlets. Just a short drive from Universal Orlando, the city's largest outlet mall is a prime destination for international shoppers, who can find shoes, clothing, cosmetics, electronics, and household goods at a fraction of their home-country prices. The massive complex at the north tip of International Drive includes hot brands such as Armani, 7 for All Mankind, Bebe, Janie and Jack, Boss, and Skagen, along with Saks OFF 5th, Brooks Brothers, Coach, Kate Spade, and Disney. Searching for bargains works up an appetite, and there are plenty of places to eat here, too, either in the well-lit food court or in one of several sit-down and highly regarded restaurants. ⊠ *International Drive, 4951 International Dr., International Drive* ☎ *407/352– 9611* ⊕ *www.premiumoutlets.com/outlet/orlando-international.*

Orlando Vineland Premium Outlets. This outlet capitalizes on its proximity to Disney (it's at the confluence of Interstate 4, State Road 535, and International Drive). Although it's easier to see from the highway than to enter (and parking is tedious and scarce), some smart shoppers have lunch on International Drive and take the I-Ride Trolley right to the front entrance (it runs every 15 minutes). The center's design makes this almost an open-air market, so walking can be pleasant on a nice day. You'll find Prada, Gap, Nike, Adidas, Tory Burch, Coach, Tommy Hilfiger, Salvatore Ferragamo, among more than 160 stores. ⊠ *8200 Vineland Ave., International Drive* ☎ *407/238–7787* ⊕ *www.premiumoutlets.com/outlet/orlando-vineland.*

SHOPPING CENTERS

Pointe Orlando. This dining, shopping, and entertainment spot is conveniently located within walking distance of five top hotels and the Orange County Convention Center. Note that it costs to park. In addition to WonderWorks (an indoor hands-on science center) and the enormous Regal IMAX theater, the complex has specialty shops such as Tommy Bahama, Hollister, Charming Charlie, and Victoria's Secret. Restaurants have become a reason to visit, with the very high-end Capital Grille, the Oceanaire Seafood Room, Cuba Libre Restaurant and Rum Bar, The Pub, Marlow's Tavern, the popular Funky Monkey Bistro & Bar, B.B. King's Blues Club, and Taverna Opa. Blue Martini and Lafayette's provide after-hours entertainment and adult beverages, and The Improv features nationally recognized comedians. ⊠ *9101 International Dr., International Drive* ☎ *407/248–2838* ⊕ *www.pointeorlando.com.*

SPECIALTY STORES

Bass Pro Shops Outdoor World. Inside a 150,000-square-foot Western-style lodge—and with fishing ponds, deer tracks in the concrete, and a massive stone fireplace—the store packs in countless boats, RVs, tents, rifles, deep-sea fishing gear, freshwater fishing tackle, scuba equipment, flytying materials (classes are offered, too), a pro shop, outdoor clothing, and Uncle Buck's Cabin (a snack bar). Check ahead for special classes, workshops, and seminars. ⊠ *5156 International Dr., International Drive* ☎ *407/563–5200* ⊕ *stores.basspro.com/us/fl/orlando/5156-international-dr.html.*

KISSIMMEE

FACTORY OUTLETS

Lake Buena Vista Factory Stores. What it lacks in curb appeal, this collection of outlet stores makes up for in selection and location. Just two miles from Walt Disney World, it has Aeropostale, Converse, Under Armour, Eddie Bauer, Fossil, Gap, Calvin Klein, Izod, LOFT, Nike, Old Navy, and Tommy Hilfiger, among others. Check out the coupons on the website, and you may find you'll need to stop by the Samsonite store to buy luggage for all your purchases, too. There is also a food court and a playground. ⊠ *15657 S. Apopka Vineland Rd. (State Rd. 535), Lake Buena Vista* ☎ *407/238–9301* ⊕ *www.lbvfs.com.*

FLEA MARKETS

192 Flea Market Outlet. If you don't want to pay full price at a theme park shop, head to this seven-day-a-week, 400-booth flea market about ten miles from Walt Disney World. It's a great place to find hidden gems and affordable souvenirs, where mostly new merchandise covers the gamut (much of it geared toward tourists): toys, luggage, sunglasses, jewelry, clothes, beach towels, sneakers, electronics, and the obligatory T-shirts. There are also wood carvings, custom candles, and vendors who offer computer and cell phone repairs. ⊠ *4301 W. Vine St. (U.S. 192), Kissimmee* ☎ *407/396–4555* ⊕ *www.192fleamarketprices.com.*

MOUNT DORA

When a major highway was routed around the town in the late 1950s, many residents thought that was the end of Mount Dora. Instead, it was preserved: The heart of the town still retains a picture-perfect retro charm with independent shops, sidewalk cafés, and quiet city parks. A short drive from the attractions, it's 45 minutes northwest of Orlando.

The Shopping Village. This busy and eclectic shopping village on the shores of 4,500-acre Lake Dora is responsible for much of Mount Dora's charm. Stroll along boutiques, antique shops, art galleries, spas, jewelers, and bookstores. ⊠ *Downtown, Mount Dora* ☎ *352/383–2165* ⊕ *www.mountdora.com.*

Renninger's Twin Markets. This may be Florida's largest gathering of antiques and collectibles dealers. Atop the hill, 700 flea-market dealers sell household goods, garage-sale surplus, produce, baked goods, pets, and anything else you can think of. Below, 200 antiques booths purvey ephemera, old phonographs, art deco fixtures, antique furniture, and more. If you have the time, hit the flea market first, since that's where antiques dealers find many of their treasures. The antiques market is open Friday–Sunday, the flea market Saturday–Sunday. On the third weekend of each month, the antiques market has a fair attracting about 300 dealers, but the really big shows—which draw about 1,500 dealers—are three-day extravaganzas in November, January, and February. Special events include swap meets for guitars, cars, and motorcycles; Civil War re-enactments, and military memorabila shows. You can spend a morning or all day at these events. Renninger's is busiest from October through May. From Interstate 4, take Florida's Turnpike north

8

to Exit 267A to Route 429 east and, eight miles later, U.S. 441 north to Mount Dora. ⊠ *20651 U.S. 441, Mount Dora* 🕾 *352/383–8393* ⊕ *www.renningers.com* 🖃 *Markets and antiques fairs free; extravaganzas $10 Fri., $6 Sat., $4 Sun., $15 for 3 days.*

WINTER PARK

Located about five miles north of Orlando, Winter Park doesn't have just a few standout stores. It has dozens. By far the most alluring area of town is downtown's Park Avenue. Akin to Worth Avenue in Palm Beach, this is definitely a shopper's heaven. Carve out an afternoon (or evening) to meander the inviting brick street lined with chic boutiques, sidewalk cafés, and hidden alleyways that lead to peaceful nooks and crannies (with even more restaurants and shops). Chain stores are scarce; instead, boutiques offer merchandise that cannot be easily found elsewhere. Renowned Rollins College anchors one end of the avenue, a charming (and historic) nine-hole golf course the other, and a few blocks away visitors take boat tours through a mansion-lined chain of lakes. Just blocks from Park Avenue, you'll find Hannibal Square, another upscale dining and shopping district, at the intersection of New England and Pennsylvania avenues. Even if you don't buy a thing, the beauty of the avenue is priceless.

Farmers' Market. If you schedule your visit to Winter Park for a Saturday morning, you can begin your day at the weekly farmers' market, which takes place from 7 am to 1 pm at the city's old train depot, just two blocks west of Park Avenue. It's a bustling, vibrant market with vendors selling farm-fresh produce, dazzling flowers, and prepared foods. Pick up locally harvested honey, locally made cheese, and freshly baked croissants. ⊠ *200 W. New England Ave., Winter Park* 🕾 *407/599–3397* ⊕ *www.cityofwinterpark.org/departments/ parks-recreation/farmers-market.*

SPECIALTY SHOPS

Charles Hosmer Morse Museum Gift Shop. The museum contains the world's most comprehensive collection of Tiffany stained glass, drawings, paintings, jewelry, pottery, and other objets d'art—so naturally shoppers come here for the representations of Tiffany glass, silk scarves with stained-glass motifs, and fine-art glass that Louis Comfort himself would have treasured. There are also many objects from world museum gift collections and a wide assortment of books about the Arts and Crafts movement. ⊠ *445 N. Park Ave., Winter Park* 🕾 *407/645–5316* ⊕ *www.morsemuseum.org/museum-shop* ☉ *Closed Monday.*

Kathmandu/Tribalasia. You'll think you're on a trek in the Himalayas instead of a stroll on Park Avenue when you spy this unique store, noticeable for its colorful, flag-festooned exterior. Items come from exotic locales like India, Indonesia, Nepal, and Turkey. Hats, turquoise and crystal jewelry, wooden necklaces, clothing, and brass figures of Indian gods are among the merchandise. Follow your nose to the smell of patchouli and sandalwood. ⊠ *352 N. Park Ave., Winter Park* 🕾 *407/647–7071* ⊕ *www.tribalasia.com.*

Shoooz on Park Avenue. While strolling along Park Avenue, your feet may tell you you need a new pair of shoes from this cozy shoe-only shop, which carries reliable designer brands including Mephisto, Taryn Rose, Rieker, Naot, Arcopedicos, and BeautiFeel. ⊠ *303 N. Park Ave., Winter Park* ☎ *407/647–0110.*

Ten Thousand Villages. This fascinating little store sells fair-trade, artisan-crafted home decor, jewelry, paintings, and gifts of all kinds from the smaller corners of the world. ⊠ *346 N. Park Ave., Winter Park* ☎ *407/644–8464* ⊕ *www.tenthousandvillages.com/winterpark.*

SPAS

MAGIC KINGDOM RESORT AREA

Senses—A Disney Spa at Disney's Grand Floridian Resort. All the senses—sound, sight, smell, touch, and taste—are engaged when you enter this Disney-designed and -owned spa near the Wedding Pavilion at the Grand Floridian Resort. Soothing fruit-based elixirs start the journey toward serenity, while soft lighting, gentle music, and the aroma of lavender encourage you to shed your stress (along with most of your clothes). Lounge chairs in separate and secluded men's and women's relaxation areas offer you a spot to further unwind as you wait. Massage tables are heated, as are the lounge chairs in the restful wet room (spend some time looking for the hidden Mickey on the wall). Swimsuits are required in all wet relaxation areas. Treatments include facials, scrubs, and many massages. A whimsical Mad Hatter chair offers little princesses a special place for a pedicure. Prices do not include the 20% gratuity. ⊠ *Grand Floridian Resort, 4401 Floridian Way, Magic Kingdom Resort Area* ☎ *407/824–3000* ⊕ *www.disneyworld.disney.go.com/spas/grand-floridian-resort-and-spa/senses-spa* ⌁ *Parking: complimentary self-parking.*

DOWNTOWN DISNEY RESORT AREA

Blue Harmony. Infused with the colors of ocean and sky, this spa lives up to its name. Its signature treatment combines exfoliation with marine salt and oil, polishing with marine salt and lavender, and a massage based on Thai techniques. Body treatments use oil-infused seawater gels to add natural minerals to the skin and end with a cozy wrap and massage. Two of the eight treatment rooms are outdoors. The serene relaxation lounge offers beverages and tea as you wait for your treatment. Bring the family, as the spa offers treatments for teens as well. ⊠ *Wyndham Grand Orlando Resort Bonnet Creek, 14651 Chelonia Pkwy., Disney Springs Resort Area* ☎ *407/390–2442* ⊕ *www.blueharmonyorlando.com.*

Senses Spa at Disney's Saratoga Springs Resort. The spa may share its name with the Grand Floridian's, but the atmosphere is quite different at this two-story, stone-and-wood spa, inspired by the legendary lodges at the mineral springs of the Adirondacks. Fruit-infused elixirs

8

and the scent of frankincense soothe you as you enter either the separate men's or women's waiting room. Signature treatments include the hydrotherapy package that combines water and stone to exfoliate, soak, wrap, and relax that stressed-out body, and the Bamboo Fusion massage that combines warm stones and an ancient technique using heated bamboo segments. There are two wet relaxation rooms, with steam bath, pool, and heated, glass-tile-covered lounge chairs. You can even bring the family—there's a couples' treatment room and a manicure and pedicure for kids ages 4–12. Swimsuits are required in wet rooms. ⊠ *Disney's Saratoga Springs Resort, 1960 Broadway, Disney Springs Resort Area* ☎ *407/939–7727* ⊕ *www.disneyworld.disney.go.com/spas/ saratoga-springs-resort-and-spa/senses-spa-saratoga.*

SOUTH ORLANDO

Mandara Spa at Loews Portofino Bay Hotel. The doors to this 13,000-square foot Asian-themed sanctuary waft you into a more tranquil world, with bamboo screens, exotic statuary, and silk hangings. Warm blankets comfort you while you wait in the relaxation lounge for one of the 14 treatment rooms. Try the Ceremony of the Hands and Feet, an indulgence that scrubs, exfoliates, and massages your extremities, finishing with a mani-pedi. The lounge and hydropool are co-ed, with separate men's and women's steam rooms and saunas. Portofino's serene sand-bottomed pool is next door, as is the fitness center. Facials and peels are available, as are full makeup, hair, and salon services. ⊠ *Loew's Portofino Bay Resort, 5601 Universal Blvd., Universal Orlando Resort* ☎ *407/503–1244* ⊕ *www.mandaraspa.com/spa/orlando-loews-portofino-bay-hotel-at-universal-orlando.aspx.*

Ritz-Carlton Spa Orlando, Grande Lakes. Prepare to be wowed as you enter this lavish, grand spa, Orlando's largest with 40 treatment rooms, a fitness center, salon, private pool, and café—which means it can get busy. Get here in plenty of time to take a tour and get your bearings, shed your tourist togs, don a plush robe, and prepare to unwind. Unisex and co-ed waiting areas with couches and chairs are available, each on a different floor, with tea, water, fruits, and snacks. Treatments include massage, skin therapy, and deep-cleaning HydraFacials that gently extract impurities from the skin. The spa's signature service is a "zero gravity" massage, in which you sway gently in a rocking hammock. A 20% service charge is added. ⊠ *Ritz-Carlton Orlando, 4024 Central Florida Pkwy., South Orlando* ☎ *407/393–4200* ⊕ *www.ritzcarlton.com/en/hotels/florida/ orlando/spa* ☞ *Parking: valet parking discounted with spa validation.*

The Spa at Shingle Creek. Most of the spa treatments feature Florida products such as citrus and cedar oils, aloe, and Everglades sugar. The Everglades scrub and body wrap begins with a brown sugar body scrub and oils infused with sweet almond, apricot kernel, and wheat germ, followed by a wrap of nutrient-rich Everglades mud with hints of grapefruit, lime, jasmine, and lemongrass. Types of massage include Swedish, aromatherapy, warm stone, and Ashiatsu barefoot massage, in which the therapist uses gravity to reach deep into your muscle tissue. A variety of facials and salon treatments are available, and, for supreme relaxation, you can even add on a 25-minute siesta where you're wrapped in hot packs after your treatment and awakened by gentle bells. Gratuity is included in the cost. Parking, either self or valet, is validated for day guests. ⊠ *Rosen Shingle Creek, 9939 Universal Blvd., South Orlando* ☎ *407/996–9939* ⊕ *www.spaatshinglecreek.com* ☞ *Parking: complimentary valet or self parking with spa validation.*

INTERNATIONAL DRIVE AREA

Eforea Spa at Hilton Orlando. From the deeply cushioned chaise longues in the waiting room, where guests relax in fleecy robes and cozy blankets, to the complimentary infused water, juices, teas, and fruits, guests are made to feel cherished from the moment they enter this big (15 treatment rooms), tropical spa. Orange blossom is the source of the oil for the signature Neroli massage, and essences of rosemary, pine, and lavender soothe the senses during aromatherapy treatments. Guests are welcome to linger in the steam room, full-body showers, or full-service salon, or to arrange to have a treatment in a cabana by the pool. Every spa guest can enjoy complimentary use of the pool and 24-hour fitness center before or after any spa service, and special services are available for youngsters and teens. An 18% service charge is added. Day pass available. Self-parking is free for nonhotel guests. ⊠ *Hilton Orlando, 6001 Destination Pkwy.* ☎ *407/313–4300* ⊕ *www3.hilton.com/en/hotels/florida/hilton-orlando-ORLOCHH/spa/index.html.*

The Spa at Hyatt Regency Orlando. Getting to this 22,000-square-foot, full-service contemporary retreat, set at the heart of a huge convention resort, can be quite a hike, so by the time guests arrive they're usually happy to shed their clothes and cares, don fluffy robes and slippers, and settle in for some serious rejuvenation. Guests have access to a co-ed relaxation lounge, while separate spa areas offer whirlpools, steam room, and showers to enjoy before and after treatments. Massages and a variety of facials and complete salon services are available. Gratuity added. ⊠ *Hyatt Regency Orlando, 9801 International Dr., International Drive* ☎ *407/284–1234* ⊕ *www.hyatt.com/corporate/spas/The-Spa-Orlando/en/home.html.*

The Spa at Rosen Centre. An intimate spa in a resort right across from the convention center caters to busy, stressed-out businesspeople as well as bridal parties, girlfriends' getaways, and spa parties. Once clothes and cares are exchanged for luxurious robes and comfy slippers in the separate locker rooms, guests move to the serene, candlelit, and aroma-enhanced separate relaxation rooms. If your muscles need a real workout, try a traditional Ashiatsu massage, where the masseuse, supported by a wooden frame, uses gravity and her bare feet to reach deep into knots. The Sheer Harmony package is four hours of indulgence, complete with a milk and honey "firming ritual" to de-stress and revitalize you before an anti-aging vitamin C facial and a mani-pedi in the salon (glass of wine included). Day pass available for hotel guests and nonguests. Parking validated for nonguests. ⊠ *Rosen Centre Hotel, 9840 International Dr., International Drive* ☎ *407/996–1248* ⊕ *www.spaatrosencentre.com.*

KISSIMMEE

Mokara Spa at Omni Orlando Resort at Championsgate. Golf courses surround this resort, which may explain why Mokara Spa offers special treatments to ease tension and soreness in stressed shoulders and backs. The Sports Massage uses muscle-warming oil, massage, and stretching to make sure you're ready for another round. There are plenty of choices for the nongolfer in the group—customized massages, deep tissue, aromatherapy, reflexology, hot stones, salt stones, and a full-service salon for hair and nail treatments. Separate locker rooms, steam rooms, and relaxation rooms ensure privacy while you wait. Packages include the Mokara Classic, a 2 1/2-hour treatment that consists of an 80-minute signature massage followed by a 50-minute facial. A 20% gratuity is added to the bill. Parking is validated if you're a day-spa visitor. ⊠ *Omni Orlando Resort at Championsgate, 1500 Masters Blvd., ChampionsGate* ☎ *407/390–6603* ⊕ *www.omnihotels.com/hotels/ orlando-championsgate/spa.*

Relâche Spa & Salon at Gaylord Palms Resort. The 20,000-square-foot spa is in the Everglades Atrium of this giant, Florida-themed resort, and guests may feel like explorers in a tropical wilderness as they make the trek toward tranquility. Soft pastels and generous chaise longues in the tearoom radiate serenity. Fresh fruit and beverages keep you hydrated while you wait, then it's on to serious relaxation. The Escape to Paradise treatment is almost good enough to eat, with a coconut milk bath for relaxation, a pineapple sugar scrub for exfoliation, and warm butter application for skin nourishment. Then you're wrapped into a cozy cocoon topped by hot stones (order a Fijian scalp massage for dessert). A 20% gratuity is added onto the bill. Day pass available for a fee. ⊠ *Gaylord Palms Resort, 6000 W. Osceola Pkwy., Kissimmee* ☎ *407/586–4772* ⊕ *www.marriott.com/spas/mcogp-gaylord-palms-resort-and-convention-center/relâche-spa/5427508/home-page.mi.*

The Spa at Orlando World Center Marriott. Finding the spa in this sprawling, multitower resort outside the entrance to Walt Disney World can be a challenge, but once you arrive, tranquility rules. Robes and slippers are provided in the locker rooms, but there are no private changing rooms. If you are modest, you must retreat to the bathroom or shower. The waiting room is co-ed. Steam rooms, pool, and fitness facility are available for use before or after a treatment in one of the 14 treatment rooms. Gratuity at guests' discretion. ⊠ *Orlando World Center Marriott, 8701 World Center Dr., Lake Buena Vista* ☎ *407/239–4200* ⊕ *www.marriott.com/spas/mcowc-orlando-world-center-marriott/spa-at-world-center/5014219/home-page.mi.*

SPORTS AND THE OUTDOORS

Updated
by Gary
McKechnie

With the sun shining virtually every day and moderate temperatures throughout the year, nearly anytime is a good time to be outdoors and active in Orlando. Surfing, horseback riding, motorcycling, and skydiving just scratch the surface of what's available.

According to folks at the Orlando Convention and Visitors Bureau, there are more than 170 golf courses and 20 golf academies in the area, and even the city's recreation department gets in on the act with country club–like golf courses that are accessible at bargain prices. Meanwhile, inside and outside the theme parks are hundreds of tennis courts, which are vastly outnumbered by thousands of lakes. Yes, around Orlando and Central Florida you can navigate more than 2,000 lakes and waterways via canoe or kayak or airboat—or even on a fishing excursion, which is something to consider when you're visiting one of the bass-fishing capitals of the world. There are also natural springs with waters flowing at a constant (and cool) 72 degrees. You can even take to the air in a sailplane or hot-air balloon or hang glider, or stay firmly planted on the ground as you explore forested hiking trails and modified rails-to-trails. Orlando's sports arena and its pro hockey and basketball teams bring in the crowds, and during Spring Training professional baseball teams come down from the frozen North to warm up at stadiums across Central Florida.

But if your vacation is based at Walt Disney World, nearly every outdoor activity you need is right at your door. Anglers get hooked on fishing charters; runners and bikers get their adrenaline rush on trails across the property, and spectators can take themselves out to the ballgame to watch the Atlanta Braves take on the competition during spring training at the ESPN Wide World of Sports Complex. But it's not just baseball. Volleyball, cheerleading, softball, track, weightlifting are just a few events held here throughout the year in a wide world of competition. For Disney recreation information, call ☎ 407/939–7529.

TOP 5 RECREATIONAL EXPERIENCES

Airboat Tours. Long before theme parks were conceived, the attractions area was a desolate setting of prairies, lakes, and swamps. Outside the parks, you can still see the beauty and wildlife of those lakes and swamps on airboat tours that put you in the heart of natural Florida.

Golf. Set aside a few hours for a round of golf, which may be (depending on your skill level) 18 holes at Arnold Palmer's Bay Hill, an easy 9 holes at the historic (and charming) Winter Park Country Club, a family round of highly themed mini golf at a theme park, or a high-tech practice session at the TopGolf driving range.

iFly Orlando. Totally safe skydiving? That's right. In this indoor chamber, a massive turbine allows you to fly like a bird without jumping out of an airplane (or even getting that far off the ground).

Seminole Lake Gliderport. There's hardly any experience simultaneously more thrilling and peaceful than being hauled to 2,000 feet in a sailplane, and then releasing the cord that secures you to the towplane in front of you. After that, it's a silent soaring adventure in the clear skies of Central Florida.

Wekiva Springs State Park. About 40 minutes east of the theme parks, this state park is centered around a crystal clear natural spring that flows into the Wekiva River. The canoe and kayak concession here offers you a chance to go with the river's flow and immerse yourself in the beauty of natural Florida.

AUTO RACING

Andretti Indoor Karting & Games. The racing legend lent his name to this entertainment facility that offers a little bit of everything: boutique bowling on black-lit lanes, a video game and pinball arcade, a sky trail ropes course with curved ziplines, Hologate (a four-person virtual reality game that takes you into another galaxy), a shoot-em-up 7-D dark ride (you have to see it yourself), and naturally, racing. Pro racing simulators add motion, vibrations, sound effects, and even add tension in the seatbelt so you feel as if you're on an actual racetrack. When you're ready to actually race, three indoor kart tracks let you whip around corners, change elevation, and zip into banked curves on small, high-torque karts. Add laser tag, a restaurant, and more than 100 screens tuned into the day's top sporting events, and you have a lot of entertainment packed into one exciting complex. ✉ *9299 Universal Blvd., International Drive* ☎ *407/374–0042* ⊕ *andrettikarting. com/orlando/* 🎟 *Racing from $19.95; ropes course from $9.95, laser tag from $8.95; other games from $8.95.*

BALLOONING

Central Florida's temperate weather is ideal for ballooning excursions, and it's not uncommon to rise early and see one—or several—balloons drifting slowly above the countryside. Prices and flight durations are roughly the same among the tight-knit community of balloonists in the

Orlando area, as is the ceremonial toast at the conclusion of your flight. But unless you purchase the entire basket, don't picture yourself with plenty of elbow room. The gondola will likely be packed with people. Still, the experience, along with the views, is unforgettable.

FAMILY

Fodor'sChoice

★

Bob's Balloons. After meeting in the pre-dawn hours at the Champions-Gate golf resort, you'll drive to one of several popular launch sites and watch as your balloon is prepared to go up, up, and away. For about an hour you'll float between the treetop level and as high as 1,000 feet, with views of farms and forest land, along with horses, deer, wild boar, cattle, and birds flying *below* you. You may be able to see Disney landmarks like the Animal Kingdom's Expedition Everest and Epcot's Spaceship Earth. Several other balloons are likely to go up near you so you'll view these colorful sky ornaments from an unparalleled sight line. There are seats in the basket, but you'll probably be too thrilled to sit down since this is an adventure that definitely surpasses the Magic Kingdom's Peter Pan's Flight. ✉ *Orlando* ☎ *407/466–6380, 877/824–4606* ⊕ *www.bobsballoons.com* 🖃 *From $175.*

Orlando Balloon Adventures. Like other ballooning services, the launch site is dependent on the direction of the breeze, although the pilots prefer to take to the skies near Walt Disney World, so you can take in an aerial view of the four theme parks. Weather permitting, they're ready to go seven days a week with a flight plan that is dependent on Mother Nature. But wherever you travel—by Walt Disney World, above fragrant orange groves, or over the as-yet undeveloped Green Swamp area—each flight is unique and memorable. If you're staying near the attractions area (Kissimmee, Celebration, International Drive, etc.), they can pick you up and return you to your hotel for a $25 fee. ✉ *Orlando* ☎ *407/786–7473* ⊕ *www.orlandoballoonadventures. com* 🖃 *From $175.*

Painted Horizons Balloons. Like their other local counterparts, Painted Horizons is ready to fly every day of the year and, like others, offers specialties like private flights (at a premium, of course), hotel pickup, and special excursions like weddings and even proposal flights (for which you are accompanied by a plane towing a "Will You Marry Me" banner). Whichever you choose, once the balloon is ready to go, you may not even notice when it lifts slowly into the air—the rise is imperceptible. After flying wherever the wind takes you, the flight concludes with a toast (champagne or sparkling cider) with pastries, cheese, and crackers. ✉ *Orlando* ☎ *407/578–3031* ⊕ *www.painted-horizons.com* 🖃 *From $185.*

BASKETBALL

Orlando Magic. The popularity of the Orlando Magic has waxed and waned since they became the city's NBA team in 1989, perhaps hitting their peak in the early 1990s when Shaquille O'Neal became the team's most recognized player and helped the Magic become the second-fastest team to advance to the NBA Finals. Now playing at Downtown's Amway Center during the October–June season, the Magic entertains locals and visitors in the multimillion-dollar, state-of-the art venue. Ticket prices vary greatly depending on where you sit and how well the season is going. Seats go for as little as $10, with courtside seats creeping up toward $1,000. ⊠ *Amway Center, 400 W. Church St., Downtown Orlando* ☎ *407/896–2442* ⊕ *www.nba.com/magic* ☞ *Tickets from $10; parking from $10; VIP parking from $50.*

BIKING

WALT DISNEY WORLD

Paved trails take you past forests, lakes, wooded campgrounds, and resort villas. If you're 18 or older, you can rent bikes at multiple locations, but you must ride them in the area where you rent them. Rental locations include Downtown Disney Marketplace (near the Rainforest Café) and nearly every moderate-to-deluxe Disney resort, including the BoardWalk Inn and other Epcot Resort Area hotels, Coronado Springs Resort near Disney's Hollywood Studios, Old Key West Resort and Saratoga Springs Resort & Spa near Downtown Disney, Animal Kingdom Lodge, Grand Floridian Resort, and the Fort Wilderness Bike Barn at Fort Wilderness Resort.

Most locations have children's bikes with training wheels and bikes with toddler seats. Surrey bikes are also an option. These look like old-fashioned carriages and are a great way to take your family on a sightseeing tour. The covered tops provide a rare commodity at Disney—shade. Rates start at $9 an hour for regular bikes ($19 for a full day) and go up to $20 to $25 per half hour for surrey bikes (depending on whether they have two, four, or six seats). Wear a helmet; it's free with each rental.

ORLANDO AREA

Thanks to the Orlando community's commitment to the nationwide Rails to Trails program, the city now has several biking, running, and in-line skating trails—converted from former railroad lines—in both rural and urban surroundings.

City of Orlando Trails. Although Orange County has created miles of trails modified from old railroad tracks, Orlando has also gotten in on the act as well, and there are always more recreational trails in the works. There's the Cady Way Trail that passes two large lakes and connects restaurants, retail, and employment centers a few miles from Downtown; the Lake Underhill Path that connects to six city parks; the 13-mile Orlando Southeast Trail that, with its location 20 miles east of Downtown, is highlighted by rural landscapes; the Orlando Urban Trail near Downtown that connects several of the city's cultural highlights (Lake Highland, Loch Haven Park, Mead Gardens, Orlando Cultural Park, and the Gaston Edwards Trail); and the Shingle Creek Trail that will ultimately stretch from Orlando to downtown Kissimmee. For a comprehensive list of trails and where they lead, check the city's biking website. ⊠ *Orlando* ☎ *407/246–2821* ⊕ *www.cityoforlando.net/ transportation-planning/orlando-trails/.*

West Orange Trail. With about 150,000 pedestrians, bicyclists, joggers, roller skaters, and skateboarders traveling some, or all, of its 22 miles every month, this is easily the most popular trail in the area thanks to its pleasingly rural setting and a route that takes it through the charming community of Winter Garden. Spanning the Orange and Lake county lines, the 14-foot-wide path rolls through the towns of Killarney and Oakland, and across U.S. 441 through downtown Apopka. Highlights are views of Lake Apopka and the butterfly garden at the Tildenville outpost. Among the trail's many access points is Chapin Station (⊠ *501 Crown Point Cross Rd., Winter Garden*), just a few blocks from what is clearly the most popular place to rest and eat: the downtown Winter Garden. With sidewalk cafés, bicycle shops, gift shops, boutiques, candy stores, a community theater, history museum, and several other interesting sights, it's the perfect place to put down the kickstand and stay awhile. ⊠ *501 Crown Point Cross Rd., Winter Garden* ⊕ *www. traillink.com/trail/west-orange-trail/.*

West Orange Trail Bikes & Blades. Bicycles—comfort style, hybrids, road bikes, kid's bikes, tandems—and in-line skates can be rented from a log cabin on the West Orange Trail just a few blocks from downtown. The facility sits right beside the trail and offers parking, changing areas, bike racks, and assistance getting the bike fitted for the ride. This center's sister shop is the Winter Garden Wheel Works, a full-service store a few blocks away in the heart of the shopping village. ⊠ *17914 State Rd. 438, Winter Garden* ☎ *407/877–0600* ⊕ *www.orlandobikerental. com* ▣ *From $6 per hour.*

BOATING

Disney has one of the nation's largest fleets of rental pleasure craft. There are marinas at the Caribbean Beach Resort, Contemporary Resort, Downtown Disney Marketplace, Fort Wilderness Resort, Grand Floridian, Old Key West Resort, Polynesian Resort, Port Orleans French Quarter and Riverside resorts, and the Wilderness Lodge. You can rent 12-foot sailboats, catamarans, motor-powered pontoon boats, pedal boats, kayaks, canoes, and tiny two-passenger Sea Raycers—a hit with children—for use on Bay Lake and the adjoining Seven Seas Lagoon, at Crescent Lake by the Epcot resorts, at Lake Buena Vista, or at the Buena Vista Lagoon. You can also sail and water ski on Bay Lake and the Seven Seas Lagoon. You'll find sailboats at the Fort Wilderness, Contemporary, Polynesian, and Grand Floridian marinas. Call ☎ 407/939–7529 for more information.

But Disney certainly isn't the only place where you can take to the waters. Head to the outskirts of Orlando, and you can see Florida's lakes and backwaters via speedboats, motorboats, airboats, and even houseboats.

Boggy Creek Airboat Ride. Just outside the attractions are creeks and lakes and swamps that comprise the headwaters of the Florida Everglades. On an airboat tour you'll explore these still wild ecosystems. Boggy Creek offers four different airboat adventures, each of which will take you into the real Florida: wetlands still populated with exotic birds, turtles, and alligators. ⊠ *2001 E. Southport Rd., Kissimmee* ☎ *407/344–9550* ⊕ *bcairboats.com* ✉ *From $27.*

Marsh Landing Airboat Ride. If you're looking for something different to do on the water, the thrill of an airboat really is something else. At this location, a fleet of 6-, 10-, and 14-passenger stadium-seating boats gives every passenger an unobstructed view of the water speeding past. With the airboat drawing just a few inches of draft, you'll skim through the reeds and near the shore to see alligators, cattle, egrets, anhingas, osprey, eagles, and deer, to name a few. Tours range in duration, distance, and cost, with the longest tour being a half-day venture into the marshlands of Osceola County. ⊠ *2830A Neptune Rd., Kissimmee* ☎ *407/624–0973* ⊕ *orlandoairboattours.com* ✉ *From $50.*

FISHING

Central Florida freshwater lakes and rivers swarm with all kinds of fish, especially largemouth black bass but also perch, catfish, sunfish, and pike, which makes this area a popular spot for fishing tournaments.

LICENSES

To fish in most Florida waters, anglers over 16 need a fishing license, which is available at bait-and-tackle shops, fishing camps, most sporting goods stores, and in the sporting goods section of Wal-Marts. Some of these locations may not sell saltwater licenses, or they may serve non-Florida residents only; so call ahead to be on the safe side. For non-residents of Florida, freshwater or saltwater licenses cost $17 for three consecutive days, $30 for seven consecutive days and $47 for one year. For Florida residents under age 65, a freshwater or saltwater license is $17 per year for each, or $32.50 for both. A five-year fishing license costs Florida residents $79 for both. Fishing on a private lake with the owner's permission—which is what anglers do at Disney World—does not require a Florida fishing license. For more information on proper licensing, contact **Florida Fish and Wildlife** (☎ *850/488–4676* ⊕ *www.fwc.com/recreation*).

WALT DISNEY WORLD

Disney Fishing Excursions. Natural Bay Lake and the man-made Seven Seas Lagoon (whose excavation helped create the foundation of the Magic Kingdom) are connected by a channel, and each is heavily populated with fish. Two- and four-hour catch-and-release excursions depart from the marinas at Fort Wilderness, Wilderness Lodge, Contemporary, Grand Floridian, and Polynesian resorts. Other waterfront resorts, including the Yacht & Beach Club, Saratoga Springs, and Old Key West, also have excursions that depart from their marinas, with the trips including a boat, equipment, live bait, and a guide for up to five anglers. Similar charters depart from the Downtown Disney Marketplace dock by Lake Buena Vista. Your guide is happy to bait your hook, unhook your catches, and even snap pictures of you with your fish. Between 7 am and 2:15 pm, guests can fish inexpensively from a dock at Port Orleans–Riverside. At Ol' Man Island Fishin' Hole, cane poles and bait are $15 per half hour for a family of up to six. You must rent equipment here to use the dock, and you're required to release any fish that you catch. The two-hour guided excursions cost $270 (for up to five people) and depart daily at 7, 10, and 1. The cost is $270 (per group) for morning departures and $235 at 1 pm. Since these are private lakes, a fishing license is not required on Disney property. ⊠ *Magic Kingdom Resort Area* ☎ *407/939–2277 fishing reservations* ✆ *From $235 per group.*

Ol' Man Island Fishin' Hole. You can fish inexpensively from a dock at Port Orleans–Riverside. Cane poles can be rented and bait purchased for a family of up to six for a single fee per half hour. You must rent equipment here to use the dock, and you're required to release any fish that you catch. The fishing hole is open daily 7–2:15. ⊠ *Disney's Port Orleans, 1251 Riverside Dr., Disney Springs Resort Area* ⊕ *www. disneyworld.com* ✆ *From $15.*

ORLANDO AREA

Although some once-great fishing spots have been affected by pollution, most have largely retained their freshwater status and remain among the area's best fishing lakes. A popular favorite is Lake Kissimmee, as well as the Butler and Conway chains of lakes, and Kissimmee's massive Lake Tohopekaliga (aka: Lake Toho)—a Native American name that means "Sleeping Tiger," which received its centuries-old name due to incredibly rough waters that kick up during thunderstorms and have sent more than a few fishermen to a watery grave. Be careful in summer when you see storm clouds. Lake Toho is held in high regard by the Bass Anglers Sportsman Society, since it is the source of the all-time record Tournament Catch. Your best chance for trophy fish is between November and April on Toho or Kissimmee. For good creels, the best bet is usually the Butler area, which has the additional advantage of its scenery: lots of live oaks and cypresses, plus the occasional osprey or bald eagle. Toho and Kissimmee are also good for largemouth bass and crappie. The Butler chain yields largemouth, some pickerel, and the occasional huge catfish. Services range from equipment and boat rental to full-day trips with guides and guarantees. Like virtually all lakes in Florida, the big Orlando-area lakes are teeming with alligators, which you'll find totally harmless unless you engage in the unwise practice of swimming at night. Small pets are more vulnerable than humans and should never be allowed to swim in Florida lakes or rivers. The key differences between the public lakes and the Disney lakes is that you have the option of keeping the fish you catch on the public lakes, while Disney has a catch-and-release policy. You'll also need a license when fishing on public lakes, but not on Disney's privately owned lakes.

If you'd like a glimpse of Old Florida (what locals recall as what Orlando was like before Disney) just head to a fish camp. With their weatherbeaten docks and rustic campgrounds, most retain an authentic look and feel that is distinctly different from the artificial visages of the theme parks and attractions. Most have general stores where you'll find a bait and tackle shop, boat rentals, snacks, beer, ice, and everything you need for a day on the water. Although there's never been a four-star fish camp, lodging often consists of cabins or trailers with standard amenities and, occasionally, kitchenettes that are convenient for long-term stays. Although basic, the appeal of a fish camp is the opportunity to see what Orlando looks like in its natural state; with picturesque lakes, quiet forests, colorful sunsets, and wildlife including deer, grazing cattle, osprey, raccoons, and bald eagles,

Guides operate out of the area's fishing camps, and you can usually make arrangements to hire them through the camp office. Rates vary, but for two people a good price is $250 for a half day and $350 for a full day. Many area guides are part-timers, who fish on weekends or take a day off from their full-time job.

Bass Challenger Guide Service. With Captain Eddie at the helm, BCG takes you wherever the fishing is best that day. It might be Lake Toho or the St. Johns River—Florida's longest and one of the few that runs north—which is a prime bass site. Indeed, bass is the only quarry. BCG also sells bait, arranges for transportation to and from your hotel, organizes multiday trips, and books area accommodations. ✉ *Sanford* ☎ *321/377–2013* ⊕ *www.basschallenger.com* 🖼 *Half-day trips from $300.*

Boggy Creek Resort & RV Park. You can see what kept tourists entertained in pre-Disney days at this camp that includes a restaurant and country store, sells live bait and propane, rents boats, and offers airboat rides. Hard to believe this much of Old Florida is just a few minutes (but several decades) away from Walt Disney World. The camp has 286 RV sites and simple, rustic cabins. Try to reserve one of their 24 cabins at least two weeks in advance in winter and spring. ✉ *3705 Big Bass Rd., Kissimmee* ☎ *407/348–2040* ⊕ *www.boggycreekresortandrvpark.com* 🖼 *Cabins from $79 per night.*

Lake Charters. This outfitter conducts trips from November to May on Lake Tohopekaliga (January through April is high season, so reserve accordingly) and has done so for more than 20 years. It's possible to catch a 14-pound bass here. Rods and reels are included in the cost, and transportation is available. You can also buy your licenses here, and an informative website will fill you in on details regarding rates and what you'll catch. ✉ *1550 Scottys Rd., Kissimmee* ☎ *407/891–2275, 877/326–3575* ⊕ *www.lakecharter.com* 🖼 *Half-day trips from $275.*

Richardson's Fish Camp. Rustic and remote, this camp on western Lake Toho is a place where time began standing still in the 1950s. The most pressing issue is whether to fish or not (you'll probably fish). Relaxing by the water, setting up a cookout, watching the wildlife (deer, osprey, eagles, and company), or catching a glorious Florida sunset are just a few of the activities you'll enjoy here. The camp has seven cabins with kitchenettes, 16 RV sites, and six tent sites, as well as boat slips and a bait shop. The camp is peaceful, quiet, and pet-friendly. ✉ *1550 Scottys Rd., Kissimmee* ☎ *407/846–6540* 🖼 *Cabins from $44.*

9

GOLF

With more than 170 golf courses and 20 golf academies in the area, it's no wonder the International Association of Golf Tour Operators has recognized Orlando as a top golf destination. Sunny weather almost year-round doesn't hurt, and though most of Florida is extremely flat, many of the courses feature hills that make them more challenging.

Resort hotels often let nonguests use their golf facilities. Some country clubs are affiliated with particular hotels, and their guests can play at preferred rates.

In general, even public courses have dress codes, so call ahead for specifics and be sure to reserve tee times. Greens fees usually vary by season, and virtually all include mandatory cart rental, except for the few 9-hole walking courses.

■**TIP→** Twilight discounts often apply after 2 pm in busy seasons and after 3 pm the rest of the year; the discount is usually half off the normal rate. Because golf is so incredibly popular, courses regularly raise rates.

GOLFPAC Travel. GOLFPAC Travel packages golf vacations and arranges tee times at nearly 80 Orlando courses. Rates vary based on hotel and course, and 60 to 90 days' advance notice is recommended to set up a vacation. Their website has convenient searchable, clickable options that let you pick the time and place for a golf outing, adding them to a cart for checkout. ⊠ *483 Montgomery Pl., Altamonte Springs* ☎ *407/260–2288, 888/848–8941* ⊕ *www.golfpactravel.com.*

WALT DISNEY WORLD

Disney has three championship courses, plus a 9-hole walking course. Any guest at a WDW hotel who checks in specifically to play golf gets free transportation to the course.

Greens Fees. Rates change frequently, so the best source for up-to-date rates is Disney itself. Disney resort guests get a price break, and you should ask about twilight discount rates. If you plan to play only once, leave the gear at home—you can rent shoes, range balls, and clubs at any location.

Tee Times and Reservations. Tee times are available daily from dawn until dusk. You can book them up to 90 days in advance if you're staying at a WDW-owned hotel, 60 days ahead if you're staying elsewhere. You must cancel at least 24 hours out. For tee times and private lessons, call Disney's central World Golf reservations line ☎ *407/939–4653.* And be sure to bookmark Disney's golf website (⊕ *www.golfwdw. com*), which contains in-depth information on the courses, layout, rates, and tee times.

GREENS FEES

Rates at all 18-hole courses are generally the same ($129 before 11 am, $115 after) but can also vary by the time of year and can change several times throughout the day. That said, the moment you know when you're ready to play, make your reservation (☎ *407/939–4653*

⊕ *www.golfwdw.com*). All fees include an electric cart, although the 9-hole Oak Trail is a walking course, and a pull cart for your bag is $6. If you've got the stamina and desire to play the same course twice in the same day, you can do so for half price the second time around, but you can't reserve that option in advance. This Re-Play Option, as Disney calls it, is subject to availability. Golf shoes rent for $10 a pair, and range balls are available between $7 to $11 a bucket. If you'd rather not pay a baggage fee to haul your clubs onto your plane, you can rent the latest TaylorMade woods, irons, and a putter for $65. If, for some reason, you have to cancel your tee time, they'll try to fill your spot, but if not, you'll be charged.

GOLF INSTRUCTION

One-on-one instruction from PGA-accredited professionals is available at any Disney course. Prices for private lessons vary: 45-minute lessons cost $75 for adults and $50 for youngsters 17 and under.

COURSES

Disney's Lake Buena Vista Golf Course. A favorite among golfers, the Lake Buena Vista course has hosted the PGA Tour, LPGA Tour, and USGA events. As you play, you'll find the course winds among Downtown Disney–area town houses and villas. Greens are narrow, and hitting straight is important because errant balls risk ending up in someone's bedroom. Be prepared for the famous island green on the 7th. This is a pleasant location surrounded by wonderful scenery. ⊠ *1960 Broadway, Disney Springs* ⊟ *From $49* ⅃ *18 holes, 6,745 yards, par 72.*

The Magnolia. One of the originals when the park opened in 1971, The Magnolia has been lavished with four stars by *Golf Digest* and was certified by Audubon International as a Cooperative Wildlife Sanctuary. The long but forgiving classic course features extra-wide fairways, and its name stems from more than 1,500 magnolia trees that line the course. While you're working to avoid the woods, try avoiding the water hazards that are found at 11 of the 18 holes. But that's not all. There are 97 bunkers spread throughout the fairway. Play here, and you're playing the course that welcomed Nicklaus, Palmer, Player, and other legends. ⊠ *Shades of Green, 1950 W. Magnolia–Palm Dr., Magic Kingdom Resort Area* ☎ *407/939–4653* ⊕ *www.golfwdw.com* ⊟ *From $39* ⅃ *18 holes, 7,516 yards, par 72.*

Oak Trail. Located across from the Grand Floridian at the Shades of Green Resort (a resort used primarily by military families), the Oak Trail was designed by Ron Garl to be fun for the entire family. It's noted for its small, undulating greens and particularly affordable fees. ⊠ *Shades of Green, 1950 W. Magnolia–Palm Dr., Magic Kingdom Resort Area* ⊕ *disneyworld.disney.go.com/recreation/oak-trail-golf-course/* ⊟ *From $39* ⅃ *9 holes, 2,913 yards, par 36.*

The Palm. Although it's not as long as the Magnolia, nor as wide, The Palm has been confounding the pros for years. The course, located across the Grand Floridian Resort, has 9 water holes and 94 bunkers—including one in the iconic shape of Mickey Mouse's head. ⊠ *Shades of Green, 1950 W. Magnolia–Palm Dr., Magic Kingdom Resort Area* ☎ *407/939–4653* ⊕ *www.golfwdw.com* ⊟ *From $45* ⅃ *18 holes, 7,011 yards, par 72.*

9

Fodor'sChoice **Tranquilo Golf Club at Four Seasons Resort.** Once known as Disney's
★ Osprey Ridge, this Tom Fazio–designed course is on Disney property
but part of the Four Seasons Resort Orlando. Sculpted from some of
the still-forested portions of the huge WDW acreage, tees and greens
as much as 20 feet above the fairways keep competitive players from
getting too comfortable. Amenities include luxury golf carts with GPS,
a Cuban-American clubhouse restaurant, driving range, and putting
green. Greens fees drop significantly for "twilight" play starting at 2
pm. Have time for only 7 holes? There's a special for that, too. ✉ *10100
Dream Tree Blvd., Lake Buena Vista* ⊕ *www.fourseasons.com/orlando/
golf/* ✉ *From $175* ⚑ *18 holes, 6,968 yards, par 71.*

ORLANDO AREA

Golf has no better hometown than Orlando. The longtime residence of
the late Arnold Palmer, with more than 170 public and private courses
along with a moderate climate and predictable weather, the city has
enticed scores of PGA professionals to make this their home as well.
Palmer's landmark Bay Hill Invitational is held here each March, and
the Daytona-based LPGA hosts several tournaments in Orlando every
year. Appearing with great frequency (every single day) are the programs and tournaments aired on the Golf Channel, which broadcasts
from Orlando. Note that the greens fees listed reveal a wide range of
prices, which can change by season and time of day. Call the pro shop
or check the website ahead of time for the current rates.

Arnold Palmer's Bay Hill Club & Lodge. It was golf legend Arnold Palmer
who helped put Orlando at the forefront of the sport, and this course
was his pride and joy. Each March, at the Arnold Palmer Invitational,
pros and visting amateurs anticipate the 18th hole here, which is considered one of the toughest on the PGA tour. Courses are open only
to those who have been invited by a member or who book lodging at
the club's 70-room lodge. But with double-occupancy rates for rooms
overlooking the course running as low as $130 for a double room in
summer, many consider staying at the club worthwhile. Keep in mind
this rate does not include your greens fees, which are necessary since
staying here in essence buys you a day of "membership" at the club.
✉ *9000 Bay Hill Blvd.* ☎ *407/876–2429, 407/422–9445* ⊕ *www.bay-
hill.com* ✉ *Varies by season, from $75 to $385* ⚑ *18 holes, 7,207 yards,
par 72; 9 holes, 3,409 yards, par 36.*

Celebration Golf Club. Talk about a great pedigree—the Celebration
course was designed by Robert Trent Jones Jr. and Sr. Located just 10
minutes from Walt Disney World, the course is paired with the master-
planned Disney community, just one mile off the U.S. 192 strip. Lovely,
wooded, and serene, the fairways are framed by natural woods and wetlands to create what the Joneses envisioned: "Every hole a hard par and
an easy bogey." Rates drop after 1 pm and again around dusk. ✉ *701
Golf Park Dr., Celebration* ☎ *407/566–4653* ⊕ *www.celebrationgolf.
com* ✉ *From $79* ⚑ *18 holes, 6,783 yards, par 72.*

ChampionsGate Golf Club. Just about 10 minutes west of Disney, as you
see this community from the vantage point of I–4, you can see that

there's some serious golfing inside the gates of ChampionsGate. The two courses here were designed by Australia's Greg Norman, and there's an on-site David Leadbetter Golf Academy. The 7,363-yard International has the "Down Under" style of Australia's coastal links, whereas the 7,128-yard National course is designed in the style of the better domestic courses, with a number of par-3 holes with unusual bunkers. Their golf shop is ranked among the Top 100, and the Pipers Grille sports lounge is a great 19th hole. At sunset step onto the veranda and watch a piper play as he walks the greens. Can't get enough? There's a four-star Omni hotel here. ⊠ *1400 Masters Blvd., ChampionsGate* ☎ *407/787–4653 ChampionsGate, 407/787–3330 Leadbetter Academy, 888/633–5323 Leadbetter Academy* ⊕ *www.championsgategolf. com* ⊠ *From $45* ⟨ *International: 18 holes, 7,363 yards, par 72. National: 18 holes, 7,128 yards, par 72.*

Falcon's Fire Golf Club. Designed by Rees Jones, Falcon's Fire has strategically placed fairway bunkers that demand accuracy off the tee. This club is just off the Irlo Bronson Memorial Highway and is convenient to the hotels in Kissimmee's so-called Maingate area. A round here includes complimentary valet parking, club cleaning, and golf carts equipped with GPS navigation. ⊠ *3200 Seralago Blvd., Kissimmee* ☎ *407/239–5445* ⊕ *www.falconsfire.com* ⊠ *From $49* ⟨ *18 holes, 7,015 yards, par 72.*

Grand Cypress Golf Resort. When it opened, Grand Cypress elevated Orlando golfing with elegant courses that spread across what once had been pasture and prairie. The four courses include the three 9's: the North, South, and East courses, and the 18-hole New Course, fashioned after a Scottish glen. In addition, the Grand Cypress Academy of Golf, a 21-acre facility, has lessons and clinics. The North and South courses have fairways constructed on different levels, giving them added definition. The New Course, designed by Jack Nicklaus, was inspired by the Old Course at St. Andrews, and has deep bunkers, double greens, a snaking burn, and even an old stone bridge. ⊠ *1 N. Jacaranda* ☎ *407/239–1909, 407/239–1909* ⊕ *www.grandcypress.com* ⊠ *From $125* ⟨ *North: 9 holes, 3,521 yards, par 36. South: 9 holes, 3,472 yards, par 36. East: 9 holes, 3,434 yards, par 36. New: 18 holes, 6,773 yards, par 72.*

Hawk's Landing Golf Club at the Orlando World Center Marriott. Located near the entrance to Walt Disney World at the monumental World Center Marriott (the world's largest Marriott), the 220-acre Hawk's Landing course includes 15 water holes, lots of sand, and exotic landscaping. As you play you'll see they've maintained the natural surroundings and enhanced the same with vibrantly colored azaleas. A good choice if you're here on business and want to get in a round. No need to pack your clubs—Callaway rental equipment is available. Need some help? Instruction is offered at the Jack Nicklaus Academy. ⊠ *Orlando World Center Marriott, 8701 World Center Dr.* ☎ *407/238–8660, 800/567–2623* ⊕ *www.golfhawkslanding.com* ⊠ *From $69* ⟨ *18 holes, 6,602 yards, par 71.*

Marriott Golf Academy. The Marriott Golf Academy is an extensive-curriculum golf school and 9-hole golf course on the grounds of the corporation's biggest time-share complex, Marriott's Grande Vista. Here you can do anything from taking a one-hour lesson with a certified instructor to immersing yourself in a three-day extravaganza in which you learn more about golf technique than most nonfanatics would care to know. The Swing Studio offers high-tech teaching methods. The course, designed by Ron Garl, is geared to make you use every club in your bag—and perhaps a few you may elect to buy in the pro shop. ⊠ *Marriott Grande Vista, 12001 Avenida Verde* ☎ *407/238–7677, 855/642–2369* ⊕ *www.marriottgolfacademy.com* ⊴ *Lessons from $99; 3-day courses from $949* ⚐ *9 holes, 2,400 yards, par 32.*

Orange Lake Resort. About five minutes from Walt Disney World's main entrance, Orange Lake has two 18-hole courses (the Legends and the Reserve), two 9-hole courses (Crane's Bend, Legends Walk), and pro instruction at the McCord Golf Academy (rates start at $65). The Legends is a signature Arnold Palmer–designed championship course; the Reserve was designed by Mike Dasher and has unique land and water challenges. Crane's Bend is family-friendly. Legend's Walk is an executive walker's course open until 9 pm nightly, where children 15 and younger play free with complimentary clubs. The signature hole for the entire group of courses is the Island Oak, No. 13, a 432-yard, par-4 hole in the Pines section (the back 9) of the Legends Course. ⊠ *8505 W. Irlo Bronson Memorial Hwy., Kissimmee* ☎ *407/239–1050, 888/640–6522* ⊕ *www.golforangelake.com* ⊴ *From $35 for resort guests; from $60 for nonguests* ⚐ *The Legends: 18 holes, 7,072 yards, par 72. The Reserve: 18 holes, 6,670 yards, par 71. Crane's Bend: 9 holes, 1,901 yards, par 30. Legend's Walk: 9 holes, 1,581 yards, par 30.*

Rosen's Shingle Creek Golf Club. Rosen's Shingle Creek Golf Club, designed by David Harman, lies alongside a lovely creek that is headwaters of the Everglades. The course is challenging yet playable, with dense stands of oak and pine trees and interconnected waterways. The golf carts even have GPS yardage systems. Another favorite for conventioneers, since Universal Studios and the Orange County Convention Center are within a few minutes' drive. ⊠ *9939 Universal Blvd.* ☎ *407/996–9933, 866/996–9933* ⊕ *www.shinglecreekgolf.com* ⊴ *From $85* ⚐ *18 holes, 7,069 yards, par 72.*

TopGolf. Way back when, bowlers would mark their own scores on a strip of paper. Then modern computers came along to track the ball's path, and scores would be tallied and automatically displayed on colorful screens. Now picture that level of technology at a driving range. At this fantastic complex near the Orange County Convention Center, golf balls are embedded with a tracking chip so you and your friends can enter your names on a computer, choose from a few dozen clubs, wait for a ball to drop out by a tee, and start swinging. Within seconds of hitting the shot, the height, distance, and course of the ball will be shown on a screen. Play for points by hitting the microchipped ball close to one of 11 targets that are spread out from 20 to 240 yards away. Multiple levels accommodate multiple golfers, and the pub and club atmosphere makes this a popular meeting place for friends— even if they've never swung a club. ✉ *9925 International Dr., International Drive* ☎ *407/218-7714* ⊕ *topgolf.com/us/orlando* 🖃 *From $30.*

Waldorf Astoria Golf Club. The Rees Jones–designed course has maintained some of the natural elements of the original landscape even while enhancing the land's existing contours. Majestic stands of pine and cypress line the fairways, and the fairways wind through a scenic wetland preserve, with bunkers reminiscent of century-old hazards. It has a five-tee system for all playing levels. ✉ *14224 Bonnet Creek Resort La.* ☎ *407/597–5500, 888/924–6531* ⊕ *www.waldorfastoriagolfclub. com* 🖃 *From $65* ⛳ *18 holes, 7,113 yards, par 72.*

Winter Park Country Club. Located in Winter Park, an upscale suburb of Orlando, this charmingly simple course frames the north end of Park Avenue, Central Florida's version of Worth Avenue in Palm Beach or Rodeo Drive in Beverly Hills. A point of pride for residents, this historic country club offers nonresidents access to its immaculate golf course. Opened in 1914, the 9-hole walking course was modeled after authentic Scottish links. Notably, within the past decade residents were given a choice to sell the golf course to developers or raise their own taxes to preserve it for the city. They chose to keep the course, which remains one of the most affordable and authentic recreational experiences in Central Florida. ✉ *761 Old England Ave., Winter Park* ☎ *407/599–3339* ⊕ *www.winterparkcountryclub.com* 🖃 *From $16* ⛳ *9 holes, 2,480 yards, par 36.*

HOCKEY

Orlando Solar Bears. Taking the ice at Downtown's Amway Center, the Orlando Solar Bears play in the South Division of the Eastern Conference Hockey League. One of three ECHL teams in the state, their season runs from October to April. ✉ *Amway Center, 400 East Church St., Downtown Orlando* ☎ *407/951–8200* ⊕ *orlandosolarbearshockey. com* 🖃 *From $12.*

HORSEBACK RIDING

WALT DISNEY WORLD

Fort Wilderness Resort. A popular activity since the earliest days of Disney World, the backwoods horseback trail rides depart from the Tri-Circle-D Ranch at 8:30 am and continue through mid- to late afternoon. Children must be at least 9 years old and 48 inches tall to ride, and adults must weigh less than 250 pounds. Trail rides start at 45 minutes; hours vary by season. You must check in 30 minutes prior to your ride, and reservations must be made at least one day ahead. Both horseback riding and the campground are open to nonresort guests. Also available are wagon rides, carriage rides, and, for the kids, pony rides. ✉ *Tri-Circle D Ranch, 4510 Fort Wilderness Trail, Magic Kingdom Resort Area* ☎ *407/824–2832* 🖃 *From $55.*

9

ICE SKATING

The Ice Factory. Ice-skating in Florida? Yup! This Olympic-class facility has two rinks and several themed evenings each week. Teens are drawn to Friday's DJ Night, and there are family-night rates on Saturday. Skate rentals are included with admission, and an upgraded pair (which costs a little extra) include extra padding (wearing thick socks is an option). Hours vary and often the rink is being used for training, so be sure to visit their website before you go for an updated schedule on public skating. And dress in layers—on the rink the temperature averages between 50 to 65 degrees year-round. Long pants and a sweater are usually fine since you're moving around. ⊠ *2221 Partin Settlement Rd., Kissimmee* ☎ *407/933–4259* ⊕ *www.icefactory.com* ⊠ *From $5; skate rental $3.*

MINIATURE GOLF

If mini golf is your game, Disney has two courses, but there are several others in Orlando.

FAMILY **Congo River.** In this clever creation, it's mini-putt meets theme park. Multilevel courses wander amid waterfalls, rocky summits, caves, and rain forests. Popular with families and, believe it or not, couples, kids are the prime audience. They love the live alligators (not loose on the course), the arcade room, and the treasure hunt. Congo River also has locations in Kissimmee and East Orlando. ⊠ *5901 International Dr., International Drive* ☎ *407/248–9181* ⊕ *www.congoriver.com* ⊠ *From $12.99.*

Fantasia Gardens Miniature Golf. Nearly every miniature golf course uses cartoon characters of some sort, but only Disney can use classic characters you'd recognize from Walt's bold experiment, *Fantasia*. Along the course are tutu-clad hippos, marching broomsticks, and pirouetting ostriches. Making things even more challenging are all the elements of a traditional golf course: sand traps, bunkers, water hazards, and sloping greens. ⊠ *1205 Epcot Resorts Blvd., Epcot Resort Area* ☎ *407/824–4500* ⊕ *disneyworld.disney.go.com/recreation/fantasia-gardens-fairways-miniature-golf/* ⊠ *$12 children, 9 and under; $14, 10 and over.*

FAMILY **Hollywood Drive-In Golf at Universal CityWalk.** With a science-fiction alien
Fodor's Choice invasion course paired with a 1950s horror movie monster course,
★ there's something for kids and fun-loving adults alike. Spectacular lighting and sound effects mean that the play is different day and night. A 36-hole Double Feature package is available, and the course is open until 2 am. ⊠ *6000 Universal Blvd., CityWalk* ☎ *407/802–4848* ⊕ *hollywooddriveingolf.com* ⊠ *From $15.99.*

FAMILY **Pirate's Cove Adventure Golf.** Two 18-hole miniature golf courses with a buccaneer theme wind around artificial mountains, through caves, beside waterfalls, and into lush foliage. The beginner's course is called Captain Kidd's Adventure; the more advanced course is Blackbeard's Challenge. In addition to this location at Lake Buena Vista (near Disney), there's a second Pirate's Cove on International Drive.

✉ *Crossroads Shopping Center, 12545 State Rd. 535, Lake Buena Vista* ☎ *407/827–1242* ⊕ *www.piratescove.net* 🎫 *From $13.50.*

Putting Edge. Another spin on miniature golfing is this course with a twist: it's indoors, lit in wildly fluorescent colors, and then further illuminated with black lights. The glow-in-the-dark universe is popular with families and date-night couples. An interactive arcade awaits after sinking the last putt. ✉ *5250 International Dr., International Drive* ☎ *407/248–0700* ⊕ *www.puttingedge.com/orlando/.*

Winter Summerland Miniature Golf. Not content to build just one themed miniature golf course, Disney built two very different courses beside the Blizzard Beach water park: one themed for the Florida summer sun, the other covered with snow that remains in a perpetual winter wonderland. The Summer course mixes things up, with surfboards, sand castles, peppermint-striped inner tubes, and palm trees decorated with Christmas ornaments. As you play your way toward the North Hole on the Winter Course, obstacles include giant peppermints, hockey sticks, and the drawbridge of a melting castle. ✉ *Blizzard Beach, Blizzard Beach* ☎ *407/824–4500* ⊕ *disneyworld.disney.go.com/recreation/winter-summerland-miniature-golf/* 🎫 *From $14.*

MULTISPORT OUTFITTERS

Fort Wilderness Resort. One of the original Disney resorts (the Polynesian and Contemporary were the others), Fort Wilderness Resort offers a number of sporting and outdoors activities. For 90 minutes you can get in some target shooting with an archery guide who oversees novice and expert marksmen (ages 6 and up). Nonresort guests are welcome to join campers, and the fee includes use of the compound bow and arrows, plus instruction. You can book up to 180 days in advance. But that's not all the outdoor activities you can enjoy here.

A two-hour Wilderness Back Trail Adventure Segway tour is done on an off-road version of the vehicle, and begins with a training session to get you acquainted with its operation. Call ahead for reservations. You must be at least 16 and carry a photo ID. If you'd prefer to rent a bicycle, stop by the Bicycle Barn where they rent for the hour or day. You can also rent fishing rods and tackle for fishing in the canals around Fort Wilderness Resort, but you must be 18 or older to rent. If you'd like to go fishing with a guide, that's possible, too.

✉ *4510 N. Fort Wilderness Trail, Magic Kingdom* ☎ *407/939–8687 Bike Barn* 🎫 *Archery from $48; Segway tour from $98; bike rentals from $12; fishing tackle rentals from $11; guided fishing trips from $270.*

RODEOS

Silver Spurs Rodeo. Many natives recall the era known as Old Florida, and that's the time before 1971 and the arrival of the theme parks. You can still find Old Florida on Disney's doorstep, right there in neighboring Kissimmee at the Silver Spurs Rodeo. Launched here by ranching families in 1944, the largest rodeo east of the Mississippi is where you'll see bull riders and cowboys competing in a variety of high-energy, high-adrenaline competitions including bull and bronco riding, steer wrestling, and barrel racing. The show is held at the Osceola Heritage Park each February and June; just grab a seat and watch in awe. Pure Florida goodness. From Interstate 4 Exit 77, take Florida's Turnpike south to Exit 244 (Kissimmee–St. Cloud). ⊠ *1875 Silver Spur La., Kissimmee* ☎ *321/697–3495* ⊕ *www.silverspursrodeo.com* ⊠ *From $15.*

RUNNING

WALT DISNEY WORLD

The World has several scenic running trails from the Grand Floridian, Polynesian, and Contemporary in the Magic Kingdom area. At the Epcot resorts, you can get your heart rate up along the promenade that circles Crescent Lake past the BoardWalk and Yacht and Beach Club resorts. If you're staying at Port Orleans, you can work up a sweat on nearby trails; Coronado Springs guests run along the resort's one-mile esplanade.

The roads that snake through Downtown Disney resorts are pleasant, and early in the morning traffic isn't too bad. At the Caribbean Beach Resort, there's a 1½-mile running promenade around Barefoot Bay. Fort Wilderness Campground has a woodsy two-mile course with numerous exercise stations along the way.

Walt Disney World sponsors many running events throughout the course of the year (⊕ *www.rundisney.com*).

SKYDIVING AND PARASAILING

Fodor's Choice ★ **iFLY Orlando.** Okay, so technically you aren't really skydiving, but you come pretty close as you float atop a cushion of air in this 12-foot-high, 1,000-horsepower wind tunnel. Letting you experience everything skydivers do but closer to the ground, the experience starts with instruction, after which you suit up and hit the wind tunnel, where you soar like a bird (or try to) under your instructor's watchful eye. It's all so realistic that skydiving clubs come to hone their skills. It's also pretty surreal as you look through the window and see people floating in mid-air. The attraction is safe for anyone under 250 pounds and older than 3. The 90-minute introductory experience includes two flights. You can purchase a video of your "jump" at the end. ⊠ *8969 International Dr., International Drive* ☎ *407/337–4359* ⊕ *www.iflyworld.com/orlando/* ⊠ *From $69.95.*

Quest Air Hang Gliding. This grassy airfield has everything you need for assorted aerial adventures. For a hang gliding thrill, you and an instructor are towed as high as 4,000 feet before releasing the line from the towplane ahead of you. After that, you're free to experience what may best be described as a motorcycle ride in the sky. The instructors will let you maneuver the glider so you can turn, bank, rise, and dip as you soak in incredible views of the Orlando countryside. Quest Air also offers "flyboarding," which requires you to strap on "jet boots" that propel you up and out and above the waters of Quest Lake, and take to the skies in tandem "Dragonflies," ultralight aircraft that let you sit comfortably as you take a leisurely powered flight. ✉ *6548 Groveland Airport Rd.* ☎ *352/429–0213* ⊕ *questairhanggliding.com.*

Sammy Duvall's Watersports Centre. Thanks to Sammy Duvall's, you can get a bird's-eye view of Disney while parasailing on Bay Lake. Flights with 450 feet of line last 8 to 10 minutes; deluxe flights with 600 feet of line last 10 to 12 minutes. You must weigh at least 130 pounds, though lightweights can bulk up with the help of a lifeguard or family member and a tandem flight (without the tandem charge). But if you want to parasail with a partner from the get-go, the cost is almost double.

At the same location, you can try your skills at waterskiing, wakeboarding, and tubing. Up to five people can go on the ski boat, which includes equipment and an expert instructor and driver. For a group that large, instructors recommend booking two hours; couples or smaller groups may want to try one hour, though half-hour rentals are available. ✉ *Contemporary Resort, Magic Kingdom Resort Area* ☎ *407/939–0754* ⊕ *www.sammyduvall.com* 💲 *From $95.*

SURFING

Surfing? Here, in landlocked Central Florida? You bet. Early in the morning, before Typhoon Lagoon opens to water-park visitors, you can hit some man-made waves with 11 other novices and a professional instructor. Run by local surf pros, the three-hour session begins with a half-hour beachside lesson on surfing moves and basics. Each session comes packed with up to 100 waves, broken into sets of 25, so the chance of learning how to master the board is pretty good. Before you know it, you're in the heated wave pool and headed for your first ride. You must be at least 8 years old, and lessons cost $165 per person. Soft-sided boards are provided. You must have transportation to Typhoon Lagoon; even if you're staying at Disney, buses don't run before the class begins at 6:45 am. The program is scheduled several days each week for up to 12 participants, but lesson days vary, so call ☎ *407/939–7529.*

TENNIS

WALT DISNEY WORLD

You can play tennis at several Disney hotels: Bay Lake Tower at Disney's Contemporary Resort (two hard courts), BoardWalk (two hard courts), Old Key West Resort (two hard courts), Saratoga Springs Resort & Spa (two Hydrogrid clay courts), and Yacht Club Resort (one hard court). Courts are available without charge on a first-come-first-served basis for resort and nonresort guests. All have lights, and most have lockers and racquets available to rent or borrow. At the Walt Disney World Swan and Dolphin hotels, you can get an hour-long private lesson on one of four courts for $90 from 7 am to 9 pm. Call ☎ *407/621–1991.*

9

ORLANDO AREA

Tennis is one of the most popular sports in Orlando, with hundreds of well-tended public tennis courts and resort hotels that offer a court or two (or more) for their guests. The city of Orlando operates more than 50 courts, some free and others reasonably priced.

Fort Gatlin Tennis Complex. Close to Downtown Orlando, Fort Gatlin has the finest city-run courts open to the public. Ten hard courts equipped for day or night play, a pro shop that's open daily, and lessons are among this beautiful facility's offerings. ⊠ *2009 Lake Margaret Dr., Downtown Orlando* ☎ *407/254–9878* ⊕ *www.fortgatlin.com/home. html* ⊠ *From $4 per hour.*

Orlando Tennis Center. Run by the City of Orlando and located near Downtown, this fine facility offers adult tennis clinics (18 and up), private lessons, and youth tennis programs (six and up). The center features five hard courts, 11 clay courts, two racquet ball courts, and three hitting walls. ⊠ *363 N. Parramore Ave., Downtown Orlando* ☎ *407/246–4469* ⊕ *www.cityoforlando.net/recreation/orlando-tennis-centre/* ⊠ *From $4 per hour.*

6th Sense Tennis Academy. Based at the Mission Inn Resort, 6th Sense is run by Olympic-gold-medal winner Justine Henin. It offers one-day, two-day, and weekly programs for adults ($120–$500) and intensive children's training ($200–$360) from March through December. The resort is approximately 40 miles west of Orlando. ⊠ *10400 County Rd. 48, Howie In The Hills* ☎ *352/435–5799* ⊕ *www.6thsenseacademy.com.*

INDEX

PHOTO CREDITS

NOTES

NOTES

NOTES

NOTES

NOTES

NOTES

NOTES

NOTES

NOTES

ABOUT OUR WRITERS

Where to Stay writer **Jennifer Greenhill-Taylor** has been a journalist for more than two decades—working as a travel editor, theater and film critic, wire editor, and freelance writer/editor. She was born in Edinburgh, Scotland, has lived in four countries and a dozen states, and travels widely for pleasure and profit. She lives in Orlando with her partner, playwright and freelance writer Joseph Reed Hayes, and enjoys sharing her extensive research on the area's hospitality with friends and family.

Orlando and Environs writer **Joseph Hayes** has informed the world about travel, food, and the arts in Central Florida for print and online publications for 20 years. He won a Florida Magazine Association Award for his work as the restaurant critic for *Orlando Magazine*. His other hat is worn in performance spaces, as an award-winning playwright produced in New York, California, Florida, and the United Kingdom, a jazz event producer, and advocate for new, original creative work for in-house and online audiences. Born in Manhattan, Hayes worked in publishing in New York before moving to Central Florida to take up writing and traveling as a full-time career. *jrhayes.net*

Gary McKechnie, who covered all of Universal and SeaWorld, knows a lot about Florida—his native state. During his student days, he worked as a Walt Disney World ferryboat pilot, Jungle Cruise skipper, steam train conductor, double-decker bus driver, and was also an improv comedian at Epcot. He wrote the award-winning *Great American Motorcycle Tours*, the nation's best-selling motorcycle guidebook, and, following years of travel and research, National Geographic's *USA 101*, which highlights 101 iconic American places, events, and festivals. Gary also speaks on America's cultural heritage aboard the Cunard Line ships *Queen Mary 2* and *Queen Victoria* and at business and tourism meetings across America.